Roger Wilkes is a newspaper and television journalist, and an expert on true crime. His works include *The Mammoth Book of Murder and Science*, *The Mammoth Book of Unsolved Crimes*, and *Scandal!*

THE MAMMOTH BOOK OF
HARD MEN

Edited by Roger Wilkes

ROBINSON
London

Constable & Robinson Ltd
3 The Lanchesters
162 Fulham Palace Road
London W6 9ER
www.constablerobinson.com

First published in the UK by Robinson,
an imprint of Constable & Robinson Ltd, 2006

A copy of the British Library Cataloguing in
Publication Data is available from the British Library.

ISBN: 978-1-84529-302-4

Printed and bound in the EU

3 5 7 9 10 8 6 4

Contents

Introduction

Roger Wilkes

Lurking within are some of the world's most notorious hard men, hard-boiled, hard-nail, hard-core hard cases, evil psychopaths and violent head-bangers, social misfits who, without turning a hair, would have committed murder (or, at the very least, inflicted serious harm) on anyone hapless enough to get in their way. Throughout history, such brutish men have used threats to control and influence their victims for, while courage is the badge of the hero, menace is the currency of the hard man. It is menace which qualifies a man to operate in the many industries of organized crime featured in this collection: mainly robbery, prostitution and the sale of illegal substances – alcohol on the streets of 1930s Chicago, heroin and crack cocaine in the London and Liverpool of today. So lest we ever confuse the hero and the hard man – as so many films and novels tend to do – consider for a moment how courage springs from virtue. In time of war it inspires the soldier to lay down his life for country, comrades, defence of the weak against the strong. And in a private capacity, where someone intervenes to break up a street brawl or when two prize fighters square up in the ring, courage is underpinned by a sense of fair play, a determination to live by the rules. Menace by contrast is the method of the rule breaker, the man unable or unwilling to control his baser instincts of rage and greed. The Kray twins – Reggie and Ronnie – indulged by their mother Violet, were rendered by nature and nurture incapable of completing the couple of years of National Service mandatory in their day: both were dishonourably discharged from the British Army.

Their aura of menace – as you will read in these pages – is the essential stock-in-trade of the hard man. It promises a willingness to inflict violence divorced from any rules of engagement, disproportionate to any offence, of a type and on a scale usually associated with the maniac. Menace, though, calculates torture and mutilation – usually meted out by the gang against an individual – as a way of securing money, power and influence.

The concept of the hard man is comparatively new; it was not recognized, for example, as recently as 1992 in American criminologist Jay Robert Nash's exhaustive *Dictionary of Crime*, and neither is it known to the *Oxford English Dictionary*. But enter the pages of this collection and discover how menace makes the hard man a distinct category of villain. Journalists and writers who have attended criminal trials down the ages often remark on the surprising ordinariness of many of those who stand in the dock accused of the gravest crimes: puny loners who hang their heads, avoiding eye contact with anyone in the courtroom, perhaps the perpetrators of rape and murder. The hard man, by contrast, retains – even when caged – great physical presence and will meet the curious glance of the reporter with a stare so confident and intense that it forces him or her to drop their gaze. Such brute strength may well have been honed in prison workouts as in the cases of Charles "Crusher" Bronson and Stanley "Tookie" Williams, both featured here.

A lack of conscience and empathy – the characteristics of the psychopath – tend to unite those you will meet in these pages. Look no further than Al Capone – perhaps the most famous – for a paradigm. In 1930, asked for his opinion of the emperor of Prohibition-era Chicago, psychoanalyst Dr William Hickson pointed out that killers like Capone pull the trigger "with no more emotion than is felt by the average man as he says good day to a friend." Like so many others, Capone was anti-social, antagonistic, the product of poor upbringing. And yet he was no hate-filled misfit, prone to random violence, but instead cultivated an image of studied urbanity. The British journalist Kenneth Allsop, who profiles Capone in these pages, writes: "He was also vain, egotistical and cold-hearted, a combination often found in people who practise excessive generosity, for the lavish distribution of gifts and favours is the only way they know to enter into relationships with others, to earn love, and at the same time to provide themselves with a substitute sensation of giving love." In one of the most horrifying incidents in this book, Capone invites three traitors to a feast and turns on them with a baseball bat.

The complete lack of rules of conduct can render the confrontations of the hard men almost comical: in 1950s London, rival villains Billy Hill and Jack Spot clashed more than once. But, in the battle for control of London's underworld, one date has burned itself into gangland lore and legend: on 11 August 1955, at the corner of Old Compton Street and Frith Street, Soho, a fight broke out that would prove the catalyst in the inexorable rise of the brothers Kray. Spot had decided to make an example of one of Hill's henchmen, Albert Dimes, and rumbled him in Soho, punching him on the chin. Dimes darted into a greengrocer's shop; Spot followed and seized a small potato knife, stabbing Dimes in the stomach and thigh. When the greengrocer's wife, a friend of Dimes, smashed a set of scales over Spot's head, Dimes grabbed the knife and stabbed Spot, who reeled out into the street and collapsed. Both men were badly slashed. The fight and its outcome are described here by Hank Janson, one of the era's top pulp writers. Less than a year later, Spot was attacked again; he and his wife were surrounded on the steps of their flat in Hyde Park Mansions by a gang led by "Mad" Frankie Fraser, wielding a shillelagh. With his screaming wife clinging to him, Spot was attacked with razors and knives and was lucky to survive: in hospital he needed 78 stitches and a blood transfusion.

But living with the constant threat of reprisal does require a discipline of sorts: Capone insisted his men stayed at their physical peak. At his Metropole Hotel HQ, reported biographer Fred Pasley, were two rooms equipped with punching bags, horizontal bars, trapezes, rowing machines and other gymnasium devices in which his staff were expected to have regular workouts. "They followed a schedule of training as methodical as that of college football athletes," Pasley said. "Experience had taught him that their professional value, based on that quality commonly described as nerve, was in direct ratio to their physical fitness. It might be only the imperceptible tremor of a trigger-finger, or the slightest wavering of an eye, or a split second of hesitancy at the crucial moment in any of a score of unforeseen emergencies; yet the cost of the lapse would have to be reckoned in lives and money."

Where do they spring from, these hard-nut hoodlums? The hard man can usually be traced back to a deprived environment featuring a dysfunctional, disrupted and insecure family life amid a daily scramble for survival. As forensic psychiatrist Ray Wyre once observed: "I have yet to meet a psychopath from a happy home."

The American gangsters of the Prohibition era were nearly all second-generation immigrants, Sicilian, Italian or Jewish, seeking the "more abundant life". Their parents had often fled oppression and hardship in their native country for the promise of prosperity in the Land of the Free. In Chicago, many found jobs in the stockyards and foundries, and roosted in teeming tenements, divided ethnically into the Jewish quarter, the Irish sector and of course Little Sicily. These slums bred Chicago's tough men, who took their pleasures in the gimcrack dance-halls, saloons, strip-joints, seedy hotels and whorehouses that festered there, just blocks away from tree-lined Lake Shore Drive with its views over Lake Michigan, playground of the city's rich and powerful. Straddling these two worlds were the professional gangsters who ran Chicago's bootlegging, gambling, prostitution and protection rackets. On the thin line dividing them lurked the neighbourhood gangs of roughs and toughs. "Gangland is a phenomenon of human ecology," one Chicago academic observed in 1927, "one manifestation of the economic, moral and cultural frontier." Columnist Max Lerner noted that the racketeer is likely to come up from the slums nursing a warped aspirational drive, "reaching for quick affluence by breaking the windows of the mansion of American success rather than by entering at the door." John Landesco, the author of a 1929 report entitled "Organized Crime in Chicago", agreed that the gangster was "a natural product of his environment". Landesco seldom encountered remorse in gangsterdom. "The welfare, standards and laws of organized society evoke no response in their hearts and minds," he reported. "They seem to have no conception of justice, of laws, and of courts, except as some external superimposed system of oppression, which they must by hook or by crook obstruct and evade."

Hard-case hoodlums often conceal unexpected reserves of native wit and sometimes even intelligence. One cannot help but admire the silky (if sinister) acumen of mobster Meyer Lansky who, while still comparatively young, exchanged the bloodied baseball bat for the business plan. We meet him here in his sun-drenched dotage, execising his Tibetan Shih Tzu named Bruiser on the beach front in Miami, along with his contemporary Tony Accardo, a man with a mind as sharp as his instinct for self-preservation. An admiring rival confided to a columnist that "Accardo has more brains before breakfast than Al Capone ever had all day", and it was his proud boast that he'd never spent a night in jail. And yet Accardo is an exception; most of these hard cases do eventually come unstuck. Someone even bigger, meaner or better organized comes along and poses a challenge or a threat, and since, like most of us, they seek approval from a wider audience beyond the criminal fraternity, they take the interloper on, and not always with success. So many of these self-regarding bombasts are in reality deeply damaged personalities inviting the watching world to hold up a mirror to their deeds, and in their desire to be admired reveal more of themselves than they intended. Al Capone, for example, finally fell foul of Uncle Sam when he was busted for tax evasion.

The 21st-century hard man can trace his ancestors back to the jazz age. In London, gangs and gangsters flourished in the so-called Roaring Twenties. Unscrupulous criminals recognized rich pickings in the holiday years following World War I, with Soho and the West End awash with money, drugs, bottle parties, orgies, nightclubs and gambling dens. Within months of the Armistice, expensive protection rackets were launched, and the vice trade flourished. After the war, a new wave of violent gangs took over the capital's prostitution, illegal betting, protection rackets and, crucially, its drugs trade, with its promise of easy and substantial rewards. Italians, Maltese, Jews and home-grown villains fought for their share of the spoils and, by the time the Krays and Richardson mobs had staked their claim to the East End and south London respectively in the swinging Sixties, crime had tripled. By the end of the century, it had tripled again.

A new breed of bad man appeared in America in the early 1930s. For loners like John Dillinger, Machine Gun Kelly and Clyde Barrow (later joined by Bonnie Parker), their aura of hardness arose from their ability to persuade people – at the point of a gun, of course – to do their bidding, usually by handing over bags of banknotes. Such desperadoes flitted under cover of darkness with a small gang of accomplices, robbing banks before hightailing it to another city, another state. They flourished briefly, between 1931 and 1936, and were confined to the Midwest "Crime Corridor" where the Border Wars of the 1860s had spawned a tradition of outlawry. But now they rode in cars, not on horseback, and they toted Thompson sub-machine guns rather than Colt .44s. In the space of a year Clyde Barrow and his gang had plundered and murdered their way into national notoriety. The couple exemplified the bandits who roamed the rural American landscape in the 1920s and 1930s and who have now disappeared.

These small-scale hoodlums and hayseeds represented the last gasp of the old West. The arrival of the automobile changed American society, creating new opportunities for the criminal. Clyde Barrow's driving skill kept his band free of capture longer than he deserved, for he was not an accomplished robber. The murders which he committed were unnecessary to his purpose and betrayed the mentality of a psychopathic killer. John Dillinger regarded the Barrow gang as bungling amateurs, and viewed their escapades with contempt. Dillinger prided himself as a skilled bank robber who planned his crimes with great care. I have illustrated his technique with an extract from John Toland's *Dillinger Days*, perhaps the best single account of the period, with well-researched material on Dillinger and his contemporaries in crime, including, besides the Barrow gang, Baby Face Nelson, Machine Gun Kelly, Pretty Boy Floyd. (Where do these names come from? As John Kobler pointed out, probably no one ever walked up to Jake Guzik and said, "Hi, Greasy Thumb." Nor did gangsters address each other as "Schemer", "Enforcer", "Potatoes" and the rest, except in films and fiction. Such sobriquets were just the result of games played by journalists. Legend ascribes many of the more picturesque tags to Jim Doherty, the Chicago *Tribune* crime reporter, and Clem Lake, a Chicago *Daily News* rewrite man, who supposedly amused themselves on slow nights by coining them.)

The exploits of the iconic Kray Twins, Ronald and Reginald, inspired a slew of books in the years since their 1969 trial. I have used extracts from the two earliest and best, Brian McConnell's *The Rise and Fall of the Brothers Kray* and John Pearson's *The Profession of Violence*. After the books came a Kray musical (*England, England*), Kray T-shirts, Kray boxer shorts and in 1990 *The Krays* film, starring Gary and Martin Kemp. These days there are various websites too. Reg Kray cashed in handsomely on his notoriety, beginning in 1988 with the publication of *Our Story*, the twins' autobiography, for which the publishers reportedly paid an advance of £100,000. Reg's solo works include *Reg Kray's Book of Slang* (£75,000 advance) and his own life story, *Born Fighter*.

Time has proved their undoing. At the dawn of the 21st century, the gangster – although one of popular culture's favourite figures – is in decline. "The Mob is probably in the worst shape it's ever been since the 1930s," reports Stephen Fox, author of *Blood and*

Power: Organized Crime in 20th Century America, and the Italian-American Mob's once-vital empires are crumbling. In America, enforcement of government statutes, a concerted federal crack-down on organized crime, and increased outside competition, has immobilized much of the Mafia's powerbase. John Gotti and Carmine Persico, unable to manage their organizations from prison, appointed their sons as family bosses and watched help-lessly as the next generation's inability to lead created disastrous internal dissent in two of New York's top Mob families. In the ultimate act of Mafia heresy, the head of a Philadelphia family broke the law of *omerta* by turning federal witness – becoming the highest-ranking American Mafia member to defect. The writing is on the wall: Dons who once seemed impervious to the law cannot withstand the vigilant pressure of state and federal officials. And along with the collapse of *omerta* as a culture, technology has penetrated the silence surrounding hard men and their activities. In the UK, some experts consider the hard man a threatened species, throwbacks to a bygone era. Scots lawyer Joe Beltrami has argued that "hard men may have been regarded in the past as 'bonny fechters [fighters]', and admired. Nowadays, they would be dismissed as hoodlums with a high pain threshold."

It's said that some hard men are simply the products of their moment in time and place: Jimmy Boyle, for instance, always argued that he had to be as he was to survive the badlands that were the Gorbals. People often say the same about those involved in sectarian violence in Northern Ireland and, although it is probably true for some, for others sectarianism offers a political front, and a useful ready-made organization, for villainy. Johnny "Mad Dog" Adair falls into this latter category. Some speculate that, had these individuals been born into wealthy homes, they may have become boardroom villains, the kind who asset-strip and sack people with no vestige of conscience. Sadly, few attractive characters have flocked to the ranks of history's hard men. (Longy Zwillman, known as the "Al Capone of New Jersey" was a good-looking guy but his favourite party trick was to produce from his wallet a pubic hair belonging to Jean Harlow, with whom he'd had a hot affair.) And yet these largely unsavoury, anti-social misfits force them-selves on our attention by sheer power of personality, their ulti-mate fate, like the one predicted for Al Capone, to be romanticized like many a pirate king. Let's meet them.

Mafia Hitman
(*Joey Black*)

David Fisher

Hard men don't come any harder than the professional killer. The man known here as "Joey Black" was a journeyman Jewish hitman whose story includes detailed accounts of what might be called his greatest hits, his chillingly "professional" murders of thirty-eight victims. As well as his career as a hired assassin, Joey was a numbers king and loan shark who in the early 1970s collaborated with writer David Fisher to lay out the rackets in gripping detail. His tone is strikingly matter-of-fact, regular-guy. On The Godfather: *". . . Actually very few mob members even have Bronx-Italian accents . . . a lot of mob people are not very tough, the people we meet and deal with are very ordinary, most of us stay home at night and watch TV, and we only shoot each other when absolutely necessary." Joey might have been the original Soprano. In 2002 David Fisher revealed Joey's identity and the incredible story of how Joey finally died. David Fisher is the author of some 40 books, including* Gracie: A Love Story *(with George Burns) and* Been There, Done That *(with Eddie Fisher).*

I've dabbled in just about every area of crime, but my specialty, the thing I do best, is kill people. I am to mob rubouts what Leonard Bernstein is to music. I am one of the most feared killers in the United States today. I'm proud of that reputation; I've worked long hours and in dangerous places to earn it.

I don't make that claim braggingly, but truthfully. I have sent 38 deserving men to their early graves. I can remember each man that I hit. I can give you the order. The details. Even the weather on the day I made the hit. Number 18, for example, was a gambler who was discovered informing on the mob. He had been arrested quietly and made a deal in order to keep himself out of a jackpot. Certain things began to kick back, and some people checked and found out my man was the source, so he had to go. I caught him in a small bar and I just walked in and blasted him with a .38. It was dark, and I was wearing a dark shirt and dark pants and when I started shooting everybody scrambled for cover. I remember him. I remember them all. You never really forget.

But it doesn't bother me, not one bit. This is my job. It is my business. I shoot people and that's it. I never think in terms of morality, although that may be hard for a lot of people to believe. I know the difference between right and wrong. By most standards of morality what I do would be considered wrong. But this doesn't bother me. I also know the difference between eating and starving. Between having a new pair of shoes and stuffing newspapers in an old pair to keep my feet from freezing. Believe me, I know.

So I don't worry about it. Because I have the ability to pull the trigger I can do what I like to do, go where I want to go, live comfortably, eat well, be what I want to be. I have no second thoughts. No recriminations. I don't even think about it because, if I did, and if I was an emotional person, I could not live with it. It would destroy me. So I do my job like a guy lays brick, a guy tends bar, a guy cuts hair.

At home, I'm not really that much different from your average bricklayer, bartender or barber. I take out the garbage four nights a week, worry about my wife when she's out alone at night, clean the outside windows every few months and complain about those ridiculously high telephone bills. Believe it or not, I'm a human being. I laugh at funny jokes, I love children around the house and I can spend hours playing with my mutt. Only one thing, I never cry during sad movies. I've only cried for one person in my life, my first wife. The day I found out she had been killed, I cried. Then I changed. So my eyes weren't even damp at the end of *Love Story*.

I've had my chances to get out of the business. One night, in I think 1966, my wife and I were driving back from spending the weekend with some relatives and there was a car pulled over to the side of the road. Regardless of my profession, when I see somebody in trouble, I stop. I pulled over, took my cannon out of the glove compartment and handed it to my wife. "If there's anything wrong," I said, "just pull the trigger."

There was a woman sitting alone in the front seat, and her husband, who turned out to be a well-known, very wealthy businessman, was sitting in back with his leg in a cast. He had broken it so he was helpless, and she didn't know the first thing about cars. I couldn't get their car going, so we drove them back to town. This guy asked for my phone number and, when I told him I didn't give it out, he gave me his card and asked me to call him.

About three days later I did call, and he invited me to his club for lunch. We really got along well, and when he asked me what I did for a living I told him straight out. "You're too nice a guy to be in that business," he told me. "How would you like to work for me?" He offered me good money, and I almost said yes. But I finally turned him down because I knew I would go out of my mind. So I stayed in the old business, doing the same old thing, killing people.

There are three things you need to kill a man: the gun, the bullets and the balls. A lot of people will point a gun at you, but they haven't got the courage to pull the trigger. It's as simple as that. I would give you odds on almost anybody you name that, if I put a gun in his hand, he would not pull the trigger. I mean, some people will go ape for one minute and shoot, but there are very few people who are capable of thinking about, planning and then doing it. To carry out an execution with the cold knowledge of what you're doing, you have to believe in nothing but yourself. That I do.

I killed my first man when I was 16 years old. The hit was offered to me by a mob guy who protected the numbers organization I worked for. The thought of killing a man had never occurred to me before. I had been a violent person and I had laid guys out, but actually killing a man just hadn't entered my mind. I was sitting on a stoop one day, and he walked over and sat down next to me. Very casually, without even looking at me, he asked if I was interested in making a hit.

I stared at him and said, "You got to be kidding." He said he was serious. I said, "You must have fifty guys that can do the same job."

He nodded. "We understand that. Just let me know tonight."

At some point you become a man or you fade. For me, this was the point. I had to make the decision whether I wanted to be dirt or accomplish something. I was very young, but I decided I wasn't going to be a piece of shit. I wasn't going to let people walk all over me. I was going to be a man.

So when he came back that night I told him okay. I had no idea what the guy I was going to kill had done. I was handed a gun, and this guy was pointed out to me. He could have been anybody; once I made the decision I knew I would stick to it. I had to plan the job myself and I wasn't too damned thorough. I waited for him one night. When I saw him on the street I just walked up behind him and blew the top of his head off. He was dead before he hit the sidewalk. Then I turned and walked away. I didn't run, I walked.

I had to get rid of the gun, but I didn't know exactly how. The first thing I did was go back to my apartment and get a little saw and I sawed the gun barrel into four quarters. Then I took the gun and the shells and got on the subway. I rode it all the way down into lower Manhattan, the Wall Street area, and I started throwing the shells down the sewers. I wasn't taking any chances, one shell to one sewer. When I finished doing that I went over to the river and heaved the pieces of the gun as far as I could. Then I went home and went to bed.

I never really got to sleep. I just tossed and turned for a few hours, going over the whole thing in my mind about a hundred times, making sure I didn't make any mistakes. I held my breath for about two days until I was positive there were no witnesses. Nothing happened.

Then the realization came to me that I was a made individual. I was a force to be reckoned with. A lot of people who had looked at me as being a snot-nosed wise-ass kid would now be speaking to me in different tones. The job paid $5,000. Five thousand dollars! It seemed like a billion. My older brother was working ten hours a day in a warehouse and bringing home $24 a week. Five thousand dollars, that's how it started.

Contrary to legend, there is no great celebration after you make your first hit. I mean, nobody throws a party for you or anything. But you are made. The word is out very quickly that you are a capable individual. That you are a heavyweight, a gunsel, a torpedo, a cannon, a hit man, a boy who will do the job. In *The Godfather* they said, "Make your bones." Now I never heard that before, but it has the same meaning.

After this first hit my career was interrupted by the army, which taught me the proper way to handle a gun – I beg your pardon, a weapon. They taught us this rhyme I remember. You had to hold your rifle and point one finger at your prick and repeat, "This is my weapon [the rifle], this is my gun [the prick], one is for shooting, one is for fun." My only problem was I never could figure out which was for which.

After I got separated from the service I kicked around in New York for a while and then went out to California and began working for Jack Dragna. Jack knew I was a wild man, but he didn't know how wild. He wanted to test me and offered me a hit.

"Sure," I told him, "why not?" After my experience in Korea I figured what difference would another guy or two make. I never did find out what number two had done either. Jack just showed me his picture and handed me a gun. He told me what kind of car this guy drove, gave me his license-plate number and explained that the guy always collected some payoffs in a certain shopping center on Monday afternoons.

The following Monday afternoon I drove over there in a stolen car and found his car parked towards the back of the parking lot. I found a spot almost directly across from his car and pulled in. I got out and sat on the trunk of my car for almost three hours, doing nothing but watching for him and listening to a transistor radio. Nobody paid any attention to me; for all anybody knew I was waiting for my wife. Finally I saw him walking down the aisle toward his car. I looked around and there wasn't another person within 70 yards. Lucky for me – unlucky for him. If I had seen anybody else I would have got in my car and trailed him and waited for another opportunity. I waited until he started to edge between his car and the car parked next to him, then I took a few steps across the driving lane and hit him. Nobody saw him go down. I put three bullets in him, then I got in my own car and drove away.

There are many reasons an individual is killed: He may be a stool pigeon, he may be too greedy, the man he is working for might suspect he is taking too much, the man he is working for might think he is too ambitious, he might be blown away because he has not lived up to an agreement he made, the job might be planned by an underling trying to take over from a boss, the target could be a mob member who has become a junkie and is therefore unreliable, it might be part of a gang war and it could even be payment for an attempted double cross. There is always a good reason and it always involves doing something you shouldn't be doing as a member of organized crime.

Innocent people, civilians, are very rarely hit. You recently saw the reason for that in New York City. You had half a battalion of mob guys killed after the Colombo-Gallo business and nobody did much of anything. But when two innocent meat salesmen in a restaurant were mistaken for mob men and killed accidentally, the commissioner almost declared martial law.

We leave civilians alone. We don't hurt them and we don't work for them. As a matter of fact, if a civilian wants to buy a hit he might be able to get someone who has done a few, but I doubt he could get anyone connected with the mob. Chances are, whoever he got, the civilian would just be taken for his money. The hit will never be made. What's he gonna do about it? Who's he gonna complain to?

Mob guys very rarely take outside work because they can't trust civilians. The police lean on a civilian and he is going to fold. He has never been battered by questions, he has never been mentally assaulted, so he's gonna quit on you. The police are experts, they can turn you up one side and down the other with their questions. And who needs to depend on a civilian?

Not me. And not any professional hit man that I know. I just don't want to mess with your so-called honest citizens. As a rule you just can't trust them.

I did come close once. Tony Bender asked me to see a civilian about doing a job for him. Tony had done me some favors, so I said I would. The civilian was a wealthy New York City socialite type. I figured maybe somebody was leaning on him businesswise. Generally civilians want other civilians hit to settle personal scores, and I certainly don't want to get involved in that. But this guy didn't want that, he wanted a broad hit in the head. I found it very unusual for a man to want a girl killed so I asked him about it. He said he had been shacking up with her and things were getting complicated.

Before giving him an answer I started doing a little investigating on my own. I found out the reason he wanted her hit in the head was that she had the nerve to get pregnant on him. I figured maybe she wanted a lot of money, but I was wrong. All she wanted was to make sure the kid was properly cared for. She didn't want no big amount of money, she wasn't looking to shake him down and she didn't want to get involved with the Social Register. Two hundred and fifty dollars a month for the kid was what she wanted. My blue-blooded friend was terrified someone would find out about

the baby and it would embarrass his family. After considering the
facts I decided I did not like this socialite's idea of the proper way
to treat children.

I went back and I told the guy, "I am going to give you some
very bad news. For one, you're gonna give this girl friend of yours
one hundred thousand dollars. And then you're gonna give her two
hundred and fifty a month until that kid is old enough to take care
of itself. And if you don't, motherfucker, I'm gonna put a bullet in
your head and I'm gonna let the whole world know why you got
killed." He went running to see Tony Bender. Tony told him he
couldn't interfere. Actually he could've, but he didn't want to.
This guy finally gave her the money. She eventually found out the
story and what I did for her. After that she left town and had the
kid. Today she is married and lives out in the Midwest. I heard
from her a couple of times, but I'm a part of her life she would
rather forget.

But you see the problem you get into when you deal with
civilians. I like to stick to my own. It's easier.

Every hit begins with a contract. If you're working indepen-
dently, as I usually do, the people who need your services get in
touch with you. A meeting is set up, and details are discussed. I'm
told what the job entails and how much it pays and occasionally
what the beef is. I'm not told who the party is, but that's not
important. The details will probably give me a good idea who he
might be, but I will very rarely ask for a name until I decide to take
the job. If I figure I might know the man, or the people he hangs
with, I'll probably say "pass". If I figure it's okay I'll do business.
On certain jobs I'm told who it is right away, like with Joey Gallo,
for instance, because the word was out all over anyway.

There is no set price for a hit. It depends on who the man is, how
difficult the job and what the results (who will gain what) will be. It
usually averages anywhere between $10,000 and $25,000 and could
go higher. The largest contract I've ever heard of was an open offer
of $250,000 payable to anyone who could get to Joe Valachi. But
nobody would take the job. If the mob could have gotten to Valachi
nobody would ever talk to the police again because it would have
completely destroyed the confidence of anybody who thought
about becoming an informer. (There's a story that Valachi was
causing problems in prison and word was sent to Attorney General
Bobby Kennedy. "Tell him to stop it," Kennedy supposedly said,
"or we'll let him go.") The most I've ever been offered was

$50,000 and I've been offered that a few times. That was the price I was quoted on Joey Gallo.

A contract is always a verbal agreement, but these contracts are as strong as any written agreement in the world. You don't have to sign a paper, you're guaranteeing it with your own life.

The money is paid in advance. The full amount. After the contract is out, the man who put it out can rescind it, but none of his money will be returned. Once I take your money I'm going to make the hit – unless you tell me you've changed your mind. That's fine, but you pay the full amount for that privilege.

There is a guarantee in the contract covering the unlikely situation that I'm caught. I will not talk. Not a word. Not a sound. Not a peep. In order to ensure that, the party with whom I've made my deal must pay all legal fees, support my family the entire time I'm in jail, and have something waiting for me the day I get out. When I came out of the Tombs (that's the Manhattan House of Detention) after sitting there for almost a full year, I was handed $50,000 for keeping my mouth shut.

That may sound like a lot of money, but it's worth it to the mob. Knowing my family is being supported and I'm earning while I'm sitting, there's no reason for me to talk. The only alternative the mob has is to try to kill me and that's stupid because, if they did, no professional would ever work for them again. Amateurs, like Jerome Johnson who shot Joe Colombo, don't get this sort of deal because no one has any doubts that, when caught, they would reveal everything. Their payment is inevitably a bullet in the head. But amateurs are very rarely used.

If you happen to be a full-time employee of a particular organization, rather than a freelancer, the contract procedure is a little different. If you're on salary and they tell you somebody has got to go, he goes. Makes no difference who he is and how close the two of you might be. He's gone. A new soldier for that big organization in the sky.

Under any circumstances, if I take your money the job is going to be done unless you decide differently. Once I take a penny, I've guaranteed that contract will be fulfilled. And so I want to make sure it gets done quickly and correctly. That's where experience comes in.

Planning a hit is not difficult. There are only a few simple rules you have to be aware of: you do not kill a man in his own home; you do not kill a man in front of his own family; you do not harm his family; you do not hit him in a church or near a church or any other place of worship; you do not torture a man (we're not his judges, just his executioners); and you do not rob him. Other than that, he's all yours.

There are three basic ways to plan a hit. The hit man will be given his intended's routine, or he'll study the man and pick up his routine himself, or the party will be brought to him at a preselected spot. I like to do as much as possible myself. I like being in total control and I'll spend as much time as necessary making sure everything is exactly the way I want it. I once clocked a man for ten days before I hit him. This guy was a numbers controller who was fingering other controllers to be robbed. He used to park his car in a gas station overnight, and I decided that the gas station would be the place. I waited in my car, which I parked in a shadow, until he showed up. When he did I walked up to his car. He didn't realize what was about to happen until I pulled the cannon. Then he realized – I'm gonna die. He started to beg, but I didn't give him a chance to get five words out of his mouth. He knew why, and it wasn't my job to sit there and give him a lecture. That gas station was the perfect spot: closed, quiet and dark.

The safest way is to have the party brought to you. If I'm told the hit is being set up this way, I get to the location early and check it out carefully. If I'm not completely satisfied with it I may not do the job. After all, it's my head in the noose. I got sent to St Louis once on a loan. They had the thing all lined up and needed an outside gun. When I got there, I said, "You guys don't mind if I take a couple of days and see if I go along with the plan, do you?" I wouldn't care if the FBI had checked it out in advance, I wanted to check it myself. They agreed, and I found their schedule was perfect and the spot they picked likewise. Only then did I agree to pull the trigger.

After you're satisfied that the proper plans have been made you can begin the execution. There are actually very few preparations that have to be made. I normally get the gun I'm going to use as soon as I agree to take the job. The gun can come from anywhere. It might be stolen off the docks or I might get a hot gun from a friend. There is a tremendous market in hot guns. Wherever I get it, the first thing I'll do is file the serial number off to make it as untraceable as possible.

If there is any chance people will see me leaving after I've done the job, I'll use a stolen car. I'll steal the car myself two or three days before the day I'm going to make the hit and just stash it away. I'll check it over carefully to make sure it's going to start when I need it to start, and if the battery looks the slightest bit worn I'll put a new one in.

Up until the time I intend to make the actual hit, my day will be very normal. I'll give you an example.

A mob guy dealing narcotics had started using them himself. He had turned himself into an addict, and the man he worked for wanted him eliminated. I agreed to do the job.

His boss gave me a pretty good idea of what his schedule was like, and I followed him for a few days just to verify my information and pick the spot. He did different things each night but always ended up at this girl's apartment. She lived in a brownstone way over in the West Forties, which is a good area to make a hit because it's dark and, in the winter, when this all took place, there are few people on the street late at night. He also parked his car in front of the same fire hydrant every night.

I got up about 11:30 the morning the job was going to be done. I made myself some coffee, and my wife and I sat down to watch the television program "Jeopardy", which is one of my favorite shows. If they would let me go on as a contestant I could win a lot of money. The only categories my wife can beat me in are "show business" and "literature".

After "Jeopardy" ended I went to a pool hall and spent most of the afternoon shooting with a buddy of mine. My days aren't what you call structured. I really never know what I'm going to be doing; it depends on what I feel like. I might go to the track, go bowling, play cards, visit some friends, see a broad. I might even stay home. But it was cold outside, so I stayed in and shot pool.

From there I went to a small Italian restaurant in the East Village named Sonny's and had dinner with some friends. I left there about 9:30 and just drove around the city till about midnight. I went over the plan in my mind a few times, but I didn't really concentrate on it. Sometimes when I've got a job to do I'll spend the night at home watching television or even go to a movie, but this night I just felt like driving. I did stop in a few different places to say hello to some friends, but I didn't stay anywhere very long.

Finally I drove up to this block and parked about three car lengths behind the fire hydrant. I looked for his car and it wasn't there, so I knew he hadn't shown up early. I have had people do that on me, which earns them an extra night of living. The only things I brought with me were a transistor radio, a thermos of coffee and a blanket. I use the transistor because I don't want to run down the battery of the car. I rarely mind the cold because it keeps you awake and alert, but the blanket is there in case it really freezes up.

This guy showed up right on time. I saw him coming in my rear-view mirror and I kind of laid down across the front seat so he wouldn't see me. While he was parking I slid out of my car and hid so he didn't see me and take off. When he turned his engine off I began the casual walk toward his car. I hit him in the head as he started to get out. Two bullets. I knew he was dead.

I walked back to my car and drove home. I was asleep within half an hour.

I usually work alone, but when you're just starting out in this line of work a backup man is normally sent along to make sure everything goes correctly. Once you're established you go out by yourself or, at worst, with a single driver. The only exception is when you're hitting someone in a crowded area and you think there is a chance you might be chased. Then you use a getaway car and a crash car. The crash car is set up to block traffic after the job is done and, if somebody tries to follow you, to "accidentally" crash into them. Under any circumstances you're only going to use the getaway car to go a few blocks. Then, depending on where you are, you're going to get out of your vehicle and lose yourself as quickly as you can in a crowd, or take some public transportation, or ride a cab, or even take another car that you have waiting.

The most important thing is to try to isolate your victim. I may be sitting in his car waiting for him and as soon as he gets in I'll blast him, or I may have made arrangements for him to be picked up by someone he trusts and brought to a destination where I'll be waiting. If possible, it's best to catch him late at night. But catching him alone is really the important thing because, if you don't, innocent people might get hurt and you don't want that, no way.

I've never had a problem with innocent people because I've always been very careful about picking my spots. But if I was on a job and an innocent person got in the way, he would have to go. I know I wouldn't feel too good about doing it, but I know I'd kill him anyway. It's part of being a professional. Other people don't take as much care as I do. Little Augie Pisano, for example, was with a girl when he received a phone call and was told to come to a meeting. The jerk brought the girl with him. Now it is a clear violation of the rules to bring a civilian with you to any business meeting. So, when he showed up, his killers were waiting for him. They had no choice – the girl had to go too. And she did.

Sometimes, though, it's almost impossible to get a guy alone. Maybe he has too many bodyguards, or maybe he's very careful. Then you have to hit him in public. On a job like this the important thing is to be cool. If you're careful there is actually very little to worry about. I've walked into restaurants in which my man was sitting and I've calmly walked over and calmly pulled the trigger and then I turned around and calmly walked out. I didn't run. I just make sure, in a situation like this, that I use a gun that's going to make a lot of noise because I want everybody in that place diving under tables. I was fortunate enough to see the police report on number 14, which I did in a restaurant. I was described by 11 different people in 11 different ways . . . and not one of them was totally accurate.

Like every professional hit man I've ever known, I've always used a gun. Always. All 38 times. I am a good shot and I know where I'm going to hit you and you are going to die. No one has lived yet. I have steady hands, a sharp eye – I don't wear glasses – and a great amount of confidence.

I prefer to use a.38 revolver whenever possible because it's not too big and I know it's not going to jam unless I have a bad cartridge in there or the hammer's busted, and I always check to make sure this is not the case. If I catch the guy by himself I use a silencer. That way the gun doesn't make any loud noises, just a small *pfffttt*. You always try to catch a guy in the head with your first shot because that ends the argument quickly.

A magnum, which is a very big gun, is nice to have around if you're putting down a revolution, but you're not going to use it in my work because it's too heavy and you need fluidity when you're doing a job. It's also not that accurate a weapon because, when you pull the trigger, you get a severe kickback. If you hold it at hip level when you fire, by the time you get through you'll be pointing at the sky.

At one point drowning was a popular way of killing people, but no more. Why go through all the trouble of taking somebody and dragging them to a spot where there is water and then drowning them when you can shoot them much more easily? Because you want it to look like an accident? Bullshit! You *don't* want it to look like an accident! You want people to know why a guy was hit. It serves as a warning to others.

The weapon I carry every day was especially made for me by a friend who is an excellent mechanic. (A mechanic is our term used to describe anybody who is great at anything.) It's a "gun" about two and one-half inches in length and about an inch wide. It's about half an inch thick and, in general, looks just like a cigarette lighter. It is actually a trigger mechanism. I have buck-shot cartridges that have been designed for this weapon. I simply screw the cartridges in and pull the trigger and, at 30 feet or less, I can make a long-division problem out of you. I can have cartridges made up for any bullet I want. As far as I know there are only about five weapons like this in existence, all made by my friend. They're great guns because there is absolutely no recoil and no markings are left on the slug or shot.

I've heard of people who have used knives, hatchets and ice-picks, who'll strangle you and garrotte you, and every once in a while someone'll use something exotic like a blowtorch. I've also heard of one guy who uses garlic. He rubs the bullets he's going to use with it. This guarantees that his target is going to die – if the bullets don't get him, the garlic will cause a slow, agonizing death by blood poisoning. I've also been told of one guy left hanging on a meat hook for three days until he died, and another guy who was heated slowly with an iron, but I don't go in for anything like that. I don't want to spend that much time with my targets, I don't want to watch them suffer. That's not my job. Of course, some people have different tastes. A midwestern hit man used alcohol and a truck. His target was a stool pigeon, and the organization did not want the police to know they were on to this guy. The guy was a heavy drinker to begin with, so the hit man and his driver kidnapped him and brought him to a small apartment. They put a gun at his head and a glass of whiskey in his hand. "Drink," the hit man said, and the target did. He kept drinking until he was completely drunk. Then they brought him down to the highway, parked his car nearby and pushed him in front of a truck. Even if the police suspected anything there was nothing they could prove.

Lately I've been hearing about a new weapon. It's a certain type of gas that you spray in someone's face. Not only does it kill him immediately, it leaves the same after effects as a heart attack. I got a hunch the two men who were involved in the trial of Newark Mayor Hugh Addonizio were killed this way. It's very strange that two important witnesses should die of heart attacks behind the wheel of their cars within a short time of each other.

I'm a traditionalist. I like using a gun. I feel comfortable with it. I doubt I would ever use anything else because I don't like to get too close to my man. I'm not looking to be sophisticated, I'm looking to do a job and not get caught, and so I never get closer than two or three feet.

Hell, if I'm within two or three feet of him, he's dead. It's important to set it up so the guy never really has a chance to move or try to protect himself or run away. The furthest I've ever had to chase a guy was about 30 yards and that was someone else's fault. This guy was brought out to a field in the middle of nowhere. He thought he was going to a business meeting. The idiot driver let him get out of the car before I was ready; he saw me and took off. I chased him on foot and, when I got close enough, I pumped four bullets into him. End of story.

He was one of the few who had that much time. Very few of the 38 ever knew what was about to hit them. I was the last thing they ever saw. I never said a word to any of them. What am I going to say? A lot of times you'll get ready to hit a man and he'll realize briefly what's happening and make the sign of the cross, or he'll start screaming, "No!" But before he can get too much of anything out it's usually all over.

Let me give you an example of a perfect hit. Number 27. At the time I was working for a particular organization, and it was decided that a man was going to die because he had become too ambitious. He was trying to move up too quickly. I was contacted and told there was a contract I was to fulfill. I had no choice in the matter. The price, I was told over pizza, was $20,000.

"Do I set up my own deal or do you set it up for me?" I asked. My employer told me I was on my own, and I began studying my man. I took about a week and by the end of it I knew what time he left his house, where he went, who he saw, what business he conducted on what days and, finally, who he was sleeping with. I noticed that this man continually drove through an isolated area and I studied this area carefully, trying to find a good quiet spot where I could pick him off. I couldn't find exactly what I wanted so I looked for another place.

I discovered he had a girlfriend who he visited on the nights he made his gambling collections, and I picked one of these nights. I used a driver but I made sure he parked about a block away so he couldn't actually see what I was doing. That way he couldn't testify to a single thing. He wasn't about to hear the shots because I was working with a silencer.

When my target came out of his girlfriend's house about six in the morning, I was standing there leaning against a lamppost. I hit him as he walked to his car. Three shots and he went down. I walked over and put another one in the back of his head. My driver dropped me off at my own car and I got in and drove home. The first thing I did that morning was get rid of the gun.

Most professional hits are similar to that one. The only time it's really different, as I said, is when a boss is involved. There are two ways to kill a boss. The easy way is to get to his bodyguard or the top man in his organization and make a deal with him.

Now the tougher way. If the bodyguard does not agree to the hit he has to go too. I was working for Meyer Lansky at one point, and some representatives of Vito Genovese invited me to a meeting. They had decided that Meyer was to be hit. An offer was made and I said no thank you. Maybe some people don't, but I believe in being loyal to an individual who helps you earn. But by saying no I made myself a target.

The only reason I wasn't killed right on the spot, after I turned them down, was because I had a gun in my hand. Whenever I go to meet somebody on business I always wear a pair of pants in which the pocket has been cut out and I can reach through to a gun I have strapped to the inside of my leg. In this particular instance we were sitting in a restaurant, me with my back to the wall. After I said no the guy said, "I'm sorry to hear that."

I pulled my cannon out and laid it on the table. "Now why is that?" I asked. He said, "We'll be seeing you," and got up and left. I made one mistake after that – I didn't tell Meyer. It almost cost me my life, but I thought I could handle it.

I couldn't. I was coming out of a bank in Miami Beach and three guys opened up on me. It's a very strange thing to be hit by a bullet. For a second there is a tremendous burning sensation, then shock takes over. Then you go into what I would call limbo – everything moves in sort of slow motion. You can feel the impact, but not the pain, when you're hit again, but you're not exactly sure what you're doing. That's when your reflexes take complete control. The next thing I remember, I had a gun in my hand and I was using it. I remember hitting one guy and seeing his head explode. I remember shooting the second guy. I never saw the third guy, he took off.

The lawyer I had gone to the bank with managed to get me into a cab. The next thing I knew I was lying on a slab in a warehouse and a doctor was cutting bullets out of me. One week later I was on a boat to Brazil where I stayed, well supported, for almost a year. So they didn't get me and they didn't get Meyer.

A few years later I was sitting in an Italian restaurant and a man walked up to me and said, "You don't know me, but I was almost your executioner." This was the third man. We talked about it. I understood. Business is business.

Normally a boss is very careful where he goes and rarely travels without a bodyguard. One mistake is all any good hit man needs. I'll give you an example. I was out in California recently and I went to visit a friend of mine who has a bakery shop. Whenever I'm out there I go see him because he's probably the only person west of the Mississippi who makes good cannoli. Of course, I'm not the only guy who knows this.

We talked in his back room for a little while, and then I got up to leave. As I walked out from the back of the place who's standing by himself at the counter but one of the biggest mob bosses in the country. He took one look at me and his face went white. His eyes opened to about the size of a silver dollar. I looked at him and smiled. "Take it easy, babe," I said. "If I was here to see you, you wouldn't have seen me." Then I reached under the counter, handed him a chocolate-chip cookie and walked out. I guarantee you he won't go to the bathroom by himself for the next five years.

In any case, whoever the victim, the first thing you do after making a hit is dispose of the weapon. Once the weapon is out of your hands, and can't be traced back to you, it's almost impossible to get pinned with a crime. No weapon, no murder raps. I break up every gun that I don't leave on the spot. I have a friend who has a little machine shop and he takes the gun and melts it down. Or I'll bring it to a junkyard and flip it into one of the compressors. Good-bye, gun. As soon as the barrel is destroyed you're safe. Once that's gone there is no way of matching the bullet to the gun.

As I said, sometimes I leave the gun right on the spot. I'll do this if it's a stolen weapon and it's completely clean. There's really nothing to worry about. The handle of the gun has ridges and won't pick up fingerprints (unless you're stupid enough to use something like a pearl-handled revolver and if you do you deserve to get caught). The hammer has ridges too, and there is always a line right down the middle of the trigger. Sometimes I'll wipe the gun anyway, just to be certain, because fingerprints can kill you. One guy blasted a target with a shotgun and left the shotgun there. Fine, except he also left fingerprints on it, so his employers decided he had to go too. Can't have him being traced back and caught, because then it gets too hot for the people who hired him.

After I make a hit, and get rid of the gun, I follow my regular schedule. I remember going directly from a hit to a wedding reception. I just forget about it.

One thing I never do is plan an alibi in advance. To me that is really stupid because, by planning, you've got to get other people involved. If you ask them to front for you they know you're going to be doing something. But if I do the job right, who's gonna know I'm there? If I have to I can always set up an alibi. I can get 18 guys to swear they were playing cards with me. Or I can get the owner of some restaurant or movie theater who owes me a favor to swear I was there. No problems.

The police don't usually bother you too much. Number one, a cop is not going to knock his brains out on a mob hit because history shows they are not going to be able to get corroborating testimony, even if they know who did the job, which they do in a lot of so far "unsolved" cases. Don't underestimate the police. They do a good job. But when a mob guy is hit by another mob guy . . . well, let's say they're not overly disappointed and don't work as hard as they might under other circumstances.

You can almost forget about witnesses. There have been very few people willing to testify in cases involving organized-crime members. Not so much because they tend to disappear, but because your average individual is a family person and he is terrified someone in his family will get hurt if he gets involved. And, second, he's just not that socially conscious. They think just like the cops, what the hell, he only killed another gangster, what's the difference. Let 'em all kill one another.

Who can blame them? The newspapers, television, movies, magazines and books have done our job for us. The newspapers in particular love to turn simple rubouts into full-scale pitched battles. I personally never check the papers after I've done a job. There is no reason for me to, I'm not interested in the publicity, and I decided a long time ago it would be a poor idea for me to keep a scrapbook. Besides, the event the papers report is not going to have too much in common with the one I remember. I quit looking after my fourth hit. It was simple and quick, I just put three bullets in the guy from close range. The papers made it sound like a whole platoon of hit men had ventilated him with submachine guns. They didn't even have the number of bullets right.

All that the communications media have succeeded in doing is scaring the hell out of people. Let me ask you a question: After seeing *The Godfather*, would you testify against Don Corleone? Shit. After seeing *The Godfather*, would you even testify against Marlon Brando?

Even when the occasional silly soul comes along and claims he has seen a crime being committed, he usually changes his thinking before the trial begins. That is exactly what happened to me – but before the witnesses realized their mistake I spent almost a year in the Tombs in New York.

The district attorney claimed he had two witnesses who had seen me pull the trigger. They were a man and a woman in their late twenties and they had been parked in the shadows near the docks making out.

Four cops came to my door to arrest me. They stood right there in the hallway and read me my constitutional rights. My wife didn't take the whole thing very seriously at first. "Now what have you done?" she kind of scolded.

"Nothing," I said. "I don't know what these gentlemen are talking about." The only person I ever discussed this with was my attorney. I sat in the Tombs for almost a year, and we finally went to trial. Amazingly enough, the DA couldn't produce his witnesses. He asked the judge for 24 hours to produce them.

The next day he came into court and he was fuming. "Your honor, the witnesses have disappeared. But the state believes the defendant had something to do with their disappearance!"

"Your honor," my attorney protested, "my client has been sitting in jail for almost one full year. He could not possibily have had anything to do with the disappearance of the DA's alleged witnesses. We're ready to go to trial. If the state isn't ready to proceed, after all this time, we ask that you dismiss the charges." Case dismissed.

I don't know what happened to the witnesses. All I can guess is they had a sudden attack of honesty and decided to go on a long vacation.

Witnesses sometimes need help to understand that things aren't always what they appear to be. In 1963 I was hired to provide that help.

A man claimed he had seen a member of a particular organization shoot down a guy in cold blood. The police put him under full protection: a squad car outside his apartment building, a cop in the lobby and a third cop in his living room. I was offered $20,000 to prove to him that the cops couldn't protect him.

I watched his place for a few days and made my move one night. Dark, no moon. I didn't want to use the fire escape because I couldn't take the chance on making noise and having someone look out their window. So I went to the roof of another building on the block and climbed across to his roof. I brought a rope – with plenty of knots tied in it to rest my feet on – and a grappling hook. I dug that hook into the roof and lowered myself down. It was only two stories.

This was in the middle of the summer and his window was wide open. I climbed in very quietly. Then I put one hand over his mouth and put my gun in my other hand, and shook him gently. "Don't make a move or a sound," I said. "There's a cop right outside your door and if he comes in here you're both gonna die. All I want to do is show you that the cops can't stop us. Wherever you go, whatever you do, we're gonna find you. We don't want to hurt you, but we think you should consider it carefully before you squeal on our mutual friend. Just do the right thing by him and you won't get hurt, I promise you. Now I'm gonna leave you. You go back to sleep. If you make a sound and I get caught, you're dead." Then I climbed back up the rope and went home.

We didn't want to kill him because that would have created a lot of heat for us. It worked out very well, he just had a sudden loss of memory. I made $20,000 and I didn't even have to pull the trigger.

Neither witnesses nor informers are hurt unless they have to be. Abe Reles, who informed on Murder, Inc., had to be. He just knew too much. He was supposedly under police protection when he "fell" out of a window and was killed. The story was that he had tried to get away from the police by tying sheets together and climbing out. The mob got to somebody and he was thrown right out the window. I assume the police who were supposedly guarding him were paid a great deal of money.

One stool pigeon who died was Arnold Shuster, the kid who fingered Willie Sutton. Arnold just had a case of bad luck. Nobody cared about Sutton, he was a freelance bank robber and meant nothing to the organization. But one day Albert Anastasia happened to turn on the television and some sort of interview was on. He looked at Shuster and said, "Kill that motherfucker. I hate stool pigeons," and a few days later Shuster was blown away. If Anastasia had not turned the television set on, Shuster would never have been hit. As it turned out his death served as a warning to other potential informers, but it also led to Anastasia's death. It was a totally unnecessary killing and it brought a lot of heat down on the mob. The other bosses never forgave Anastasia for this.

About the only thing you have to think about, after the gun, the witnesses and the police, is the body. Most of the time it's best to leave it where it falls, but some people prefer to have victims simply disappear off the face of the earth. No body, no police. What the hell, they're paying for it. One organization brings its leftovers to a junkyard that has a compressor and makes them part of next year's Lincolns. Another uses a furnace in the backyard of a New Jersey estate. And there are still some undiscovered farms with lots of shallow graves fertilizing the plants. I suppose the most popular places are construction sites. The organization finds an area where concrete is about to be poured and they put the body in there. Some guy comes to work the next morning and, what does he know, he pours the concrete. Here's a helpful hint, though – always pour lime over the body or, when it starts decomposing, it's going to smell just terrible.

This point was proven just a few years ago by some people in the Canarsie section of Brooklyn. They had the bodies of two recently departed individuals on their hands and they did not want them discovered by the police. These victims had been linked to a business everyone thought was legitimate, and the mob didn't need that. So they made an early deposit in what was going to be a bank. They showed up one night in February and stuck the bodies in the foundation. Unfortunately, they neglected to cover them with lime. This was fine in the winter, because the bodies froze and nobody knew they were there. But by the time the bank opened in August the bodies were decomposing and nobody could walk in or out of that place without losing lunch.

I've only broken one rule in my career. I have killed three men for revenge – and I made them suffer when I did it. Normally you're supposed to get permission, but I didn't bother. When I think back on it, it seems like a plot for a bad motion picture. I remember in *Nevada Smith*, Steve McQueen tracked down the three guys who killed his parents and, when he found the third one, he just couldn't kill him. That's the difference between real life and pictures. There wasn't a man on this planet who could've stopped me.

It was 1958 and I had made a private deal to bring narcotics into the country from Mexico. My cut was supposed to be $40,000, but instead of paying me the party thought it would be a great deal cheaper to kill me. Unfortunately, when he sent his goons to my house I wasn't there. My wife was there and four months pregnant at the time. They came into the house looking for me and when they realized I wasn't home they got abusive. One of them kicked my wife in the stomach and they left her lying on the kitchen floor. She started hemorrhaging. She was dead by the time our neighbors got her to the hospital.

They caught up to me in Reno, Nevada. I had just come out of one of the casinos – at this point I didn't know what happened to my wife – and I started to cut through this alley over by some railroad tracks. The lights blanked out. I was smashed over the head with a blunt instrument.

Ten days later I came to, paralyzed from the neck down, in the Washoe Medical Center. The doctor manipulated my vertebrae and managed to restore some feeling in my body. The next day some friends came by and they told me what had happened to my wife.

That was the day I stopped caring whether I lived or died. That was the day I lost all fear of death. All I had within me was hatred. I would not have gone after the three men for what they did to me – business was business – and I would have simply settled with the head man. But they were dead the moment they kicked my wife.

We had only been married a few months. When we got married I didn't know if I was going to stay in this business or not. I certainly never would've stayed in as a hit man if she had lived; I even like to think I would have quit. You talk about your life changing around because of a woman . . . mine did. She was a real clean kid. And she was mine. For the first time in my life I had found someone who made me completely happy. Until that point, I didn't know what happiness was. All my life I had been a taker, everything I owned I had had to grab. Finally I had found someone who was willing to give simply because she liked me. There were never any threats, any wild shows, any violence; she liked me just because I was me.

Then my whole world exploded. It just came apart. It changed me radically. Before this I was sometimes wild and crazy, but I just wasn't mean. This made me mean. As soon as I could move I got on the telephone and called the guy who had set the whole thing up. He picked up the phone. All I said was, "You made a mistake, fuck. I'm still alive."

I laid in the hospital for eight months, and one day the doctor walked in and said I could either lie there like a vegetable for the rest of my life or risk an operation. I asked him what my chances were.

"Even," he said. "You'll either walk out or be carried out." I didn't give a damn either way, so I told him to start cutting. Seven months later I walked out of that place. And went after the three men who had killed my wife.

I started to hunt them down. I carried .22 long-range flatnosed bullets because I wanted them to suffer. At short range they won't kill you, but they will smash your bones and make you bleed. I found the first one in California. I killed him very slowly. I had trapped him in a garbage-filled alley and he started swearing he had nothing to do with it. There was no way I was going to listen. I just started to pump bullets into him methodically. First into his legs so he couldn't move. Then into his rib cage so he would bleed. Then into his shoulders and then I shot his ears off. I just kept reloading the gun; I was having a good time. Then I left him there to die.

I found the second one in Mexico and killed him the same way. I had never known anything as sweet as these killings. They were wonderful sights. And I could smell the fear. If you've ever wondered why an animal attacks someone who's afraid of him, it's because the fear just pours out of him and creates an odor. I saw it. I smelled it. I loved it.

I had to chase the third one completely across the country. He knew I was after him and he tried to hide. It took me almost a year to find him, but I did, in New York City. He went down just like the first two. Then I got on the phone to the boss. I said two words, "You're next," and then I hung up. But before I could get him he was arrested on a narcotics charge. That bust saved his life. I guarantee it. And, if he lives through it, the day he walks out I will be standing there waiting for him. I swear it.

Why do I do it? Why do I kill people? There are a number of reasons. Obviously, the money. I like money. I like what money can buy, what it can bring you. I remember when I didn't have it.

I like the status it brings. I'm somebody. Straight people like to associate with me. They like to be able to brag that they know a real live killer, or that this guy can "do things" for people. And girls, when they meet me, they want to find out what it's like to be with an individual who has killed people. They want to go to bed with you. Don't ask me why, but they do. They feel you're going to be different than anybody else. You're not, and they're disappointed when they find out, but the idea of being with an animal really appeals to a lot of people. Believe it or not, there are "hit man groupies". I like women being attracted to me. I didn't have what you would call a normal social life when I was younger; I didn't do too much dating. And I know I'm not the best-looking guy in the world either, so if it's being the tough killer that turns women on, I'll play that role. I'll be as tough as they want. Usually, though, after they ball you, they get sick. They feel they've corrupted themselves.

I also see killing as a test of loyalty and courage.

In business terms the ability to pull the trigger is vitally important. If you expect to progress in the organization you have to be able to do it. I would say almost every man who has ever become a boss has pulled it somewhere along the line.

And, finally, I guess I do it because I enjoy it. I like having the power of knowing that I am it, that I can make the final decision of whether someone lives or dies. It is an awesome power.

Don't try to analyze me or any other hit man either. I would guess there are maybe 1000 men still working at it throughout the country. But except in New York there hasn't been much work lately, so I guess you could call us a dying breed. The thing about hit men that is so unusual is that they are so usual. A man that is sadistic, that is crazy-wild, that is a troublemaker, that has strange habits or stands out in a crowd, he can't make it. He'll be disposed of.

Hit men differ in a thousand ways. Some are friendly, some moody, some tall, some short, some bald, and, lately, some even have long hair. You would never be able to pick one out of a crowd but, then again, you won't have to. A hit man is only known to those people who have to know who he is.

What makes a good hit man? Pride and confidence. A good hit man goes out, does his job, comes home to his family and can sit down and eat his dinner without any problems. After all, no one likes to bring his work home with him.

Hostage Taker
(Charles Bronson)

Charles Bronson

Armed robber Charles Bronson has been labelled Britain's most dangerous convict. During more than 30 years in jail, he has forged a fearsome reputation as the prison system's only serial hostage taker. "If you're going to come at me," he warns, "you'd better be prepared to knock me unconscious or kill me. I fear no one. Violence just makes me madder and stronger." Bronson, real name Michael Gordon Peterson, was born in Luton in 1952. He's spent more than a quarter of a century in solitary confinement, locked in dungeons, in iron boxes anchored in concrete and, famously, in a cage like the fictional Hannibal Lecter. He is always held under maximum security, in a spartan cell furnished only with a fireproof bed and a table and chair made from compressed cardboard. When he is unlocked, up to a dozen prison officers, sometimes in riot gear and with dogs, are standing by. In his epic prison career he has been moved 150 times, often trussed up, naked, in a body-belt. His prison life began in 1974 when he was jailed for seven years for robbing a Liverpool jeweller. He has since known only 69 days of freedom. In 1978 Bronson was certified insane, sectioned for life and sent to Broadmoor, but returned to a conventional prison when the authorities realized how much it was costing to repair the damage he was causing. Released in 1993, he was back inside within eight weeks, this time for an eight-year stretch for yet another robbery. He received a further ten years for various misdemeanours, including roof-top protests, assaults on prison officers and hostage-taking. An unlicensed fist-fighter, Bronson claims to have survived mob-handed beatings by prison staff and a potentially fatal attack when he was repeatedly stabbed in the back by fellow convicts. In 2001, in prison, he married a woman who'd written to him after seeing his picture in the paper. The late Lord Longford was his best man. Bronson says his spectacular roof-top protests and hostage takings – such as this 1994 incident recounted in his memoirs – are his way of fighting back against the system.

Taking hostages for me has become a dangerous game. They want me to fuck up, they want me to take another one. It would suit them fine for me to take one a day, take a hostage a day to keep the penal system away, but you know what the outcome would be – death. They'd shoot me and it would be a case of shoot to kill!

I've got to tell you about one particular hostage-taking situation because it's special, very special. My best siege of all time is the one in which I took a governor hostage; it was the best one for pleasure. Governor Wallace at Hull Special Unit became my fly, wrapped up in my web.

4 April 1994, just after breakfast, I made my move. Deputy Governor No 2, Adrian Thomas Wallace, became my hostage. He upset me; he was arrogant, big-headed and had to be right all of the time, no matter what. He upset me over some little thing, which multiplied.

There were only four cons on the unit; we were all considered too dangerous to put on the wings with other cons. There was Ed Slater, a lifer; Paul Flint, a lifer, Tony McUllagh, a double lifer and of course yours truly. I told them all to stay out of it "cos I'm gonna wrap Wallace up!"

He walked into the unit like a lord. I pushed past the other guys in front of me as soon as I saw him and grabbed him by the neck. There were screws about but I'm so fast that they didn't see it coming, whoosh! I pushed Wallace towards the wall and put my forearm under his chin from behind him; I pulled his head back and applied pressure to his throat. "Don't come near me or I'll snap his neck," I shouted to the screws. I chinned Wallace and dragged him backwards into the TV room. I kept my back to the wall and, once in there, I tied him up, using his own tie to do so. I sat him down on a chair in the middle of the room, facing the door, while I barricaded the door with tables and chairs.

I spoke to one of the screws, Roy Kirk, through the windows. "He's nothing but a bastard and nobody likes him!" I told Wallace that I'd snap his neck if he moved. I noticed he had a personal phone! So I called them up and said, "I want a fillet steak, French-fries, mushrooms and a tin of dog food for Wallace." The mush-rooms meant a lot to me 'cos I had a quarter of a pound of them nicked from my cell and I know it wasn't cons. At the time Wallace did fuck all about it. This part of the siege wasn't mentioned in his subsequent statement used in evidence. Poor memory this guy has?

He was lying a maggot, "Please, Charlie, please don't hurt me." None of that went into his statement, either, proving what an arrogant sod he is. He had this blue pinstriped suit on while I was dressed in tracka [tracksuit] bottoms, a vest and prison boots – worlds apart. I slapped him across the chops a couple of times and this knocked him to the floor; it was just to show him who was boss. I grabbed him by the neck like I was holding a puppy and threw him back on the chair and told him to "fucking shut up".

I kept telling him he was a bag of shit and how I was gonna kill him. I was starting to get really pissed off and told Wallace that police marksmen would be brought in and if I was gonna get it then he'd get it as well, as they wouldn't give a fuck.

I rifled through his pockets and put all the stuff on the table in front of him and then started to chuck it all over the room. None of it was any use to me. Credit cards and other shit, his money; I tore it all up! I pulled his keys out of his pocket and with a yank it ripped his trousers down the leg – a new fashion style by the House of Bronson. He looked really cool in this little number.

He really got to me, this guy, and as I spotted an iron I felt like taking it to his face and reshaping it – a bit of plastic surgery never goes in wrong – but I'm not a cold hearted bastard. Although I came close and held it to his head, then threatened to stave his head in with it, I didn't. Doesn't that show you the type of man I really am? I could've done it, but the look in his eyes, the fear, the terror and the tears stopped me.

I swung Wallace around in the chair he was in, turning him away from the door and the windows, as he was seeing too much for my liking. They're a crafty lot, this mob, winking and twitching to each other. The room was about 10 feet square: I kept pacing up and down, making decisions and kicking furniture around that was getting in the way.

I told Wallace to shut up, but I had to ask him to get on his radio and I gave my demands to him. "Tell them that we're to leave the prison together and if there's any SAS or Royal Marines in the prison then they'd better shoot us both." Wallace complied and he also told them that I'd done jungle warfare and I wasn't fucking about.

Roy Kirk was still watching through the window during this time. I was becoming bored with it so I turned the TV on to the pop station and turned it up full blast – yeah, this suited me down to the ground. I asked for a cuppa and, being the gent I am, asked Wallace if he wanted one too, which he did. Wallace shouted to the screws what we wanted and, shortly after the tea arrived, I moved the barricade just enough to let the cups fit through.

This Wallace fella's a clever guy. He asked for his hands to be untied so as he could drink his tea and I obliged. His free hand, I told him to keep in his pocket. I'd told them that I wanted my demands met by 11.00 a.m. or Wallace would get hurt.

I despised Wallace because he's power crazy, he hates cons and he's a coward and I'll tell you why soon and then you'll know why I made that remark. Also, I'd been writing to a female inmate at Durham's "She Wing", Avril Gregory, a lifer. It was agreed that a one-day visit would take place at Hull or Durham prison for the pair of us to meet as I'd been writing to Avril for a while. Who agreed to that visit? Governor Wallace and the guy in charge of all of the CRC units in this country.

Great, I was built up to this visit. Wallace and Goulds had agreed fully to this visit going ahead. It'd made my day and I was really looking forward to meeting Avril and then, you know what? The fucking bastards cancelled it. You know what they told me? That it was some problem at Durham! I knew then that I'd been lied to by these bastards once again, I'd fell hook, line and sinker for it all over again. I took it calmly, very calmly. There was no point in being awkward over it as I'd need time to think what I was gonna do.

When you're banged up with people, you get to feel that they'll stand by you and you all work as a team. But as I took Wallace hostage I heard Eddie Slater and Paul Flint saying, "Come on, Charlie, there's no need for this, come on – not this way, Charlie." What a fucking mob of turncoats.

Roy Kirk was my personal officer and I even worked out with him in the gym and I had my own special diet that the others on the unit also followed. There was 34 screws to look after us four. I'm not kidding – work out the wages spent on that little lot in a month and I bet all of your debts would be paid off and some more! I started to trust Kirky and, credit where credit's due, he started to mix with me. But I'm used to how they go about it, although I sensed something different about him, like he cared.

This man called Goulds told me to apply for accumulated visits down south and I would be transferred, so here I was, having all my hopes built up again. A move was on, it looked good, but – guess what? – yeah, I was knocked back again at the last fucking minute. By now I was starting to lose it.

I was supposed to go to Belmarsh so I could be closer to Lorraine and Andy. Wallace loved it when this was stopped, fucking arsehole. There's one thing to get a KB [knock back] but when they gloat over it then that deserves a slap. Wallace stopped equipment coming into the unit from the education department; he upset Eddie Slater, one of my fellow cons, over a claim for lost property. I cleaned the unit spotless, I worked hard to achieve positive things, but he never once respected it.

I tried to smash one of the windows in the TV room so as to be able to speak to Kirky. I tried with wood and then I bashed it with the iron and would it fuck go. By this time I was losing it badly but Kirky indicated he would remove the small glass from the room door. Why didn't I think of that? Kirky was shouting at me to calm down. "It's this cunt's fault," I told him. Wallace was put down by Kirky's words, but I knew he was trying it on with me and that was starting to get to me, as I'm not an idiot and I know you don't get to be a governor without having some brain cells in your head.

I wrote a note saying I wanted to speak directly to Goulds and to get a phone so I could call his London office. I demanded a blow-up doll, but a one with blonde hair, not black. I was starting to worry about the SAS, as they drill through walls, so I strapped a chair to the front and back of Wallace – clever, eh? I grabbed him by the neck and we marched to the next room, another TV room, as we had two rooms that accommodated two TV channels, one for each room.

"I'm in charge, I'm gonna die today and if anybody tries anything, they'll join me!" I got Wallace on the door and tied a sheet around his neck and I asked for two more cups of tea – it's thirsty work this hostage taking malarkey. I sat at the back of the room, behind Wallace. The lights were out and the TV was on; it gave me some cover as I stayed in the darkness as the light from the TV glared at them looking in.

As I said earlier, I like to sing to get rid of tension, so I started to sing into the radio. I told them I wanted this song recorded and for it to be played at my funeral as I knew I was gonna die that day. I was prepared for it coming my way. I sang "I Believe" and I belted it out, it was my swan song – or so I thought! This steak and chips was taking a fucking long time to come. The room service stunk – they weren't going to get a tip, that was for sure.

I was behind Wallace and I wanted a piss. I pissed in the waste bin. I knew Wallace would be thinking that I'd pour it over him and it was that which gave me even more pleasure in not doing it. His day would've been made if I'd done it, but by not doing it kept him in suspense. I was playing mind games with in reverse with him. To really humiliate him I should've pissed over him but I saw it as a waste of my piss. Why piss on a dog? I read in Wallace's statement later on that he'd thought I was going to sexually abuse him when he heard my zip opening. What a fucking pervert. Here's me wanting a piss and all he can think about is sex.

I heard all the other screws coming over the radio and it was starting to do my head in, so I told them to close the prison for the day and go home. My blow-up doll hadn't arrived so I got Wallace to get on the radio and ask for it and I wanted it dressed in a black skirt with black tights. My last hostage situation, when I took Andy Love, my demands weren't met. So here I was again, simply asking for a blow-up doll, but when that failed to turn up my demands became heavier. I wanted an Uzi machine gun with 5,000 rounds of ammo.

I had the keys to the whole damn prison and I wanted to know which key fitted what door. I had to get out of that fucking room somehow. I wrapped the sheet around Wallace and me. If anyone was going to shoot they'd have to have fucking x-ray eyes to see through the sheet so as to get a clean shot at me.

I got back on the radio. "I know I'm gonna be shot by one of them fucking coppers' bullets. Make sure you send a recording of that song to my solicitor in London." I then started singing some Christmas songs and hymns and, for good measure, I tore the TV from its stand and smashed it to the ground near Wallace. I was getting claustrophobic and my life was running past me, and it's not like they tell you. All what I could see was liquid cosh, beatings, body belts, pain, kickings and worse – hell!

I had to get out of this room; it was starting to kill me. I pushed Wallace out and I kept my back to the wall. We're sheeted together, I headed back for the first room we'd been in, fuck knows why. I grabbed for the handle, but we started to fall over as I was off balance.

Footsteps come running and I was overpowered. Wallace was snatched from me like a baby. "All right, it's over," I said. I was cuffed up and still on the ground when I felt an almighty smash, like my brain had exploded. What the fuck was it? I twisted my head around and from where I was held I could see Wallace's foot coming in landing for a second time. It made contact with my jaw, crunch! You'd have thought I was eating boiled sweets from the noises that were coming out of my jaw. He kept kicking me in the face and body.

Wallace's statement was a load of lies. He said he got to me before the other screws come running. How the fuck could he, when he was sheeted in with me and I was under him on the floor and the screws were only a few feet away from us? Wallace went on to say that he was grateful that he'd been dragged away otherwise he felt he'd have done some harm to me. Look! A man of my size isn't gonna lie there taking it from a fucking arsehole like Wallace, am I? I was fucking cuffed up and held down for him to do his dirty work on me, like a coward does.

Guess what else Wallace said in his statement? He said he felt as if he was being pampered and didn't want all of the hassle after he'd went to the governors' office. The first two screws to jump me were Kirky and David Lloyd Jones. Jones mentioned nothing of Wallace kicking the shit out of me, and neither did Kirky. Jones conveniently lost his notes he made immediately after the event, saying they were left in the TV room – fucking liar. I had the shit kicked out of me and Wallace's statement confirmed it when he admitted kicking me, yet not one of the other statements mentioned this. A screw called David Purvis jumped on me as well and his statement didn't even mention the kicking I got.

In a conflicting statement issued by Wallace, he went on to say that as we went down, "I whacked him one." He went on to say, "I thought to myself 'He's still there', and I can recall Roy Kirk on him and I whacked him again and then there were a lot of officers on top of him, and I can recall George White shouting 'get out of here'. Dave Purvis then grabbed me visibly . . ."

Wallace, in this statement, admits whacking me and says that I was held by a screw when he did it. The truth of the matter is he kicked seven bells out of me while I was cuffed up and held down. He was right, though, when he says I was held. If I hadn't 've tripped this day then who knows what the real ending would've been! Maybe it was to have been a marksman's bullet.

Cutting a long story short, when it all came to court, I pleaded not guilty to the Andy Love hostage taking at Woodhill, in a trial that lasted less than two days. I didn't dispute any of the facts and I was given a total of eight years to run concurrent. On the Wallace hostage taking I was given a whole load of domino numbers that amounted to a total of 15 years, which included the Woodhill sentence and one earlier of robbery where I had a loaded sawn off shotgun, remember – 1993?

Well, it looked all roses and there was nothing left for it but to get my head together for some serious thinking. What did come out of it though was that Judge Laurence Marshall, who tried my Woodhill hostage case, asked that he be kept informed of my movements as he was concerned at my being moved some 28 times in the space of only 21 months! Judge Marshall of Luton Crown Court said he would be asking Probation Services to keep him updated so that he could monitor what was happening. Since then I've been moved quite a bit, yet I can't see Judge Marshall paying any interest. That's how it's always been – people making the right sort of noises and leaving it at that. Another let down. If a judge can't do as he says then how can I ever expect a prison governor to?

The Big Fellow
(Al Capone)

Kenneth Allsop

The most famous and feared name in American gangsterdom, Al Capone (1895–1947) possessed a thunderflash temper, and when angered could exact terrible punishment on his rivals. To Capone, killing was second nature. He personally executed three Sicilians for disloyalty, first entertaining them to a lavish and raucous banquet at a hotel in Cicero, just outside Chicago, before pushing back his chair and letting a glacial silence fall over the room. His biographer John Kobler noted that

> Capone had observed the old tradition. Hospitality before execution. The Sicilians were defenceless, having, like the other banqueters, left their guns in the checkroom. Capone's bodyguards fell upon them, lashing them to their chairs with wire and gagging them. Capone got up, holding a baseball bat. Slowly, he walked the length of the table and halted behind the first guest of honour. With both hands he lifted the bat and slammed it down full force. Slowly, methodically he struck again and again, breaking bones in the man's shoulders, arms and chest. He moved to the next man and, when he had reduced him to mangled flesh and bone, to the third. One of the bodyguards then fetched his revolver from the checkroom and shot each man in the back of the head.[1]

1 *Capone: The Life and World of Al Capone* by John Kobler (Michael Joseph, London 1972)

Capone was evil, ruthless and corrupt, a violent killer who personally murdered dozens of rivals himself and gave orders for the elimination of hundreds more. Raised in Brooklyn, the son of Italian immigrants, Capone worked as bouncer and bartender at the roughhouse hotel in Chicago owned by Frank Yale, US head of the Unione Siciliana, a secret criminal society linked to the Mafia. Slashed on the left cheek for insulting a woman, Capone detested his Scarface tag and, as his fame grew, masked the ugly wounds with talcum powder, taking care to present photographers with his right profile. Only his intimates were allowed to call him Snorky, street slang for "elegant". His crime career started in 1919 when he fell in with Chicago gangster Johnny Torrio, 17 years his senior, who hired him as a bodyguard at his Four Deuces casino-cum-whorehouse at 2222, South Wabash Avenue. Capone used his massive fists on Torrio's gangster rivals, who were taken to his cellar and tortured until they talked. "Then they're rubbed out," one informant reported.

Following the murder of Jim Colosimo, the first of Chicago's great gangster overlords to be assassinated, Torrio and Capone expanded their territory and developed gambling and brothel interests in nearby Cicero. When Torrio went to Europe for an extended holiday, Capone headquartered himself at the Hawthorne Inn on 22nd Street, installing steel shutters at every window and an armed lookout at every door. In 1924 he hunted down a man who'd offended him, found him in a bar and emptied a six-shooter into his head. By this time, Capone's word was law in Cicero. He surrounded himself with bodyguards and sharpshooters like rifleman Phil D'Andrea, who could split a quarter in mid-air, and "Machine Gun" Jack McGurn, whom the police suspected of 22 murders. (As a post-mortem gesture of contempt, he would often press a nickel into his victim's hand.) In 1925, Capone's syndicate opened a new brothel containing a death chamber, although Capone himself was already at pains to cultivate a more respectable image. "I don't hurt nobody," he explained. "Only them that gets in my way." But among the Chicago mobs, Capone's brutal reputation was legendary. When Bugs Moran escaped the St Valentine's Day Massacre by minutes in 1929, he knew who to blame: "Only Capone kills like that."

Capone's fortune bulked as large as his fame. A compulsive (and unlucky) gambler, he seldom staked less than $1,000 on a *dice roll, and would think nothing of wagering $100,000 on the spin of a roulette wheel or horse race. This finely tuned portrait of Capone's heyday comes from a history of Chicago's boot-leggers by Kenneth Allsop (1920–1973). Allsop began his journalistic career in Fleet Street before becoming one of the first anchormen for BBC current affairs programmes including* Tonight *and* 24 Hours. *Having lost a leg to tuberculosis during World War II and battling daily tubercular-related pain for the rest of his life, he produced a vast quantity of journalism and numerous diverse books, as well a Broadway play.*

At the door of Cook County Jail on an October morning in 1931, which, unbeknown to him then, was the last meridian moment of his singular career, Alphonse Capone paused on his way inside to issue a statement to the press. It was a sentence that, in its poignant bafflement and hurt, classically expressed the attitudes that set the psychotic criminal irreclaimably apart from society.

"It was a blow below the belt," he said, "but what can you expect when the whole community is prejudiced against you?"

Capone had just stepped down from the dock after receiving an eleven-year prison sentence for tax evasion, a sentence he managed to postpone until the following May, during which time he remained on bail pending appeal. Until that summer, when, only by the most stubborn persistence had the Federal Government of the United States of America hauled him into court, Capone had been one of the most obviously powerful men in the world. In this year of 1931 Mussolini had been dictator of Italy for nine years; the National Socialists had just won a hundred seats in the Reichstag, and it was only months ahead before Hitler became chancellor and constituted the Third Reich; Stalin had been supreme head of the Soviet Union for seven years. All, in this developing age of rule by violence and victimization, were more sombrely fearsome by far than an American gangster whose ambitions were neither political nor nationalistic, but who used politics obliquely as a means of obtaining money and the power through which more money was obtainable. Yet perhaps all of them were part of the same pattern of that darkening time, an age when enforcement of policy by gun, cruelty and oppression, in contempt of the theoretical canons of law, became naked and ubiquitous. Capone himself seemed hazily conscious of inherent similarities. As he walked, handcuffed, from the courtroom to his cell through volleys of exploding flashbulbs, he said with melancholy pride to Eliot Ness, the F.B.I. prohibition agent who was largely responsible for his conviction: "Jeez, you'd think Mussolini was passin' through." And, in 1931, when Hitler was aged forty-two, Mussolini forty-eight and Stalin fifty-two, Capone was but thirty-six. For a comparatively young man, a slum delinquent of foreign birth and little schooling, his accomplishments up to that year had been prodigiously impressive.

The President in status and several hundred industrialists in material possessions were mightier and more influential Americans than Capone, yet not by so great a margin, and, in concentrated autonomy, were much less so. Probably no one man since Cesare Borgia's rule of Rome had so inexorably controlled a city for purposes so piratically self-interested and contrary to principles of government in the society of which he was a member. In his four years of total power, between 1927 and 1931, Capone's authority ramified beyond Chicago and beyond the state of Illinois. "He was," wrote Paul Sann, "mayor, governor and machine boss all rolled into one. He gave the orders; the people's elected servants carried them out and kept their mouths shut. His authority was so great it could not be measured." The gross income of his business in liquor, gambling, prostitution and assorted rackets ran into millions of dollars annually. Chicago's twenty thousand speakeasies operated, with only sporadic and ineffectual interference from the Federal Prohibition squads, openly and busily for years. He ran an organization which owned or had stakes in breweries, distilleries, warehouses, truck-companies, garages, bars, nightclubs, dance-halls, restaurants, brothels, race-tracks and casinos, and which was beginning at the time of his retirement to infiltrate its extortion racket into unions, film production and dozens of trades and industries. He amassed a fortune of twenty million dollars – an incredible sum that is not my estimate but that of the Internal Revenue Office. He was the commanding officer of a private army of seven hundred storm-troops, and for auxiliaries had call upon an estimated sixty percent of Chicago's police force who were on his pay-roll. In that four-year period there were 227 gang murders; there were no convictions. (In the forty-year period from 1919 to 1959 there were 929 gang murders committed in Chicago. Only seventeen culprits were convicted – and several of those were freed on appeal to the Supreme Court.) He took over the suburban district of Cicero with a military efficiency and converted it into a vice-reservation, a day-and-night resort of 161 cabarets, call-houses and dice-parlours, and when he seized control of the town of fifty thousand people he nominated his own group of bought politicians and posted squads of gunmen at the polling stations to ensure their election. His influence extended into journalism; there was certainly one reporter – Jake Lingle of the Chicago *Tribune* – on his pay-roll, and probably others in regular receipt of patronage in return for sympathetic coverage. Even during his prison term the headlines rang with fond concern: CAPONE GAINS ELEVEN POUNDS and CAPONE DOESN'T GO TO CHURCH ON SUNDAY. He was a celebrity swelling into a legend. Citizens scurried to the kerb to stare when his three-and-a-half ton armour-plated Cadillac, with bullet-proof glass and tail-gunner's movable back window, passed with its escort of two armed scout-cars. Lucky out-of-town and foreign visitors among the crowds had their stimulating glimpse of the famous face, stuck with cigar, in the dim haze of silken cushions, perhaps the quick glint of one of his famous diamonds, behind the bodyguard in the front seat with Thompson sub-machine-gun handily across his knees. Tourist buses had "Capone Castle" – his Hawthorne Inn headquarters in Cicero – and his Metropole Hotel city headquarters on their itinerary. A press photograph of him with Jack Sharkey, the boxer, and Bill Cunningham, former All-American football player, which was nationally circulated by an agency, was captioned "Gangland's King". When he attended a prize-fight or race-meeting the fact was mentioned by the sports columnist. In 1929 the London *Daily Mail* despatched Mr Edgar Wallace to Chicago to write a series of articles about the Capone régime, and he was only one of many European journalists who were hastening towards a tastily juicy story of smoking guns and brazen daring, an improbable Wild West melodrama here for the harvesting in a modern city. The articles, interviews, biographies and personal reminiscences proliferated, and accuracy of detail was not allowed dingily to stifle the rich potentialities of such material. If one collated all the alleged direct quotations from Capone himself that were printed at that period, a curious portrait of a garrulous but primly stilted Boy Scout would emerge. This watchful and wary crime-syndicalist, who, except when angry (which was rare to see) or relaxed with wine (which was not often in the presence of outsiders), confined his conversation outside the confederate circle to pleasantries with reporters, would seem, from the printed records that remain, to have been able to discourse learnedly upon philosophy or Napoleon's tactical errors ("the world's greatest racketeer, but I could have wised him up on some things"). One 1929 newspaper report of his activities during his short prison sentence in Philadelphia described him as "a stern highbrow" and cited his "favourite authors" as Shakespeare and Shaw; another dispatch reported that he was occupying himself by reciting Balzac and Victor Hugo. He was even, in one odd publication in 1931, *Carrying a Gun for Al Capone* by the sculptor-painter Jack Bilbo – who later admitted that he had never been to Chicago – represented as being a reader of Robert Louis Stevenson and Karl Marx, and as talking like a ruminative cardigan-clad don in an English repertory drama: "Sentimentality is the main danger which threatens us in life. One either has to rid oneself of it or one is entirely in its power. The day will come when our softness will rise up and we will flounder in it." Most of the myth-making that was then beginning had at least a few more roots in reality, even if it was as fatuous as Edward D. Sullivan's description of him in a 1931 book, *Chicago Surrenders*, as "the best billiard player in the Greenpoint section of Brooklyn", but there was also a vast quantity of glamour-endowing mawkishness about Capone in Sunday paper serials, in "detective" magazines and in quick-turnover booklets, lavish with those smudgily sinister pictures of corpses sprawled beside fire-hydrants. One of these, *X Marks The Spot*, published in 1930, is a fair specimen of the tone of excited, fulsome admiration thinly veneered with moralizing that was current then. Beside a full-page frontispiece ran this caption: "Here is an excellent likeness of Alphonse Capone, the big boy of Chicago Gangland, and the greatest that ever lived. When King Al poses for a photograph, which isn't often, he always turns his right cheek to the camera. The left one is disfigured by an ugly scar. Legend has it that Capone was struck by a machine-gun bullet when he was a soldier in France." (That, as will be seen later, is one little Capone-inspired legend that collapsed.) Within, the story of Capone's life, which was on the level of the "official" biography of a film star in a fan-club circular, began: "He is a glamorous figure, an actual part of the American scene. Legends are already springing up around him. The magazine stands are aflame with underworld stories about the man with the gat who wears a tuxedo and has a liveried chauffeur. With no intention to eulogize him, Capone unquestionably stands apart as the greatest and most successful gangster who ever lived. The difference between him and all other gangsters is that he is possessed of a genius for organization and a profound business sense." All the documentary comment induced was not quite so banally degenerate as that but there were more sober and grudging tributes to his talent. An internal revenue officer, charged with investigating his tax dues, told Pasley: "Capone has exceptional business ability and would have gone far in any legitimate line. If he had only been honest, what a hero he would have made for a Horatio Alger tale." Capone and his régime also brought about novels such as W. R. Burnett's *Little Caesar*, plays such as Ben Hecht's *The Front Page* and Edgar Wallace's *On The Spot*, and a cycle of brilliantly harsh gangster films of which *Scarface*, directed by Howard Hawks and with Paul Muni as the psychopathic hoodlum Tony Camonte, a name with, perhaps, a deliberate onomatopoeic quality, was the best. (In 1932 in America it was billed, deludingly, as "The Shame of a Nation", when there was, in mass unemployment and hunger, a far more bitter shame abroad. In Britain it was extensively cut, banned completely by the Manchester Watch Committee, and the Council of the Cinematograph Exhibitors' Association recommended that it should be sent back to the censor for "further consideration because of its morbidity and bloodshed".)

Fact was inextricably scrambled with fiction. It was fact that this new dignitary, the paunchy pallid-faced Big Fellow who was beginning to tower above the officially eminent with a unique glitter and who was giving Chicago a peculiar global fame, was among the committee appointed to welcome Commander Francesco da Pinedo, Mussolini's round-the-world goodwill pilot in 1927, together with Leopold Zunini, Italian Consul-General, Dr Ugo M. Galli, Chicago Fascisti President, and Judge Bernard P. Barasa, representing the Mayor. It was a fact that he was lionized by the smart – it was cute to know Al; that he entertained at his Florida estate seventy-five guests at a time, many of them fashionable and famous; that he rebuked and instructed politicians and judges over the telephone from his Metropole Hotel office; that on the occasion of the second Dempsey–Tunney fight he threw the biggest, and wettest, party seen before or since in Chicago – it blinded on for three days, the liquor bill (even at his wholesale rates) was fifty thousand dollars, and it was attended by socialites, movie stars, politicians and theatre and boxing celebrities from all over America.

So it may well have also been a fact that – as he once bragged – in seven years he "fooled away" ten million dollars, pocket money on gambling. He customarily shot craps for fifty and a hundred thousand dollars a throw, and never for less than a thousand unless with impoverished friends; he bet a hundred thousand at a time on a horse race (but would not gamble on the stock market – "Wall Street is crooked"). Appropriate to his station, he lived a sybaritically luxurious life. His custom-built car cost thirty thousand dollars, his ring, an eleven-carat blue-white diamond from the South African Jagersfontein mines, fifty thousand dollars. His casual munificence with his thickly wadded bankroll became one of the romances of that hard-bitten city where nothing had ever previously been for free. He was once charged – and paid without wincing – a thousand dollars for a round of drinks in the Country Club, an exclusive New York speak run by Belle Livingstone, dubbed by the papers "the Most Dangerous Woman in Europe" when she was the outstandingly lurid playgirl of the Edwardian age. His personal gratuity rates were five dollars for a newsboy, ten dollars for a hat-check girl and a hundred dollars for a waiter. There were many such heart-warming stories as that of the hard-up hat-check girl who, decent but desperate, pleaded for a position in one of his brothels to support her ailing mother. "Forget it. Not a nice girl like you," said Al, peeling off a hundred dollars for her. At Christmas he spent a hundred thousand dollars on miscellaneous gifts. All the year round he distributed diamond-inlet belts to his new friends and ruby-set gold cigarette cases to politicians and business associates, whose cellars were also kept stocked with wine and champagne (not the speakeasy brands). During his only other prison term – a sojourn in Philadelphia in 1929 for carrying a gun – he bought a thousand dollars' worth of the convicts' handiwork, ship models, cigarette boxes, carvings and other *objets d'art*, and posted them to friends as Christmas presents. He sent 1,200 dollars to a deserving Philadelphia orphanage. With probably no traditional knowledge to draw upon, he regarded this huge industrial city as his estate and assumed the function of a squire, a benevolent despot capriciously distributing largesse among his villeins. In hard winters the poor of Cicero could draw all the groceries, clothing and fuel they needed from coal depots and department stores on the Capone account. His individual acts of charity, from a fifty-dollar loan to an outright gift to a destitute Italian family, were many. He paid the hospital bills of a woman bystander wounded in a street gun-battle. It is not altogether astonishing that today there are many respectable citizens in Chicago who speak glowingly of Capone's philanthropy and particularly point out that in the early Depression days it was the Capone gang who set up the first soup-kitchens and block-restaurants for the distribution of free food on Thanksgiving Day.

When this real-life Robin-Hood appeared at a North Western University rally, ten thousand Boy Scouts, young eyes a-sparkle with hero worship, spontaneously set up the yell, to the embarrassment of their troop leaders: "Good old Al". Older people, too, made Capone what Pasley described as "the object of a sort of hero worship". Upstanding citizens sorted out the opportunity in public places of grasping his hand. A Chicago civil engineer, on a business visit to Philadelphia during Capone's stay in the Eastern Penitentiary, requested an interview with him, introduced himself, shook his hand and told him: "Al, we're with you."

Perhaps one should remind oneself, however, that this one-man welfare state had at his disposal for his good works the lion's share of the 150 million dollars, which was the sum estimated that marauding and extortion cost the State of Illinois annually.

At one point, around the time that he had been described as "a cancer" and "America's Nineteenth Amendment", and was saying mournfully: "There's a lot of grief attached to the limelight," Capone considered hiring Ivy Lee, the publicist who pulled off the most formidable assignment in public relations, that of popularizing the loathed, union-smashing millionaire John D. Rockefeller, Snr. This did not come about, possibly because Capone recognized that his own instincts for publicity were as sound as any advice he could buy from Lee. By 1930 he was a celebrity of a size rare in the pre-television age. Pasley, writing at that period, described him as "America's Exhibit A. Al had grown from civic to national stature. He was an institution," and Pasley grouped him in a small glorious host in the annals of enduring Americana with Will Rogers, Henry Ford, Rin Tin Tin, Babe Ruth, Charles Lindbergh, Texas Guinan and Al Smith.

As it has turned out, Pasley sold Capone short. I suspect that today although Ford and Rin Tin Tin might be known to many children in Europe, Africa, the Far East and even perhaps the Soviet Union, most would instantly recognize one name only among that list and that, if language was a barrier to explanation, they would be able to communicate their knowledge with a levelled finger and a staccato rat-a-tat-tat.

He outlasted four chiefs of police, two municipal administrations, three United States district attorneys, and a regiment of Federal prohibition agents; he survived innumerable crime drives, grand jury investigations, reform crusades, clean-up election campaigns, police shake-ups, and Congressional inquiries and debates. He killed between twenty and sixty men himself – there is no way of ascertaining any nearer tally – and was responsible by delegation for the murder of at least four hundred others, and was never charged with one of them. His ultimate arrest and commitment to jail on 24 October 1931 came about from the doggedness of the Intelligence Unit of Elmer Irey, chief of the United States Treasury Enforcement Branch; but it was not really the forces of law and order that defeated Capone. When he was struck down his strength and menace were failing. Capone had been defeated by three unexpected things: the approach of repeal, which was to dissolve his black-market in booze; depression, which dried to a dribble the easy money of the golden days; and disease which was eating him from within.

Now, thirty years after that febrile and predatory era, it is evident that Al Capone will have a more durable, definitive place in history, both popular and serious, than any of those other candidates for immortality with the possible exception of Henry Ford, although even that revolutionary will never be preserved in the same glare of popular fascination.

As the years go by Capone stands out more palpably as a phenomenon and a symbol of a sort. He cannot be summarized by all the conventional terms of disapproval, that he was evil, ruthless or corrupt, although he was all those things. The splendour of his dispensation to the needy and the greedy cannot be allowed to admit him back to grace, although he did practise a flashy generosity which, although doubtless paranoically vanity-feeding, was no mere fable. In only a decade he ascended from squalid poverty to a status, which, if no less squalid, was unique in its power and scope. He was, after all, a pioneer of a kind, for nobody before had done quite what he did, and in him there were undoubted qualities of imagination, forcefulness and ingenuity.

Sources of information about Capone's early life are scanty, even about his first years in Chicago. The reasons are obvious. Most of those who knew him best have died, usually abruptly and with their shoes on, and, because of both a lack of educational training and a deep distrust of volunteering any facts, were not men disposed to leaving behind personal journals and written reminiscences. The Italian-Sicilian circles in which he lived all his life are, in any case, famously tight-lipped about their private circumstances. Capone was watchfully guarded in what he revealed about himself – although it pleased him to hint at romanticized or downright falsified events of his younger days – and during the years of prosperity his family was shuttered out of the blaze of publicity that enveloped his public life, unobtrusive in the marginal shadows of respectable domesticity where a good Catholic-Italian family belongs. Nor is his background appreciably filled out by official police records. In 1929 Landesco remarked upon "the meagre records of Al Capone and his two brothers, Ralph and John" and elsewhere observes laconically: "Most Capone men have no records whatever." It seems deducible that bribes had bought the necessary Orwellian "memory-holes" down which irritating documentation could be consigned to oblivion.

Capone was born in 1895, although he liked to whittle five years off his age and usually gave 1900 as his year of birth. He was also sensitive about his foreign blood. In 1931 he stated: "I'm no Eyetalian. I was born in New York thirty-one years ago." He also declared with bellicose patriotism: "I'm no foreigner. I'm as good an American as any man. My parents were American-born and so was I." None of this was strictly correct. Although often described as a Neapolitan, and sometimes as a Calabrian, Capone was born on 6 January 1895 at Castel Amara near Rome and christened Alphonso. His surname was then spelled Caponi. His father was Gabrielle Caponi, a shopkeeper. His mother, who already had a two-year-old son Ralph, was named Theresa. The year after Alphonso's birth his father obtained immigration visas and the family filtered insignificantly, in the great European exodus of the late nineteenth century, into the United States of America, the new world of liberation and opportunity for Europe's oppressed. One immigrant who was spectacularly to fulfil the dream and the promise was the Caponi baby who went steerage to New York.

The family vanished into the congested Italian quarter of slum tenements in Brooklyn, where the father worked variously as grocer and barber, without ever financially getting out of the gutter on to those golden sidewalks of New York. Of the five more children born, four brothers and a sister, all but one also entered the underworld, sister Mafalda's connexion having been to marry one of the Maritote clan who were prominent in Chicago's Italian community. Ralph, known as Bottles, Frank and John joined Al in his Chicago enterprises. John, now known as Martin, still lives in Chicago. Frank was killed in the 1924 Cicero election. Ralph went to jail on a three-year sentence at the same time and on a similar tax-charge as Al's. Matt, the youngest of the brood and for whom Al planned superior things – he sent him to the exclusive Villanova University in Philadelphia – was later tried for murder. The fourth brother, Richard, soon after the First World War detached himself from the family and became a law officer under the name of Two Gun Hart, in Nebraska, where he died in 1952. Gabriel, the father, died in 1920, never to know of Al's world fame to come; but he was not altogether left out of the family bonanza. When the beer profits were foaming in, Al had his father's remains exhumed from their drab Brooklyn grave and reburied with great pomp in the Capone enclosure in Chicago's Mount Olivet Cemetery. Theresa saw the whole rise and fall of her second son: she lived until the age of eighty-five, dying in Chicago in December 1952.

It was a rich harvest of delinquency, bound with family solidarity, that had sprouted in that particular Brooklyn backstreet apartment. The childhood of Al seems to have been classically parabolic in its conditioning and logical in its course: the case of the second son is exceptional merely in that the trajectory of his career described a higher curve than is normal. At fourteen, before reaching top class, Capone was removed from school and put to work to bring in money for the family. During his term in Alcatraz twenty years later he was adjudged to have the mental age of a thirteen-year-old, but this seems to require some qualification: his educational standard may have remained at that stage, but the facts of his career do not support any inference that he was retarded.

Nevertheless, when he left school he read poorly and his spoken English – unaided in a household where Italian was used – was bad. It is a familiar context, and one which is just as relevant today in New York's Puerto Rican ghettos – the dead-end kid, fiercely resenting a sense of inadequacy and oddness that he cannot change or subdue, graduating into the hostile delinquent. Capone, according to the pattern of instability, zigzagged from meaningless job to meaningless job, and in the meantime was integrating with the street gangs that then, as now, found scrapings of self-respect, strength and importance in unity and preservation of territory, their "turf", their few blocks of decaying buildings and garbage-littered streets, and found substitute excitement in the tensions kept permanently taut by the clashes and rumbles with adjacent gangs. Capone, a hefty thick-set youth with fast boxer's feet, was already developing the calm and deadly shrewdness which later characterized him. Today he would be said to be cool, for it is still the same quality of deadpan, controlled menace that stamps the most successful hoodlum in any Western city teenage gang. But, at this point, Capone had not realized his potential; his gang activities were mostly violence for violence's sake, with casual felony exploited when the opportunity turned up for shop-breaking and the looting of parked lorries. At twenty-two he was employed as a meat-cutter in an Atlantic City butcher shop. This was in 1917 and upon America's entry into the war he was summoned to the Army.

In newspaper interviews in later years he attributed to his war experiences the two parallel three-inch scars on his left cheek, of which he was inordinately self-conscious and which earned him the nickname of Scarface (one which was never used by his henchmen and never used in his presence by anyone else who wished to retain his goodwill). "I got those scars fighting for my country overseas," he related. "I was eight months in France with the famous Lost Battalion of the Seventy-seventh Division. A burst of shrapnel caught me in a battle. I was operated on four times in a base hospital and laid up for two months before I got back to the front lines again." He somewhat modified this account during his trial, when, as he stood under oath, he was directly asked by the prosecuting attorney what his war service had amounted to. More briefly this time, he answered: "I was certified in the draft but never called." In fact, the scars were the outcome of a knife-fight in a New York saloon with Frank Gallucio, another Brooklyn hoodlum, after Capone had made a slighting remark about Gallucio's sister. Later Capone resumed his friendship with Gallucio and at one stage employed him as a bodyguard, but continued to the end sensitively to turn his left cheek away from any camera pointing in his direction.

He also on occasions paid tribute to the American Army for planting the seed in his mind of the machine-gun as a piece of business equipment ("The sergeant told me that one man with a

machine-gun was master of fifty men with rifles and revolvers," he
told a reporter. "You know something? That guy was right") but
as his only brush with the Service was at his medical-board, that
idea presumably germinated later.

Not avidly seized upon by the Army, Capone went back to his
odd-jobbing and promiscuous rough-stuff. He was now carrying a
gun and a blackjack, and was acquiring a local reputation as a
felicitous adept with both. By 1920 he had become initiated into
full-time professional criminal society, but still comparatively,
when one looks forward only a few years, at the most submerged
level. He was then given a job in a Coney Island cabaret with an
atmosphere of resounding academic stylishness, since it was named
the Harvard Inn and run by a Mr Frank Yale. However, Frankie
Yale's real name was Uale, and he was the rackets and liquor boss
of Brooklyn, a gunman mercenary and national head of the Unione
Siciliana, and the Harvard Inn was a tough waterside honkytonk,
handily adjacent after Prohibition began for the reception of
bootleg consignments from the rum fleet plying off the Long
Island coast. Doubtless Capone was happy to be meeting the right
kind of people after drifting aimlessly for so long around the edges
of quality crime, but nevertheless he was not so young – he was
twenty-five – and the job Yale gave him did not have much
splendour or status. He became, in the Harvard Inn, a dishwasher
and part-time bartender, who operated also as a bouncer if dis-
agreements with customers occurred. During that year he developed promisingly. He was enrolled into the notorious Five Points
Gang, which had been formed by an Irish thug named Paul Kelly
with a horde of 1,500 young tearaways in the early years of the
century and which reigned in the sector bounded by the Bowery
and Broadway, and Fourteenth Street and City Hall Park. (Charles
Dickens, in his *American Notes*, described the Five Points slums as
"of the utmost depravity", "all that is loathsome, drooping and
decayed".) The Five Points steel-hardened not only Capone but
also such other celebrated cadre men as Gyp the Blood and Lefty
Louie (the suspected killers of Herman Rosenthall, the gambler, in
1912) who ten years earlier had been recruited by Big Jim Colosimo, the prostitution tycoon of Chicago, as a bodyguard against
Black Hand persecution. In 1920 Capone was questioned in two
murder cases. Wary at the attention being paid to him, he wrote to
Torrio in Chicago, an eaglet from Torrio's old eyrie asking for the
opening to spread his wings in new country.

Capone did not know it then, but the timing could not have been more propitious. It was 1920 and Prohibition was just floundering into existence. Colosimo, the aging, antiquated vice-boss, flabby from too much easy money for too long, bemused by his infatuation for a young girl singer, and unable to see the stupendous bullion waiting to be carried off by organized booze-traffickers, was about to topple. Torrio, the modern man, the murder-planner rather than the operator who pulled the trigger, and now the burgeoning business executive, began to see what might, with the techniques of cartel and organization, be extracted from this new situation. Colosimo was not to be persuaded. "Stick to women," he said. "There's no future in bootlegging." On 11 May 1920 Colosimo was struck by two bullets in the lobby of his restaurant. When Torrio heard of his death he wept. "Me kill Jim? Why, Jim and me were like brothers." According to the police, Frankie Yale, who had been visiting Chicago, left that night just after collecting ten thousand dollars from Torrio.

It was at this point that Torrio received the letter from Brooklyn. He knew Capone's reputation was that of a hard-headed, dependable and ruthless yeoman, and Torrio was building his shock-troops for the imminent action. He sent for him. Capone, with the Irish-American wife, Mae, whom he had married at fifteen, and his baby son, took the train west and to an abundant future.

That this was to be the case was not immediately apparent. The job Torrio had for Capone in one of his Burnham brothels – a unique establishment which straddled the state line and had one entrance from Indiana and another from Illinois – was, once again, as chucker-out. His zeal and dedication made his probationary period brief. Torrio recognized in him business talent similar to his own, and within a few weeks Capone was appointed to the management of the Four Deuces, a vice emporium which took its name from its street number, 2222 on South Wabash Avenue, which contained whores on the third floor, gambling chambers on the second, business offices on the first, and a bar, cabaret and restaurant at street level. It was a tough spot, where twelve unsolved murders had been committed, and was not much visited by socialites from Lake Shore Drive. Capone moved into a corner shop next to the Four Deuces, stocked it with an imaginative range of articles including a piano, furniture, carpets, books (among which was a copy of the Holy Bible) and a glass case displaying

leather wallets and purses, and had the sign painted up: SECOND
HAND FURNITURE DEALER. It may not have had much turnover but it
served as a cover of ordinariness.

It is interesting to look back upon the obscurity of Capone's
early years in Chicago. In only four years he was to ascend
through a welter of blood, slaughter and conspiracy, to become
the overlord of the city's vice, a multi-millionaire and a symbol
throughout the nation and beyond the seas of a startling new era
of autocracy in which crime and politics were partners. But then,
in that first year of Prohibition, Capone still looked the slum
tough from the Five Points district. He played pinocle with other
rankers in Amato Gasperri's barber shop and ate his spaghetti in
Esposito's Bella Napoli Café. He wore a cloth cap and cheap
clothes. The unguent urbanity of manner that later characterized
him had not matured, nor had he assumed the striped yellow
suits, spats, velvet-collared overcoats and white fedoras that were
to make him the prototype of all film gangsters. He had by then
slightly adapted his name. Alphonso Caponi had become Alphonse Capone, but he was more widely known – and continued
until the end of his life to be generally known in the underworld
– as Al Brown. Apart from the hated nickname of Scarface, he
also was known to his most intimate associates as Snorky. The
Capone, he insisted in his pursuit of complete assimilation,
should be pronounced Capohn. How unimportantly he was rated
by newspapers and police is indicated by the mistakes that
usually occurred on the rare occasions that his name went on
to paper. He was more often described as Anthony or Alfred than
as Alphonse. It was not until August 1922 that he broke into the
news for the first time. He was the subject of a City News Bureau
item, which was evidently assessed to be of such trivial moment
by the copytasters that only one Chicago paper used it, as an
inside down-page story. It ran:

Alfred Caponi, 25 years old, living at the notorious Four Deuces, a
disorderly house at 2222 South Wabash Avenue, will appear in the
South Clark Street court today to answer a charge of assault with an
automobile. Early this morning his automobile crashed into a Town
taxicab, driven by Fred Krause, 741 Drake Avenue, at North
Wabash Avenue and East Randolph Street, injuring the driver.
Three men and a woman, who were with Caponi, fled before the
arrival of the police.

Caponi is said to have been driving east in Randolph Street at a high rate of speed. The taxicab was parked at the curb.

Following the accident, Caponi alighted and flourishing a revolver, displayed a special deputy sheriff's badge and threatened to shoot Krause.

Patrick Bargall, 6510 South Claremont Avenue, motor-man of a south-bound street-car, stopped his car and advised Caponi to put the weapon in his pocket, and the latter then threatened him, according to witnesses.

In the meantime, the Central police had been notified and they hurried to the scene, arresting Caponi. Krause was given first aid treatment by an ambulance physician.

Not only did the City News Bureau err with Capone's name but also in the charges preferred against him. In addition to assault with an automobile, he was charged with drunken driving and with carrying a concealed weapon. It made little difference. In the hours between the tipsy fracas and his appointment in the South Clark Street courtroom certain concealed events took place. What representations were made by whom and to whom can be only guessed at, but the case never came to trial, and the charges were dropped. Capone did not appear in court. The misdemeanours of the Special Deputy Sheriff of Cook County were expunged from the record. (Even as late as 1929 he was still described as Caponi – in reports of March of that year when the Federal authorities were trying to persuade him to return from Miami to be questioned about the St Valentine's Day Massacre.)

Yet within three years of that first trumpery news item about an unknown hoodlum, there was always a fresh anecdote circulating Chicago about the power and pull of the newly risen boss. There was the story told on the police network of the prisoner who escaped from the Criminal Courts Building and who was searched for in South Side gang hang-outs. A party of young and newly enrolled patrolmen burst into the back room of a café and surprised a gathering of bootleggers, who shed their pistols and sawn-off shot-gun on to the floor. The policemen collected these and delivered them to their chief, who said: "Take that stuff back. Who gave you orders to confiscate them?" That was not the end of the incident. They were told that Capone was irritated by their brash zeal, and that they had better call and put themselves right with him. He received them at the Metropole Hotel. "Well," he

said, "I understand your captain wasn't to blame, and that you
boys just made a mistake. I'm going to give you a break. After this,
don't pull another boner." They left chastened and grateful for the
kindness. Another story was related by a reporter who was talking
with Capone in his office when he was informed that one of his
gunmen had just been brought up in court in defiance of his orders
for a release. Angrily Capone got the judge on the telephone and
yelled at him: "I thought I told you to discharge that fellow?" The
judge explained that he had been off the bench, had written a
memorandum to a fellow judge but that his bailiff had forgotten to
deliver it. "Forget!" shouted Capone. "Don't let him forget
again!"

His wealth and influence waxed. After he had bought his Palm
Island estate three miles outside Miami – a deal that was conducted
without his identity being revealed – that part of the coast became
the winter playground of Chicago's gang-chiefs. Terry Druggan
and Frankie Lake took a neighbouring estate, and Hughey Stubby
McGovern another large villa at which a non-stop house party was
held and to and from which bootleggers and mobsters and girlfriends streamed. There were big and convivial meetings at the
Hialeah horse-track and the Miami dog-tracks, and much money
surged into Florida from the Illinois bar and brothel trade. Capone
had also moved his family – his wife, son, mother, sister and
brothers John and Matthew – into a pleasant, plain, quiet residential house on Prairie Avenue, on Chicago's South Side; he had
there as neighbours two policemen and a police sergeant. The
Capones, the only Italians on the block, were liked by the other
Prairie Avenue householders, who included, as well as the police
element, a druggist, a publisher, a draughtsman, a Presbyterian
minister and a clothing manufacturer. Capone's sister, Mafalda,
was then attending a girls' private school, to which at Christmas
time Capone drove up with his car laden with gifts for all the pupils
and teachers, and turkeys and fruit for the term-end dinner.

He was encouraging, and enjoying, his reputation as a free-
spender and good guy. When he attended a prize fight he bought a
hundred dollars' worth of extra tickets, which he handed out to the
youngsters who milled around him calling "Hi, Al!" Such munificence was increasingly easy. The daily – and nightly – scene at the
Metropole Hotel was indicative of his swelling importance. A
description by a reporter who knew it at that time was this: "It
was garrisoned like Birger's blockhouse in the woods in Bloody

Williamson county. The Capones occupied as many as fifty rooms on two heavily guarded floors. They operated their own private elevators and maintained their own service bars. Gambling went on openly and women visited the floors at all hours of the day and night. The aroma of highly flavoured Italian foods brought in from the outside permeated the corridors. Nearly every hotel rule and regulation was violated daily. On Sunday mornings especially the lobby was a beehive of activity. Prominent criminal lawyers and high officials of the police department, along with politicians and dive-keepers waited their turn to consult with the Big Shot. Policemen in uniform streamed in and out. A blind pig operated in the lobby by a semi-public official did a land-office business. In an underground vault, specially constructed, was stored 150 thousand dollars' worth of wines and liquors. The stock was constantly replenished. It was for the gang's private use. Capone himself occupied rooms 409 and 410, overlooking the boulevard. The hallway was patrolled by sentinels, posted at regular intervals as in an army. In an ante-room of the Capone suite was the body-guard, equipped with the latest type of fire-arms."

Two blocks away Capone had more private and intimate quarters, at 2146 South Michigan Avenue, where there was a small plate on the door bearing the name Dr A. Brown. This was the strongroom of the syndicate, the business cell that was overseen by Jack Guzik, the financial head and man of solid and weighty status in the underworld (and so he still was twenty-five years later when the Kefauver Committee examined his gambling activities and reported that the reformed Accardo-Guzik-Fischetti Chicago crime ring was then "one of the two major underworld organizations in the nation"). Jack Guzik and his brother Harry (a convicted, but unpunished, pimp who was pardoned prior to serving sentence) had been associates of Torrio since 1916. Jack Guzik was Capone's appointed dictator of gambling in Cook County, and accountant for all the prostitution, liquor and assorted rackets. When a relative of his was married in 1929 a report was carried by a morning newspaper under a two-column picture; guests included Bathhouse John Coughlin, First Ward alderman; William V. Pacelli, Bloody Twentieth Ward alderman; Captain of Police Hugh McCarthy; and Bottles Capone. The value Capone placed upon Guzik is indicated by the round-the-clock guard that he stationed at Guzik's bed when he was ill in Michael Reese Hospital. His concern for the well-being of Guzik became understandable after the raid instigated by Mayor Dever on the medical premises on South Michigan Avenue. Behind the reception room was the surgery. It contained rows of bottles, ranging from phials to quarts, containing various coloured liquids. These, a sniffing detective found, contained samples of all the types and brands of alcohol that could be offered to customers by the Capone bootleg organization, and which could be taken away for a chemist's analysis. Under Guzik's administration, an office staff of twenty-five ran the syndicate's auditing system, the machinery of "a super-trust operating with the efficiency of a great corporation" (Pasley). The records contained the names of more than two hundred well-known Chicagoans and hotels and drug-stores supplied by the syndicate, the names of police officers and Prohibition agents on the bribe list, a transportation plan for running in booze from Canada, Miami, New Orleans and New York's Rum Row, personnel lists of four breweries owned by the syndicate and producing most of Chicago's beer, brothel income ledgers, and an alphabetical register of the Illinois saloons and speakeasies buying the syndicate's drink.

It seemed, fleetingly, as if Dever was right when he announced triumphantly: "We've got the goods this time." The evidence of graft among police and Prohibition agents, and of vast illegal trade, was conclusive. Next day, before the documents could be turned over to the Federal authority as the basis for prosecution, they were impounded on the orders of a municipal judge. Sixteen hours after the Federal office at New Orleans asked for a transcript – a request which was not granted – the judge, at a special and unnotified hearing, had them returned to Capone. United States District Attorney Edwin A. Alson handed to the press his letter of protest to the judge demanding that he withhold a decision until an investigation and an inspection of the records. The letter was ignored. The judge was unscathed – except by public knowledge of his conduct – and Capone and Guzik continued their business from safer quarters. It was not until after Capone had been seized for tax evasion that Guzik was similarly overtaken by belated retribution – in 1932 he was sentenced to five years in the Leavenworth, Kansas, Penitentiary and fined 17,500 dollars for nonpayment of taxes on income of 1,538,155 dollars from gambling houses.

Mad, Bad and Dangerous to Know
(Johnny "Mad Dog" Adair)

David Lister and Hugh Jordan

Short and muscle-bound, Johnny "Mad Dog" Adair, once the leader of the Ulster Freedom Fighters, one of Northern Ireland's loyalist paramilitary groups, was among the most feared men in the troubled Province. A target of rival IRA attacks for many years during the Troubles, Adair narrowly escaped death in 1993 when the Provisionals targeted him with a bomb planted in a fish and a chip shop on Belfast's loyalist Shankill Road. Adair was imprisoned for 16 years in 1996 for directing terrorism, but released in 1999 under the Good Friday agreement, only to be rearrested the following year because he posed a threat to the Northern Ireland peace process. Released again 21 months later, the Shankill Godfather sought to persuade his detractors that he was a changed man; he took a job as a prisoners' welfare co-ordinator, a £16,500 p.a. post funded by the British taxpayer. He fell out with his old supporters, moved to England with a few loyal colleagues, set up home in Bolton but finally moved to Scotland when his marriage broke up, and was last heard of living on benefit in Troon. He also has plans for a drama based on his life as one of the most recognisable faces of terrorism in the 1990s. From his years in a skinhead band to his bloody reign as a loyalist thug, Adair's career was charted by two British journalists, David Lister and Hugh Jordan, in a biography Mad Dog *published in 2003.*

B y the time he was 16, Johnny Adair had left school and joined his father as a wood machinist in the Ulster Timber Company in Duncrue Street in Belfast docks. Although the work was menial it gave him enough money to buy drink and to finance his new hobby: music. With their dark suits, pork pie hats and shades, the ska band Madness caught the imagination of many British teenagers and Adair and his best friend, Sam "Skelly" McCrory, were no exceptions. But Adair's love of ska was only a warm-up to a style of music that was far more direct and aggressive. By 1980, the skinhead revival was in full swing. On street corners across Britain, shaven-headed young men and women, angry at rising unemployment and immigration, stood in packs drinking and sniffing glue. Their music, known as "Oi!", was as blunt as their image. Among the bands Adair enjoyed and admired were The 4-Skins and Infa Riot (pronounced "In For A Riot"), but the one he and Skelly listened to most was Skrewdriver. A neo-Nazi group that openly proclaimed its support for the National Front (NF), it was so right-wing that its lead singer, Ian Stuart, made speeches between songs attacking immigration. A leading member of the Blackpool branch of the National Front, Stuart was even pictured on the cover of one album shaking hands with a Ku Klux Klan grand master in full ceremonial dress.

The anti-immigration outbursts meant next to nothing to Adair and his friends in Northern Ireland, where there were hardly any black faces. But for Protestants living under the shadow of the IRA, there was one message above all that hit home with a vengeance. "It was the Britishness thing," said one former skinhead. "The first song I ever heard was 'The Voice of Britain' by Skrewdriver. It gave you a sense of pride, that you were a British skinhead, that you were proud to be a Protestant." Like many other Protestant youths from the staunchly loyalist Shankill Road, Adair and his friends were swept up by the skinhead scene. As well as shaving their heads, they sniffed glue from plastic bags and listened to "Oi!" music in a community centre on the lower Shankill estate. Called The Ultimate, it cost £1 to get in but you were allowed to bring your own drink. According to one skinhead who hung around with Adair and his friends: "All the skinheads would have went there and we used to then go into the town and fight with the Fenians (Catholics)."

Like his friends, Adair was often getting into fights, and to this day his head bears a number of scars that date back to these years.

More often than not knives were produced and bottles thrown. Though Adair knew how to fight, he was small and less physically intimidating than Skelly and Donald Hodgen, another close friend who'd known Adair since his schooldays. But his friends looked to him as their leader. "He would say and do crazy things," said one old friend. "You'd all be starting to walk home from the town and it would be Johnny who would suggest going up the (Catholic) Falls Road and cutting across rather than walking back up the Shankill. At that stage you would never have thought about walking up the Falls but, because Johnny suggested it, you did it."

Adair was often accompanied by his girlfriend, Gina Crossan, a slim, dark-haired girl from Manor Street. She was three years younger than him; they started dating in 1980, when Gina was just 14, and would stay together on and off for the next two decades. Gina, too, was a skinhead, sporting just a tiny tuft of hair at the front of her shaved head. But by far Adair's best friend was Skelly. By now the pair were extremely close, and throughout their youth they would often hug and hold each other, provoking constant speculation about the nature of their friendship. To this day Skelly remains a complex personality. A thug and a bully, he also has a soft side and is openly gay. Even by his teens the contradictions were obvious. One moment he was in the thick of a skinhead brawl and the next he was going to bingo, as he did every week, with a bisexual man.

By 1980, Adair and Skelly had formed a skinhead band together with Brian "Watsy" Watson, who lived around the corner from Adair, and Julian "Tarzan" Carson. Although Adair likes to claim responsibility for founding and naming Offensive Weapon, in reality the idea came from Watson. The only talented one among them, Watson played lead guitar and wrote most of their songs. Adair played bass guitar, although he would later claim that he was the band's lead singer. He only opened his mouth to back up Skelly, who delivered the band's incomprehensible lyrics with a growling rage.

Between 1981 and 1984, Offensive Weapon played around 20 concerts. The venues included the loyalist club in Romford Street, off the Shankill Road, the Buff's Club, the White Cross Inn in North Street and the Times Bar in the loyalist Tigers Bay district.

Several of their songs were borrowed from English bands, including "Sorry" and "Evil" by the 4-Skins. Skelly's rendition of the latter went down especially well:

> I like breaking arms and legs
> Snapping spines and wringing necks
> Now I'll knife you in the back
> Kick your bones until they crack
> (chorus) Evil, evil, evil, evil (x4)

No Offensive Weapon concert was complete without their popular song "Bulldog," which provoked hysteria whenever it was played. The song shared its name with the magazine of the Young National Front. It was invariably preceded by Nazi salutes from the band and chants from the audience of "Sieg Heil! Sieg Heil!".

By 1983, the links between Protestant skinheads and the National Front were becoming increasingly close. A number of NF supporters came from England to attend Offensive Weapon concerts and seized the opportunity to hand out leaflets. Some time in 1983 Adair attended a meeting at the Ormeau Road Library in south Belfast, which had been booked in the name of a local fishing club but was in reality a cover for the NF. They were preparing for a big day intended to launch their campaign for support in Northern Ireland. That day came on 3 September 1983, when Adair and his friends were among up to 300 who took part in the NF's first ever rally in Northern Ireland. Dubbed the "glue-sniffers' march" because it consisted almost entirely of skinheads, it set off from the loyalist Sandy Row district and proceeded through the city centre before stopping on the Shankill Road. It was denounced by Sinn Fein as an ultra-fascist and sectarian show of strength. Protestant skinheads did not echo this view. "It was class. All you would have seen was Union Jack after Union Jack," said one. "There was all this stuff about blacks, lefties and Britain for the British."

Adair himself never took the NF's anti-immigration views terribly seriously. Like other youths on the Shankill, he went along with the politics because of the NF's anti-IRA stance and because it was an exhilarating movement that swept up many from the same background. As well as the Belfast march, he attended an NF rally in Coleraine the following year. Along with Skelly, Donald and four other Protestants from the Shankill and nearby Tigers Bay, he also spent a weekend in London, where they attended a National Front "tea party" and met Ian Stuart of Skrewdriver. According to one of the group, while in London they beat up and mugged a black man.

But in truth Adair was an unlikely NF supporter, and throughout his life he has enjoyed reggae music and apparently had a fascination with black women.

Although the Belfast rally attracted reasonable support, the conditions did not exist in Northern Ireland for an anti-immigration party to have any great success. As well as being almost exclusively white, the Province's main loyalist paramilitary groups, the Ulster Volunteer Force (UVF) and the Ulster Defence Association (UDA), viewed any pro-Nazi display as a direct attack on the United Kingdom. "What you have to remember is that a lot of people in the paramilitaries would have had relatives who fought in the war," said one skinhead. As a result, the link between far-right groups in Britain and loyalist terrorists never took over, although informal connections remain up to the present day.

For Adair and Skelly, the most important thing was their music, and neither had anything to do with either the UVF or the UDA. Adair in particular was proud of being a member of the first skinhead band on the Shankill. He was delighted when the group was mentioned in an article in the Belfast *Telegraph* on 14 June 1983. In January the following year Adair told a reporter from the Belfast *Sunday News* that he wanted a harder head because he was getting in so many fights. "I've been hit over the head with a hammer, a crowbar, a cider bottle and a hurley stick," he disclosed.

"Anyone want to help us do a bus?" The words caught some of Johnny Adair's friends by surprise as they stood drinking cider outside the Buff's Club on Century Street, a spot where many of them hung out and harassed passers-by.

Adair and Skelly had just returned from a meeting of the Ulster Defence Association's C8 team and the pair, egging each other on as usual, had volunteered to hijack a bus and set it alight. C8 was one of up to 18 "teams" of between 30 and 60 people which, between them, formed the UDA's "C Company" on the Shankill Road. Their commander, Andrew "Doodles" Calderwood, had made the instructions short but clear. "We want the peelers [police] to know we can take them on," he had told them. "John", a childhood friend of Adair's, recalls: "About 20 of us piled over to the bus stop facing the Buff's Club, the bus came up and we jumped on and said it was a hijack, but your man [the bus driver] just laughed at us. We told your man to drive across the road, but somebody poured the petrol over one of us rather than the bus."

According to one of Adair's C8 superiors, the hijacking descended into a farce. "They weren't successful in their operation, let's just say that," gibed the C Coy veteran. "They all got on the bus, but they didn't have a lighter or a match between them to set it on fire with. That's been a common joke on the Shankill over the years."

Adair's first operation had ended in embarrassing failure, with police recovering the bus before serious damage could be done to it. The date was 15 August 1984, and the Shankill was entering several nights of ferocious rioting, the worst in a Protestant district for a decade. Earlier that day a scuffle had broken out in the Crumlin Road Courthouse between police and nearly 50 loyalist terrorists fingered on the evidence of the UVF supergrass, William "Budgie" Allen. Relatives of several of the accused pelted police with bags of urine, and in the mêlée eight RUC men and several defendants were injured. That night more than 500 loyalists took to the streets, setting two shops on fire. A stream of rioters tore up paving stones and hurled them at police. Although most of the violence was orchestrated by the UVF, the UDA was also involved. Over the next four nights Protestant mobs torched cars and threw petrol bombs and anything else they could lay their hands on. For the first time in ten years loyalists opened fire on the RUC, who responded with plastic bullets.

Although Adair was still a skinhead, the movement was dying a death and Offensive Weapon had come to the end of its natural life. He had swapped one gang for another, joining the UDA several months earlier after it drew up a list of nearly 20 people, all of whom it considered to be a nuisance in the area. Not surprisingly, the majority belonged to Adair's extended circle of friends. Word had reached the UDA that they had been attacking police officers and breaking into new houses in the Oldpark. They were told in no uncertain terms to join up or take a bullet in the leg. Most were known as rioters, and by 1984 Adair had a criminal record that was typical of many youths from his area. Since 1979 he had been before the courts an average of three times a year.

It was little surprise that Adair and his friends were attracting the attention of their local paramilitaries. But there was nothing to suggest that any of them would go on to do anything more sinister than rioting. "We were all rioting," said one childhood friend who later moved away from the Shankill. "The Johnny Adair I knew is not the Johnny Adair that emerged later. I can put my hand on my heart and say that, although he was occasionally slightly crazy, he was not a psychopath. Where that came from I don't know, but it must have been something that happened in his early twenties."

Neither Adair nor his friends had previously even toyed with the idea of joining the UDA or the UVF, the two main loyalist paramilitary groups. The UDA was formed in 1971 as a network of vigilante groups, with at one point more than 40,000 members. It was born on the Shankill and retained a strong power base there, but in the early Eighties most youths regarded it as little more than an overgrown working men's club. To the disgust of many nationalists, the UDA was able to recruit openly because it was still technically legal, and remained so until 1992; however, its killing arm, the Ulster Freedom Fighters, was illegal. Adair was sworn in on a Friday night in an upstairs room at a C Coy social club. Four masked men stood in front of a table draped in a UDA flag, on top of which was a copy of the Bible and a 9mm pistol. The UDA's solemn oath was read to Adair and slowly and deliberately he repeated it:

"I, Johnny Adair, am a Protestant by birth and, being convinced of a fiendish plot by republican paramilitaries to destroy my heritage, do swear to defend my comrades and my country, by any and all means, against the Provisional IRA, INLA, and any other offshoot of republicanism which may be of similar intent. I further swear that I will never divulge any information about my comrades to anyone and I am fully aware that the penalty for such an act of treason is death. I willingly take this oath on the Holy Bible witnessed by my peers."

Adair and his friends went straight into C8. "They all wanted to join C8 – it was the most militant and the most popular because it was all headers in it," said one C8 veteran.

Like most volunteers in the Eighties, Adair did relatively little to begin with. He paid his dues and attended C8 meetings, but was otherwise busy with the arrival of his first child, Jonathan, who was born on 23 August 1984, just days after the riots ended. In the middle of 1984, Adair and Gina Crossan, his girlfriend, moved into 10 Beechnut Place, off the Oldpark Road. It was a tight-knit community and just around the corner from his parents in Century Street. At this time Adair was still working at the Ulster Timber Company in Duncrue Street in the docks area. "He was leading an ordinary life," said Ian Truesdale, a C9 member, two years older than Adair. "He didn't just join the UDA and go straight into being a gunman.

"You have to work your way up. He'd have gone to the meetings, started to know who was who, sat back and done his homework before saying, 'I want a piece of the action.'"

Adair himself is vague about his early UDA career, and his memory of these years has been badly damaged by years of glue-sniffing. During his first two years as a UDA foot soldier, the most he was involved in was shooting at police, taking part in punishment beatings, robbery and arson. But for most of the Eighties, Adair's bread and butter was still rioting, and there was plenty to keep him busy. On 15 November 1985, Margaret Thatcher and Garret FitzGerald, the Irish Prime Minister, signed the Anglo-Irish Agreement at Hillsborough Castle outside Belfast. For the first time, Dublin was given a direct say in the internal administration of Northern Ireland and a "secretariat" for Irish government officials was established at Maryfield, Co Down.

Britain had committed the ultimate betrayal. On 20 November Tom King, the Secretary of State for Northern Ireland, was attacked by a crowd of loyalists as he visited Belfast City Hall. On 23 November Adair was among more than 100,000 people who attended a huge "Ulster Says No" rally outside the City Hall. Over the next few months civil unrest swept loyalist areas.

Since the early Eighties, the UFF, the UDA's military wing, had been virtually nonexistent, particularly in west Belfast, where the level of military operations was kept to a minimum by Tommy "Tucker" Lyttle, the UDA "brigadier" who was also a paid Special Branch informer. But the Anglo-Irish Agreement was to change all that. "I noticed a lot more activity within our own ranks – preparing for assassinations, preparations, training and more recruiting," said William "Moe" Courtney, a former ally of Adair and C Coy veteran. "The training at that stage got more serious. We went off on training days outside Belfast – Co Derry, in that direction."

The exact location was a farm about two hours' drive from Belfast. It was not used for weapons instruction but rather for teaching a series of basic military and survival skills, initiative tests and fitness training. Above all, it was intended for young volunteers who had been singled out as "officer material" by the UDA's hierarchy and selected to join a special outfit called the Ulster Defence Force (UDF). In the words of one UDA "brigadier", "The UDF was meant to be like Sandhurst or something. The idea was that the people in it would have no criminal record and a squeaky-clean image, but the training camp became more of a physical thing than anything else."

Among those who blagged their way on to the course by lying

about their brushes with the law were Johnny Adair and several of his friends. "Johnny got his silver wings before he was kicked out – Big Donald (Hodgen) and Skelly did as well," said one C Coy veteran. "At one time just about everyone was getting up for a weekend."

Many young UDA militants were now convinced the time had come for more than training.

The inevitable finally happened on 26 August 1986, when Paddy McAllister, a 47-year-old Catholic with four children, was shot dead as he watched television in his home off the Falls Road in nationalist west Belfast. It was C Coy's first "hit" in nearly five years. He worked as a black-taxi driver, an occupation that marked him out as a republican sympathizer in the eyes of loyalists.

By the time McAllister was shot dead in 1986, Johnny Adair was just starting to take part in C Coy murder bids. In the summer of 1985, William "Winkie" Dodds had been released from jail after serving six years for robbing a post office. The 27-year-old Oldpark man started running C8 and shortly became C Coy's military commander. A quiet, thick-set man with a pistol tattooed on his left forearm, Dodds was a dedicated sectarian "operator".

Dodds was keen to bring on Adair and his friends, most of whom he knew from growing up in the Oldpark. It was Winkie who showed Adair how to fire a gun. According to "John", a C8 member close to Adair, "We never really got any formal weapons training. I think once we were shown how to use a gun in a community centre."

In 1986, "John" went out on his first murder bid, accompanied by Adair: "It was Johnny, me and [one other]. It was up the Oldpark. Somebody supplied information on a republican and we went out with a shotgun and a Magnum and we rapped the door and your man came out but he slammed the door shut.

"There was a wee windie down the door and he was shot through the windie but didn't die."

It was a difficult time for Adair. Badly injured in a fight, he lost his spleen and punctured a lung, and spent several days in intensive care. In February 1985, another old friend, Mark Rosborough, had been found dead on a rubbish tip after being savagely beaten by three UVF men.

In 1986, Adair lost another friend, this time through his own doing.

Maurice Drumgoole was one of several passengers in a car Adair was driving when it crashed just outside Belfast. Adair had no licence and was also drunk. According to one former colleague, "It affected Johnny very badly."

On 19 November 1986, Adair appeared at Antrim Magistrates' Court and was convicted of reckless driving, driving while under the influence of drink and without insurance or a licence. He was sentenced to six months' imprisonment, banned from driving for three years and fined £150.

After losing an appeal, he was jailed at Crumlin Road Prison in Belfast in February 1987. When he came out in June, Adair vowed to devote himself to his family and keep a low profile. It was fine in theory, but the lure of his friends was too great to resist. Within weeks, he was going out on regular murder attempts.

Adair and his friends, all in their mid-twenties, were racing each other for their first kill. They did not have to wait long. On 9 September 1987, two UFF gunmen shot dead Patrick Hamill, an English Catholic, at his home off the Falls Road in nationalist west Belfast. According to police intelligence, the killers included a C8 volunteer who was one of Adair's oldest friends. Aged 29, Hamill was shot in the forehead as his wife nursed their 11-month-old baby, while her three-year-old sister played on the floor. Within hours of Hamill's murder, a Protestant lorry driver, 38-year-old Harry Sloan, was shot dead in retaliation by the IRA.

Over the next year C Coy members were involved in several murders and attempted murders. The murder of Gerard Slane was particularly gruesome. In the early hours of 23 September 1988, the 27-year-old was gunned down at his home off the Falls Road. At around 4 a.m. Slane's wife, Teresa, heard noises outside the house and got up to see what it was. She later recalled: "I remember waking up with this commotion going on, with Gerard running up the stairs shouting, 'Teresa, it's the Orangemen.' Then they opened fire on him."

Most of Slane's face was blown off and one bullet had ripped off his nose.

His neighbour heard the shots and looked out of the window to see Slane's "little boy, his son, in his pyjamas, and in such distress that he was jumping up and down in the front garden, lacerating his feet on the broken glass from the front door where the killers had smashed their way in".

In later years, Johnny Adair recounted in graphic detail how he had shot Slane. One friend said, "I remember Johnny telling us,

'Your man stood at the top of the stairs and as I went up after him I sprayed him from top to bottom, started on the legs and then worked my way all the way up, just cut the f***** in half.'" It was typical of Adair's bragging, which was usually intended to instil in his audience a mixture of fear and admiration.

In fact, the boast was a total lie. Adair was not even at the scene of the murder, though he sat and listened with an expression of childlike awe as one of the killers talked him through the gory details. "What did he look like?" Adair asked. "Where did the blood go? Did he say anything? Did you look in his eyes?" Two of his oldest friends had already been "blooded" but not him, and that hurt his ego. He saw no reason for facts to spoil the image, which he sought to promote at every opportunity, that C Coy's Johnny Adair was a ruthless killer.

Every time Johnny Adair was held in Castlereagh barracks he complained to his closest friends that police tormented him about two of his sisters, Lizzie and Etta, both of whom suffered from severe learning disabilities.

It was a pity, then, that his brotherly compassion did not extend to others with similar mental problems. On a freezing December night in 1993, Adair changed into a smart black jacket and black shoes before entering a derelict flat in Boundary Walk, just a few doors down from the C Coy shebeen, an illegal drinking den. There, with a young UDA member standing alongside him, he stood in front of a large man on his knees and declared, "The Ulster Freedom Fighters finds you guilty of treason and, as such, sentences you to the ultimate penalty – death." He tapped the silencer on his Magnum 10 Pistol, put it against the man's head and squeezed the trigger. Despite his boasts, Adair's big secret – which only his closest friends knew – was that he had never killed anybody. He had seized control of C Coy three years earlier and was now the UDA's "brigadier" in west Belfast, but although he was the mastermind behind a wave of killings, he had not murdered anybody by his own hand. Despite his many attempts to take life, this was the first time he had shot someone from point-blank range in the head and for a brief moment he did not know what to do. He walked out of the flat, where Gary McMaster, another C Coy man, was waiting. "Move!" he barked as he handed him the gun.

At 9.30 a.m. on 13 December 1993, a neighbour, hearing groans from the flat, pushed open the front door to reveal an appalling sight. More than 12 hours after he had been shot, 26-year-old Noel Alexander Cardwell lay in a pool of blood, still alive but only just. It had been so cold during the night that his blood had been prevented from flowing at a normal rate, delaying his death and prolonging his agony by a few extra hours. After being rushed to hospital, he died at 10.20 a.m. McMaster was later given a life sentence for his role in the murder, though Adair has never been charged with the killing. In a telephoned admission of responsibility, the UFF said Cardwell had been executed by the terrorist group's "Special Assassination Section".

It said he was a Special Branch informer and blamed him for a series of recent weapons finds. The claim was a lie. Noel Cardwell had been assassinated because Adair could not resist the opportunity to look ruthless in front of his men. Even if he had wanted to, Cardwell would not have been able to disclose much to police because he was not a UDA member.

There was also one other fact that made him an unlikely candidate for a police informer: he had the mental age of a 12-year-old. "He used to play about with the kids outside," said a relative after the shooting. "He would do anything they asked, he was so soft."

Jackie Robinson, Adair's former girlfriend and fiancée, remembers "Big Noel" as a harmless young fellow who collected glasses in the Diamond Jubilee Bar on the lower Shankill. "All he wanted was to be in with the big boys. He was very simple-minded," said Jackie. "He just wanted to be liked and he thought it was great to be around Johnny and his clique."

Cardwell had been abducted by two C Coy henchmen earlier that day shortly after checking out of the Royal Victoria Hospital on the Falls Road, where he had spent the night after some of Adair's friends spiked his drink in a bar, in a typically callous prank. While in hospital, however, Cardwell received a visit from the police, who, due to the suspicious circumstances under which he had been admitted, were keen to find out who he had been drinking with. Not thinking that he was doing anything wrong, Cardwell named two UDA men who were then arrested, questioned and released without charge. Cardwell's simple-mindedness cost him his life. After being picked up from the hospital by his sister he headed to the Buff's Club on the Oldpark Road for a quick game of snooker with his friends. He never made it home.

Murder at the Blind Beggar
(Ronald Kray)

Brian McConnell

The Kray twins became icons of post-war Britain. Ronnie Kray (1933–1995) was a dangerous, unstable schizophrenic, the brawny half of a terrifying killing partnership that dominated the criminal East End underworld of the 1950s and 60s. With his brainier twin brother Reg (1933–2000), Ronnie Kray spent most of his national service in the glasshouse for assaulting NCOs or going AWOL. On his discharge, Ronnie (known as "The Colonel") was already showing signs of the unbalanced personality that became the twins' strength and weakness; Ronnie's sudden violent mood swings inspired fear in rival criminals, but also embroiled them (and their elder brother Charlie) in pointless violence for which the three Krays served more than 70 years behind bars. In 1956 Ron was sentenced to three years for GBH and two years later was certified insane. In 1966, he murdered fellow villain George Cornell, shooting him in the Blind Beggar pub in the East End. At first, all the witnesses were too frightened to give evidence and it seemed for a time that the Krays were untouchable. The following year, Reg butchered Jack "The Hat" McVitie, a small time crook and disrespectful Kray irritant, and again, it looked as though the twins would get away with it. But when Detective Superintendent Leonard "Nipper" Read spearheaded a huge police operation to bring them to book, witnesses eventually testified and the twins were given life sentences with a recommendation of 30 years. This account of Ronnie Kray's murderous visit to the Blind Beggar is by the journalist Brian McConnell (1928– 2004) who wrote a book about the twins based on reports of their trial in the Daily Mirror. *In March 1974 he was shot during an attack on Princess Anne by a crazed gunman in The Mall. The man had planned to kidnap the princess and demand a £3m ransom. Brian McConnell, travelling in a passing taxi, was presented with the Queen's Gallantry Medal for his role in helping to foil the kidnap.*

For more than three hundred years, old women have wept at the tale of *The Blind Beggar*. Young lovers have sighed at it, and children have been put happily to sleep by it, for it is that kind of story.

Originally a ballad by Percy, the sixteenth century writer, and included in his work *Reliques*, it was written-up into a heart-rending, tear-jerking play, *The Blind Beggar of Bethnal Green* by Chettle and Day in the year 1600. In 1834, playright Sheridan Knowles took the story as the basis of yet another melodrama, and thus it became a legend, part of East End folklore in poetry, in songs, and on the boards.

The story itself is simplicity. Bessee, a beauteous damsel of Bethnal Green, or Bednall Green as it was originally called, was pursued and courted by four suitors at once. They were each young men of substance: a knight, a gentleman of fortune, a London merchant, and the son of an innkeeper from Romford, Essex. Each in turn asked for her hand in marriage, and to each Bessee said, "You must ask my father's permission." When they learned that her father was a blind beggar, three of the four abandoned their suits and vanished. Only the knight still wanted to marry her. Her father agreed, and gave one hundred pounds for her wedding gown and three thousand pounds for her dowry.

At the wedding feast, the finale of the story, the blind beggar explained that he was not just a poor sightless alms-seeker. He was in fact Henry, the son of the great Simon de Montfort, father of the English parliament. When Simon was slain on the battlefield at Evesham, his son was not, as history has it, slain with him. He lost his sight in the battle, but was cared for by a lady who found him and tended his wounds and, as a result of this sick-bed ministration, bore him a daughter, the beautiful Bessee of Bethnal Green. And so they lived happily ever after . . .

Shortly after 8.30 p.m. on the night of 9 March 1966, the new story of The Blind Beggar of Bethnal Green was to enter the pages of East End folklore, but not with tears of happiness. Instead of romance it became a tale of brutal, horrible murder which, on the face of it, had no apparent or obvious motive, and no arrestable culprit. It was, however, a gang murder for power, prestige and pride, and was carried out by Ronald Kray.

When most of the members of the Richardson gang were taken into custody, into hospital or placed under surveillance following the shooting affray at Mr Smith's one member of the gang remained at large. And this was not just an odd man out, but an active lieutenant of the gang who had escaped the law's net. This was George Cornell of the South London mob, a key figure in the torture and extortion racket operated by the Richardsons. Whilst he was at large he could organize another gang, carry on the work of the Richardsons, and be a threat to the enterprises of the Kray firm, to their authority, and to their prestige. Worse than that, he was a tough villain who did not fear anyone, certainly not the Krays nor their henchmen.

That is why he thought nothing, on that March night of 1966, of crossing the River Thames by way of London Bridge, from South London to the East End, to have a quiet drink in the centre of what police and criminals alike acknowledged to be the Kray manor.

The word "manor" used by policemen since times immemorial to describe the beat and the territory they covered, and popularised by the late Edgar Wallace in his crime novels of the 1920s, was also the term adopted by the Krays. To them it meant more than just a criminal territory. It meant literally, a feudal domain. Just as the medieval lords kept their manors, comprising their homes and the surrounding lands for their own personal exploitation and use, so the Krays intended to keep and to exploit their manor in every particular.

Consequently, for Cornell to enter upon their domain and sit and drink there with his henchmen was a provocation and a threat in itself. The quintet from the other side of the river drove through Aldgate, spanning the actual square mile of the City of London, and pulled up at the Mile End Gate, the invisible boundary of the commercial capital marked by the beginnings of Bethnal Green. Car parked at right angles to kerb on the wide road, they crossed the ample pavement to the terraced public house, The Blind Beggar.

The pub had always been a local landmark, but in appearance it was not very prepossessing, with its flat frontage below an upstairs bow window and two entrances into two long bars, which were joined into an overall "U" by the rear Snug. This was the layout: Saloon on the left, Public Bar on the right, Snug at the back, private living quarters above, cellar down below.

In the East End, they say criminals use Saloons and pensioners the Public Bars, and this is how it was – at least for the most recent arrivals – on this midweek evening. Only one customer, an old-age pensioner and a regular, was sipping his Guinness in the Public Bar. Into the Saloon went Cornell and his comrades for "five light ales, mate", as they told the cellar-boy. Up came the "lights" and Cornell took a stool, not against the counter but out in the middle of the floor, while his companions formed a semi-circle in syco-phantic deference around him.

They had not sipped long before first one and then another of his unidentified companions left the party and left the pub. It was about then that the finger was put on George Cornell and the telephone rang in The Lion in Tapp Street, a mere half a mile away in the hinterland behind the Whitechapel Road: only a few min-utes' drive for a car. It was Ronald Kray that the telephone rang for. He was wanted – and urgently.

It was a typical scene in the pub known popularly as "The Widow's", or "Madge's" with the mob fawning on the twins. Big "Scotch Ian" was there as the principal minder of the night, and when Ronald came back from the phone a tough Glaswegian had joined the group.

"Got your car?" Ronnie asked the newcomer, short, stocky John "Scotch Jack" Dickson.

Told that it was outside, Ronnie promptly made up his mind on his course of action. "Take Ian and me down the Whitechapel Road to the London Hospital," he ordered with native caution, and off the trio went. Ronnie, immaculate as usual in a dark suit, white shirt and discreet dark tie, followed by John "Ian" Barrie, tall, muscular and fair haired, and by Dickson, the one-eyed driver.

"We won't be long," Ronnie tossed over his shoulder as they went out, as if he was only disappearing for a second to wash his hands.

Out in the grey Ford Cortina, down the rainswept streets to the Whitechapel Road, they went, and Ronnie ordered Dickson to pull up beyond the hospital at The Grave Maurice public house. "Won't be a minute," said Ronnie as he jumped out of the car and dashed inside. A few moments later he rejoined his Scots companions and told the driver to move on to The Blind Beggar. There, Dickson was to turn the car around and wait with the engine running. And this time Ronnie was accompanied by Barrie when he got out of the car, and both men had guns in their possession as they walked quickly into the Saloon Bar of the Beggar, which was hung around with gay fairy lights.

The cellar-boy had gone home to his supper, leaving only a part-time barmaid on duty. She was a one-night-a-week employee, earning a little extra money to keep her two children, and that evening she was finding custom scarce and her work monotonous. To enliven the dull atmosphere in the pub she switched on the record-player, choosing the then current top of the hit parade, the Walker Brothers' rendering of *The sun ain't gonna shine any more*, and as she turned from the record-player she saw Ronnie and "Scotch Ian" walk into the Saloon. They strode straight forward until they were directly in front of Cornell on his mid-floor stool.

Cornell was a big, bull-necked fellow in his mid-thirties, no older than his visitors, but his face looked as if it had more years and experience and wisdom and knowledge than theirs. His mouth, thin and tight, was drawn up into the permanent sardonic sneer of one who was liable to say something objectionable to anyone who challenged him. And this time was no exception.

He looked up at Ronnie Kray and, with effortless sarcasm, said "Well, just look who's here". They were the last words that Cornell ever spoke.

Ronnie had pulled out a 9mm Mauser pistol, and Barrie produced a .32 revolver from his raincoat pocket. While the Scot blasted off warning shots which ricocheted from the ceiling to the floor, smashed against the fancy wrought ironwork of the Snug and left tell-tale holes in the furniture and the wall, the Kray twin looked down at the seated Cornell and fired just once. The bullet smashed into the South Londoner's forehead just above the right eye and emerged, spent, from the back of his neck, toppling him from his high stool seat of honour. Without a word, the gunmen had arrived and fired. Without a word now they left, and the needle of the record-player at that moment stuck on the tune's key phrase: "*The sun ain't gonna shine any more . . . any more . . . any more . . . any more . . .*"

The barmaid hurried round, cradled Cornell's head, and removed the cigarette which had fallen from his tight lips onto his shirtfront where it was burning both shirt and body.

By the time the police arrived the killers and their chauffeur had vanished. A police constable removed the offending arm of the record-player, and an investigation began. But as in so many other criminal cases in and around the East End, the first barrier to be surmounted was one of silence. For it soon transpired that it wasn't only the Beggar which had been blind that night. So had every possible witness to the shooting, the barmaid particularly. She had, she said, been in the cellar at the time, and had returned to find Cornell lying on the floor. No, she wasn't able to assist in identifying the killers because she hadn't seen them. Nor could she help in identifying the men who had been drinking with Cornell when the shooting began. The last two companions, like the first two, had vanished.

Two perfectly respectable businessmen, who had been in the Snug, claimed quite rightly that they couldn't see what had gone on in the long Saloon Bar. Besides, they had promptly dived for cover when the first shots rang out. As for the elderly gentleman in the Public Bar sipping his Irish beverage, he was only too glad to talk to the reporters outside and to tell them that no-one, but no-one, could see anything which transpired in the Saloon Bar from the depths of the Public, in which he had been devotedly minding his own business.

Dickson, meanwhile, had driven his passengers back up Whitechapel Road and through the back streets to the Tapp Street railway arch beneath the Bethnal Green railway station, and had parked diagonally opposite The Lion pub.

All that was said on the journey came from Ronnie. "Dead men don't tell any tales."

But was George Cornell dead? Fast moving ambulancemen whisked his crumpled body into a waiting vehicle and over to the London Hospital, where a casualty officer promptly diagnosed a head injury which would require brain surgery. Back into the ambulance, Cornell was taken with an escort of police squad cars and motorcycle outriders, their blue lights flashing and klaxons wailing, to the Maida Vale Hospital. There, a complete theatre staff were waiting to perform whatever operation was necessary to his survival. But it was too late. The receiving surgeon at the Maida Vale Hospital looked at his last-chance patient and shook his head. "Sorry," he said. "This man is dead."

But Ronnie Kray was going to have to wait some time for this information to reach him. Back at The Lion pandemonium was the customer. "Ronnie had just shot George Cornell," gasped one of the group. Back came Reggie's rejoinder: "Ronnie does do some funny things." But the exchange, though outwardly calm, masked an undercurrent of panic.

Reginald rushed out of the pub and, seeing three brothers whom he knew getting out of their car, shouted to them to take Ronnie away with them. "Drive off the manor!" he yelled. "And drive careful. We don't want a pull."

What he meant was a pull from the arm of the law for a speeding or other traffic offence. One by one the cars left until the widow's pub was deserted.

Off the manor meant away from the Krays' usual haunts. But not so far away as to be out of touch. Ronnie, identifiable if a witness to the killing could be found, had changed his dark smart suit for an ill-fitting pair of trousers and a jersey which was far too big for him. One member of The Firm asked: "What's wrong?" Back came the answer: "I hope he's dead."

The brothers' car headed eastward for six miles to the High Street, Walthamstow, and to The Chequers, a big three-story pub on a corner which had more than the usual amount of accommodation. There, in a private room at the rear of the ground floor usually reserved for parties, The Firm held a council of war to decide just where Ronnie and Barrie should stay until the heat was taken out of the police investigation into the shooting at The Blind Beggar. Something had to be done, and done fast, for everyone knew that it wouldn't take the smartest police officer in the metropolis to deduce that the shooting of a South London gangster in the East End must be the work of an East End gangster who was, at the very least, in some way connected with the Kray twins.

And while members of The Firm wrestled with the knotty problem that all of this posed Ronnie Kray went out to a washbasin and, while Reggie held his head down, was violently sick. Sick with the sight of the blood bursting out of George Cornell's head, sick with panic, or sick with travel? He was certainly sick with worry about one thing: was George Cornell dead? There was only one way to find out. The landlord of the pub was summoned and asked if he had a radio upstairs and if the twins could listen to the news bulletin at midnight. "We want to hear all the football results," said Reggie. And upstairs they went.

Closing time had long since been called. The minutes dragged
slowly by as the late night music programme brought a rhythmic
end to the day for ordinary listeners. Then, at last, came the final
news bulletin:

"Manchester United won the Quarter Final of the European
Cup tonight by beating Benfica five–one. United won the contest
on an eight-to-three aggregate. Tonight, Manchester's goals came
from George Best, who scored twice, and from Connelly, Crerand
and Charlton. Benefica's goal came when Brennan, the Manchester right back, deflected into his own goal."

There followed news that, in the same competition, Real Madrid
had beaten Anderlecht four goals to two, and Partizan Belgrade
had beaten Sparta Prague five–nil, after which the results of the
Cities Fairs Cup and the Football Association fifth-round replays
were announced.

The audience in The Chequers grew increasingly restive.

Even when it was announced that the East End side, West Ham,
had beaten West Bromwich Albion two goals to one in the first leg
of the Football League Cup, the East Enders showed only im-
patience. They were waiting for something else, and this was
neither the Third Division nor the Fourth Division results.

They had to listen to the outcome of all the matches being played
for the Scottish Cup and to the results from both divisions of the
Scottish League before they heard what they had so long awaited.
"A man," said the newscaster, "was shot dead in an East End
public house tonight. He was later identified as Mr George
Cornell, of Camberwell Green. After the shooting he was taken
to Maida Vale Hospital for brain surgery, but was found to be dead
on arrival."

The usual formula followed about the police seeking a man – or
men – who could help them in their inquiries, but what was known
to the police and the populace was hardly admissible in a British
court of law.

It seemed that everybody knew that a Kray had killed Cornell,
but because the beggars were blind and the witnesses both deaf and
dumb no-one could ever prove it. After hearing the glad news of
Cornell's death, Ronnie left The Chequers with one of the brothers who had driven him there and – together with Barrie – stayed
with the man's wife and children while the police investigation into
the killing proceeded. He kept in touch with events by posting old
Bill Exley, a member of The Firm, with a shotgun at the family

house in Vallance Road. If the police called, he would let the twins know by telephone. If anyone called seeking revenge for Cornell's death, he would use the shotgun to protect the Kray property.

In their bolthole the two fugitives from The Blind Beggar and other members of The Firm made merry. They even held a party at which was performed the then popular dance of Zorba the Greek. "When Zorba dances everybody dances" was the legend of the film of that name, and when the Krays said drink and have a party everyone drank and had a party. As the music of Zorba quickened and the beat became more frenetic a neighbour complained by banging on the wall and when, in response, the music only got louder the neighbour called the police.

A uniformed policeman thereupon visited the hideaway flat and asked the occupants if they would turn their music down because it was disturbing their neighbours, and this they then obligingly did. And, throughout, Ronnie Kray remained in that party room, still in hiding.

But staying in hiding soon began to pall. Every hour of every day stretched out endlessly, and the family on which the fugitives from the police had imposed themselves began to show in a thousand-and-one little ways that they were outstaying their welcome. So Ronnie Kray moved on. He moved to a place above a barber's shop in Lea Bridge Road, Leyton, still on the edge of the Kray manor where the action was, and there the police found him and, at separate times, asked him and his twin to accompany them to separate police stations to answer some pertinent questions. Later, they were allowed to go, and that was the day reporters from Fleet Street newspapers finally ran Ronnie to earth.

He had visited a police station, and he had returned, so why could he not tell the public what was happening? Detective Superintendent "Tommy" Butler, chief of Scotland Yard's Flying Squad, had interviewed him and, apparently satisfied, had allowed him to leave. Wouldn't Ronnie now give his story to a waiting world? Surely, he had nothing to hide?

Ronnie agreed to talk about his experiences, and invited the reporters into his temporary home above the barber's shop. A minder on the door pointed up the stairs and said: "The Colonel's up there. He'll see you now." And upstairs was Ronnie, but not as smartly turned-out as usual. Instead, he was wearing a grubby white shirt tucked into his slacks, looking as if all the laundries were closed. To those surprised at his appearance he explained that this was the shirt he had been wearing when he had gone to Commercial Street Police Station, and that he had not had an opportunity to bathe or to change.

"We were having a little bit of a party in here when they picked me up," he said. "They took me to Commercial Street, and my brother, Reggie, is still inside at Leyton. The coppers didn't ask me hardly any questions at all. They told me it was about the George Cornell affair, The Blind Beggar shooting. And I was there all day yesterday and half of today, thirty-six hours in all. There was another bloke on the parade but I don't know who he was or anything about him. Two witnesses walked by the identity parade and I heard one of them say 'There's nobody here'. The other one nodded his head."

As Ronnie spoke, five men formed a semi-circle about him, silent and acquiescent. The Colonel had the floor. "I was kept in the cells," he continued, not complaining but a little regretful at having to admit it. Then he added respectfully: "Mr Butler came to see me. The police looked after me. They gave me sausage-and-mash and a pie, and tea when I wanted it. I don't know what they wanted to charge me with. Murder? Could have been murder. I just don't know what they wanted to charge me with. It may have been murder. I just don't know. They didn't tell me. That's all I can tell you."

The Colonel had spoken. The interview was at an end. And Ronald Kray had followed his recent success at Commercial Street Police Station with a competent repeat performance before an audience of equally critical reporters. But the investigation into the murder of Cornell did not end with police and reporters. Someone else had a very deep, personal interest in the killing. And that person was equally certain and satisfied that at least one of the Krays had had a hand in it.

Mrs Olive Cornell, George Cornell's widow, had less chance than anyone of proving the truth, but she tried. She suspected one particular truth with feminine intuition: that the barmaid at The Blind Beggar had seen the killers and had witnessed the murder, and was now too terrified to talk. So Mrs Cornell followed in the footsteps of her husband and went to the pub and tackled the barmaid. But that lady stuck to her story. She had been in the cellar at the time of the shooting. She had seen nothing.

If hell hath no fury like a woman scorned, then no woman scorned has the hellish fury of a woman widowed. Mrs Cornell was determined that the world should know who had murdered her husband. She went one night to the Krays' home in Vallance Road – the impregnable Fort Vallance with its armoury of weapons and its tough bodyguards – and there she announced to the street that it was the home of a killer.

Doors and windows sprang open as if by magic along the street – but stealthily, so as not to give offence to the Krays. And to make sure that the inhabitants of the street were left with no illusions whatever as to who she was shouting about, she ended her tirade with a screamed statement of fact: a Kray "killed my husband in cold blood". With that, she hurled brick after brick at the front of Fort Vallance until every window facing onto the street was shattered.

Mrs Violet Kray came out, and in tears protested innocence. "My lovely boys would never do a thing like that," she told Mrs Cornell. But the charge had reached a wider audience than the rebuttal, and even in the confines of Cockneyland the story began to be whispered, and promptly to grow. For her behaviour, Mrs Cornell was taken by the police to the magistrate's court and charged with causing wilful damage to the Kray home, and she was fined one pound which she promptly paid. But Mrs Cornell – though no Amazon – was not going to give up.

Many people asked then, and later – and are still asking now – what ordinary folk who lived in the same street as the Krays, but who were not part of The Firm, thought of the outburst. The answer is clear. They were horrified by the accusations, and although they did not altogether disbelieve them they were reluctant to commit themselves one way or the other, and certainly refrained from openly passing them on.

Some were frightened of the Krays, knew their fighting ability, knew – or suspected – their capacity for brutality, and didn't want to get involved. Others still believed the Krays to be what they had always pretended to be: charitable, generous boys. They could remember countless acts of Kray benevolence and generosity; how the twins had sent Christmas gifts each year to the children who were in the same classes of the same schools they had once been in themselves; and how when the British Empire Cancer Campaign Appeal was announced as the beneficiary of the proceeds of an amateur boxing tournament the twins had purchased two hundred pounds' worth of tickets.

The Krays had not even waited for charities to come begging.

They went to see the Mayor of Bethnal Green, Councillor Robert Hare, a van driver with the then London County Council meals-on-wheels service. Spending his life ensuring that the old folk received a hot meal as often as possible, he was touched by the Kray twins' kindred sympathy for those in need of help. "Nice, able local boys" was his opinion of them, and he was in many ways correct. For when they were not invited, or did not take part in any charity show, the attendances were down and the takings suffered considerably.

One could hardly expect the ordinary folk who lived around them to be able to work out why it was important to them to give to charity. Even when the brothers invited the stars of the Cockney comedy *Sparrers Can't Sing* to their old Double R Club to arrange yet another charity performance, who could be so ignoble as to suggest that their intervention on charity's behalf had anything but the most charitable of motives? Anyone who, in fact, had suggested such a thing would have been regarded as an unspeakable cynic and not nice to know. When they invited their friends the famous boxers – and they were indeed famous – to charity functions, and the charities benefited, they were above and beyond criticism in the eyes of the ordinary people who lived around them.

When Cassius Clay was once asked to join in their charitable endeavours, the extraordinary heavyweight declined – unimpressed by their imposing list of more accommodating pugilistic friends such as Joe Louis, Sonny Liston, and other earlier world champions. Clay the clown promptly rattled off a witty quatrain:

> *Kray, Kray, Kray,*
> *Want me to go an' stay,*
> *But while I punch and flay*
> *Who makes the hay?*

Cassius – "the lip" – might be a painful poet, but the point he was making was shrewd enough. The charities concerned undoubtedly got every penny intended for them, but were there not side-benefits for the Kray twins? Their image became even more beneficent, their influence ever more renowned. They packed the halls with the people whom they persuaded to buy tickets. No-one, apparently, could refuse the Krays anything.

Vicars, curates, church workers and social welfare helpers were all amazed at their industry. One East End woman told the Krays how difficult it was to collect for a good cause and was promptly asked to let them try on her behalf. She was amazed when they returned with armfuls of gifts, but would probably have been even more astonished to know that not all of the donors concerned had given of their merchandise willingly. The Krays were a different kind of collector to the registered charity worker. No-one would – or could – refuse them.

Of all the Kray twins' mighty and magnificent charitable gestures none was so odd as the Benefit Night they arranged for Ted Berry. An ex-boxer, Berry had been shot in the leg whilst walking near his Hackney Road home and the limb had to be amputated. Throughout the police inquiry which followed, Berry insisted that he did not know the identity of the gunman, nor any reason why anyone should want to shoot at him, and his friends and all who knew him maintained that same view. Yet many, many people in the East End knew – or could easily discover – the identity of Berry's assailant. Most certainly, just one word from the Krays would have been sufficient to produce that information. But the East End remained silent; the one word from the Krays was never uttered.

Nevertheless, the Krays felt charitably disposed towards ex-boxer Ted and arranged for the Spitalfields Porters Association to promote a mock boxing night at the York Hall swimming baths. Former boxing stars clowned away the night, and a currency note and silver collection produced a handy five hundred pounds for the bewildered Berry.

Police patronised that exceptional night out, and came away with an apt piece of philosophy: never had there been assembled so many charitable people whose charity apparently did not extend to assisting in the arrest, conviction and punishment of the criminals – obviously well known to them – who had maimed Ted Berry, their alleged friend.

As the *Sunday Times* once remarked of the Krays: "As philanthropic fund-raisers, their background may not be entirely conventional, but nobody can deny their remarkable persuasive powers."

All of which might well have been above the heads of the Krays' neighbours in Vallance Road as they heard George Cornell's widow screaming that a Kray was responsible for her husband's death. Even so, they had good reason to be grateful to the Krays themselves, for on one remarkable occasion the twins did not seek any publicity for their do-gooding. No reporters and no photo-graphers were invited when the twins sent around a vanload of gifts for the surprised and grateful pensioner members of the Good Companions Old People's Club in Vallance Road. Charity begins at home, and then – but only then, presumably – it should be anonymous.

Mrs Cornell, fresh from her demonstration in Vallance Road, had no illusions about the kind of benefit she herself was likely to receive as a result. "From that moment outside their house it was as if I was a witness to my own husband's murder. Because I had spoken out, my life was in danger. I knew from that moment – the moment I had offended their mother – that although I knew what I said to be the truth I would be on the Krays' list of victims. But I took precautions for my own safety. I also knew I wouldn't rest until they paid for George's murder."

Nor did she.

Mrs Cornell's defiant penetration of the East End became a hunt for the Achilles heel in the body of local silence. The weak point had to be another woman: the terrified barmaid who would not speak out. To Mrs Cornell she maintained her story of denial, but every time she had a visit from the widow the quiet, patient policeman, Detective Superintendent Harry Mooney, would sub-sequently drop in for a chat. He would stop by unobtrusively, talk about the weather and her two children, and enquire if she was frightened of anything. If she was frightened she had only to say so, and the police would give her all the protection necessary.

If she was afraid for the safety of her children, she had only to say so and arrangements would be made to protect them at school and at play. If she was frightened because people knew her identity and where she lived, then arrangements would be made to change that identity, and to find her a new home and a new school for her children. She had no reason, no reason at all to continue living in fear. If she had anything to add to her story about what had happened on the night of the shooting she could say what it was without fear of reprisals from anyone. That was the promise.

For with witnesses silenced by fear, or by favour, there could be no evidence, and without evidence there could be no prosecution, and without prosecution there could be no justice.

It is doubtful whether the ever-vigilant Ronald or the ever-quizzical Reginald heard – or, if they did hear, whether they fully understood – what was going on behind the scenes. If they had ever heard of Tintagel House, the high rise office block on the south side of the Thames, they showed no appreciation of the activity that was going on inside it. For if they had known what was afoot in that building overhanging the river between the Vauxhall and Lambeth bridges they would probably have forthwith broken the bonds that held them to Cockneyland and gone into hiding – perhaps for ever.

Tintagel House was the headquarters of the specially selected team of detectives which was to bring about their ultimate downfall.

The twins had certainly heard the names of the senior police officers investigating their activities, but they clearly had no idea of their strength. They had survived an investigation by Superintendent Butler, and another by Detective Superintendent James Axon. More recently, Detective Chief Superintendent Fred Gerrard and Detective Superintendent Leonard "Nipper" Reed had probed their activities, and still the Krays had survived. So contemptuous of the police, in fact, had the twins become that they described any investigating officer as a snake, and on one occasion sent to Harrods, the world-famous Knightsbridge store, for a suitable reptile for them to christen. Back came a pet boa constrictor of South American origin hopefully broken of the habit of crushing of death any casual acquaintance, and they promptly named it "Gerrard".

When "Gerrard" disappeared, they sent another message to Harrods for advice on how to find it. Back came the expert prescription: buy a second boa, and he will find the first. This they did, and the second snake, named "Reed", promptly discovered the first one snug in the airing cupboard.

To celebrate the occasion, not once, but fortnightly, the twins invited friends to a party to watch them feeding white mice to the snakes who swallowed them whole.

The real police, as distinct from the boas, were not so hasty, however. They did not swallow every piece of information with which, over the months, they were fed. Every scrap was carefully examined, and checked and counter-checked before being digested. With painful slowness, but infinite thoroughness, a reliable case against the Krays was built up.

The detectives involved in this operation had a task which – as was later revealed – was very different from anything previously known in the annals of criminal investigation. They knew of a series of crimes, and they knew the identities of the criminals responsible for their commission, but they had no evidence, no real evidence supported by witnesses, to sustain their knowledge to the point of securing convictions in a court of law.

So, while the detectives went about their business, the Krays – free as any Cockney in his restricted manor can be – went about theirs.

And a part of that business was murder.

The English Godfather
(Owney Madden)

Graham Nown

No one who met Owney Madden ever forgot him. Even as an old woman, Mae West would lift the corner of her mouth at the mention of his name and purr: "Hmmm. So sweet – and so vicious . . ." Madden was once declared America's most dangerous public enemy, and was certainly among the most influential godfathers of organized crime. Born in Leeds and raised in Liverpool, at the age of 11 he emigrated with his family to America, taking with him his northern accent and a lifelong love of racing pigeons. Settling in New York's notorious Hell's Kitchen, he was soon drawn into a life of petty crime and gang violence. He rose to prominence as the owner of the world-famous Cotton Club in New York, where he was known as the Duke of the West Side, presiding over a network of underworld bootleggers, corrupt police, judges and politicians. In 1933, to escape prosecution, Madden exiled himself to the wild gambling town of Hot Springs, Arkansas, in a million-dollar deal so secret that it was never officially recorded. There, he married the postmaster's daughter, Agnes Demby, and settled down to a life of quiet respectability. His biographer Graham Nown (1944– 97) recalled Madden's quiet, self-effacing manner. "The toughness came from within," wrote Nown, "a rock strata compressed in the Lancashire coalfields, Liverpool's dockland and the mean streets of Hell's Kitchen . . . In ten years he built up a fearsome reputation, equal, some say, to Capone's in Chicago." On his

*way to fame and fortune as "the English Godfather", Owney
Madden led a vicious street gang called The Gophers, who spent
their time raiding freight cars in the sprawling marshalling
yards at New York Central. At the age of 21, Madden was
already earning himself a hard-knock reputation as a street-
fighter and ruthless assassin.*

After a night at the movies, Owney Madden loved to saunter
down 41st Street, the heartland of Irish tribal anarchy. He
was a familiar figure, walking with his chest out, like one of his own
prize pigeons, or a duke doing the rounds of his estate. His manner
once prompted an old sergeant at West 37th Street police station –
the "Hell's Kitchen Precinct" – to call him "a banty little rooster
from hell." As he strolled along he would take everything in. He
watched faces in the crowd, noting which shops had changed hands
– absorbing every detail with the alert, restless eye of a born
survivor. An urge to know everything that was happening pre-
occupied him. At home he would read every column inch of the
newspapers, marking up items which caught his eye, and putting
them to one side for reference. Even on his deathbed, his attorney's
secretary sat for hours reading every page of the New York dailies
to him, while he nodded knowingly at one story or another.

Hell's Kitchen Precinct was one of the city's most violent police
postings. Locals called the place "the Slaughterhouse", because of
the shouts and disturbances which emanated long into the night, as
officers worked out on uncooperative young bloods to keep their
hand in. One of the most formidable characters ever stationed at
the fortress-like precinct house was Officer Patrick H. Diamond,
known throughout the West Side as "The Iron Claw." A man so
hard that he regarded police-issue revolvers with contempt, and
was never known to draw a firearm while making an arrest.

"He was reported to wear out a couple of night-sticks [trunch-
eons] a week," Hell's Kitchen historian Richard O'Connor related.
"When his weapon broke in his hands, he would hand out a cargo
hook – hence his sobriquet – and 'continue the argument', as a New
York *Sun* reporter noted." When Diamond finally retired, five
hundred gangsters and policemen joined forces to treat him to
dinner at the Old Homestead restaurant on 23rd and 8th Avenue.
They raised their glasses in salute and genuinely mourned the
passing of an era.

Hell's Kitchen officers – many of them from Ireland themselves – had to wage a running war to make their presence felt against the brawling warlords from vast families of Gallaghers, Brennans, Malarkeys and Mulraneys. Protection rackets flourished openly, houses were ransacked in broad daylight, and anyone with a hint of cash in his pocket ran a serious risk of being blackjacked to the ground.

"When he was in a mellow mood (he rarely ever drank much, but he could unbend) he liked to talk of the old days when he and his wild hellions ravaged the West Side from 42nd to 14th Streets," Stanley Walker wrote of Owney in *The Night Club Era* in the 1930s. "In retrospect these lads would appear not as bruisers, loft thieves, pickpockets or whatnot, but as good-hearted lads full of the spirit of fun and horseplay. 'Wildest bunch of roosters you ever saw,' is how he remembered them."

Burglary was one of Owney's early specialities but, despite many arrests, he was never brought to justice. The New York District Attorney files reveal a typical case in 1910, when a patrolling policeman spotted him boarding a 10th Avenue trolley car at 3am in the company of three other men. Owney and another Gopher, Eddie Jordan, were each carrying heavy bags which aroused Patrolman Collins' suspicions. He leapt onto the moving car after them and drew his revolver. Jordan threw the bag at him and all four escaped in the confusion. Owney and Eddie were later arrested and charged with stealing $43 worth of scrap metal, three watches and 160 foreign coins from a lock-up junk shop on West 33rd Street. Both pleaded not guilty when they appeared before city magistrate Paul Krotel, and were acquitted. How they managed to achieve this remarkable feat will unfortunately never be known, as the court records have since been destroyed.

The West Side gangs feared no one and displayed a strutting confidence in the power of the knife and club. One Lung Curran, a former Gopher leader, and one of the wildest figures on the street, believed that anything which caught his fancy was his for the taking. High among the legends about him, which ran like bush fires through the sawdust saloons, was the cold winter's day he strolled along with his girlfriend on a street west of 8th Avenue. The girl shivered in the freezing wind gusting up the riverside canyons, until the gallant Curran decided to do something about it. He ambled over to a patrolling policeman and, without exchanging a word, clubbed him to the sidewalk and tore off his blue serge tunic.

Curran's girl bundled it up and took it home. After a few hours
at the kitchen table with scissors and thread, she had cut it down,
nipped the waist and altered it to fit her. Even among the mixture
of styles parading Hell's Kitchen it was an instant talking point.
She wore it with a swagger and, hanging onto Curran's arm,
imbued him with new authority. Soon, no law officer could feel
safe. Gangs waylaid them at every street corner to beat them up
and take home uniforms as trophies for their girlfriends. It was
around this time, when patrolmen were forced to walk in twos and
threes, that the authorities described that the blatant rampage of
the Irish warlords could not be allowed to continue.

The Gophers – in Hell's Kitchen they pronounced it "Goofers"
– earned their name because they tended to congregate in cellars
and basements, like their subterranean namesakes. Owney was
proudly English; however, with Irish parents, his credentials were
good enough for the Gophers. It may have been a slightly eccentric
pedigree but, in the gang's rigid code, was infinitely preferable to
being Jewish or Italian. The boy was small and wiry, with a raw
nerve and self-reliance which quickly won their admiration. He
made his early reputation with a curiously Victorian weapon – a
length of lead pipe wrapped up in newspaper. It was an English
novelty in Hell's Kitchen and remembered for generations.

The factor which set him apart, perhaps more than any other,
was that from the age of fifteen he was one of the very few
hoodlums anywhere on the West Side to carry a gun, and use it
with deadly efficiency. Owney, with his well-oiled .38 Smith and
Wesson, was regarded from the East River to the Hudson as "the
finest shot in New York". It was not until the First World War,
when many of them were conscripted and trained in weaponry,
that firearms became fashionable on the streets of Hell's Kitchen.

The Gophers defended their territory with clubs, knives, brass-
knuckles and blackjacks against hit-and-run raids by rivals. The
Gas Housers, the Five Pointers, the 14th Street Gang and, above
all, the Hudson Dusters were their sworn enemies. In times of
emergency the Gophers could muster up to 500 street fighters to
put the opposition to flight. Skirmishes were bloody and ferocious,
occasionally resulting in death, as they defended rich pickings
provided by the freight cars waiting in depots along 11th Avenue.
Some nights the cars strung out, loaded with commodities, almost
the entire length of Manhattan, from the Battery to Riverside
Drive at 72nd Street, protected by battle-weary railroad guards.

Gophers regarded work with disdain. They were lazy and lived well, kicking their heels until the dancehalls and movies opened, or darkness gave cover for their raids. During one of Owney's many spells in Hell's Kitchen Precinct House (he was said to have been arrested more than 140 times, and convicted only twice) a sergeant asked him about his movements. A curious reporter hanging around the desk, had put the officer up to it. Owney, amused by his growing notoriety, obliged them by borrowing a police pad and writing:

Thursday: Went to a dance in the afternoon. Went to a dance at night and then to a cabaret. Took some girls home. Went to a restaurant and stayed there until seven o'clock Friday morning.

Friday: Spent the day with Freda Horner. Looked at some fancy pigeons. Met some friends in a saloon early in the evening and stayed with them until five o'clock in the morning.

Saturday: Slept all day. Went to a dance in the Bronx late in the afternoon, and to a dance on Park Avenue at night.

Sunday: Slept until three o'clock. Went to a dance in the afternoon and to another in the same place at night. After that I went to a cabaret and stayed there almost all night.

There was, of course, no mention of any crime. Freda Horner, a blonde with bobbed hair who hung around with the gang, was one of several steady girlfriends. She was what came to be known in the early 1920s as a moll – a breed of steel-hard girls, often with gang mottoes, such as "death before dishonour", tattooed on their forearms. They carried their boyfriends' guns in their clutch bags, in case of a police shakedown, and were known for putting up a formidable fight when arrested. Freda, like many of them, was attracted to Owney's growing reputation. He was also more of an attentive ladies' man than his rough-and-ready Gopher associates. They liked his generosity and were aware that, beneath the polite exterior, he could command authority with just a look.

Stanley Walker recalled him in the 1930s – less of the wild rover in those days, but still possessing a magnetic charm: "Ladies who heard of him were thrilled at meeting him – to some he appeared cute. His forehead was not high, and it receded a little. The nose was a fierce beak. He had that first requisite of leadership, 'a bone in the face.'

"His mouth and chin dropped away almost straight to the neck.

No offense meant, but, when viewed from the front, there was something fishlike about the way the mouth drooped at the corners. His face was sometimes pallid, and sometimes flushed.

"His body bore the scars of many bullets, and the condition of his lungs always made him fear that he would die of tuberculosis. His hair was black and sleek. His eyes were blue, a very bright and piercing blue. Sometimes they were friendly enough, and in repose they were even sad, but usually they were hard, and shining, and they saw everything."

No one who met him ever forgot him. Even late in life, before her death in 1980, Mae West would lift the corner of her mouth at the mention of his name, and purr: "Hmmm. So sweet – and so vicious . . ."

Owney would take Freda, or any of the other girls he picked up round the crowded dancehalls, back to his apartment. Freda had several sexual partners and, like her best friend Margaret Everdeane, contracted a mild form of syphilis. Freda's medical records at Bellevue Hospital noted that it was "not infectious, and that no person is in danger of contracting the said disease." Margaret, who came from a well-to-do background, was less fortunate and had to be admitted to hospital for prolonged treatment.

Freda saw less of Owney when he married another of his girlfriends, Dorothy "Loretta" Rogers, in 1911. For a while they lived at his apartment near 41st Street and 8th Avenue, where Dorothy gave birth to a baby girl, Margaret. The marriage, by all accounts, lasted barely two years. Owney's turbulent street life was unsuited to domesticity and Dorothy moved in with her mother on West 42nd Street. She remained on the fringe of the Hell's Kitchen scene, and was later reported to have drifted into bootlegging. For almost twenty years they remained man and wife on paper. Owney, chastened by the experience, never considered remarrying until he met Agnes many years later in Hot Springs. He had Dorothy traced in order to obtain a Reno "quickie" divorce, and she disappeared again, cushioned by a $75,000 cash settlement, a yacht and a house in Yonkers to ease the discomfort of old memories. Margaret grew up in New York barely knowing her father.

Freda Horner reappeared on the scene when Dorothy moved back with her mother, in a rekindling which Owney was to regret for the rest of his life. Freda had thrown over a wild gunman named Patsy Doyle to move back with the Duke and, for a while, it was apparently like old times. Later, when Doyle was to be fatally cut down by two gunmen after being lured into a saloon, she pointed the finger squarely at her lover. Owney clearly had an ability to arouse the strongest emotions in the opposite sex.

Gopher troubles in the early months of their marriage undoubtedly contributed to the breakup with Dorothy. At the time, he was a fast-rising, able lieutenant, and the gang, facing its darkest hour, desperately needed his services. The New York Central Railroad Company was not amused by their nightly forays and decided that the Gophers' days of unchallenged power were numbered. Thousands of dollars' worth of freight had been looted and a number of company patrolmen seriously injured. If the police were unable, or unwilling, to handle them, New York Central decided, then the time had come to take its own preventative measures. Under conditions of great secrecy the railroad company assembled a huge squad of handpicked security men, all chosen for their willingness to take on the Gophers. Some were keen to settle old scores, others hard men simply hungry for a rumble to relieve the monotony of normal railroad work.

After many tactical discussions they were ordered to attack the very heart of Gopher country, and take the gang by surprise, rather than ambush them in the darkened confusion of the freight yards.

A few weeks earlier the police had launched a concerted show of strength against the West Side mobs by staging co-ordinated assaults on their respective neighbourhoods. The battle left the Gophers winded, but far from defeated. When the police withdrew, a semblance of peace returned, leaving the gang unprepared for a raid by the railroad company.

Among the casualties of the long pitched battle with New York's police were Gopher leaders Marty Brennan and Newburgh Gallagher, who had been captured and hauled away to Sing Sing prison. Other passengers in the fleet of trucks which carted away bleeding prisoners included Willie Jones, boss of the Gas Housers, Itsky Joe Hickman of the Five Pointers, and Al Rooney, who ran the fearsome 14th Street Gang.

The railroad swoop was planned at a time when the walking wounded felt demoralised by the loss of their leaders. The special force divided into groups and fanned through Hell's Kitchen, smashing down the doors of Gopher hangouts and beating them senseless with nightsticks. A bloody battle raged over several hours, with residents fleeing the streets. When some gang mem-

bers followed Owney's example and pulled out firearms, they were
stunned to be met by a hail of accurate gunfire. The railroad police,
anticipating tough opposition, had trained specially for the occasion.

Over the next few weeks wave upon wave of fresh attacks broke
the hoodlums' resistance. One patrolman, watching impressed
from a street corner, reported that the Gophers had been "clubbed
from hell to breakfast."

"Many thugs were wounded and several sent to prison," gangland historian Herbert Asbury was to recall a decade later, "and
there was scarcely a Gopher who did not receive a sound thumping. Within a few months the new force devastated Hell's Kitchen
with clubs and blackjacks, and thereafter the Gophers avoided
railroad property as they would a plague. To this day a New York
Central watchman is regarded as the natural enemy of a Hell's
Kitchen hoodlum."

Owney was seen in the thick of the fighting but somehow
managed to avoid arrest. As Richard O'Connor remarked, "He
had the cherubic smile and general appearance of an altar boy, so
he might well have been overlooked." The Gophers, broken and
decimated, convened a conference and decided to split into two
main gangs – one commanded by a roughneck known as Buck
O'Brien, the other by Owney.

He had now been in America just nine years, and was on the
threshold of achieving impressive gangland power. In the process
he had run up a long arrest record for assault, burglary, carrying
burglar's tools and petty larceny, without once being jailed. Rival
gangs, circling like vultures for the pickings offered by Owney's
new territory, considered the Gophers a spent force. The young
Englishman knew that his leadership was about to be tested. To
give himself breathing space, and time to consolidate his weary
troops, he entered into a peaceful agreement with Tanner Smith,
leader of the Marginals, who controlled the streets to the south of
his domain. The Hudson Dusters, the Gophers' oldest enemies,
showed interest in a similar arrangement. "Unlike the old Gophers, Madden's gang refused any peace treaty with the Dusters
and often battled in the streets with them," O'Connor noted.

It was a period when gangs were evolving all over New York,
waging territorial wars which occasionally turned to gun battles on
the streets. East Side and West Side, neighbourhood racketeers
and petty criminals emerged from the age of innocence before

Prohibition to run organizations more profitable and influential than legitimate corporations. As Meyer Lansky was to later proudly tell his syndicate: "We're bigger than US Steel." The single factor which provided the means to help major figures such as Owney to awesome power was the misguided intentions of moralists who wanted to see America alcohol-free. The organizational flair and business talent of these master gangsters stemmed from apprenticeships in the crude street rackets of their youth. Hell's Kitchen, like similar slum areas across the city, became a proving ground in which only the strongest managed to survive.

As a warning to the Dusters, and to raise his standing among his own men, Owney shot a young Italian, Luigi Mollinucci, on the corner of 11th Avenue and 30th Street. He stepped out onto the sidewalk, and calmly squeezed the trigger, in full view of passers by. It was a cold-blooded slaying, and detectives were convinced they at last had a case against him. As the weeks passed by, proceedings had to be dropped when several key witnesses packed their bags and vanished from the neighbourhood. Owney, arrested on suspicion of homicide, was freed.

His leadership of the Gophers instilled a fear in the Dusters which was never quite forgotten. Many years later, when Owney was investing heavily in fighters, he called in to see Joe Jacobs, an old promoter who shared an office in New York's Putnam Building with his partner William McCarney. Bill Corum, the *Chicago Herald-American* columnist, heard the story in 1946 and ran it under the headline: "When A Duster Tasted Dust." McCarney told him:

"One day a slight, soft-spoken man came in and asked for Joe. I told him that Jacobs wasn't around but that he might be in later.

" 'Mind if I wait?' he asked.

" 'Not at all,' I told him.

"There were a lot of fight pictures on the wall if you recall, and pretty soon the visitor got up and started walking round looking at them. I could see the pictures interested him and, of course, with me a story went with every one of 'em. I started telling him about the various fights and some of the angles and situations that had come up in my, if I may say so, varied experience.

"I guess I must have gassed him for almost an hour, when he interrupted me and said, 'I'm afraid I'm taking up too much of your time, Mr McCarney.'

"I told him he wasn't. That I had nothing to do, so I cut up some more old fights, with him only asking a question now and then to keep me going.

"Finally, when he got up to leave he said, 'I've enjoyed this. I'm sort of out of action these days. Would it be all right if I drop in again sometime when you're not busy?'

"So a couple of weeks later he comes again and it happens that, again, I'm the only one in the office.

" 'This is the second time,' he said, 'that I have sat around here talking fights with you without introducing myself. My name is Owney Madden.'

"Well, if he had said he was King Tut I couldn't have been more astonished. My mouth opened up so wide I almost swallowed my cigarette. I'd read a lot about Owney Madden in the papers and the picture I had formed of him wasn't anything like this almost shy fellow that just seemed to want to fan about boxing."

In his article, Bill Corum went on to describe how Owney told the elderly promoter that, if he could ever be of any service to him, not to hesitate to ask. A short time later Owney took a suite of offices in the Putnam Building. A few floors below, William McCarney – known in boxing circles as "the Professor" – was paid an unexpected visit by an unsavoury mobster named Linky Mitchell:

"Mitchell walked in and demanded, 'Where's the Monkey?'

" 'We don't have any monkeys here,' the Professor told him. 'Who is it you wish to see?'

" 'I want to see that monkey Jacobs. I've just taken over ten per cent of his fighters, and I'd better see him quick if he knows what's good for him.'

" 'That's funny, I'm his partner and he didn't tell me.'

" 'He don't have to tell you, I'm telling you,' sneered Mitchell, and he patted himself lightly under his armpit. That was where McCarney phoned Madden. Three minutes later Owney was in the door.

" 'Get out of here,' ordered Owney Madden.

" 'Yes sir, yes sir,' Mitchell mumbled and started sidling towards the door.

"Madden still filled most of the doorway, and the man made himself so thin he scratched his back against the jamb as he eased out and went away from there.

" 'He won't bother you again,' Owney promised the Prof as The Link sneaked off down the hall. Nor did he.

"Linky Mitchell was a supposedly tough member and trigger-happy hood of a West Side New York gang that had once been called the Dusters."

The slaying of Luigi Mollinucci took place in September 1911, just three months after Owney's marriage. Devoting his energies to diversifying the Gophers' interests meant spending less time at home, and there are indications that he and Dorothy were beginning to lead separate lives. Six months on, Owney was having an affair with someone else – some say Freda Horner, taking advantage of the separation. His relationships were rarely casual, and in return he expected a certain loyalty from his lovers. Throughout his life, until his second marriage, Owney's girls were treated royally by the underworld and given a wide berth by those who knew how protective he could be towards them.

George Raft and Owney ran into each other regularly and had slightly differing views on women. Georgie, with slick hair and polished shoes, had become a small-time dance celebrity around town. He had a fast way of talking and an amusing line in flattery which won hearts wherever there happened to be a dance contest. The handsome young man with the flashing feet and Valentino looks had no interest in pursuing steady relationships. The tango, waltz and jazz dancing provided an endless supply of willing partners. By night he was a dancehall sensation – a friend recalled a typical Raft routine to biographer Lewis Yablonsky: "The hall was dark. Suddenly there's a spotlight on George. He had a jaunty look. Jet black hair, wearing a black suit with flared trousers. Over one eye is a sharp derby. He got a tremendous ovation even before he began his dance because he looked so perfect."

In the afternoons he worked tea dances for two dollars plus tips. Often, the female clientele were interested in paying for private sessions of a more intimate nature.

Owney would listen to tales of his conquests and laugh until it seemed he would never stop. Throughout their lives they were to meet up and yarn away the hours together. George's escapades always amused him, and the young gigolo enjoyed relaxing with his childhood hero. On Gopher ground he knew he was safe, but Raft encountered girl-trouble in other gang areas, where they were as keen as Owney to protect their women.

His dancehall companion of the time told Yablonsky about a memorable trip to Yonkers with ten friends: "George was just unbelievable with women. This one attached herself to George – a beautiful girl. Then three tough guys came up to me. One said: 'Your friend's dancing with my girl.' Next he pulled a knife and said: 'I'm going to get him. Not now. In a little while.' Then they walked away. I told George and he said: '—him.' He was just carried away dancing with this girl. Finally the last thing I remember is the whole crowd of us running down the street trying to catch the streetcar for New York City. The guy with the knife and his gang were after us. We just about made it onto the rear of the streetcar. It scared the hell out of us and I felt certain that George, and all of us, had just escaped with our lives."

Owney was occasionally known to warn off the opposition in a similar fashion. According to Jay Robert Nash, author of *Bootleggers and Badmen*: "Madden was girl happy. Any girl he knew was his girl. Any man who made a pass at his girl was beaten senseless."

In February 1912, when he was leading the Gophers and ruled a vast tract of New York, only a fool, or someone far removed from the world of crime, would have made advances to a girl he was known to show affection for. The reckless – or naive – man in question was a clerk named William Henshaw. By all accounts, Owney had warned him off with his usual quiet understatement, though one version says they argued. Henshaw, either through stubbornness or misunderstanding, did not take the advice of the Duke of the West Side.

Owney watched him drop the girl off at her home in uptown Manhattan after a date, and waited until Henshaw boarded a trolley car. As the trolley passed the corner of 16th Street and 9th Avenue he swung aboard, levelled his Smith and Wesson coolly at the clerk, and shot him in front of a dozen passengers. Before alighting, Owney paused on the rear step and tolled the trolley car's brass bell in a sinister death knell. A moment later he vanished into the night, leaving the passengers in turmoil. Those who rushed to help Henshaw detected faint signs of life, and he was quickly taken to New York Hospital. Before he died he managed to tell detectives the identity of his killer.

After the shooting the Duke went to ground, lying low in various Gopher apartments, until he was sighted ten days later, emerging from the doorway of a Hell's Kitchen tenement block. Three detectives who had been watching the neighbourhood gave pursuit when he disappeared back into the building. Owney made for the fire escape and a long, desperate chase ensued over the rooftops of

10th Avenue. High above the streets, where he kept his pigeon lofts, was a world "as familiar as the inside of his pocket." He was finally cornered when reinforcements were brought in to surround the area, and arrested. The police, for the second time, were convinced they had a watertight homicide charge against him, and he was on his way to the electric chair. However, by the time Owney appeared in court two days later, relaxed and untroubled, they discovered that key witnesses from the trolley car had decided to leave town and the case was dismissed.

Oddly, despite the killings, Owney never quite achieved a murderous reputation among those who knew him. "Old playmates of his say he wasn't so homicidal as the authorities made him out to be," Richard O'Connor concluded.

From 1911 to 1914, Owney built the Gophers into the most powerful criminal organization on the West Side. After the railroad raid his first priority was to establish an unassailable headquarters, and to spread the gang's interests beyond a dependency on freight cars. A building was found soon after the Henshaw killing; the grand plan took a little longer and included links with influential Democrats which led to a close, lifelong association with men of political power.

Owney's two close escapes from prison encouraged him to keep a low profile and devote more time to diversifying the Gophers' activities. Three experienced killers – Eddie Egan, Bill Tammany and Chick Hyland – carried out his orders, overseeing rackets which terrorized new areas of the community, and provided Owney with a personal income of $200 a day. The Madden family, in a way none of them could ever have anticipated, were at last living the dream they believed America would provide for them. Mary had a vague idea what her son was involved in, but tended to turn a blind eye. As far as she was concerned Owney was loyal, loving and looked after the family as his father Francis always hoped he would.

Owney joined forces with his new ally, Tanner Smith of the Marginals, to invest in a secure new headquarters. After touring the neighbourhood they settled on a suite of rooms two floors above a blacksmith's shop, and turned it into a bar and bistro called the Winona Club. Owney kept a small apartment there and the inevitable pigeon loft on the roof.

Looking after his collection of prize birds was becoming so time-consuming that he paid one of the Gophers $75 a week to feed and clean them out. "Owney liked pigeons almost as well as blondes," one journalist recalled. "In his spare time he would potter about the nests or do a bit of flying with them. All the hoodlums in Hell's Kitchen knew Owney's pigeons, and they were immune from bullets. You could kill a Hudson Duster, but lay off Owney's pigeons. Owney didn't even have the heart to eat squab under glass."

Owney's well-protected pigeons were, however, not beyond causing trouble themselves. "He spent much money on them," one observer noted, "Nun's Caps, Hollanders, Buda-Pesth Tiplitzes and other breeds. These birds used to fly round New York, enticing birds from other coops to come home with them, and many fights ensued."

Perhaps only one other man wielded as much power as Owney did on the West Side. His name was Jimmy Hines, a chisel-featured blacksmith turned city alderman. The two met as their respective careers were blossoming. Owney instinctively saw, like generations of later gangsters in all the great cities of America, that a powerful, tightly-run political machine, which controlled the police and judiciary, could be of enormous advantage. In New York it happened to be the Democrats, and their fastest-rising star was Jimmy Hines. Party politics in such matters were secondary to personalities and power.

Hines, at times ambitious to the point of desperation, was a vastly different character to Owney, but their backgrounds and outlook were largely similar. "Hines was a man who commanded loyalty from others by giving loyalty," wrote Craig Thompson and Allen Raymond in *Gang Rule In New York*. He never deserted a pal, and he never, if he could help it, refused the granting of a favour. He believed, as those who worked for him and supported him believed, that in his lifetime he did "a lot of good".

"Whether it went for good things or bad, the undeniable fact is that of the enormous financial return that came into his hands through crime, relatively little of it stayed with him. Certainly a large percentage of this blood-stained money was scattered by him in service of the poor. He gave it lavishly to men and women who said they needed food, or coal, or rent, or hundreds of other things that required money they did not have. That was the system to which he adhered, in which he was raised, and he served it without apology or much deviation. That he left his people to be preyed upon by those who operated the rackets was a fact he never looked in the eye."

Electioneering in the roughneck days before the First World War was a bloody, street-corner business. Hines had vowed to wrestle the influential office of district leader from a tough Irish plasterer called Jimmy Ahearn, who was equally determined to hang onto it. The bitter campaign began in 1907, with Hines suffering two narrow defeats before a third, all-or-nothing attempt in 1912. The two candidates, accompanied by hired toughs, would stand on the backs of open wagons and harangue each other from opposite sides of the street. Ahearn was the more accomplished orator, and made capital of his rival's lumbering way with words. Hines hated to lose anything, and had a quick temper which was easily roused. On one occasion, in the 1907 round, Ahearn shouted a jibe from his platform, leaving Hines speechless at his own inability to come up with an appropriate reply. He stormed across the street and landed Ahearn a right hook which knocked him from the wagon.

Listening intently to these heated exchanges from a street corner was a small, bright young law student called Joe Shalleck. He had already formed a college Democratic club at Columbia University to back the re-election of New York's Democrat Mayor Bill Gaynor, and had been studying Hines' campaign from the side-lines with interest. As Jimmy climbed down from the back of his wagon, Joe shook his hand and said:

"Mr Hines, I listened to you. You have some very good ideas. But you are unquestionably the lousiest speaker I ever heard."

For a second Jimmy looked as if he might floor him, then asked: "What's your name?"

Joe explained who he was and about the support he had given Bill Gaynor. He appeared confident and was highly articulate.

"All right," said Hines finally. "From now on you're going to be my speechmaker."

Joe's skill, which later made him one of the most successful criminal lawyers in New York, began to have a marked effect on Hines' popularity. When Shalleck graduated from law school one of his most celebrated clients was the other silent partner in Hines' team, Owney Madden.

In his first two attempts for district leadership Hines had the advantage of a powerful speech writer, but his Gopher muscle yet lacked the benefit of Owney's leadership. They were unruly and unpredictable and failed to appreciate the importance of organization and timing in the run-up to the polls. The flow of voters had to be carefully monitored at each polling station, and a constant record kept of Democrat fortunes. If the pendulum began to swing the wrong way, steps had to be immediately taken to rectify it, either by keeping the wrong voters out, persuading them to change their minds, or bringing more of the right voters in. In emergencies votes were cast on behalf of the dead, or someone who had not turned up to register. If the hapless voter did materialize, they would hotly accuse him of trying to vote twice, usually with the admonition: "What do you think this is, bud – a personality contest? Get the hell outa here."

On the credit side, the Gophers were good with their fists, and in the stormy first round of the contest with Ahearn, little else mattered. Each street-corner campaigner carefully picked his own protection squad. Ahearn's hired muscle was led by a stone-faced pugilist called Spike Sullivan whose hatred for the Gophers made a bloodbath inevitable. Several Gophers were beaten up in the scuffle which followed Hines knocking Ahearn from the wagon, and immediate retaliation was considered essential.

"Degnan's saloon was on the same corner, and Spike Sullivan, apparently unaware of what had gone before, made the mistake of entering the bar room alone," gangland historians Thompson and Raymond recorded. "The Hines gang went in after him. In the carnage that followed, chairs, tables, beer mugs and many another quick weapon flew wildly. The battle surged into the bar. The place was wrecked and so was Sullivan, who did not get out of hospital in time to do any voting. Had he been able to get around, Hines would probably have lost by more than he did – Ahearn kept his control by forty-seven votes that year."

Hines lost the next election by twenty-seven votes, the narrow margin making him even more determined to succeed in 1912. By this time Owney, as boss of the Gophers, had honed them into an efficient and highly effective election force. To cover his overheads Hines mortgaged his smithy and borrowed the rest, raising $4,000 for what proved to be a profitable investment. With shrewd presence of mind, and an awareness of the wealth political power could bring, he had already closed his bank account, leaving no evidence of the vast income which was to come his way in the years ahead.

Hines, with Owney's tactical advice, planned his 1912 campaign following the basic rule of West Side political warfare: "The more an opponent's hoodlum resources were crippled in advance of a day of voting, the less opportunity he then would have of winning at the polls."

With Shalleck's eloquent speech-writing and Owney's battle skills, Hines swept to victory by a margin of 1,500 votes. The memorable and exhausting campaign forged a relationship which operated to their mutual benefit throughout the 1920s and 1930s. When the celebrations were over Joe acted as Jimmy's political manager while building up his law practice. Hines moved into the haulage business and, with a fleet of trucks, obtained lucrative city contracts. Owney returned to expanding his rackets empire, knowing that he could now call on Hines' friendship at any time.

Glasgow's Ice-Cream Gangs
(Arthur Thompson and Paul Ferris)

Richard Whittington-Egan

One night in 1960s London, the capital's famous crime twins, the Krays, were holding court in their busy nightclub, Esmaralda's Barn, when they were told somebody wanted to see them. The demand in itself was presumptuous enough but the sequel beggared belief. There, on the Krays' home turf, the stranger who had made this bold request pulled a sawn-off shotgun from under his coat and demanded that Ron kiss his brother Reg's backside. As Ron knelt and complied, the grim-faced man smirked and, in a strong Glasgow accent, announced, "Ma name's Arthur Thompson, ye'll remember me!" Backing out and still holding the gun, Thompson jumped into a waiting cab and sped off. Arthur Thompson ruled Glasgow for 40 years, serving a criminal apprenticeship as bouncer and heavy for the mobs, and graduating via much-feared enforcer to become Glasgow's Godfather of crime. Eventually he met his nemesis in the shape of a young man called Paul Ferris, whom he'd recruited as a bagman, debt collector and equalizer. With his capacity for extreme violence and his undoubted intelligence, Ferris was the Godfather's heir-apparent. But when gang warfare broke out on Glasgow's meanest streets, Ferris quit the Thompson clan to stand alone. They gave him weeks to live. While Ferris was caged in Barlinnie Prison's segregation unit on a charge of

murdering Arthur Thompson's son Fat Boy, two of his friends
were shot dead the night before the funeral and grotesquely
displayed in a car on the route of the cortege. Against all the
odds, Ferris was acquitted of murder, as the prolific crime
historian Richard Whittington-Egan (b. 1924) recounts in this
survey of the Glasgow gang scene.

A balmy West Coast June day in 1992. After a 54-day trial –
Scotland's longest in a criminal cause – on charges involving
drug-dealing and its orbital satellites, murder, attempted murder
and kneecapping, the twenty-eight-year-old Glasgow hard man
stands, surrounded by an immobilized phalanx of certainly not
laughing "polis" men, on the Justiciary Court House steps. Arms
outstretched like a missionary about to emit a benediction, his
shrewd eyes survey the scene of his freshly-laundered triumph.
Look, he has come through the judicial cleansing machine;
emerged clean as a whistle, Sanforised by fifteen men good and
true. The cameras click like rapid-fire false teeth in a film-star
burst of flashes. Vindicated, jury-certificated upright citizen, Paul
Ferris "smiled twice", as they have it in Glaswegian parlance –
once like everyone else, then an involuntary encore presented by
the "chib" memorial scar, snaking from the right side of an
ungenerously lipped mouth to the shadow below a firm-set jaw-
line. A final significant gesture . . . Then it was off to a cham-
pagne-supper celebration.

No corks popping, though, for the almost biblically nicknamed
Blind Jonah, only thirty-six, his face described variously as "a hot
cross-bun of knife-work," and "a sort of flesh map of the gang
battles of Glasgow." Mr Jonah McKenzie is a walking object-
lesson in survival. Not that he walks too well after the knife attack
that severed the leg muscles. Reputedly one of Young Arthur's
Team, aka the Thompson Gang, the opposition to Mr Ferris's
Barlanark Team, he is said, by Mr Ferris, to have brought a great
many of his troubles on himself, by lending a hand in the murder of
Arthur Thompson, Junior, and by kneecapping William Gillen, a
Barlanark aide. Blind Jonah has been made the (head) butt of
unfeeling hard-man humour:

Question: What kind of weapon does Blind Jonah use?
Answer: A Braille gun.

No fizzy either at Mr Ferris's festal free-for-all for Limpy Willie Gillen aforesaid, a turncoat Barlanarkian barnacle who had the rash temerity to nominate his whilom boss as his kneecapper. Not so, said Mr Ferris's jury.

And there was no celebrating at locally dubbed "South-fork", two stone-cladded-into-one council houses, garnished with Spanish patio, satellite dish and refined ornatures of that ilk: the Provanmill Road home of the man they call the Godfather of Glasgow, Arthur Thompson, Senior, whose thirty-one-year-old son, "Young Arthur," aka "Fat Boy", was into wholesale heroin as a dealer before being dealt out by a blowaway job – fatally shot while enjoying an innocuous weekend furlough from an eleven stretch in jail. The jury had likewise pronounced seven-times-libelled Mr Ferris unconnected with this sad event.

Who wiped out the Fat Boy? Melted him down? Echo answers who. But, deservedly or undeservedly, two hard men of Mr Ferris's Barlanark Team, Joe "Bananas" Hanlon and Bobby Glover, were scythed down by the grim reaper on the very morning of Young Arthur's funeral. Bananas and Bobby stood not upon the order of their going. In point of fact, they lay, cherubic, side by side, death did not divide them, in their car, parked outside the earthly valhalla of a favourite pub, twin bullet holes in the napes of their necks and, for good measure and as a reminder (to others) of the importance of rectitude, even in a life of crime, a carefully aimed bullet apiece up the rectum.

Both the Thompsons and the Ferrises hail from Blackhill, an abysmally drear scheme (*écossais* for Council Estate) to the north-east of the city centre. Thompson, Senior, is a man with a chequered past – convictions for assault, housebreaking, robbery, safeblowing and extortion – which he does not deny. But, for nearly a quarter of a century now, Mr Thompson has steered well clear of little malfeasances of the sort in which he had permitted himself to indulge in the 1960s. Standing, in recent times, below the security camera limpeted upon the stucco of his fortress home, he pooh-poohed the notion of his being the Glasgow Godfather. "I would have to start talking like Don Corleone," he chaffed merrily, adding, with less twinkle, "It's pure nonsense."

As the 1980s mounted, so did the spiral of violence. The temperatures of the participating factions climbed way out of control. It was in 1985 that Young Arthur had been sentenced to eleven years for trafficking in heroin. While he was inside, battle had to be joined for the preservation of his outside trading territory. A first major indication of the flaring of the drug war came when, in 1986, Old Arthur was wounded in the groin while innocently tinkering with his motor. For the record: in 1989 Young Arthur's sister, Margaret, died with a heroin needle in her arm – a cruel irony which brings no moralizing gratification in its wake.

Drug rivalries came bursting, literally, into the open in 1990, when a hand grenade was rolled into the pub where Ferris's Barlanarks did their drinking. Hard on the heels of that, Arthur Thompson, Senior, was put into hospital after being the victim of a most determined hit-and-run car accident.

Repercussively, Paul Ferris's father, Willie, a cripple already, who walked with two sticks, came in for some pretty rough handling with hammer, baseball bat and razor. Following one such attack he had more than a hundred stitches. His tyres were slashed and his car with its "disabled" label subsequently torched.

Torched, too, was Joe "Bananas" Hanlon's ice-cream van, salespoint also for heroin. And later his XR2 was blown up and he was shot in the penis.

Then, in August 1990, came the rubbing out of Young Arthur and the consequent erasure – or execution – of Joe and Bobby.

Hard-line humour:

Question: What is the favourite song on Glasgow's karaoke machines?
Answer: Yes, we have Joe Bananas.

It took three bullets to fell Arthur Thompson, Junior. Number one nicked his cheek. Number two chipped his ribs. Number three hit bang smack home in his heart. Famous last words, to his sister: "I've been shot, hen. I'm going to collapse."

The whisper is that a £30,000 contract is out on Ferris. Hard-folk joke:

Question: What's the difference between Paul Ferris and Elvis Presley?
Answer: Paul Ferris is definitely dead.

Mr Ferris himself treats this maleficent ribaldry with all the contempt an innocent man naturally feels for such manipulative fat-chewing.

And yet . . . Glasgow is no kingdom of empty threats. Dark promises are kept, bloody vendettas kept up. The plain truth is that this roaring nineties Runyonland north of the Border preserves the ancient order – or, rather, *dis*order – hymned by that thirties prose bard of the Gorbals, A. McArthur, and his *No Mean City* accomplice, H. Kingsley Long.

Who today knows anything of McArthur, the little Gorbals grocer who set himself the task of immortalizing the blood-frothed spilth and sport of the razor gangs of his local streets, and succeeded in it so magnificently? Not great literature, but he produced a wondrously powerful manuscript – no mean feat considering his tenuous literacy – which, after being shorn of sundry stylistic quiddities and licked into grammatical shape by the co-author, very likely a relative of his London publisher, John Long, *No Mean City*, published in 1936, became a bestseller. It has to date sold upwards of 17 million copies. McArthur set to – with a co-author again – hoping to repeat his success with a sequel, *No Bad Money*. Sadly, there was to be no second small miracle. What modest confidence McArthur had built up in his writing ability pitifully swiftly drained away. Depressed, he pitifully swiftly drained away the contents of far too many bottles. They found him dead on the banks of the Clyde, full of methylated spirits.

But the gangs of Glasgow had come into being a good half-century before McArthur began his basically accurate but, even so, highly coloured, chroniclings. The first named collection of organized Glaswegian hooligans to take shape out of the fogs and rain-mists of the remoter reaches of the past was the Penny Mob, who were brawling around the Townhead district in the 1880s. This earliest, recorded as such, gang, numbered about three hundred, and took its name from the fact that every member had to chip in a penny a week to a kitty which provided money for the payment of fines imposed on members of the mob by the courts. The leaders of the Penny Mob packs were known, rather oddly, as "Chairmen" – the title bestowed upon them actually in court reports of the time. The Penny Mobsmen would be encountered lolling on street corners, prowling among the sprawling East End tenements looking for mischief, and making nuisances of themselves in and around city pubs. Quite a sizeable proportion of Penny Mob violence was, it seems, the Dead Sea fruit of religious intolerance.

The next collection of unworthies to figure with any prominence on the Glasgow roll of dishonour were those young turn-of-the-century tearaways, aged mainly between sixteen and twenty, who banded themselves together in gangs of a hundred or more under such bizarre banners as the Hi Hi, operating in the Northern Police Division area; the Ping Pong, in the Eastern Division; and the San Toy, the Tim Malloy, the South Side Stickers, and the Village Boys in the Southern District. These gangs attached great importance to territoriality, identifying themselves with specific tracts and sections of the city which they regarded as their exclusive preserves. The San Toy Boys, particular rivals of the Penny Mob, came from Calton, rather nearer to the city centre. Extremely belligerent, their war-cry as they charged into street battle was: "We are the young Santoys and we can fight the Tim Malloys."

None of the early twentieth-century gang members carried razors, knives or bicycle chains. They were weaponed up with knuckle-dusters, heavy, old-fashioned bolts shaped like small, lethal dumb-bells, a brass rod with a hefty doorknob at the end, and, a great favourite this, a small poker carried hidden up the sleeve.

The young gangsters would waylay folk coming out of places of entertainment and demand money with menaces, go into shops for cigarettes and public-houses for drinks, all to be handed over, of course, without payment.

Whatever, with ego-boosting grandiloquence, they called themselves, the hooligans were originally known to everyone else in Glasgow as "Keelies" – a Keelie is defined in the Scots dictionary as "a street-arab; a pickpocket" – but for many years now the name has been changed to "neds". No one seems to remember how or when the term originated. The dictionary definition is: "a donkey, a simpleton."

In the years leading up to the Great War, the Glasgow gangs proliferated. The Redskins was one exceptionally vicious gang, numbering among its members several young girls, one of whom was the legendary and truly formidable Aggie Reid, who lived in a women's hostel in Trongate. Her record of arrests for assault was both long and alarming. It took at least four policemen to get her into a van. Boasting an organized membership of a thousand, the Redskins took over the East End, vanquishing the Hi Hi and the Calton Black Hand, and seeing off also the Hazel Bells from Mile End and Bridgeton, the Baltic Fleet from Baltic Street, and the Kelly Boys from Govan.

Fisticuff fighting was despised. Battle was waged preferably with meat-cleavers. Failing that, with hammers. Protection money was extracted from shopkeepers and other tradesmen, and the gangs did not think twice about openly attacking and robbing people in the street in broad daylight. Leaders were no longer "Chairmen" but "Kings", and there were also "Queens", invariably the prettiest, and not uncommonly the wildest, under-twenty-ones. If any Redskin found him or herself in trouble, a special loud, quick, tuneless whistle would bring rapid relief reinforcements.

Throughout the Great War (1914–18), gangland activity subsided. There was fighting of a different kind to be done; a new arena for the channelling of brute energies. Meanwhile, for those keeping the home fires burning, peak production demands at the shipyards and in the munition factories reduced that unemployment out of which street violence and idle-hands villainy had arisen and been recruited.

With the war's end, however, all the old spectres – unrequited slumland hunger and thirst, dizzy new heights of unemployment – stalked the streets where the surviving heroes who had fought to make Scotland a land fit for heroes to live in, sold matches and boot-laces. So, ill-shod feet came marching back to the sounding of drumbeats calling up the old troops of Redskins and Calton Black Handers, and conscripting willing new "soldiers" to new gangs which would replace those which, through loss of leadership, attrition due to the passage of time and war, had simply dwindled away. And gradually the hoodlum body was revitalized. In his memoirs, *Life Begins at Midnight*, the late Detective Chief Superintendent Robert Colquhoun remembered 1923 as a vintage year for Glasgow's gangs. The Cheeky Forty and the Black Diamonds were his very particular *bêtes noires* in his bailiwick, St Rollox. Elsewhere in the town, he says, the Redskins, the Norman Conks and the Billy Boys were entrenched, and a new outfit, the Beehives, was just beginning to buzz.

Three more names to conjure with.

The hostility between the Norman Conks (unexpectedly erudite corruption of William the Norman Conqueror in conjunction with the fact that the gang's headquarters was in Norman Street explains the nomenclature) and the Billy Boys, more prosaically doffing their nominal caps to that other King William, of Orange, aka King Billy, both stomping the East End, was a matter more than territorial. Glasgow, it must be understood, and many things

Glaswegian, are shot through with the steel thread of religion. It goes back to the impact upon the native Protestant Scots of Irish Catholic immigrant workers, brought over at the time of the Industrial Revolution. The old rivalry survives, even though the initial cause of that rivalry has diminished as religion withers nationally. It was former Chief Constable of Glasgow, Sir David McNee, who said that one of his senior officers described the football matches between green-shirted, Catholic Celtic, from the East End, and blue-shirted, Protestant Rangers, from the South, as "the biggest outdoor religious festival held anywhere in the world."

The Norman Conks were led by a ferocious character named "Bull" Bowman, under whose sanguineous command they ported their favourite arms, 42-inch-long pick-shafts, weighing close on three pounds, backed up by a variegated weaponry of swords, hatchets, and lovingly sharpened bicycle chains, worn like a rosary round the necks of their Queens, because they knew the police hesitated to search girls for fear of accusations of improper assault. For hand-to-hand infighting, beer bottles were the first choice. Favourite target of these favourite weapons were, of course, the Billy Boys.

The Billy Boys' boss was William (Billy) Fullerton, who used to work in Gilmour's Club in Olympia Street, Bridgeton. The gang, eight hundred strong, had kept up the Penny Mob tradition of exacting a weekly payment and, allowing no doubt for inflation, a tuppence per week contribution was marked up on all membership cards. The resultant nest-egg, tucked safely away in the local bank, provided funds for fines and also for the bringing of small comforts to wives whose men were, for reasons not unconnected with the courts, temporarily out of circulation. At one stage the nestegg, to which, incidentally, local shopkeepers were also "invited" to donate, topped well in excess of £1,200, and Fullerton lifted about half of this sum to kit out a flute-and-drum band. Rabid Orangemen, the Billy Boys were henceforth able to taunt the Catholic arch-enemy by marching down Norman Street on Saints' and Holy Days, fluting and drumming lusty Orange airs. The Conks' religious response was a hail of pick-shafts, bricks, bottles and bucketfuls of ordure. The tale is still told of how on one such occasion, when things had really got out of hand and attracted a full-scale charge of mounted police, a quick-thinking Billy Boy, Elijah Cooper, took a smart header into the big drum he had been beating and rolled off hidden therein to avoid the drumming hooves of the police steeds.

The Beehive Corner Boys – so christened after their meeting-place, subsequently abbreviated to the Beehive Gang – developed along different lines from most of the other gangs, whose main objects were to display ego-building machismo to their Queens, maintain a firm hold on their territory, and bash, slash and generally mutilate a respectable quota of the enemy. To them, heavy crime was incidental, happenstance, peripheral. To the misbehaving Beehives, however, serious crime was very much an integral part of their agenda. Thieving, housebreaking, shop-breaking, safe-blowing, hold-up jobs and intimidation were all on the menu; which meant that the Beehive was thus posing a greater threat to the respectable citizenry.

Beehive organization was, moreover, formidable – almost army fashion – with young recruits enlisting in the cadet branch, earning promotion to auxiliary membership and final enrolment to the hard, inner core attained only after success in various tests and trials.

Weaponry: razors, hatchets, chains and bottles.
Footwear: fighting boots with carpenter's nails projecting wickedly from the toe-caps.
Headgear: cap with razor-blade stitched in the peak.

Their King was Peter Williamson, powerfully built, in his early twenties, a legend in his own lifetime, as the cliché has it, for his prowess with his fists. Second in command was his friend, Harry McMenemy. The real mastermind was said to be a character named Howie.

The Beehive did not survive the Second World War. Peter Williamson did. He went into the army and was soon made up to sergeant. Demobbed, he returned to Glasgow . . . and safe-blowing . . . and Peterhead Prison.

The Beehive territory was especially the Cumberland Street area of the Gorbals, and by 1931, when, following his gang-busting success in Sheffield, my good friend Sir Percy Sillitoe was ap-pointed Chief Constable of Glasgow, the Beehives were the un-doubted rulers of their chosen domain.

Over the preceding decade, the gangland scene had undergone inevitable changes. The Billy Boys were still in there, battling away against the Norman Conks. Also in the East End were the Romeo Boys, the San Toy and its Gallowgate subsidiary the Bridgegate Boys, the Stickit Boys and the Derry Boys from Bridgeton and the Antique Mob from Shettleston. The legions from the South Side numbered among them the Black Diamond Boys, the Hammer Boys and the Dirty Dozen. Govan contributed the Kelly-bow. A state of open warfare was disastrously ongoing between the South Side Stickers and the San Toy Boys.

The Parlour Boys – so called because their headquarters was the Bedford Parlour Dance Hall in Celtic Street – was another of the smaller, but perilous to ignore, gangs. Their leader, twenty-six-year-old James "Razzle-Dazzle" Dalziel, was so self-consciously macho that he sneered at dancing with girls as effeminate, and would only take the floor with another burly male member of the gang.

In the Glasgow of the 1930s, it was a case of one thing laughing at another, for while, civic pride in full swell, "Glesca toon" was boasting, and boosting, itself as the Second City of the British Empire, life for the painful majority was no picnic in the grim valley of the Clyde. One man in three was out of work. Times were rough and things got rougher.

It was the Gorbals that in these years introduced a new weapon to the skirmish scene – the open razor. The phrase "razor-slashing" started to appear in the public prints. The regular pitched-battles for transient supremacy raged. Pathetic, cloth-capped young men, the losers, were carted off, bloodstained bundles, to lock-up or casualty. Older, more cunning men, veteran survivors of the war to end wars, began, first to infiltrate, and then to take command of the war to end want – their personal want – on the crustless streets. The gang battles, the internecine warrings, escalated to pretty terrifying proportions. Gurkha knives and bayonets were added to the armoury; souvenirs, no doubt, in some cases, of previous combative engagements overseas.

Sillitoe countered with an even rougher offensive. Using without compunction the toughest men in his force, on the poacher-turned-gamekeeper principle, he had them conveyed under cover, in furniture vans and suchlike inconspicuous transports, to the site of the hasslings and there unleashed them with wink-as-good-as-a-nod permission to bring to play whatever exercise of strength they liked to sanitize the streets. And Sillitoe was winning when, in 1939, the Second World War interrupted his street-gang sweeping campaign. He relinquished his Chief Constableship in 1943.

The 1939–45 war that coffined and buried so many of the old ways, good and bad, brought in its wake changes of catastrophic dimension. Socialist City Fathers occupying the chambers of civic power decreed a New Order for auld Glasgie. The noisome, festering, massively overcrowded old sandstone tenement slums – the Glasgow ghettos, McArthur's Land – were to be razed. Bulldozers should do what the blitz did not. New schemes "amid the green hills far away" on the virgin fringes of the city. Bright new dormitories for the deserving. But the idealists should have listened and been warned. Did not their own national poet caution, "The best laid schemes . . . Gang aft a-gley"? And these, it has with hindsight to be admitted, were not the best. Oh, the houses, acres and acres of look-alike, balconied grey battleships breasting the green wave-crests of the circumjacent hills, were fine. Nothing a-gley there; the baths and indoor toilets were all present and correct, the paint was bright, the wallpaper cheery, roofs water-tight. But, and it was a very big but, the enthusiastic, well-intentioned planners forgot to graft a heart into the place. Essentials, basic and more, had been remembered and supplied, but amenities had been forgotten. No places of sport or entertainment had been laid on. There was even a dearth of shops. Bus services to the city centre were poor. Boredom and depression became the next-door neighbours of the inhabitants of the new, cut off, Robinson Crusoe townships. Easterhouse, Drumchapel, Castle-milk and Pollok . . . the names droop off the tongue like a litany of despair. Here, in this concrete and chrome heaven turned to hell, was a splendid new breeding ground for the fresh gangs. Mean-while, those left behind – those not yet included in, and encom-passed by, the rural–urban drift – found idle hands' solution to relieve the novel boredom and frustration. The inner city infra-structure might be crumbling but, despite decimated territories and depopulated streets, it was still tough enough to support a thinning scatter of gangs, whose members, in their bewilderment at the disintegration of the environment and cognate eco-system, sought security of identification in the redoubling of self-expres-sive violence.

So it was that, in the late 1950s, the old, if not venerable, Glasgow tradition of street gangs and territorial violence came back with a terrible new vivacity. Even more disturbing was the speedy revelation that the use of the considerably more lethal knife had replaced the horribly mutilating but far less life-threatening razor as the weapon wielded with a new ruthless disregard for fatal consequence.

The gang names, new names, started to appear. Alongside the Tongs from Townhead, the Cumbie from the Gorbals, the Fleet from Maryhill, the Govan Team, there came the Buck and the Drummie from Drumchapel, the Toi and the Young Team from Castlemilk, the Bal Toi, the Torran Toi and the Bar L (named after Barlinnie Prison) from Easterhouse, and the Shamrock from Blackhill – that same Blackhill which spawned the Thompsons and the Ferrises.

The wings of the new breed of hoodlums were well clipped by Lord Cameron and his fellow-judges at the High Court, who handed out hefty exemplary sentences. But the containment of the mayhem and the ferocity was destined to be utterly shattered by the emergence in the early sixties of the drug problem. This was to become so grievous and far-reaching in its consequences, especially among the young, that the increase of other crimes – such as the opening up of local shebeens, illegal money-lending at extortionate interest rates, as well as the traditional bread-and-butter villainies of theft and protection racketeering – paled.

The 1970s and 1980s have witnessed a dramatic upsurge in the statistics of murder and serious assaults committed by gang members, although, oddly, the number of weapon-bearing gangs actually out on the streets has decreased.

The first half of the 1980s will always be remembered for the ferocious Glasgow Ice-Cream Wars, and their terrible culmination in what has been frequently described as Scotland's most horrific mass murder. Despite the long and strongly whispered rumour that drugs were at the back of it all, the best authority – and I am including in this the statement of the campaigning journalists Douglas Skelton and Lisa Brownlie, the authors of *Frightener* (1992), a close-focus study of the ice-cream scene – denies this. At the root of the trouble was the good, old-fashioned, Thatcherite profit motive gone obscenely wrong.

In order to understand, which is not to say to sympathize with, the market pressures leading to inevitable commercial battlings, all one needs to appreciate is that the struggle was for control of the "runs" or sales pitches of the numerous ice-cream vans operating on the various council estates. These sales of ice-cream, sweeties, soft drinks, crisps and cigarettes were not peanuts. Without overexerting yourself, you could rake in profits ranging between £200 and £800 a week, the higher figure if you were prepared to reset (receive) stolen wares.

Theoretically, anybody could enter into this free enterprise. There were two routes: you could buy your own van and pay to garage it at the premises of such cash-and-carry firms as Fifti Ices, who would also sell you stock, or you could lease a van by the week. If you chose the latter course, you had a choice of three hire firms – the Marchetti Brothers, Capaldi & Sons, and the Viking Ice-Cream Company. You would pay £50 to £60 a week for the vehicle, the hire company being responsible for all the costs, other than petrol, of keeping the van on the road; that is to say, maintenance, insurance, tax and so on.

As realization of the rich pickings to be had from this nice little earner dawned, insalubrious interests were raised, insalubrious characters muscled in, and feuding over the best runs broke out. Each side was, according to the police, backed by well-known criminals. Out came the balaclava-ed strong-arm men, wielding baseball bats and shotguns, and fifty-seven varieties of scare tactics were put into force, including discretionary torchings.

The ultimate torching was the setting on fire, in the small hours of Monday, 16 April 1984, of the top-floor flat of No 29 Bankend Street, in the district of Ruchazie, where Andrew Doyle, eighteen-year-old driver of an ice-cream van put on to the disputed Garthamlock run by Marchetti, lived. Six people perished, including Andrew and an eighteen-month-old baby.

The gangland boss identified as responsible by the police was thirty-one-year-old Thomas Campbell, a hard man's hard man known shuddersomely throughout the underworld as "T. C". His lieutenant in the matter was said to be Joseph Steele, hitherto qualifying as nothing more nefarious than a petty thief. Tried in September 1984, these two received life sentences. But there are those, the authors of *Frightener* among them, who believe that Campbell and Steele are the victims of a miscarriage of justice. This does not *necessarily* imply innocence – indeed, the word on the street at the time was that they were guilty – but what it does suggest is that, innocent or guilty of the act libelled, the position is unacceptable if false evidence was used to secure the convictions. A key prosecution witness, William Love, has sworn an affidavit that he lied at the Glasgow High Court trial. An independent public inquiry into the way the police investigated the Doyle murders is currently being sought.

What, one may ask, is the outlook for Glasgow, erstwhile City of European Culture, city with a drink problem three times as high as anywhere else in Britain and generally acknowledged to be the alcoholic capital of Western Europe –

Hard-folk joke:

Question: What is Glasgow's favourite drink?
Answer: Kneecappuccino.

– home to 900,000, of whom 12,500 are main-lining H (for Heroin, not Hard) men and women, and addicts of a hotchpotch of other junk for junkies? More than somewhat unhealthy.

There's only one way out: gang up on the drug gangs.

Axe Man
(Frank Mitchell)

John Pearson

Frank "Mad Axe Man" Mitchell was a vicious, simple-minded giant and an old friend of the Krays. Although mentally retarded, he was enormously strong, and could lift two 15st men and hold them aloft at arm's length. He could lie beneath a full-size billiard table and lift it with his massive hands. A persistent escaper from penal institutions, Mitchell kept himself super-fit with a punishing self-imposed regime of physical jerks, so that his body was outstandingly well-developed. He was put in a straitjacket, dumped in a bath of cold water, and lashed with the cat-o'-nine-tails, all of which he shrugged off. For attacking prison officers, he twice received the maximum fifteen strokes of the birch, showing off the weals as though they were stripes of office. The prisoner no prison could hold was declared insane and transferred to Rampton for treatment, but Mitchell broke out and in a two-day terror spree tried to burgle a house, wounding the occupant with intent to murder, stole two hatchets and armed himself with a shotgun and cartridges.

In 1967, nine years into a life sentence, Mitchell escaped from Dartmoor with the help of Reggie Kray and vanished, apparently into thin air. In prison, Mitchell had been a "trusty" who was allowed out on working parties and who regularly visited pubs on the isolated moor to buy beer. Now free, he holed up in a hideout provided by the Krays in East London, not far from their own house in Vallance Road, Bethnal Green. They also laid on an attractive nightclub hostess, Lisa Prescott, to share his bed. The Krays had regarded Mitchell as a key enforcer in their power battle with the rival Richardsons, whose principal strong-arm man was "Mad" Frankie Fraser. But once they'd helped spring Mitchell from Dartmoor, the Krays realized he was an embarrassment and arranged to have him killed. His body was never found. Mitchell's escape and mysterious disappearance is related by John Pearson (b. 1930) who probably knows more about the Krays than anyone living – or dead. Before they were arrested, the twins commissioned him to write their joint bio-graphy. The result, The Profession of Violence, *became an international bestseller, and reputedly the most popular book in British prisons after the Bible. It also became a cult book among the young and unwittingly helped turn the Kray Twins into living criminal celebrities.*

In 1966 one of the potentially most dangerous prisoners in Britain was Frank Mitchell, the so-called "Mad Axe Man". Gaoled originally for robbery with violence, he had spent eighteen of his thirty-two years in detention. He was immensely strong, but prison and the punishment he had received for violence had numbed what scant intelligence he had. His body bore the scars of birchings for attacks on prison officers. He earned his nickname when he threatened an elderly couple with a felling axe while on the run from a hospital for the criminally insane, and was detained at Dartmoor during Her Majesty's pleasure.

By now he seemed to have accepted life in prison. Handled with understanding he was easy to control, and during the four years he had spent in Dartmoor, warders had come to like him. The prison governor, Mr Denis Malone, took a particular interest in him and always called him by his Christian name. He saw that it was useless to impose too strict a discipline on Mitchell – warders would get hurt and Mitchell was strong enough to take any amount of punishment. He would just end up more rebellious and brutalized than ever.

Instead of this the governor allowed Mitchell a loose rein. He was given the blue arm-band of a trusted prisoner and promised that if he behaved himself the governor would do everything he could to get him a release date from the Home Office. Mitchell seemed happy with the arrangement, and Dartmoor became something of a home for him. He spent hours in the gymnasium improving his extraordinary physique and during the day seems to have had more freedom than anyone in Dartmoor. Most days were spent on the moors in working parties guarded by a single warder, who often let big Mitchell wander away on his own. Mitchell liked this. He had a way with animals, taming the wild moorland ponies and riding them for miles. Wearing his shirt and denim trousers he was quite free to visit isolated Dartmoor pubs and often brought a bottle of Scotch back for the evening. He bought a budgerigar for his cell, and even had a mistress for a while, a village schoolmistress he used to make love to in a deserted barn. Each night, when he was locked up in his cell, he did his press-ups and his weight-lifting and went off to sleep dreaming of the release date which the governor would get him.

Another reason for Frank Mitchell's peace of mind came from knowing he had friends outside and was not forgotten. It was ten years now since he first met Ronnie Kray in Wandsworth, but the Krays still kept in contact with him. They visited him and wrote quite regularly. The radio which Reggie brought him allowed him to listen in to the police and the prison authorities' short-wave conversations and he was well supplied for money. Kindness apart, Mitchell was a legend among long-serving prisoners and the life he led in Dartmoor was a good advertisement for the twins' "Away Society". This was one reason why they had taken such care of him when he was charged with the attempted murder of another prisoner during his period at Wandsworth. Word was passed round the prison that Frank was a friend of the Krays and that anyone giving evidence against him did so at his peril. Nemone Lethbridge, the attractive female barrister who appeared for Ronnie in his car-stealing case in 1961, was briefed to defend him. And Ronnie even got his tailor to make Frank a suit so that he would look his best at the trial. After Mitchell was acquitted, he always spoke of the twins as "the two best friends a man could hope for".

During these ten years there was one thing the twins never did – encourage Mitchell to escape. It would have been no problem for him to get away from Dartmoor, but they agreed that much his best hope was to rely on the governor's ability to get him a release. They also knew that if he escaped he could never stay at liberty alone; his size made him conspicuous, his simple-mindedness a liability.

Then suddenly they changed their minds. A few months after George Cornell was shot they told Mitchell that they were going to get him out. Mitchell was thrilled. If the twins told him to escape it must be right. From that August on he thought of nothing else and began planning on his own account.

This strange decision of the twins has never been explained. In court the only explanation offered was that the twins required Mitchell on the Firm as a strong-arm man. This is absurd. They had all the strong arms that they needed and Mitchell's would have been superfluous. But the twins' own account, that they were "simply feeling sorry for Frank", is equally implausible. They had been feeling sorry for him now for years. The truth is that the whole idea of helping Mitchell to escape began as a simple exercise in underworld public relations, a gesture of the sort the twins could not resist – especially that summer when it was clear that something needed to be done.

For, contrary to Ronnie's arguments, the Cornell murder had backfired, scaring their friends more than their enemies. Business was suffering. Payne and Gore had both left town. Even the protection business seemed to be suffering. London's top gambling club, which the twins had "minded" for three years, decided that they were far too dangerous to have around and offered a £10,000 lump sum to end the arrangement. Something was needed to convince the underworld that the twins were more than trigger-happy murderers. The idea of using Mitchell for this purpose seems to have come from one of Ronnie's friends, "Mad" Teddy Smith. Smith was an unusual gangster. The BBC had recently accepted a play he had written about a bank robbery and he was tending to see life in somewhat dramatic, televisual terms. He had been interested in Mitchell's story for some while and asked the twins to let him visit the Axe Man. He found him starting to get worried about his release date and formed the idea of helping him to get public sympathy.

Smith put his plan to the twins. Mitchell should be helped to escape, then kept in hiding. While in hiding he could write letters to the press, pointing out the hardship and injustice of his case and promising to surrender if his sentence were reviewed. There was a new Labour Home Secretary and a current mood of sympathy for the underdog. Mitchell would be sure to get his case looked into, and most of the credit would belong to the twins.

The twins were easily convinced. This seemed the sort of coup they needed, something to restore their image as benevolent, responsible public figures. Ronnie began to think of several journalists and politicians he could put pressure on to back up the campaign. And Mitchell was informed that he would definitely be home for Christmas.

But this remained an awkward period for the twins; reactions to the Cornell murder were making life uncomfortable for both of them. Ronnie saw potential traitors all round him and wondered whom to shoot next. Reggie was drinking heavily. Most nights they slept at Vallance Road and one night Cornell's widow came and smashed the windows, shouting that the twins were bloody murderers. Violet was upset that anyone could say such things about her boys.

In fact nobody was talking to the police, but the twins had grown so jittery that when they heard rumours of fresh police evidence about Cornell they fled the country. They had had an escape route ready for some time and a private aircraft was waiting for them in a field near Bognor. This flew them to a landing-strip near Calais, where they were picked up by a car and driven to Paris just as dawn was breaking. Tickets were waiting for them both at Orly under assumed names and they flew without incident to Morocco. Here they spent three untroubled weeks and for the first time since his marriage Reggie enjoyed himself. Billy Hill was there, a respected figure with a big white car, to show them round. They spent most of their time in Tangier, drinking and swimming and lazing on the beach; Ronnie enjoyed the Arab boys, Reggie invited out a blonde hostess from the Latin Quarter Club in London. During her fortnight with him he never once referred to Frances or the East End. Instead he spoke of settling in Tangier and buying a small club. The girl agreed to join him. Reggie was wondering how to break the news to Ronnie when the police saved him the embarrassment. The chief of the Moroccan police arrived in person at their hotel to tell them they were undesirable aliens. Two seats were booked for them on the next plane back to London – this time in their right names.

They returned expecting Butler to be waiting for them to charge them with the death of George Cornell. Instead the Yard had got no further with the murder and they walked through the airport free men. Their departure had naturally caused something of a panic in gangland. Their safe return meant that they had work to do, repairing the damage. Members of the Firm who had prudently made themselves scarce resurfaced and were greeted as if nothing had happened. Fresh warnings were put out against talking to the police about Cornell. Arrears of protection money were collected, fresh deals for marketing a new batch of stolen American securities arranged. When someone in the Firm asked Ronnie if they were still proceeding with the Mitchell escape he replied, "Of course" – Frank was his friend.

That same week in October 1966 Frances Kray made her first attempt to kill herself, locking herself in the front room of her parents' house in Ormsby Street, putting a rug against the door and lying on a cushion by the gas fire with the taps on. Her father, who came home at midday, found her just alive. When she revived in Bethnal Green Hospital she was murmuring, "Leave me in peace. Why can't you let me sleep?"

That night Reggie visited the hospital but was refused admission to his wife. Later he finished off a bottle and a half of gin and dropped off, muttering that he would have to kill his in-laws.

Mitchell was counting off the days to his escape and had made a mask from a piece of his girl-friend's black nylon nightdress in readiness. Various members of the Firm visited him to discuss the final plans. He would escape from a working party. Two of the Firm would pick him up in a car and drive him to London; 12 December was fixed as a provisional date, but at the crucial moment Ronnie involved himself in a curious case with a senior policeman.

According to the twins a police inspector had offered Ronnie the use of an East End pub with guaranteed police immunity for a regular £20 a week. The last thing the twins needed was fresh involvement with the police, but Ronnie was unable to resist a chance of scoring off the Law. He laid his preparations cunningly and hired a private detective to bug the pub and wire Ronnie up with a tie-pin microphone and shoulder-holster tape recorder. Prepared for anything, Ronnie invited the inspector for a discussion. A few days later Ronnie lodged a formal complaint against the police and tapes from the recorders found their way to the office of the Director of Public Prosecutions. For some weeks nothing happened; then Ronnie was informed that the inspector would

be prosecuted. Ronnie was required as prime witness for the
Crown. The trial would start on 28 November.

Ronnie insists that all that he could do was disappear. It was a
matter of principle. "I'd do most things, but I'd never go in no
witness-box for the Law to get someone put away – not even a
copper."

The squeeze was put on to a Mayfair property man to find the
twins a suitably discreet flat; within a few hours Ronnie had what
he needed – a five-room furnished flat in a quiet road in Finchley.
The day before he was due in court he moved in and for the next
eight months remained officially on the run.

Ronnie was quite sincere about refusing to appear in court, but
he could hardly have found a worse moment to disappear. He went
to ground completely and had soon turned his flat into a fortress. It
was crammed with guns and he kept one of the machine-guns
under the floorboards. The curtains were kept drawn and he never
ventured out. Instead he got the Firm to bring stocks of food and
gin and bottled beer so that he could stay hidden for weeks on end.
Codes were invented for the telephone and letters. He played
Italian opera on the gramophone and had a fresh boy every night.
During the day he would be busy working out who needed
murdering.

As usual in the twins' crises, everything fell on Reggie – running
the Firm, coping with Ronnie, worrying about Frances. On top of
this 12 December was approaching. His brother Charlie said that
he was mad to think of springing Mitchell at a time like this. Reggie
agreed, but Ronnie wouldn't hear of letting Mitchell down. As
usual Ronnie got his way. But nothing was properly planned now.
Reggie was forced to improvise as best he could and he asked
several members of the Firm if they had relatives prepared to put
up Mitchell for a week or two. Predictably, none had. Someone
suggested a man called Lennie Dunn, who kept a bookstall in the
East End.

Lennie had trouble – with his nerves, his business and his wife.
He lived alone in a ground-floor flat in Barking and was sufficiently scared of the twins to do as he was told and keep his mouth
shut. Reggie ordered him to expect a visitor.

Then came a fresh problem. Mad Teddy Smith and Albert
Donaghue, another member of the Firm, had both agreed to collect
Mitchell in a car; neither possessed a valid driving licence. Reggie
had to borrow one so that they could hire a car. Someone else

produced clothes for an extremely large man. Then 12 December arrived.

Mitchell was wearing his black nylon mask as he came lumbering through the moorland mist towards the green Vauxhall parked on the Princetown road. Donaghue told him to change his clothes and take the mask off to avoid attracting attention. Nobody was interested in the car as it sped back to London. It was to be another four hours before Mitchell was missed. By the time the police were checking the roads from the moors Mitchell was eating steak and chips in Lennie's flat in Barking and feeling faintly disappointed. He had expected something grander, a hero's welcome from the twins, a great party with champagne and girls and the congratulations of the underworld. Instead Smith had to explain as best he could that the twins were unable to see him that night and that Scotch Jack Dickson and Lennie Dunn would be taking care of him. Just for a few days he would be the most wanted man in Britain and must make no attempt to see anyone or contact his family. He must be patient, lie low, trust the twins.

Mitchell was reassured. The twins were his best friends and they were very smart. Now that they had freed him he had nothing to worry about. They gave him more to drink; he brightened up. When they turned on the television news at 10.00 p.m. and watched marine commandos combing the moors for him he laughed until the tears came.

"If they try coming for me now, I'll kill the lot of them."

"You won't have to, Frank," said Dickson. "Now that the twins are looking after you, no one will ever find you."

"But I'd kill anyone rather than go back to prison. Anyone at all. Even you."

They gave Mitchell the back bedroom with the double bed; Dickson took the front bedroom; Lennie swallowed two sleeping pills and stretched out on the living-room sofa. At 3.00 Dickson was woken up by Mitchell, who was standing by his bed with a knife. He said he was restless and couldn't sleep. Dickson made him tea and they talked – about his family, about his friends and the animals on the moor, and about the twins. He hero-worshipped them, Ronnie especially. Ronnie had told him that when everything was sorted out they'd live together, just the two of them, in a beautiful rich house in the country. He could keep all his animals there. He loved animals, particularly little ones – birds, mice and kittens – anything he could be gentle with. Ronnie had promised him all the animals he wanted; Ronnie was an animal-lover too.

He waited all next morning for him, but no Ronnie – Reggie came instead. Rather than say that Ronnie too was in hiding, he told him he was away and would soon be coming. In the meantime Teddy Smith would help him write his letters to the press and the twins would see that he had Christmas with his family.

Mitchell was reassured by this. Soon he was suggesting one of his favourite games, a trial of strength. To humour him, Reggie took off his jacket, sat down at the kitchen table and gripped Mitchell's enormous hand with his own. Reggie was exceptionally strong in the arms and shoulders, but Mitchell smiled and pushed and slowly Reggie's arm went back until his knuckles touched the table. Mitchell was delighted.

"See what I used to do in Dartmoor," he said, and picking up Dickson and Lennie Dunn by the belts, lifted them, one in each hand, until their heads touched the ceiling.

"That's what I'd do with anyone who tried to catch me."

That afternoon Mad Teddy and the Axe Man worked on the letters to the Press and the Home Secretary. Mitchell had learned to write in prison but was slow and lacked the literary touch which, as a writer, Mad Teddy thought the letters should have. After some false starts they agreed on a rough outline and, with Smith dictating, Mitchell laboriously penned his letter to the *Mirror* editor and to the Home Secretary, care of the editor of *The Times*.

Sir, the reason for my absence from Dartmoor was to bring to the Notice of my unhappy plight, to be truthful, I am asking for a possible Date of release, from the age of 9 I have not been completely free, always under some act or other.

Sir, I ask you, where is the fairness of this. I am not a murderer or a sex maniac, nor do I think I am a danger to the public. I think that I have been more than punished for the wrongs I have done. Yours sincerely,

Frank Mitchell

While Mitchell waited patiently for Ronnie, Ronnie was having troubles of his own. His depressions had begun and he was spending most of the day behind drawn curtains, armed and watching the road for the police. One of the Firm had brought

his favourite records of Churchill's speeches; he played them
endlessly and drank a lot.

Sometimes he ordered a full meeting of the Firm and talked
about the future – further link-ups with the Mafia, control of a
London-centred narcotics network, a Kray representative running
the rackets in every major British city, an international strike force
ready for villainy anywhere in the world. Ronnie was thinking big.
At other times he was obsessed with private grievances and wanted
someone hurt. A boxing manager had been impolite about a young
boxer he fancied; a villain they occasionally employed called Jack
McVitie was becoming unreliable; Payne was suspiciously silent.
What was he up to?

Sometimes the strain of hiding seemed unbearable and even
Churchill's wartime speeches were no help. All he could do was
drink himself insensible or lie in bed taking more Stematol until
the depression lifted.

Time passed slowly for both prisoners. While Ronnie had his
nightmares in Finchley, Mitchell in the basement flat in Barking
still talked endlessly about him and the life they'd lead together.
He would be Ronnie's right-hand man; they would become in-
separable, the greatest criminals of the century. He would willingly
die for Ronnie – that was the one way he would like to go. But when
could he see him?

For more than a week Dickson and Lennie made excuses; then
Mitchell seemed to understand that Ronnie would never come and
stopped talking about him. Two men were always with him;
Donaghue and the ex-boxer Billy Exley took turns with Dickson
and Lennie. All they could do was try to make the time pass. For
hours on end they played cards with Mitchell; he was no card-
player but they always let him win to keep his spirits up. He ate
hugely, cleaned his teeth a dozen times a day and constantly
combed his hair, examining his looks in the mirror. He was
inordinately vain.

There was a day's excitement when *The Times* and the *Mirror*
published his letters, both of them in full. The *Mirror* included an
appeal from its editor for Mitchell to give himself up. Then
nothing happened. Reggie called in the next day, but he had no
news, only fresh promises that Frank would see his family for
Christmas. Mitchell became restless. This was worse than prison.
A few nights later he threatened to go out and find himself a

woman. He was beginning to groan in his sleep. Dickson told
Reggie that if he didn't get a woman soon, there would be trouble.

They brought a girl for Mitchell in a taxi at 2 a.m. With Reggie
was Tommy Cowley, a little gambler with pale eyes and short red
hair who always seemed a cut above most members of the Firm.
The girl was thirtyish; Cowley said they could count on her
discretion. He and Reggie picked her up at Winston's Club in
New Bond Street, where she was a hostess. In the taxi they had
informed her of her duties. Reggie said that if she did as she was
told she would have the gratitude of the East End. She replied that
gratitude was all very well: she preferred cash. Reggie agreed.

She had a lot of blonde hair and a good figure. Her name was
Lisa. She was expensive. When she entered Lennie's flat in a long
black dress and heavy make-up Mitchell was all for having her at
once. He appeared almost childish in his enthusiasm, but Lisa was
no child; since Reggie had gone on to Vallance Road without
paying the £100 she wanted, she told the Axe Man he would have
to wait.

Mitchell could have forced her. Nobody would have stopped
him. Most girls in her position would have done as they were told.
But Lisa had her professional pride, and Mitchell wanted someone
he could love, not rape. She kept her dignity and her black lace
dress, and both of them sat in the kitchen, drinking tea, while
Scotch Jack Dickson drove round to Vallance Road for her fee.
Reggie grumbled but paid – a hundred old notes in a carrier bag;
Dickson gave them to her, less twenty for expenses. Reggie had
promised that if she kept Frank happy there would be more to
come. And on this tender note Lisa and her Axe Man went to bed.

They stayed there for the next two days, curtains drawn, the
glow of the electric fire providing the only light, and Mitchell
sometimes leaping out of bed for fifty press-ups. Mitchell was an
enthusiastic lover – "His virility was greater than that of any man I
have known," the girl wrote later. But even sex was no real answer
to the twins' dilemma. It was soon obvious to everyone that he
would not remain cooped up in the flat much longer. He was
becoming moodier; only the girl could quieten him. On 20 December he gave Lennie £5 and asked him to buy enough drink for a
small party as he was going to ask his family over before Christmas.
The twins had promised he could see them.

Lennie and Scotch Jack Dickson had been guarding Mitchell for
ten days now; both were afraid that he would break out soon.

Rather than this they asked Lisa to try persuading him to give himself up. The first time she mentioned it he said that he would do whatever the twins thought best. Next day she spoke about it, but the idea sent Mitchell into a rage, shouting about the eighteen years he had spent inside and how he would kill anyone who tried to get him back. She tried calming him, but he went on shouting, and for a while the others thought he would make a dash for it.

"Give me your gun," he yelled at Exley, who was too frightened to argue. The gun calmed Mitchell.

"I'll hang on to it," he said. "It's nice to know it's there in case I need it."

Next day, 22 December, Mitchell woke later and appeared cheerful, knowing he had a gun. Later his mood began to change. By afternoon he was weeping, shouting and saying he would go out and shoot the first policeman that he saw. When he was quieter he told Dickson that he wanted him to take a letter round to Reggie.

It took an hour to write; in it he said that unless the twins got him away at once he would get in touch with his parents. If anybody tried to stop him, he had a gun and would use it. Reggie was visibly annoyed at Mitchell's letter. "Who does he think he is? He's got everything he wants, even a bloody woman, but he goes telling us what to do." Then he asked Dickson more about Exley's gun and Mitchell's threats to leave. This clearly worried him.

"Jack. Go back to Mitchell and tell him he'll be all right. Tell him not to do anything silly and he'll be out of the flat in forty-eight hours. I think it's time I had a word with Ron."

The twins and several members of the Firm discussed what should be done with Mitchell that night at the flat in Finchley. Although Ronnie was cut off, he had been getting regular reports on Mitchell. He even knew about the gun, and according to one story he had heard Mitchell was threatening to go round to Vallance Road and use it on the Kray parents.

Certainly the Colonel's attitude to his old friend had changed dramatically: suddenly he seemed to understand just what could happen if the police caught him. The twins and many of the Firm would be involved. Mitchell could destroy them.

That night as the twins discussed what should be done, Frank Mitchell was no longer a friend but a threat.

Next day a further complication: Frank Mitchell was in love.

"Wherever they're taking me to in the country, Lisa must come as well. We'll never be apart again."

Later the girl whispered to Dickson, "He can think I'm going but I'm not. Just tell the twins I'll keep my mouth shut and that's that."

"OK, but don't say anything to Frank. If he thinks you don't love him, he'd really do his nut."

When Reggie came, Mitchell asked him about the girl. Of course he could take her. It was a lovely place the twins had ready for them, with animals and servants. Lisa and Frank could both be there together.

Reggie gave Lennie Dunn money to buy Mitchell fresh clothes for the journey; his friends were calling for him the following evening. Mitchell was thrilled; to show how happy he was he put his arms round the piano and lifted it right off the floor. Everybody laughed. Reggie looked relieved, shook hands all round and promised to be down to visit Frank and Lisa for Christmas.

It must have seemed the most exciting Christmas Eve in Mitchell's life: for the first time in nearly twenty years he would be spending Christmas Day in freedom, and with the girl he loved.

Reggie rang during the morning saying that Donaghue would be calling around 8.30 pm and that Frank was to be packed and changed and ready to leave immediately.

Dickson asked what was planned for the girl.

"Don't worry about her. Albert will see to her."

Mitchell and the girl got up around midday. She cooked them all a late Christmas Eve lunch. Afterwards everyone exchanged cards. In his Mitchell wrote, "To Lisa, the only one I've ever loved", and she wrote back, "Darling Frank, may this Christmas be the best you ever had". They kissed, drank to the future and went to bed for the last time in the flat.

At 7.30 pm the telephone rang twice, then stopped, the sign that Reggie was on the line wanting to talk to Mitchell. Was he packed? The friends would soon be round.

Just before 8.30 Donaghue arrived. A big grey man with thinning hair, he was one of the enigmas of the Firm. He was a drinker and a fighter and an Irishman but he never talked much, never gave himself away. The year before, Reggie had shot him in the foot during an argument in a pub off Vallance Road. Since then they had made it up and "Big Albert" was regarded as Reggie's

man, but he still limped. Mitchell trusted him because he had
helped him escape; Donaghue said Reggie's friends were outside
with their van, the Axe Man laughed and asked where they were
taking him.

"Kent, Frank. A farm in Kent."

"That means we're driving through the tunnel under the river,"
said Mitchell to the girl.

"You know your way round pretty well for a man who's done the
time you have, Frank," said Donaghue. "Got your things ready?"

Mitchell had nothing much to carry and was anxious to be off.
He shook hands with Dickson, then with Lennie Dunn, promising
that Ronnie would be sending him £500 after Christmas for all his
trouble.

"Get your coat now," he said to the girl. "They're waiting for
us."

"I'm not coming yet, Frank."

"That's right, Frank. Ronnie's orders. It's risky enough getting
you there on your own. We don't want her involved, do we, if
there's any trouble? Cowley will bring her down in his car. She'll
be there as soon as you."

There was no time to argue; Mitchell nodded and kissed the girl
goodbye.

"See you at Ron's place, then. Don't be long."

At a sign from Donaghue, Lennie turned the lights out. A few
moments later Mitchell stepped through the back door. There, in
the Barking Road at 8.30 p.m. on Christmas Eve 1966, the story of
Frank Mitchell, the Mad Axe Man, officially ends. As far as the
police know there was no farm in Kent; if there was they have no
evidence to suggest that Mitchell ever turned up there alive.

All that is known is that ten minutes or so after seeing Mitchell
off the premises, Donaghue returned and helped Scotch Jack
Dickson and Lennie Dunn to clear the flat of all trace of him.
The girl hung on to the prison comb and the Christmas card he
gave her. Otherwise his few belongings went – the beret and mask
he wore during his escape, a pair of shoes and a couple of paper-
backs he had been reading. Every surface in the place was cleaned
of finger-prints.

Then a car driven by another member of the Firm arrived for
Donaghue and the girl, and they ended up together at a Christmas
Eve party in Evering Road. Reggie was there and took the girl
aside. She was to forget all she had seen and heard during the last

five days. She had never heard of a man called Frank Mitchell. If she mentioned him to a living soul the twins would hear of it and in the end they'd deal with her, wherever she was.

"I'll forget all right, and the sooner the better." She drank a lot, did her best to enjoy the party and spent the night in bed with Donaghue. After Christmas she was back at Winston's, demure as ever in the same black lace dress. For her, as for everyone who came into Frank Mitchell's sad and violent life, he had ceased to exist. She kept the card that said she was the only woman he had ever loved, but those were the only words he ever wrote to her. None of his few friends nor his family ever heard from him. Lennie Dunn never received his £500.

The months went by and the police continued their search. The twins had told the Firm to answer any inquiries about Mitchell by saying he had gone abroad. There were reports that he was seen in Melbourne, in Casablanca and the South of France. A postcard supposedly written by him was received from Tangier.

But more persistent were the underworld rumours that Frank Mitchell was dead.

If Frank Mitchell's grand escape did end in death, his remains were disposed of with some thoroughness. For two years later, when the Kray brothers and a South London gang leader called Frederick Foreman were accused at the Old Bailey of murdering him, the prosecution had to admit that they were alleging a murder without the evidence of a body.

The case was long and complicated. The Krays admitted responsibility for helping Mitchell to escape and for harbouring him; that was all. The absence of any trace of a corpse threw doubt on the prosecution, and Frederick Foreman and the Krays were finally acquitted. But it was during the evidence for the prosecution that the girl Lisa, Lennie Dunn and Albert Donaghue gave their own versions on oath of what happened during those ten minutes after Frank Mitchell left the flat and how the story of the Axe Man ended.

Lennie Dunn and the girl both said they remained in the darkened flat, and their evidence was essentially the same. Both claimed to have heard loud bangs from the street outside, two or three minutes after Mitchell left. Lennie Dunn took them for a car backfiring, but the girl was hysterical and screamed out that they had shot him. Later when Reggie Kray told her to keep her mouth shut she did so because she "knew the Krays and what they could do".

But it was Donaghue's evidence that created the greatest stir in court. In the first hearing at Old Street Magistrates Court he had been in the dock, along with Foreman and the Krays, accused of murdering Mitchell. But by the time the case reached the Old Bailey he had turned Queen's evidence. The murder charge against him had been dropped and he went into the witness-box to give his version of what happened between 8.30 and 8.45 p.m. that Christmas Eve.

According to him, the Krays were desperate to get Mitchell away from Barking before he landed them all in trouble, and Reggie Kray and Donaghue had a meeting with Foreman, an old friend of theirs, to arrange the move. Foreman had said he would lay on a van and a driver to take Mitchell down to the country. It would be waiting outside the flat at 8.30, and as Donaghue was one of the few people Mitchell trusted he was told to bring him out.

To start with, said Donaghue, everything went as expected. When he led Mitchell out of the flat a dark-painted Thames van was waiting, double-parked, twenty yards or so down the main road. There were three men inside, including Foreman. One of them opened the back door and Donaghue and Mitchell got in, Mitchell sitting on the wheel casing on the right-hand side of the van and Donaghue going to the front beside the driver.

Continuing his evidence, Donaghue described how the doors slammed to, the van drew away, and Foreman and the man beside him drew their guns, Foreman a silenced automatic and the other man a revolver. Mitchell made a dive towards the driver, but before he could reach him he had been shot several times in the body and collapsed, groaning, with his knees doubled up under him. By now the van was travelling down Ladysmith Avenue, a turning off the main Barking Road, and three more shots were fired into Mitchell's chest in the area of the heart. For a moment, said Donaghue, he lay still. Then he lifted his head. Two final shots, claims Donaghue, were then fired into his head and everything was over.

This was Albert Donaghue's story from the witness-box of the Old Bailey. He said that he telephoned the news to Reggie from the flat, telling him briefly, "The geezer's gone", and according to another witness who was there, Reggie Kray wept when he heard the news.

As for the disposal of the body, Donaghue alleged that Foreman later told him they had to hold on to it for five days over Christmas, before taking it "down to a man in the country" for disposal. He also described how Foreman told him that they took the body to pieces, that the heart was ripped open and three bullets found in it, and that he had a tiny brain – "He cupped his hands to show me just how small it was." Donaghue believed the body had been burned.

All this was strenuously denied by Foreman and by the Krays, and the judge ruled that under English law, Donaghue's evidence required independent corroboration before the jury could accept it, as Donaghue was himself criminally involved in Mitchell's escape. There was no corroboration. Frederick Foreman and the three Krays were found not guilty of the murder of Frank Mitchell, and to this day the Axe Man is still officially on the run, one of the few men in history to have made a successful getaway from Dartmoor.

The Clown Who Killed Boys
(*John Wayne Gacy Jr*)

Clifford L. Linedecker

America's most prolific serial killer, John Wayne Gacy Jr, sexually tortured and murdered 33 young men and boys over a three-year period in the 1970s. None of his friends and neighbours suspected anything. He was popular in his neighbourhood, and occasionally entertained local children in his guise of Pogo the Clown. But Gacy was a Jekyll and Hyde figure who led an outwardly normal life, while brutalizing dozens of youths before killing them and hiding their bodies beneath the floorboards of his house in a Chicago suburb. The American crime writer Clifford L. Linedecker (b. 1931) lived near Gacy's murder beat in the 1970s and knew the territory and people associated with the man accused of some of the 20th century's most horrific crimes. In his 1980 book about the case, Linedecker described the ordeal of Jeffrey Rignall, who was lucky to escape death at Gacy's hands. Rignall survived an encounter with Gacy in Chicago's raffish New Town district in March 1978 but at great physical and mental cost.

Jeffrey Rignall shivered as he stepped away from the apartment building into the post-midnight chill. He liked Chicago. It was nice to be home, and the stay in Florida during the winter had provided an opportunity to return to the city with an unseasonable tan that gave his slender face a healthy beachboy look under his curly mop of sandy hair.

But New Town wasn't Florida. It was late night on 21 March and it was cold. The crisp, dark sky was punctuated with the merest flecks of clouds and a brisk breeze off the lake whispered through the streets, scattering discarded papers onto lawns and ruffling his hair like a capricious hand. Even though the temperature had inched a couple of degrees above freezing, Rignall's sinewy frame shook in the frigid air.

He first noticed the sleek, black late-model Oldsmobile with spotlights on the side after it had slid quietly in front of him, blocking his path. Rignall began to step around the car when a heavyset man with genial features and a Santa Claus smile leaned out the rolled-down window and complimented him on his tan.

New Town is a friendly neighborhood where people often talk to strangers. The hum of activity and the music and laughter drifting from discos and taverns can provide a false sense of security and trust, and many meetings are by chance. Rignall replied good-naturedly that he had picked up the tan in Florida.

When the stranger invited him to share a joint and take a ride, the twenty-seven-year-old bachelor didn't give it a second thought before popping inside the car. He was thankful to get out of the cold, and looked forward to loosening up with some marijuana. The decision was instantaneous – and fateful.

Rignall began to relax as he pulled the soothing smoke into his lungs and leaned back into the comfort of his seat. The cigarette was passed a couple of times. He was contented and off guard when the big man suddenly whirled and shoved a rag over his face. Rignall tensed, flailing his arms and legs in alarm and drawing in his breath. Then he passed out. The rag was soaked with chloroform.

There were moments of fuzzy semiconsciousness during which he remembered opening his eyes and being dully aware of brief chimeric visions of street signs and a familiar expressway exit before the rag was once more pressed against his face and he lapsed again into total darkness.

Sometime later he experienced a dreamlike feeling of being carried in powerful arms into a house, through another doorway and down into a lowered room. As the veiled darkness began to clear from his mind and his eyes focused on the confusing miasma of shapes swimming in front of him, he realized he was lying on a couch, fully dressed. The rag was pressed to his face again. The next time he regained consciousness he was naked. His wrists and

neck were locked in a pillorylike rack. The man who had chloroformed him was standing in front of him, also naked, his huge,
hairy belly bulging obscenely. Several whips, chains, and dildos
were lined up on the floor.

Rignall was groggy, but his eyes widened in alarm as the stranger
told him in cool, even tones exactly how each of the implements
was going to be used. The words rolled off his tongue like an
incantation. Then the torture began.

Rignall was in the power of a sadist who used one instrument
after another, waiting before each new assault until he saw the
young man's face bleach gray in fear and pain, then smiling and
applying the chloroform again. As soon as Rignall regained consciousness, the torture resumed.

Between the sessions of physical abuse and unconsciousness, the
big man bragged that he was a policeman. He once said that he
would just as soon shoot his pain-wracked victim as look at him.
The abuses being performed on Rignall were so horrible and
excruciatingly painful that there were times when he didn't care
if he died. But at other times he pleaded for his life and babbled to
his tormenter in mindbending terror that he was from Florida and
would return there if he was freed.

Once as he was being tortured during a period of groggy semiconsciousness, Rignall was aware of a light being turned on in the
kitchen area. He vaguely wondered who was there, allowing the idea
to crouch on the edge of his consciousness until the pain and the
chloroform caused the blackness to close around him again. He
didn't expect to live through the night. Finally, after the darkness
had enveloped him for the last time, he forced his eyes open and
realized that he was sprawled under a statue in Lincoln Park near the
lake. He was fully clothed but dishevelled, and his body was
trembling from the shock of the ordeal he had just undergone, as
well as from the chill of the early morning air. He had his billfold and
his money, but, oddly, his driver's license was missing. It was just
after five o'clock, and although it was still dark, birds were already
beginning to stir and fill the crisp air with their cries.

Rignall stumbled a few blocks to his girlfriend's apartment and
collapsed on the bed. Several hours later he reported to police that
he had been kidnapped, tortured, and raped. Policemen took him
to a hospital for treatment. He was there six days. The chloroform
had permanently damaged his liver, he had facial burns from the
chemical, and was bleeding from the rectum.

Police told him that they were pessimistic about finding his attacker, because of the scarcity of information. Rignall had no name for the man, no license number, and no address.

He wasn't willing to permit the matter to drop, however. He had been kidnapped and his body outraged and permanently damaged by the unnatural trauma of the assault. It took courage to report the rape in the first place. It is estimated that as few as one heterosexual rape in ten is reported, and only one homosexual rape in one hundred, primarily because of embarrassment. Rape can also be one of the most difficult offenses to prove. But Rignall was hurt, and he was angry. He decided to do his own detective work.

He remembered the vague images he had become aware of while being driven along the Kennedy Expressway, of the road signs that teased his consciousness with foggy visions of Bryn Mawr and Cumberland Avenues. Other images were even more clear, those of the hulking sadist who had abused him, and of the black Oldsmobile with the spotlights.

Rignall rented a car and drove to the expressway exit he remembered from the night of his abduction and rape. He spent four to fifteen hours a day for about two weeks searching streets in the area for the car or sitting by the exit, sometimes accompanied by friends, waiting for it to drive by. His patience finally paid off when the black Oldsmobile turned off the expressway one day and passed him. He jotted down the license number and followed the Oldsmobile. The car turned into a driveway at 8213 West Summerdale Avenue in unincorporated Norwood Park township, a few blocks from the expressway.

The amateur sleuth's next steps were to check the license number and real-estate records. Rignall was familiar with real-estate records because he had managed real-estate properties and did other work in the field for a law firm.

The records turned up the name of John Wayne Gacy, Jr. Rignall took his information to Chicago police.

Police subsequently informed him that Gacy had a criminal record from Iowa, where he was convicted for sodomy. It would take about three weeks, they said, to obtain a photograph of Gacy. When the photograph was available, Rignall picked it out from among a thick book of pictures they showed to him. He swore out a warrant for Gacy's arrest, but police took their time acting on it.

It appeared that Gacy was developing a pattern of getting off easy after young men had accused him of kidnapping, physical abuse, and rape.

In December 1977, approximately four months before the assault on Rignall, an agitated nineteen-year-old told police that Gacy had kidnapped him from the north side at gunpoint and forced him to engage in unnatural sexual acts.

In a news article by John Gorman in the *Chicago Tribune*, the boy was quoted as saying that police treated him as they would someone who was high on drugs when he complained about Gacy.[1] He believed they were influenced against him because he had been arrested three months earlier for possession of marijuana when police found three joints in his pockets.

Police reported that Gacy was taken into custody and admitted to the sexual encounter, including the brutality, but insisted that both he and the teenager were willing participants. He claimed the boy tried to blackmail him and was angry because the attempt failed.

Officers later pointed out that they were faced with two people telling conflicting stories, and there were no other witnesses. Authorities refused to file charges because of lack of evidence. Off the record, investigators noted that current permissive attitudes toward sexual conduct have also made it difficult to prosecute sex offenses.

Gacy's associates never saw him with a gun. But he talked about guns a few times. He told Czarna that he had sealed a handgun he claimed belonged to his former mother-in-law in the concrete stoop at the back entrance to his house. He didn't explain why.

And Art Peterson said that Gacy once made a veiled threat about a gun in an attempt to frighten him. Peterson was a strong and supple twenty-five-year-old when he knocked at Gacy's door late in 1977 and asked for a job. The contractor invited him in for a beer.

Recalling the incident, Peterson said that one of the first things Gacy did after handing him a beer was to announce that he was a bisexual. Then Gacy suggested that since the young job seeker hadn't immediately punched him, that he (Peterson) might also be interested in men.

They debated bisexuality over their beers for about fifteen minutes before Gacy tried to molest him. When Peterson pulled

1 *Chicago Tribune*, 7 January 1979.

away, Gacy became angry and said he had a gun collection. It would be an easy feat to kill someone, roll the body in a carpet, and dispose of it in a trash dumpster, Gacy warned. The contractor added that he had in fact already killed people. Peterson didn't believe him.

Gacy eventually calmed down, and Peterson worked for him for a few days. During that time Gacy offered him three hundred to four hundred dollars to engage in sexual relations, and also offered him nine or ten dollars an hour to be his traveling companion on business trips, Peterson said. He wasn't interested in the extra-curricular activities and quit his job after a few days because he was dissatisfied with the pay. Before he quit, however, Peterson asked where all the bottles of pills and capsules came from. Gacy replied that he got them from pharmacists.

Both Peterson and Dominique Joscziniski, who worked for Gacy for about two years, said many of the employees were propositioned and that they regularly joked about their boss's sexual peccadillos. Josczinski said that Gacy had made sexual advances to him, but he rejected them. Gacy didn't try again.

On 30 June 1978, the nude body of a young man washed ashore in the Illinois River near the Dresden Locks in Grundy County. The name "Tim Lee," tattooed on his upper left arm, was the only identifying mark on the body.

Jeff Rignall, meanwhile, was becoming impatient waiting for police to act on the warrant for Gacy's arrest. In early July the plucky young man drove to the house in Norwood Park and knocked on the door. An elderly woman answered the door and said she was John Gacy's mother, and that her son was away but would be back soon. She inquired if Rignall was planning to come to her son's Italian theme party. It was going to be a big one with hundreds of guests.

Rignall said he wasn't interested in the party, but would return later. He walked to his car and parked it nearby, to wait for Gacy's arrival so that he could telephone Chicago police and ask them to serve the warrant. The police arrived before Gacy showed up, but when they got there they realized they could not make the arrest. The house was outside the city limits, and thus outside their jurisdiction.

While the men were standing outside their cars talking, Rignall was approached by a soft-spoken man about his own age who had driven up in a late-model red Chevrolet with a white vinyl top. The newcomer, who was neatly dressed in clean working clothes, asked Rignall not to mention the rape complaint to Gacy's mother. The problem could be handled without bringing the woman into it and needlessly upsetting her. The stranger didn't mention his name, and identified himself only as a friend of Gacy's.

Rignall saw the man once again a couple of months later when he showed up at a scheduled court hearing. The mystery man said that he worked for Gacy and his boss needed a continuance because he was out of town. He left without his name being entered in the court records. Rignall and Fred Richman, Rignall's attorney, followed to obtain his license number, but he drove away in a van owned by PDM Contractors, Inc. Rignall was intrigued by the possibility that the man might be the individual who had been in Gacy's home the night of the assault, and talked to police about his suspicions.

Gacy had always been considerate of his family. He kept in close telephone contact with his mother and visited at least twice a year. He never forgot birthdays or Christmas and was generous with his sisters and their children. When his older sister's home needed repairs, he gave her money to help with the expenses. And when his younger sister's deep freeze broke down, he purchased her a new one. He was always available with help when family members needed it.

During the Thanksgiving holidays in 1978 he traveled to Arkansas to visit with his mother and his sister's family. It was a relaxing break in his busy schedule and he went Christmas shopping with his sister to buy presents for his nieces and nephew, his mother, and other family members.

The family of James Mazzara also spent Thanksgiving together. Like Gacy, James was a considerate and loving son who remembered birthdays and holidays and called his parents at least once a week. But he slept only occasionally at the family home in suburban Elmwood Park – preferring to exert his independence and stay with friends.

Carrying 110 to 120 pounds on a five-foot, two-inch frame, he was small for a twenty-year-old, but he had been taking care of himself by working at a variety of part-time and unskilled jobs since dropping out of Elmwood Park High School a couple of years before. The youth, who was called "Mojo" by his buddies, was good-looking, healthy, and genial, and it appeared that there was still plenty of time to get serious about carving out a career. So it was a happy occasion when he sat down to Thanksgiving dinner with his family. When he left that evening it was with the understanding that he would be home again for Christmas, if not long before. His older sister, Annette, didn't begin worrying about him until well into December after James hadn't telephoned or visited his parents' home. She asked a few of his friends if they had seen him recently, and when some of them replied in the affirmative, she was somewhat relieved and settled down to wait for Christmas or earlier to hear from her errant, dark-haired brother.

Meanwhile, Rignall's persistence was beginning to pay some dividends in his drive to elicit satisfaction from Gacy for the 22 March abduction and rape. Police had finally arrested the contractor on a misdemeanor charge of battery of 15 July. They refused to file a more serious felony charge, despite the urging of Rignall and his attorney Fred Richman. It was explained to the perturbed young man that if he had been chloroformed as he claimed, it would be difficult for him to positively identify his assailant even though he had talked with the man outside the car and for several minutes while smoking the marijuana.

Rignall had also moved, through Richman, to recover some of the expenses he was piling up for medical attention. He was continuing expensive treatments for the liver damage, he had lost forty pounds, and his vitality was sapped as a result of the ordeal. He was admittedly saddled with serious emotional disturbances and was facing financial ruin. There were nights when he would awaken at 3 or 4 a.m. and sit staring blankly at the wall of his bedroom. When he went to the hospital for the shots that were making road maps of his arms and legs, he fidgeted, his nerves humming like hot wires, as he struggled to understand why he had been singled out to be the victim of a madman.

Richman notified Gacy that he planned to file a civil suit on behalf of his client to collect for the medical bills. Gacy at first suggested that they meet to talk things over in a west suburban restaurant, but later agreed to come to Richman's office. The attorney had arranged for Rignall to wait in the outer office. As Gacy walked in, Rignall got his first good look at him since 22 March. Rignall was certain he recognized the man he believed to have attacked him. But Gacy gave no indication that he recognized his reputed victim.

At the meeting, Gacy assumed an air of muddled innocence as he listened to a reading of the proposed suit. When he left he indicated that he wasn't worried about the possibility of the suit being filed, but in a subsequent telephone conversation advised Richman that the matter had been referred to attorney LeRoy Stevens. Stevens was the registered agent for PDM Contractors, Inc.

When Stevens talked with Richman, he reportedly remarked that he didn't believe Gacy was capable of carrying out the acts described in the proposed suit. Nevertheless, about ten days later Gacy offered a settlement of $2,800 through Stevens if Rignall would promise not to file the suit. At that time, Rignall had already run up $7,000 in medical bills and he had no medical insurance. He was worried that without police cooperation he would have difficulty proving that Gacy was the person who had attacked him. After negotiations, he agreed to accept $3,000. He also obtained a promise that Gacy would drop a counter-complaint charging him with battery. The battery charge against Gacy, of course, still stood.

Gacy continued to maintain his usual facade of self-confidence, but privately he may have been beginning to feel the pressures of the problems building around him.

Even his reputation as a man who could always hold his drinks was beginning to slip. It was late fall when Zielinski ran into him at the Harlem-Irving Park Plaza Shopping Center a few blocks from Gacy's home. Gacy was drunk, Zielinski said. When Zielinski asked his friend how business was, Gacy replied that it was good. Zielinski should have continued working for him, Gacy said, because he was paying his employees big money.

Lillie Grexa had a short conversation with her neighbor at about the same time. He told her that his house was becoming too small for him and he was thinking of building on another floor and adding three rooms.

That was foolish, she said. If he felt that way he should sell the house and buy a bigger one.

Perhaps she was right, he agreed, nodding his head in assent. It might be better to sell the house and move on.

Gacy's secret life was finally exposed a few days before Christmas 1978. Police investigating the disappearance of 15-year-old Robert Piest were told that he was last seen, with Gacy, outside a pharmacy in Des Plaines. Detectives checked Gacy's record and were suspicious when they saw his conviction for sodomy in Iowa. They obtained a search warrant for Gacy's home but an initial search only turned up some jewellery and documents. The search team did notice a terrible smell emanating from the crawl space beneath the house but believed it to be a cracked sewage pipe. The detectives soon realized that what they had found was of great significance. The jewellery included a high school graduation ring that belonged to the missing Robert Piest, together with a receipt that Piest had been given shortly before he disappeared. As police prepared to conduct a second, more exhaustive search of the house Gacy confessed to killing dozens of boys and young men. "There are four Johns," he told detectives. There was his businessman personality, his political operator side and his volunteer charity worker character. But the fourth personality, which he called Jack Hanley, was responsible for the murders. This was Gacy's attempt at building an insanity defence by claiming to suffer from a split personality. It did not impress the jury at Gacy's trial, who took only two hours to find him guilty of the murder of 33 people. Sentenced to death in 1980, he spent fourteen years on Death Row before his appeals finally ran out. Clifford Linedecker adds a specially updated postscript to the Gacy story:

A few minutes after midnight on 10 May 1994, fourteen years after he was sentenced to death following the murder of 33 young men and boys, John Wayne Gacy, Jr, was executed at Stateville Correctional Center in Illinois.

Seeing justice done and carrying out the will of the people was a long, frustrating process that the blustering serial killer took advantage of to milk every possible bit of continued notoriety and attention from a fascinated public.

Like a handful of other condemned men before him, he became a prison artist. After thumbing through a few art books in his cramped death row cell at the Menard Correctional Center in the far southern end of the state, the unrepentant sexual predator grandiosely announced that after studying some of the great masters such as Michaelangelo and Leonardo DaVinci he had developed a painting style all his own.

He began turning out canvases of clowns, Mickey Mouse, fairy tale characters, Indian chiefs – even a portrait on felt of previously executed serial killer Theodore "Ted The Troller" Bundy. But his favorite subject among the more than 500 paintings and pencil drawings he produced was his own alter-ego, "Pogo The Clown", from the days when he dressed up and entertained children at parties near his suburban Chicago home.

Gacy's work more closely resembled "paint-by-the-numbers" canvases than the old masters he claimed to admire, and the appeal of the paintings and drawings was linked more to the infamy of the artist than to the art. Yet, years after his death his works were still being offered on eBay for as much as $1,300. Actor Johnny Depp owned one of the clown paintings for a while, before selling it.

The paintings provided plenty of income to support prison commissary purchases and for postage stamps, which he used to carry on spirited correspondence with death row groupies and other pen pals from around the world. One of his pen pals was a twice-divorced single mom, who explained that she took her small son with her on visits to the condemned sex slayer because she thought it would be good for the boy to be around a strong male role model.

While Gacy was painting, romancing groupies and filing interminable appeals, death row was filling up and the population expanded from five men when he was first sentenced to 60 when his time finally ran out.

In the interim, Illinois had abandoned the electric chair, and when Gacy was transported from Menard to the death house at Stateville where executions were carried out, he was destined to die from lethal injection. Still ranting and claiming he was an innocent man, on the last full day of his life, the loudmouth bully began his deathwatch in a 6-by-12-foot cell at the end of the East Wing only 20 feet from the execution chamber. The tile walls were covered with reinforced steel plating.

For his final meal, served at 9 p. m., Gacy ordered a bucket of fried chicken, deep-fried shrimp, French fries and fresh strawberries. The "Original Recipe" chicken was purchased at a Kentucky Fried Chicken restaurant, and the rest of the food was prepared by a gourmet-trained chef at Catcher's Tap in the nearby town of Crest Hill. The bill for the entire meal, including tax, was $18.26. The condemned man ate most of it.

Exactly at 12:01 a.m., Gacy was taken from his cell, strapped to a gurney, a tube was attached to one arm, a saline solution was injected into a vein, his hands were cuffed at the wrists, restraints were fasted around his chest and waist and a white sheet was placed over his body.

Only his head was showing when he was wheeled through the

door with the "Exit" sign and into the death chamber. In moments the saline tube was removed and replaced with an intravenous line attached to drug-filled syringes in a delivery module mounted on the wall. At a word from the warden, two men selected as executioners simultaneously pushed buttons on a machine that released the flow of the anesthetic sodium pentathol, pancuronium bromide to paralyze the respiratory system, and potassium chloride which stopped the heart. Only one of the buttons pressed by the executioners actually released the lethal drugs. The machine made the random choice. Approximately ten minutes later, Gacy was pronounced dead.

But when the man convicted of more serial killings than anyone else in the history of the United States finally checked out, he left snarling. His last words, uttered to one of his guards were: "You can kiss my ass!"

Boss of Britain's Underworld
(Billy Hill)

Billy Hill

A dead ringer for Bogart, complete with trenchcoat and snap-brimmed fedora, Billy Hill (1911–84) was a vicious London criminal who set up his Camden Town Gang in the 1930s. Specializing in violent robbery, Hill taught his men how to "stripe" with a razor, cutting downwards rather than slicing across an opponent's face, so scarring for life instead of severing an artery. Birched in Borstal as a young tearaway, Hill served jail terms totalling 17 years for safe-cracking and thievery, including a four-year stretch in Dartmoor for robbery with violence. On his release in 1947, Hill merged his gang with the Elephant Mob from south London, Benny the Kid (a bookie's enforcer with his own gang of thugs) and several minor villains. Together they overthrew the Black gang, the reigning London mob, a coup Hill celebrated by leading 200 thugs armed with razors, knives, axes, hammers and hand grenades into Soho in a show of force. To consolidate his grip, he embarked on a sustained campaign of robberies and protection rackets, culminating in the Great Mailbag Robbery of May 1952, in which Hill masterminded the snatch of a staggering £287,000 from a sorting office off Oxford Street. The haul stood as a record until the Great Train Robbery in 1963.

Billy Hill was rattled by the emergence of a new pretender to his title, Jack "Spot" Comer, with whom he conducted a venomous feud. Hill sent some of his henchmen to "chiv" (slash)

Comer's face; one, "Mad" Frankie Fraser, was given a seven-year prison sentence for his pains. Shortly after a gold bullion heist in 1954, Hill retired to Tangiers where he dictated his memoirs and sent them to London, where the shady crime reporter Duncan Webb knocked them into passable prose. Hill's great boast was that he was King of London's Underworld, a claim Webb reinforced in a celebrated series of articles in the People newspaper. One of Hill's confessions was that he'd refused an offer of £5,000 to murder Webb. In fact Duncan Webb died young, aged only 41, after being suddenly taken ill with a blood infection. Hill himself emigrated to Australia and opened a beer garden in Sydney. But the authorities promptly closed him down and sent him back to the UK. "I've been rejected," Hill complained, "by a bunch of cons." Hill lived to be 73, dying peacefully in Bayswater in 1984 and reportedly leaving an ill-gotten fortune of £1m.

Stand in any part of Piccadilly Circus, at any hour of the day or night, and not an hour will go by without you being spotted by at least six of my men. Walk for a mile in any direction from that spot and it will be impossible for you not to pass a dozen of my mob somewhere along the line.

Piccadilly is the centre of London, the British Commonwealth – and my territory. It is the centre of my empire, the district from which I rule the underworld of Britain.

Walk up Shaftesbury Avenue and ask the first gangster you see. Ask him who runs the underworld. If you don't know any gangsters, and it's odds on that you don't, then stop a copper and ask him. He'll tell you. He'll tell you that Billy Hill is the guv'nor. And, if he knows anything about crime and the under-world, he'll most likely mumble to himself, "And a good job too." Continue your stroll through the hub of the Common-wealth of British Nations and turn left from Shaftesbury Avenue. You'll pass my headquarters. No, it's not a club or a speiler. Nor is it an office or a café. It is an ordinary flat on the first floor of a building. It is tastefully furnished with all modern comforts and a sprinkling of antiques and little knick-knacks. It is as similar to the popular conception of a gangster's flat as a drawing-room in Mayfair.

If you could walk in you would most likely see me there, perhaps dressed in my pyjamas or dressing-gown and sipping a cup of tea. A discreet buzz would make you look round to realize that my coloured telephones in every room are equipped with toneless buzzers instead of bells. If you heard me speaking it is a safe bet that you would not understand a word of what I said. That is, unless you were of the underworld, or of the police. I would be talking in underworld jargon.

For my telephones are tapped by a monitor system which records all conversations on to tape-recording machines. Post Office officials, Scotland Yard, the Home Office, can listen to these recordings at will.

I would like to see the faces of some Post Office officials when they listen to my conversations. Our language of the underworld was not evolved for Post Office clerks! It is a jargon which has been forced upon us so that such people as those who would have our guts for garters don't know what we're talking about. An emphasis on one word is something which cannot be translated into any other language. A reference to "the other feller" could never mean anything in a witness-box. Modern armies could well copy the underworld for security arrangements such as I have been putting into operation for a few years.

Thirty years of battling with the law have taught me something about security. They say you learn by your mistakes. Well, I learned plenty. Because my mistakes have been numerous. I've spent seventeen long, weary and bitter years behind bars for those mistakes. My prison sentences total more than twenty-three years. That's ample time in which to lie on a straw bed in a locked peter thinking things out. By the time I was half-way through my twenties, I was getting to know a thing or two about not getting caught. Since then I've made security pay off. I've earned plenty and I think I'm entitled to it.

I've been crooked since I was thirteen years of age. I was first convicted when I was fourteen. I've been in and out of gaol fifteen times. And, believe me, I've not wasted a moment during the time I've been out. Every time I was caught I went over where I had gone wrong. I saw myself doing that job again. I went over every small movement. I asked myself how I made that last mistake. I never made the same mistake twice. Then, as the years walked with me, I realised that it's one thing to earn a living by being crooked, but in the end you've got to earn more than a living if you want to remain crooked. And the first step to pulling off a big job – you know, the big job that pays off for life – is to get hold of a team of blokes you can really trust and rely upon.

Now the jungle that is the underworld is as near to the African bush in a way of life as any human community. The laws, perhaps, are a bit tougher for crooked people than they are for lions and tigers. You've got to be tough to be able to give it and take it. You've got to be more. You've got to be able to make tough mobsters, screwsmen, bandits and gangsters want to do as you tell them. If they don't want to do it they won't. So you have got to get them to rely on you, to trust your judgment, to know your mind and to realise that by obeying your orders a job will come out right.

That's why, all my life, I've always given everyone a square deal. Society, the law, Parliament, can brand me as a criminal, as a gangster, what they like. But not one crooked person in the world can say I've doubled on anyone, or that I've screamed or grassed to the law, or that I have not kept my part of any bargain I've made. I wanted to be like this with my own people. Only too often did I know what it was to be double-crossed or to be sold out to the law. When I started thieving as a boy, a burglar or thief of any kind was like so much dirt to society, the law, and even the underworld. We were dead ducks for being blackmailed by almost anyone who cared to demand money from us. A thief had to pay many sorts of people, in the way of bribes and sweeteners, to survive. He did not mind paying the law so much, or even straightening a snout out now and again. But there always was a rebellious feeling against the racing mobs who blacked all thieves right and left whenever they saw them.

In those days the Sabini mob ruled the race-tracks of Britain. They were led by the notorious Darby Sabini and his brothers from the Saffron Hill area of London near Clerkenwell. They were Italians, and some people had it that Darby Sabini was a member of the Mafia, the dreaded Sicilian secret society. Their game was to blackmail bookmakers who stood up at the tracks. They went round the rails with a bucket and sponge and wiped the book-makers' boards. That cost the bookies money. Plenty of dough. I remember in those days one or two were stupid enough not to pay. Their stands were wrecked, they and their men were beaten up, and they dared not stand up on a track again. The pickings from this game were so much that other gangs were always trying to muscle in. The result was the race-course gang fights which you may have heard about so much during the 1920s.

Somehow the Sabinis always seemed to win. There might be as many as a hundred tearaways having it off with razors, choppers and hammers. The green grass of Brighton track might be red with blood, and the local hospitals full of broken heads and arms. But the next day only the other gangs would appear in court on various charges. Never a Sabini. They were bad days in more ways than one. There were more crooked policemen about than there are today. The Sabinis received protection from certain elements of the law. If a thief or pickpocket was seen on the course a Sabini man would whiten the palm of his hand with chalk and greet the thief with a supposed-to-be "Hello". In doing this he would slap the thief on the shoulder, just like a long-lost friend. The whitened hand-mark would identify him to the law. They then knew without doubt that this man was safe to be nicked for being a suspected person. In this way the Sabinis ingratiated themselves with the law so much that they more or less had things their own way.

From the race-tracks alone they earned bombs in dough. The dog-tracks of London and the Home Counties must have brought them in fortunes over and over again. You would have thought they got tired of stacking money away. Did a hungry horse ever get tired of eating? We thieves didn't mind so much the Sabinis grafting as they did on the race-tracks. But they did not stop there. They had London in the palms of their hands.

In those days Soho and Mayfair, which is the West End of London, was like a combination of Broadway and the Bowery of New York. That square mile of London which is known as "Up West" had more money in it than Fifth Avenue and Beverley Hills put together. It was in the days of Jimmy White the millionaire, Mrs Meyrick's notorious 43 Club in Soho, George Edwardes's lavish musical shows, Edgar Wallace's thriller plays, when the Charleston was all the rage, and the aristocracy and society thought they were going slumming when they rolled from Curzon Street to Gerrard Street in their then modern Rolls-Royces. The bottle party was all the rage too. Every cellar in Soho was occupied, and packed. Cafés and restaurants, run mostly by aliens from the Continent, flourished. Speilers turned over more ready cash than did the Riviera casinos. Every club, every speiler, many small cafés, had slot machines operating in them. These slot machines, adjusted properly, would earn a fortune in one night's play. A fortune for the owners, not the proprietor in whose premises they were installed. The owners never got their fortunes, however.

Darby Sabini and his boys managed to "win" too often on those machines. And if they were not paid up in hard cash the machines were wrecked along with the premises.

The tills of public-houses never ceased clanging. There were more streetwalkers on the pavements than ever London had known. Their trade was conducted not only in their dingy little rooms; they also earned a lucrative livelihood from steering mug clients into thriving afternoon drinking-clubs and the speilers which operated at night.

From all these sources of immense wealth the Sabinis were drawing revenue. Bottle parties, clubs, public-houses, cafés, restaurants, even ordinary shops, had to pay protection money to the Sabini extortionists. None dared refuse. If they did, the Sabinis gave information to the police which compelled the law to act for some broken petty regulation. Individuals connected with the premises were attacked in the streets. Proprietors of businesses finished up in hospital. The streets of Up West were literally paved with gold for the Sabinis. They also ran with blood. The blood of their victims.

Burglars and thieves had no chance. If they wandered Up West they had to go mob-handed. And they had to be prepared to pay out if they were met by any of the Sabinis. If they went into a club, it was drinks all round. The prices were usually especially doubled for their benefit. If they did go into a speiler they never won. They knew better than to try and leave while they were showing even a margin of profit. If one word was spoken out of place, it was all off. The Sabinis, who could rustle up twenty or thirty tearaways at a moment's notice anywhere Up West, stood for no liberties, although they were always taking them. Night after night some thief or other was cut, or his head was bashed in. Merely because he was a thief, and not only a tearaway. Probably because he did not have enough loot on him to pay the Sabinis when they put the bite on him. That was the West End in the 1920s, when I was a kid. It was the glamorous, mystical life which I knew only from a distance or from the mouths of people like Eddie Guerin or Brummy Sparkes, two of the best burglars of their day. Naturally it attracted me later on in life, like Mecca pulls at the heart of an Arab.

It was some years before I was to venture into the mysterious stronghold that was Up West. By then I had plenty of form behind me. I had done more than enough of my share of bird. I was learning from that great teacher, the professor of mistakes. And I had come a long way in my own right. When the last war broke out in 1939 the Sabinis, being Italians, were interned. Overnight the Blacks took over. They were a gang of hoodlums run by five brothers named Black. Some of them had been in their time thieves and burglars, but they had neither the guts nor the brains to do any good at it. Very early in life they realised that the safer way to get a living was from the same game as their name implied, blackmail. They looked at the Sabinis and came to the conclusion that there was room for two at that game. They nearly got away with it. At least, they made room for one and a half. They became a rival mob to the Sabinis. And, because they were not on top and therefore did not have the facility of merely nodding their heads for what they wanted, they had to go out and get it the hard way. The war was a godsend to them. It automatically destroyed the vast empire which had been built up by the Sabinis, and left the huge gap to be filled in by the first comers. The Blacks were already there.

They took over the horserace-tracks and the dog-tracks concessions. They continued the blackmail of club owners, café proprietors and publicans. They even ran some of the brasses on the streets and got them to steer the mugs into their speilers and drinking-clubs. Then let a mug win at a game of dice or cards and let him try get out of a speiler with his winnings. He might get as far as half-way up the stairs, but by the time he was reaching for the top step the workman on the door sent his boot crashing into the mug's face. A strong foot would be inside that boot, and a muscular leg would have driven it into the mug's face with enough force to send him toppling back down the stairs into the speiler. He didn't want his money so much after that. Or let the mug in a drinking-club complain about being overcharged, or the brass ask for a glass of champagne or a large Scotch instead of a beer.

The position was then reversed. His money was taken from him and he was then kicked down the stairs. That is why the thieves had to go Up West mob-handed. All they wanted was to buy a drink at club prices, or have a speil with an even break. No gangster would dream of going into a speiler alone and hoping to come away with profits. But in the end the Blacks put it on the thieves just too much.

All through the war years they had it all their own way. No one could open a drinking-club or speiler in the West End without the Blacks' permission. And their permission usually meant the payment of a dollar-in-the-pound out of the takings.

At that time I had my own manor. I was guv'nor of Camden
Town, that part of London that is bordered by Regent's Park,
Hampstead Road and King's Cross. The Blacks came out of
Islington, which is next to King's Cross. So you can see they
did not have much love for me. Most of London was split up into
various dominions. The Elephant mob from over the water had
South London running their way. That included Brixton, Cam-
berwell and New Cross. Over at Notting Hill and Shepherd's Bush
another mob was in command. Down in the East End Benny-the-
Kid had become king.

Benny was not a thief. He was just a tearaway. He would fight a
copper with his bare hands, but he would never nick as much as a
cigarette. All sorts of jobs are put down to him or to his planning.
But if Benny was in a bath full of soap and water he could not blow
a bubble, let alone blow a peter. He is Jewish and was born and
reared in Mile End, well east of Aldgate Pump.

As a boy he began to work for various bookmakers. He organized
street pitches for them. He worked hard and got on well in the
business. Then he was given a job running a club in the East End
on behalf of a wealthy bookmaker named Moshe Cohen. Moshe
was a powerful man. His name is not known to the public. He is not
a tearaway or a thief or anything like that there. He's just a shrewd
businessman who's made a stack, and has kept it. And now that
he's got a stack he can do with money what money always does.
Buy services. Cohen can buy the services of most things, and men.

He bought Benny-the-Kid. He paid him a couple of centuries a
week to look after his bookmaking interests and run speilers.

By the time the war was over, and the real big money in London
was flying about, Benny was the guv'nor of the tearaways in the
East End. The Blacks couldn't do a thing about it. They tried to.
They went looking for him. They went looking for him because he
was earning a few quid. So they went after him to knock him out of
business before he got too big.

At about this time I was creeping into the West End myself.
There was so much going on there in those days that it became
almost impossible for the Blacks to run it all on their own. In any
case I had my own mob, probably the toughest team of screwsmen
ever to be formed in the United Kingdom. We were called the
Heavy Mob by the underworld, by the Flying Squad, by everyone
who knew about us. There was not a peter in Great Britain we
could not screw in one way or another. There was not a bank or

warehouse safe from our skill, if we wanted to go in. For about ten years I had had it all my own way as a screwsman and, with the team I had behind me, the Blacks would have had to think twice before tackling me.

It did happen several times when I was out enjoying myself Up West. But there weren't enough of them. They could come with their choppers and chivs. They could bring their iron bars and razors, but I always managed to leave my trade-mark on a few of them before they scarpered. That mark is a long, thin red line on the face of the men I cut. I still am one of the best chiv merchants in the business. The Blacks seemed to have a sort of healthy respect for me. They knew my game was then thieving. Thieving anything from a safe weighing a ton or more to a lorry-load of silk. They knew, too, that we had a few good blags to our credit. It takes nerve to make robbery with violence pay. And they knew I had made it pay. They also had a sort of suspicion that I had been involved in certain kidnappings which had taken place in London just after the war. So they were not keen to upset me. After all, I was not a petty thief. I was a guv'nor in my own right. And I knew that if the need arose I could become guv'nor of a bit more than I already had. So they did not take many liberties with me.

There is an indefinable arrangement in the underworld whereby if you want to find someone you get hold of someone who knows someone else and send word out that you want to see him. It is a sort of contact system reaching down the line by a series of messengers. The Blacks used this system to challenge Benny-the-Kid. They said he was getting too powerful. What they really meant was that he was becoming too prosperous.

As soon as Benny got the challenge, all the underworld knew about it from the grapevine in the speilers and drinking-clubs. Everyone was saying, "The Blacks have challenged Benny-the-Kid." So those on the rails waited to see the race. Bets were laid and taken. In some cases odds were offered and accepted.

And, as soon as Benny got to hear about it, he came to see me. I was then thirty-six. The Kid was thirty-five. It was in the summer of 1947. We both had come up the hard way. The Kid had only done six months for a GBH job, but I had then done getting on for twenty years of prison sentences. I had paid dearly for my graft and my wages. I had done my bird. Not that I was complaining. After all, I was on top. I had a good following, the rightest team ever anyone had for thieving, and I was making a good living. I had got to where I was because I had earned it. But I had not forgotten the beltings the Black mob had put on our boys in the past. Only too well did we all remember the number of times the Blacks had grassed on us to the law. I felt too that if the Blacks beat Benny-the-Kid they would then want to take me apart. Or else put it on me with the law so that I was out of the way again for a few more years.

Therefore I told the Kid that it was OK by me if he wanted to go for the Blacks and have it out with them. You see, it occurred to me that if the Blacks were out of the way the West End would be cleaned up overnight. Club owners, café proprietors, small tailors, speiler-runners, bookmakers, publicans, could get their living without the Blacks' protection. Anyone would be able to go into a drinking-club or speiler without having it put on them by the Blacks. We ourselves could even get into the West End and make a fair living without getting into trouble. And that meant without extorting protection money at that.

It would also mean that we could go Up West and enjoy ourselves without having to pay three ways for it.

So Benny got his boys together and went looking for the Blacks. At the same time, the Blacks, hearing about this, went looking for Benny in a big way. They ganged up in sixes and sevens and roamed round the West End in private cars, hired taxis, shooting-brakes, any vehicle that was handy to them. They were armed with choppers, hammers, pick-axes, knives and razors. Benny got his armoury out too. Then the Blacks got out the shooters. Lugers, Smith-Wessons and Colt revolvers. They slung handfuls of ammunition into their pockets. That was when the guns came to London. It was like two opposing armies marching towards each other. Snouts from each side were whispering information so that it would reach the other side. And the underworld watched and waited.

Then one night the Kid's boys found one of the Blacks alone. With Benny were Little Georgie, Terrible Ted and Big Sam. They carved the Black boy up so much that he was taken to hospital. He nearly died. In accordance with our code he did not talk, and for being a good boy he was paid a monkey for his trouble. He was so grateful that he later left the Blacks to join us.

Not within living memory had one of the ruling racing mobs been cut-up by thieves and ordinary tearaways. And got away with it. If the other preliminary business had been all words and messages, this one incident was a challenge which must be acknowledged and dealt with by the Blacks. And at once. If they let it go without doing something about it, they would never get another penny from a thief, or anyone else for that matter. The first opportunity they had for reprisals happened to be on one of my boys. Now he was not a thief, or much of a tearaway for that matter. But he was in my mob, and therefore one of us. He was Up West minding his own business when the Blacks came across him. They almost belted the life out of him.

That was it. That was all I wanted. For years the Birmingham mob, the Sabinis, and now the Blacks had put it on us thieves in every way. For generations men, and their sons and grandsons, had been sent away for years of bird because of the Blacks and their like.

Now the Blacks were not content with challenging an East End tearaway. To show how clever they thought they were they had taken a liberty with my man. He had been done mob-handed without opening his mouth. I sent a message to Benny to come and see me. I told him to bring his boys to make a meet with my mob. When the other thieves and burglars heard this, they all fell in behind me.

The generations of repression, extortion and blackmail were remembered vividly by the sons of men who had spent years in gaol because of the race gangs. At last they saw a chance to revenge themselves for their fathers and uncles and grandfathers. I saw, at last, a chance to clean up the West End.

So the Elephant mob came my way, and over the bridge from South London with them came the teams from Brixton and Camberwell and Southwark and Rotherhithe. From Shepherd's Bush and Notting Hill the burglars came, and the King's Cross gang and the Holloway team joined in. The Paddington and Kilburn lot fell in behind as well.

The Blacks got scared when they heard this. Bill Black, the boss, got together a team about a hundred-handed. They all had their shooters and chivs. In their cars and vans and taxis they came up to Camden Town looking for me and my boys. Unfortunately I was out in the West End looking for them.

So it came to nothing that night. Then the other mobs from down East said they wanted to join us. Timber Jim and Wooden George from Ilford came along with their team. Bugsy Reilly brought the Upton Park mob along. A handy gang from Dagen-

ham turned up. Then Fido the Gipsy from Essex joined in. If
necessary Fido could have brought along 1,000 gipsies with him to
settle this argument. He did not bring 1,000, but he brought a good
number. Even the diddikies would not stand for the Blacks. You
see, the gipsies have to make a living on the race-tracks, and even
they had to pay out to the Blacks when it was put on them. Fido
had with him his favourite weapon. It was a tailboard chain from a
greengrocer's cart. It was neat so that it could fit into his pocket
without any trouble. It was easy to handle and manipulate when
wiping it round a man's face. It left terrible injuries. After Fido
had been known to use it once or twice, villains did not pick fights
any more. They feared that tailboard chain wrapping itself round
their faces.

Then the thieves from the docks and many of the dockers
themselves joined in. They brought their stevedores' hooks with
them. If they manage to catch you in the back of your neck with
one of those hooks you won't quit, because it's then too late to quit.
So you just take what is coming. And, with dockers, when they're
roused, that's plenty. From East Ham, Custom House, Canning
Town, they came to reinforce us. From Hammersmith, Acton,
Ealing and even Clapham they came to Camden Town to fall in
behind my banner.

In the end we were more than 150 strong. "All right," I said to
the Kid. "We'll meet tomorrow night and go out after them."

When the Blacks heard about this unusual assembly they swallowed it. They had never reckoned on so many thieves and tearaways getting together under one roof. Their mob dispersed. They
put their cars away. Their taxis went back to plying the streets.
And the six leaders of the gang went into hiding.

We met the following night in a boozer which I used as my
headquarters in Camden Town. Every man had his own weapon.
They had chivs, choppers, chains, razors, knives, hammers, iron
bars and coshes. But we knew the Blacks had shooters.

I decided that, no matter what villainy mobsters and tearaways
got up to in London, I was not going to stand for guns. We were in
business to live and enjoy life, not to shoot the town apart like a
bunch of film-star "gangsters". The Blacks had therefore to be
defeated at their own game. So one of my women brought some
artillery to us. Revolvers were easy to get in those days. We had a
good assortment which I handed out all round. Another of the
women brought in a bag full of ammunition. It was all .45 stuff.

One shot for one man was all that was required. I handed it out by the handful. Then another woman brought along a bag full of Mills bombs. Benny and I took charge of these and gave them to Bugsy and Butch Conlon to look after. As if that was not sufficient Nifty Charlie called me outside, and in one of the cars he showed me a machine-gun, all belted up and ready for firing.

"If we see them first we'll let them have it," he said. From Camden Town to Hyde Park Corner we spread out, combing every club and speiler that existed. From Aldgate Pump right through the City and up to Islington we looked in every pub, club and café.

The West End of London and its outer parts was a strange place that summer's night in 1947. The rubbers were empty. None of the usual customers dare show out in case they got involved in the battle. Pubs used mainly by members of the underworld were occupied only by the odd stray local going in for a quick one. The pimps and ponces kept well out of the way too, and the brasses were only too pleased to grab the first client and give him a long time instead of a short one. If the Flying Squad or Ghost Squad were out and about they must have wondered what was on. Usually they know where to pick up a tealeaf, if only for a drink and a talk for the purpose of trying to find out something. But that night there was not a thief or burglar to be found in his usual haunts. As the law realized that there was something on, and reported back to their various stations or to the Yard, they tried desperately to find out what it was all about. But there were no villains to find out from, and those left in the various clubs and boozers were too scared to talk. Even to a cozzer.

If the law had locked the doors of my Camden Town boozer on that summer's night they would have had under lock and key most of the tealeaves in London. And Greater London at that.

We were an army which had operated for years, but never before had we all been under the same roof. There were more hardcase villains in that pub that night than there were in the Moor or on the Island. We talked the matter over quietly as we stood next to the bar. Bugsy stood behind Benny. Strong Arms Phil was with me. Our head men were not far away.

Meanwhile, the other mobs stood about sipping beer and talking quietly among themselves. Each of them had their eyes on us all the time. It only needed a look from me, or a nod from the Kid, and each leader of each little mob made his way through the crush to ostensibly have a chat with what looked like an old pal.

Quietly I murmured my orders to each head man. It needs few words in our language to say much. And these boys were only too eager to understand what I meant when, for instance, I said to Bert the Dip, "You take your five blokes along Marylebone Road as far as Baker Street. If you find them, give us a whistle on the blower."

Without a word he strolled back to his boys. They drank up and left. Then a nod to Meathook Harry from Custom House. He walked over to us, gently pushing his way through the throng. It appeared as though we were buying him a beer. We did, and as I was handing it to him, I murmured, "Go with Ironjaw Jack. Take five of your boys with yer. He'll take you down through Gray's Inn Road and along Holborn as far as Tottenham Court Road. Leave the City out of it. As soon as you see or hear anything give us a whistle."

So our army moved off. Like beaters in the bush a dozen teams of six or seven heavily-armed men combed London, trying to flush the hidden game. They were determined men. They were desperate. For once there was murder in their hearts, and for once we were all armed to kill. If the Blacks had stood up to us there would have been mass murder in London that night.

St Valentine's Day in Chicago would have looked like a girl guides' picnic.

Throughout the West End I had snouts quietly moving from one rubber to the other seeing if they could put their finger on any of the Blacks. One or two of our women combed the boozers. We even had some of the West End toms on our side, ready to phone us if they could find out where any of the Black mob were to be found.

All night long our teams combed the streets, clubs, pubs and speilers. One or two of the more skilful burglars even brought short-wave wireless sets with them to keep in touch with one another. But the Blacks were not to be found. We sent messengers out openly to tell them, and the world at large, that we were ready, and waiting.

They were not able to deliver their messages. The Blacks had gone underground and wanted to remain there.

Then they sent a messenger to us asking us to call it off. "There's room in this town for everyone," they said. Our views had changed by then. "Everyone but the Blacks," was my reply. For his trouble their messenger was given a cut on his face just to show that we were not being kind any more. Then we put it on him to tell us where they were. He screamed all right. He could not scream fast enough by the time we had finished with him.

That was all I wanted to know. Taking Bugsy, Strong Arms Phil and Butch with me, and making sure that my shooter was in working order, I went up to a small flat in Islington.

We did not wait to ring the bell. We blew the door down and went in. There they were, crouching by the wall. Six of them. Afraid to walk the streets they had terrorized for so long. I took hold of Bill Black by the scruff of his neck and lifted him from his crouched position. Then I held his head over the fire, close to it so that he would know, for once, what it felt like to have the heat put on him.

He hooted and hollered for a bit. Then he screamed like a stuck pig.

"Well!" I said quietly. "What's it going to be?"

"Billy, Billy," was all I could get out of him.

"From now on," I said to him, "you're working for me."

So I gave him a kick in the guts which sent him sprawling across the room. Bugsy pushed the flat of his hand into two of the others' faces. We took their shooters from them. I said, "All right. So I'm the guv'nor now. You'll do as I say, or else."

We stripped their pockets of a few nicker. They might have had a grand between the six of them. We took it to give to the boys who had come along to massacre them. Then we returned to Camden Town.

"It's all right," I said to Benny-the-Kid, "we won't need shooters in this town any more. Get 'em off the boys and get rid of them."

They collected the shooters and bombs and the machine-gun and destroyed them. They were actually thrown down a manhole.

We had a few drinks on the house, for which the landlord was paid plenty.

And I was the boss of Britain's underworld.

Getting Gotti Good!
(John Gotti)

Jeffrey Bloomfield

As head of the feared Gambino family, John Gotti (1940–2002) was the most powerful Mafia leader in New York in the 1980s. His sophisticated tastes in tailored suits, luxury limousines and the best restaurants concealed an inner ruthlessness: he threatened his own henchmen if they crossed him, and conspired at the murders of many of his gangland rivals on his way to the top. He first came to notice as one of Carlo Gambino's entourage who avenged the murder of the old man's nephew, Manny Gambino, in 1972. He went to prison for seven years, and was rewarded on his release with his nomination as one of the Gambino family's top bosses. A violent feud with New York union boss John O'Connor reached a climax when Gotti hired four gunmen to assassinate O'Connor. The plot failed, but two of the hired assassins, from a violent Irish street gang called the Westies, turned informant and Gotti was arrested in 1989. Despite the admissibility of 28,000 taped telephone conversations recorded between March 1985 and May 1986, which portrayed Gotti as the undisputed boss of the Gambino mob, the jury at his trial found him not guilty. Once again Gotti had earned his nickname The Teflon Don, against whom nothing seemed to stick. The story of how justice finally caught up with John Gotti is told here by Jeffrey Bloomfield (b.1954), a miniaturist of American true crime whose essays appearing in various US and British academic journals are regularly anthologized.

A merica has always prided itself on its reputation as the "land of opportunity", where poor immigrants find that "the streets are paved with gold". In fact, most immigrants find life a hard struggle, and live in the lower third of the economic spectrum for the first generation or so. How quickly they rise out of poverty and the ghettos depends largely on their racial and religious background. Currently, an immigrant from Latin America or Africa is more likely to be kept down than any from a European, Japanese, or Chinese heritage. But it was not always so easy for Europeans . . . at least, those from eastern or southern Europe. One of the groups that found it very hard to make a beachhead here were the Italians. In the first century of our existence as a nation, Italians were a curiosity and rarely seen, not even in major cities. But after Italy was unified in the 1860s, many Italians began coming to the US, hoping to find that promised land with the golden streets.

It is always very tricky talking about other peoples, because there is the danger that statements you make about them may sound bigoted. Therefore, let me say that Italians are hard-working, honest, and law-abiding people, who are *possibly* the most maligned in the world. The popular image, at least since the 1890s in the US, is that of wine-guzzling spaghetti-eaters, in garish clothing, who are oversexed, worship a faith that is full of obsolete superstitions and dogmas, and make a living in well-organized gangster mobs. That this image exists, despite the fact that Western society has derived benefits from the Etruscan, Roman and Renaissance Ages that came from the Italian Peninsula, is due to hatred and envy directed at a whole group: a hatred that carefully picks out certain bad examples and ignores the conditions that enabled them to grow into being.

Because of the grinding poverty faced by Italians when they landed, and the really low-paid, humiliating jobs they had to take, *some* of them became criminals. The first criminal gangs preyed on the Italian immigrant communities themselves, levelling blackmail by threats of death or destruction of property. These gangs would often leave written threats which had a "signature": an inked hand – hence the term "Black Hand". Initially, to the non-Italian public following the doings of these gangs in the yellow press, most of the crimes were ascribed to "Black Handers". However, a new term entered the lexicon in 1890. On 15 October of that year, David Hennessy, the Chief of Police of New Orleans, was shot to death in that city. Hennessy had made something of a career going after criminals of Italian background, even making international head-lines in 1881 when he brought one back to the United States for trial. He was a man with many enemies, and not all the details of the events leading to his death are certain. However, he had been looking into the possible presence of Italian criminal gangs on the New Orleans waterfront. In the process, for the first time in American history, the term "Mafia" for a Sicilian criminal orga-nization was revealed. As Hennessy was dying, he told a friend that he had been shot by Italians. Eleven were arrested for the murder, but all were acquitted (possibly due to bribery and intimidation, though it must be said that much of the evidence against them was weak). On 14 March 1891, a mob of citizens lynched the Italians. The ensuing international furore led to a break in diplomatic relations between the US and Italy, until President Benjamin Harrison (after his own inquiry) paid an indemnity to the families of the dead Italians.

The original "Mafia" had been set up to protect native Sicilians from oppressive foreign invaders. Never disbanded, it gradually changed its character into an oppressive one. Like other secret societies, it has its own initiation rules, and lives on a code based on total respect for the entire body and membership (known as *la cosa nostra*). In theory, the members are pledged to respect each other in the hierarchy of the guiding families that have divided up the various territories. The foot soldiers owe allegiance to an immedi-ate boss, the *consiglieri*, who owes allegiance to the *capo*, the head of the family.

But that is only the theory. It is inevitable, with so many violent men involved, that some of them are going to get tired of taking orders, and will want advancement. Also the heads of families might have expansion plans at each other's expense. Finally, every now and then the head of the largest mob in a city may feel entitled to the title of *capo di capo* – chief of chiefs. Some of the other mob leaders will resent this, and a bloody war can break out. One in New York City in 1930–1 only ended when junior mobsters killed the two mob leaders who were fighting for the title.

After that incident, the New York City area was "straightened out" by gangsters "Lucky" Luciano, Frank Costello, Albert Anastasia, and Vito Genovese. Taking their cue from big business, instead of cutting each other's throats, they formed a board-room type of arrangement, in which five Italian families ruled all the rackets. This set-up actually worked very well until the 1980s.

Leaders of the families might change (Luciano was deported, Costello "officially" retired, Genovese died in prison, and Anastasia was murdered), but the basic family units remained intact.

That is no longer the case, because of one man: Mr John Gotti. He achieved the title of *capo di capo*, but he may very well have destroyed the Mafia in the process.

John Gotti was born in 1940, the fifth of thirteen children of poor immigrants. His home was in the East Harlem area of Manhattan, which was an Italian enclave then. It was a rough area, and Gotti became a tough street-fighter, as did some of his brothers. Although he was never interested in school, he had an IQ of 140. The family made several moves as he grew up, in the hope of finding a better life in another district. Unfortunately their moves were from one slum to another. Young Gotti continued fighting while at school, and learned other illegal activities in areas like the Brooklyn waterfront. Their final move was to the "East New York" section of Brooklyn, which was notorious as the headquarters of Albert Anastasia's and Louis Lepke's "Murder Inc." Although that organization was broken up in 1943–4 (with the electrocution of Louis Lepke for murder – he was the only major crime boss ever executed in the USA), the area had many illegal gambling shops and other illegal activities going on. One more step in Gotti's education.

Gotti dropped out of school, joined a local gang, and by force of personality (including a violent temper), became its leader. At fifteen, he was running an illegal gambling operation. He got to know other young punks. One was Wilfred "Willie Boy" Johnson, who became a close associate. A local Mafia "soldier" noticed Gotti, and hired him to run errands. Thanks to his good memory, he was extremely efficient as a collector for local loan-sharks. Then he was arrested in 1957 for disorderly conduct. The charges were dropped, but the police had now noticed John Gotti.

He had moved into the gang of Carmine Fatico, in which he was an enforcer, a hijacker, and an occasional killer. The police were aware that Gotti had beaten up a salesman who had insulted Fatico, and who disappeared soon afterwards. No charges were brought in this 1967 incident, probably due to a lack of any evidence of a murder. It would not be the last occasion, nor the most notorious, that Gotti's name would be linked to that of a man who disappeared. Meanwhile, Fatico had moved his operations into the Ozone Park area of Queens, using the Bergin Hunt & Fish

Club as his headquarters. Gotti and his criminal brothers were among the closest associates of their boss.

Since his first arrest in 1957 Gotti had been arrested many times, but no charge was ever successfully pursued. Then he and his brother Gene made a mistake: they were caught trying to steal $30,000 worth of electronic goods and women's clothes at JFK Airport with forged papers. In 1969 they were convicted and sent to Lewisburg Federal Prison in Pennsylvania. It was a four-year sentence, but Gotti got out on parole after three years. He had met many Mafiosi in the prison, and learned much about how the Mafia was organized. In particular, he had learned the inner workings of New York City's largest "Family", that of Carlo Gambino.

When Gotti was released, he was put in charge of Fatico's gambling operations. This was somewhat ironic, for Gotti's biggest weakness (aside from power-hunger) was gambling. But because of his own weakness, he knew precisely how to batten on other gamblers. Gotti was also learning about business racketeering, the pornography business, and the fencing of stolen securities. One might think that he would have been satisfied with his success within the system, but he was ambitious to go right to the top of the mob family.

In January 1973, a son of Carlo Gambino was kidnapped. The kidnapper, one James McBratney, must have been remarkably stupid, because he took $100,000 and still killed the boy. Gotti was one of the men picked to punish McBratney. Actually they fumbled the job: they went to Staten Island to capture him, but he gave them trouble and one of them shot him dead. The police arrested Gotti. Gambino made some deal with the Staten Island District Attorney, and Gotti pleaded guilty and was given only four years for attempted manslaughter (he had not fired the gun). He spent this prison sentence at Green Haven, a New York prison, and was paroled again in 1977. Now he had paid his dues to the Mob, and in the summer he was formally inducted into the Mafia.

Because of later repercussions, I have to digress here about Mafia rules. I mentioned earlier the code of respect that is at the base of the organization's hierarchy. In practice, there is rivalry about who has control over what, but if the territories are clearly delineated by all the heads of the families, nobody dares to question their decision. Also, there is a rule of never raising a hand against a fellow member. Now this rule too has been broken in the past, but usually when the heads of the families have concluded that the fellow member has acted in such a way as to cease to merit the rule's protection. In 1957, Albert Anastasia, a founding member of the five families, had begun invading the territories of other members. He was given several "friendly" warnings to abide by past agreements, but refused. He ended up being shot to death in a hotel barber-chair. That was a rare occasion. Normally, to avoid violence that was of no productive use, the Mafia favoured some kind of compromise. Carlo Gambino was a master of this type of diplomacy. But he died in 1976, one year before John Gotti was inducted into the organization.

Gambino's passing has an important symbolic value to this story. In 1931, when the five families were set up, the leaders were all first-generation Italian immigrants. So was Gambino. All had been born in Italy, and had some strong concept of respect for rules and hierarchy and honour. I know this may sound strange, for we are discussing murderous thugs, but that first generation valued their past, and were able to graft it with American business methods to make it work. But the generation of John Gotti, born in the United States from 1940 onwards, knew nothing of the sense of *noblesse oblige* which was part of the original Mafia's strength. It had tied the heads of families to their underbosses and soldiers with bonds of loyalty. Gotti and his generation would give lip-service to these ideals, so that the old mobsters would be pleased, and advance them – but once they were in the positions of real power, they would drop these ideals as so much useless baggage. What is more they would willingly turn on the old bosses.

After Gotti's first prison term was over, when Carmine Fatico put him in charge of the gambling operations, he was told that the Gambino Family frowned at money made in the drugs trade. Gotti nodded his head, as though the message was accepted, and then created a system where he could appear to have nothing to do with drugs, while his associate, Sal Ruggiero, did the dirty work. The mobsters above Gotti were taken in by this facade.

As a rising underboss in the Mob, Gotti moved to the Howard Beach area in Queens with his family (he had married Victoria DiGiorgio back in 1960, and they had two sons and two daughters). Here, despite his occasional displays of violent temper, he seemed to be finding an element of stability. His older son, John Jr, was a disappointment, being a violence-prone model of himself, but the younger one, Frank, was an intelligent boy, and the hope of his father in achieving a set of respectable, middle- or even upper-class heirs. Like many mobsters, Gotti yearned for his family to break free of their evil, poverty-stricken roots. Frank Gotti looked very promising, but on 18 March 1980, the boy was killed in a car accident.

If ever anybody was born under an unlucky star, that person was John Favara, a neighbour of the Gottis. Driving home that day, Favara had the sun in his eyes. Frank Gotti darted out from behind some garbage cans, and was hit by the car. Favara quickly learned how serious his position was: he attempted to pay his respects to Mrs Gotti, and apologize for the accident, only to be hit on the head by the lady with a bat. She began to goad her husband about letting their son's "murderer" live, and erected a shrine in memory of Frank Gotti in the house. Actually, there was little need for her to press her husband, who was in a state of emotional anger far beyond his normal bad temper. Soon Favara's car was stolen. It was located wrecked, with the word "murderer" written on it. His house was vandalized, and his mailbox found to contain a funeral card with a picture of the dead boy. There were furtive looks and whispers whenever he appeared. When he asked the police for protection, they said they couldn't give him any, and could not act against Gotti; they suggested that he should either kill Gotti or sell his home quickly and move out of the state. Favara had actually put his home up for sale when he was confronted by three men, knocked out, and driven away in a van. That was in May 1980. John Favara has never been seen since. Rumours of his fate are reminiscent of the film *The Texas Chainsaw Massacre*.

Tragic as is the destruction of this hapless man, one has to admit that the New York City Police happened to be right about their inability to help him. The only thing that could have been pushed was an assault charge against Victoria Gotti for hitting Favara with the bat, and no court would have been hard on her because she would have pleaded that she was distraught over her son's death. Nothing actually linked Gotti to the stealing and wrecking of the car, the vandalism, or the abduction. Common sense could find a connection, but common sense without evidence is worthless. The Favara incident was simply one more item for the police to add to their growing record of Gotti's career.

The regular course of business kept Gotti busy for the next few years, but meanwhile he was watching the changing shape of New York City's Mafia power. After Carlo Gambino's death, the press had pinpointed one Carmine Galante, a bald-headed old thug with a perpetual frown on his face, as the new chief mob boss in the city. Actually this was an exaggeration, though Galante would have liked to make it true. In 1979 it became a moot point, when Galante was gunned down while eating lunch at a Brooklyn restaurant. Now the man generally conceded as filling Carlo Gambino's shoes (if for no other reason, as head of the Gambino Crime Family) was Paul Castellano. Like Gambino, he was of the older generation, believing in the original sense of honour and respect for members that the Mafia stood for (in theory). Castellano was not as over-enthused about Gotti as other *consiglieri* were. He could sense the ruthless ambition and the lack of control in that young Turk.

Castellano never failed to watch Gotti and to look for any breach of Mafia rules. In 1981, he reiterated the ban on drug deals. Whether Castellano knew of Gotti's involvement at the time is not certain, but it is likely that he soon learned of it. As mentioned, Gotti had put his close friend, Sal Ruggiero, in charge of the drug business. Sal's brother Angelo was a party to all the secrets of the business, and unfortunately, he happened to talk too much. Castellano heard. He could not act quickly, as he had pressing legal difficulties with the government, but by 1985, having given a number of veiled warnings to Gotti, all ignored, he decided to arrange the execution of the latter. However, Gotti had been busy too, making a valuable alliance with Castellano's underboss, Frank DeCicco. Castellano had a conference with DeCicco on 14 December 1985, setting up arrangements for a meeting with Gotti at Stark's Steak House in Manhattan in two days' time. It seems likely that Castellano either hinted at or openly stated his intention to kill Gotti. No doubt, as a good friend, DeCicco told Gotti what was planned. On 16 December, Castellano was driven to Stark's by his chauffeur, Thomas Bilotti. Both were shot to death by assassins, waiting in a nearby car.

The police immediately suspected Gotti, though (again) they had little real evidence. Gotti spent the next year solidifying his control over the Gambino family, establishing his henchmen in the main positions of power. His success in that regard was not due to brilliant politics. Most of his opponents were old men who figured that acquiescence was the healthiest policy; they all wished to be allowed the chance to die in bed, not untidily in a street like Castellano. Had Gotti taken a moment to consider what his success was based on, he might have questioned how real it was. Not only was it based on the fear felt by a set of old men who would soon be dead or retired, but Gotti had just demonstrated that the head of the mob was a figure with feet of clay: if Castellano could be killed by Gotti the Young Turk, what was to prevent some other Young Turk from killing Gotti? Loyalty had protected the likes of Luciano, Costello, and Gambino – but Gotti, by his own actions, had shown the true value of loyalty among thugs and thieves. His throne was already insecure.

Soon afterwards, an unanticipated act should have tipped him off about the effect of his ambitious actions. As a reward for betraying Castellano, Frank DeCicco was made Gotti's underboss. In April 1986, DeCicco was blown up by a car-bomb. The killers were never caught, but it appears that they were hired by the family of Thomas Bilotti, the chauffeur-bodyguard murdered with Castellano. The killing shook Gotti's confidence in a way nothing had before.

It is very odd, when discussing mobsters in real life, how frequently the truth repeats the scripts of those old Hollywood crime films with Edward G. Robinson or James Cagney. Like the ancient morality stories, the start of a tale follows the central figure as he advances in material wealth and power, usually at the expense of society, and then reaches a high point: now he can go no further, and at this point the fates decree that he should begin the descent from power and prestige to disgrace. For John Gotti, the high point was the year 1986, when he replaced Paul Castellano as *capo di capo*. That year marked the start of the series of trials that was to end with him in a federal prison for life.

The destruction of John Gotti was started by a man he considered a friend. When Gotti began his street-gang career in the 1950s, one of his closest associates was Willie Boy Johnson. Gotti was unaware of it, but Johnson subsequently held a grudge against Carmine Fatico, Gotti's old patron: it seems that Johnson agreed to take the blame for an armed robbery, which entailed a three-year spell in prison, on the understanding that Fatico would take care of Johnson's family; Fatico failed to do so, and Johnson came out of jail to find his wife and children on welfare. Johnson became an informant to the FBI and the Queens District Attorney's Office. How Gotti, with his sources and connections, never knew this until it was too late is one of the minor mysteries of the story. Not only did Gotti fail to latch on to Johnson's treachery, but he relied on the man to commit many important crimes for him: Johnson was one of the three men who abducted John Favara.

In 1987 the Queens District Attorney's office brought racketeering charges against Gotti and eight associates, including Johnson. Apparently, they hoped that Johnson would prove to be a fully cooperative witness, if faced with probable conviction; they also thought that the FBI would be glad to cooperate. They were wrong on both counts. The FBI has always been loath to share information with state authorities, fearing that its operations will be compromised. As for Johnson, as the trial approached he was given reminders of the recent deaths of Castellano and Bilotti, making him fully aware that it would be distinctly unhealthy to testify against the new Boss of Bosses. Gotti hired Barry Slotnick, the famous defence attorney, to represent him. He also decided to maintain his public image, which this trial would soon enhance.

The old-time mob bosses had, for the most part, been very low-key in public. They did not court the eye of photographers; well-dressed and groomed, they looked like successful middle-class businessmen. The two glaring exceptions to this had been Al Capone and Bugsy Siegel, the former flaunting his power even for newsreels, the latter frequently getting his picture taken with show-biz stars. In both their cases, the public image did them harm: Capone looked as if he was too powerful, almost inviting another government trial; Siegel's spend-thrift methods of developing Las Vegas shook the confidence of his associates, forcing them to have him killed. But that was in an earlier time. In the 1980s, Gotti, with his thousand-dollar wardrobes, his swagger, his (for the public) smile, looked perfect for the media. He cultivated the image of a misunderstood nice guy: his press releases emphasized that every Fourth of July he put on a giant fireworks display for his neighbourhood; he could guarantee that a crowd of neighbours (many of them members of the Bergin Club) would come down to the courthouse and voice their disapproval of the legal "persecution" of their beloved friend.

The Queens trial was a fiasco. One witness spoke of Gotti's bragging of murders and the planning of other crimes, but the witness was so unsavoury himself as to render his testimony worthless. A second witness, confronted by demands that he testify against the new head of organized crime, claimed that an assistant district attorney had offered sexual favours if he would lie about Gotti. Willie Boy Johnson's position would have been comical had it not been for the danger he faced. Though he kept denying that he was ever an informer, he was treated as a hostile witness, which meant that information that only he was privy to was produced in court: even if he demonstrated an unwillingness to tell the truth about Gotti, the latter was fully able to see what he had been up to. On Friday, 13 March 1987, the jury found Gotti and his fellow defendants not guilty. In August 1988, Willie Boy Johnson was shot to death. When informed of the "mysterious" death of his one-time friend, Gotti said, "Well, we've all got to go sometime."

The 1980s was the period of the Presidency of Ronald Reagan. It was called the "Teflon Presidency" because the President was so well liked that, no matter what scandals arose, he maintained his "clean" fatherly image. Gotti, with his rapid advance to supreme power in the New York City Mob, and now his acquittal on a serious legal charge, became the "Teflon Don". It looked as if nothing could or would ever be successfully laid against him. Judging from his confident mien, his arrogant comments, he began to believe this nonsense himself.

And it is here that the real controversy of the case of John Gotti appears for the first time. As we read of his career, we are aware that (1) the *evidence* needed to convince any jury of his guilt was woefully non-existent; and (2) the sordid *details* were there, to convince any rational person that he was as evil and guilty as the state and federal governments claimed. Despite his pleasing public persona, his "good neighbour policy" in Howard Beach (*pace* Mr Favara), he was not a desirable person to have out in society. With every successful evasion of a legal charge, Gotti was defying the government. No government will suffer such treatment indefinitely, since to do so renders it contemptible in the eyes of the public. Whether, had his operations occurred during a period of national domination by the Democratic Party, he would have found his successes more easily "stomached", is an interesting question. As it was, Gotti's misfortune (as it was for his predecessor, Al Capone) was that the Republican Party dominated the national level of government.

The Republicans have had scandals and corruption, but they tend to have less tolerant views than Democrats regarding the criminal actions of certain minorities: these minorities (Italian, Jewish, African-American, Latino) tend to be the ones who vote for Democrats. Under the Reagan Administration, the President's policies were so involved in dismantling the administrative structures set up since the New Deal (by Democrats) that he gave little real consideration to the Mob. This attitude was less apparent under his successor. George Bush made lawlessness a keystone of his 1988 Presidential Campaign, culminating in the unfair commercials showing one Willie Horton, an African-American released from a Massachusetts prison while Bush's opponent was Governor of that state, and who then committed another crime in Maryland. Bush had an extremely ruthless streak in him, one that stood comparison with Gotti's. As President, he seemed determined to nail Gotti once and for all.

In December 1990 the Federal Government arrested Gotti for murder and racketeering. The new trial demonstrated the full extent of demoralization within the Mafia. In the 1987 trial there was a distinct lack of willingness to testify against Gotti, based on fear; the murder of Willie Boy Johnson should have cemented this fear. But in 1990 another close Gotti associate, Sam "the Bull" Gravano, willingly testified after his sister was shot by masked gunmen. Others too were soon singing. The ancient fears and loyalty of the system had been demolished by Gotti's own actions on the way up; he had only himself to blame.

Even so, the behaviour of the Federal Government in "getting Gotti good" in this trial leaves an unpleasant feeling in many of us who despise the man. Barry Slotnick was not the defence counsel in this trial, but Gotti's normal legal expert, the brilliant and smooth Bruce Cutler. In the preliminary rounds of the Federal trial, Cutler made considerable inroads into the prosecution case by questioning the motives of witnesses like Gravano. Then, suddenly, the Federal Government stopped the trial to protest the continued appearance of Cutler as defence attorney. The prosecution had bugged Gotti's headquarters, and had tapes of him and Cutler talking about Mob business, so that it was argued that Cutler was potentially a defendant or witness himself. The court agreed, and Cutler was replaced by Albert Krieger. Krieger is a fine criminal lawyer too, but there is a tradition of a defendant having the lawyer of his or her choice, especially in a trial that may result in a long prison term. The action of the Gotti court, if it is accepted (and it looks as if it may be, as the Supreme Court of the United States is loaded with Republican appointees), is not a good precedent for the future. Curiously enough, after Gotti's trial ended on 3 April 1992, the Bush Administration made no effort either to prosecute Cutler or to use him as a witness. It seems that the Clinton Administration is not planning to prosecute him either.

The Teflon chipped that day in April 1992. Gotti was found guilty of five counts of murder and racketeering. He is now imprisoned for life, but his lawyers (Krieger, Cutler, and the civil-rights activist, William Kunstler) are appealing. One's reactions are distinctly mixed. The thought of such a "good" neighbour and businessman back in society is sickening. But the thought of a government riding roughshod over any legal right (to show who really is "Boss") may be worse.

Afterword

On 2 April 1992 John Gotti was convicted of 13 counts of murder (six counts alone), conspiracy to commit murder, loan sharking, racketeering, obstruction of justice, illegal gambling, and tax evasion in the United States District Court in New York City. He was formally sentenced on 23 June 1992 to life imprisonment without possibility of parole. He was sent to the Federal Penitentiary in Marion, Illinois. His sentence included 23 hours of solitary confinement each day.

Of course, as I mentioned, he appealed. It did not help. The "Teflon" finally chipped. Teflon is an artificial man-made compound, and such compounds are not self-replacing. They can only be replaced by anyone interested in doing so, with time on his or her hands, and with a smooth surface to apply it upon. In Gotti's case it was just impossible. Once the dents in the Teflon were made, the underlying surface revealed so many holes and scars and rough spots that they could not be recovered.

In a sense he became a "poisonous tree", whose fruit would spread to others, both family and foes. The most notable casualty was his son John Jr. The "Junior Don" turned out to have even less ability to lead than was expected. He has already served some time in prison. At the present moment (as of this writing in spring 2006) Junior is fighting the Feds as his old man did. They had charged him with several counts of racketeering and one of kidnapping and attempted murder last year. The racketeering was accepted by the jury as proven, but the charge regarding the kidnapping and attempted murder led to a hung jury on that point alone. The target of the kidnap/murder plot was Curtis Sliwa, a popular, vigilante-like crusader against organized crime, and radio personality. Sliwa was badly wounded in this 1992 kidnap attempt, which he claimed was due to his having attacked Junior's dad on his radio show. Rather than just accepting this solitary defeat, the Federal Government decided to retry Junior on the kidnap/attempted murder. This trial is still going on.

The testimony revealed more dirty linen, including an affair the "Teflon Don" may have had that resulted in a love child. To her credit Mrs Victoria Gotti took it in very good (at least for public consumption) stride. She said she would treat the little child well, because John Sr loved his children. Whether this illegitimate child story is true or not is another matter, as it is part of the testimony of a former Gotti mob member, Michael "Mickey Scars" DiLeonardo, who is testiying against Junior. However, most of DiLeonardo's testimony seems to hold up. Junior, by the way, also may have a "love child".

DiLeonardo's predecessor in testifying against the Gotti family, Sammy "the Bull" Gravano, turned out to be a mixed blessing to the Federal Government who forgave 19 murder charges against him for his testimony. Put into a Federal protection program, Sammy was sent to Arizona, but soon got bored being under the watchful eye of his protectors. He voluntarily left the program in 1995. He explained that he felt inhibited in his freedom by the program. Maybe so, but one wishes he had defined "inhibited". In 2000 he was arrested for having masterminded a gang in Arizona that sold the illegal drug "ecstasy". He was prosecuted by State and Federal Governments, ending up with a 19-year sentence to prison in Colorado. Things could have gotten worse. The notorious mob hitman, Richard Kulinski (known as "the Iceman") told authorities in prison that Gravano was responsible for the 1980 murder of a policeman named Peter Calabro. Sammy was indicted in February 2003, but then (in 2005) Kulinski died. The charges were dropped.

The "Teflon Don"'s daughter Victoria Gotti (named after her mother) did show a streak of originality. She managed to get a cable television network to put on her television show, *Growing Up Gotti*, which starred her and her children. It lasted about one season or so. One admires her grit and gumption to try such an experiment, but it makes this writer wonder what would have happened if John Wilkes Booth had operated in 1995 rather than 1865. Would Wilkes be staging award-winning dramatic productions in prison (perhaps *Marat/Sade* would have been the hit of his season)? Americans (unfortunately) do like their sensations and frequently go too far with them.

The Federal Government is now under another President named Bush (the son of the one who did get Gotti). One might make a comment on Homeland Security and the tamping down on civil rights, but it is a trifle unfair because of the situation that has existed to bedevil the world since 9/11/2001. But even so, one wonders how distant from actual pre-9/11 intentions are the current curtailments on civil rights. It is perplexing and quite disturbing.

John Gotti Sr did not live to see the misadventures of his surviving heir and namesake, or of his daughter's interesting television career. If he noted what happened to Sammy "the Bull," or about 9/11, we have not heard his remarks. Gotti developed cancer of the head, neck, and throat while in prison. He was transferred to the United States Medical Center for Federal Prisoners in Springfield, Missouri. John Gotti Sr died there 10 June 2002. He was 61 years old.

The Man of a Thousand Cuts
(*Jack Spot*)

Hank Janson

Jack Spot (b. 1912) was the closest Britain ever came to a Jewish Godfather. In his heyday, during the Second World War and five years either side of it, Spot dominated the East End's protection rackets, gambling joints and the illegal drinking dens known as spielers. Spot's recruitment methods were novel. To test the physical toughness of a potential henchman, he would lead them to the lavatory and knock them cold. "That was my surgery," he recalled. "I used to go to the toilet and Bomp! Leave them in the piss." Against his various adversaries, Spot's principal weapon was the razor, creatively stuffed into unlikely household items including bottle corks, the rims of flat caps and, in the defence of Cable Street against Sir Oswald Mosley's Blackshirts, potatoes, which, with three or four blades stuck into them at odd angles, were lethal when hurled. Spot sliced his way from bookie's runner to sharp-suited gangster with a Kensington address solely on the strength of his skill with a razor; though his own face was often rearranged in revenge. King of London's underworld in an era of choppers and razors, Spot never actually killed anybody, and when a pair of psychopathic twins, also Jewish – the Krays – started to edge in on his manor in the 1950s, he didn't stand much of a chance. They were prepared to kill and ended up killing, and their taste for weaponry went beyond blades of steel.

Spot's reign ended abruptly in a London street when, armed with a knife, he went after Billy Hill's right-hand man, Albert

Dimes. "I was here and Albert Dimes was here," he recalled. They tumbled into a greengrocer's shop on the corner of Old Compton Street, where Dimes grabbed Spot's knife and stabbed him in the side. He woke up in hospital, encased in plaster. Spot didn't walk properly for nine months, then "this other mob got me. They reckoned I might rise up again, see. Thirty men with razors and choppers and bars of iron." Comer also made an enemy of Billy Hill's amanuensis Duncan Webb, famously breaking his arm with a knuckleduster. When Spot was fined a paltry £50, Webb sued in the civil courts and won £700, hounding Spot through the bankruptcy court for his money. Hank Janson was the pseudonym of Stephen D. Frances (1917–89) who, searching for a name with a hardboiled American ring to it, chose Hank because it rhymed with Yank. Between 1946 and 1953 he wrote a series of hugely successful pulp novels that were little more than soft-porn tales under the guise of gangster novels. He wrote a couple of dozen of them, in a ludicrous "American" style that was even then seen as hilariously off-key. In his heyday Janson enjoyed large sales in the UK, despite his cornball writing style, entirely because of their lipsmacking descriptions of female bodies and sex scenes that went as far as a British writer dared to in those days of strict censorship. Jansen managed to escape prosecution under the Obscene Publications Act by flitting to Spain; his publishers weren't so lucky and went to prison. Frances continued writing into the 1970s, although the last Hank Janson novel reliably attributed to him was published in 1963. He died in 1989, at his home in Spain. In his characteristically hard-boiled style, he describes the showdown on 11 August 1955 in Frith Street, Soho, between Jack Spot and his nemesis Albert Dimes.

"I want you, Dimes," I panted.

He was a big man but I'm even bigger. He looked at me apprehensively.

"You've been talking big," I snarled. "You've been spreading the word around I'm to come and see you. You've been talking like a strong-arm guy."

"Take it easy, Spotty," he soothed. "Don't blow your top, Spotty."

"You've been talking too big," I panted.

"Let's go somewhere quiet and talk it over."

"You can't treat me like a nobody. I've had my troubles. But I'm still a big man. I'm bigger than you'll ever be."

Dimes said quietly: "Face up to it, Spotty, You're finished!"

"We'll soon see if I'm finished!"

He said it again: "You're finished, Spotty. What's more, it's about time you're finished. You've had your day. It's about time somebody took over from you. And this is your final warning. Get out."

As he spoke he gave me a shove.

It wasn't much of a shove but it was all that was needed to bring my anger to boiling point.

I hit out at him, and automatically my hand dropped to my pocket. But the gesture was futile. Because ever since Smokey, I hadn't had the heart to carry it around with me.

But the precious split second I'd spent feeling in my pocket gave Dimes time to recover. He came at me punching viciously and I hit back at him. Then suddenly a woman nearby screamed loudly as Dimes' hand went up in the air.

Instinctively I raised my arm protectively and felt the sharpness. I closed with Dimes, grappled with him and, locked together, we fell over some vegetable boxes displayed outside a greengrocer's shop. I managed to get his right hand twisted round, but as I did so he pulled his arm round and I felt a sharp pain in my side.

We broke away from each other, closed, grappled and, locked together again, staggered inside the shop. Men's voices shouted, women screamed and hands plucked at us. But all the sounds were only a background to Dimes' heavy breathing, my own breath rasping in my throat and the sharpness that hit me again and again.

I wrested the knife from him, felt it rip through cloth, felt him suck in his breath and knew he would kill me if he could.

I struck out again.

This wasn't just a matter of a simple cutting. This was a duel to the death. We were two men fighting with the desperation of wild animals, each man obeying the instinctive law of self-preservation and trying to save his own life at whatever cost. There was the sharp pain, again and again. I still grappled with him but my strength was ebbing from me as the sharpness deepened and twisted cruelly. And then suddenly, miraculously, he broke away from me.

I watched him as he loomed massively in the doorway, leaning exhaustedly against the door jamb before he stumbled outside on to the pavement.

The pain was a searing burning in my side, and warmness was flooding down my leg and filling my shoes, and there was blood on my hands and clothes.

Momentarily I thought of Rita, saw her beautiful, trusting and anxious face and heard her pleading with me. "Don't go today, Jack. I've got . . . a premonition."

I knew I was seriously wounded, but as my memory of Rita blurred and greyness began to nibble at the outer edges of my brain I knew dully that I must get away.

I staggered out of the shop, vaguely noticing that the staring faces flinched away from me. Unsteadily, swaying like a drunken man, I stumbled along Frith Street. I thought numbly: "*I'm all bloody. I must get clean.*"

I saw the striped pole of a barber's shop some fifty yards ahead. I concentrated upon it, forced my rubbery legs to move, and stumbled ever onwards, obsessed now with but the sole ambition of reaching that sanctuary.

I got to the barber's shop and leaned against the open door for a moment while white and startled faces looked up at me from the barber's chairs. Then I staggered across to the laundry rail. There were starched white towels hung ready for use. I reached out and saw the crisp whiteness suddenly stained by the brightness of blood. I dabbed the towel at my bleeding face, then the room began to swim.

My head made a hollow detached sound when it hit the floor. Then I was staring up numbly at a ring of white faces and from a long way off a voice breathed: "Good God, Spotty! What's *happened*!"

I didn't know myself then what had happened. And I didn't find out until some time later.

But I had been destroyed!

I had nine stab wounds. One stab had punctured my lung and another had driven the blade of the knife within a quarter of an inch of my heart. I'd been punctured so many times blood had run out of me as though I was a sieve, and air seeped into my belly, that is normally a sealed-up capsule, until I was swollen up like a half-inflated balloon.

I knew none of these things, of course. I was unconscious and hovering close to the point of death while the doctors worked desperately. As they operated there were blood transfusions, X-rays, delicate probing instruments and a final sigh as the surgeon turned away from the operating table and said quietly: "I can do no more."

I hovered in a grey, twilight world, punctuated by sharpness, the smell of anæsthetic and constant nausea.

Awareness was a long time coming back to me. But it did come finally. The memory of Dimes' wild and desperate eyes, the sharp pain, the barber's shop swimming until I was staring up at the whiteness of the ceiling, the sickly sweet smell of anaesthetic and the grey man sitting beside me.

The grey man who sat beside the hospital cot was patient and silent. He grew into consciousness with me. Long before I knew who he was and the significance of his sitting there, his stern and serious face had become a part of my consciousness.

He was a cop, of course.

And as soon as the doctors told him I was well enough to be questioned he fired them at me.

"I don't know," I told him. "I don't remember."

"You were stabbed," he insisted. "You *must* know who stabbed you."

I closed my eyes wearily. "I don't remember."

The full significance of my position grew upon me slowly. When you wake up in a hospital and find a cop waiting beside you it's a hundred to one the police are going to charge you with something or hope to ferret useful information out of you. At first I wasn't worried. I didn't want to talk and I knew there was no power on earth that could make me talk.

But slowly I began to realise the real truth. It wasn't merely that I had to keep my mouth shut to protect Dimes. It was *what might happen to me!*

When I began to look at everything from the point of view of the cops, I began to sweat. I was a self-made man, the Boss of the Underworld. I was famous and I'd wielded enormous influence. I'd been the guiding, master mind for the operations of experienced criminals.

And now, stupidly, I'd got myself mixed up in a squabble. And the cops had something on me. Not much – but *something*. In the past, from time to time, projects had gone wrong and a man or two who'd been playing his tiny part in a large-scale robbery had got caught and sent to jail. Of course, going to jail is part of the business. If a man's unlucky he merely resigns himself to being locked away until good conduct reduces his sentence by a third. Prison is not exactly a luxury hotel. But at least a man knows that while he's serving his time, his pals on the outside are carrying on with the good work and putting something aside for him each week so he'll have a sweetener when he comes out.

I'd never been arrested for robbery. Indeed, in all my years of activity the only guilty verdict registered against me was when I bashed up the Fascists.

British law requires evidence of a man's guilt before he can be charged before a jury. And nobody had ever produced any scrap of proof to show I was ever in any way connected with crime.

But the cops *knew*!

Plain clothes detectives mingle with the old lags and criminals of the underworld. There are, too, the police informers, the scum who drop a discreet word now and again to obtain protection for their own nefarious crimes.

Also, for years, like a Chicago gangster I'd strutted insolently around Soho, spending money like water, flamboyantly displaying my wealth and shouting aloud to the whole wide world that I was the master mind directing successful criminal activity.

And now, recklessly, I'd committed a final indiscretion and allowed a Sunday newspaper to publish my life story, wherein I'd described myself as the Boss of the Underworld.

It had been madness. But I hadn't realized it then. I'd been so vain, so proud, and so cocky.

But the cops, smarting from the blistering criticisms of their superior officrs, had glowered impotently, powerless to prevent me boasting to the whole wide world that I was the Boss of the Underworld and how the police couldn't touch me.

But now I'd slipped.

In three mad, enraged minutes I'd thrown away a life-time of carefully planned precautions.

The cops had me!

They didn't have me for much. The most they could accuse me of was fighting in a London street. I had a good defence too. Every man has the right to defend himself from attack, especially when a weapon is used that might result in his death.

But if the cops could make a charge of assault stand up in court and get a conviction registered against me, I was a dead duck.

I might even get sent to prison!

It would all be quite legal. It would be because of my vainglorious strutting and boasting.

I turned cold inside when I thought of it. They might even send me away for nine months. With good conduct, I'd be out in six months. But on top of all my other worries, six months locked away would ruin me!

I'd spent money like water right up to the last minute and I'd staked everything on my last big plan. But I couldn't carry on with that now I was in hospital, and for the first time in many, many years I was desperately in need of a few quid.

Rita came to see me. Just seeing the tragic sadness in her eyes hurt me a thousand times more than the pain of my wounds and the sickening apprehension inside me.

For the first time I saw clearly what I'd done to Rita. She was a good, decent girl and I'd married her and dragged her into the shadow of my own bad luck. Now my two poor kids, my home and my family were all exposed to public scorn. Rita was branded as the wife of a Soho gangster. And I was a thug who'd brawled like a hooligan in the streets of London. The shame of it all was in Rita's eyes as she stroked my hand and told me not to worry.

She told *me* not to worry!

While I didn't even have the money to pay next week's rent.

"Don't worry, Jack," she told me. "Just get better. That's all that matters."

"What are you going to do?" I asked desperately. "How are you going to live? You've *got* to eat. You've got to look after the kids."

She said quietly: "Don't worry, Jack. I've a little money."

I stared at her unbelievingly and then squirmed with remorse.

I was a swine. I'd believed I was on top of the world and that I could go on for ever. I hadn't cared how I'd spent money. I hadn't considered Rita and I hadn't thought about the kids.

I didn't speak. I just held her hand tightly and tried to swallow the lump in my throat.

"We need you, Jack," she whispered. "We want you to get better quickly."

I gulped. I could see everything so clearly now. I knew the cops might make it bad for me and I knew I could only drag her down.

"The newspapers will crucify you and the kids," I warned her. "We mustn't let it happen. Do you hear me? We mustn't let it happen. Now you do just what I say. Go away somewhere. And quickly. Leave right away, forget about my trouble and don't come near me until it's all over. Do you understand? It's important."

She nodded. "Don't you worry, Jack. I'll do what's right."

I knew I had only to upturn my palm and she'd give me everything. But although I was in trouble and needed money desperately, I became soft. I told her to keep the money!

The next day a solicitor came to see me.

"I don't want *you*," I sneered. "I've got no money to waste on lawyers."

"That's all right. Arrangements have been made for settlement of my professional fees."

That startled me. "Who's paying you?"

"Your wife."

"She's mad," I choked. "She hasn't any money. She *can't* pay you."

He smiled. "Mrs Comer anticipated you would refuse legal assistance. I should make it clear that with or *without* your active co-operation, I have still been retained to act for you."

That was how Rita destroyed herself along with me.

She could have cut herself free from me and escaped the misery and the heartbreak that pursued us in the months that followed. Rita had her chance. But she threw it away because of her loyalty to her husband. To a man of my position! To – a failure!

On the twelfth of August, 1955, the newspapers reported that detectives remained at the hospital bedside of both men who had been involved in the fight in Soho. Dimes was reported to be in a serious but not critical condition. I was no longer in danger after my operation.

On the twentieth of August Detective Inspector Eric Sheppard came to see me in hospital.

"I'm taking you down to West End Central Police Station," he told me.

"If I'm going anywhere," I grated, "it's where I can do something useful. I'm getting out of here now. They've been threatening my wife."

"I'm taking you to the station," said Sheppard quietly. "I'm arresting you for causing grievous bodily harm and possessing an offensive weapon. A knife."

As soon as I was charged at the police station I sent for my solicitor. We had a long talk together, and while I waited hour after hour in a lonely, drab grey cell to appear before a magistrate on the following Monday, I had plenty to think about.

I lay awake with cold sweats breaking out all over me. This was the chance the cops had been waiting for. All these years they'd been waiting to get their hands on me. And now at last, in three minutes of madness, I'd walked right into their clutches.

The charges against me were serious. *Very* serious. Me and Dimes weren't being treated like schoolboys who'd scrapped in the street. It had been assumed that we had tried to kill each other. And Authority was trying to prove *both of us* guilty. Not just Dimes. But *me too*!

And if they succeeded?

That's what gave me cold sweats. Every time I thought of what they could do to me I curled up with misery. The legal punishment for serious crimes isn't just a few months in prison. The maximum can be years.

If I was found guilty of rough-housing with Dimes, it could put me behind bars for seven, or perhaps ten, years.

That long, lonely weekend in the cells wrought a great change in me. I wasn't any longer the Boss of the Underworld. I wasn't any longer a vainglorious, strutting and self-important petty dictator.

Instead I became a badly frightened man, a cringing, broken shell of a man, who cried with self-misery every time he thought of his wife and kids. In the depths of my misery I even thought of desperate, fatal ways to escape the long years behind iron bars which would swallow up most, if not all, of the life left to me.

On Monday the 22nd, me and Italian Albert appeared at Marlborough Street Police Court and were charged. We stood in the dock together with cops sitting between us. I looked slyly at Albert, wondering how he had taken all this and wondering if we should fight together to defend ourselves.

But Albert wouldn't look at me.

And when the case was remanded for a week, Divisional Detective Superintendent Sparks opposed bail. He said he was afraid I would abscond, and that he had reliable information that there would be intimidation of witnesses.

My solicitor worked hard on my behalf. But I knew already he was wasting his time. I'd never get bail. They had me now. I was in their clutches and they'd never let me go again. *Never*.

Bail was refused.

I spent another week of mental agony in jail waiting to come up again before the magistrate's court. I can't begin to describe the mental agony of waiting for the slow hours to pass, when every minute of each long hour is terrible mental torture and doubt.

I wanted to get it over quickly. I wanted to know the worst. But nobody else was in a hurry. Everyone was content that everything should drag on sluggishly while I was driven to the point of smashing my head against the cell wall to escape the mental agony of uncertainty.

Then, when I appeared again on Monday the 29th, I saw clearly the way things were going.

Mr MacDermott, the prosecuting counsel, told the court I'd stabbed Dimes with a knife. Then, he said, Dimes stabbed me and we continued fighting inside a greengrocer's shop.

Next the prosecutor asked the magistrate if witnesses might write down their names and addresses instead of announcing them in open court. My solicitor immediately demanded to know the reason. It was then said that the identity of the witnesses should be kept a secret to safeguard them.

I could feel the subtle web being drawn tightly around me. Who was supposed to be intimidating the witnesses?

They meant me!

It didn't matter that I had no money, nor that I had been driven out of the underworld and was scorned by even the dregs of the criminal world. My own vainglorious cockiness and strutting was coming home to roost. The whole wide world wouldn't hesitate to believe that Jack Spot, Boss of the Underworld, was using hired assassins to intimidate witnesses.

The web was drawn even tighter. A witness described the fight and stated bluntly that *I* attacked Albert Dimes. He identified me as the assailant and Dimes as the innocent, attacked man.

Sitting there in the courtroom and hearing one damaging piece of evidence after another was like an awful nightmare coming true. My solicitor worked like a Trojan. He challenged the witnesses searchingly and practically accused them of having been rehearsed in the evidence they were giving. But he couldn't shake them.

But the real drama wasn't to reach its climax in Marlborough Street Police Court. After all the witnesses had been heard, the prosecuting counsel requested that I should be committed for trial.

Me and Dimes weren't going to be treated like most other lawbreakers. The magistrates' courts have the power to impose only light sentences.

Something special was prepared for me!

The charges against me were transferred to a court where the maximum sentences of the land can be handed out.

I was committed for trial at the Old Bailey.

The Central Criminal Court!

Anybody who is involved with the Law can't avoid knowing about the great injustices that take place and which are calmly accepted as a *normal part of legal procedure*.

I was an innocent man. Some evidence had been shown to indicate that *I might be guilty* of a crime and I was arrested on the 20th of August.

But it wasn't until the 19th of September that I appeared at the Old Bailey.

Bail had been consistently refused me. In the eyes of the law I was still an innocent man. But they locked me away like a criminal. They shut me in a stone cell and forced me to associate with criminals. Most of them I knew and they treated me like a leper.

The word had spread through the underworld like a prairie fire. I was untouchable. I was an outcast.

But the law, still proclaiming its magnificent impartiality, was keeping me locked in with men who hated me. And locked away with the bitter and agonising thoughts and memories that were driving me mad.

I abandoned all hope. Everything and everyone was against me. Truthful witnesses of what happened that fatal day in Frith Street had failed to come forward on my behalf.

So, slowly but inevitably, I was being driven towards that fateful day in the Central Criminal Court when the foreman of the jury would solemnly intone the verdict of Guilty. Then the judge would take a deep breath and announce my punishment.

And my punishment would be a living death. Perhaps even twelve years.

Twelve years for being stabbed and brought close to death!

I sat in the dock at the Old Bailey like an automaton. The long weeks of waiting had sucked from me nearly all emotion. What was happening around me went on like a theatre. All the actors knew their parts and were playing now to the public, performing all the rituals, swearing in witnesses, showing the jury exhibit A and referring to their learned colleagues.

All this dramatic ritual was being used to destroy me. The red-

robed judge and the twelve honest men seated in the jury box, the
be-wigged and be-robed counsel who shot questions across the
court-room and the public in the gallery above were all a part of it.

All this had been prepared for *me*. All this expense, all this drama
to pave the way for the inevitable verdict.

This was my last moment of awful glory. But I alone would have
to pay for these trimmings. Not in money, but in years off my life.

On the second day of the trial, the powers-that-be decided
they'd been doing everything wrong. They decided Dimes and
me should *not* be charged together but separately. The judge
ordered the jury to bring in a verdict of Not Guilty against me
and Albert Dimes. Then he dismissed the jury and I was immediately charged separately with intent to wound Dimes and
cause him grievous bodily harm and being in possession of a knife
without legal justification.

Dimes was charged with just one thing. Wounding me with
intent to cause grievous bodily harm. That left Dimes' defence
intact. His counsel could now claim that Albert Dimes had been
attacked and had wounded me only in self-defence. But it made *me*
the accused attacker and would-be murderer!

Back I went to jail. I still had not been proved guilty but was
treated as though I had been.

Rita came to see me while I was on remand. I pleaded with her
desperately. "You've got to go away," I told her. "Go right away
with the kids. You can't do anything for me now. I'm finished.
They've got me where they want me after years of waiting for this
moment. I've played right into their hands and I'll never get away.
I'm finished."

I could see further than Rita. I could see her savings draining
away on solicitor's fees and defending counsel's professional
charges. The cost of just those two days of abortive trial in the
Old Bailey had been enormous. And now it had to be repeated all
over again. And every day while the lawyers talked the fees rose
higher.

I tried desperately to make her realise this. "The money's being
wasted," I panted. "The lawyers can do nothing for me. Nothing!
Understand? *Nothing*. Can't you see it? I'm going away. For a long,
long time. So all that's worrying me is you and the kids. Don't
waste another penny in my defence. Save it for yourself and use it.
You *must* have some money."

She just nodded quietly and reassuringly with a sweet, understanding smile on her face. "Don't give up hope, Jack. Don't give up hope."

On Thursday, the 22nd of September, I found myself in the dock at the Old Bailey again. Alone this time. I was put into the witness-box and asked about my fight with Dimes. I explained it simply, just the way it happened. But I was like a robot now, without emotion and without interest. It was ironical, in a way, that I was being obliged to act my part, too, in this magnificently-staged drama in which I would be the one and only victim.

Then followed the witnesses. Sebastean Boonacore, who said he was a commission agent, said I started the fight by pushing Dimes.

Hyman Hyams, who was in the greengrocer's shop, said he was nervous of me, but the police had reassured him. He said I chased Dimes into his shop with a knife in my hand.

His wife, Mrs Sophia Hyams, said I grappled with Dimes, who had nothing in his hand.

The next day in court the evidence followed the same pattern. Every word spoken in that court was a nail in my coffin. And when Dimes' statement was read in court I knew I had no chance. I knew I was finished. I was no longer Boss of the Underworld. I wasn't even a petty crook. I was just a beaten shell of a man, broken on the wheel of his own vanity, who was at last paying the full price for his way of life with his liberty and the happiness of his family.

Then came the turn of the defence to have their say, and as the court usher shouted a name, I looked up in surprise at my counsel, Miss Rose Heilbron.

She was standing serenely in the well of the court, serious and dignified and quietly watching the witness who now entered. I, too, looked at him and blinked in amazement.

He was an aged and feeble parson, stumbling into the courtroom with the dazed look of a lost child. He smiled benignly at the court usher who indicated the witness-box, and blinked up in bewildered, awed surprise at the red-robed judge who sat high above him.

The parson gave a tiny, courteous bow to the judge. The judge graciously acknowledged the bow by gently inclining his head.

Then the parson stepped up into the witness-box, looking around him curiously and just a little nervously. The public knew at once from his manner that he'd never before been in such an awful place as a criminal court and had not the slightest idea how it operated.

Miss Rose Heilbron was gentle with him, drawing out the facts that he was the Rev. Basil Claude Hudson Andrews, a retired clergyman who had volunteered to give evidence and who had been in Frith Street on August 11th.

I listened to him in astonishment. Then a wild surge of desperate hope flooded through me as he gave his evidence.

He'd actually been in Frith Street and seen the fight between me and Dimes. He had seen Dimes holding a steel implement with which he'd struck at my head. He described how I brought up my arm to shield myself and had been wounded in the arm.

Such an unpleasant scene as a fight with a knife was very upsetting for him, he explained. He hurried away before the police arrived. But later, when he read in the newspapers that *I* was accused of being the aggressor, he knew it was not true.

"It astonished me and I thought: dear me, this is entirely wrong. The darker man was the aggressor. He attacked the fair-haired man!" the parson told the judge.

The parson then identified *me* as the man who had been attacked, and Italian Albert was brought into the Court and the parson immediately identified him as being the man who had attacked first.

When the parson stepped down from the witness stand the palms of my hands were sweating with excitement. I saw hope now. Real hope. Slowly and ruthlessly the evidence against me had been built up. But the witnesses had been challenged every step of the way. And now the Rev. Andrews, completely of his own accord, had come forward to give evidence that completely vindicated me.

Miss Rose Heilbron summed up for the defence with many telling points. Of the two men who had taken part in the Soho duel, medical evidence had shown clearly that I had suffered much more grievously than Dimes. If Dimes was really the victim instead of the aggressor, how could he have inflicted such terrible wounds upon me? It had been proved that I could not have had the knife and hidden it where it was subsequently found, and it was suggested that Dimes knew a great deal about this knife which mysteriously appeared sixteen days after the duel.

Then finally it was the turn of the judge, Sir Gerald Dodson. He spoke a long time, summing up the evidence for and against me, and a lot of the time I didn't understand what he was driving at.

For example, he referred to me describing Dimes as a strong-arm man. "The inference is raised," he said. "Why, on going to interview a strong-arm man, did he (Jack Spot) not arm himself?"

It was as though the judge was saying I shouldn't have gone to see Albert without taking a knife along with me. But I couldn't imagine a judge believing that, since it's a crime to carry a knife if you're thinking of using it on somebody. Then Sir Gerald Dodson went on: "He is entitled to defend himself, and if a knife is being used, he is entitled to turn it on the assailant." Then he weighed up the evidence against me and compared it with the evidence given by the parson. And all the time the judge was talking I was growing more and more hopeful because what he said seemed to me to be all in my favour. Finally the jury was ordered out by the judge to consider their verdict.

Two warders took me downstairs where I sat and sweated for sixty-five minutes.

The jury came back, and when I again stood in the dock and faced the judge, the fateful words were asked: "Members of the jury, what is your verdict?"

The foreman climbed to his feet, licked his lips, glanced across the court at me and then back again at the judge.

He said slowly and clearly: "Not Guilty!"

I was a reprieved man!

I wanted to kiss Miss Rose Heilbron, slap each of the jury members heartily on the shoulder, wring the parson's hand and give the judge my deepest thanks.

It was too wonderful to be true.

At the last moment I had been reprieved.

Despite everything, Justice had prevailed.

The Man who Invented Las Vegas
(Bugsy Siegel)

Dean Jennings

Benjamin "Bugsy" Siegel (1906–47) was the man who invented Las Vegas. He clawed his way to the pinnacle of gangsterdom to become a kingpin mobster. Handsomely chiselled and socially assured, he enjoyed a flamboyant lifestyle, mingled with film stars, politicians, criminals, columnists and socialites, but died as violently as he had lived, his body riddled with bullets. Mark Gribben, an American historian of organized crime, describes Bugsy Siegel as a textbook sociopath. "He took what he wanted when he wanted it and the emotion of remorse was alien to him. In his mind, other people were there to be used by him, which was demonstrated by his long record of robbery, rape and murder dating back to his teenage years." After a career as Meyer Lansky's number two in the 1920s and early 30s (they formed the Bug and Meyer Gang, reputedly the most violent of the Prohibition mobs outside of Chicago), Siegel was forced to flee New York. In 1935, indicted for shooting one of Dutch Schultz's henchmen, Siegel flew to California where he linked up with Jack Dragna, capo mafioso of Los Angeles, to launch a series of spectacularly successful rackets. They were helped by Mickey Cohen, a psychotic killer on Dragna's payroll who later funded Richard Nixon's first political campaign. Siegel personally assassinated Harry "Big Greenie" Greenberg, a former Murder Inc. killer, before he could squeal to the FBI. In 1945 Siegel took a $3m loan from the Syndicate, added $3m of his *own, and began building the Flamingo Hotel (so-called because it was his pet name for girlfriend Virginia Hill) in Las Vegas, Nevada. The Flamingo, and the dozens more hotel-casino-nightclubs that followed, made Las Vegas the entertainment and mob capital of America. Siegel's fatal error was his reluctance to repay the loan from the Syndicate. Lucky Luciano's second request for settlement was refused. On 20 June 1947, an unknown gunman entered Virginia Hill's house and shot Siegel dead as he sat on her chintz sofa. His murder is recalled by author and journalist Dean Jennings (b. 1905), whose biography of Bugsy Siegel appeared in 1968.*

I n Beverly Hills, Police Chief Anderson got a tip. In Chicago the mob men said Virginia Hill had gone to Europe to get a reprieve for her man from Lucky Luciano. Lee Mortimer spotted some notorious Eastern gunmen in a Beverly Hills hotel – or so he wrote long afterward. They told him they were there for a little talk with Ben Siegel, and they were going to ask him what happened to their money in his casino. Meyer Lansky arrived at the Flamingo, and Siegel introduced him to Paul Price.

"This is my old friend, Mr Lansky," Siegel said. "He's staying with us for a couple of days."

Meyer Lansky was not officially registered at the Flamingo, and he was not seen outside his room. But the gangsters in town knew he was there.

Ben Siegel went about his daily business, trailed by Hymie Segal and Dave Berman and Fat Irish Green. He was more irascible than ever, and sent word to the major bookies in Nevada, California, and Arizona that he wanted them in Las Vegas for an important conference.

They showed up as he had ordered and, during a stormy meeting in the hotel, he told them he was doubling the price of his wire service. There was open rebellion, and many of the small operators claimed that Siegel was forcing them to pay for the big losses at the Flamingo. The mutiny was so flagrant that even Hank Greenspun and Paul Price, who had carefully avoided direct contact with the underworld elements, heard threats against Siegel from half a dozen sources.

On 13 June, when the bookies had gone home grumbling, Siegel phoned Price at home and said: "I have to fly to LA on some money business, Paul, and I want you to come along. Meet me at the airport."

Price glanced at his watch and saw that it was almost midnight.

They landed in Glendale about two a.m. and found the airport deserted. It took some time to get a taxi, and they were taken directly to the Linden Drive house. They sat around for an hour in the living-room talking business. Chick and Jerri were not home. Siegel made fresh coffee for Price, and he himself sipped a small glass of Remy Martin.

"I never saw a man more calm in my life," Price recalled. "The curtains were all pulled away from the windows in the house, and he walked right through the front door with no hesitation. If he had any fear, do you think he would be out alone at night with just a Press agent? He had as tough a crew as you'll ever see, and they were always around at the Flamingo. But that night he was wide open for it. I was convinced all the rumours didn't mean a thing."

Siegel and Price returned to Las Vegas the following afternoon, and once more his personal gunmen followed him. If there were killers nearby, they couldn't have hit him with a cannon.

In Beverly Hills the next evening, Chick and Jerri were asleep on the first floor of the big white house. Just before midnight Jerri suddenly shook Chick into wakefulness and whispered: "Chick! I hear someone downstairs!"

Chick leaped out of bed, grabbed his gun, and went to the head of the staircase.

"Who's down there?" he called.

As he had hoped, his voice was heard by the unknown intruder, and the silence was broken by the sound of someone running. He snapped off the safety on the gun, switched on the lights, and went down to the living-room. He felt a current of cool air, walked to the kitchen, and discovered the back door wide open. He locked it every night.

There were scratches indicating the prowler, whoever he was, had forced the latch.

He stood there for a moment, listening for sounds in the darkness outside. Then he closed the door, left the lights on there and in the living-room, and went back to bed.

"I don't like it, Jerri," he said. "I don't like it a bit."

Just before noon on June 19, four men who looked like underworld gorillas marched into the Flamingo Hotel, and demanded to know where they could find Siegel. When one man pulled a gun they were told the boss usually came in around 2 p.m. The men left, and Siegel was notified at once. He sent Hymie and Dave into downtown Las Vegas on a frantic search for the tough guys. They had disappeared.

All through that day there were long-distance calls for Siegel, and when he answered the phone a voice would say, "Bugsy, you've had it," and then hang up. Siegel finally asked Dick Chappell to have the hotel operators trace the calls, and he left word at the switchboard that he would not answer unless the callers were people he knew.

Siegel also had a curious session with Little Moe Sedway that day. He did not discuss it with anyone, and it was not mentioned until 1951, when Sedway was on the stand at the Kefauver hearings. Sedway, who was keenly anxious to be identified with the respectable people in Las Vegas, was chairman of the United Jewish Appeal campaign that year, and claimed he and Siegel were together at the Flamingo to discuss a fund-raising dinner to be held in the hotel.

"Siegel said he thinks he can get Al Jolson down for the dinner," Sedway testified, "and I said that would be a big thing for us."

"Did he say anything that might indicate he was in fear of his life?" he was asked.

"No, he never said anything. He was supposed to call me the next day about Jolson. He never did call me."

One suspects that this conversation between Siegel and Sedway never took place at that time. Sedway was No. 1 on Siegel's black list in Las Vegas, as everyone knew, and he was not permitted inside the Flamingo under any circumstances.

Early in the afternoon on June 19, Siegel phoned Chick Hill.

"I'm coming down tonight with Swifty Morgan," he said. "I've got a meeting with Paul Price at Joe Ross's law office in the afternoon, and I want to get my clothes. Don't wait up for me because I'm not leaving here until after midnight."

About 8 p.m. Siegel went into his private office, and sent for Fat Irish Green. The fat man, who was not only one of Siegel's bodyguards but also employed as a timekeeper, came in and sat down.

Siegel opened a briefcase and let Green see that it was jammed with currency. Green later said it was only $60,000, but Government investigators believe there may have been as much as $600,000.

"I'm going to Los Angeles for a couple of days," he said. "I'm leaving this bundle with you, Irish. Nobody in Vegas knows you've got it."

"What's going on, Ben?" Green asked.

"Nothing. I'm leaving it with you – just in case," Siegel said. "If anything happens to me you just sit tight and there'll be some guys who'll come and take the money off your hands."

At midnight Siegel joined Swifty Morgan, and they were driven to the airport. Swifty looked more and more like a leprechaun, with his long moustache and his little goatee, and he was full of gags as usual as they boarded Western Air Lines flight 23 for Los Angeles. The plane took off at 12.53 a.m. and landed at Mines field in Los Angeles about 2.30. Siegel and Swifty called a cab and went directly to the Linden Drive house.

Chick was awake when they arrived, but Siegel was too tired for conversation. He went upstairs and took Swifty to a guest room. The largest of the four rooms on that floor overlooked the street. It contained Virginia's antique four-poster bed, with a canopy over it, and the safe which was concealed by a swing-out panel. Siegel looked in there out of habit, then went to his own room next door. He went to sleep at once.

In the morning, Siegel, Chick, Jerri, and Swifty were served breakfast by Virginia's Chinese cook, Lee, and shortly afterward the phone began ringing steadily. Siegel had long conversations with many people. Chick does not know their names because he was not in the bedroom where Siegel was using the phone. He does recall that Siegel eventually came downstairs and said he was going to Mickey Cohen's house in Brentwood. Siegel took Allen Smiley with him, but when they got there it was obvious that he wanted to see Mickey alone.

"Take a walk, would you, Al?" he said.

Smiley knew what that meant. "I'll wait in the car," he said.

Siegel went into the house after Mickey had looked at him through his front door peephole, and he said: "Mick, I hope this place isn't bugged."

"Not this one," Mickey laughed. "It's been tried."

"I don't want to take any chances," Siegel said. "Let's go outside." They went out through the back door, and Siegel said: "Mick, you got any guys with equipment?"

"Well, Hooky Rothman's in town. Woody may be here, too. They can both handle a rod pretty good."

"Ask Hooky to see me tomorrow," Siegel said.

"I'll have Hooky call you," Cohen said. "What's up, Ben?"

"Nothing much," Siegel replied casually. "I'll see you."

Reconstructing this brief exchange later, Mickey said he had never seen Siegel so knotted up.

"I should have asked more questions," he said, "but Ben was the kind of guy who told you only what he wanted you to know. If I'd had any idea what was coming up, I'd have hung around closer myself."

En route back to Virginia's home, Siegel drove to the George Raft house in Coldwater Canyon, and found the actor starting breakfast. Raft was shocked by his friend's pallor and his jerky speech and movements, and he said: "You look terrible. Why don't you get out in the sun more? Take a vacation. Get away from the hotel for a while."

"I'm tired, Georgie," Siegel said. "And I am going to get away for a few days. My two daughters are coming out from New York by train in a couple of days, and I promised to take them to Lake Louise up in Canada." Siegel glanced at his watch. "How about having dinner with me and Al Smiley tonight? We're going to a new place – Jack's at the Beach."

"I wish I could, Ben," Raft said. "But I'm trying to start a picture company of my own, and I have a date with some people."

"Maybe you can drop around at the house tomorrow."

"Will do," Raft promised.

At 2 p.m. Siegel walked into Drucker's barber shop to meet Paul Price, and he took what Price calls "the full treatment" – shave, haircut, manicure, neck and shoulder massage, and shoe-shine. They left there together and walked to Joe Ross's law office, a few blocks away.

Siegel was alone with Ross for perhaps an hour, going over account books and discussing legal problems in connection with the hotel. There was probably also some talk about Virginia, because at the time Ross was not only preparing her income tax returns, but also receiving money on her behalf from Joe Epstein in Chicago. During one four-year period cashier's cheques from Epstein to Ross totalled $10,000. Ross also disclosed later that Ben Siegel had given him approximately $50,000 which he had turned over to Virginia on various occasions.

"I don't know where Miss Hill gets all her money," he said once, "and I don't want to know."

That day Ben Siegel probably wished he had the $50,000. He was being crushed in a financial vice, and was so touchy about it that he quibbled with Paul Price about a small expense account that afternoon in Ross's office.

Siegel pulled out his wallet, counted out three one hundred dollar bills, and stuffed them into Price's hand. "Now you're not busted," he said. "Forget it."

Siegel and Price agreed to meet at the airport the following day for the return flight to Las Vegas, and went their separate ways. It was now 4 p.m.

Siegel drove back to North Linden Drive, and joined Chick in Virginia's bedroom. The warm sun touched the gun lying on a bedside table. Siegel turned slightly to keep the reflection out of his eyes, fingered the gun he had taken from the safe only moments before, and spoke to Chick, who was lolling in a chintz-covered chair.

"Chick," he said, "put the rod back in the safe and lock it up, will you?"

Chick uncoiled himself from the chair, smoothed out his brown alpaca sweater, and walked past the big bed with its gold damask spread.

"Don't you want the rod, Ben?" he asked.

"Hell, no," Siegel said. "Who needs it here?"

Chick closed the door of the safe, spun the dial twice, and then swung the concealing panel in front of it.

"You know Tab's jewels are in that safe, too," he said. "They cost her a hundred grand, and it makes me nervous having them in there."

"That's your sister's worry, kid," Siegel said. "I got enough on my mind."

"The stuff's not insured."

"So it's not insured. You think this is some Alabama hillbilly town? You're in Beverly Hills, where the cops come along this block every half-hour." Siegel glanced at his watch. "Let's go in my room," he said. "I want to make some calls."

The telephone was ringing just as they stepped into the room, and Siegel answered the call.

"Hello," he said. "Oh, it's you." He listened for a moment as the other party talked, and Chick saw Siegel's face darken. "You son of a bitch!" he bristled. "Over my dead body you will! You haven't got the guts!"

He dropped the receiver into its cradle.

"Trouble, Ben?" Chick asked.

"Just some wise guy who thinks he can take me," Siegel growled.

"Anybody I know?"

"You know him. Look, Chick, leave me alone for now. I got urgent business."

Chick went back to his own room, trying to guess the name of the man whom Siegel obviously did not want to identify. He never mentioned the incident to the police or any other official, and he is still guessing.

In New York City, Police Chief Clinton Anderson of Beverly Hills got into a police squad car on the afternoon of 20 June with New York Police Lieutenant Francis Phillips and a uniformed policeman, and started out on Riverside Drive heading towards the Bronx. In Beverly Hills, some months before, a robber had held up Mrs Samuel Genis in her apartment and taken $114,000 worth of jewellery. When Chief Anderson let her riffle through a stack of mug shots, the usual procedure in such cases, she quickly picked out one photo.

"That's the man who did it," she said.

"Albert Greenberg," Chief Anderson said. "A tough ex-con. You're sure?"

"I'm positive," Mrs Genis said. "I'd know that face anywhere."

Greenberg was eventually traced to New York and was found in a Bronx apartment. Tough or not, Greenberg put up no resistance when the three policemen walked in that day, and he quietly admitted his identity. Later, when Chief Anderson questioned him, he said: "I didn't do that caper, Chief. I wasn't even in Beverly Hills."

"Where were you?"

"At the Flamingo in Vegas. I was there two days before the robbery, and two days afterward. Never left the joint."

"Anybody see you there all that time?"

"Bugsy Siegel himself saw me there. He'll be my witness."

At 7 p.m. on 20 June Ben Siegel phoned the Hollywood office of *Daily Variety* and asked for Florabel Muir, who was then doing a column for the show business newspaper.

"I just want to thank you for your review of the Flamingo floor show," he said. He told her he was planning a major advertising campaign, and had booked the Ritz Brothers for a September opening. "I'm paying them $25,000 a week, but I think they're worth it."

At 7.30 Allen Smiley pulled up at the kerb in front of the house in his new powder blue Cadillac convertible.

Siegel said, "Hi!" to Smiley and then turned to Chick. "Chick," he said, "your car's parked in the driveway, so we'll go to Jack's in Al's car. Tell Jerri we're all set."

Siegel sat in front with Smiley driving; Chick and Jerri were in the back seat. The night was warm, and there was a soft but cooling breeze from the sea when they reached Jack's restaurant in Ocean Park. They had a leisurely sea-food dinner, and Siegel seemed cheerful for a change as they watched the slow rollers snaking in from the sea, and breaking up in foam on the sandy beach.

Shortly after nine o'clock Siegel paid the bill, tipped the waiter, and walked out to call for the car. While he was standing there, someone handed him a copy of the morning *Los Angeles Times*. Chick does not remember whether it was Sonny Meyes, one of the owners, or the cashier. On the front page was stamped: *Good night. Sleep well with the compliments of Jack's.*

Siegel tucked the paper under his arm, and as they started for Beverly Hills he said to Smiley: "My nose feels a little stuffy. Stop at the Beverly-Wilshire drugstore and I'll get something." Minutes later Siegel went alone into the pharmacy, and bought a bottle of Campho-phenique. He came out, holding the medicine in a small paper bag, and Smiley drove on and parked in front of the Linden Drive house.

Siegel reached into his pocket for the solid gold key Virginia had given him, unlocked the front door, and switched on the hall light. He stopped suddenly, sniffing the air like a hunting dog.

"Chick," he said, "there's a very strong odour of flowers in here. Like carnations."

"I don't smell anything," Chick said. "There isn't a flower in the house."

Siegel ignored Chick's remark, and looked irritably at Jerri Mason. "Can't you smell them, Jerri?"

"No, I can't, Ben," she said. "If your nose is stopped up I don't see how you can smell anything."

Siegel went into the big living-room and sat on the chintz-covered divan.

"I'm going to talk to Al for a while, Chick," he said. "But take a look round. Somebody must have sent us some flowers. I can still smell them."

Chick went from room to room, but found no flowers.

He remembered something his mother had told him when he was a little boy in Alabama.

"When someone smells flowers and there aren't any in the house," she had said, "it means they're going to die. That's what it means, Chick. They're going to die."

Cars sped along Sunset Boulevard in Beverly Hills, taillights spattering the dark like tracer bullets, glowing pale red as the traffic flowed, changing colour when the traffic signals showed yellow, and the stream slowed. Just east of the Benedict Canyon intersection, where the curved driveway of the Beverly Hills Hotel makes its exit, Arthur Day, Jr., sat at the wheel of his Yellow Cab, listening to music on the radio. Business had been slow that evening, but later, when dances and parties were over, he would be busy rolling through the tree-lined streets, driving fares to apartments and homes.

He was twisting the tuning knob when he heard a voice outside his window, calling, "Hey, Mac!" The street corner was bright with overhead lights, and alongside the kerb he saw an old Pontiac sedan with crumpled wings and dents in the body – not the kind of car usually seen in the streets of this prosperous neighbourhood of shining Cadillacs and Lincoln Continentals. In the front seat, looking at him, was a stout, black-haired man who wore a seedy snap-brim hat pulled down over his eyebrows. The man at the wheel was in the shadows, but there was a third rider on the back seat, whose dark hair was long and unkempt, and whose white shirt was open at the neck. All three, Day decided, were Italian or Mexican.

"Hey, Mac," the man nearest the window said again, speaking with a Brooklyn accent, "how do we get to North Linden Drive from here?"

"You're almost there," Day replied. "You keep going three blocks to Whittier Avenue. You make a left turn there, and Linden is the first street coming into Whittier from the left. You can't miss it."

"Thanks, Mac."

The man in the back muttered, "Let's go," and the battered old car moved on. Day turned up the volume on his radio, but his mind was on the three strangers in the Pontiac, and he said afterward he had never seen three tougher-looking characters in that street.

Twenty minutes later he heard the sound of sirens, and two police cars shot out of Canon Drive to his left. The sirens screamed, red lights flashed their warning, and in an instant the cars were out of sight. He said to himself: "Some poor slob's in a jam."

At midnight, tuning in the news, Arthur Day heard a bulletin that shocked him, and it brought back the gruff sound of a man's voice. "Hey, Mac!" He shivered a little, because now it was all very clear. He was suddenly afraid, but he knew what he had to do.

Ben Siegel and Al Smiley sat side by side in the living-room of Virginia's house, and as they talked the *Los Angeles Times* was spread open, like a napkin, across Siegel's lap.

Despite Virginia's expensive redecorating, it was not an attractive room, and the flowered sofa seemed incongruous in the Moorish-style setting. There was an oil painting of a dowager on one wall beside the fireplace, and a small bronze statue of Cupid beside the fireplace tongs and poker. The curtains were parted, and a scant twenty feet away was a plant-covered latticework frame separating the property from the driveway of the house at 808 North Linden, owned by Martin and Anna Belousoff.

There was a car parked at the kerb just ahead of Smiley's Cadillac. Ben Siegel did not see it. There was a man outside the window, standing behind the lattice frame. Ben Siegel did not see him.

There was a .30–30 carbine resting in a notch of wood, and the finger on the trigger was trembling. Lined up in the sights was Ben Siegel's handsome face. He did not see death; neither did he hear it, nor feel it. Here in the peace and stillness of the night he was safe. In thirty-five years there had been only two killings in Beverly Hills, and both were quickly solved.

"We have a unique community in this respect," Chief Anderson has said. "The streets are patrolled every half-hour, and strangers are quickly detected. It is a safe and pleasant place to live."

The first slug crashed through the window glass into Siegel's skull and drove his right eye fifteen feet away and plastered it to the tile floor of the dining-room. Baby Blue Eyes, George Raft had called him. His long eyelashes were sliced from the eyelid, and were later found glued to the door jamb. The second bullet broke up the rest of his face, driving into the neck and out.

There were seven more bullets. One of them ripped through the sleeve of Allen Smiley's coat. Another hit the painting on the wall. There was a little figure of Bacchus on the top of Virginia Hill's piano, and the white figure fell apart and bits of marble dropped on the ivory keys. Siegel's head rolled away from his neck and rested against the back of the sofa, and his flowered necktie was sticky and red.

"It was like firecrackers," Chick Hill said later. "We didn't know he was dead. We didn't know a goddam thing. Smiley yelled to douse the lights, and I did. And when I turned them on again there was Smiley inside the fireplace. I don't know how he got in there. Maybe he doesn't know himself. Jesus Christ, we were scared!'

Chick ran back toward the stairs, and Jerri Mason was standing there, staring, stricken dumb by blood and death.

"Call the cops!" he yelled at her.

She ran to the phone. She riffled through their phone list with fumbling fingers, found the "P" section and dialed the number marked Police. But it was not the police number; it was the emergency phone for Barney Ruditsky's private detective office, and she screamed at the man who answered, and he said: "I'll be right over."

The instant she picked up the phone Chick remembered the safe in Virginia's room. He bounded down the hall, opened the panel, and unlocked the steel box. His hands came out with a handful of fire – Virginia's $100,000 cache of jewels – and he stood wondering where to hide them before the police showed up. He went to the laundry chute and dumped them inside, and they landed on the dirty linen piled up at the bottom of the chute.

Then he began to shake, and fell into the nearest chair and waited. He did not want to go downstairs again.

Good night. Sleep well with the compliments of Jack's.

Life After Life
(*Jimmy Boyle*)

Lynn Barber

As a young man, Jimmy Boyle was a gang-leader in Glasgow's notorious Gorbals district. He once said that the only way he knew how to survive the drinking, fighting and thieving of 1950s and 1960s Gorbals was to fight and steal himself. The son of a Glasgow hard man, Boyle worked as a teenager for a loan-sharking operation, charging 25 percent interest a week. Defaulters were threatened by Boyle armed with a bayonet wrapped in a copy of the Glasgow Herald. *After attacking two men with a broken bottle, one of whom lost an eye, Boyle was involved in another fight, during which a man was scalped. A charge of murder against him was dropped. Following the killing of Glasgow gangster "Babs" Rooney in 1966, Boyle fled to London where he was sheltered by the Kray Twins. Traced to an East End pub, he was returned to Scotland and sentenced to life imprisonment for murder. While in prison he wrote a book,* A Sense of Freedom, *which was made into a play, a TV documentary and a film. He was freed in 1982. Boyle helped create a Gorbals matrix of a hard-drinking, violent community, dominated by greed and selfishness. At his murder trial, he was described as a man "of unbridled savagery and unprecedented violence". During his incarceration, he maimed a prison officer during a riot and spent five years in solitary confinement, much of the time living naked in his own excrement. Now a reformed character, Boyle married Sarah Trevelyan (daughter of the*

*former British film censor) and pursued a career as a writer and
sculptor. With her hallmark insights and candour, as well as
bruising honesty, Lynn Barber (b. 1944) ranks among Britain's
best-known journalists. She has won five British Press Awards,
more than any other interviewer, and is credited with rescuing
the so-called celebrity interview from the doldrums of deference.
She has published two collections of her interviews; although she
now works for* The Observer, *she wrote this profile of Jimmy
Boyle during her time at the* Sunday Express, *three years after
his release from prison.*

There are a lot of people in Scotland who believe that Jimmy
Boyle should have been hanged. Preferably drawn and quar-
tered as well. The taxidriver who drove me to Jimmy Boyle's place
in Edinburgh said I should not even be talking to a man like that –
"Once a villain, always a villain."

The first time Jimmy Boyle came up on a murder charge, in
1965, he *could* have been hanged – capital punishment was still
extant – and they cleaned out the Death Cell in readiness for him.
But that time he got off. The second time he came up on a murder
charge he got off again. But the third time, in 1967, he was found
guilty and sentenced to life imprisonment. The judge said he was
the most dangerous man in Scotland, and should serve a minimum
of 15 years. He did.

He was released in October 1982. He is married to social worker
Sarah Trevelyan, and they have a daughter, Suzi. Sarah is the
daughter of John Trevelyan, the former film censor, so Jimmy
Boyle makes an appearance in Debrett's, where he describes
himself as a "writer and sculptor". His sculpture has been ex-
hibited in Edinburgh and London; he has written two books about
his prison experiences, and co-authored two plays.

His main work now, though, is running a rehabilitation centre
for drug addicts in Edinburgh called the Gateway Exchange. It
was there that I met him. I don't know what I expected an ex-
gangleader and murderer to look like but it certainly wasn't like
Jimmy Boyle. He has a soft, almost babyish face, and he smiles a
lot. He looks younger than his 41 years. He has charisma – he has
sex appeal – and he knows it. He holds himself on the balls of his
feet like an athlete and he walks with a strut, hands on hips to
emphasize his beefy chest.

There is a deep ugly-looking hole in his neck, residue of a knife fight in the Gorbals. There is also a newer, redder gash on his cheek and he fingers it tenderly. "That was my daughter Suzi. She was cross when I took her off Sarah and she scratched me with her fingernail – she was real shocked when she saw blood!" He says this with a doting Dad smile; he is nothing if not sentimental. He says he loves changing nappies, he loves helping with housework; he missed out on all that with his first family (he had two children by a former girlfriend in his twenties) because he was inside all the time they were growing up. In the 1980s the elder daughter got married and the teenage son James managed to come off heroin.

Jimmy Boyle ("call me Jimmy") takes me on a guided tour of the Gateway Exchange, delivering what is obviously a well-rehearsed speech. The tour goes so smoothly, I feel a bit like Princess Anne being shown round a new factory or something. No messy heroin addicts get in our way – indeed, there are very few people in the place – though Jimmy does warn me not to leave my handbag lying around. He talks quietly and seriously, like a good PR man, about the problems of drug abuse and the way the Gateway is tackling them.

The emphasis is all on creativity. He refuses to have dart boards or pool tables in the building because "I want to stimulate people on a much more fundamental level: you've got to replace the buzz of heroin with the buzz of life." He believes that the energy which is wasted on drugs or crime can be channelled instead into art. It would all sound like pie in the sky were it not for the fact that Jimmy Boyle has done it.

His first book, *A Sense of Freedom*, recounts his prison experiences (it was also made into a television documentary and a film), and what makes it so powerful is the sense of rage it expresses. That is why it is so difficult to reconcile the blazing Jimmy Boyle of the book with the smooth-talking PR man of today. The Jimmy Boyle of the past belonged to the Gorbals slums. His father was "away", his mother out at work all the time. Inevitably, he was drawn into the gang life of the streets.

By his early teens he already had his own gang busily engaged in shoplifting, breaking and entering, and fighting with other gangs. He did spells in approved school, in Borstal, in prison, graduating up the criminal career ladder. He was really proud of himself when, at 18, he was sent to Barlinnie men's prison – the youngest prisoner there. "I thought that I'd arrived."

Between the ages of 12 and 38 he spent just 12½ months out of prison. He was a recognized underworld leader, a sort of Glaswegian Ronnie Kray, building up his "contacts" in prison and exploiting them on release. His special business was money-lending – lending cash at 25–50 percent interest *a week*. He claimed, he even *still* claims, that this was a useful service fulfilling a well-established public demand. It was only necessary to "put the frighteners on" defaulting debtors once in a while. It was putting the frighteners on Babs Rooney – by slashing him open from forehead to abdomen – that got him sent down for murder.

He took pride in being a "hard man". Once, a rival gang trapped him in a dark alley and set about him with hammers and hatchets till both his kneecaps were crushed and half his guts were hanging out. He regained consciousness in hospital. He immediately discharged himself, called up some friends, got them to patch him up a bit and dress him and carry him to the pub so that he could be sitting there, grinning, when his assailants came in to boast that they had finished Jimmy Boyle. No matter that the blood was splashing down his legs – he was being a hard man.

He remained a hard man for the first six years of his life sentence. He attacked other prisoners, warders, policemen, even the Prison Governor, because he felt that, serving life anyway, he had nothing to lose. He smeared himself and his cell with his own excrement to stop the warders coming in and once, when he was put in a brand-new cell block, he managed to demolish six walls overnight. He was consigned to the "Cages" at Inverness and, treated like an animal, he behaved like one.

All this changed in 1973 when he was transferred to a new experimental Special Unit designed to cope with unmanageable prisoners. On arrival at the unit, he was handed a pair of scissors to cut the string round his parcel of clothes and he almost fainted with shock – he had forgotten that scissors were intended for any other purpose than stabbing people.

He was deeply distrustful of the whole set-up at first, but gradually started joining in, talking to prison officers and other prisoners, taking up sculpture and writing his book. But it was a hard struggle – his young brother came to visit him and told him, "You're going soft. Don't give in, Jimmy, don't give in!"

But then there was a new influence: Sarah Trevelyan read his book and wrote asking to visit him. They conducted their courtship in prison and outside – unknown to the press at the time,

Jimmy Boyle was often let out for weekends. He claims now that
there were "queues" of middle-class girls waiting to sleep with
him, plus "all the usual weirdos who hang around prisoners". The
party ended when he was transferred back to a conventional prison
in Edinburgh for the last two years of his sentence. It was back to
one-hour-a-week visits through a grille, and having to ask to go to
the toilet. But by now he was married to Sarah and she set up a flat
for them and laid the foundations of their future respectable life.

The Jimmy Boyle of the present is *so* respectable, so assured, so
word-perfect in the lingo of social concern, it is hard to believe he
is the same man. After the guided tour, he takes me to "a nice little
place I know" for lunch. It is pure Jean Brodie – a wonderfully
genteel front parlour of a restaurant with potted palms. The lady
owner rushes over to greet Jimmy with squeals of delight – she had
a famous QC in the other day, she says, who was talking about
Jimmy Boyle and his fine work for the community. Jimmy in turn
tells her that I am a journalist, and that the girl he brought last time
was Cubby Broccoli's daughter – "He's a famous film producer,
you know."

We debate the merits of cockaleekie and "happy herring" while
all the other lunchers whisper, "That's Jimmy Boyle. That's Jimmy
Boyle." He is a real celebrity in Scotland, recognized everywhere he
goes. "But I refuse to give autographs. Except once – it was to a lady
in a wheelchair – I felt I couldn't refuse." Saccharine smile. He
mentions that he met Leon Brittan at a dinner party a few weeks ago,
while he was still Home Secretary – "I just wish he had tried a bit
harder to be the person he really was, but he didn't have the courage
– he capitulated to his career. It's real sad."

There is something so incongruous about the idea of sitting here
among the potted palms listening to an ex-gangster commiserating
with the plight of an ex-Home Secretary. I keep wanting to pinch
myself. Instead I ask, nastily, whether he ever bumps into any of
his former victims. "Almost every week," he says evenly. "And
. . .?" "They say 'Hi, Jimmy', shake my hand."

He himself had the weird experience of bumping into the judge
who sentenced him the first time he was let out of prison on parole.
"Actually, I've got friends who know him, Lord Cameron: they
say he talks about me a lot."

All this sweetness and light and universal forgiveness has the
effect of making me feel more acid and I ask if he has ever read
Tom Wolfe's book *Radical Chic*. He hasn't, so I explain: "It's

about the sort of trendy scene where you have terrorists and murderers going to cocktail parties, and being treated as celebrities themselves."

He takes a deep breath before replying. "Look, let me tell you. I could move into London tomorrow but I don't want to get into all that trendy shit. There's all these middle-class trendies and academics who think they've got the answer to everything, and meanwhile they just leave people on the scrapheap while they stand around having intellectual arguments. But really the only people who can find the solution is the scrapheap, and I'm right in the thick of it, working at street level. *Yes*, I have acquired middle-class tastes, but my roots are still in the Gorbals and I wouldn't be doing the work I'm doing if they weren't."

A good answer, though any pretence of friendliness between us has now hit the dust. "Why are journalists so cynical?" he keeps asking. "Because it's our *job* to be cynical," I keep telling him. But what is extremely irritating is that he interprets any criticism, or even questioning of himself and his work, as cynicism. He is so sure he is right. He *knows* about poverty, he *knows* about crime, he *knows* about prison, he *knows* about drug addiction – how can a mere journalist understand these things? And he himself is a walking advertisement for the success of his own ideas.

Everything he says about the way people can change must be true because here is the proof – look at me, look at me, look at me!

I put it to him that yes, sure, he has done all these things but not everyone in the world can do the same. After all, he was a natural leader in the Gorbals; he rose to the top as a criminal at a very young age, but most people never rise to the top in any field. It must be just wishful thinking to believe that all the kids who come into the Gateway can be transformed into sculptors or artists and pillars of society.

"They *can*, they *can*," he punches back. "*Anyone* can change. Even you! If I had you at the Gateway for six months I'd have you doing things you wouldn't believe!" It is an alarming thought – six months doing pottery with a lot of heroin addicts. Does he mean it as a joke? No, he has no sense of humour; he means it for real. He may not be a hard man in the gangster sense any more but, by golly, he is a hard man to have an argument with.

As we emerge into the street, with a new flurry of compliments from the lady restaurateur, he visibly softens. The sun shines, the streets gleam, passers-by say, "Hi Jimmy," and smile in recognition. Has he changed, I ask, in these three years of freedom? "Yes, I've softened a lot, especially since Suzi was born – I just melt over her.

"These three years have gone so quickly. But I still feel that sense of freshness, of freedom. I feel it at this moment when I walk on the street, I still think, 'It's marvellous to be here.' It's like coming back from the dead."

Little Big Man
(Meyer Lansky)

William Schulz

The thinking man's gangster, Meyer Lansky's ability to re-member complex numbers without writing them down earned him the title of "accountant to the mob". The son of Jewish Polish immigrants, Lansky (1902–83) grew up toughing it out in Manhattan's Lower East Side. Lansky worked hard to promote a non-violent image, but as a mobster in the 1920s he and Bugsy Siegel organized the brutal Bugs and Meyer gang, a forerunner of Murder Inc., said to be the most violent of the Prohibition mobs in the American East, available for beatings and contract killings known as "slammings" and "rub-outs". Biographer Robert Lacey described Lansky's "hard, sinister power", wielded in spite of his underwhelming physical presence; at a very short 5ft 3in, Lansky wore heel-lifts, but he was totally unfazed by bigger men. "He was just cold-blooded," one Miami cop remembered. "There wasn't an ounce of fear in his eyes." Lansky was the brains, sophistication, and hot money of orga-nized crime, and for 60 years remained virtually untouchable by the law. But in retirement in Miami Beach, Lansky found himself targeted by federal agents trying to uncover his fortune, estimated at between $100m and $300m. In 1970, Lansky was the subject of this unflattering profile by William Schulz, an associate editor of Reader's Digest *magazine.*

"**A** perfect gentleman," says a wealthy neighbour at the posh Seasons South, an ocean-front high-rise in Miami Beach. "A quiet guy with simple tastes," observes a long-time associate. A "retired investor" he says of himself on his tax forms. And 67-year-old Meyer Lansky acts the part. A slightly built man with thinning grey hair and a pinched face, he dresses conservatively in custom-made suits. He lives quietly with his second wife, shuns night life, tips modestly. He drives a rented Chevrolet and his idea of fun is a leisurely walk along the Miami beach front, his miniature Tibetan Shih Tzu dog "Bruiser" at his heels.

But there is another side to Meyer Lansky. To a veteran New York prosecutor he is a "ruthless mobster whose brains and guile have made him a major underworld figure since the Roaring Twenties." To the *Wall Street Journal* he is a financial genius who "has shaped the organized crime syndicate into a well disciplined operation." And to a leading government Mafia expert, he is Public Enemy No. 1.

Government authorities put Lansky's wealth at more than $100 million, almost none of it in his own name. His holdings include gambling casinos from the Caribbean to the Middle East, New York clothiers, New England race tracks, Miami hotels – and millions upon millions in foreign banks and US stocks.

Born Maier Suchowljanksy in Grodno, Poland, Lansky emigrated to Brooklyn at the age of nine. He dropped out of school after finishing eighth grade (he earned As and Bs on his report card), and joined a gang of thieves on Manhattan's Lower East Side. He graduated quickly to the big time, and in the late 1920s, during Prohibition, hooked up with another young hood, Bugsy Siegel, to form the Bugs and Meyer Mob. Their gunmen guarded illicit booze shipments between Chicago and the East Coast. They were partners – with Joe Adonis and Frank Costello, rising stars in the Mafia – in at least three illegal distilleries. Their criminal interests grew to include casinos, narcotics and a nationwide bookie network.

During the early 1930s, *La Cosa Nostra* (LCN), or the Mafia, formed a "Commission" to bring its warring factions under a supreme council. As a non-Italian, and a Jew, Lansky was ineligible for LCN membership. But his power was such that he became an *ex-officio* member of the commission. His financial genius was eagerly sought by LCN big shots. They, in turn, allowed him to expand his empire.

Working with an outsider is one thing. Trusting him is another. Always, LCN kept a "watchbird" with Lansky, just to make sure that his split with them was honest. For many years, the Lansky watcher was Joe Adonis, a *capo* (captain) in the "family" of New York's Vito Genovese. When Adonis was deported in 1956, the job was taken over by Vincent (Jimmy Blue Eyes) Alo, another Genovese *capo*. Alo remains one of Lansky's closest companions.

Lansky was a very rich man by the end of World War Two. He and his brother Jake ran 24-hour-a-day casinos in Florida's wide-open Broward County, north of Miami. His gambling dens and lotteries boomed in New York, New Jersey and Lousiana. In Las Vegas, Lansky was building a multi-million-dollar casino, to be run by Bugsy Siegel.

The early 1950s brought a temporary setback. US Senate crime-busters, led by Tennessee's Sen. Este Kefauver, exposed the dimensions of Lansky-financed corruption in Florida and New York. The Broward County casinos were shuttered, and Lansky received the only jail term of his long criminal career – three months for operating the plush Arrowhead Inn, an illegal gambling emporium in Saratoga, NY.

But in 1952, Fulgencio Batista, back in power as dictator of Cuba after several years in Florida exile, had laws passed giving Lansky and his associates a complete monopoly on Cuban gambling. The purpose: to convert Havana into a glittering mecca for US tourists. After Batista was overthrown in 1959, the mob tried to work out an "understanding" with Castro. But the end came, a Lansky intimate has disclosed, when Che Guevara sent his gun-toting men into the casino counting rooms to make sure that the regime was getting an honest tally on the taxes due. Lansky & Co. thereupon fell back to Nevada, where the counting rooms were, in the words of one operator, "sacred, inviolate," off limits to tax collectors and government agents.

In Las Vegas, the Lansky Group – Lansky, a few associates and front men – controlled at least four major casinos: the Flamingo, the Fremont, the Horseshoe and the Sands. Three times a day, at the end of each eight-hour shift, the casino chiefs totted up their winnings. Government authorities cheerfully took their word on what taxes they had coming. Thus, the stage was set for a killing.

In 1960, the Lansky Group began a process known as "skimming". The FBI discovered what was going on when agents bugged the Fremont Hotel in 1962. In each casino, huge sums of money – as much as $280,000 a month – were simply lopped off the top of the winnings. No taxes, state or federal, were paid on the skim. It just vanished from the counting rooms, carried by teams of bagmen to Lansky in Miami. Lansky kept the lion's share – approximately 60 percent. The rest was delivered to New Jersey's Gerardo (Jerry) Catena, a *capo* in the Genovese family, which has long shared racket profits with the Lansky Group.

Week after week, FBI agents pieced together details. On 6 January 1963, for instance, they listened as two members of the Lansky Group, Edward Levinson and Ed Torres, discussed the delivery of $115,650 to the boss. Worried that G-men were tailing Benjamin Sigelbaum, a long-time Lansky aide, Levinson suggested that the money be carried by someone else – Ida Devine, the matronly wife of Las Vegas racketeer Irving (Niggy) Devine, another Lansky associate.

Torres: You want to give Ida the money?

Levinson: She'll go down on the train.

Torres: She'll never leave the stateroom. So give it to her.

Torres: Safe as could be.

On 8 January, Ida Devine packed the money in a black bag and left for Chicago, where she switched trains and continued on to Miami. She delivered the package and returned to Nevada – all under the watchful eye of federal agents.

By the middle of 1963, Attorney General Robert Kennedy was waging all-out war on the skimmers. Couriers were tailed, tax agents pored through casino records. With the heat on, the Lansky Group sold out its Las Vegas hotels and turned its attention to the sunny Bahamas. Legalised casinos opened there in 1964. Whereupon month after month, couriers carried suitcases stuffed with illegal skim across Florida Strait to Lansky and his cohorts.

A government investigation of Lansky's Bahamian interests alerted authorites to his latest sleight of hand, by which "black money" was transformed into legitimate capital, through the use of Swiss banks. An expansive Benny Sigelbaum explained how it worked. "Let's say," said Sigelbaum, "that Mr X puts a big sum in a numbered account in Switzerland, then wants to invest it in the stock market. The bank buys the stock in its own name. The dividends are credited to account of Mr X. He's got an interest in the company, but his name never appears on the books or records as a stockholder."

The same scheme, completely legal in Switzerland, shielded

members of the Lansky Group when their deposits served as collateral for Swiss bank loans to enterprises in America. The records show only that the loans came from a Swiss bank. What isn't shown is the Lansky skim that made the loan possible.

It has been more than three decades since Lansky helped create the national crime syndicate. Of the mob's founding fathers, he alone survives. The others – from Frank Costello and Joe Adonis to Louis (Lepke) Buchalter and Bugsy Siegel – have been murdered, toppled from power, jailed or deported. How has this frail little refugee shown such remarkable staying power? Here are some clues:

Despite his carefully nurtured image of peaceful legitimacy, Lansky is by nature as violent as any LCN terrorist. But he learned early to delegate the dirty work to others. In 1928, for instance, he attempted the liquidation of John Barrett, an underling he believed to be a police informer. The unsuspecting Barrett was taken for a ride, and Lansky opened fire at point-blank range. He succeeded only in grazing Barrett, who dived from the car and was found by police. Charged with "suspicion of homicide", Lansky arranged for the delivery to Barrett's hospital room of a roast chicken stuffed with strychnine. Barrett, who tossed the poisoned fowl out the window, got the message. He refused to testify, and Lansky walked out of jail a free man.

From that day on, Lansky left the strong-arm tactics to trusted lieutenants. In 1931, his hired gunmen mowed down the No. 1 Mafia boss, Salvatore Maranzano, enabling the Young Turks – including Lansky and Lucky Luciano – to consolidate national control of the rackets. In 1947, Lansky's "hit-men" executed his long-time partner, Bugsy Siegel, less than 24 hours after the two had argued violently about Siegel's management of the Flamingo.

In Nevada, the casino skimmers shelled out "campaign contributions" to political candidates and to officeholders, to big shots and to small fry. On 9 November 1962, Ed Levinson, of the Lansky Group, sat down with an aide in the bugged Fremont Hotel to fix the amounts of some of their contributions: $1,000 to Sen. Alan Bible, $500 to Rep. Walter S Baring, $500 to the Mayor of Las Vegas, $500 to a candidate for lieutenant governor, $300 to a legislative hopeful, $300 to a county commissioner, $200 to a candidate for justice of the peace.

Other casinos made similar contributions. One hotel reportedly poured $20,000 into the campaign coffers of then Gov. Grant

Sawyer – who later echoed Sen. Howard Cannon's denunciation of
the FBI's "Gestapo-like" bugging of the skimmers. Cannon even
went to President Johnson to protest the bugging. Asked if he
received campaign contributions from Levinson and other casino
operators, Cannon said he could not recall, but would be "disappointed" if he had not.

Lansky apparently has allies in many places. On 24 April 1963,
the FBI delivered a top-secret report on the Las Vegas skimmers to
the office of Attorney General Kennedy. Based on electronic
surveillance, it spelled out the theft of millions of dollars. On
27 April, agents listening to the Fremont bug were astounded to
hear Levinson and Devine leafing through the FBI report, page by
page, reading it aloud. Levinson exclaimed, "My God, Niggy,
they even know about Ida."

Government officials have still not determined how the report
travelled from Kennedy's office to the skimmers in less than 72
hours. But this was not the only such happening. On 23 August
1963, Ben Sigelbaum walked into the plush Miami offices of
attorney Alvin I. Malnik, one of Lansky's trusted money-movers.
"Greetings and salutations," he said, tossing a document on
Malnik's desk. "This is from the Justice Department."

Indeed it was – a top-secret report that jeopardized the identity
of a key government informer.

Lansky himself has dropped an occasional hint about his influence. Once he bragged of arranging the transfer of a federal
investigator "who was giving me a bad time".

Lansky's greatest protection is undoubtedly The Group – the
trusted associates who surround and insulate him, who hold his
property in their names, carry his millions to secret Swiss banks,
and who balance his books at the Eden Roc hotel's Cabana 169.
Among them are such men as Hyman Siegel, 65, a heavy-fisted
third-grade dropout whose criminal record dates back to the
1920s, oversees Lansky's investments in the New York garment
district and his interests in a number of crooked unions. Blumen-
field, alias Izzy Bloom, alias Kid Cann, long-time Minneapolis
gambling boss, has been convicted of white slavery, tax-evasion
and bootlegging. He fronts for Lansky in at least four Miami Beach
hotels – the Singapore, the Aztec, the Kimberly and the Hawaiian
Isle.

In recent years, Lansky has pumped new blood into The Group.
Alvin Malnik is an example. Recruited out of the University of

Miami Law School, Malnik is known to his neighbours as a successful young attorney, investor and socialite. He has a lovely family and belongs to the best clubs. But his real job is that of a Lansky banker. Accompanied by Lansky bagmen, he flies regularly to Canada, meets with Swiss contacts and arranges the handling of skim. His future is predictable. "Members of the Lansky Group have lifetime contracts, with no cancellation clause," says one federal agent. "If they get tired or afraid, the mob has its own way of closing out the association – permanently."

The illegal and untaxed enterprises of Meyer Lansky deny the government millions in needed levies. His infiltration of legitimate business constitutes a deadly poison in the nation's economic bloodstream which affects every taxpayer. As a leading lawman says: "This man represents what we're talking about when we use those familiar words, 'public menace'."

Federal authorities are currently exploring every avenue that could lead to nailing Lansky. His tax returns are examined and re-examined. US officials have applied pressure to open the secret records of Swiss banks. Perhaps one of Lansky's silent associates will decide to talk. Perhaps Lansky himself will slip up. Fortunately for him, the FBI tapes spelling out the great skimming conspiracy are inadmissible as court evidence. Until Meyer Lansky *is* brought to justice, his blood-and-theft rise to riches is a story that should shame and concern every US citizen.

Shortly after this article appeared, in 1970, Lansky moved to Israel but was denied citizenship and wound up back in the US. He underwent several federal trials as well as heart bypass surgery. In 1976, having beaten all charges, he finally retired to Miami Beach, and died in 1983, leaving a trust fund for his wife and handicapped son that proved to be almost worthless.

Public Enemy No. 1
(*John Dillinger*)

John Toland

Like the old-style outlaws of the wild West, but toting Tommy guns instead of six-shooters, John Dillinger (1903–34) blazed a trail of death and destruction across America, propelling himself, in the space of just over a year, from obscurity to national infamy. Insanely reckless, contemptuous of careful planning, Dillinger and his gang blasted their way into bank after bank, killing tellers, guards, cops, and innocent bystanders without hesitation or remorse. His wild career soon became the stuff of legend, glittering with breathtaking escapes and stunning reappearances, crowned by his final betrayal at the hands of a woman, stoked by improbable stories of his sexuality and rumours that he may, after all, survived the police ambush that put an end to his villainy.

Born in Indiana, Dillinger was a petty crook before his metamorphosis into a public menace, bursting out on a crime spree with a gang of gunmen drawn from the ranks of the most vicious killers of the day. Jailed for multiple bank robberies in Lima, Ohio, Dillinger was freed by an armed band of his friends, among them Harry Pierpont and Charles Makley, who shot the local sheriff dead. Pierpont and Makley were caught, but Dillinger, with his girlfriend Billie Frechette, shot his way out of a police trap; the Chicago authorities promptly slapped his name on their list of public enemies and organized a 40-man Dillinger Squad to bring him in. In January 1934, Dillinger led *another gang who stole $20,000 from a suburban bank in East Chicago, Indiana, killing a cop called O'Malley as they fled, taking the bank president hostage and using him as a human shield. As the bullets flew, Dillinger and another outlaw, John Hamilton, were wounded, but the gang escaped, only for Dillinger to be arrested in Tucson, Arizona, where the fugitives had regrouped.*

Extradited back to Indiana for trial, Dillinger hired a self-taught lawyer called Louis Piquett. Piquett's defence strategy was to bribe a prominent local judge to smuggle a gun into Lake County jail in the sleepy town of Crown Point. Dillinger was housed in a newly built wing, said to be escape-proof. Half a dozen barred doors and 50 guards stood between him and freedom. Locals joked that not even Houdini could escape from Crown Point now. But Dillinger proved them wrong, as the American historian John Toland (1912–2004) recounts. Toland won the Pulitzer Prize for his history of the Japanese empire before and during World War Two, and his 1976 biography of Adolf Hitler became a huge best-seller. His vivid chronicle of Dillinger's career includes this account of the notorious outlaw's daring prison breakout in March 1934.

D illinger was planning to escape the next day. He had $14 and a gun. That was all. He didn't even know the complicated layout of the building but he was sure it wouldn't take him long to find out when the time came.

The following morning it was raining. After breakfast Dillinger and the fourteen other prisoners in the felony cell block began exercising in the second-floor corridors of the new part of the jail. Another routine day had started.

A few minutes after 9:00 a.m. Sam Cahoon, an elderly attendant, unlocked the barred door leading into the cell block and let a group of trusties – trusted prisoners – enter for the morning clean-up. Cahoon was a good-natured, well-intentioned man who knew more about his jail than most attendants, having often served time here for drunkenness. Soon he would be characterized by a judge as "good for nothing" and "not a responsible person".

Dillinger casually walked up to the unsuspecting Cahoon, rammed a gun against his stomach, and nodded toward one of the opened cells. "Get in quick or I'll kill you."

Cahoon didn't move but the trusties obeyed the order. "I don't want to kill anyone," said Dillinger quietly. "Now you do as I tell you." He shoved the resisting Cahoon into the cell with the others and, keeping one hand on the gun in his pocket, he began questioning Cahoon.

Once he had a mental picture of the building's layout, Dillinger brought Cahoon to the stairs leading down to the old jail on the first floor. Dillinger cautiously descended a few steps, then looked carefully up the corridor of the old jail. He saw a man. "Call that fellow back here," he said.

Cahoon did, and Deputy Sheriff Ernest Blunk, the fingerprint expert and an appointee of Judge Murray, approached without suspicion. Dillinger jumped from behind Cahoon and pointed his gun at Blunk. He now brought the two hostages back up to the second-floor jail and locked them in with the others.

From Blunk he learned that Warden Lou Baker, the only experienced jailer at Crown Point and the man most likely to prevent the escape, was downstairs in his office. Dillinger led Blunk back down the stairs to the corridor and said, "Call Baker."

"Come on, Lou," shouted Blunk. "Someone back here wants you."

Baker, a slight man, was an inch shorter than Dillinger. Before the Depression he had been a jeweler and his favourite joke was, "I used to sell watches, now I watch cells." When he heard Blunk he was at his desk in the jail office near the front of the building. He walked back to Blunk, who was standing at the foot of the stairs leading up to the new jail. Suddenly Dillinger grabbed him from behind by the collar, poked a gun in his back, and told him to walk upstairs.

Dillinger felt more relieved once the warden was locked up but there were still about thirty other guards in the building, and he now forced Blunk to decoy three of these, one by one, from the outer rooms. Before he could make a break for freedom, however, he first needed more firepower. After some questioning he learned there were machine guns in the warden's office and once more forced Blunk to go downstairs with him. They crept up the corridor of the old jail toward the front of the building and finally came to the receiving room, which was separated from Baker's office by a barred door. Dillinger stuck his gun through the bars at the turnkey, who unlocked the door without any argument. Incredibly enough he was a trusty, in for petty larceny.

As Dillinger stepped in, he saw a National Guardsman standing just beyond the office and, in a whisper, told the turnkey to face the wall with hands up, then motioned Blunk to call the soldier.

The unsuspecting Guardsman entered, to find himself facing a gun. Dillinger picked up two machine guns lying on the window sill. Now he was ready to escape – and freedom lay only a few feet ahead, out the front door of the big building.

But a dozen guards were stationed there and Dillinger knew it. He would escape the long way – out the rear.

His luck held and the way was still clear as he marched Blunk, the turnkey, and the Guardsman back upstairs to the new jail.

Once there, he gave one of the machine guns to Herbert Youngblood, a big Negro from Gary awaiting trial for murder, and asked if anyone else wanted to go with them. Only two inmates accepted the invitation. Dillinger led the group to the rear of the building but when they came to the kitchen door, he ordered Blunk to go in first. Here they surprised three farmer vigilantes sitting at a table having coffee. Dillinger ordered them to join the party, took two of their raincoats, and quietly led everyone down the stairs to the jail garage. Youngblood brought up the rear.

At the bottom of the stairs the three vigilantes ducked into a washroom and were followed by the two would-be escapees. Dillinger didn't care – they were, in effect, locking themselves up where they could do no mischief. He was too busy capturing an assorted group in the garage: the jail cook, kitchen helpers, several trusties, and Warden Baker's mother-in-law, matron for the women prisoners.

Dillinger ordered the matron into a Buick. When he saw the keys weren't in the car, he asked Blunk where they were. The frightened fingerprint man said he thought Warden Baker had them.

Dillinger was once more only a few feet from freedom but he could think only of the Buick – it seemed such a perfect means of escape. He decided to press his luck and go all the way back to the jail. Leaving Youngblood to guard the hostages, he retraced his steps upstairs and asked the incarcerated warden for the car keys. Baker pretended he didn't know where they were and Dillinger, realizing he had already wasted too much time, hustled back down to the garage. Now all he could do was pull the ignition wires from the police cars and try to find other transportation.

Just above, in the warden's apartment, Mrs Lou Baker heard a strange rattling noise. She went to the clothes closet, looked through a peek hole, and saw her husband rattling the bars of a cell.

"Irene," he called, "has the car left the garage?" She didn't know what he was talking about. "Call for help. John Dillinger is out."

She picked up the phone connected with the jail switch-board but for some reason there was no answer. Then she remembered her mother, the matron, had just gone down to the garage. She went to the bedroom window overlooking the street behind the jail, saw a mailman and shouted, "My God, John Dillinger is out!"

He looked up in puzzlement.

She ran down into the garage and saw Deputy Blunk with a man holding a machine gun. "John Dillinger is out," she told them. The man with the gun walked toward her. "Oh, no," she said. "You're not Dillinger."

Dillinger took her arm. If he hadn't, she would have fallen.

"Mrs Baker," said Blunk, "you do as he tells you."

Dillinger led her to the laundry where Youngblood was guarding her mother and the kitchen help as well as several trusties who were debating whether they too should escape. Mrs Baker ended their parley when she told them the building was surrounded by heavily armed guards.

Dillinger put on one raincoat, handed Youngblood the other. Then he pushed Blunk out of the side door and followed him to the street. Behind him he left the escape-proof jail and a score of locked-up jailers. He was pleased with himself – even Jesse James had never put on such a one-man exhibition.

There was not a single guard patrolling the rear of the building. Nor, at the moment, were there any on the right side of the jail. Otherwise they would have seen the trio walk behind the Criminal Courts building and into the back door of the Ford Garage.

Blunk and Dillinger approached Ed Saager, a mechanic working on a generator. The sight of a gun was common in Crown Point and even when Dillinger asked which was the fastest car, Saager thought they were a posse.

"The V-8 Ford." It happened to be Mrs Holley's car.

Dillinger told Saager to get in the car but the mechanic said he was working. "Better do as he asks," said Blunk. Saager, imagining he was being deputized, resentfully got into the back seat.

"Get in and drive, Blunk," said Dillinger, climbing in front. Youngblood silently got in the back seat with Saager.

Robert Volk, a mailman, had just parked his truck inside the garage. Recognizing Dillinger, he ducked behind the truck as the Ford started moving. A salesman came out of the showroom.

"Keep still," warned Volk. "It's Dillinger." The salesman froze. After the car lunged out of the garage and speeded north on Main Street, Volk picked up a phone and called the Gary police. Their reaction angered him: they said only that they would check into the matter. He ran to the first floor of the Criminal Courts building.

"Dillinger's escaped!" he said.

The armed guard said he was nuts and shooed him away. Volk ran across the alley to the jail and pressed a bell. There was no answer. Finally one of Estill's deputies looked out a third-story window of the courthouse and asked what was going on.

"Dillinger's escaped!"

At Dillinger's direction, Blunk drove through a red light in the middle of the business district but there were no police on hand to notice. Once out of town, Dillinger turned, grinned at Saager, and briefly showed a pistol. "It's a wooden gun. That's what got me out." Saager at last realized this was Dillinger, not a lawman. The gun looked real enough to him.

Dillinger nudged Blunk. "You wouldn't think a guy could make a break with a pea shooter like this, would you?" He laughed and put the gun – a real one – in his pocket.

They continued on a zigzag course into Illinois, stopping only once – to unscrew a red police light from the front of the car and put chains on the two rear tires so they could navigate the back roads turned muddy from the rain.

As they drove on, Dillinger sang, "I'm heading for the last roundup." Youngblood didn't join in; so far he hadn't said a word. When Dillinger noticed there were no telephone poles and therefore no way to report their position, he told Blunk to stop. He handed Saager $4, shook hands with the two hostages, and said apologetically, "I'd give you guys more but that's all I can spare."

He directed Youngblood to hide between the seats – together they could be too easily identified. Then he grinned at the hostages standing on the road and said, "I'll remember you at Christmas." As the car churned off through the mud at a conservative speed, chains clonking, he waved.

When Prosecutor Robert Estill drove up to the Criminal Courts building not long after the escape, a deputy sheriff shouted to him,

"Dillinger's got away!" He found Mrs Holley in tears. No one apparently was in charge and guards stood outside talking to spectators. Estill immediately filed charges against Blunk and Cahoon, ordered them arrested. He wouldn't know for some time that an hour after the escape only three phone calls had been placed from the jail – to local police stations. Apparently it never occurred to anyone to inform the state police.

In Chicago Captain Stege, who had just disbanded the Dillinger Squad, had to alert it again to be on the watch for a Ford V-8, license number 679,929. "What's the use of arresting Dillinger if we can't keep him in jail," he told a reporter. "I'm sending squads all over the city to nab him if he tries to cross the Indiana border. But even if we do get him, it will probably be the same thing over again. I'm disgusted."

When Dillinger drove into Chicago that afternoon no one stopped Mrs Holley's Ford. It seemed only a fitting climax to the day's mistakes that the wrong license number had been passed on to Stege by an excited Crown Point official.

The first thing Dillinger did in Chicago was to phone Piquett and tell him to be at a designated location on Belmont Avenue at 4.00 p.m. He wanted money.

Piquett found Dillinger lolling in the driver's seat of the car. Youngblood was still crouched in the rear.

That night newspapers all over the country ran headline stories of the wooden gun escape. A nation, fascinated by Dillinger's impudence when he was brought back from Tucson, was now outwardly appalled. Secretly, however, many were titillated by this dramatic and unexpected turn of events; it was a welcome relief from the realities of the Depression.

When an *Indianapolis Times* reporter told the news to the elder Dillinger tears rolled down his cheeks and he said hoarsely, "And he got away!" He alternated between smiles and tears. Finally the man, who had once thought his son was hopeless, said with a touch of pride, "Well, he was pretty tricky. He's no fool."

The day's events certainly had proved that John Dillinger was far from a fool. Yet he had committed one small mistake: driven a stolen car across a state line. He had stolen other autos before he joined Pierpont and nothing had ever happened but now he had violated this federal statute in a sheriff's car and with the eyes of the world on him. This was all the FBI needed. Now they could join the hunt.

By Sunday morning, 4 March, there was no doubt at all that Dillinger was America's Public Enemy Number 1. People imagined they saw him everywhere. Reports came from dozens of towns and cities in ten states, some as far east as Pennsylvania.

If the rest of the United States was fascinated and even entertained by the escape, the citizens of Dillinger's home state certainly were not. They had been humiliated and demanded an immediate investigation. The hunt for scapegoats began. A former judge of Circuit Court said Dillinger could not have escaped without help outside the jail. "In my opinion the entire prison organization at Crown Point needs a cleaning out." A Criminal Court judge suspected that "corruption and cowardice" played a major part in the affair. A former U.S. District Attorney said, "John Dillinger's escape is one of those things which should never have happened. It is disgusting."

The Republicans, of course, blamed Governor McNutt. Hadn't he paroled Dillinger in the first place? McNutt in turn ordered Attorney General Lutz to conduct a thorough investigation. "The nation is horrified and shocked at the escape of this notorious bank robber," said Lutz, "and I am surprised that Lake County officials let him get away."

Those Wisconsin authorities, recently accused by Lutz of conspiring with Dillinger in Tucson "under conditions smelling of bribery and corruption," could not hide their delight at the Indiana Attorney General's embarrassment. One said, "In view of what happened [at Crown Point], I wonder on whose side the bad odor lies."

In Chicago Captain Stege of the Dillinger Squad said, "How in the name of common sense could a prisoner go through six barred doors to freedom? . . . But I told them it would happen. I pleaded with Governor McNutt's secretary to put him in the penitentiary.

"Now bright and early Monday Dillinger will rob a bank to get funds. Then when he gets together with John Hamilton, the two of them will raid a police station some place and get guns and ammunition. Then maybe they'll come back, to Chicago for another game of tag."

It was a remarkably accurate guess. At that moment Dillinger was in Chicago trying to form a new gang, so he could rob a bank on Monday or Tuesday at the latest – but he was having his troubles. While Pierpont and Makley had carefully picked their gang over the years, he needed money at once and had no time to be selective.

For his first lieutenant he chose Hamilton, who appeared so steady but had shown at East Chicago that he could be as reckless as Dillinger himself. Their selection for chief torpedo was Lester Gillis, the sour-natured young man, better known as Baby Face Nelson, whom Pierpont and Mary Kinder had considered such a poor touring companion on the trip to Tennessee. He was a stocky five foot five and his innocent, boyish face hid a vicious temper. He was the first of Dillinger's associates who enjoyed using a gun. Dillinger, Hamilton, and Pierpont had all killed rather than be captured but Nelson, like the Barrows, was addicted to violence and had only one thing in common with Dillinger. He liked women and was rarely without the company of his pretty wife, Helen – or an attractive substitute.

Baby Face had been brought up in the Chicago packing-house district and graduated from stealing cars for thrills to crime for profit. After serving a term in the St Charles School for Boys he began to rob banks, was caught and sent to Joliet. While returning to prison from trial, he escaped and fled to California, where he became a bootlegger. But this paid poorly and he had recently returned to his home town.

Dillinger had one more good contact – his old companion at Pendleton and Michigan City, Homer Van Meter, who was then in St Paul and had been robbing banks in the Northwest for several months. Dillinger, Billie Frechette, Hamilton, and Nelson drove to the Twin Cities on 4 March and within a few hours of their arrival Van Meter introduced them to Eddie Green, an associate of Harry Sawyer and well-known as a jug marker – one who knows which banks to rob. Green already knew the bank they should hit first and it was in Sioux Falls, South Dakota. He also could supply the sixth member of the team – an expert machine gunner named Tommy Carroll.

Dillinger suggested they follow the same procedure as that used at Racine. Hamilton vouched for its efficiency and the others quickly agreed. That is, all but Nelson, who had his own theories of robbing banks – he liked coming through the front door shooting. Van Meter laughed sarcastically and the short, squat Nelson moved toward him. For a moment it appeared as if the gang would disintegrate as fast as it had been organized but Dillinger stepped between the two good-humoredly.

Though the crisis was over, Dillinger was rightly concerned – trouble could break out at any moment between two such temperamental antagonists, but there was nothing he could do about the situation now. He desperately needed cash; not only for himself but for Pierpont, Makley, and Clark, who were waiting in the Lima jail to be tried for the murder of Sheriff Sarber.

The following morning, 6 March, the new Dillinger gang drove into Sioux Falls in a new green Packard, and a few minutes before ten parked in front of the imposing Security National Bank and Trust Company.

A pretty bank stenographer jokingly remarked to a clerk, "There's a bunch of holdup men." The clerk was not joking when he replied he didn't like the way they looked and, as they got out of the big car, he put a finger on the burglar alarm button in readiness.

It was a cold, clear day. Hamilton remained near the Packard. Carroll, a happy-go-lucky ex-boxer, stationed himself in front of the bank, a machine gun hidden under his overcoat, while Dillinger led the other three inside. Suddenly Nelson, right behind him, pulled out his machine gun and began shouting in a shrill voice, "This is a holdup. Lay on the floor."

The clerk pushed the button and the burglar alarm on the side of the building clanged. Dillinger paid no attention to the noise and walked into the cage of the head teller, Robert Dargen. Laying his automatic on the counter, he completely ignored Dargen and began to scoop up the bills. Dargen debated about grabbing the gun, decided not to, and a moment later Dillinger asked, "Is that all of it?" It was. Dillinger now escorted the head teller back to the vaults. But Dargen had trouble with the complicated five-way combination of the money vault.

Van Meter ran up, jammed a machine gun into his side and said, "Open it up, you son of a bitch, or I'll cut you in two."

Dargen said he would if Van Meter would take the gun out of his ribs. Dillinger stood by calmly but the tall, skinny bandit talked and threatened constantly, until the door finally swung open. Van Meter eagerly pulled out about $14,000, then ordered Dargen to open the next vault.

The head teller said he didn't have the combination and that it contained only bonds. Van Meter immediately began shouting for the bank's president.

At the police station the desk sergeant got a telephone call about some trouble at the bank but the caller didn't mention that the alarm was ringing and the sergeant, figuring some drunk was bothering the customers, sent a patrolman to quell the disturbance. When this man walked into the bank a few minutes later, he was disarmed and told to lie on the floor with the customers.

Baby Face Nelson was hopping around the lobby like an enraged bantam rooster. He wanted revenge on the one who had set off the alarm. Bounding up to the front of a cage, he stuck his machine gun at the teller and said, "I'm going to kill the man who hit the alarm, and I know you did it!"

The teller argued that the alarm button in his cage was up and if he had pushed the alarm, the button would now be down. Dillinger, still behind the cages, called out, "Forget it and get the money."

The next moment Nelson looked through the side window and saw a man in a khaki uniform getting out of a car. It was an off-duty policeman, Hale Keith, drawn by the growing crowd around the bank. The alarm was still ringing as Keith hitched up his belt, a habit of his.

Nelson, thinking Keith was going for a gun, hurdled a waist-high railing, jumped up on a desk, and began firing through the plate-glass window. He saw Keith fall, then hopped off the desk and shouted, "I got one of them!" His face was yellowish, his eyes wild.

Out front, Carroll was standing in the middle of the street. He had already captured and lined up two carloads of police, including the chief, without firing a shot. A fascinated crowd of about a thousand was pressing around the bank, filling the streets.

Melvin Sells, Sheriff of Minnehaha County, was in his office at the courthouse talking to a court reporter when the phone rang and some man asked if they had any guns. Sells, thinking it was a joke, reckoned they had a few.

"Better bring them up to 9th and Main." The informant hung up.

Sells said he thought he was being kidded but he handed the reporter a machine gun and took a rifle. They walked somewhat sheepishly out of the courthouse, half expecting some practical joker to appear.

Several blocks from the bank Sells saw a mob, with hundreds peering down from upper-story windows. It looked like a fight. Then Sells saw Carroll standing in the center of the streetcar tracks, brandishing a machine gun at a line of police officers. The sheriff and reporter headed for the second floor of a hotel, hoping to get a clear shot at the robbers.

By now they had collected over $49,000 and were rounding up some ten employees as hostages. Those who were too slow got a sharp kick from Van Meter, who was still chattering. The hostages were ordered to surround the gangsters. As the group neared the front door, Nelson, who had wanted to enter with guns blazing, decided to exit, at least, on his own terms. Quite unnecessarily he shot the glass out of the front door.

Once outside, still acting as if he were the leader, he selected five girl hostages and told them to mount the running boards of the bandit car. One said she couldn't hold on and was allowed to step off.

As the Packard started south with the four girls and Leo Olson, a teller, riding outside, Patrolman Harley Chrisman, who had just found a rifle in a hardware store, shot a hole in the car's radiator. When the motor sputtered after a block, the Packard stopped and the hostages jumped off the running boards.

"Come on back here," shouted one of the robbers, firing a shot in the air – and everyone hopped back. One girl told Olson she couldn't hang on and he put an arm around her. Somehow the Packard was started again and a few minutes later it turned right, then left. A car containing Sheriff Sells and three other lawmen was now in pursuit but still out of sight, half a mile to the rear.

Olson, who had always imagined a getaway car would careen at top speed, marveled at the Packard's leisurely, careful pace of less than twenty-five miles an hour. The car turned into Dakota Avenue, slowing cautiously to pass a milk wagon drawn by horses. At a dip in the street it again slowed and before long they were on Route 77, the main highway to the south. There were no police yet in view but Dillinger knew they would soon arrive and he told the driver to stop, so that large roofing nails could be scattered on the road.

"The girls are freezing," called out Olson.

"Well, come in the car," said Dillinger. The four shivering girls crammed into the back seat, sitting on the laps of three robbers.

"What about me?" asked Olson. In spite of the cold, his shirt was soaked with perspiration. When Dillinger told him, "You're through," he stepped to the road, thinking he would be shot.

But Dillinger merely told the driver to get moving. After four miles the damaged radiator began to steam violently. The robbers waved down a Dodge and told the owner, a farmer, to get into the fields until they were out of sight. While the four hostage girls waited fearfully on the road, gasoline cans were transferred from the disabled Packard to the Dodge.

Only one car passed. A woman driving south slowed down when she saw the two stalled cars, thinking there had been an accident. She called to the four girls standing on the highway, warning them they'd catch their death of cold without coats. They hadn't even realized they were shivering.

At that moment Sheriff Sells and his three companions, who had been delayed by punctures from the roofing nails, approached. They stopped a hundred yards from the three parked cars but were afraid to fire for fear of hitting the girls on the road and simply watched the robbers scramble into the farmer's Dodge. They saw Nelson make a move to grab a hostage, then saw Dillinger pull him, protesting, into the Dodge.

Now an all-out chase began with several exchanges of fire whenever the police drew within range. It led almost into Iowa but within two hours the pursuers lost the trail. By this time Dillinger was heading back east and before midnight arrived in Minneapolis. The gang went up to Green's apartment to count the money. Nelson, who had been incessantly complaining because Dillinger hadn't stopped to let him get a good shot, began arguing with Van Meter about who had contributed most to the success of the operation. Nelson insisted that he had saved everyone by shooting Keith through the side window while Van Meter claimed credit for getting the head teller to open his vault.

The bickering stopped when Nelson saw Green laying the money on a table in six equal piles. Grabbing his machine gun, he wanted to know who the hell Green thought he was.

"Let Lester count it," said Dillinger diplomatically.

Nelson scooped up the money and piled it on the floor. Like a petulant child who insists on marking the rules of every game, he slowly, methodically made six heaps, the others watching in silence.

Once Dillinger had his share – about $7,600 in currency and bonds – he phoned Louis Piquett that he now could help Pierpont and the others pay their attorney and suggested that Mary Kinder, recently freed after being held twenty-eight days in the Indianapolis jail on suspicion of aiding the Michigan City break, be sent at once for the money. She could be trusted.

For the first time Dillinger had been the leader in a major robbery but, ironically, the law refused to believe he had even been in Sioux Falls. The few witnesses who said they could identify him were not believed and the possibility was even ridiculed by the man who headed the combined inquiry, the chief of the northwestern bureau of the Burns Detective Agency.

Bancorporation, a holding company for over a hundred banks in the Northwest, didn't agree, their underworld contacts insisting not only that Dillinger was the leader but that the new mob was going to strike another bank in the same area soon. Explicit warnings were sent out to banks in Minnesota, South Dakota, and Iowa.

Bancorporation was correct: Dillinger was planning another robbery. Green and Van Meter were scheduled to leave that night for Mason City, Iowa, where they would room at the local YMCA and spend the day wandering around the neighborhood of the First National Bank.

A few hours before their departure Mary Kinder arrived from Indianapolis, called the phone number Piquett had given her, and Van Meter made arrangements to meet her several hours later on a deserted road. The two had little regard for each other since Mary shared Pierpont's low opinion of the erratic Van Meter. He told her curtly that Dillinger was too tired to come himself but she didn't believe it. And when Van Meter added, "Johnnie doesn't want to see you because he's afraid of women," she believed it even less.

She said she wouldn't leave without seeing Johnnie and Van Meter finally admitted that Dillinger hadn't been identified at Sioux Falls and wanted to stay under cover. He handed her an envelope from Dillinger containing $2,000 in bills, a good part of his cash share of the robbery.

In Lima Pierpont's trial was being conducted in a carnival atmosphere in a crowded courtroom only a few hundred feet from the scene of Sheriff Sarber's murder. The prisoner was in shackles, guarded by machine guns, and the constant target of movie cameras.

Pierpont's attorney, Miss Jessie Levy, had tried to prove he was at his mother's farm at the time of Sarber's murder but this defense was completely exposed by a surprise witness. Shouse, the man kicked out of the gang in Chicago, took the stand and was telling everything he knew.

Lima was almost in a state of siege. The courthouse was heavily barricaded with sandbags and guards patrolled the surrounding streets. It was feared that Dillinger would attack any minute with a new, heavily armed gang and break his friends out of the same jail he had been freed from.

Since the county had neither the money nor personnel to guard its jail, Governor George White had ordered General Harold Bush, an artilleryman, to form a defense with a contingent of National Guardsmen. Bush, nicknamed "Whispering Willie" because of his booming voice, had already set up three .30 caliber machine guns at strategic spots. Seven dummy guns made of wood and a barrier ten feet high between the sheriff's quarters and the courthouse rounded out the defenses.

The climax of the trial came on the morning of 11 March when Pierpont himself was put on the stand by Miss Levy to testify that he was not in Lima on the night of the murder. But his words had little effect in the face of Shouse's factual account. Pierpont seemed to realize that his testimony had not changed anything but he remained calm, almost detached. In an effort to goad him into disclosing his violent nature, Prosecutor Ernest Botkin began taunting him during the cross-examination, claiming that Pierpont, who had been brought to Michigan City from Tucson, had agreed to leave the prison and stand trial only to get out of the hole.

He had touched Pierpont's most vulnerable spot – his pride. The defendant shouted angrily, "I was in the hole twenty-one months one time!" and a moment later leaned toward Botkin and cried out, "An umpire can win any ball game!" He ridiculed Botkin's ability, charging that the prosecutor had built a fake bank robbery case, "brick by brick", against his brother, Fred. "You framed it right here in your own courthouse and you caused his arrest," he shouted.

When Botkin accused Pierpont of engineering bank robberies that had netted $300,000 in the short time since he'd escaped from prison, the bandit grinned and said truthfully, "I wish I had." Then he added, "Well, at least if I did, I'm not like some bank robbers – I didn't get myself elected president of the bank first."

The crowd burst into laughter and the judge ordered the last few lines stricken from the record.

"That's the kind of man you are, isn't it?" prodded Botkin.

"Yes," retorted the prisoner, encouraged by the audience response. "I'm not the kind of man you are – robbing widows and orphans. You'd probably be like me if you had the nerve."

Late that afternoon Jessie Levy delivered her closing argument. After a plea for mercy she said, ". . . and I now leave the fate of Harry Pierpont in your hands and, 'Even though I walk in the valley of the shadow of death, I fear no evil.' I know God is with me, with the defendant, in the hearts of every one of you." For the first time Mrs Pierpont was sobbing. The defendant and his father sat with heads lowered. "So I hand him over to you, and I pray God in His goodness will show you the way to do the right thing."

In his closing argument Botkin remarked, almost as an aside, that if it hadn't been for a tip from a certain informer, they "probably would not have been able to round up this gang."

Again Pierpont reacted, rising part way from his chair and shouting, "Yes, and if you had never heard of Matt Leach, you wouldn't have heard of me. Matt Leach gave you my address!"

Later when Botkin said Mrs Pierpont was "partly responsible for her son being in crime" the heavy-set woman who sat beside Pierpont at the defense table outdid him. She leaped to her feet and yelled, "I'm glad you're not the judge!" Across from mother and son, the elder Pierpont sat, frail and subdued.

Botkin demanded the death penalty. "If this evidence doesn't require the chair, I don't know what I'm talking about. . . . It is our duty to uphold the law, impose the proper sentence. Members of the jury, if you'll do this, you will have nothing to fear or regret. The only thing you need to fear is violation of that thing that your conscience tells you to do."

After deliberating only fifty-five minutes the jury returned with a verdict of guilty – and no recommendation for mercy. Pierpont sat quietly with a half smile on his face, Judge Everett said he would pronounce sentence later and asked if the prisoner had anything to say.

"No, not a word."

Photographers swarmed around the defense table but Mrs Pierpont held a scarf in front of her son's face. He whispered something and kissed her. Then he was unchained and led through lines of National Guardsmen to the jail. Here Makley called from his cell, "Well, Pete, what was it?"

"Well, what would it be?"

The next day General Bush announced he had just been warned that Dillinger was on his way to Lima. "I'm not going to call out a regiment," he told reporters. "I think we're set."

Chicago police thought the threat serious enough to transfer Pierpont immediately to the state penitentiary. They believed that Dillinger was hiding in Chicago – only two days before there had been a gun battle in Schiller Park.

Just after Makley's trial began that morning, Judge Everett added to the tension in the courtroom by mysteriously declaring, "We have received direct word that Dillinger is on his way here with armed men."

In Columbus Governor White and his daughter were put under heavy guard for fear Dillinger might kidnap them and demand Pierpont's freedom as ransom. This precaution seemed justified when police in northwestern Ohio were alerted that night to watch for an Illinois car containing three heavily armed men, one presumably John Dillinger.

At about 7:00 that same evening Harry Fisher – assistant cashier of the First National Bank of Mason City, Iowa, and the man responsible for opening the main vault every morning – was reading the *Globe-Gazette* when his wife came from the kitchen and said someone was looking in the front door.

It was Eddie Green, Dillinger's jug marker. Fisher came to the door and Green asked if this was 1228 North President.

Fisher, a small man of fifty-nine, said 1228 was a few doors up the street.

"Oh." Green looked intently at the key man in Dillinger's plan. He had to recognize him the next morning. Then he left without saying anything else and walked off in the wrong direction.

13 March was cold and though the sun occasionally shone through clouds, there were flurries of snow. After lunch Green and Van Meter checked out of the YMCA, a location appealing to the latter's sense of humor, and drove their Buick almost four miles to the southeast of town where they parked in a sand pit just across from a rural school. Soon a large car came from the north;

Dillinger, Carroll, Hamilton, and Baby Face Nelson got out and transferred to the Buick. At about 2:00 P.M. they headed toward town.

Mason City was a prosperous community of 25,000, typically Midwestern in appearance and manner, eventually to be immortalized by one of its native sons as the setting of *The Music Man*. In addition to being a center of rich farmlands, it had withstood the Depression better than most Iowa towns because of the local cement plants.

On that day the First National Bank had almost $240,000 in cash within its vaults, an astounding sum in 1934 for such a relatively small city. Eddie Green had done his research well and if this robbery succeeded, the gang would have enough to afford the best equipment, lawyers, judges, politicians, and police spies. With this one robbery they could possibly insure themselves a long and safe career in crime.

But Dillinger had already decided on a far different future. With his share, some $40,000, he would at last be able to do what he and Jenkins had spent so many hours talking about in prison: escape to Mexico or South America to "live like a king".

The officials of the First National, like those of the other banks associated with Bancorporation, had been warned they might be robbed any day, but they weren't particularly concerned. Robbery was like death; it happened to someone else. Besides they felt well protected. Some fifteen feet above the lobby on a balcony attached to the front wall was a seven-foot-high steel cage. Within this shield sat Tom Walters, the bank guard. Through its bulletproof window he could survey everything below and at the first sign of trouble he was to fire his gas gun half a dozen times; within minutes the robbers would be overcome by fumes. That was the plan, and the man upon whom it depended was experienced and determined.

At 2:20 p.m. Harry Fisher, who had been visited by Eddie Green the night before, was at his cage waiting on a customer. He had completely forgotten the odd incident. Suddenly he heard a wild yelling "like Indians on the warpath". Looking up, he saw three men, resembling well-dressed salesmen, waving guns. He ducked down.

The gunmen were Green, Hamilton, and Van Meter. The latter was looking for the bank president, Willis Bagley. When Van Meter saw Bagley sitting at a desk facing the other direction, he walked briskly up, machine gun at the ready.

At that moment Bagley swung around in his swivel chair. Seeing the wild look on Van Meter's face, he thought a "crazy man" was loose and ran toward his private office, a few yards away.

"Stop," shouted Van Meter. The president ducked into the little room and started shutting the door but Van Meter thrust the barrel of the gun forward against the jamb, preventing the door from closing. For a moment it was a stand-off. Then Van Meter yanked the gun free. Bagley slammed the door and locked it. Van Meter fired once through the door, the bullet grazing Bagley's chest. Frustrated and angry, Van Meter began rounding up hostages for later use.

In the meantime Hamilton, armed with a pistol, had gone behind the cages and ordered the employees into the lobby where Green, waving a machine gun, was shouting, "Everyone on the floor!"

Margaret Johnson, the switchboard girl, was standing on the mezzanine balcony at the back of the bank, about to go downstairs to check some calls when she heard the first yelling. Almost simultaneously she saw Bagley chased into his office. She opened up the switchboard so the president would have an outside line, and then pressed the Western Union button, hoping it would attract their attention.

At that moment a call came in from the wife of a teller. "You can't talk to him," said Margaret, "the bank is being robbed."

On the balcony across the room Guard Tom Walters had thought the first noise was a customer complaining about a loan. He rose from his chair inside the steel cage, looked through the thick window, and saw Green cradling a machine gun. He picked up his tear-gas gun and fired through a horizontal slit in the cage. The eight-inch-long pellet hit Green in the back and began releasing its 25,000 cubic feet of gas.

Green swore in pain, anger, and surprise.

"Get that son of a bitch with the tear gas," called Hamilton from behind the cages where he was already scooping money into a sack.

Green grabbed a bank director, swung him around as a shield, and fired a burst at the steel cage, several bullets spitting through the gun slit. Walters, nicked in the right ear and chin ducked down. He tried desperately to pry the swollen, empty shell from the gas gun with his jackknife blade but couldn't budge it. Finally the blade snapped. He reached for gas candles but there were none. The plan for defense had bogged down.

The auditor's assistant, however, was already running back into an office off the mezzanine balcony. He found a gas candle, pulled the fuse, and threw it down to the marble floor. Fumes began shooting out of perforations as the candle rolled across the lobby. An elderly man lying on the floor kicked it away. Another elderly customer kicked it back. It was like a game and a few intrigued spectators on the balcony almost laughed.

Margaret Johnson was also looking down at the coughing choking customers. She stood half paralyzed, half fascinated. "I said everybody down," Green yelled, then loosed a burst of shots over her head. She and a book-keeper started crawling back to the storeroom. En route the middle-aged book-keeper noticed his companion had lost a shoe and gallantly went back for it. But she hurried to the window overlooking the alley behind the bank, completely unaware she had only one shoe. "Hey, you," she called to a short man wearing a cap and brown overcoat. "Get to work and notify somebody. The bank is being robbed."

Baby Face Nelson looked up, pointed his machine gun at her. "Lady, you're telling me?"

By now Van Meter had rounded up a dozen hostages from the lobby and was conducting them to the sidewalk in front of the bank. Here Dillinger, dressed in gray fedora, gray overcoat, and striped muffler, lined them up as a living shield. This done, he left Van Meter in charge, ducked into the bank building and entered the investment department – opposite the lobby – where Lydia Crosby, a young stenographer, and several others were hiding on the floor. She had hated to drop down; her dress had just been cleaned.

Dillinger ordered them all outside and, when Lydia hung back, tapped her on the arm, telling her to hurry along. As these new hostages went out the revolving door, he said, "Stand close to me." They hesitated and he chided mildly, "Come on, get up around me." They too were lined up on the sidewalk, hands in the air, backs to the bank, but they soon tired and their hands dropped. Dillinger was like a scolding school-teacher. "Can't you get your hands up any higher than that?" A machine gun was strapped to his right arm; he held an automatic pistol in his left.

A driver, not realizing why the cars ahead of him had stopped, swung his car around the stalled traffic and went past the bank.

Dillinger fired into its radiator with his pistol and no other cars tried to run the gauntlet.

A large crowd was gathering across the street. Some of them had no idea the bank was really being robbed. A freelance cameraman had been shooting motion pictures of the business section that morning, and now they thought a film of a robbery was being made. So they eagerly shoved forward to get a better look at the movie stars.

Van Meter was recruiting more human shields from the nearby Nichols and Green Shoe Store. About half a dozen obeyed. The rest retreated to the stock room.

About the time Dillinger entered the bank for hostages, Enoch Norem, city editor of the *Globe-Gazette*, was ordering his reporters to go out immediately and get at least one city brief apiece. He bawled them out for not bringing in enough local items. Reporter Carl Wright was heading up a side street toward the center of town to get his brief when he heard shooting and saw Baby Face Nelson standing on the sidewalk near the rear of the bank. Across the street, in front of the Prescription Shop, was a second machine gunner, Tommy Carroll. Squarely between them, blocking traffic on the side street, was the bandit car.

Nelson saw the reporter and fired a few warning shots. At that moment an auto went past Wright, innocently heading toward the parked bandit vehicle. Nelson fired at the car, which stopped with a scream of brakes and backed up full speed for three blocks, miraculously hitting nothing.

The reporter ducked into a bookstore, telephoned his skeptical city editor, and ran outside again just in time to see R. L. James, the School Board secretary, completely unaware of the danger, casually walking toward Nelson. Baby Face suddenly turned and fired again. James, hit in the leg, slumped to the sidewalk.

Chief of Police E. J. Patton, in civilian clothes as usual, heard the first shots when he was walking toward the court-house where he'd been subpoenaed for a trial. As he crossed into Central Park and saw the large crowd, he too thought movies were being made.

Then he heard someone say, "They're robbing the bank!" He cut through the park and saw people across the street lined up in front of the bank, hands in air. He ran into the Weir Building, a structure with a vaguely Japanese flavor, one of Frank Lloyd

Wright's early designs. The chief climbed to a second-floor office and saw Dillinger walking back and forth behind a line of people, but it was too dangerous to risk a shot. Then he noticed one of his patrolmen dart across the park toward the bank with a sawed-off shotgun.

Dillinger fired his pistol, and the patrolman ducked behind a meteorite, a Civil War monument. He stuck out his gun menacingly but, like his chief, he was afraid to pull the trigger.

"Stand up and shoot it out like a man," called Dillinger from across the street and hit a parked car with a bullet.

He was safe from the police but there was one man who decided to take a chance. John C. Shipley, an elderly police judge, was peering almost straight down at Dillinger from his office on the third floor of the bank building. He disappeared and came back with an ancient pistol. He took careful aim and pulled the stiff trigger. Dillinger clutched his right shoulder, whirled and fired his machine gun up at the window but the judge had disappeared once more.

In spite of the pain, Dillinger calmly told Van Meter to get inside and warn the others that it was time to leave. The skinny bandit ran into the lobby and excitedly shouted out Dillinger's order.

"Give us three more minutes," answered Hamilton. He had collected only $32,000 from the cages. The big money was in the vaults. He pressed a gun in Harry Fisher's back and said, "Now you come on back and open up." The assistant cashier was trying to figure out how he could keep from surrendering the money in the vault. There was a fortune there, over $200,000, and he didn't want to be the one to give it up. Hamilton kicked him in the buttocks. "Hurry up, damn it!"

The great round door of the main vault was open and Fisher stepped inside with Hamilton just behind. The cashier went past the safety boxes to the barred door leading to the money vault. After unlocking this door, he pushed it open and automatically reached for a heavy bag of pennies he used as a door stop. Hamilton beat him to the pennies, then deposited them – a treasure, he thought – into his big sack. Fisher could hardly believe his luck. He stepped inside the vault and released the door. With no bag of pennies to hold it open, it slammed shut and locked. Now there were bars between Hamilton and Fisher.

Fisher went up to the safe where the money was kept. He could simply have pulled open the door but instead, he spun the dial, locking it. "I don't know whether I can see to work this combination," he called out to Hamilton, who was standing impatiently on the other side of the barred door. Tears from the gas were streaming down the faces of both men.

"You'd better open it goddamn quick," warned Hamilton.

The cashier fumbled for another minute and finally opened the safe; then he turned, took hold of the barred door and shook it. "Now this door is locked and I can't open it," he said.

Hamilton was so anxious to get the money he forgot Fisher had unlocked it a moment before with the key that was still in his pocket.

"All I can do is shove the money out through the bars," said Fisher. Hamilton told him to do it quickly. Fisher returned with ten bundles of one-dollar bills and slowly shoved each package, one at a time, through the narrow opening of the bars. After he finished he made a second deliberate trip for more ones.

"If you don't hurry up, I'm going to shoot you," said Hamilton.

Outside, the crowd was growing and Dillinger, seeing the situation might soon be out of hand, told Van Meyer to order those inside out at once. Van Meter ran in, shouted the message. "Just gimme another minute," pleaded Hamilton. When he saw Fisher getting more ones he said, "Gimme the big bills!" Fisher, pretending he didn't understand, kept handing out packages of one-dollar notes.

Van Meter ran in a third time. "We're going!"

"It's hell to leave all that money back there," complained Hamilton. Of the almost $200,000, Fisher had doled out only $20,000. Hamilton picked up the sack weighted with the heavy bag of pennies and, with his free hand, grabbed Francis De Sart of the Savings Department, the Scoutmaster of Troop 13. "C'mon," said the bandit, "let's go." The two went out the front door.

Lydia Crosby saw Hamilton come out, tears running down his cheeks. Then she heard Dillinger tell the hostages to move around the corner.

The robbers, surrounded by citizens, began turning left down the side street just as Judge Shipley – the self-appointed deputy – again peered out of his third-story window and got off a hasty shot at the last robber to turn the corner. Once more his aim was remarkable. The bullet struck Hamilton's right shoulder.

The first thing Dillinger saw after he rounded the corner was

James, the school secretary, bleeding on the sidewalk; he knew Nelson had shot him. "Did you have to do that?" he said, then ordered the hostages to crowd onto the running boards of the Buick. It was Sioux Falls all over again except that this time there were almost three times as many hostages and it was hard to see how they could all get aboard.

Baby Face Nelson jabbed at the assistant cashier, Ralph Wiley, called him a "bald-headed son of a bitch", and told him to climb onto the back bumper and hang onto the back window frame – the glass had been carefully removed. With Wiley were Lydia Crosby, Scoutmaster De Sart, Emmet Ryan – another bank employee – and the white-coated owner of the Mulcahy Prescription Shop.

Women – some were bank employees, some depositors or shoppers – were herded into the back seat of the Buick. Other women and men filled the two running boards. Two men were even perched on the front mudguards. Lydia Crosby counted twenty-one on and in the auto, Wiley twenty-three and De Sart twenty-six. Whatever the figure, it looked like a comedy car in the circus.

When Chief Patton, from his vantage point in the Weir Building, saw the bandits drive away he got a sawed-off shotgun at the police station and set off in pursuit in an unmarked car with two of his officers. By now the freelance cameraman, H. C. Kunkelman, was finally taking movies of the excited crowd around the bank.

The Buick ponderously proceeded north at less than fifteen miles an hour. De Sart saw some girls he knew coming out of a beauty shop and resisted an impulse to wave at them. The car began to turn west at the Kirk Apartments. Miss Minnie Piehm, an elderly hostage hanging desperately on at the right side, cried hysterically, "Let me out! This is where I live!"

As if it were a bus, the Buick stopped and Miss Piehm got off. Wiley also descended but someone inside shouted sharply, "Get back on, you." He did and the Buick started off again, this time at a more rapid pace – twenty miles an hour.

Chief Patton's car was held up by the traffic. "They turned at the Kirk Apartments," a boy yelled; so the police vehicle also turned and, by the time the Buick swung west onto Highway 18, was only a block behind. "Don't get too close," warned Patton. "They can shoot us. We dassent shoot at them."

A little later a man taking his wife and daughter for a ride turned onto Highway 18 and saw the overloaded Buick ahead. Thinking it was a "merry party" or a wedding shivaree, he became curious and drew closer. A bullet suddenly struck his car and, splitting in three parts, wounded him three times.

Baby Face Nelson had also begun shooting at the police with a high-powered rifle. At the top of the hill near the city limits the Buick stopped. Nelson jumped out and again fired. The police car turned off the highway into a farmer's driveway.

Nelson, holding the rifle under his arm, started to sprinkle tacks on the cement road but did it so excitedly that many bounced under the Buick.

Dillinger leaned out and said in a remarkably calm voice, "You're getting tacks under our own car." Nelson kicked several out of the way and said, "Those cars following! We'll shoot 'em!" Dillinger ordered him to get back in.

The Buick continued almost a mile on the highway, then turned south on a dirt road. About this time it was discovered that one of the hostages, Bill Schmidt, who had been en route to a customer with a paper sack of sandwiches, was still clinging to it. The bandits ate the sandwiches. As they were crossing Highway 106, one of the women inside said she was getting sick.

"For God's sake," said Dillinger, "let her out." They stopped near a farmhouse.

As she stepped to the road, Baby Face shouted, "You phone the law. Tell them if they don't stop following us we're going to kill everyone in this car. That's some law you got!" Then he jumped out again and spread more tacks on the dirt road.

A woman on the running board said hysterically, "I don't want to die this way." Dillinger told her to get off and the Buick resumed its journey through the open country, carefully avoiding bumps and holes. Soon it turned east, back again south and once more east, never at a speed of over twenty-five miles an hour.

The hostages clinging to the car were suffering from the cold. Sharp flurries of snow spit in their faces and Lydia Crosby was sure her glasses would blow off any moment. She wondered how much longer she could hang onto the rear window frame and considered quitting her job at the bank. It wasn't worth such trouble.

In the last forty-five minutes they had driven almost thirteen miles but were only three miles due south of Mason City. They stopped soon after crossing Highway 65 and Nelson jumped out, ordering everyone to get off and raise their hands so he could search them for weapons. When Emmet Ryan, the paying teller, stared at him, Nelson said, "Don't look at me, you son of a bitch!" Ryan ignored the order and kept on staring.

One woman was kept in the car as a hostage and a woman friend insisted on staying with her. Then the Buick headed for the sand pit where the other bandit car was parked. Several minutes later the last two hostages were released and the gang headed toward St Paul in two cars.

They arrived close to midnight. First-aid bandages had been put on the shoulder wounds of Hamilton and Dillinger but, since there was a strong possibility of infection, Green promised to get a doctor. He went into the Green Lantern Café on Wabasha Street, where he found Pat Reilly – formerly mascot of the St Paul baseball team and presently a waiter for Harry Sawyer – who agreed to help. Reilly's wife was one of three sisters with similar tastes; the other two were married to Tommy Carroll and Alvin Karpis.

Reilly took Dillinger, Hamilton and Van Meter to the home of his family doctor, N. G. Mortenson, the city's health officer, and told him Dillinger and Hamilton had been wounded in a shooting scrape in Minneapolis. The jittery Mortenson removed the dressings and examined the wounds. "They're not dangerous," he said and hastily reapplied the bandages. He was frightened and, claiming he had no first-aid kit at home, told them to come to his office at eleven the next morning if they wanted further treatment.

As they were leaving, the doctor noticed a machine gun sticking out of Van Meter's overcoat. Now he was sure they were gangsters and started to telephone the police. But he hung up. They might come back and kill him.

In the aftermath of the Mason City robbery, Youngblood was killed by police in Port Huron, Michigan; in Lima, Ohio, Pierpont and Makley were sentenced to death, and Clark to life imprisonment. Dillinger himself shot his way out of two further police traps and, with a reconstituted gang, robbed another bank in Indiana, killing a policeman in the process. He was finally betrayed by a prostitute, Anna Sage, fearful of being deported to her native Romania, who told the Dillinger squad that their quarry would be attending a movie at the Biograph Theatre on Chicago's Lincoln Avenue on 22 July.

The FBI and Chicago police set an ambush, and when Dillinger emerged from the cinema he was shot in the head and died within minutes. Conspiracy theorists have suggested that Dillinger was never killed, and that a petty criminal was set up by the authorities to take his place.

Britain's Triple Police Killer
(Harry Roberts)

Keith Dovkants

*In 1966, Harry Roberts became Britains's most wanted crim-
inal, hunted, captured and jailed for the murder of three London
policemen. He shot them at point blank range when they tried to
search the car which he and two fellow criminals were driving in
a quiet street in Shepherds Bush, west London. The judge at his
trial said Roberts should serve at least 30 years. The UK's most
reviled police killer has now served 40. Roberts is a complicated
personality. He was raised by a lone mother, who worked hard to
send him as a boarder to a private Catholic school in south
London. He repaid her by punching her in the face and splitting
her lip. In jail in the late 1950s, serving seven years for robbery
with violence, he acquired City and Guilds certificates for
bricklaying and plumbing, coming top of his class; at the same
time he developed a violent temper and a capacity for epic sulks.
While in solitary confinement on a diet of bread and water,
Roberts attacked a prison officer for killing his pet spider,
screaming and with his eyes bulging with hate. Harry Roberts
shot the police officers while cruising the streets with two
criminal cronies, John Witney and Jock Duddy. Showing no
remorse, Roberts blamed his victims for having the temerity to do
their job searching a suspect car. After the killings, Roberts
vanished and Britain's biggest-ever manhunt ensued. A reward
of £1,000 and broadcast appeals by his mother failed to flush
him out; after several thousand reported sightings, Roberts was*

finally cornered in Epping Forest, where he'd been living rough for three months using survival skills learned during his time in the Army. At his trial the judge called the murders "the most heinous crimes to have been committed in this country for a generation or more." Keith Dovkants was chief reporter for the London Evening Standard *when he visited Harry Roberts in prison in 1995.*

The prison door slams shut. A crop-haired guard conducts a delicately intimate body search, takes away my bag and stamps an ultra-violet marker on the back of my right hand. Ahead is a bare exercise yard open only to the sky, another steel door, more cacophony of keys, more guards. There is a deadening, hermetic hush. No one, all this seems to say, is going to spring Harry Roberts.

It makes you wonder: why bother? Not since his elderly mother tucked a pair of bolt-cutters into her brassiere and smuggled them into Parkhurst has anyone tried to help him escape. His gangster friends are mostly dead now. The rest are banged up or washed up, arthritic and living on income support.

Harry Roberts is a killer. He put a bullet into a policeman's eye, then shot another in the back. He watched an accomplice shoot a third officer in the head. It is still the most devastating crime visited upon the Metropolitan Police in modern times. Get him out? Why would anyone want to do that?

Harry Roberts sits at a table, relaxed, smiling. He has been in jail for 29 years and yet the heavy-lidded eyes are instantly recognizable from that photograph on the wanted posters. When he went in, Harold Wilson was prime minister, London was in mid-swing. Colour television was beginning to catch on; space was unconquered.

He is powerfully built and looks fit. The face is craggy, the hair thinning and grey, but there is something that makes you think of that old-fashioned phrase "well-preserved". He is 58 and you wonder if sequestration has allowed a kind of suspended animation, a slowing of the usual processes.

Roberts was sentenced to life. Although it is an open-ended sentence, many prisoners serve a "life" term in as little as eight years. For others, like mass killer Jeremy Bamber (and, currently, 14 other lifers) it means they will die in jail.

Die in jail. The very phrase has a satisfying sonority, a finality that many demand for those crimes which place their author beyond earthly redemption. Yet it is a relatively new idea. Roberts was sentenced in the immediate afterglow of the repeal of capital punishment, in an era when 30 years was reckoned by many to be a civilized alternative to the rope.

Since then murders have multiplied and behind each fresh gust of outrage has been a muted, almost unconscious, groping towards some suitable penalty. In a society increasingly traumatized by murder, yet unwilling to punish in kind, the concept of locking up killers and throwing away the key has taken firm hold.

This leaves Roberts staring into the abyss, a fate many would say is all he deserves. You tell him this and he laughs, and counters with a point to support his contention that one day, not necessarily soon, he should be released. Soon our conversation becomes a disputation: he argues his case, ranges arguments he has had more than 14,000 days to consider.

In the grey courtyard, the shadows beyond the steel bars lengthen. Another of those days is vanishing. I find myself returning again and again to the question – why would anyone want Harry Roberts free?

The life that may or may not end in jail began promisingly enough. His mother Dorothy had a small café and prospered as a black marketeer during the war. He was a boarder at St Joseph's College, a Catholic school in Beulah Hill, south London, and was considered quite bright. One of his schoolmates told me, with nostalgic awe, how Roberts would impress the other boys by showing them the 10-shilling note he received as weekly pocket money. The lure of even bigger money led to crime and Borstal. When he was 18 the Army took him in as a national serviceman and he was posted to Malaya. According to him, this was where he first killed. His victims were communist insurgents, shot in the line of duty.

That, of course, is what they say about his police victims. There were three of them, Detective Sergeant Christopher Head, PC Geoffrey Fox and Detective Constable David Wombwell. They stopped Roberts and his accomplices, John Duddy and Jack Witney, in a street near Wormwood Scrubs just after 3 p.m. on 12 August 1966, in what was described as a routine check.

This is what happened, in his words:

"DC Wombwell was talking to Jack through the window of our

van. He was shouting and trying to get the door open. Jack said, 'Let the slag have it, Harry.' I shot him point blank with the Luger, one shot at the bottom of his eye.

"As Wombwell fell I turned towards DS Head on the other side of the van. He started running back towards their car. I aimed quickly and got him right in the middle of the back. He fell but he wasn't dead. I ran up and aimed at his head. I pulled the trigger. It misfired. I pulled the trigger again. It misfired again.

"He got up and staggered to the car, but fell down in front of it. PC Fox tried to drive off but he jammed DS Head under the wheels. Then Duddy shot PC Fox in the head."

His hands are spread out, palms down, on the gaily coloured plastic table. A young prisoner walks past, gives him a respectful nod.

"It was over in seconds. Once it started it was not going to stop until it was over." Over? "Until they were dead."

His voice is flat, emotionless. It bears not the slightest trace of remorse. I ask anyway: does he feel sorry?

"You have to understand the circumstances. I'm not trying to make excuses but really, remorse is the wrong word. I can understand someone being sorry for killing someone they love, someone they care about. But these men were strangers. It wasn't personal.

"Don't you see the difference? I feel sorry for their families but we were in danger from those men. We had guns. If they'd nicked us I'd have got 10 years.

"I believed I had a right to be a criminal, that it was my free choice. I don't hate policemen but for a professional criminal like me they were the enemy. They did what they chose to do and I had to do what I chose to do." The hands are fists now, loosely clenched on the tabletop. The right hand relaxes, slowly. I realize I'm staring at it, thinking of Chris Head, one bullet in his back, staring up at the Luger as that hand squeezes the trigger; once, twice.

How, I ask, do you expect to get out of here if you frankly admit you don't feel remorse? He gives me a very hard look. "Listen," he says, "I am being honest about this." I smile and he starts laughing. "That's my trouble," he says. "I'm too honest.

"Psychos (prison psychiatrists) don't understand that. They don't understand me and they don't understand my crime. I would never dream of robbing working-class people, or hurting children or raping someone.

"If I was a rapist I'd be out of here in a flash. Psychos love them. They say, 'Why do you hate women? Was it your mother?' You say yes, it was my mother. You go in for a bit more chat like that then they say, 'Do you still hate women?' You say no and they say you're cured. Off you go. It's like drug addicts. They have courses and to show the courses work they have to say they are cured and let them out.

"But what about me? I'm not a pervert and I don't use drugs. I'm a professional criminal and they can't understand that. They want to break me and rebuild me in a way that suits them. I could lie and make them think it was working but I don't. I'm too honest."

You might imagine a plangent tone in all of this, a kind of pleading whine. Not so. Roberts delivers his case in a harsh staccato. If there is any self-pity, I don't detect it.

At one point he says he believes the police should be given guns, that his one big regret is that he shot unarmed men. And he scoffs at the recent move to equip policemen with body armour. It would not have saved his victims.

Roberts is quite fit and still, by his own account, tough. Certainly he makes the current crop of punks look more like pranksters than gangsters. But he insists he can go straight. Witney, released three years ago, has dropped out of sight. The third man, Duddy, died in jail. "I'm not going to get into trouble again, am I?" says Roberts. "Nobody would want to work with me, for a start. I'm too hot. I'm finished with all that and they know it. I've even stopped trying to escape. I haven't tried to get out since 1980.

"I'm too old for action now. I just want to quietly retire; spend my time fishing." He would be unlikely to manage an anonymous retirement, even if he wanted it. In certain circles Harry Roberts is a cult hero. Football crowds use his name to taunt policemen. There is even a chant:

> Harry Roberts, he's our man.
> He shoots coppers, bang bang bang.

His name features in recent graffiti. Even without this he would be a dangerous item to handle and he knows it:

"This is how the Home Office works. Some civil servant gets a piece of paper pushed in front of him with 'Harry Roberts' release' on it. What's he going to do? There's nothing in it for him if he signs it, but it could cost him his career once the *Sun* gets wound up.

"You think [the then home secretary] Michael Howard's running the prisons, don't you? Well, you're wrong. The *Sun* does. Anyone who lets me out has to have the balls to take on the *Sun*."

So what can the argument be? Where is the answer to that central question: who would want him free? He diverts the question, asks me to think about his predicament. Is it fair, he asks, to carry on day after day not knowing how long he can expect to serve, or even if he will ever get out?

"That," he says, rummaging for the phrase, ". . . is cruel and unusual punishment. I don't mind life being life if it applies to everyone. There are people carefully planning to kidnap children, rape them and murder them. Premeditated, evil murder. They get out in 12 years. I can't even find out how long I'm in for.

"If it's 35 years, all right. If it's 40, well, sod it, I'll do my best. Every day is a day less. But when they don't let you know, it's torture."

Deep inside the building someone slams a door, the crash echoes through the corridors. He is looking at me. There is no sympathy for you out there, I say. He lowers his eyes, murmurs. "I know that." He tells me two more things: every time a policeman is killed his chance of freedom slips further away and that by any measure he has already served a lifetime.

The word sticks in my head, across the exercise yard, out into the street. Lifetime. It makes me think of Philip Walters. He was born, grew up, became a policeman and was shot to death in a London suburb, all in the 29 years Harry Roberts has spent in jail.

Yes, it has been a lifetime.

America's Worst Nightmare
(Stanley "Tookie" Williams)

Chris Summers

*Stanley "Tookie" Williams spent nearly a quarter of a century
on Death Row awaiting execution for four murders. Sentenced
to death in 1981, his reputation for violence and mayhem went
before him. A huge man with powerful muscles and a stone-cold
stare, Tookie and his friend Raymond Washington founded the
Crips gang in 1971. It became the most notorious criminal gang
in Los Angeles, before spreading its tentacles to cities and towns
in 43 US states as well as Canada, South Africa, Germany and
even Britain. Raymond Washington was shot dead in 1979, but
Tookie remained the Crips' spiritual leader, according to the
California Department of Corrections. The authorities estimate
that each year there are some 240 gang-related murders in LA,
where there are 12,000 Crips, 5,000 rival Bloods and another
30,000 Latino gangsters. Tookie Williams came to earn the
description of "America's worst nightmare". He was California's original black "gangsta". His murderous robberies were
brutal and senseless. In the first he shot a store worker in the back
at point-blank range. Two weeks later he broke down the door of
a motel and blasted the owners and their daughter to death.
Since the killings, thousands more have died in the violence
spawned by the Crips, their rivals and imitators. Bizarrely, the
man who founded the most feared street gang in California was
nominated for the Nobel Peace Prize in 2001. Chris Summers
(b. 1968), works as a journalist for the BBC News website,*

where he specializes in covering crime both in Britain and abroad. As a local newspaper reporter in Gloucester in 1994, he covered the Cromwell Street murder case and the dramatic trial of Rose West, who was given 10 life sentences. Since joining the BBC in 1997 he has focused on organized crime and various miscarriages of justice. Chris Summers visited Tookie in the condemned cell in 2003, two years before he was finally executed.

San Quentin prison is one of America's oldest jails and has housed some of the most notorious killers in history. It was perhaps inevitable that Stanley "Tookie" Williams, one of the founders of the notorious Crips gang, would end up incarcerated on its Death Row. The Crips started as a bunch of raggedy-arsed youths hanging around on street corners in their native south central Los Angeles. The name was a corruption of their original moniker – the Avenue Cribs, meaning a junior gang allied to the Avenue Boys gang. The gang's co-founder Raymond Washington was shot dead in 1979 and Tookie was convicted of four murders in 1981 but the Crips went from strength to strength. They had created a Frankenstein's monster which mushroomed out of control.

The Crips now have affiliated gangs all across the United States as well as in Europe and South Africa. Despite renouncing violence in the early 1990s and eschewing the "gang banger" lifestyle, Williams remained the "spiritual leader" of the Crips, according to the California Department of Corrections. Until shortly before Christmas 2005, when he was executed by the state on the orders of Governor Arnold Schwarzenegger, the former actor and star of films such as *The Terminator*.

I visited Tookie two years earlier, in the summer of 2003, long before anyone in Britain had ever heard of him. The visit was arranged by Barbara Cottman Becnel, Tookie's friend and most staunch supporter, who co-wrote several books with him in which he criticized the gangs and warned youngsters not to join them. These books earned him a Nobel Peace Prize nomination in 2001.

Ms Becnel had warned me of the do's and don'ts of visiting Death Row. "You can't wear jeans or any denim – because it looks like prison uniforms – and you can't wear green, yellow or orange (the colour of prison overalls) or T-shirts with motifs on them," she said. Also out were sunglasses, keys, matches, cigarettes, cameras, pens and notebooks. I parked the car and congregated with the other visitors – who appeared to be mostly wives, lovers or mothers – in a hut known as "the tube". We had to leave all our possessions in lockers and could only bring in money – up to $30 – in $1 bills.

Several of the women were fretting about their choice of clothes. A notice pinned to the wall of "the tube" warns against transparent blouses, trousers with slits above knee level or any clothes which showed off too much cleavage. Presumably the fear is that inmates, starved of female company for years, would be unable to control themselves at the sight of a scantily clad woman. "I always bring a change of clothes in the car in case they reject what I'm wearing," one woman told me as we waited.

So I was surprised when, after walking through an airport-style metal detector and having an ultra-violet pen painted on my wrist, I was free to walk up to the Death Row block itself. As we approached Ms Becnel pointed out the chimney which used to lead from the gas chamber – lethal injection has since replaced cyanide as the means of execution – and the green and red lights used to indicate when an inmate has been dispatched.

We entered the building through an airlock-type door and, after leaving my passport as a deposit, I was led through to the visiting room. Vending machines – serving fried chicken, potato chips, sodas, chocolate milkshakes and candy – lined one side of the room. "The food they get in the prison is not very good and while the vending machine food is not gourmet by any means, they really look forward to it," said Ms Becnel, as she busied herself buying chicken pieces and sticking them in a nearby microwave oven.

The centre of the room was full of white metallic cages, no more than eight feet long and five feet wide. It was a sweltering California day and San Quentin's budget does not run to air conditioning. Hands cuffed behind his back, Williams stood sweating profusely in one of the cages as he waited for us to be allowed in with his food.

Tookie, who suffers from high blood pressure, had already undergone the indignity of a strip search – and would have to undergo another one after the visit – and his mood was further strained by rumours about a note which claimed Crips would start killing guards if he was executed.

When we were finally showed into the cage, and his cuffs were removed, there was an awkward silence as he sat for several

moments seething with frustration, and muttering: "This place!"
Eventually we broke the silence with introductions and he told us
of the prison authorities' attitude towards him: "I'm always going
to be their Al Capone (who, after being jailed for tax evasion, spent
years on Alcatraz in nearby San Francisco). Anything that happened, especially involving blacks, is supposed to be to do with me.
But my 'gangbanging' days have been over for a decade."

At almost 300 lbs – years of weightlifting bulked up his arms and
chest, although weights have since been removed from all California prisons – Williams was an impressive and intimidating
presence. His greying beard was neatly trimmed and his hair
was held in two braids which hung down over his powerful
shoulders. The dark brown eyes were deep and sad and his voice
soft and persuasive. His language was scattered with words learned
from the thesaurus (one of his favourite books) and there were
none of the profanities so common with the younger generation.

"I spend my time praying, exercising, reading books and studying the dictionary," he explained.

Williams refuted suggestions by the authorities that "as recently
as June 2000 he was considered leader of the Blue-note Crips."
Tookie said: "They've kept me fossilized in the amber of a gang
past. They thought of me as irredeemable and they thought I
would not change." But he said his disillusionment with the gangs,
and his decision to actively campaign against them, was a gradual
process and not an "epiphany".

There are now an estimated 12,000 Crips, around 5,000 rival
Bloods and another 30,000 Latino gangsters in Los Angeles alone.
Each year there are around 240 gang-related murders in the City of
Angels. The Crips have spread, like a plague, to cities and towns in
43 US states, as well as Canada, South Africa, Germany and even
Britain. Originally founded in black communities of South Central
LA, Crips now include as members white farm boys in states like
Tennessee and Arkansas.

Much has also been made of the Crips' use of the colour blue but
Williams said this had mundane roots. "One of my friends was into
colour co-ordination. He used to wear a blue rag (bandanna), a
blue hat, blue sneakers, so we followed him. People have a
tendency to romanticize and sensationalize some of these things,"
he said.

As Crip gangs began to pop up all over LA in the 1970s non-
Crip gangs such as the Pirus and the Bounty Hunters formed an

informal alliance called the Bloods. But Williams said the Bloods were never a proper gang, like the Crips. "They would say, 'Yo, Blood,' to each other, while we'd say, 'Yo, cous(in)' because we were like a big family," he said. It is this feeling of belonging which attracts so many rudderless youths to join gangs. He also claimed his son was a Crip affiliate who was serving time in another California jail.

Tookie was sentenced to death in 1981 and spent seven years in solitary confinement after prison officials were warned about a gang war about to erupt behind bars. But gradually he realized the error of his ways and in 1993 began work on a series of books, with Ms Becnel. In 2001 he was nominated for the Nobel Peace Prize by Swiss MP Mario Fehr because of his "extraordinary youth violence prevention and intervention work", which includes his own website.

But Williams' struggle for redemption may have come too late to save his life. He was convicted of murdering cashier Alvin Owens, 26, in a February 1979 robbery at a 7–11 store which netted only $120. Two weeks later he is said to have killed Robert Yang, his wife Tsai-Shai and their daughter Ye Chen Lin at the LA motel they ran. Williams always denied all four murders. He blames his predicament on "bad karma" caused by the numerous "atrocities" he committed against members of the black community, mainly rival gangsters.

Williams, who was born in Louisiana and moved to LA in the 1960s with his mother, claims many urban blacks have unconsciously inherited a "slave mentality" from their forebears. He says modern-day slave traits include dropping out of school or college, dealing drugs and committing other crimes and abandoning babies which they have fathered. His zeal in urging young people to reject these traits would appear to impress even the most conservative Republican but he failed to persuade those, like Governor Schwarzenegger, who insisted he should have apologized to the families of Alvin Owens and the Yang family.

Williams responds: "Why should I apologize to these people when I didn't do it? That is an oxymoron."

As we talked, and Tookie munched on his fried chicken and potato chips, a guard brought an electric fan over in an attempt to combat the stifling heat.

When Ms Becnel first visited him he had been approached by several publishers who were keen for a sensationalistic "warts and all" book about the life of a top gangster. But by then Tookie had renounced the gang life and he wanted to write a book instead which would warn American youths of the evils of the gangs in an effort to convince them not to join.

He denies it has been a public relations exercise designed to spare his life and pointed out the appeal court was only allowed to consider the facts of the case and not the behaviour of an inmate after his conviction. "Anyone who doesn't know that is ignorant of the law," he said. Williams said his conviction was based on "hearsay" and witnesses who claimed to have heard him "bragging" of the crimes had either been beaten or bribed into making their statements.

He has written a series of books – known as the *Tookie Speaks Out Against Gang Violence* series – which are aimed at pre-teen children. In the books, which are dictated over the phone to Ms Becnel from his cell, he uses street slang like "down" and "homeboy" to challenge the glamorous aspects of gang life. In one book, entitled *Gangs and Weapons*, he writes: "Many kids carry guns like we did. Some kids bring them to school . . . Some kids even believe that carrying guns makes them grown up.

"Kids think they have lots of reasons to carry guns. But there are no good reasons. They all lead to violence, death and sadness."

Williams criticized the Hollywood movie, *Colors*, starring Sean Penn as "bogus" and said while Spike Lee's film *Boyz N The Hood* was more true to life their lives were far more violent than their big-screen portrayals.

When our time was up and Tookie went back to his cramped cell – it measures the same size as the visiting cage but also has a bed, a toilet and a sink in it – I shook his huge hand and wished him all the best.

As we left Ms Becnel pointed up: "You see that light there on the roof? That light goes red to signal an execution has taken place."

She hoped she would never see the red light.

Two years passed without me hearing anything more of Tookie. Then in the autumn of 2005 I read that his appeals were all but exhausted and Schwarzenegger was hinting that he would not exercise his right to grant clemency to Tookie. Suddenly the case became a major talking point in the United States, sparking debate about the nature of redemption. Williams' supporters include rapper Snoop Dogg – himself a former Crip – actors Jamie Foxx and Susan Sarandon and human rights campaigners Rev Jesse

Jackson and Bianca Jagger. Foxx had played Tookie in a film, *Redemption*, which can be found on the shelves of most British DVD shops.

In their petition for mercy Tookie's lawyers wrote: "This is about redemption, rehabilitation and hope. It is about a single man, a prisoner for a quarter century, who found purpose while facing death by execution."

Governor Schwarzenegger said he agonized over the decision, but in the end denied clemency.

Williams was executed by lethal injection in the early hours of 13 December 2005.

Howway!
(Ernie Bewick)

Stephen Richards

Here's a (hard) slice of life from the north of England, a portrait of one of the region's hardest men, Ernie Bewick. Fiercely anti-drugs, his world is one of burly club doormen, gun-toting, drug-dealing villains, "straighteners", internecine rivalry and the constant fear of ambush and even death. In 1997 Bewick killed another man in a fight outside a Sunderland pub. He admitted a charge of manslaughter and was jailed for six years. He is now a free man. Stephen Richards, the maverick investigative journalist, has had many of his 40-plus books serialized in the national press and magazines. He has appeared in many crime-related documentaries on national and international TV. He acts as a literary agent for crime writers, produces and directs crime documentaries and also promotes members of the crime underworld on his website www.crimebiz.com. Stephen Richards writes in a distinctive vernacular style that's exemplified here.

Ernie Bewick has been called a "gangland killer" and an "enforcer" but I can tell you he's one of the most forgiving men I've come across . . . okay, that might shock some of the family of Tony Waters and it might shock the people that have been spoonfed lies and deceit, but it's the truth and I always try to give you the truth until I find out otherwise.

For those of you that might not have heard of Ernie Bewick I'll fill you in with the details. 7 December 1997 was to be the last day in the life of convicted drug dealer Tony Waters. As a result of a fight Waters, 44, lost his life outside the Eastender pub, in High Street East, Sunderland.

Waters deliberately went looking for Bewick with the intention of doing him some damage over an incident that took place the previous night between Bewick and two other men in Sunderland's Luciano's restaurant. Ernie Bewick was pursued head on in a confrontation that was designed by Waters and for that reason it goes against all of those that have advised since the death of Waters that he just wanted a quiet life since his release from prison some four years earlier. It would seem that some would want to paint Waters as a whiter than white character and if that had been genuinely so then you'd be reading a very different view point here but as it goes I cannot write anything else.

Waters left behind a family that grieve him to this day and of course the time of year (Christmas) of his death compounds the pain and hurt they must feel for the loss of their loved one, but without fear or favour such sentiments should be put to one side for a moment in order to reveal the depths of Waters' resentment for Bewick. Bewick was and still is anti-drugs; Waters was pro-drugs and was well known within the drug fraternity of the north and saw Bewick as a stumbling block to dealing his drugs in the pubs under Bewick's charge so any excuse for a confrontation would help in ridding Bewick from the area.

Bewick, not a man to underestimate, was fully aware of the way Waters was dealing drugs and knew that he was the difference between Sunderland being flooded with drugs or being kept relatively drug free and so long as he was in charge of certain pub and club doors it would remain that way. In a similar way to how Viv frowned upon drugs so did Bewick and just as similarly as others wanted rid of Viv so that they could deal in his patch on Tyneside it looked to be the same way in Bewick's territory on Wearside. Bewick and Graham had a lot in common although I would have to give Bewick the slight edge over Graham in his handling of matters and his ability to sense danger.

Waters, a terrier-tempered person, met his untimely end as a direct result of his desire to wheel and deal drugs in Sunderland, although first I give you an insight into Ernie Bewick so that you can make your own mind up as to whether you agree with what I write. Directly from Ernie Bewick the story unfolds with his account of the two fights he had with another northern hard man, Billy Robinson from Gateshead. Here, Ernie Bewick accounts for the night he was working on a door when Billy Robinson and his party turned up:

That night I was called to the door (The Blue Monkey) and they said that Billy Robinson was at the door and he wanted to come in. Well, on that particular evening it was the type where everybody had to pay when they came in so I went up and I really didn't know Billy at the time and I explained that everybody had to pay to get in. His henchmen standing beside him said, "Do you know who you're talking to," and things like that. I said, "I'm sorry you know but you've got to pay in."

If anybody had asked me the same thing I'd have said, "Fair enough," so then I was being called a little shit type of thing and abuse like that thrown at me so I said, "Look, you can't come in." So he said, "Right, you little thing, get round the corner, you little shit," I said, "Well, fair enough." So then Billy slapped me across the face and I went forward to go into him, he tried to punch me so I ducked over the punch and gave him a right cross and an upper cut and knocked him out.

Then his friends were there, his big henchmen suddenly seemed to deflate and I said, "Right, get him up and fuck off and don't ever come back here any more," so they went but obviously by then all the talk starts to generate so obviously there were a few scares that they were going to come through team-handed at the door and there was a couple of times we had to prepare for what might have happened.

Months later I heard rumours that I was going to be set up and different things so one day Keith Bell (who changed his name to Keith Collins) come knocking on my door, trying to go on as though he was a friend, and he says, "Look, Billy wants to have a go at you and he wants to see you as soon as possible for a one to one (straightener)," so I said, "Fair enough I'll come now." He replied, "Well, can you not make it later on tonight? You know where I live, you've been to mine before, can you come through?" We went through and it went on a couple of hours while they were talking so I got something to eat at Keith's.

Later on the fight was arranged at a gym in Jesmond, which was owned by Andy Webb (a former Mr Great Britain). Andy Webb was a gentleman, Viv was a gentleman, they were all nice and friendly. I came through by myself. (Staggering to think that Ernie was fearless in turning up to such a venue on his own, but he did!) I never brought anyone with me I walked in their camp on my own, there was a few of them there and Viv got on the phone to tell Billy I was there and I was kept waiting a further hour and half to two hours before he came.

I remember feeling cold (due to the lengthy waiting process) and Andy Webb was very good towards me and he gave me a cup of tea to warm me because by the time Billy had arrived they'd been talking for about twenty minutes around the corner. So I more or less explained to Viv that if I sort it out over a cup of tea without any trouble then that's the way I preferred it. (Again, staggering to think that Ernie was as calm as a cucumber wanting to talk things over a cup of tea and obviously the others there might have seen this as a sign of weakness, but Ernie's just that sort of guy and not for one minute should he have been underestimated – it wasn't for nothing that his fists were called the "peacemakers".)

I didn't want any trouble but at the same time I went through because if that was the way to solve it fair enough and Billy obviously wanted the fight on so fair enough. So I went through where they had the fight arranged, it was a small compartment, there was a little bank that went up and obviously I realize now that was suited for Billy's needs; with me being a lot lighter he could get me into the corner or if I ran up the bank I would slip or fall over, which I did at one point when I was fighting but I got out of that anyhow.

Billy came up to me and he was a gentleman when he approached me. The first thing he said to me was, "Ernie, I want to shake your hands now before we have this fight and I'm going to shake your hands after the fight." So I shook his hand then we got on with the fight.

Billy sort of stood in a boxer's stance, I didn't underestimate him because he's got a powerful punch and later on as we became friends we had a bit of trouble with someone and he has got a powerful punch. So my strategy was to wear him out and then go in for it, that was my strategy before I even went through there. I stood there and I jumped about a bit and I was flicking punches at him trying to egg him on to come forward. The punches weren't really very hard; to be honest I wasn't even properly warmed up because I'd been standing waiting all that time in the cold.

So Billy was throwing lefts, coming forward with lefts, straight lefts and trying to catch me with them but obviously I was jumping about a little bit, flicking a punch here and there, getting him to move and at one stage Billy got on top of me, but I managed to quickly escape from underneath his arm and I was back up on my feet in no time because I was only $13\frac{1}{2}$ stone at the time and I was pretty fit and agile and I could jump about a little bit. (Wow – don't let Ernie fool you here, he's still very fit and looks like he could walk through a barn full of troublemakers.)

We stood, we bounced about a little bit again, he was trying to get his punches and I noticed he was open for a left hook. But something inside's telling me to hold that left hook back so now I'm throwing right hands all the time and now I'm warmed up and they're coming over strong and I even said during the fight as a bit of hype, "Right, I'm warmed up now, I'm starting the fight off now."

I don't know how long I was fighting, I cannot say if it was five minutes, but it wasn't half an hour or three quarters of an hour, but when you think five minutes could be a long time for most fit fellahs. Anyhow I never took any punches, I might have had to a little bit but nothing really hard and I came in with a right hand all the time, I've thrown a right hand and caught him with a left hook, so now I'm coming in to finish the job off. (It would seem that Ernie was cruising in like a battleship.)

Billy's moving around but as he's staggering over, I'm thinking, "Whoa, I've been caught with an upper cut," by then I fell over, it was a good punch, one of my hands was on the ground, in fact it was the left hand, and then Keith Bell come around and he got hold of my hand. I was embarrassed because I thought they were stopping the fight because I'd been knocked over, I thought Billy was now going to run in and kick me because he would have been desperate and I was going to roll around and spring back up, that was the theme that went through my mind, you're confident that that was the way it would go.

So I knew I was vulnerable because he could have run at me and kicked me. I got up and that was the point I went berserk, I tore into him, split all his lips and that and literally went mad and shouted, "COME ONNNNNNNNNN!" and just literally went straight at him as if to say I'm not getting beat off anybody, I was really hyped up.

Then I went forward and Viv grabbed me shouting, "HOW-WAY ERNIE. HOWWAY ERNIE," and things like that. So they stopped the fight and I was dead confused because I'd realized Billy had knocked me over, but they said, "Howway, you've beaten him fair and square." So then Billy went that way and Viv went the other way and I was confused so I followed the way Viv went.

Remember, walking away from that I'd been involved in a fight and I'd been hit and things like that and for a minute my mind went a bit blank so as I walked through the door I remember walking into Viv and he was sitting on the seat and he was saying, "Look, I want no trouble, I want no trouble in this gym, mind." I said, "Look, I'll stand here with you." I folded my arms and stood beside him. Andy Webb was standing there and Andy Webb's head was down like that, I don't know why. I thought it could be because of what Viv said or he was embarrassed with the way Viv went on because he seemed to be like an honourable type of person and was nice towards me and made me feel comfortable.

I can remember that I went to the toilet, came back and then shook Viv's hand and everything and we were alright, as I walked towards the door and went out I could feel Viv watching me from behind, I knew without turning my head. When I got out Billy was at the other side of the door so he must have walked around and out some other way. He come up to me and hugged me and I hugged him back and we shook hands and everything and just like what he said before the fight that he'd shake my hand after the fight he kept his word.

I'd previously boxed Viv Graham and I beat him in the ring, I was too strong for him pound for pound. I remember when I was young I used to idolize Rocky Marciano and when I used to fight in that ring I didn't want to box and I used to think it clever to take punches so I knew I could take a punch even though I'd boxed a few times. At that time I was silly, I was young and it was daft the way I went on at that time. At 17 to 18 we go through all sorts of phases when we grow up, don't we? Looking up to Rocky Marciano gave me strength; if I wanted to beat anybody I just used to think of Rocky Marciano, he had a head like a bowling ball and you couldn't hurt him and that's the way I thought so really a little bit of that was still in me.

Anyway getting back to the fight with Billy, as I was getting back into the car Keith Bell said, "You know, Viv shouldn't have stuck that sly punch on you." I said, "Ah, I see what you mean," and then I realized that it wasn't Billy that gave me that walloping uppercut and it all fitted into place then. I got out of the car and went back into the gym and Viv was on the phone and I think Keith was in the other room although I'm guessing about that. When Viv finished he came over and said, "Ernie, look, Billy was like a dad to me he really brought me up when I was younger." I said, "Look, it was only a daft punch, forget about it." Viv said, "Is it okay if I come through?" (to Sunderland). I said that it would be all right, but I'm always like that; even when I got out of prison I forgave certain people for what they'd done against me.

But I can forgive people and I realize everybody's got good points and everybody's got bad points, I try to motivate the good points in people which isn't a bad thing is it, but be careful because the bad ones will take over. Marciano is portrayed as a good man, his mother went to church and prayed for him, he come from an Italian-type of family where his mother didn't like him getting into the ring and he didn't like his mother knowing he was getting hurt so I suppose in a way when you're reading books like that as a kid maybe it's been reflected in me and kept me off the drugs and off the streets and got me into the gym training. People wanted to be like Marciano but now people want to be like Tyson.

After the fight with Billy I maintained some links with Viv and we had a few discussions on the phone about it because I'd heard rumours going about that I'd been knocked out for ten minutes, I'd discussed that with Viv and Viv explained, "Look, I haven't said anything like that, Ernie." He told me that he had lots of respect for me and I came through there on my own.

Billy Hardy went through to Newcastle and he met with John Davison and Viv and all them and he turned around and said, "Look, all of them through there they've got loads of respect for you." But I was also hearing stories, what happened once was that Gavin Cook was asking me about what went on and he said, "I've been in his (Viv's) company and he says he knocked you out for ten minutes." I said, "Look, if Viv ever wants his go at me . . ."

I heard Viv was very supportive towards me over a few things because I've had trouble with the Sayers; we've chased them from Sunderland when they came with guns one night. There's a load of lads will tell you the truth about what happened there. They come barging in, it was Gary Rob who had the "After Dark" (club), and what happened was Gary said, "Look, they've all barged in." Ashy (Paul Ashton – now serving a total of 31 years' imprisonment) was there, I said, "Don't worry we'll get them out," I went up to the two Sayers (Michael and Stephen) and said, "Look, there's all of us, are you daft or something?"

There were some big hefty blokes with us so I turned around and said, "If you want trouble, we'll do it that way, then!" They turned around and said that they had guns so I said we also had guns. "He's got one there," I said, pointing to one of the men with me. I was only bluffing but sure enough one of them did have one as well, he actually went to his car, came back and told me he had one but I never saw it, but I spread that about. I'm not a bloke that would like to use things like that, but from my point of view it was a bit of bluff and I wanted to get them off the premises and they offered me violence and I said, "Okay, then, I'll have you two together and I'm offering you two violence." In other words if that's what you want, but there's loads of scenarios happened like that around the town. Anyway the bluff worked with them and they cleared off.

Some time later there was talk that one of them (Sayers) was going to come through and have a go at me now; I heard that Viv went up to him and he turned around and told the lad that was with the Sayers that he was going to get knackered if he had a go at me, so one night when he come through to Sunderland I sat and waited and confronted him and said, "I hear you're going to have a go at me?" "Nah, nah, I don't want any trouble with you," was his reply so I just left it.

I built up a friendship with Viv and actually went through to his house and had a cup of tea with him and had a discussion over different things. I remember Gavin Cook was working with Viv through there (Newcastle) and he came through and said, "I've told Viv that you're not bothered about him and I'm keeping out of it, so here's his phone number." He must have been match making and I said, "Look, I'm not going to back down from him, Gavin." So I pulled Viv up and said, "You're the one going around telling everyone that you knocked me out for ten minutes." He replied, "Ernie, I've never said that, I've got nothing but respect for you and all I want is your respect." I replied, "Look, Viv, you've always had my respect, I've heard a lot about you although the only thing that put me off was when you punched me but you've always got my respect, but now you're going around saying you knocked me out."

Anyway Viv denied saying it to the end. I remember meeting one of Viv's friends called McNally from around where Viv had once lived in Rowlands Gill and he said, "Honestly, Ernie, Viv Graham had lots of respect for you," and he went on to tell me that Viv was telling everyone I was "a man" and how I'd went on my own to the fight. There was another lad training with me in the gym and he said, "You know something, Ernie, you should never take notice of what some people say, I was training with Viv once and he's got loads of respect for you."

I ended up getting on well with Viv but you've always got to remember that there's still a dividing line and you do hear Chinese whispers and all that. I'd heard stories, how true they were I don't know, but he'd come and have a drink with you, he'd take you to the bar when he was ready and as you go in he'll put his arm around you and all of a sudden it's BANG, BANG and he's on you.

Other stories were that he wouldn't take his coat off and stand in front of the man, it would be something like "You alright, mate," and then BANG so I was advised to be wary of that sort of stroke so I kept that little bit of doubt in my mind and I was very careful of how I went about it if I ever socialized with him, because he did want to come through here. I'd also heard that Viv liked to have an audience around him when he kicked off with a couple of lads who he might knock out and then the word spreads, "Viv knacked three lads the other night, you should've seen him." I mean, anybody can go and do that, but that's just the image . . . but anyway it mightn't be true because you hear all kinds of stories about me, you'll hear some good and you'll hear some bad.

There ends the interview relating to the Billy Robinson fight and it goes to show what kind of a man Viv was in the sense that he broke a code of conduct for his friend and mentor, Billy Robinson, when he punched Ernie in order to give Billy some time. Billy wouldn't have approved, had he had time to say so, because afterwards he congratulated Ernie on a fair and square win.

Maybe that's not the way it was meant to go but it did and I believe that when Ernie felt Viv's eyes burning into his back after the fight that Viv may have been overawed at Ernie's resilience to his punch and it maybe showed Viv that if he ever had a toe to toe with Ernie then, as had happened in a past boxing match between them, then it would be Viv who would come off the loser.

Ernie was forgiving towards Viv and that clearly shows the type of characteristics he learned from his hero Rocky Marciano. As for Viv spreading rumours that he'd had Ernie knocked out for ten minutes, it fits in with some rumours I'd picked up elsewhere but of course such bravado helps maintain a hard man image, and what better way to do it than to perpetuate the hard man image by embroidering on the truth, as Viv seemed to do.

Ernie is the classic hard man, Viv was the new breed straddling the line between past and present, but Viv didn't have the inherent safety reflex that's bred into city dwellers and that is what I believe Viv lacked and was to cause his eventual downfall.

The delicate matter of Ernie being on prison licence made it difficult to talk about the Tony Waters murder but the story I've heard time and time again was that Tony had it in for Ernie and he'd made a cocked gun gesture with his hand and pointed it towards Ernie, indicating that Ernie was going to be shot. From a third party I was able to get the picture of the build up to Tony Waters' death. That night Ernie was hit over the head with a bottle and his head was bleeding. The night before that Ernie had a fight with Scott Waters when Ernie tried to eject him from a restaurant because he was being abusive.

Word was spreading around town that it had taken seven of them to sort Scott Waters out, a rumour apparently started by Waters. Ernie was in one of the pubs that Waters was in and people were looking to Ernie to see what he would do to scotch this rumour and it looked like Ernie was sucked into a vacuum of deceit and lies and reacted in a way that was out of sorts with his character and he decided to approach Scott Waters. Ernie was maybe forced into this option in front of the very same crowd that had told Ernie about the rumours Waters was spreading and because he couldn't back down he confronted Waters head on. Ernie, as a consequence, knocked out Scott Waters.

Further rumour has it then that Waters went back and told Tony Waters and a number of others that he was getting the better of Ernie Bewick and in fact had supposedly decked Bewick twice when seven others intervened and jumped him. This twisted story was to be the death of Tony Waters and the following day police intelligence reports suggest that people were walking about with guns looking for Ernie Bewick, looking in all the wrong places it would seem, which gives rise to the fact that they probably wanted word to get back to Ernie Bewick that they were looking for him over the previous night's fight.

They wanted to send a message of strength and into the bargain they wanted to frighten Ernie Bewick into staying away so that they could sell their drugs. Certain people were advised to stay away from the town centre because there was "going to be trouble". Ernie, being Ernie, wasn't going to stay away because it was his territory and he had to show others that he wasn't going to hide away over something like this. My own intelligence gathering suggests that Ernie Bewick was told that there was trouble in a pub; although there wasn't any trouble at all, it was the perfect way to entice Ernie into another confrontation, designed by Tony Waters in order to get Ernie Bewick to show.

On entering the Eastender pub Ernie saw Tony and they acknowledged each other and the story goes that Tony asked what had happened the night before and in Ernie's understated fashion he told the truth but Tony was having none of it and gave Ernie an insult that was designed to cause further trouble, he called Ernie a "liar".

Scott Waters wasn't a fighter and it would go against such a man as Ernie Bewick's own code of conduct to hand out the thrashing Waters said he received, but it didn't pull any weight with Tony and Ernie was told to get outside the door, obviously for a one to one, but as Ernie walked towards the door he had a bottle thrown off his head and a scuffle ensued; but all was in control and Ernie then approached the man, Tony's stepson, who had thrown the bottle off his head, but the man's mother got in between her son and Ernie and became protective towards her cherub of a son who had just stotted the bottle off Ernie's head.

The altercation seemed to have settled and one of the doormen, Ritchie Laws, had taken over the dialogue of settling everyone down, but Tony's stepson had now thrown another bottle and this time it hit Ernie square on in his face. It beggars belief that Ernie didn't retaliate, he'd taken so much and yet here he was still in control, which takes some doing considering the force with which a grown man can throw a bottle off someone's head and face.

My inside source is able to tell me that Ernie pleaded with Tony to go and to forget about it. Surely two bottles stotted off Ernie's head should have been repayment enough but Tony was shouting at a lot of people and wouldn't leave and he was now making a show in front of people and was walking to go out and then would make to go back inside, asking Ernie to come outside with him. Ernie by this time was telling Tony's wife the story of how it was only him and Scott Waters that had the tousle and that Scott had been lying about the "seven" others.

Tony Waters came back in for the third time and during this time Ernie was explaining things to Andrea Chesum and remonstrating that she should ask the man that accompanied Scott about what had actually happened.

During this time Tony was shouting that Ernie was going to be shot and the argument continued down the stairs and when Ernie followed Andrea down Tony was physically poking his finger into Ernie's face and yet still Ernie didn't retaliate.

Outside the pub . . . well, Tony Waters met his death in a fight that was ferocious by any man's standards but when you consider my findings as to how Tony had conducted himself and the provocation Ernie was under, I believe that was far more than my words can convey. Ernie didn't intend for Waters to meet his untimely ending in such a fashion and was genuinely taken aback when he was charged with murder.

Ernie was Sunderland's 4th Emergency service and the similarities between how he and Viv worked were uncanny; although no doubt every major city in the UK can boast a Viv Graham character I don't believe many can boast an Ernie Bewick character modelled on Rocky Marciano. Where the police couldn't protect people's businesses from being taxed by criminals, Ernie Bewick could protect them, and many a time the services of Ernie were called upon to resolve certain issues that the police stayed away from.

Ernie now faced a murder rap and his club and pub doors were open to being poached by others seeing this as a power vacuum that they could fill. Davie Binks was a name suggested as one of the people interested in taking over Ernie's doors, but they were soon won back into Ernie's realm with the help of Ritchie Laws. One of Ernie's men was jumped on by five others and rumour has it that Ritchie stood up to Davie Binks, although for the sake of protecting both from prosecution let's just say this was a fairy tale I was told from one of my Chinese whisperers. We've got two very big men here as well as a man we'll call Wayne.

Wayne, although young, 23, is very mature and powerful for his age and a fight breaks out where he ends up doing well and again rumour has it that he told Ernie on a prison visit that no one was taking his doors. Ritchie won some of Ernie's doors back in Sunderland and Newbottle and all of this happened during Ernie's period of prison remand, which was for a period of some 14 months. With such loyalty behind him Ernie had more support than Viv had when he was murdered and that indicates the difference in terms of Ernie and Viv . . . yes, Ernie was a lone wolf, just like Viv, but when the cards were on the table Ernie's loyal supporters would always be there for him.

For those interested in further rumour there is a story that Ronnie Bestford went to a pub called the Sun Inn and told Davie Binks that he'd have to go and he wouldn't be picking money up any more and with this Ernie's friends, continually of their own free will, gave their support to ensure Sunderland wasn't taken over by outsiders.

Initially, when Ernie was on remand, Joe Freeman and a few others helped secure peace for the city of Sunderland and eventually Graham Potts was brought in to work with Joe as well as Brian Loughlan and many others safeguarded Ernie's doors. Of course Ernie was still on remand while all of this was going on and little did he know what was to be the outcome of his trial where he was to face the charge of murder.

What I was able to ask Ernie was about the current scene and how things had changed and keeping within the confines of his parole licence he was able to tell me that a lot of the trouble has died down and a lot of the "bad lads" have split up and how Paul Massey from Manchester (serving $17\frac{1}{2}$ years, reduced to $13\frac{1}{2}$ years on appeal) had been able to help avert a gangland war in the city of Sunderland over the death of Tony Waters and because of this Paul Massey must be given credit for his part in smoothing things over in respect how people were fed rumours as opposed to fact.

I suppose while the police intelligence were oblivious to what troubles were brewing in Sunderland it was down to Ernie Bewick's ability as a "peacemaker" to avert a serious takeover of the city from outsiders and with the backup and support of those brave enough to step out into a city ready to burst with violence a very serious situation was avoided.

Ending on a high note it would seem that Sunderland is a pretty well mannered city and things have settled down. Ernie Bewick deserves some credit for how he handled things when he was actively involved in running the doors; his followers deserve some credit for how they conducted themselves and maintained a calming atmosphere.

I could have plastered this chapter with violence, but you know sometimes it's better being understated than overstated and that's what I believe Ernie Bewick is all about. He's not a brash and egotistical man, he doesn't stick his chest out and spit on the path to give himself a hard case image – in fact Ernie is the total opposite of what you'd expect such a hard man to be and that's what makes him hard; he doesn't have to try; there's no need for such dramatics as I've often seen displayed by drug or drink-fuelled louts.

Ernie doesn't even swear, he says f'd instead of fucked, which fits in with the way a lot of the London chaps go on. With Ernie you get what you see, there's no hidden agenda beneath his calm exterior and you can imagine him going about his business as if it was an everyday occurrence. Comparing some so called hard men to Ernie makes them look like common thugs and I feel we're not going to see the likes of these characters ever again. I mean, what role model do kids use these days – steroid-filled athletes, whinging and argumentative tennis players, booze-filled darts players . . . you can keep the lot of them because there's only one Rocky Marciano in Sunderland.

Rocky Marciano helped evolve Ernie's style while a controversial character helped destroy it and because of that you'd expect Ernie to be a bitter man, but he's not. Throughout his prison sentence he only lost eight days in remission, that shows his strength of character and he did his time the right way, which I believe many could learn from.

Paul Massey is classed as the Godfather of Manchester's criminal underworld and to many that is how he will always be remembered but to some a debt of gratitude has to be acknowledged towards him for his swift intervention on behalf of Ernie Bewick and the city of Sunderland.

Paul is serving $13\frac{1}{2}$ years for a nightclub stabbing in which he denies all the allegations thrown at him. Even though the injured party stood in the witness dock and told the court that the man in the dock, Paul Massey, was not the man that stabbed him, Massey was found guilty. The court decided that the injured party was far too eager to make his testimony in defence of the defendant and for that reason found against Paul, but just imagine for one moment that it was you, the injured party, wouldn't you stand in the witness box and strenuously defend an innocent party if you knew the man in the dock wasn't the man who had attacked you with a knife?

The original sentence imposed of some $17\frac{1}{2}$ years defies logic. Justice must be seen to be done, but how can it when court rooms are made into gunned fortresses and the press are gagged with Public Immunity Interest (PII) Orders slapped on evidence by judges too fearful that the truth will come out?

Little Boy Lester
(George "Baby Face" Nelson)

Myron J. Quimby

Despite his "Baby Face" tag, Lester Joseph Gillis (1908–1934) possessed a thoroughly unsavoury disposition, characterized by one social commentator as "something out of a bad dream". Every writer on American gangsterdom has remarked on his innate cruelty. As a boy, he roamed the Chicago streets with a gang of juvenile hoodlums. By the age of 14, he was an accomplished car thief and had been dubbed "Baby Face" by members of his gang on account of his juvenile appearance. Nelson's early criminal career included stealing tyres, running stills, bootlegging, and armed robbery. He grew to be one of the toughest and most pitiless of the Depression-era criminals, a cold and brutal psychopath. "Where outlaws such as Pretty Boy Floyd and the Barkers would kill to protect themselves when cornered, Nelson went out of his way to murder – he loved it," observed the crime historian Jay Robert Nash. "His angelic, pear-smooth face never betrayed his instant ability to kill." Richard Lindberg added: "Standing only five feet four inches, Gillis compensated for his physical limitations with a murderous temper and a willingness to employ a switchblade or a gun without hesitation or remorse for the intended victim." In 1929 he began working for Al Capone. He assumed the name George Nelson, but everyone knew him as "Baby Face"; the nickname belied his reputation for carrying out vicious killings. Later, Nelson joined the John Dillinger gang and took part in

several bank robberies before being killed in a police shoot-out
with FBI agents in November 1934. His story is told here by
Myron J. Quimby Jr (b. 1923) as part of a true-crime account
of notorious criminals of the 1920s and '30s. Quimby achieved
still greater success with his book about American place names
and their derivation: Scratch Ankle, USA.

In the history of American crime, there has been no single individual more vicious, or who got more of a thrill from killing, than Mrs Gillis's little boy Lester. Once a small child, with a cherubic face, he eventually grew into a bantam-sized, hoodlum-killer, with a baby face. At full growth he would never tower above five feet, five inches.

Lester was born in Chicago, Illinois, 6 December 1908, of Belgian immigrant parents. His father died while he was still very young; thus he was denied the needed guidance and companionship only a father can give to a son.

Lester's mother, Mary Gillis, had to work very hard to provide for him and his sisters. As an unskilled worker, she earned very little money, and the children had to fend for themselves during the day.

Lester grew up in the packing and stockyard district of Chicago. This was a rough slum neighborhood, ruled by a local mob of young toughs known as the Five Points Gang. They were a kind of local crime wave, and stole from practically everybody.

With his small stature, baby face, and the meek-sounding name of Lester, he had to learn the art of self-defense at an early age. One look at him, and the members of the Five Points Gang wanted to start a fight with him. He fought back, and soon became most proficient with the "poor boy's equalizer" – the switchblade knife.

It was about this time that he met a pale, pimpled-faced young kid with a leaky heart, and the impossible name of Francis Albin Karpoviecz, who was also unacceptable by the Five Points Gang. This young man interested Lester, so the two of them teamed up. Lester taught the young Lithuanian all he had learned about stealing cars, and stripping them. Then the sickly kid got sicker, and had to leave Chicago. Lester was alone again. He didn't mind really, for he would get used to the loneliness. He didn't trust anyone, and felt that he needed help from no one. Yet, his ostracism by the members of the Five Points and other gangs did cause him some resentment, and increased his bitterness.

When his legs failed to grow to the length demanded by society, and his delicate features failed to mature, he became even more incorrigible. Mary Gillis had lost complete control of her son, and he of himself. His temper became so ferocious that members of the Five Points Gang came to fear him.

In 1922, Lester was arrested for auto theft while attempting to sell some of the accessories he had taken from the car. His vicious attitude toward the arresting officers, and his complete refusal to cooperate, earned him harsh punishment.

He was sentenced to an indefinite term at the St Charles Reform School. Then, in April 1924, he was surprisingly enough paroled for "good behavior". In September of the same year, he was back as a parole violator. In July 1925, he was again let out on parole – apparently in an expense-cutting maneuver – but he was returned again in October.

Not ones to give up easily, the authorities again paroled him, in July 1926. Now old enough to be sent to the penitentiary if he misbehaved again, he would not return to the school.

Lester never once looked upon these years in the reformatory as lost ones. He had spent the time getting an education from its inmates. He had real professionals as teachers; this was his education, and he made the most of it. He learned new methods of stealing cars, how to blow a safe, and even held debates with the older boys about the merits of bank robbery, as opposed to burglary.

When he left the Reformatory, Lester hung around his mother's house, on Marshfield Avenue, for a time. He was 18 years old now, but he never gave serious thought about getting a good formal education, or looking for a job. He was going to live the good life, with plenty of money, girls, cars, and excitement.

Mary Gillis gently tried to hint to her son that he should get a job and help out a little with the expenses. His sisters came right out and told him that he was a dead beat, and that he should help pay his way. Lester, however, was unimpressed.

Finally, disgusted with their incessant "nagging", Lester left Chicago, and started roaming across the country. He had stolen a car for transportation, and held up lonely filling stations for his expense money.

He lived in Reno, Nevada, for a short while, getting a job (his first) as a chauffeur for a small time gambler. Here he saw the easy money flowing across the gaming tables; but it eluded him. Still, he saw how the big gamblers, and the little gamblers, were living, and he wanted to live that way too. He was no professional gambler, though, he knew this, so he continued his travels Westward, looking.

He drifted into the Los Angeles area, where he settled for a while, and tried his luck at bootlegging and rumrunning. All it took was a small investment, and a lot of nerve; Lester had both. This occupation paid quite well, and no one seemed concerned with his small stature or his baby face.

Still the big money was eluding him, so he decided to move up north into the San Francisco Bay area. San Francisco was a wide open seaport town, where prohibition was just a nasty word. Up and down the Embarcadero, out on Market Street, and throughout Chinatown, swanky speakeasies drew large crowds, and the booze and money flowed.

Bootleggers and rumrunners here were making good money, with little or no interference from authorities. This was just what Lester was looking for: a wide open town, with plenty of opportunities for an enterprising young hoodlum.

By the end of 1928, Lester had earned enough money to return to Chicago in style. He was most anxious to show everybody in his old neighbourhood, and particularly the members of the Five Points Gang, just how much of a big shot he had become.

His return was sweet, and many people were impressed with the lavish way he threw his money around. Unhappily for Lester, the old Five Points Gang had changed; it was now controlled by an entirely new crop of delinquents who had never heard of him. Still, they were impressed, and so was a petite Polish girl who worked in the local five and ten.

Blue-eyed Helen Wawrzyniak was indeed five feet, two. She weighed about 94 pounds. She was a brunette, very pretty, and only 16. But she knew what she wanted, and now it was that strutting, swaggering, pint-sized Lester Gillis.

Against the violent objections of Helen's parents, they were married, and he spent lavishly to make her happy. Then they settled down for a while in Chicago, where he tried to make a go of things. But Lester didn't inspire much confidence with the local gangs, and he could seem to make an inroad into the Chicago Underworld.

Disgusted and disappointed, Lester packed up his new bride and moved back to the West Coast. They settled in the small village of

Sausalito, on the east side of Golden Gate, the entrance to San Francisco Bay.

Here and in the Bay Area, Lester tried to reestablish his once flourishing bootleg enterprise, and pulled several small-time robberies in the meantime, to pay the rent. It was in San Francisco that he was picked up by the police for carrying a gun. A short time later he was arrested again, this time on suspicion of holding up a gas station, but was released without prosecution.

Through various criminal activities, he and Helen managed to put together a bundle, and then they felt the call of home. There were two children in the family now. Ronald was born in 1929, and Arlene was born the following year. Lester Gillis, who was now using the name George Nelson, hadn't wanted any children, and they were proving a nuisance to both himself, and Helen. So, when they got to Chicago, they unloaded both of them on their grandmother, the long-suffering Mary Gillis.

Here Arlene would stay, and eventually would come to know her mother only as "Aunt Helen." Ronald would later be sent to Bremerton, Washington, where he would live with a married sister of Helen's. Neither of the children would ever come to know their father.

Things were always a bit rough for "George Nelson," because he just didn't look like the bad man he wanted so desperately to be. His tough talk and egotistical boasting sounded like the crow of a bantam rooster to most of the hoodlums he wanted to work with.

Eventually Nelson did find a couple of bank robbers who were more desperate than they were choosy about the help they hired. He was given a minor role as a lookout and wheelman in the robbing of a bank in Spring Grove, Illinois.

His cut of the take was niggardly, but he now had a foot in the door and he could properly call himself a "bank robber." This, to him, was the most important part of the operation. And, sure enough, the boys called for him again, and he helped them loot the First National Bank of Itasca, Illinois. Things seemed to be looking up for George Nelson, and Helen was also elated.

Time passed, then Nelson and a couple of other hoods hit the bank in Hillside, Illinois. Nelson, feeling cocky, shot a bank guard. The guard wasn't killed, but the news media screamed for vengeance; so the three of them divided the $6,250 in loot, and separated.

With this fabulous wad, the Nelsons went on a spending spree that wouldn't stop until they ran out of money. Helen bought jewels, furs, exotic perfumes, and all the clothes she could carry. They also purchased a Ford V-8, and wined and dined in the most fashionable speakeasies in town. Then suddenly there was no more money, and George Nelson had to go back to work.

The newspapers, reporting on the Hillside bank job, with its subsequent shooting of the bank guard, described one of the hoodlums as "a young man with a baby face." Now some of his acquaintances began to call him "Baby Face Nelson" and, although it had a distinct ring to it, he didn't like it one bit. Helen calmed his ruffled feelings, however, and told him she thought it was kind of cute. He grew to hate this name passionately.

Helen had bought some of her jewelry at a small shop just off Michigan Avenue. At that time, Nelson had learned that it was owned and operated by one old man. So on 15 January 1931, Nelson entered the store, and told the old man, "This is a holdup."

On the way out, his pockets filled with loot, Nelson walked into the arms of the police. They, too, had been impressed with the store's vulnerability to robbery, and had staked out the place. While Nelson had been casing the store for a hit they had been casing him, and when he made his move they made theirs.

Booked in the station downtown, as Number 5437, George Nelson, alias "Baby Face Nelson," alias Lester M. Gillis, was charged with armed robbery. At the jail, during a routine lineup, someone remembered the story about the baby faced bandit, the Hillside bank job, and the shooting of the guard.

Witnesses were brought in, and Nelson was positively identified as one of the three bandits who had held up the bank. His refusal to cooperate by naming the other hoodlums went hard on him, but he couldn't help that. He knew that if he became a "stoolie" it would upset all his future plans for a career in crime.

On 15 July 1931, he was found guilty, and the judge gave him the maximum sentence of from one year to life in the Penitentiary, and he entered Joliet on 17 July 1931.

Living in Joliet was miserable to say the least and, with his rebellious nature, Nelson did nothing but antagonize both guards and inmates. He was in one fight after another, and was placed in solitary for long periods of time. This only served to make him more defiant, and more vicious, if that was possible.

During the waning days of 1931, Nelson tried to escape, but the attempt failed miserably. All it got him was an additional sentence, and again brought him to the attention of authorities.

These authorities, in reviewing his case, discovered that he matched the description of one of three holdup men in a bank robbery in Itasca. This identification, and news stories, led authorities into the habit of referring to him as "Baby Face Nelson".

Nelson, now formally accused of the Itasca bank job, was taken from Joliet Penitentiary, and placed on a train to Chicago. Upon arrival there, he was transferred by automobile, to the DuPage County Jail at Wheaton, Illinois, to await trial.

The trial took three days, and he was again found guilty of bank robbery, and sentenced to from one to twenty years in the state penitentiary (Joliet). Now he knew he would never get out of prison unless desperate measures were taken.

On 15 February 1932, he was put aboard the Rock Island Special, in leg irons, and handcuffed to his guard. Then they headed back to Joliet. They debarked from the train in downtown Joliet, and his guard hailed a cab to take them to the penitentiary.

Strange as it might seem, this action was not unusual, as guards had standing instructions to take cabs if a prison car was not waiting for them. This, authorities believed, reduced the possibility of escape, which would be compounded by loitering around the depot awaiting an official car.

Nelson, still handcuffed to his guard, and still wearing the cumbersome leg irons, entered the cab first. This placed him right behind the driver, with the guard on his right. As soon as the door of the cab was closed, and the cab started away from the curb, *Nelson pulled a gun!*

He disarmed his guard, and then placed his pistol to the back of the cab driver's head. He instructed him to drive out of town, and to avoid attracting any attention, otherwise, Nelson assured him, he'd be a dead hero. Then he turned his attention to his guard again, and ordered him to remove the irons.

The nervous driver started speeding toward the outskirts of Joliet, and Nelson warned him to slow down. He told him, "I'll blow your damn head off, if you don't slow this cab down!" The driver slowed down, and the three quietly cruised into the suburbs, where Nelson noticed a cemetery on his left. It was a nice quiet and secluded place so Nelson ordered the driver to pull over and get out.

The guard got out first, prodded by Nelson's pistol, and Nelson knocked him unconscious with a rap on the head from his gun. Then Nelson led the terrified cab driver deeper into the cemetery and told him to turn around. Scared witless, the driver started to run, but Nelson also struck him down with his pistol.

Nelson then stripped the cab driver of his hat and coat, put them on, and drove away in the cab. No one had been killed, but the driver did catch pneumonia from lying on the frozen ground, and the guard awoke with a bad headache.

How Baby Face Nelson got his pistol was never established, though there have been many theories. It could have been slipped to him, as he brushed against someone on the crowded train, or delivered to him as he and the guard walked down the station platform. Both the guard and the cab driver were cleared of any suspicion of complicity in the escape.

One thing was certain – Helen Nelson had somehow gotten a gun to her husband. He had no gang, and with the exception of Helen there was no one who cared if he stayed in prison or not. He didn't have enough money to buy a friend or his freedom.

From this moment on Nelson would never see the inside of a jail or prison again. Yet the police would come to know him as Lester Gillis, Alex Gillis, Lester Giles, Big George Nelson, Jimmie Nelson, Jimmy Burnett, and of course, Baby Face Nelson.

Nelson fled back to San Francisco, where he used the name of Jimmy Burnett. Here he again entered the waning trade of rum-running and bootlegging. For a while he worked at these occupations industriously, trying to earn enough money to send for Helen.

Most of the criminal activities in and around San Francisco were syndicated by a gang under the direction of a hoodlum named Joe Parente. Parente's operations covered most of the San Francisco Bay area, but stretched as far south as the San Joaquin Valley.

"Burnett", because of his past bootlegging connections, was allowed to join the gang, which was then engaged in many diversified activities, and earned enough money to send for his wife. She arrived, bringing their daughter Arlene with her. She told Nelson she had done this to throw off suspicion, and that a kid would make them appear more like a regular family. Though this made good sense, Nelson didn't like the idea.

While working for Parente, Nelson met two other characters who would later play their part in the drama of his life. One was a two-bit hoodlum called Fatso Negri, who was not too heavy in the brain department, but more than made up for it elsewhere. He would do anything for a buck, and this made him valuable for use as an errand boy.

The other was a tall, dark-eyed, dark-haired bootlegger named John Paul Chase. He was destined to become Baby Face Nelson's lieutenant. Chase's parents were native Americans, and had come to California from Omaha, in 1901. That same year their son was born, and they gave him the patriotic name of "John Paul".

Before Chase could finish grade school he quit and went to work ranching, farming, and also held a job as a chauffeur for a Reno gambler. Later he got a job as a machinist's helper in a railroad shop, but in 1926 he was fired, and this ended his career as a working man.

Chase became a bootlegger and, with his suave manner, and small, trim mustache, was also something of a ladies' man. He was ambitious, industrious, and anxious to make a lot of money, but he lacked the brains or intelligence to funnel this energy into the proper channels. What John Paul Chase had need of was a leader.

He became strangely attracted to this short, baby-faced character, who strutted around as if he were six feet tall. His interest increased sharply when "Burnett" confided in him that his real name was Nelson, and then told of his escape from the law, and of his many bank robberies. Perhaps he laid it on a bit thick, but he thought he might be able to use this charming, none-too-bright, hoodlum in the future.

Chase had heard of Baby Face Nelson and was smitten with a kind of hero worship. He would sit around and listen to "Big George", as Chase called Nelson, while he bragged of his past glories, and told of his grandiose plans for the future.

Things were going real well for Burnett, but one day poor, dumb, Fatso Negri, reading his favorite detective magazine, came across a picture of Baby Face Nelson. The accompanying article told of Nelson's fantastic escape, and mysterious gun.

Any rational hoodlum would have quietly called the article to Nelson's attention, and then let it go at that. But not Fatso. He took an extreme delight in showing it to every hood he knew, and all at once everybody in the area seemed to know that Jimmy Burnett was really Baby Face Nelson. The Nelsons fled.

In Vallejo, California, there was a seemingly respectable hospital, which was really operated by and for criminals. For an extremely high fee the gangster could have bullets removed, his fingerprints erased, or even his face changed.

The hospital was owned and operated by a retired bank robber, safe blower, and burglar, Thomas C. (Tobe) Williams, whose real name was Thomas C. Cohen. He was known throughout the West Coast, in the underworld, as "The Goniff from Galway".

Helen Nelson entered the hospital here for a serious operation, and it was performed successfully by an underworld doctor. Nelson, as he sat around fidgeting, decided to have a small operation himself, so he had his fingers burned with acid to get rid of his fingerprints. The operation, of course, was a dismal failure, and it cost him a bundle.

When Helen could travel, Nelson began to make plans. He wanted to form his own gang so as a beginning he offered a position to John Paul Chase, who accepted immediately. His first assignment was to purchase an automobile that couldn't be traced.

Then Nelson, Helen, and Chase drove across the country to the city of Minneapolis, where they rented an apartment. From this base of operations, Nelson hoped to form a gang, fan out across the Middlewest, and hit some of the fat little farm banks. In the meantime he and Chase hit the bank in Brainerd, Minnesota in October 1933, and got their first big money: $32,000.

The two of them split the money down the middle, then settled back to enjoy it. With $16,000 apiece, they didn't have to work for a while. In those depression days, this sum of money was a fortune.

Repeal came suddenly on 5 December 1933, and thousands of hard-working bootleggers, rumrunners, hijackers, and other allied professionals were thrown out of work. Many of these would be forced to find other ways to make a dishonest buck.

For reasons which have always remained vague, on 4 March 1934, Baby Face Nelson shot and killed Theodore W. Kidder, 35, a paint salesman. Kidder worked for the National Lead Company in St Paul.

Kidder was with his mother-in-law, and they had just come from attending a children's party in Minneapolis. Although the police did not find out why Nelson killed him, they did have an excellent description of him and the car, with its California license plates. Kidder was Nelson's first recorded murder victim.

In the days that followed, the story was splashed across the nation's newspapers, together with a picture of Baby Face Nelson.

Also included was a complete description of the Ford sedan, with its tag number: 6-H-475.

The seemingly senseless killing aroused the people in the Twin City area, and the newspapers played it up, but then it was suddenly bumped off the front page by another, more exciting story. The day before, John Dillinger had pulled his sensational escape from the Crown Point jail using a wooden gun, and the details were just now being released.

Running scared the Nelsons and Chase fled from Minneapolis to Bremerton, Washington, where they hid out with Helen's sister for a time. Here Nelson read about the escape of John Dillinger, but it made no impression upon him. He didn't know Dillinger, and had no personal interest in the whole affair.

Intuition told Nelson that it was time to move again. He feared the authorities might trace them here, so they drove down to Reno where he and Chase both had friends. In Reno, the hoods greeted them with open arms. They needed the help of the two hoodlums.

A couple of the local boys were in real trouble, and were most anxious to get rid of a witness before he could testify. They asked Nelson and Chase if they would help. The pay was high and they needed money, so Nelson agreed to take the contract.

Nelson did the actual killing, while Chase drove the murder car. After they had disposed of the body, Nelson decided the car was too hot so he instructed Chase to drive it to San Francisco and get rid of it. They made a date to rendezvous later in Chicago.

Chase took the car to California, where he disposed of it, and the Nelsons then took a train to Chicago, where they awaited Chase's return.

While in Chicago, Nelson bumped into Tommy Carroll, who had worked with him on a couple of bank jobs. He told Nelson that a friend of his, one John Dillinger, was hiring gun hands.

This was big news for Nelson, for John Dillinger was now the talk of the land. He was really big time, and Nelson knew that he himself was still small potatoes. He believed that this man could open a whole new future for him, so he told Carroll he'd like to meet him.

Huddled around a table in a hideout in Chicago were Dillinger, Red Hamilton, Homer Van Meter, Eddie Green, Tommy Carroll, and Dillinger's latest girlfriend, Billie Frechette. The men were in the middle of planning a bank hit when Nelson arrived.

The proposition was simple, and the offer curtly made. Dillinger needed another man for the bank job, and he wanted to know if Nelson was interested in joining them. The split, he told Nelson, would be equal shares for all. Nelson agreed at once, and then joined them in the planning.

The only member of the gang who had worked with Dillinger before was Red Hamilton, but the rest had agreed to follow his orders. Carroll, Van Meter, and Billie Frechette knew Nelson from past experience, and none of them liked him. Nelson didn't like anybody but Nelson, so this presented no problem.

6 March 1934, the Dillinger gang arrived in Sioux Falls. As soon as they entered the Security National Bank and Trust Company, someone set off the alarm. This robbery meant a great deal to Nelson, and he was sure it would go off without a hitch with the "great" John Dillinger leading them. Nelson had also been fooled by the Dillinger publicity.

Now Nelson's temper took over, and he nearly threw a fit. Employees and customers later reported that he raved and ranted, and told them of the terrible things he was going to do to that "son of a bitch who set off that alarm". The only trouble was he never did find him.

A little later, while the other members of the gang were grabbing the money, the maniacal little killer shot Hale Keith, an off-duty motorcycle cop, seriously wounding him. Then he did a kind of "Lindy-Hop" around the bank, eyes glistening, and screaming "I got one of them! I got one of them!"

In all probability, if Dillinger or others in the gang had witnessed any of these shenanigans, this would have been Nelson's last job. This business of holding up banks was a serious one, and they couldn't tolerate any nuts.

Taking their hostages, the gang, with its loot, wheeled out of town and headed back to Eddie Green's apartment in Minneapolis.

When it came time to count and divide the loot, Eddie Green started to officiate. The sight of this infuriated Nelson, who violently disliked Green. Impulsively, Nelson snatched up a machine gun laying nearby, and pointed it at Green, demanding to know who the hell had made him the official counter.

Dillinger, not wanting any dissension in his newly formed gang, told Eddie to let Lester count it. "It'll come out just the same," he assured Green.

So Nelson, like a petulant child, and spitefully taking his time, eventually divided the loot of $49,500 into six neat piles. Out of Nelson's split would come a smaller one for his protégé, John Paul Chase, money for expenses, such as weapons and bullet proof vests, and protection money.

No one was in more of a hurry for money than John Dillinger, so the gang was again called together on 12 March, and they hit the First National Bank of Mason City, Iowa, the following day.

Nelson had a ball here, as they decided to leave him on the outside, stationed near the rear door of the bank. While here, he took a particular delight in firing bursts from his machine gun at the crowds of curious people. It was one of these playful bursts that cut the legs from under R. L. James.

Tommy Carroll, who had been posted across the street from the bank, couldn't find a thing to shoot at during the same time that Nelson, at his post in the rear, had used almost a full drum of ammunition.

Upon leaving, a sniper managed to shoot both Dillinger and Hamilton in the shoulder. The take was also only $52,000, and it should have been a lot more, according to the newspapers. Nelson began to wonder if the "great" John Dillinger was as great as he had once thought. As far as he was concerned both bank jobs had been dismal failures.

With two of the gang wounded, the members voted to split up for a while. This would give Dillinger and Hamilton time to heal their wounds, and allow the rest of the gang time to seek rest and relaxation. Nelson found no argument with this decision.

Returning to Chicago, Nelson picked up Helen, and parked John Paul Chase. Then they headed to Milwaukee, away from the others, so they could really enjoy their ill-gotten gains. Meanwhile, Dillinger and Billie went to St Paul, where they moved into the Lincoln Court Apartments.

Secure and safe in Milwaukee, Nelson and Helen read, with mild interest, the latest news from St Paul. It was 31 March 1934, and the FBI had caught up with Dillinger at his Lincoln Court address, and with a St Paul detective had tried to take him. There had been quite a gun battle, but John, Homer, and Billie had escaped. One of them had been wounded, however, for there was blood on the scene. Nelson wondered, idly, who it was.

Then, on 3 April, the FBI shot and killed Eddie Green, in St Paul, and Nelson laughed about this. "Now," he told Helen, "that SOB won't be dividing any more money."

Next came the arrest of Billie Frechette and Doctor Clinton May, who had been enlisted by Green to treat Dillinger. They were charged with harboring a fugitive.

Still feeling safe, Nelson tickled his wife, Helen, by going around the apartment, whistling and singing, "Those FBI agents are breaking up that old gang of mine." He was cocksure of himself, and had never given the FBI a serious thought.

On 17 April, Nelson got the word, through Chase, that Dillinger was gathering the gang together and wanted to see him. He had been spending his funds freely, so he was ready to go back to work. Helen went with him, then dropped off in Chicago.

In Cicero, the gang presented a sad sight. Dillinger was limping, and his shoulder was still sore. Hamilton had never fully recovered from his shoulder wound, and didn't seem to be interested in anything. Homer Van Meter and Tommy Carroll were both followers who couldn't lead a gang, and nobody was willing to follow Nelson, whom they all believed to be a neurotic.

Under the circumstances, someone suggested that they all go to a resort in northern Wisconsin for a rest, and then later, maybe, they could come up with an idea for a job. The place was called Little Bohemia, and was primarily a summer lodge. It was located on Little Star Lake, not far from Mercer. Since it was a summer lodge, but open in the winter, they were sure of having it all to themselves.

While the rest of the gang settled down in the main lodge building, the Nelsons preferred to keep to themselves. The owner had a few separate three-room cabins nearby, so they took one of these.

Mr and Mrs Emil Wanatka were delighted to have so many free-spending guests in the off season. Mr Wanatka had remained open in hopes something like this would happen. He was carrying a heavy mortgage on the place, and could use the extra money.

His happiness soon changed to terror when he finally figured out who his guests were, and he got word to the FBI. On Sunday night, 22 April 1934, the agents surrounded the lodge, and before long a full-fledged battle was in progress.

Nelson and Helen were in the main building when the shooting began, and Helen ran into the cellar with the rest of the women. Dillinger, Hamilton, Van Meter, Carroll, and Nelson all escaped through a back window, but the sounds of battle stimulated Nelson's interest so he circled the lodge, hoping to get a clear shot.

According to Melvin Purvis, Special Agent in Charge, Nelson did spot him, and churned up the dirt in front of him with his machine gun. But when the agents returned the fire, Nelson fled.

While Nelson was having his fun, his comrades were churning up some dirt of their own, but with their feet. When they reached the banks of the lake, they turned to the right and escaped along the shore. By the time Nelson got there everyone had gone, and he turned to the left.

He stumbled along the left bank of the lake for a while, but he soon got winded. Living the easy life of wine, women and song, he wasn't in the best of condition. Finally he cut away from the lake, and crossed through the woods.

Presently he came upon a store operated by Mr and Mrs Alvin Koerner. They also ran the telephone exchange for the area. Nelson ran inside, wild-eyed, and waved his tommygun at Alvin Koerner.

Nelson's words were curt and to the point: he wanted to know if Koerner owned a car. Koerner, his eyes glued to the waving machine gun, said there was a car outside, but it didn't belong to him. "To hell with that," Nelson spat, "get out there and get in – we're going to take a ride."

Outside Koerner tried to reason with Nelson but Nelson told him, "Get in and shut up, I gotta think." Just as they had gotten into the car and Nelson had switched on the lights, they saw another car coming. He immediately shut the lights off, and told Koerner to keep quiet.

In the other car were a local constable, Carl C. Christensen, Special Agent Jay Newman, and Special Agent W. Carter Baum, of the FBI. Christensen was showing them the way to Koerner's store so they could call the FBI field headquarters at Rhinelander for more agents.

Nelson just sat there calmly waiting for the other car to arrive. He was fingering the machine gun in his lap nervously, and thinking dark thoughts. He had had just about enough of being chased, and was about to lose his vicious temper. He wasn't thinking about getting away now, but only about getting even.

When the car got close enough so Nelson could see the pistol in Agent Newman's hand, he opened the door of the car and began to spray the FBI car with a deadly fire. Agent W. Carter Baum had a machine gun in his lap, but he never got a chance to use it.

According to Christensen, he tried to duck down behind Baum, and Newman tried to duck down behind him. Baum fell out of the car, then he got up, and tried to run but fell across a fence. He had been hit in the throat. Then Newman was hit in the head by a bullet and he rolled out.

Christensen then jumped out of the car and started to run, but Nelson's bullets slammed him to the ground. Christensen was very bitter in his story, as he said, "I tried to crawl to Baum, who had fallen across the fence. I could still hear him breathing, but he died before anyone got there. They let us lie there about an hour before anyone dared to come!"

Then Nelson jumped into the car the officers had driven to the scene, and sped away into the night, leaving behind him two badly wounded men and one dead one. Special Agent W. Carter Baum, 29, died, draped across a fence. Christensen had eight bullets in him, and Special Agent Newman had been shot in the forehead, but both would live.

Koerner, who had jumped from the car, raced into his store. Here he immediately telephoned the police in Mercer and reported what had happened. They, in turn, got in touch with the FBI, who eventually got agents to the scene, but it was too late.

Nelson drove the car as far south as Squaw Lake, where it quit on him. Then he fled into the woods on foot but, having no sense of direction, he headed north to the vicinity of Lac du Flambeau.

Here he stumbled upon the hut of an old Indian called "Catfish", a full blooded Chippewa. Still carrying his machine gun he convinced Catfish to act as his host for three days. The old Indian had no idea who he was, but tolerated him and his weapon.

When Nelson decided that it was safe enough, he left the Indian Reservation, and made his way to the small town of Fifield, in Price County. Here he stole a car, and sped back to the safety of Chicago.

In Chicago he called Chase and sent him on errands – buying food, guns, ammunition, and a bulletproof vest. He remained in the hideout, where he kept his ear glued to the radio. Before long he had a pretty good idea of the situation. All of the gang had gotten away, but Helen – his Helen – Marie Conforti, and Jean Delaney had been captured. He felt the loss of Helen rather strongly for the moment, for he was beginning to get a little scared.

The next day Dillinger and Van Meter were speeding toward St Paul in a stolen sedan, with Red Hamilton asleep on the back seat. Two officers recognized the car from a description they had, and started out in pursuit. When Van Meter speeded up they fired at the car, and a lucky shot entered the back seat, then entered Hamilton, mortally wounding him.

On 30 April 1934, three policemen recognized Baby Face Nelson, Chase (who they thought was Hamilton), Van Meter and Harry Fox. They pursued them and finally cut in front of Nelson's car; but before they could make their move, Nelson was out of the car with a machine gun in his hand.

Getting the drop on the three officers, he ordered them out of their car. As the driver emerged, Nelson beat him to the ground, then ordered the other two to start running.

The two officers, their hands still raised, started off up the high-way, and Nelson cooly raised his machine gun and took deliberate aim at their backs. Both Chase and Van Meter pleaded with Nelson not to shoot; they told him they were already too hot as it was.

Nelson lowered the gun, but he was plainly disappointed. Then to vent his pent up anger, he suddenly whirled and blasted the police car with his machine gun, shooting out most of the glass, and disabling the automobile.

Bad news came on 7 June, when Nelson heard on the radio that Tommy Carroll had been killed in a shootout with Detectives Emil Steffen and P. E. Walker, of Waterloo, Iowa. He hadn't particu-larly liked Carroll, but the killing hit too close to home. Then came the good news: Helen, Jean Delaney, and Marie Conforti had been sentenced to two years, then let off with probation. In less than a day, Helen joined Nelson in Chicago.

During the waning days of June, Chase brought the news that Dillinger and Van Meter were planning to rob the bank in South Bend, and wanted their help. According to Van Meter, who was the expert in such matters, this bank held enough money to put them all on easy street for a long time.

On 30 June 1934, the quartet hit the Merchants National Bank of South Bend, with Dillinger and Van Meter performing the actual robbery, while Nelson and Chase remained on guard outside.

Dillinger, showing the strain of past events, sent an angry burst from his machine gun into the ceiling of the bank. Nelson, had he seen this, would have been proud of John. But he was too busy with his own problems to take notice.

A jewelry store owner, Harry Berg, heard the machine gun fire, and peered out of his shop window. When he saw Nelson with his gun, he instantly knew what was happening, and decided to become involved. He came charging out of his store with a pistol in his hand. Taking careful aim, he fired at the unsuspecting Nelson, and Nelson spun from the impact of the bullet. His steel vest had protected him, and he was only bruised.

As he recovered from the impact of Berg's bullet, his temper took over, and he poured a torrent of bullets at his assailant, who prudently ducked back into his store. The shots shattered the shop's front window, and a ricochet bullet plowed into the leg of Jake Soloman, a customer. Another citizen, Samuel Toth, who was sitting in his automobile across the street, was struck in the head by a stray bullet. Then Patrolman Harold Wagner showed up, drawn by the noise of the shooting, and Nelson promptly killed him.

While Nelson was trying to look in all directions at once, a most extraordinary thing happened. A 16-year-old high school boy took a high flying leap and landed on Nelson's back! Around and around they went, with Nelson's machine gun spitting out sudden death. At last he shook off his tormentor, and then fired his remaining shots at him. The kid fell against a store window, shattering the glass, and one of Nelson's bullets passed through the palm of his hand, and he fainted.

By now Nelson was in a dour mood, and he must have reflected briefly upon the wisdom of following this man Dillinger. His gun was empty and he had no idea who would attack him next.

When Van Meter and Dillinger came out of the bank with several hostages, Nelson was more than ready to leave this crazy city. A gun battle with a jewelry store owner and a wrestling match with a school kid was about all he could take in one day. He felt no emotion over the killing of Patrolman Wagner.

They all loaded into the car, placing hostages on each running board. Then law officers came from everywhere, and everybody started shooting. The police succeeded in shooting two of the hostages, and they wounded Van Meter slightly.

Fleeing the town with their $28,000 in loot, they left behind one dead policeman, and five wounded citizens. The bank robbery had been a total failure as far as Nelson was concerned. The gang split up at once, with Dillinger going back to Chicago, Van Meter to St Paul, and Chase to Gary, where he had a girlfriend. Nelson picked up Helen and they went to a hideout he had arranged in Barrington, Illinois.

Then the inevitable happened, and on a muggy Sunday night, in

Chicago, the FBI and East Chicago, Indiana, police caught up with the "great" John Dillinger, and killed him. Dillinger didn't even get a shot off.

Nelson didn't feel any remorse over the death of Dillinger, whom he now rated as a third-class bum. He did feel anxiety, for now he became the FBI's Public Enemy Number One. Now he would have all those Federal Officers on his trail.

Mrs Gillis's little boy Lester had come a long way since the days of the Five Points Gang. He was now the most wanted man in America, and he felt an overpowering sense of doom.

He was the leader now, and he decided to see if he couldn't supervise a bank job without it turning into a disaster. His bank jobs would be thoroughly cased before he pulled them. To hell with this "playing it by ear". That was just plain foolishness!

Nelson knew that he would have to leave this part of the country soon, so he made plans to return to the West Coast. They would need money – plenty of it, Nelson said – so he sent Homer Van Meter, who had accepted his leadership, north into Minnesota. His assignment was to look over the fat little banks in the Iron Range district. He was to see if he could locate two banks that they could hit in the same day.

Van Meter looked over the field, but he wasn't too happy with the prospects. The roads left much to be desired. They were narrow, twisted affairs, which made it too easy for the law to set up roadblocks. He thought it better to stick to the flat country, so he headed to St Paul for a look-see, and to visit his girlfriend.

It was 23 August 1934, and the gang was about to lose another member. Four St Paul officers recognized Van Meter and called him to surrender. He took off, sprinting down the street, and into an alley where they killed him. For all practical purposes, this finished the Dillinger gang.

With this new development Nelson decided the time to leave the Chicago area was now. To hell with money. He rounded up Chase and Helen, and they started Westward.

Traveling the country roads, they made their way to Reno, being careful not to exceed the speed limits in the states they crossed. Helen always rode in front, while Nelson or Chase ducked down in back. This made them look like a couple out for a drive.

In Reno, Nelson looked up an acquaintance, Frank Cochran, a garage owner and airplane pilot. He told him their troubles, and Cochran got them a secluded cabin, where they enjoyed the fishing and hunting. Another acquaintance, Henry O. (Tex) Hall, a Reno gambler, promised to keep them informed of any police or FBI activity. It wasn't long before he sent word by Chase that Reno was filled with FBI agents who were questioning everybody.

Leaving at once, they fled to California, where they headed for the criminal hospital in Vallejo. Tobe Williams wouldn't even let them come in the door. He handed Nelson a thousand dollars and told him to keep going; he was too hot to handle.

Frightened, the trio gingerly threaded their way back towards the Chicago area. It was the only place they had left to go.

The underworld wanted Baby Face Nelson out of the way as much as did the police and the FBI. He was bringing too much heat down on their heads. The FBI was everywhere, peering, prying and probing. It was getting so a hard-working hoodlum couldn't ply his trade without an FBI agent stepping up to him to ask if he knew where Baby Face Nelson was hiding. Crime was a business, and Nelson was bad for business. He had to go.

Somewhere along the way back to the Chicago area, an informer saw the Nelsons and Chase. He notified the FBI, and also gave them a description of Nelson's car, and the license number.

All FBI agents in the Chicago area were immediately alerted to be on the lookout for a Ford V-8, bearing Illinois license plates Number 639–578. Agents were also watching a house in Barrington, where Nelson had hid out after the South Bend job.

On 27 November 1934, one of the agents watching the highway leading to the house saw Baby Face Nelson drive by in a car. He immediately called the nearest FBI field headquarters for assistance. Two special agents, Thomas M. McDade and William C. Ryan, were sent to investigate.

Then, a one-in-a-million event happened, and Nelson's car passed the FBI car, which was headed the other way. Nelson grew suspicious of the car as soon as he saw it and, when they came abreast, he saw one of the agents straining to get a better look at him. That settled it. He yelled to Chase, "That guy in that car. He was a Fed. I'm sure of it, and we're going to take another look."

With this he swung the car around, and the agents found themselves being pursued by Nelson. Chase, seated in the rear, told Helen to duck, then he started shooting right through the windshield at the agents' Ford Coupe. They fired back, pulling on ahead; then they saw a turn-off, and took it. Stopping their car, they jumped out, took up defensive positions, and waited.

Nelson was cursing again as his Ford coughed to a rolling stop. "They hit something," he said, "the car has quit on me." Just at this moment another car came speeding up from the rear with Inspector Samuel Cowley and Special Agent Herman E. Hollis inside; they, too, were looking for Nelson.

They saw his stalled car, and immediately recognized him. Hollis slammed on the brakes, but the momentum of the car still carried it on ahead for about 40 or 50 feet.

Inspector Cowley and Agent Hollis got out of the car, and looked for cover. Cowley, with a machine gun, ran over to the roadside, where he took up a position in a ditch. Hollis, armed with a shotgun, elected to stay with the car.

Nelson yelled at Helen to get out of there, and he and Chase took up defensive positions. Helen ran out across a plowed field, then fell to the ground, covering her head with her hands.

The battle began at once, with Cowley and Baby Face Nelson dueling with machine guns. Hollis swapped shots with Chase, who was using a high-powered rifle. Suddenly Hollis was given a clear view of Nelson's legs, and he fired at them; Nelson staggered. Then, in pain and anger, Nelson fired a long burst from his machine gun at Cowley, who pitched forward on his face, but not before he fired again at Nelson.

Hollis, his shotgun empty now, threw it aside, and clawed at his pistol as he ran toward Cowley and the machine gun. Nelson, crazed from his wounds, staggered into the open and emptied his machine gun at Hollis, who spun around, and fell head on into the ditch, near Cowley.

With both FBI agents now dead or dying, Nelson turned his attentions toward getting away. He expected the other agents to return at any moment, so he yelled to Chase, "Get Helen, and let's get the hell out of here!"

They both knew their Ford was useless, so they all loaded into the Hudson Hollis had been driving. Then, as an afterthought, Chase got out again and went back to their own car and got a blanket and the remainder of their guns. He tossed the blanket to Helen, then slipped in behind the wheel, and they drove away from the bloody scene.

Special Agent Herman E. Hollis had been killed instantly, but

Inspector Samuel Cowley was still alive. The entire battle, while savage and brutal, had lasted only a few minutes.

State Patrolman William Gallagher, who had stopped at a gasoline station, gave his version of the battle: "The cars stopped on the northwest highway about 500 feet west of state road 63. I sensed that it was a case of police authorities after hoodlums of some sort.

"As the agents advanced with drawn guns, instinctively I pulled out my rifle. When the shooting started, I started firing at the desperados. There were about fifteen people getting in my line of fire, and I had to stop. The people in the other machine got out too; swinging a machine gun, its muzzle flaring lead. Then, with the agents lying on the ground, they jumped into a machine and roared away." Just how Gallagher determined who were the "hoodlums," and who were the FBI agents, he didn't say.

On his way to the hospital, in Elgin, Illinois, Cowley was fully conscious, and kept insisting upon talking to Melvin Purvis. Just before they gave him ether for an emergency operation, he asked, "Did you get Purvis? I must talk to Purvis before I die." By the time Purvis got to the hospital, Cowley was unconscious, and was undergoing an operation.

Cowley regained consciousness three times following the operation, but he was unable to talk clearly. He died at 2:40 the following morning.

That same morning, Baby Face Nelson, with 16 slugs from Hollis's shotgun in his legs and thighs and at least one bullet from Cowley's machine gun in his side, also died. The machine gun bullet had ripped through his stomach, liver and pancreas.

Philip Sadowski, a Niles Center undertaker, protested that he needed more information. He had received a call at 7:55 a.m. from a woman who told him to go to Lincoln and Harms Avenue, and pick up the body of Lester Gillis. She refused to elaborate and hung up.

He then called Chief of Police Axel C. Stollberg, and reported the mysterious call. When he told the chief that the name of the dead man was supposed to be "Lester Gillis" Stollberg exclaimed, "My God, man, don't you know who that is? That's Baby Face Nelson!"

Stollberg immediately notified the FBI of the mysterious call. They dispatched 12 agents to check it out, as it was only 15 miles from the site of the battle, near Barrington. They found no body, but they did find a pile of bloody clothing, an empty money belt, and a laundry bag stamped with the name of a Chicago hotel, the Pratt Lane.

Slowly searching, in an ever-widening circle, the area had grown to almost $2\frac{1}{2}$ miles. They were just about ready to give up the search when one of the agents shouted – he had found it.

And there he was, in a drainage ditch, where he had been dumped. His arms and legs were twisted, and his cherubic face contorted, giving grim testimony to the fact that he had died in intense agony.

In an attempt to bind the gaping wound in the little man's side, a crimson-soaked blanket had been wrapped around his middle. Under the blanket was a knotted handkerchief, which had been used in a hopeless attempt to stem the bleeding.

Baby Face Nelson sported a blonde moustache, and his finger tips were scarred by acid, but little difficulty was encountered in establishing his identity by his fingerprints. Also, most of the FBI agents had spent a great deal of time committing his face to memory, following Special Agent W. Carter Baum's death.

The following day, the stolen FBI Hudson was found on a Winnetka side street, where it had skidded into a muddy ditch. The body of the car had been severely damaged by bullet holes, and its steering wheel almost completely blasted away. It was a wonder that Chase could have steered the car at all. There was no report of any automobile having been stolen in Winnetka recently, so authorities decided that Helen and Chase had made their escape on foot.

The papers screamed the headlines that Helen Nelson Gillis was now the first woman to be listed as Public Enemy Number One. They also carried the story that orders had been issued to shoot her on sight. What the FBI had said was that it would not withhold fire because she was a woman.

A radio station, capitalizing on the bloody events, persuaded John Wawzynak, Helen's father, to go on the air with an emotion-filled plea for her to give herself up before she, too, was killed. It may have been a little overdramatic, and a bit on the sensational side, but it apparently worked.

Two days after the demise of her hoodlum husband, Helen surrendered to the FBI. She would eventually be returned to Madison, Wisconsin, where her original two-year-probation –

following the Little Bohemia fiasco – would be revoked. Later she would escape a more severe penalty, by "ratting" on her husband's lieutenant, John Paul Chase.

On 1 December 1934, Baby Face Nelson was laid to rest in the St Joseph's Cemetery, at River Grove, Illinois. Mrs Gillis's little boy Lester would kill no more.

Life with Gino
(Messina Brothers)

Marthe Watts

As London's premier pimps, the five Messina Brothers – Salvatore, Alfredo, Eugenio, Attilio and Carmelo – were the capital's uncrowned vice kings during and after World War Two. The brothers thought nothing of making dire threats against anyone who crossed them, but the most ruthless of the five was Eugenio, known as Gino. Although they were born in Egypt, their father was Italian and not, as they claimed, Maltese; confusion over their nationality played an important part in their long immunity from prosecution. The brothers' heyday began after the war, when they began importing girls from Belgium, France and Spain to work in London as prostitutes. "Like Professor Higgins," recalled one Scotland Yard chief, "they could apparently transform any girl, whatever her background, into a fashionable young lady, supplying her entire outfit, and installing her in a flat in the heart of the West End." While the police were aware of what was going on, they were powerless to act, the girls being too scared of reprisals to testify against the Messinas, who controlled them ruthlessly. In 1947, a rival Maltese gang tried to muscle in, demanding £1 a day protection money from the Messina girls. Gino Messina fought the leader of the interlopers, cutting off the tips of two of his fingers. Messina was subsequently jailed for three years. In 1955, the Belgian authorities arrested him again on charges that included the procuring of Belgian girls, and received a much heftier jail term. His younger brother Carmelo was freed but was refused admission to England. When he entered the country illegally he was imprisoned and deported to Italy, dying there in 1959. Finally, some of the Messinas' vice girls were persuaded to give evidence against another brother, Attilio, despite his threatening to "cut them up". He was jailed for four years and subsequently deported. Marthe Watts (b. 1913), who worked for the brothers as a prostitute for 15 years, lived with Gino as his mistress. Having married an elderly English alcoholic, Arthur Watts, she arrived in London from her native France in 1937. In the course of plying her trade on the streets of the capital, she had more than 400 convictions as a common prostitute and was twice convicted of keeping a brothel. One newspaper called her "the wickedest woman in London". Gino, her vicious pimp, beat her with electrical flex – "tasting the electric wire" – but insisted on spending three nights a week with her, dividing the rest of the week between his French wife Andrée (known as Collette) and another of his street girls, a woman known as Anita. A fourth bedmate, Jeanne, was fitted in on the occasional afternoon. "I found many opportunities to regret my folly in joining the Messinas," wrote Marthe Watts, who reckoned she earned £150,000 for Gino Messina between 1940 and 1945. "I will only say one thing in my own defence, namely that, if it had not been for the War and its difficult circumstances, I would never have gone in with the Messinas in the first place." The Messinas and their evil empire were finally exposed in September 1950 by the crime reporter Duncan Webb (1917–58) in the People *newspaper. This extract from Marthe Watts's remarkable memoirs begins in late 1941, when her flat in Jermyn Street was hit by a German bomb; she was out and the next day took another apartment in Bennett Street. Two weeks later, that too was bombed, and this time Marthe lost everything she owned:*

This happened one Saturday evening when, according to his usual custom, Gino was with his wife and I found myself staying at Lansdown Street with Anita and Jeanne, for Gino had managed to convince me that during the weekend I should go and live with his two other girls. I ought to say that we lacked for nothing in our establishment, for despite the rationing Gino had no difficulty in finding ways and means to buy food in the black

market. There was butter and meat in abundance and all the drinks
we wished, and what was curious also, the three of us were far more
in accord with each other during the weekend when we were left on
our own, than we were when he was there during the week.

During my first few weeks with him, apart from the fact that I
had to put up with Gino and his various disagreeable traits, which
had started to reveal themselves, life was not too bad. I did not go
out to work until late in the evening, and when it was my turn with
Gino for the night, he took me back with him early. Even when it
was not my turn, he always arranged to pick me up in the car and
we would do a tour round the town before he went to find the one
whose turn it was to spend the night with him.

But after that everything started to change. First of all, after I
had lost my flat at Bennett Street, I had to work with the other two
at Shepherd's Street and we were no sooner together than the
quarrels started. I was not accustomed to be chased round as if I
was in a regiment. I soon found to my distress and amazement, that
Gino's strictest instructions were that I could not spend more than
ten minutes with a client at a session, even if the latter spent a great
deal of money. This was a rigid time limit. It brought me many
slaps and blows for, if I stayed with a client even eleven or twelve
minutes, it led to scenes, as the two other girls made it their
business to time my movements as if by a chronometer and
reported them back to Gino. More than that, apart from my work,
I was not allowed to speak to anyone whom I had known previously. While on the other hand none of the other girls in the West
End, whom I had known previously, would any longer come near
me, because no one at all, even in the underworld of prostitution,
had any affection for the Messina family.

I could never go out alone. (This did not apply to me alone, but to
all three of us.) I could not even go out to the corner shop along in
Shepherd's Market without either Anita or Jeanne coming along too;
and that again caused a good many quarrels, as I resented this stupid
type of restriction, while not only were the two other girls both more
accustomed to working with Gino than I was, but undoubtedly they
had decided to gang up against me on account of their jealousy of a
newcomer. They would repeat to Gino without fail everything that I
did or said. According to him, I was far too friendly with the
customers and that alone made me liable to reprisals!

Another very strange thing was that none of us was allowed to
put on either blouses or dresses of a décolleté or transparent kind,

but always had to wear everything right up close to the neck, so that we did not show any portion of our skin. Moreover, we were never allowed to look at the cinema or film magazines in which there were pictures of male film stars in an undressed state. This may seem, perhaps, rather comic in the light of all the men whom we saw during our day's work, but I can assure my readers that it was so. The reason was, I imagine, that Gino was afflicted with an inferiority complex and was evidently afraid of our comparing these wonderful people with him. It was probably for a similar reason that he would not let us stay too long with a client, for fear that we might find someone with more prowess than his own in bed. While, in regards to our speaking to anybody, he undoubtedly wanted to make quite sure that we would not find any other man who could go to our heads in rivalry against himself.

As Gino was still uncertain of me and had it in mind that perhaps, when the war was over, I would leave him for someone else, two months after I had been with him he compelled me (and I myself was stupid enough to consent to this) to have his name tattooed on my left breast. I had no sooner had this done than I was utterly ashamed of it and I remained so during all the time that I was with him. For instance, even when I went to the doctor, I would always hide this stupid thing with a plaster. The first thing that I did when I eventually left him was to have this disfigurement removed by a small skin operation – to my immense relief.

I should add that we were, of course, not allowed to smoke either.

From time to time I was liable to scenes of jealousy. Sometimes we would be sitting in a restaurant and Gino would become angry with me because, according to him, I had looked at another man. I thought at first that this might be merely an act in order to make me believe that he was jealous of me and had a special regard for me; but I soon discovered that I was not the only one who had this sort of treatment. Each of the other girls told the same story.

The only thing that Gino never bothered to try to make me believe, because he knew well enough that I would not believe it, was that he would end his days with me and would marry me, as was his custom to do with so many others of the less experienced girls whom he subsequently made work for him. He could not do this in my case because, even before I went with him, I knew that he was married. Of course his other women found out too about his wife, but he usually managed to convince them that he had forged the marriage papers and that his marriage was a false one. But, as he was well aware that I knew all the lies that a man of his kind could tell to a woman to keep her in his power, he did not bother to try anything of this kind on me.

The three of us stayed some while working at Shepherd's Street. Gino had moved from Berkeley Square, as the house was requisitioned for offices, and had come to live in a house in Park Street. Anita and I, according to our turn, would go and sleep at Park Street with him, while the two others slept at Shepherd's Street. The Park Street house was not very comfortable and Gino did not stay there long. The apartment was large enough, but it was a dismal sort of place and lacked electric light during all the time that we were there. Moreover we would from time to time hear noises as if the house was haunted and this made Gino nervous. This was a pity, as this apartment was lucky for us and we all did good business.

Gino now found a flat at Lowndes Street that he took under another name. I imagine that, like his brothers, he was keen to cover up his activities and it was their habit to use a variety of names as it suited their purpose. Gino would be Edward Marshall – or, on occasions, Eugenio du Bono, his mother's name, Carmelo would be Charles Maitland and Attilio would be Raymond Maynard. This was a simple, but effective expedient for throwing dust in the eyes of whoever wanted to pick up their tracks.

On the move to Lowndes Street first of all we had a small apartment where we stayed six months. During this time Gino and I had a most terrible quarrel, for I had begun to think that I had had enough of family life with this particular family and I wanted to leave. I had stumped out of the flat, but, not knowing this part of London very well (for I had arrived at night by car and any time I had been out of the district it had also been by car), I soon lost myself in the maze of streets. I had, however, not gone too far before I spotted Gino, who was out in his car looking for me – it was as if he knew instinctively which direction I had taken. He got out and waylaid me on the pavement, pleading to me to return. At the same time he generously gave me a day off so that we could make the peace.

On the same floor as the small flat at Lowndes Street, there was a larger flat free. It was a very pleasant one and so we moved into it and settled down afresh there. Gino started to order the decorations to be done all in gold: gold had gone to his head, for, not content with gaining a considerable amount of it, he spent his time thinking of it as well. At last, however, our gold decorations were finished. We now had an immense lounge with columns support-ing the ceiling and this was done in gold the same as the rest of the flat. We also had a dining-room, two large bedrooms, two bath-rooms and a maid's room and also another small room which Gino took for his office. He had by then bought a large safe which was so heavy that six men were hardly sufficient to carry it and it was necessary to roll it along on wheels. This safe was placed in his office: in order to have it there, he had to have special authorisation from the estate agents and insurance company to take it upstairs on account of the risk of it being too heavy for the structure of the house. Then he furnished the place lavishly throughout, spending an idiotic amount of money on furniture and carpets.

So, at this stage in his career, you might have seen Gino amidst these luxurious gilded surroundings in the Lowndes Street flat like a spider in the centre of his web: the evenings would find him sitting at his desk in his office working at his carefully kept account books in which he meticulously recorded all our earnings in his own handwriting in the manner of an old-time merchant prince.

Gino also made himself a hiding place. (I imagine that he was afraid that they would get him for the Army, as it was always a mystery to me why he could pass himself as a British subject and not be called up.) When he was young he had worked as a carpenter with his father and he was very clever with his hands. He con-structed a piece of furniture with several planks of wood which was the height of the walls of the flat. It had several shelves just like a bookcase and in the bottom shelf he left enough space to fit his own body, while the final plank lifted up in a way that no one knew about except himself. He placed this bookshelf structure in front of a wall cupboard after he had removed the door from this and then fixed it in place. As soon as anyone rang the bell – that is, anyone whom we were not expecting – Gino would lift up the bottom plank, enter the cupboard, close the shutter from the inside – and disappear.

One day a friend offered him a big price for this flat. He therefore sold it and went to live in Porchester Gate, Bayswater, in a house which he had taken under yet another of his repertoire of names.

At Shepherd's Street business had been good but, amongst the other things we were forbidden to do, we were not allowed to go with the Americans. When they first started to arrive in London, Gino had not wanted us to take up with them, though I really don't know why. Seeing that the other street girls seemed to prefer them, we took the other men. It was the same with the French and Italians. These too were forbidden to us, though perhaps in their case he was afraid that I might find some old acquaintance amongst them.

An unhappy occurrence took place one evening at Shepherd's Street. I had met a very generous client whom I had known previously. I did my best to please him, but my best was not good enough for him to find satisfaction in ten minutes and my client could not understand my attitude towards him at all in the light of our previous happy times together. This particular evening Gino was with Anita. He arrived at Shepherd's Street in company with her while this client was with me. He then waited in front of the door until I had finished; scarcely was the client out of the door than Gino came upstairs furiously and slapped my face.

This time I was equally furious with anger myself.

"Leave me alone," I shouted, "I can't understand why you are so angry and I won't put up with it!"

On this occasion, strangely enough, he calmed down and became quiet as a lamb and very gentle.

Another time Jeanne took a Chinese as a customer. He was not satisfied at the end of his allotted time and started to make a rumpus. I came to help Jeanne and a terrible fight started. I can only think that this particular client was a judo champion, for the result of it was that he threw me down a whole flight of stairs, then stepped over my prostrate body at the bottom of the stairs and went quietly out, leaving me black and blue for several days afterwards.

Finally the lease of the house at Shepherd's Street ran out and we were not able to renew it. Certainly the proprietor must have been glad to see the last of us. Then we went to live in Duke Street, St James's, in exactly the same apartment where I had lived when I had first come to London and where the police came for my poor Georges. It made me sad to go back there, for it reminded me so much of the happy days when Georges and I had been together. This apartment was a maisonette. Gino had bought the lease of the house and had made two separate apartments in order to avoid trouble with the police. Two of us would now go out, while the third looked after the house and did the housework, the cooking and washed the lingerie for the others.

We still had plenty of trouble though. The reason was always this question of the time limit on the client's length of stay, regardless of whether he got what he wanted or not. After my first disputes with Gino, I had no alternative but to do as he wanted and when the allotted ten minutes were up I would, if necessary, leave the room and leave the client to himself. It was this which frequently caused the battles and hardly a day passed without our having to call the police to make the clients leave.

One Saturday evening I had most terrible trouble with a guardsman. I understood very well that this man had given me £3 and that this was a great deal for a simple soldier and naturally he wanted satisfaction. But I did not manage to give him this and the police had to come in to make him go out. He left for several minutes, but then he came back and sat the whole evening outside the door. No one could go out because I truly believe that, if we had opened the door, he would have torn any one of us to pieces. He only left, I imagine, when it was time for him to return to his barracks.

The week passed and I had quite forgotten the guardsman by the following Saturday, having plenty of other troubles on hand. However, when next Saturday came and I went out to start business, I saw the same guardsman at the side of the door and I had just time to open and close the door again quickly. This again lasted several hours until it was time for him to return to duty.

When the first Saturday's event happened I had told Gino all about it on the Monday when I saw him.

"What a pity I was not there to deal with him," he said bravely after I had explained the whole incident in detail. "I would soon have got rid of him for you."

During the following days, however, the matter appeared to escape his attention: he made no attempt to rearrange his week-end plans to deal with a repetition of the incident. So we went on the same way for some three or four Saturdays, at the end of which time the soldier fortunately failed to return.

By this time it had become Gino's custom to drive round and round the streets in his car in order to supervise us while we were working. Petrol rationing presented no difficulty to him in this; as it was an essential part of our own duties to cadge petrol coupons from our clients under various pretexts of hard-luck stories – these

coupons, of course, went straight to Gino. Alternatively, if he
wanted a little exercise he would walk round with one or other of
his brothers, but never alone.

We stayed for almost a year at Duke Street. At the end of that
time the police had doubtless had more than enough of us and had
started to realize that there were three of us in the house: one
Saturday evening the police officers arrived and we found that we
were raided for keeping a brothel. Anita was charged and had to
stay at the Police Station for the weekend, the Inspector refusing
even to allow her bail. Finally, on the Monday she came before the
Magistrate and was remanded for a week and given bail until that
time.

Anita went before the Magistrate again the week following and
had to pay a fine. After this we left Duke Street and went to St
James's Place where we continued the system of two of us being
out on the streets looking for clients while the other stayed inside,
each one taking her turn to be outside or inside day by day; though
I did not relish very much at any time having to act as maid for the
others. This was all the more so as the house in St James's Place
was next to other houses which had been damaged by bombs and
were now deserted and full of rats, of which I was much afraid. I
preferred to be out in the streets.

This house was completely empty apart from ourselves, as it
also had suffered bomb damage and did not, for instance, have
any glass in the windows. The doors too were in rickety condition
and we could not even put the lights on in the entrance or on the
stairs owing to the black-out, as we were, of course, afraid that
the clients would leave the door open when they left and would
get us into trouble. We lived up at the top of this rather derelict
house: and we first of all occupied the top floors which consisted
of two large rooms on the third floor together with the fourth
floor which had a kitchen and bathroom, also a dining-room and
another little room. The two of us who were on duty started to
work in the rooms on the third floor, when Gino realized that it
would be better if we could take the lease of the floor below. I am
sure that the estate agents at this time were only too pleased to
find a tenant for a house in this state. Accordingly I took over the
second floor for myself. This consisted of two large rooms: one
had a wash-basin, but only one of these rooms had any sort of
furniture, comprising a bed and a dressing-table, a chair and a
small electric fire, which we hardly ever put on owing to our fear

of fire; it is not surprising that the clients frequently complained of the cold.

It was at St James's Place that we eventually started to take the Americans and this improved our financial returns considerably, for these Americans were very generous. But under Gino's direction, with this golden harvest about for the picking, the length of our hours of work also started to increase at the same time. We would start at 4 o'clock in the afternoon and not finish until six in the morning. These were our regular hours and it needed a constitution of iron to stick them. All the time we were under the supervision of Gino and his brothers. Punctuality was expected of us, just as if we were in a factory: if we were five minutes late in starting in the afternoons, then we had to stay on duty for an extra five minutes when it came to knocking off in the early morning: it was as bad as that.

As I have said, Gino was now living at Porchester Gate. His flat was a large one on the seventh floor with a big balcony, overlooking Hyde Park. There were four bedrooms, three bathrooms, a big lounge, a dining-room, another little room, and a very large kitchen. The three of us would go back there every night after finishing work and we each had our room in this flat, as we still shared Gino in the same way as we had been doing. The one of us who had the night with Gino would spend it in his room while the two others would sleep in their own rooms. When we came back in the early hours of the morning Gino had prepared our food for us and we would put it on the table for ourselves. The girl whose turn it was to have the night with him would retire and make her toilet. Then Gino would pay a visit to the two others, each in turn, to say goodnight and hear about the incidents of the day's work. Then in the morning the two who were not in his room with him would prepare breakfast for the family and do the washing-up of the night before.

Gino was desperately frightened of the bombs and particularly so when the flying bombs started to descend on London. He had had a shelter in reinforced cement specially constructed and had obtained authority to put this shelter in the basement, where the common shelters of the house were already, so that he was able to be in a shelter inside the normal shelter. During this time towards the end of the war we would return from work much sooner because Gino did not want to go upstairs at all; he would spend his time in his shelter when we were out on Piccadilly and so was not available to bring us back by car. We accordingly had to take the last Underground to get back home. This lasted for four or five months. We would have our beds in the shelter, where we would all sleep through the night. We would then go upstairs about 8 a.m. and would go to bed once again in our normal beds in order to continue our night's sleep.

This arrangement continued until one Sunday morning when a flying bomb fell opposite where we were. This was, of course, during the time when Gino was with his wife. All three of us had been in the shelter and had gone upstairs in the usual fashion at seven in the morning. The incident happened at midday when we had just got up in order to start the housework. All the windows were broken, the doors were torn off, the furniture overturned and we were fortunate that our rooms were at the back of the house, otherwise we would have been seriously injured. As it was, we were badly dazed and, when the rescue squads arrived, they were not a little surprised to find three almost nude women running around in a bewildered state.

A little later, when we had recovered from the shock, we telephoned Gino's parents, so that they could get into touch with him, as we had no idea what to do. It was impossible to leave the apartment unguarded as everything was open to the four winds. Gino's father accordingly came along to see us then telephoned Gino and spoke to his wife. Colette, his wife, knew quite well that we were with Papa Messina and also knew us quite well, but she did not wish to hear anything we said. I imagine that Gino did not want us to lose a single day's work in any circumstances and it was eventually arranged that his father should stay at the apartment to keep an eye on it while we were to go out to work.

After this we no longer went down into the shelter as Gino decided and we ourselves agreed that it was as well that we should stay out and sleep at our place of work in St James's Place. The safe, about which I have previously told, was also removed from the flat as it was too heavy and the estate agents would only give permission for it to be down in the basement. It therefore came to rest in the reinforced concrete shelter: it was, naturally, far more precious than we were.

We remained at St James's Place until the end of the war. On the V.E. Day celebration we were out on the streets as usual. Indeed this day is a memorable one for me, as I took more clients than I

ever had on any other day during my life in London. The number
of clients started to mount towards fifty and I stayed until after 6
a.m. in the morning to find the fiftieth in order to make a round
number; but this last one eluded me and I had to be content with
forty-nine.

It was, as everyone knows, in the immediate post-war years that
the Messina family reached the height of their fortunes. In 1946
Gino took over the lease of Number 7 Stafford Street and shortly
afterwards bought the house. At the same time he acquired his first
Rolls-Royce. The atmosphere of contempt for law and order that
characterised those days suited him and he knew it. "London
belongs to me" was, so to speak, his slogan.

Stafford Street, the narrow street between Bond Street and
Dover Street, now became our regular place of work. At first
Anita and I went out and Jeanne stayed in the house, but we too
were going up in the world and we started to employ a maid. Poor
woman, what a time she had with us! For now we took the clients in
our rooms, but we scarcely gave them their ten minutes before we
were out again, leaving the maid to get rid of them. We would still
have frequent recourse to the police to help us, but they began to
get rather tired of us, for we were the only women in the business
to keep calling on them without any let-up in the way that we did.
We were also the only ones who had so strict a time limit for our
clients, as even the girls who worked for the other Messina
brothers did not work on the same system as we did.

It was soon after this there occurred the first of the cases in which
the Messinas started to figure in the public eye. This was when
Gino was charged in Court with unlawfully wounding an old
enemy of his, Carmelo Vassallo, and was sentenced to three years
imprisonment at the Old Bailey on 24 June 1947. This case and the
publicity accompanying it also drew the attention of inquisitive
Members of Parliament who started to ask questions why he had
not also been charged with offences in connection with prostitution. During the course of these it became obvious that the legend
of the Messinas was already building up when the sum of £500,000
was quoted as Gino's personal fortune – not to mention the
restaurants and other businesses which he was supposed to own.

The next two years were spent by Gino in Wandsworth Prison
and it is, at least, to his credit that he did not waste his time there.

Amongst other things, he started to improve his mind. Incredible as it may seem, despite his worldly success and the ease with which he took to high living, Gino still wrote in a childish handwriting and could only read with difficulty. This was his opportunity to improve these elementary attainments. Throughout the time he was in prison he was very conscientious in writing to us, improving his handwriting as he went on by modelling it on our own in our letters to him. We would receive a letter from Gino each in our turn, couched in the tenderest terms, but just the same not forgetting to give us full instructions as to how we should carry on our work. He would send these letters out always in the same name to Carmelo's address, marking them with a special sign different for each girl. Carmelo would know these secret signs and give the letter to the girl to whom it was written. We would also go and see him once a month, with two of his brothers, leaving him a stock of intellectually improving books in the French language on each occasion.

This lasted for no less than twenty-six months, during which time we continued to work the same as if he was still supervising us nightly, while, like the silly idiots we were, we put all the money on one side for him for when he came out. Each week we would put the money we had earned in the big safe in his apartment in the presence of two of the brothers, who each had his combination key to open the safe, the combination being such that one key could not open it without the other.

We had been looking forward to a great celebration when he came out and had arrangements in hand to meet him at the gate of the prison. However, he was released three days sooner than we had expected, at an early hour in the morning, so that he suddenly arrived on us one morning when I was at the apartment with Anita. We telephoned the family straight away to give them the news, and all the brothers hurried round happy to see him again.

We then went out to celebrate at a restaurant. Here, Gino suddenly developed toothache and we had to take him to his dentist. Then, after he had had his tooth seen to, we went to Carmelo's place, but Gino felt no better. He accordingly went to bed early and, since it was my privilege to stay with him this first night, I have to confess that I was only too relieved that he was not feeling well.

The next morning we woke early, for of course he had acquired the habits of the prison routine. He felt better and lost no time in asking me for my accounts. I was very pleased with myself when I told him that, during his absence, I had put on one side no less than £22,000. But Gino did not appear too satisfied with this, for evidently he had already formed the opinion that, while he had been away, I had been buying too many shoes and too much lingerie. It was not long before he had worked himself up into a furious temper at the thought that I had been spending too much altogether; moreover, he had heard that I had been going out by myself. This started our quarrels once more and, after that, the slaps and blows which invariably followed.

However I was spared further trouble as he went on to fulfil his other obligations – a day with Anita, a day with Jeanne, and then on to his wife's place, where he stayed several days.

Then, to celebrate his release, he bought himself a new Rolls-Royce with special bodywork for the price of £8,000. This bodywork was yellow so that now he could make quite a sensation in and around town, as he drove round in it. He also took a flat in South Street, in his alternative name of Edward Marshall.

A little later he came to the conclusion that we each of us deserved a present for the way we had looked after things in his absence. I had a mink coat, a brooch and a pair of ear-rings, while the others also had similar presents, including, I imagine, his wife. We went out on the streets in our usual fashion wearing all these adornments, and everyone looked at us as we were quite a spectacle. Carmelo too earned a diamond ring worth £700 in thanks for looking after us.

Life began all over again just as it had done in the past. We would start our work early, then Gino would come and find us to give us each our turn with him, according as it was our evening. Indeed he now started to tour up and down almost without ceasing in his new Rolls-Royce, in the quarter where we had our beats. First of all in order to let himself be seen and admired, and also in order to exercise proper surveillance over us.

I think, however, that I am best quoting from an independent observer to give the picture of the Messina organisation in the late nineteen forties. I do so from some jottings by the late Duncan Webb which are in my possession.

"Going to gaol did not do any harm to the business Eugenio Messina had built up. His brother looked after his side of it, and Carmelo even went so far as to bribe a warder in Wormwood

Scrubs goal to provide certain favours for his elder brother while he was inside. For this Carmelo got three months imprisonment.

"But nothing was done by the police to book any of the gang for organizing vice, and by the time Eugenio Messina had done one year in prison, his brothers were openly boasting of how they had defeated the law in running their vice business. They were laughing at the Home Secretary's answers in Parliament, and chuckling when one Member of Parliament suggested that the gang had coined millions from their proceeds from prostitution.

"So brazen did the Messinas become that when someone got in their way they no longer exposed themselves to the fate of Eugenio by indulging in knife and gun play; they framed false charges against them, usually with some success. There was a succession of cases in the courts in which accused persons pleaded that they had been framed by the Messina Gang. Magistrates expressed their annoyance with this, what they thought to be empty plea and only increased the sentence.

"In fact, by 1949, the Messinas had become so much of a legend in London that they were accepted as part of the London scene. So many fantastic stories were told about them that persons in authority attributed such stories to mere gossip, multiplicated anecdote, and in some cases romantic and wishful thinking.

"I am sure, from some of the remarks passed by some magistrates, that they did not believe that there was such a thing as the Messina Gang. They certainly did not when Sally Wright was charged in Court by Rabina Dickson Torrance with assaulting her with a knife. Sally Wright pleaded in Court that Torrance was a Messina woman, that the whole charge had been framed by the Messina Gang, and that she was innocent. She should have known what she was talking about, for she had been a Messina woman herself for some years, and knew more about the gang than most people.

"She was by no means the first person who had not been believed after pleading that she had been victimised by the Messina Gang. It seemed that when anyone upset the Messinas all they had to do was enlist the aid of the Courts, apparently with police assistance, and that someone was conveniently imprisoned, and incidentally discredited for life."

This was the state of affairs as Duncan Webb describes it when, as the crime reporter of *The People*, he was briefed by his editor to investigate the Messinas. As he says, his editor may as well at that time have ordered him to jump over the Empire State Building. He describes how he pursued his investigations in his book *Crime is my Business*,* so I must return to my own story and tell of our own reactions when Duncan Webb started to follow us everywhere and to observe all our acts and movements.

At first we did not know that it was a journalist doing this, as we naturally thought it was the police. After almost a month, we eventually had some idea who it was, but still without having any conception of the scandal which the papers were capable of causing and which, of course, it was their intention to cause.

At the height of his power, when Gino had felt secure, he would thrive on the Press comments about himself. "Vice King" and such like epithets, which the newspapers used and which might have been obnoxious to many people, were meat and drink to his already inflated ego. He would read them out to us with an obvious sense of pride and elation. Now, however, he started to take alarm and instructed us to take a note of their numbers whenever we saw strange cars hanging about. We would then report these to him and he would make it his business to find out who was the owner. He certainly gave himself a good deal of work, as the journalists would often change cars three or four times a day, knowing that they were being watched in turn. Moreover, Duncan employed several assistants and they would follow us everywhere. Even when Jeanne and I, as we had started to do at that time, were taking driving lessons and the instructor took us into quiet streets out of the traffic, we still saw the same cars behind us, which would follow us back to our apartments and then to our work in Stafford Street. Indeed our earnings began to drop, as we were so busy watching the cars that we hardly had time to take any clients or make any money.

Gino also gave us strict instructions that we were not to allow ourselves to be photographed, or even be approached by a photographer, under the threat of his gravest displeasure. But that was no easy matter, as Duncan Webb and the photographers seemed to appear round every corner. We became so frightened of the photographers that even the fine summer evenings never saw us without our umbrellas, which we would open out to protect our faces at the least sign of a strange car – passers-by who did not know what was happening must have thought that we were mad.

* Published by Frederick Muller Ltd.

Photographers, as I have said, seemed as if they were everywhere. There was one in Stafford Street who had stationed himself in the window of the first floor in the house opposite. On one occasion I was surprised by another who came out from between two cars stationed opposite the house. I chased this man with my umbrella and ran after him as far as Dover Street where he leapt into a car that was waiting for him round the corner: he was a little man, but he just ran fast enough to escape me.

Gino, hearing of all this, realized that the papers were shadowing us in earnest and no longer toured round in his yellow Rolls. He was nervous of being deported if a scandal was raised: and he decided to lead his army from behind. He satisfied himself with boasting that, if only he had the opportunity of meeting Duncan Webb on the Continent, he would take the pants off him: and, in the meantime, he instructed me that it was my job to go and beat up Duncan if I saw him about. Obedient to Gino's will as ever, I am ashamed to say that this is what I did on more than one occasion. My poor friend Duncan, whom later I came to know so well, describes in his book the occasion when he was in one of the bars in Stafford Street with another man when I spotted him. I had to wait almost two hours before at last he came out at closing time. I then cornered him against the door of the bar. He said nothing at all to me, but I began to insult him and slap his face, so that his pipe and his glasses fell on the pavement. Then I walked away without giving Duncan the chance to say a word.

But then came that dreadful Sunday of 3 September 1950, when the *People* blew up with their revelations about the Messina family. There was this awful scandal on the front page of this paper, which sells its many millions of copies, with all our names and the photographs of the houses in Stafford Street and elsewhere. This by itself was shocking enough, but the next thing that happened was that people came from here, there, and everywhere to watch us and look at the houses, as if it was a pilgrimage. I am given to understand that Londoners love a spectacle: if so, we were from now on their spectacle. On Saturday and Sunday men, women, and the children as well, gathered to admire us and watch our movements.

Gino now appreciated that London was not a particularly healthy place for him and on 10 September 1950, he got into his Rolls-Royce, headed it towards Dover and left the country, and as far as we were aware, never came back again. Though I have heard that he was seen elsewhere in England in early October, in which case he must have come back without telling us – which he was, of course, quite capable of doing.

Even when Gino had left, Duncan Webb still continued his articles. Each Sunday we would wait anxiously for the *People* to appear to see if there were any fresh revelations or photographs of us in its pages. The situation had its amusing side, for amongst the readers of the *People* are a good many of the male sex, who would promptly either come to see us, or write us letters, sometimes offensive and scurrilous ones, and others begging us to give up our way of life, and still others putting money inside for the worthy purpose of helping us to do so. Needless to say, this money, like the rest, finished up in the pockets of Gino.

Gino had not profited from his new apartment at South Street. The decorations had just been finished, and he had had special paper put up and bought some beautiful furniture. But now he had to leave all this for the use of us who stayed in England. On the day of his departure the curtains had not yet been put up, and these were left to us to complete and enjoy.

Gino spent most of the subsequent months travelling round the Continent with Carmelo, staying in large hotels in the south of France and Italy – the Duomo Hotel, Milan, the Miramar Hotel, San Remo, the Bristol Hotel, Genoa, were all stops in this pilgrimage – with Duncan Webb tailing them, and reporting their movements for the edification of the readers of the *People*. There is the entertaining little story of how Duncan (who had heard of Gino's boast) obtained entry to the bedrooms occupied by the brothers Messina at their hotel in Genoa, abstracted a pair of Carmelo's trousers and then posted them back with his card attached.

When, at the end of a year, Gino saw that he could not return, he made us let the South Street apartment and we were forced to live in the flats where we worked. By this time he had settled in an apartment at Paris, where he employed a chauffeur together with his wife who acted as housekeeper. He had sold one of his Rolls-Royces, but took the other over to Paris with him.

Even here he did not enjoy uninterrupted peace, for one morning, when I was on holiday in Paris and was at Gino's place with him, there was a telephone call for him. This was the French police, who were waiting to see him in the entrance hall of his block of flats. He went down, stayed a little time, and then came back, telling me to dress myself in good style in order to go along with him to the prefecture, because the police wanted to question us. He made me put on my mink and my jewels, and when we went down to meet the two inspectors waiting for us in the hall with myself looking like this and then were met at the door by the chauffeur with the Rolls, the two officers could scarcely hide their surprise. Gino sent his chauffeur away and drove his car himself to the prefecture, where we were questioned for some two hours, but really about nothing out of the ordinary.

What did I do in London?

Had I known Gino a long time?

These, and other simple questions of this kind, were all that were put to us, and then we were allowed to go. I stayed a few days longer in Paris without being further disturbed and then I left for London.

Once he had become accustomed to the Continent Gino adapted himself to it in the same way as he had done to life in England. Indeed, with his flair for turning all the circumstances in which he found himself to his own advantage, he developed his stay into an almost non-stop campaign for further recruits for the ever-growing "family". His favourite hunting grounds were tea dances in the popular dance halls where young girls of an idle and pleasure-seeking nature are apt to congregate with only a small number of the male sex to entertain them. During his last year or so in London he had already become a frequenter of the Palais de Dance at Hammersmith where he had made a number of conquests.

So now in Paris he developed the habit of visiting tea dances several times a week and it was on one such occasion that he found sitting at a nearby table a *petite* woman of about thirty-two years, and not particularly good-looking. However, Gino's friends, who were with him, knew her as she was a waitress in a restaurant where they all went to eat, and it appeared that a good many of them had tried to get an angle on her, but had not succeeded. It was, in fact, a mystery to them how she managed to be so well-dressed. However, they now bet him that he would not be able to seduce her, as she clearly knew the form well and was not an easy proposition.

Gino, of course, could not resist the temptation of seeing if he was cleverer than the others and started to pay attention to her. In the event his conquest was all too easy for when Augustine, as she was called, saw the Rolls-Royce and found that Gino was able to take her to eat in the most chic restaurants, she thought that this indeed was *la grande vie*. She allowed herself to be flattered, as the rest of us had been, into doing what he wanted, above all because Gino, according to his usual form, promised her mink, cars, jewels and everything else.

Before long Gino had taken an apartment in Augustine's name in the Rue de la Faisanderie, and lived with her there. This, for the information of those who do not know it, is in the very classy part of Paris and was quite near where the Duke of Windsor lived. It was a common thing to see Gino's car and that of the Duke of Windsor parked side by side. Augustine kept house and did the cooking for him and, in fact, did everything, for the chauffeur and his other housekeeper had left. Then, before long, she appeared in London as the first of his long string of recruits from the Continent.

In August 1955 police raided the Messinas' main brothel at 39 Curzon Street. Gino and Carmelo were arrested in Brussels and put on trial there "smiling, powdered, brilliantined in their usual fashion", Gino having his photograph taken for the English Press with his pretty Belgian lawyers. Gino was jailed for six years and Carmelo for two.

Hell's Archangel
(Sonny Barger)

Bel Mooney

Sonny Barger is the founding father of the international Hell's Angels, said to be the world's fastest-growing organized crime group. As the world's most infamous Hell's Angel, immortalized by Hunter S. Thompson as the motorcycle outlaws' Maximum Leader, his rap sheet ranges from drugs possession, tax evasion, firearms violations, and conspiracy to transport explosives across a state line. At the end of the Sixties, Barger was on stage at the Rolling Stones' Altamont concert when Meredith Hunter was stabbed to death in the front row during "Sympathy for the Devil". By the early 1990s, police believed the Hell's Angels were involved in drug trafficking, contract killing, extortion, prostitution, money-laundering and credit card fraud. Like the Angels themselves – with their history of riots, chain-whippings and gang rapes – Sonny Barger's reputation is an ugly one; to straight society, he's an unholy thug, a convicted felon, a man whose life has been devoted to violence and crime. The Hell's Angels reportedly have established links to the Triads, the Cosa Nostra and Colombian drug cartels. Their Oakland gang, founded by Barger in 1957, is said to be the movement's "mother chapter". Bel Mooney (b. 1946), who met Barger when he visited Britain in 2002, is a highly-regarded novelist, children's author, journalist and broadcaster. She writes a weekly advice page for The Times *which is read all over the world. Her latest novel is* The Invasion of Sand.

T he entrance to the London Hell's Angels' clubhouse, in East London, is deliberately forbidding. The metal nameplate is decorated with a full-on skull, and the echo of the massive door knocker might well be heard across the Styx. There's a peep hole, which they use every time; presumably the Hell's Angels have enemies in other "outlaw" fraternities, in any case, they take no chances. And today they have a VIP guest, so everything must run smoothly. The legendary Ralph "Sonny" Barger – head honcho of the USA Angels, founding father, the "President", the man Hunter S. Thompson called "the Maximum Leader" – is in town. To Hell's Angels worldwide this man is a hero, to straight society a violent ex-convict. All his adult life Barger has been respected and feared in equal proportions.

The contrast between the exterior and the interior of the club-house is a fitting symbol for the way the Hell's Angels have changed – very subtly – since the days when the young Sonny Barger raised hell, fought, spent a total of thirteen years in prison (usually narcotics and firearms charges) and snorted enough co-caine to decorate a Winter Wonderland set. I'm sitting waiting for him in a spacious, immaculate leisure/meeting area which leads on to a decked patio complete with green sunshades and planters tumbling pink and white flowers. On the walls are Hell's Angel memorabilia, beautifully framed. A spiral staircase leads past a magnificent backlit stained glass panel, showing the winged death's head which is the club's precious logo, down to the huge bar area containing the kind of furniture you'd find in any chic little West London venue patronised by models and advertising executives. There's chardonnay and champagne in the fridge. There's only one word for this: civilized.

What's more, I'm shown around by Hell's Angel Andy, who is the highly intelligent and articulate security manager for a large, well-known company. Andy was one of the leaders of the bikers who (with his beautiful wife riding pillion) roared down the Mall during the Queen's Jubilee Parade, to the evident delight of Prince William – and the great pride of the "brothers" in the club. There's a new sophistication about the Angels. Before he died in a bike accident two years ago journalist-Angel and PhD Maz Harris was one of those who were most keen to bridge the gap between the Hell's Angels and the public – notably through the annual Bulldog Bash bikerfest, organized by the Angels with zero crime. But how does all this new PR square with the bad guy image?

Sonny Barger's reputation precedes him. In 1968, for example, a bunch of renegades were foolish enough to steal his Harley, and when the club rounded them up they were beaten until they cried for mercy, then had their fingers broken with hammers. The man himself is smaller than you expect, but with arms well-toned from working out. He has the presence of somebody used to attention, and when he speaks attention is required, since his voice nowadays is a quiet rasp. In 1982, after thirty years of smoking three packs a day of filterless Camels, Barger discovered he had throat cancer. He survived the laryngectomy, and then a heart attack, but lives with a blocked artery and talks through a valve in his throat. With unaffected sincerity Barger smiles, "The best thing that ever happened to me is – I woke up this morning."

In 2000, Barger co-wrote his autobiography with the writing twins, Kent and Keith Zimmerman, who did the same job for Johnny Rotten. That volume, *Hell's Angel*, gave a unique insight into the formation and ethos of the club, including an account of the infamous incident at Altamont in 1969, in which neither the Angels nor the Rolling Stones appear as anything other than obnoxious. In 2002 came a new book, a collection of personal tales from the motorcycling fraternity, including non-Angels and women – because the writing team wanted to produce a book which might go some way to explain the motorcycling mystique to the general reader.

The fact that the book is likely to confirm the prejudices of those who detest bikers doesn't bother Barger. We agree on the truth of the sticker I have on my own motorcycle helmet: "If I have to explain, you wouldn't understand." Barger says, "I don't know if you've taken acid but it's like trying to explain how it feels – like those movies where they do swirly shots?" I admit I haven't, but know what he means about the buzz of being on a motorcycle. Barger still rides 30–40,000 miles a year, and describes a ride from Sedona to Flagstaff, Arizona with a faraway look of pure pleasure: ". . . about forty of us riding out, doing 110 . . . and the women love the speed."

Sonny Barger was perfect "outlaw" material: deserted by his mother at four months, brought up by his alcoholic teamster father, dragged through school, signing up for the army while still underage, always anti-authority, always in trouble. Growing up in East Oakland made him hard – a "street tough", who identified with the character played by Lee Marvin in *The Wild*

One. He was nine years old at the time of the notorious 1947 Hollister fracas which was the basis for that movie, and it was just eight years later that he joined his first bike club. At this time Barger was beginning to evolve what would become the Hell's Angels mindset: "I needed a close-knit club of men who could jump on their bikes . . . and not abide by the rules of clocks. I needed a second family."

It simply isn't interesting to dismiss all Hell's Angels as violent drug-dealing murderers and rapists, although they certainly didn't get their reputation from singing in church choirs, and the hopped-up Hunter S.Thompson take on the Angels obviously contains some truth. Sonny Barger's life is inextricably entwined with the history of his club, and the key to both is the camaraderie of the military. The Hell's Angels (and Satan's Slaves, Road Rats and the rest) derive their history and ethos from a military past.

The term "Hell's Angels" was first used by a squadron in World War One; from then on bomber units and divisions of soldiers thought up cool names to indicate their toughness. In addition, motorcycles played an important role in both wars. Then after World War Two, the brotherhood of military life was missed by the young men who returned with a swashbuckling taste for danger, "unafraid to ride full-throttle and kick ass", as Barger puts it. The ground was ready for the Hell's Angels. The (copyright) winged Death's Head that appears on the back of every Angel jacket can be traced back to similar insignias on the 85th fighter squadron and the 552nd medium bomber squadron. Those men flew into the likelihood of death each time they pulled back the joystick and rose into the equipoise between heaven and hell. Their pose was rough and tough; their swaggering mateship the means to keep terror at bay.

Similarly, Hell's Angels see themselves as an elite: the epitome of toughness, masculinity, freedom – the image of the frontiersman or anti-hero. This idea is deep within the American psyche. Sonny Barger's autobiography explains how the biker finds identity through the club and through the Harley: "motorcycles are the be-all, end-all of what this club is all about". At 100 mph-plus, with nothing between the rider and the road surface, a patch of wet might mean instant oblivion, and there is transcendence in the danger. The fact that the Angels must (according to the rules) ride out together means the danger is often shared. That ethos of brotherhood annihilates alienation. Wearing the patch, the colours, necessitates acceptance of a system as strict as any Masonic lodge, with the same guarantees of support.

Barger explains that now, with more and more people riding motorcycles, the Hells' Angels are becoming more accepted than before. "People fear what they don't know. As for the bad guy image – well, we're only bad if you force us to be. Everything I've done I did because I had to. Some people'd say that instead of rounding up those guys who stole my bike I should've gone to the police. If I had they'd have laughed in my face, and I wouldn't have got my motorcycle back. I did what I had to do."

He explains the old mistrust between the Angels and straight society as a two-way street: a mutual pushing away into dislike and distrust. Now he sees the taking part in the Queen's Jubilee as symbolic of the shift: "I thought it was pretty nice." But it doesn't mean the Angels are pussycats: "Just because we do some of the things other people do, doesn't stop us being us." Angel Andy adds that their club is the hardest to join in the world. The fact is that even if an accepted outsider asks one question too many the clamming up is perfectly affable, but immediate.

Sonny Barger sums up his 46 years with the club neatly. In the late fifties they formed "to party and ride". Then in the sixties they started mixing with trouble, in the seventies were into crime, in the eighties doing time, in the nineties getting out of prison and settling down, and since 2000 they are having fun again. And Barger seems to be revelling in his new status as Grand Old Man, "branded" by his lawyer Fritz Clapp, with the writing talent of the Zinnermanns. He's co-written a biker-thriller called *Death in 5 Heartbeats*, the tale of a Barger-type outlaw called Patch Kincaid and his club "The Infidelz." After that will come a volume, probably called *Freedom*, containing Sonny's pithy rules for existence – to be sold in the self-help area of bookshops.

The mind boggles. At the same time the Sonny Barger website will sell you the range of hot sauces (the "Hellfire" line), a "signature" electric guitar, T-shirts, hats, pins, stickers and wallets, a motorcycle accessory kit, and "Sonny's Beer" – strong or "lean". A "signature" motorcycle is in development, as is the movie of *Hell's Angel*, with Fritz Clapp as producer. Barger is laconic about becoming an icon who is also a commercial "property". What matters most to him is, "Now, because of the books I get paid to ride my motorcycle." The signings and public appearances are endless, and his energy seems undiminished despite the fact that he can't jog any more and his doctor wonders why he is still here.

Barger doesn't believe in God, only in fate – and that you will die when it is the right moment. When his time comes he would like to be buried in the military cemetery in Phoenix, because there's no grass, "only dirt" – and he loves the desert. As the London rain rattles against the clubhouse windows, far from his beloved Arizona, we talk of the War against Terror. The opinion of the man who became a GI at sixteen because there was nothing else for him, and who once wrote to President Johnson volunteering Angels to fight in Vietnam, is exactly what I expected. There's nothing soft about this national monument. "What happened in our country on 9/11 – we can't let that go. When people do something to you, you have to hit them so hard they'll never ever do it again. You have to retaliate. You have to hurt them. It's like when those guys stole my motorcycle all those years ago."

The Most Dangerous
Man in Britain
("Mad" Frankie Fraser)

Frankie Fraser with James Morton

In the 1960s, Frankie Fraser was a notorious torturer and hit-man for the Richardson gang of south London criminals; he spent 42 years behind bars before achieving a certain cult status in later life as an author, after-dinner speaker, television pundit and tour guide. His enduring nickname "Mad Frank" derives from his violent temperament which caused him to attempt to hang the governor of Wandsworth prison (and the governor's dog) from a tree, and to be certified insane on three separate occasions. At least two Home Secretaries considered Fraser (b. 1923) the most dangerous man in Britain, an image which, in old age, he has only half-heartedly sought to dispel. Although he was never convicted of murder, police reportedly hold him responsible for 40 killings. Physically slight at only 5ft 4in, and invariably wearing a smile and – in retirement – a sharp Savile Row suit, Frankie Fraser was nevertheless a ferocious and brutal hatchet man. He shot, slashed, stabbed and axed. An early nickname "Razor Fraser" reflected his penchant for "chivving" his enemies' faces with a cut-throat blade. An unrepentant villain of the deepest dye, Fraser's greatest moment of national notoriety came in 1967, during what the media billed as the Torture Trial, in fact a series of trials that became one of the longest in British criminal history. The two Richardson brothers were convicted and the elder, Charles, sentenced to 25 years. Fraser, tried separately, was jailed for ten. In January 1965 a London club owner called Benny Coulston was hauled before Charles Richardson for swindling him out of £600 over a consignment of cigarettes. In grisly detail that still resonates more than 40 years on, an Old Bailey jury heard how Frankie Fraser tried to pull Coulston's teeth out one by one with a pair of pliers. Shortly afterwards, Fraser kidnapped Eric Mason, a member of the rival Kray gang, outside the Astor Club in Berkeley Square, with even direr consequences. When Mason demurred, Fraser buried a hatchet in his skull, pinning his hand to his head. Mason was found, barely alive, wearing only his underpants and wrapped in a blanket, on the steps of the London Hospital in Whitechapel. "Eric wasn't a bad fellow," Fraser later explained, "but that particular night he was bang out of order." Frankie Fraser spent literally half his life behind bars. He was moved from prison to prison more than 100 times because he was virtually impossible to control. In 1969, he led the Parkhurst prison riot on the Isle of Wight and found himself back in court charged with incitement to murder: he was acquitted. Fraser was defended by a young solicitor called James Morton, who later became an author and wrote a history of London's gangland. The book upset some of those mentioned in it, and Morton was dismayed to arrive home one evening to find a message from Fraser on his answering machine, demanding to speak to him urgently. Morton (b. 1938) was relieved that, rather than remonstrating, Fraser wanted him to write his life story. In this extract from Mad Frank: Memoirs of a Life of Crime, *which appeared in 1994, Fraser recalls his return to prison at the end of the Torture Trial; he was already serving five years for his part in the notorious 1966 brawl outside Mr Smith's Club in Catford, the incident that broke the Richardson family's grip on south London.*

The day after I was sentenced I was taken to Durham from the hospital at Wandsworth. I was walking properly by this time, although I still had my stick with which I had been hoping to get a bit of sympathy from the jurors. It didn't take long for me to get into more trouble. By the time I went there in the July, I had done over twelve months as a convicted man. Charlie Richardson had only done a week, and the rules then were that you couldn't watch a bit of television unless you had served so many months. I kicked up a fuss and got the other prisoners to join in. As a result the screws had to let Charlie and Roy Hall, who was with us, look at the telly after that.

There was always sheer hatred for London prisoners from the Geordie screws, and in 1967 when I went back hatred was more inflamed than ever. They didn't like the southerners in any event. Tensions built up between prisoners and the prison officers, and I'd only been there about a month or six weeks when a mob of prison officers came and took me to the punishment block. When I got in the cell they came in with escapers' patches. In the security wing at Durham you wore the ordinary prison clothes because it was then considered escape-proof, although later John McVicar got out and Wally Probyn and Joey Martin nearly made it. I refused to wear them. Apart from that time as a kid I'd never tried to escape even once, because when any good escape attempts were being hatched or were ready to go I'd been transferred. I am a very practical person that way. By that I mean I didn't want some fancy scheme which you knew full well would fail. If I was going to try to escape, then I wanted a reasonable chance of success, but I was never in a prison where I could see that chance. The Alfie Hinds scheme was all right, but it was the only one I heard of and as I say he was moved before anything could be done.

I was left in my cell with just my pants on. An hour or so later I heard a voice shouting out from another cell, "Frank, Frank." It was a prisoner called Ronnie Piper, serving a sentence for manslaughter, who also had refused to wear the escape outfit. He said he wasn't going to eat either. We weren't on report. Knowing we'd refuse the patches and so would therefore be on punishment all the time, the screws were trying to make an example of us and intimidate the rest of the prison. We were both taken before the Governor for refusing to obey an order, and given bread and water as well as loss of remission and solitary confinement. The bread and water didn't make any difference because we weren't eating anyway. We were then put on report again for refusing to sew mailbags in our cells. We got more punishment. After three or four days I had a visit from Doreen, and Piper asked if she would make a complaint on his behalf as well when she did for me. I said I'd do my best. She went to see his wife, and went to the Home Office and protested. After seven days a prison officer came and said my friend was now sewing and had put on the patches. I burst out laughing, I thought he was kidding me. When he shouted out that evening, I told him what the screw had told me. He said it was true. I said he shouldn't have started in the first place if he was going to give in. He said the Deputy Governor had promised him he'd go into the wing, and that when his wife visited he'd get a much better visit – not just twenty minutes. I said yes, but you knew all this before you started and you'd have to suffer. Why do it in the first place? I said he was weak, and he more or less started crying. A day later they let him up. I carried on and after about twenty-eight days they took me to the hospital. I had refused to go and so I was strapped down and was taken over in a body belt. I was forcibly fed. They forced my mouth open, put a block of wood in and put the tube through the wood. After a day or so the doctor said, "You've won. You'll go back on the wing and you don't have to wear the escape patches." My wife came to visit me in the hospital and I was told I'd get a two-hour visit.

On the previous visit I'd asked Doreen to write to Mr Bainton as he was now Director of the Prison Service. She went to see him and he told her it would be best if I was transferred. I was now eating and three days later I was put back on the wing. People cheered and shook my hand. After two days my door was opened and there was an escort from Leicester to take me to the security wing there. What Durham never said was that my wife had told them that she was coming to visit me that day, so she came all the way for nothing.

So in October 1967 I went to Leicester. The screw who took me had had a straightener with Jack Rosa in Birmingham in 1948 or so. Jack got eighteen of the Cat for attacking him with a weapon, but it had been a straight fight. He knew I knew this, and that I didn't like him for it. He was the type of screw who fancied he was a street fighter who could hold his own, but he'd underestimated Jack. He'd come to Jack's cell and got done. That was a bad start for me and Leicester in a way. A straightener with a screw wasn't common but it wasn't completely unknown. For example old "Dodger" Mullins, after the Dartmoor mutiny, had had a straight fight with a screw and then the screw had said he'd attacked him. The same thing happened with Jack McVitie, but no one ever offered me one. I'd have taken the chance it was genuine if a screw had offered it.

When I got to Leicester it was a shambles; only the main part had been built. The security wing was on the ground floor. People in the basement couldn't look up, and you were separated from the first floor as well. Workmen were still putting doors and electricity in. Tommy Wisbey, Bobby Welch, Jimmy White from the Train, Joe Martin who'd been in Durham and had tried to escape with John McVicar, and Frank O'Connell who was doing fifteen years for manslaughter, were all in the security block. After Buster Edwards arrived I can remember him telling me that Tommy Butler and Frank Williams had been to see him in the cells at Nottingham to say they never went crooked on him. Williams had given evidence to say that Buster should have burned the Farm down and that he hadn't been on the Train Robbery proper. This supported Edwards' evidence and the judge, Milmo, who'd acted for the *Empire News* in my libel action, must have half believed him. By getting only the fifteen, it did open the gates for the others to get parole.

There was always conflict at Leicester. There were prison officers who wanted to make it hard and tough for the prisoners, and at that stage in the Prison Service they were predominant as opposed to the ones who were intelligent and wanted a liberal regime. They could manipulate the Governor, Clay, who was known as Cassius. You never knew where you were with them. One moment they would be all right and the next they'd want to clamp down. In the meantime, with the works going on the noise was terrible.

One day Tommy Wisbey, me and Micky Morgan, who'd been nicked for murder at Wakefield and was doing life, got into trouble and had a row with prison officers and were put on report for it. We got our punishment and when we managed to get together again we were riled about what had happened. Even by prison standards it was a liberty. I suggested we shouldn't waste time with the officers and rather go for the Governor, and they both agreed. So we did the Governor, rather gently in a way I suppose. You had to take turns at cleaning the submarine, which is what we called our landing, and me and Tommy and Mickey would do it once or twice a week between us. We would leave five buckets spread discreetly round the wing. These buckets would be full of filth, dirt, urine, dog-ends, and it was the Governor's luck on that happy day to fetch round the Chief Probation Officer for Leicestershire. There would be a chief officer, possibly with eight or more officers clustered round him. You'd hear him saying proudly, "I've got the Train Robbers,'' because they were world famous. Out of the blue came the three of us with buckets. We pushed everyone aside and tipped them all over the Governor. Tommy Wisbey was magnificent. As he was taller, he could tip the bucket actually over his head and ram it down. It had to be pulled off him. It may read or sound terrible to people who don't understand prison life, but to prisoners it meant a lot. You were only doing things the prison officers do to you down the punishment blocks. We were jumped on and locked up. The Governor had to have a shower and a suit brought over for him he was in such a state. It was wonderful fun. We lost remission, were given bread and water by the magistrates, and we did it happily. We weren't transferred immediately. I was the first one to go, and I was sent to Brixton three weeks after the arrest of the Twins.

It was the day Manchester United won the European Cup and I remember being driven down the M1 and seeing all the scarves and pennants flying from the car windows as they passed us. Shortly after I arrived in Brixton, who came in but Tommy Butler who'd arrested me over the Mr Smith's fight. This time along with him was James Earl Ray, who was later convicted of shooting Martin Luther King. I shouted out abuse at Butler – the screws had to fight to get me away – as he had fitted me up for the murder of Dickie Hart.

They had Ray in a room which had been used as an office and which in effect was two cells knocked into one. They'd cleared the office out and had him with two officers. Now it really was rather like he was in the condemned cell, with the one slight difference that you could actually speak to him whereas in the condemned cell no other prisoner could speak to or even see that man.

He was on the landing underneath and occasionally I could nip down and have a word with him. It wasn't permitted but the screws turned a blind eye. The officers would tell me to go away, but they didn't want to enforce the order. Their main role was to see that he wasn't assassinated rather than to prevent his escape. There was a big black population in Brixton itself, as well as a high percentage of prisoners. In fact a black civilian worker, a stoker in a boiler house, was, I think, suspended until Ray was sent back to the States. They were concerned in case there was a riot. Once the officers realized I wasn't trying to attack him they weren't too worried about me talking to him. As I had been in so much trouble prison officers, for once, weren't tempted to rock the boat. Ray wasn't fighting the extradition; he didn't deny his involvement to me or anyone else that I knew. All he did was run down the black people in the south of America, seeming to try to justify his action. He called King a man who stirred up trouble for the whites.

I was only in the wing for three months. I could also see Reggie or Ronnie to get a parcel of food sent in. They were already there, and I used to have the odd conversation with them. First, they asked me about Charlie Mitchell who was charged along with them. They had a gut feeling he was going to give evidence against them. Mitchell was a good dog doper, and he had been a good thief in his time. Did I think he would give evidence? I said I didn't think he would but I wouldn't trust him. He was very rich and he could use as much money as he needed to get himself out of it. He did give evidence at the committal, but he didn't turn up for the trial. He went abroad, where he was later killed in a fight.

What the police were trying to do in the Kray case was to get to as many people as possible, and if a man of Mitchell's standing in the underworld gave evidence that would encourage many others to do the same. That part of the prosecution succeeded. The Twins then asked if I would help with their defence, and I said of course I would. Ronnie had just been charged with Cornell's murder and asked if I would give evidence to say they were very friendly with him. In fact I may have suggested it to them, I can't really remember. We couldn't have really long conversations, just pieces here and there, because with me convicted and them on remand we weren't supposed to be able to mix, but of course we did.

Then in August 1968 I started fighting with the officers in the security wing in Brixton. I was injected, put in a straitjacket and put in the padded cell in the hospital. Twice they did this, and it was on the second occasion after I was taken out of the straitjacket I was moved to Wandsworth down the punishment block. The needle must have been dirty because I got yellow jaundice. If you're on punishment a doctor has to see you every day. Usually they just look in your cell, go "All right" and move on to the next, but this day a hospital screw looked at me, said "You've got jaundice", called the doctor back and in no time I went over to the hospital where I was treated.

Some months later I was taken from the hospital to see the Deputy Governor. A solicitor representing the Krays wanted to see me, would I see him? I said of course, but the Deputy tried to talk me out of it. I told him to get on his bike and mind his own business. A solicitor came and took my statement and I was produced at the trial to give evidence.

After completing my evidence, as I went through the dock back to the cells I shook hands with Ronnie and wished him the best of luck, said that I knew he was innocent. It was all a bit of show. It didn't do any good, but I did me best and they appreciated it. It really infuriated the prison authorities. I think that everyone else had been frightened off by them.

I was then immediately taken to Leicester security wing. I rather fancied going back there. However, Eva had bumped into Rene Wisbey, told her I liked the idea, and she passed the message on to Tom who said to tell me to forget it. After the attempted escape, life was murder there and I should stay away. I thought it was just that they had a good number going and they didn't want me messing it up.

What had happened in August 1968 was a very daring escape from the security wing, six of them in all including Tommy Wisbey, Joey Martin, Bobby Welch and Little George Elliott. They tied up the screws, made two makeshift ladders, one to go over the fence and the other to be pulled up and pushed on to the wall – Leicester prison's wall is the highest in the country, always had been. Unfortunately for them they had had to guess the measurement from the fence to the wall. The ladder missed the wall by an inch or two and it crashed. They didn't have time to lift it up and try again. The security wing cameras had seen, and in seconds armed police was in. They were arrested and charged in the prison and were all punished. A new Governor was brought there. He was called Steinhausen.

It was sensible advice from Wisbey, but like a fool I took no notice. Whilst I was in Wandsworth, Beisty – that was the Governor's name – had brought the Prison Director round and I'd asked him if I could go to Leicester. It's unusual to get where you want to go, but sometimes they agreed with what you asked. Plus I'd written a petition about the dirty needle, and I think they may have sent me where I wanted to keep me quiet. Generally wherever they say you go, you go. If you refuse, you get to go in a straitjacket.

I arrived in March 1969 and I'd only been there two days when I arranged to go and see the Governor. Micky, an Irish guy, agreed to come with me.[1] It was decided we would see the Governor and ask for better visits, because when you had them there were screws breathing down your neck the whole time in case you planned something. We hadn't been there at the time of the escape and we thought it might carry more weight. The screws took us out the workshop into the wing and took Mick in first. Unbeknown to me, Mick had a row with the Governor and he chinned a Principal Prison Officer. I'm marched in to the Governor and I could see everyone was tensed up. With prison instinct I knew something was wrong. The Governor was still arrogant, but he did listen and then completely dismissed the application.

Later when Mick told me what had occurred with him, he said he would attack the Governor the next day. I said that since it had been my idea to see the Governor, on principle I had to do it. I told the rest and they said, "Don't. Don't get in trouble." I said, "No, it's got to be done." The next day when the Governor came into the workshop I went into the toilet, came out, washed my hands, gently eased my way past a throng of officers and slung him a beautiful punch. Many a prizefighter would have been quite proud of it; he had about eight stitches below the eye. I was engulfed by officers and I shouted to the prisoners not to get involved in any circumstances. They said they wouldn't as long as the officers didn't beat me in front of them – all they could do is restrain me. Blood all over him and I managed to spit in his face. It doesn't sound nice, but that's what I thought I should do. I was put in a body belt, and when the screws brought food in they deliberately spat in it and one said he'd pissed in it. I kicked it out of their hands all over them. I was taken in front of the Governor, this time in a body belt, and was charged with gross personal violence to the Governor. He really shouldn't have heard the charge, he shouldn't have taken part. When he remanded me to the Visiting Magistrates, by a superhuman effort I slung myself, dived over the table and nutted him. Half of me is on the desk and half is on him. I got paid properly for that and was back in the strong cell in minutes.

I wouldn't eat or drink for about ten days. It was a miracle how I lived. I was then taken out of the security wing and put into the punishment block of the prison proper.

1 Some time later, Micky was on a motor-bike on his way home when one of the police cars escorting the Queen when she was visiting Clapham knocked him down and killed him. His wife got a letter from the Queen expressing her sympathy.

In the meantime, that bent copper Walter Virgo was head of prison security.[2] I didn't know it then, but Virgo was trying to contact Jimmy Humphries, the Soho porn king, to touch him for a few quid. He knew that in 1951 Humphries had been arrested with me and been acquitted of the burglary of the hotel in the Aldwych when the juror had given Jimmy the nod. Jim Humphries and I had gone a long way back. When Humphries got married to his first wife, Eva and Jimmy Brindle put them up in a room in their house until they could get on their feet; so Jim Humphries had a great regard for them both.

Virgo got in touch with Humphries to say that the authorities knew I was going to have a knife smuggled in on a visit, stab the Governor and smuggle the knife out. Virgo had also told him that all my visits were tape-recorded. Jimmy must have realized all this was complete rubbish. For a start, we were surrounded with screws during a visit and you couldn't pass over a cigarette paper let alone a knife. Anyway, visitors had already been through an electronic survey before they were allowed to see me. I was just the excuse and a cover for him to get in touch with Humphries, and Jim did get a message to me.

When Eva and Doreen arrived at Leicester in early April for a visit, they're marched into the Governor's office where there's a screen. They're told they won't see me unless they strip. Rightly they refused, and the visit was cancelled. They went to the Post Office and sent me a telegram explaining what had occurred and then they went to the *Leicester Mercury*. I was given the telegram the next day and the *Mercury* printed the story of the search.

I had been on hunger strike about twenty-eight days in protest about the treatment of Eva and Doreen when the Director of Midland Region came round. He had one leg and one arm. He slung the screws out and asked me if I wanted to go to Broadmoor, which he said would be much better for me. I wouldn't have minded but I couldn't say yes. Francis, my youngest son, was at school and I couldn't have him being teased that I was in Broadmoor; it was bad enough for him me being in prison. I'd promised Doreen I wouldn't go to Broadmoor again if I could avoid it and so I said I'd like to go to Chelmsford. He gave a very definite "No".

2 Commander Wally Virgo, who was head of the Porn Squad, received twelve years' imprisonment. He and a number of other officers had been taking money from Humphries and others in the Soho porn industry. Virgo's conviction was later quashed on appeal.

I then said what about Parkhurst? He went "Maybe" and that was the end of the conversation.

Away he went and a few days later I was transferred to the Isle of Wight. There had been plenty of trouble at Parkhurst in the 1960s. The prison had been built in 1838 and was really well over-crowded. There'd been trouble with warders taking things home for themselves, and fights between them and prisoners. The *Daily Mail* had published an article the year before I got there, saying that prisoners were being beaten by the screws and there would be a riot if something didn't happen. The laundry got set on fire, and just before I got there prisoners sent out a round robin letter to the *People* newspaper saying they were being beaten up.

I went straight into the hospital and saw Dr Cooper there. He said to me I was to eat little but often, and I did so. I was on the punishment wing, but when it finished they still kept me down there. Alistair Miller was the Governor, immaculately smart but not as strong a governor as some and someone whom the prison officers could manipulate but he seemed the perfect gentleman. A new Deputy Governor, Hawkins, arrived, but again he was a bit weak and not particularly nasty. He spoke to me quite pleasantly. I'd got on reasonably well and it was agreed now I'd done five months down the punishment block I would go into the prison proper. About three weeks or so later, in October, a prisoner engineered a marvellous escape; out of his cell, over the security fence, over the wall and just missed the ferry. He was then running round the Island. He was the first man to get out of his cell in thirty-five years. Everyone was chuffed. Prisoners were torment-ing the screws – we should have known better – and there was a lot of news coverage. The officers were fuming.

Right out of the blue the officers got into the Governor and he gave an order that all Category A men would be moved from their cells and on to another landing. A cell is a prisoner's home, and when he has to move home when he'd not been in trouble it's a very important thing. If you've been a prisoner you'll understand. We went to see the Governor and he pooh-poohed our complaints. Added to that, the final straw came on the Wednesday before the riot when a prisoner was taken ill in the recreation area. The screws wouldn't get him a doctor, and so some of us stayed over until medical help did arrive.

We agreed we'd have a sit-in at 7 o'clock at the end of association on 20 October 1969. There'd been a similar one in Durham the year before, and at the end of it everyone had been given a bath and a meal before being sent back to their cells, and the Governor had come and listened to what they had to say. Ours was to be like that. There would be up to twelve officers with us, and we had to do it very quickly so they couldn't stop us. There was to be no violence. That was to be all there was to it.

We asked every prisoner who would be on association if they would join in, and if not would they stay away from association that night. It had to be done, but it was dangerous because of the risk of a leak. As it was, six of the prisoners went to the authorities. They went sick that afternoon, and once they were taken out of the workshops they'd ask to see the Chief Officer. This type of sit-in had been talked about for two years but on each occasion, when it came to it, the prisoners had done nothing. Their nerve had gone. This time, with the reports from the grasses, the screws took it serious. All officers' leave at Albany was cancelled, along with all association at Albany and Camp Hill. Officers arrived from Winchester and Portsmouth. At 5 p.m. everyone was locked up there and groups of prison officers were drafted in, twenty here, thirty there, forty in the bathroom. Riot sticks were issued, but the prison officers on our association weren't told. If the screws had wanted to stop the demonstration they could have done so easily. All they needed to do was to cancel association that night, or the Governor could have sent me and a couple of others down on Rule 43 for twenty-four hours. They didn't do either of these things. Instead they allowed more prisoners than usual into association that night. They were just spoiling for a fight.[3]

I gave the order at 7 p.m. The barricades were up and they was on us. There was tremendous fighting, literally in minutes. There's been riots enough since, but I doubt that even to this day there has been such fighting as that half hour. The order was to go in and get us come what may. Quite a lot of prisoners who did nothing were knocked about. The officers turned it into a bloody, violent confrontation when it needn't have been. They say they were fighting for their lives, but so were we. Inside half an hour it

3 Where it appeared desirable for the maintenance of good order or discipline, the Governor could invoke Rule 43 and order that a prisoner should not associate with other prisoners generally or with specific prisoners. This could last for twenty-four hours, after which a member of the Visiting Committee could continue the order which could be renewed from month to month.

was all over. They had six of us in the table tennis room. We were all unconscious and as we came to, there lined up were officers in riot gear with sticks – tough guys taking the piss out of us. I said, "I'll have a fight – keep the stick or not." They all said, "You're mad." Then in comes the screws' hero, a big brute of a man built like a barn door – in he come, sleeves rolled up. They told him what I'd just done. He come forwards, and I must admit I was frightened but I had to challenge him. It was the road I'd gone down. When it came to it he was a coward like the others; said I was mad. The officers were stunned with disbelief. As he walked into the corridor someone who hadn't been rounded up threw a billiard ball at him and knocked him out.

As we were walked down the steps from the association room there was a gauntlet with riot sticks – like an arch at a wedding. One screw had got a meat cleaver; others had bars of iron. The officer at the top of the steps was in charge. He would shout out "Smith coming down" and the inflexion in his voice meant you can give him a clout but it doesn't matter if you don't. If there was a growl it meant give him a few clumps, but if there was a stern voice it meant see to him. Then "Fraser coming down" meant anything goes. From the association to the punishment cells was about a hundred yards with officers all the way along, so by the time I got to the punishment cell I couldn't stand. Then I was just slung in there. When the doctor came round two hours later the floor was smothered with blood and he immediately ordered I be taken to hospital in a wheelchair. That's where I was kept for six weeks until after the trial. And most of that time I was still in the wheelchair.

Cooper, the doctor, was good to me and to the other prisoners as well. It wouldn't be right to say otherwise. He did have sympathies and asked to be told exactly what happened. Cooper was really my mentor; he wanted me to go back to Broadmoor, and he brought a South African doctor from there to see me. Again I had to say no because of the promise I'd given to Doreen. It was a promise which did me no good. I'd have been much better there. Broadmoor was improving by leaps and bounds. When I was there in 1955 no one got remission. All that now was done away with: they were only too pleased to get you out.

Finally nine of us were summoned over the riot including me, Martin Frape, Tony Blythe, no relation of Billy, Timmy Noonan, Mickey Andrews, Stan Thompson, Peterson, and Andy Anderson, the one who'd escaped with Ronnie Biggs and landed up at Atlantic Machines. I had about eleven summonses including incitement to murder as well as GBH on the screws. There was no point in actually charging us because we were already serving sentences. Eva got me a lawyer – the one who'd defended her over that conspiracy to pervert in the Torture trial – and he briefed Billy Rees-Davies, who was known as the One-Armed Bandit and who was an M.P., and also Ernle Money who was then a Tory candidate. Unfortunately the election came up and they couldn't continue with the case, so my lawyer suggested I got George Shindler. He telephoned me at the hospital in Parkhurst – I was called into the doctor's office to take the call – and Mr Shindler said he had prosecuted my son David when he got seven years for a security van. He was very honest, he didn't have to tell me. He said that one day he prosecuted and one day he defended, but I just didn't feel on principle I could have him and so he defended Anderson instead. To my delight he got him found not guilty, but it was also a bit of dismay because he might have got me a not guilty and all. Eventually I had Richard Harvey, who was known as Don, a big, nice Irishman who wrote *Harvey's Industrial Relations*. He was very good but he was a bit soft when it came to it.

One of the problems, since we were all separated and in solitary, was preparing our defence. Jimmy Robson was a red-band by now, and used to come to my cell window and we could have a chat. I could give him instructions saying I'd like to call this witness, ask him if he'd mind. I wanted their permission to pass their names on to my lawyer. If they said they didn't want to, then I wouldn't get them involved. Out of the blue Eddie Richardson, who was in the security wing, came over the hospital to report sick from a cold. Whilst me and Jim was talking at the window we could hear the dog barking. Eddie would normally wave and I thought he'd do it that day and Jim would get caught. Fortunately no one noticed.

Messages used to be left in the chapel font, but the screws found this out and brought it up at the trial. There was one which was intercepted saying we wanted to get a barrister called Guy Willett to defend, and the message read he was "shit-hot". When it came up at the trial Mr Willett stood up and said, "My Lord, I have to tell you I am not."

First, we heard the judge was going to be Mr Justice Lawton, and we were very upset and were going to appeal against him, but then we were told we were going to have Mr Justice Bean, and what a difference he made in the end. Then we were told that we were going to have the trial on the Isle of Wight, which was something we didn't want because we thought a jury would be prejudiced against us and favour the screws. What we didn't know was that the screws at Parkhurst weren't generally popular on the island. Mr Justice Bean's son came and watched the trial, and he was sitting near us. We all heard who he was and Timmy Noonan wrote him a note: "Tell your Dad to see we get a fair trial and to find us all not guilty." The boy had a sense of humour. He wrote back, "What's the point. Because if you're all innocent why should my father have to find you not guilty?" We sent him another saying, "Tell your Dad to do his best." He turned round and gave a charming smile. He was a nice boy.

It was a funny trial. It was the first they'd ever had on the Island. They didn't want to transport us to Winchester for security reasons and so they converted the upstairs of the Town Hall where they'd held the committal proceedings. There was no room for our relatives and at first there was a tannoy system into a room outside the court, but then when we protested the judge said that our families could come in and sit behind us.

About the second day when we went back to Parkhurst, there on the cell floor was Andy Anderson's radio, the screws had smashed it whilst he was gone. As a result, we stayed away from court. The judge sent a note to all of us saying we would be welcome back any time, and when we heard the trial was being fair we did so. But what was best was all the barristers in the case, including the prosecution, had a whip for a new radio for him. It was terrific what they done. Another time the prosecution, Sir Tim Molony, treated one of the prisoners to a pack of twenty cigarettes. We used to break in the morning for coffee and there was no time to send us back to Parkhurst and no room to separate us from the barristers outside the court, so they used to give cigarettes to those of us who smoked during the adjournment and then go straight back to cross-examining us afterwards. And that included the prosecution. Patrick Back, who was for Martin Frape, was especially good. He used to come and spend hours with him in an evening calming him down because Martin was really on edge. At the end of the trial when Mr Back came in to see Martin we all sang, "For he's a jolly good fellow." I would say, for that time and day I've never seen barristers and solicitors work so hard and diligently for the people they were representing. I think they felt, "Yes, there is something wrong here."

Every night when I came back to the prison hospital Dr Cooper would come to see me, and the day he gave evidence for the prosecution he told about our injuries. That night he showed me a card he'd received from the wife of a prison officer saying he would be killed, and another one saying he was a dog. The next day I told my counsel and when it was put to Dr Cooper he never denied it. The night after he was cross-examined I apologized, but he said it didn't matter and it was the truth. He was very very good.

In a way the judge summed up for us. He told the jury that we had been hit by the screws after the riot. "Injuries to prisoners in the Parkhurst Jail riot permitted no other explanation than the excessive use of riot sticks," is what he said.

When it came to it the jury was decent. I was acquitted of incitement to murder but convicted of the main charges. I got another five years added on to the fifteen I was already doing. But if I'd gone down on the incitement to murder I don't think I'd ever have come out. In its way it was a result.

Angel of Death
(Dr Marcel Petiot)

David Rowan

While posing as a prosperous French physician, Dr Marcel Petiot (1897–1946) was in reality a sadistic monster. On his own admission, he murdered and dismembered no fewer than 63 people at his home in Paris, not far from the Arc de Triomphe. Two psychiatrists who examined Petiot judged him to be "without scruples and devoid of all moral sensibility", yet ruled that he was sane. As a boy Petiot enjoyed torturing animals, once dipping his pet cat into boiling water and, on another occasion, poking out the eyes of trapped birds with a needle before looking on in amusement as they hurled themselves against the sides of their cage. Petiot's mass killings were uncovered towards the end of World War Two in March 1944, when foul-smelling smoke was seen pouring from the chimneys of his house at 21 Rue Lesueur. Police found dismembered human remains not only burning in the copper but also in a pit of quicklime in the cellar.

The wanted man was named as Dr Marcel André Henri Félix Petiot, a forty-seven-year-old physician. He used No. 21, Rue Lesueur, as his main surgery, having a smaller consulting-room in his flat at No. 66, Rue Caumartin, just behind the Opera. Police descended on the flat within an hour of discovering the murders, but they were too late. Everything was in confusion. The dark-haired, intense-looking doctor, with his wife and seventeen-year-old son, had hurriedly packed two suitcases and fled. It was then that a neighbour thought he remembered seeing Dr Petiot calmly cycling down the Rue Lesueur that afternoon, just as the fire brigade arrived . . .

Despite a nation-wide man-hunt on an unparalleled scale, Petiot had vanished without trace. Throughout March 1944, there were rumours that he had been arrested in Paris, seen on the Metro, found drowned in the River Yonne, near Fontainebleau. Two water-diviners, in districts of France about 200 miles apart, each claimed to have found his body. And the enemy radio added fuel to the flames by announcing that Petiot had been interned at a German camp, where he was the medical officer; similar crimes to those of the Rue Lesueur had been discovered in Germany, the announcer added, and it was suspected that Petiot might be responsible for them, too.

In the first week of April, the search rose to fever pitch in and around Auxerre, Petiot's birthplace, ninety miles south-east of Paris. Forty-nine cases of clothes belonging to his victims had been found in a bicycle shop in the nearby little town of Courson. But the doctor was no longer there. Every corner of France was combed, from the lonely mountain regions of the south-east to the teeming industrial cities of the north, from the vast forests south of Bordeaux to the sloping vineyards along the Rhine. Nothing. And all the time the hunt was overshadowed by the fear that there might be more victims to come.

However unsuccessful their desperate efforts to find Petiot, the detectives did not take long to establish the motive and method of his crimes. They proved beyond all doubt that he had made a fortune from his victims, whom he had found by posing as an agent for a Resistance escape group. Through friends, he had let it be known that he could help anyone in danger from the Gestapo – particularly Jews doomed to forced labour in Germany, or worse – to escape from Occupied France into Spain. The victims were told to report to his surgery in the Rue Lesueur after dark, and to bring a small suitcase containing their clothes and all available money and jewellery. They were never seen again. But their families were not disturbed at hearing no news of them, merely assuming that it meant they had been successful in getting out of the country. Until that foul-smelling black cloud told the true story, that is. Then the police reports struck terror in their hearts.

Adjoining the consulting-room, the police revealed, was a small

triangular room in which Petiot's victims spent their last minutes
on earth. His system was simple and unvarying. When a fugitive
arrived, he or she accompanied the doctor into a well-furnished
front room. There they sat side by side, in two large armchairs,
discussing the escape plans. At a suitable point in the conversation,
Petiot told the fugitive that it would be necessary to have an
inoculation before making the trip. He produced a hypodermic
syringe and the job was quickly done. Then Petiot led the victim –
not yet feeling the effects of the poison he had injected – into the
small triangular room. The victim was told to sit down and make
himself comfortable, and did not become anxious when Petiot left,
locking the door behind him, for on the other side of the room were
two folding doors through which the rescue "guides" were to
enter. He was not to know that these doors were fixed in front of a
solid brick wall for the sole purpose of reassuring him while he was
dying. Nor could he know that his death agonies, now inexorably
upon him, were being watched to the end by Dr Petiot – through a
periscope. The doctor had bored a small hole high up in the wall
for this purpose, using the periscope so that he could see into the
death chamber without being seen.

When it was all over, Petiot came back into the room and
stripped the body of all clothing and valuables. His next step
was to dispose of the corpse, and for this, too, he had planned down
to the last detail. Behind No. 21 was a small courtyard, overlooked
by the backs of three other houses – all then unoccupied. The only
outside point from which a small part of the courtyard was visible,
in fact, was the top storey of a neighbouring apartment house. But
Petiot, missing nothing, had had a wall built to block this view.
Nobody could see him dragging his victim across the courtyard
into the basement opposite. From there he pushed the body into
the cellar and, with an elaborate chain and pulley system, lowered
it into the limepit. If the bath was already full, or any of the
remains proved unduly obstinate, he dissected the body and
burned it piece by piece in the stove or the copper.

Nobody knows how much Petiot made from his satanic scheme,
but it may well have run into six figures. Among his victims was an
entire family, the Knellers; the coup brought him their hoard of
£15,000 in gold.

Strange as it seems now, the first reports about the so-called
"death cellar" were greeted sceptically outside France. It was
suggested that the Germans had cooked up the story to help divert

public attention both from the Russian victories in the spring of 1944 and from thoughts about the inevitable Allied "Second Front". (France was still under German occupation, and Paris was not to be liberated for another five-and-a-half months.)

At Free French headquarters in London, several searching questions were asked. Why was the German radio giving such disproportionate publicity to the murders? Why were the French radio stations – particularly that of Paris, which would have been in close touch with the police – some hours later than the Germans in giving the wanted man's name? There were hints that the unknown Dr Petiot might really be a Resistance patriot and that the hue-and-cry had been started by the Gestapo as a means of trapping him. An expert at the Institute of Medical Psychology in London was quoted as saying that, on the evidence up to that point, "the whole thing sounds like a put-up case."

In some ways, the sceptics were nearer the mark than might be imagined. Doubtless the Germans *were* glad to distract attention from their recent military defeats – and there seems little doubt that the Gestapo had a very good idea of Petiot's activities, as we shall see later.

Within a few days, though, even Free French H.Q. could no longer doubt the fact of the murders, whatever the German motives. On 13 March, a German Overseas News-agency broadcast produced "the woman who was to have been murdered at 3 p.m. today". The woman was Mme Parisinot, a sales assistant at the *Printemps*, one of the largest department stores in Paris, only a stone's throw from Petiot's flat. She had a pain in her wrist the previous Saturday, she said, and a chemist advised her to "consult Dr Petiot in the Rue Caumartin, as she had dislocated the wrist bone". After waiting fifteen minutes in the doctor's reception room, she was received by a man who "looked like a labourer, since he wore no tie and his clothes were splashed with lime".

Mme Parisinot went on: "I held out my wrist. A shiver ran down my spine as he touched me. His black eyes bored into me with such impertinence that I thought he was mad. He X-rayed the wrist. 'You have dislocated the bone all right,' he said. 'Your bones are very delicate, my dear, and you need calcium.' He then told me that he could carry out only a cursory examination in his consulting-room but that he had other consulting-rooms at the Rue Lesueur, where better X-ray apparatus was installed. Petiot then gave me another appointment for Monday at 3 p.m."

Fortunately for Mme Parisinot, that black cloud of smoke intervened . . . She was the first, however, to mention the doctor's strange eyes and give a clue to the eerie hypnotic power with which he must have influenced some of his victims.

A few hours after this broadcast, police made their first arrests in the case. Those detained were Petiot's wife, Georgette, and his brother, Maurice. They were found at Maurice's home in Auxerre (a lead which later led to the discovery of the victims' clothes at Courson). The couple were charged with being accomplices, though Mme Petiot claimed that she knew nothing about the murders and that she had never visited the house in the Rue Lesueur. Deathly pale with shock, she sought desperately to find some justification for the doctor's acts. In a statement quoted by Berlin Radio, she said: "Possibly my husband hoped to eliminate people who had been described to him as traitors."

Maurice Petiot freely admitted having brought quantities of lime to No. 21, Rue Lesueur, giving the somewhat unconvincing explanation: "My brother wanted it for whitewashing." Both he and Mme Petiot, however, were eventually freed. The Petiots' young son was at no time implicated.

Meanwhile, alarming evidence was also being gathered about the wanted man's earlier life. It is easy to be wise after the event and point to his intense appearance, his broad brow and small chin, his thin, cruel lips, his jutting eyebrows and deep sunken eyes – all forming a picture, perhaps, of an intellect on nodding terms with madness. Such features, though, could be a description of many perfectly harmless individuals. Again, one might think that Petiot could have got away with his crimes for so long only in the confused conditions of an occupied country. But what is really astounding is that he was as much as allowed to continue his medical practice, *in view of his record before the war*.

Petiot showed criminal tendencies even at school, where it was proved that he had stolen from his classmates. In 1917 he joined the French Army as a medical orderly. But before the war was over, he was accused of selling morphia, at black-market prices, to drug-addicts in the town of Dijon. The morphia came from the military hospital to which he was attached. Petiot, too, is believed to have fallen into the drug habit by then. Not for the last time, though, he managed to escape the consequences of his crimes. Instead of receiving a heavy sentence, he was discharged from the Army and given a pension – with free treatment for psycho-neurosis!

After the war, he resumed his medical studies, qualifying as a doctor in 1921. It seems amazing that he was able to do so, and testifies to his undoubted brain-power. For between 1918 and 1921, he lived partly in an asylum and partly with his mother, who said that he never studied!

Petiot first came to police notice in 1928, but only for the petty offence of robbing his electric-light meter. He was then mayor of the little town of Villeneuve, in the Yonne Department, not far from his home-town of Auxerre. Two years later, however, he lost the post. There were grim chuckles when questions were asked about this later and a shopkeeper from Villeneuve said that the doctor "was always good to humble folk". Then why, he was asked, was this "model mayor" removed from office? The shop-keeper replied: "Some people at Villeneuve persecute those of good ideas . . ."

Possibly a far more sinister affair during Petiot's term as mayor remains unexplained to this day. Two maidservants employed by him at that time were rumoured to have vanished suddenly over-night. There may have been no mystery about it, but the fact remains that they were never seen in the district again.

No more was heard of the doctor until World War Two, when he was again convicted of drug-trafficking, and was once more stated to be an addict himself. Inexplicably, he got off with nothing worse than a £10 fine.

That, then, was the record of the Dr Marcel Petiot whom detectives were hunting in every corner of France in the spring and early summer of 1944 – until their efforts were temporarily directed elsewhere by the Allied landings and the liberation of Paris. In those first, jubilant days of freedom, the confusion was indescribable. Traitors were being rounded up, fugitive patriots were coming out into the open for the first time in years; the whole vast process of running the country was having to be started again almost from scratch. For a while Petiot was all but forgotten.

But in October 1944, France was reminded of him again, with a shock of surprise. For there, in the newspaper *Résistance*, was a letter supposedly signed by Petiot himself! In it, he claimed that he had been imprisoned by the Gestapo and that, while he was in gaol, his house was used as a dumping-ground for their corpses. He had long been a member of the Resistance movement, the letter went on, and was still working for it. Echoing the earlier sceptics, he said that the Gestapo's motive in making such a song about the discovery was to divert public attention from the Russian victories in the spring of 1944.

Was the letter a fake? There was only one way to find out. The writer's statement that he was still a Resistance officer was noted by the Free French commander of the Paris region, Colonel Jaques Roll. Immediately Colonel Roll sent for the original manuscript of the letter and had it compared with examples of Petiot's handwriting in the police dossier. There was no doubt that Petiot really was the author. At once the handwriting was carefully compared with that of all officers enrolled with the Free French forces in Paris. It was found to "fit" exactly with the writing of a Captain Henri Valéri, who was serving as an investigating officer in the Free French barracks at Reuilly. On 2 November, Captain Valéri was arrested as he was leaving the Metro station of St. Mandé-Tourelle, in the extreme eastern outskirts of Paris. His trapped expression left his captors in no doubt that they had found the right man. The manhunt was over.

And where had Petiot been all this time? No, not in some remote part of France, nor even safely hidden in the Auxerre district, but right under the noses of the Paris police . . . In fact, one local police station even received a complaint about him! He had taken refuge in a small, three-roomed flat in the Rue du Faubourg St Denis, just off the *grands boulevards*, the capital's main thoroughfares. To disguise himself, he grew a bushy beard and wore dark blue glasses. He remained indoors all day, venturing out only at twilight, but could not resist standing at the open windows of the flat to get a little fresh air. Because of this habit – or rather, the fact that he invariably stood with his hairy chest bare – he became known among the neighbours as "Tarzan" and a protest was made about his somewhat alarming mien in such undress. But a man could hardly be deemed a criminal because he liked going around his home bare-chested, and no action was taken.

When he was not scaring the neighbours, Petiot passed the time by playing patience, reading crime stories and books on sociology, and making abstruse calculations with a queer set of dice that he had designed himself. The man who sheltered him was a fifty-six-year-old housepainter, Georges Redoute, who lived in the flat with his twenty-two-year-old adopted daughter. Both were out at work all day. Redoute told the police later: "One evening after an air raid, I met Petiot carrying two heavy suitcases. He said to me: 'My wife has just been killed in the raid. My home is destroyed. I have nowhere to go.' I knew the doctor, so I offered him a home and let him sleep on a mattress in my room. Petiot told me that he had been working for the Resistance and had shot sixty-two Germans.''

During the seven months he stayed with Redoute, however, Petiot gave no indication that he was still working for the Resistance and did not even seem to be a particularly good patriot. The fact is significant, not just for itself, but because it shows the extent of his ability to persuade and impress people, no matter how implausible his story.

It is quite possible that he would have escaped completely in the post-liberation turmoil, if he had been content to remain in the shadows. But Petiot, bolstered by his immense vanity, was certain that he was too clever to be caught. British criminal experts, discussing his case, said that, with a maniacal killer of his type, "absolute secrecy is essential to the satisfaction that he gets from his deeds." Though that was undoubtedly true, he also had the exhibitionism and feeling of invincibility characteristic of many less intelligent murderers. He could not resist letting everybody know that he was still alive. So it was that he wrote to *Résistance* – wrote the letter that was to lead him to the guillotine.

After his arrest, Petiot was taken to the Quai des Orfèvres – Paris C.I.D. headquarters, on the Île de la Cité – where it was established that he had been carrying on his masquerade as "Captain Valéri" since 27th September. He had entered the Resistance barracks with a full set of papers establishing his identity as a patriot. The papers included an Army paybook.

During his brief service, he seems to have made quite an impression. He refused to wear uniform, unless ordered, was always boasting about his medical knowledge, and, as an investigating officer, was highly successful at making prisoners talk without using force. "He never hit anyone," it was reported. His secretary at the barracks, twenty-five-year-old Mlle Cecile Dylma, a former actress, stated: "He was always a very gentle man, but now and again a queer sadistic look came into his eyes. Sometimes he would stride nervously up and down the room. He had a craze, too, for telling horror stories. It was his hands and eyes that scared me." But with best respects to Mlle Dylma, perhaps she, too, was being wise after the event . . .

On the evening of Petiot's arrest, he was interviewed by newspapermen at police headquarters. Here are some of the questions and answers:

Question: "How, Dr Petiot, do you explain the presence of those bodies in your cellar?"

Petiot: "They were put there while I was in prison. The Germans had the keys of my house."

Question: "How is it that your wife and other members of your family are stated to have been wearing clothes belonging to victims found in your cellar?"

Petiot: "That statement was made by the Germans. As to the fact that suitcases believed to belong to the dead people were found in my brother-in-law's house, there is a simple explanation. He was asked to collect some furniture from my house in the Rue Lesueur and he took these suitcases at the same time."

Question: "What motive could anybody have had for putting those bodies in your cellar?"

Petiot: "I would rather not make any statement about that at present."

Question: "You wrote a letter to *Résistance*, saying that you were innocent and that you were working with the Resistance movement. In that case, why didn't you come forward and explain everything to the police?"

Petiot (after a moment's hesitation): "Because I believed the work I was doing was more urgent than having an inquiry made into this affair."

After this interview, Petiot – who had previously undergone lengthy questioning by the head of the C.I.D., Chief Commissioner Pinault – was interrogated until a late hour by an examining magistrate, Judge Mariotte. (Under French law, an examining magistrate fulfils much the same functions as a Grand Jury in the US; he does not try criminal charges, but makes a detailed judicial investigation into them to decide whether or not there is a case to answer; his report usually forms the basis of the prosecution case at the trial proper.) The volume of work on the case was so great that three examining magistrates took it over in turn. At the end of November, it was confided solely to the third, Judge Goletti, who was relieved of all other duties. By then, the Petiot dossier already weighed more than 50 lbs!

Inconsistencies in Petiot's various statements were quickly apparent. In one of the earliest, he was reported to have told the police: "Thirty of the bodies were German soldiers and the rest were either German or French Gestapo men. I executed them in different places round Paris, sometimes in lonely parts in the outer suburbs, and then brought them to my cellar." This was certainly at variance with his answer to the newspapermen on the evening after his arrest.

He told yet another story when Judge Goletti asked him – for the nth time – how the bodies came to be in his house. Petiot replied: "You know I am an old member of the Resistance movement. I imagine the bodies were brought to my house while I was detained at Fresnes Prison by the Germans. Without doubt, it was a practical joke played on me by my pals. However, as I did not want to have any bother with the police, I was obliged to dispose of the bodies – so I made them disappear."

This time, then, it was not the Gestapo who had dumped the bodies, but his "pals". To lend strength to his story, he told the magistrate that, during his detention, Gestapo torture experts filed his teeth and forced him into a bath charged with electricity. As a Resistance worker, he fought Gestapo informers, while helping patriots to escape. In this way, Petiot said, he had killed "Francois the Corsican", "Joe the Boxer" and "Adrian the Basque" – all Gestapo informers.

Up to a point, Petiot was telling the truth here. Among the bodies police succeeded in identifying were those of a few undesirables, of whom "Adrian the Basque" was one. Unfortunately for the defence, however, it was also proved later that the Basque was carrying nearly £10,000 worth of stolen jewellery when he disappeared . . .

There is no doubt, either, that the doctor did fall into Gestapo hands in 1942–3. The reason for his arrest has never been established. It may have been for drug-trafficking, but some evidence supports another, much stranger story. This evidence goes to suggest that the Gestapo learned quite early about Petiot's supposed willingness to help fugitives escape from France and that they set a trap for him. An old Jew, due for execution, was told that he would be reprieved if he went to Petiot as a would-be escapee and then told the Germans exactly what happened. The man did so – and promptly vanished. Petiot, of course, was arrested immediately.

It is significant that he was not held for long. Possibly he managed to convince the Gestapo that he had no means of helping people to escape, even if he had wished. But it is equally possible – indeed, more likely – that they found out the whole story. Their cynical minds would have been vastly amused at the idea of Jews and other unfortunates eluding their grasp, only to land in Petiot's death cellar. So the doctor was released and allowed to carry on his "good work".

This version was supported by a statement made in July, 1945, by a man right outside the case. The man, Charles Beretta, was arrested in Paris as an alleged collaborator. He told the police that he had tried to flee to the Argentine during the Occupation, but that the Gestapo arrested him before he called at Petiot's house. The Gestapo, Beretta was quoted as saying, told him of his narrow escape. They expressed admiration for the "death cellar" and let Petiot continue his activities. In the difficult days immediately after the war, it was impossible to substantiate this statement, or even whether those were Beretta's actual words.

But there is another small pointer – a requisition order which Petiot received at the beginning of March, 1944. He was told that he must vacate No. 21, Rue Lesueur, by the middle of the month, when it would be taken over as a hostel for Gestapo drivers. (A garage, subsequently used by the British Embassy is just opposite the house.) Petiot was desperate; the limepit was full and there were still many bodies to be destroyed. To get rid of them, he crammed the stove and copper to overflowing – and so caused the black cloud that betrayed him. But what seems really surprising is that the Germans gave him as much as a fortnight's notice to quit. Usually they did not hesitate to requisition premises almost over-night. Could it be, therefore, that the Gestapo tried to make sure he had enough time to clear up the mess?

Although that seems very feasible, the investigators were unable to find conclusive proof one way or the other. The long inquiries dragged on through 1945, through the German surrender, Hiroshima and V.J. Day. For a while, Dr Marcel Petiot was forgotten yet again. In November, still as arrogant as ever, he refused to answer any more questions from Judge Goletti – because, he complained, no notice had been taken of him for the previous six months!

Finally, on 18 March 1946, more than sixteen months after his arrest, Petiot entered the dock in the vast, ornately painted Seine Assize Court, in the heart of Paris. To one side of the dock, behind the Clerk of the Court, was an enormous pile of suitcases, trunks, brown paper parcels with clothes bulging from them, wicker baskets and wooden crates – the property of the doctor's victims. A long glass case held medical instruments, lengths of wire, pulley-wheels and other apparatus which he had used to dispose of the bodies.

Petiot had shaved off his bushy black beard for the trial and looked surprisingly smart in a mauve pin-striped suit with bow tie and a tweed overcoat. From the first, his hypnotic black eyes bored into the jurymen in a clear attempt to dominate them. The Clerk of the Court took more than an hour to read the statement of the accusation against him. He was accused of murdering twenty-seven people – all that the police had been able to identify – but himself insisted that the correct total was sixty-three.

It was not long before Petiot set the stormy note of the whole trial, which several times had to be suspended because of public feeling and the violent insults hurled between the various counsel. Losing his temper with the President of the Court, Judge Leser, he bellowed: "Yes, it's true, it's true! I killed them! But I killed them to help the Resistance movement. You will acquit me for these killings, and when I have been acquitted, I will give you the names of other victims for whose deaths you will also acquit me!"

Petiot claimed that he belonged to the "Fly Spray" group, a Maquis organization formed to wipe out Gestapo agents. He had been trained by "a Resistance agent from Britain". (When Petiot first mentioned this to the examining magistrate, police were unable to find any survivors of the group in France; a detective was sent to London in December, 1944, to search for a member of it – again without success.)

"I was concerned in the Resistance," he declared, "from the moment the Germans arrived in Paris."

Judge Leser: "Do you believe there *was* a Resistance organization in Paris in the first days of the German occupation?"

Petiot: "I think there were certainly some Resistance men in Paris even in those early days."

The judge: "There was none!"

This comment by the judge aroused shouts of protest from many parts of the court. Indeed, any mention of the Resistance was liable to cause trouble, for this was no ordinary murder trial. Behind it, and constantly overshadowing it, lay the whole dark conscience of France – the treachery and fears of the Occupation, now exposed so nakedly through the agency of this maniac doctor.

When the protests died down, Judge Leser continued sarcastically: "Well, if you were a member of the Resistance, if you were a hero of the Maquis, give us the name of the men with whom you fought." Petiot remained silent, and the State Prosecutor, M. Dupin, leapt to his feet and joined the judge in shouting, for a minute on end: "Give us names! Give us names!"

At last, crouching in the dock, his eyes blazing and face strangely twisted, the accused spat out a reply. "No, no! I will not give you the names! I will not betray the men with whom I fought! The purge in France has not yet ended. There are too many followers of Pétain, too many traitors still at liberty in my country."

The "Fly Spray" group, he said, seized Germans or collabora- tionists and "took them for a ride", usually in the Bois de Marly (a wood to the west of Paris). They had killed sixty-three people altogether.

How many of those, asked the judge, did you yourself kill?

Petiot: "I myself killed only two German motor-cyclists. I killed them with my silent secret weapon, which leaves no trace."

It was not the first time Petiot had mentioned this "secret weapon", said to be a form of long-distance syringe. He claimed that he had killed Germans with it from 100 ft. away and that he had offered it to members of the American Embassy in Paris. But when pressed to describe it or produce it in court, he replied: "I will give details of this weapon only when I am convinced that to disclose them publicly would be in the interest of France."

Describing the scene at Gestapo H.Q. after his arrest, Petiot broke down and sobbed: "I saw my own Resistance comrades being beaten up, with some lying dead on the floor." He was released after eight months, he said, on paying 100,000 francs. The judge's request for the names of these comrades, however, still met with refusal. "As soon as I am acquitted, I will give names," Petiot said defiantly.

With this smokescreen of mystery, and his skilful playing on Resistance emotions, Petiot's defence appeared to be making some headway in the first few days of the trial. The turning point came when the doctor, denying that he had killed for gain, said that four men and five women among the victims were "bad Frenchmen and bad Frenchwomen, who were selling their country to the Nazis", and that their money and jewels were still in their pockets or sewn inside their clothing. The packed court was deathly silent as nine suitcases were taken down from the pile and their contents thor- oughly searched. There were no diamonds, no gold, no money.

From that moment on, Petiot knew that he was doomed. His manner became more contemptuous and domineering than ever.

At one point, the State Prosecutor accused him of killing an eight-year-old girl for her ration-book, adding "You refused to answer the examining magistrate about this."

"That's a lie!" Petiot shouted. "A fine thing, your so-called justice!"

Then, above the ensuing uproar, he shrieked: "I won't talk to idiots – I want jurymen."

By now the whole court was in confusion, with judge, counsel and prisoner all shouting at the top of their voices and a number of free fights in the public gallery. Proceedings were so out of hand that finally Judge Leser banged his gavel and suspended the hearing "to let tempers calm down".

The high point of the trial came on the fifth day, Friday, when the entire court transferred to the Rue Lesueur for one of the most extraordinary crime reconstructions in legal history. More than fifty armed police manned wooden barricades at either end of the street as the scarlet-robed judges, black-gowned lawyers, jurymen and journalists trooped into the tightly-shuttered house. Chalked on the outside double carriage-door of number twenty-one was a swastika and the notice: "Here lie the ashes of many martyrs," a grim reminder in face of the gay spring hats in a milliner's shop-window across the way.

Despite a cold drizzle of rain, hundreds of women clustered behind the barricades and every window in the narrow street was packed. When Petiot emerged, bare-headed, from a police lorry, the crowds burst past the guards, with brandished fists, and shouts of *"Assassin!"* – and a few coarse jokes. He smiled cynically, without looking round.

Inside the house, the doctor explained his way through each room, for hour after dreary hour. Dust and whitewash marked everyone's clothes and the rain soaked them as they crossed the courtyard, heightening the all-pervading sordidness of the whole scene. Steadily, Petiot became more and more haggard, though he flared angrily when a detective, Inspector Sannie, demonstrated the features of the triangular "death room" (which the jury were able to enter only by instalments). The room was supposed to have been used for giving ultra-violet rays to patients, the inspector explained, but it was much too small for that purpose. Petiot cried out: "I tell you, I made this room for ultra-violet rays, and any medical expert will say it is big enough!" He had another outburst of anger when the inspector said he had erected a ten-foot wall to prevent neighbours looking into the courtyard. "Listen!" he shouted fiercely, "I paid 40,000 francs to have that wall built so that children could not throw stones and break my windows. The neighbours could see what I was doing, despite the wall."

But his anger vanished when the court visited the cellar, with its sinister lime pit. He was so overcome that he fainted . . . On coming to, he explained quickly: "I'm tired – that's all."

Back in the Assize Court, Petiot faced a barrage of questions from jurymen about the house. When he denied that the triangular room was used for "executions", one juror asked: "Why were electric switches and a lock fixed outside the room? Why were there holes in the wall?" Petiot answered that he bought the house in 1941, at the worst period of the Occupation, and had difficulty in installing gas, electricity and water.

The verdict had long been certain, but the trial dragged on for another thirteen days. Slowly, relentlessly, the last threads of his defence were torn away.

His claims to have been a Resistance worker were finally destroyed when he was brought face to face with a Maquis officer, Captain Henri Boris. Petiot glared at him, insulted him, then argued with him about the extent to which Britain helped to arm the Maquis and the way in which British-supplied explosives were used.

The doctor had previously stated that he took part in experiments "with an explosive plastic used in the Maquis". When Maître Veron, a lawyer representing the family of one of Petiot's victims, asked him to explain exactly how he used the explosive, he went into a long, confused account – in no way tallying with that which Captain Boris gave later. Petiot added that a parachutist from Britain was sent to demonstrate the plastic explosive. But Captain Boris told the court: "The way to use the British explosive was clearly explained in the instructions and there could be no doubt about it."

As the days passed, the accused lost his arrogant air. His eyes dulled and his powerful fingers twitched nervously. Once he rose to question a witness, crouching low over the dock rail; the judge reprimanded him, "Stand up properly," and immediately he straightened himself. Sometimes, as a long, sad procession of his victims' relatives passed through the witness-box to give evidence against him, he babbled unintelligibly. But at no time did the defence show the slightest sign of trying to save Petiot on the ground of insanity.

Two of the witnesses were men who had last-minute escapes from his "death-cellar". The first, Michel Cadoret, a thirty-three-year-old decorator, told the court: "I suspected him as soon as I saw his dirty hands, so unlike the hands of other doctors I knew."

After making his decision to escape from France with his wife and child, M. Cadoret said, he met Petiot through a Mme Kahan. "He talked vaguely about diplomatic papers, about the need for British and American money, about being inoculated against certain diseases to satisfy the South American aliens' regulations.

"Petiot told me: 'Bring all your money with you.' That struck me as suspicious, because Resistance men didn't usually demand large payments for their help. It was then I noticed his hands . . ."

The second witness, Joseph Scarella, said that Petiot asked for £2,000 to help him get out of the country. Fortunately for him, he decided to remain in France after all.

Dr Paul, France's leading pathologist, gave evidence that skin had been removed from the faces of some of the victims so that they could not be recognized. They were apparently scalped in Indian fashion, he said. Petiot affected a modest smile as Dr Paul commented: "The bodies were obviously cut by an expert hand, by someone who knew where to put the knife."

There was a shout of macabre laughter when another expert witness, Professor Paul Gourriou, an eminent French psychiatrist, was questioned about the accused's medical qualifications. "In his examination for dissection," Professor Gourriou told the court, "Petiot was marked 'mediocre'. . . ."

Fierce arguments between the State Prosecutor and the defence counsel, Maître René Floriot, broke out anew when a red-haired Rumanian actress entered the witness-box and the lawyer alleged that she had been in Gestapo pay. "You should be ashamed of yourself for defending such a foul cause," the prosecutor shouted. Yet again Judge Leser had to suspend the trial until the tumult died and the prosecutor withdrew his "harsh words".

The actress in question, forty-eight-year-old Mme Kahan, was the woman through whom Michel Cadoret said he met Petiot. Tears poured down her face as she told the court that she had considered Petiot a "god" because of the "work he was doing for the Resistance movement and for the good of humanity". He had told her to bring her Jewish friends to him and he would help them to escape to South America. "I am Jewish myself. In all good faith,

I introduced my friends to him. We had tea parties at my home in the Rue Pasquier. Petiot was extremely entertaining."

Under cross-examination, she denied that she had accepted commissions for introducing fugitives to him or that she had ever worked for the Gestapo, but admitted that she had a Nazi officer lover during the occupation, adding in extenuation: "He was an Austrian."

At last the trial entered its third week and rolled ponderously to a close. Though he must have known that he was lost, Petiot's hopes were momentarily revived by his counsel's final, five-hour speech to the jury. As the judge and jury filed out to consider their verdict, he turned to his guards with a look of triumph in his eyes and exclaimed: "I shall not die on the guillotine. France will not behead a man who killed nine German agents. I put my trust in my country. I shall not die . . . I shall not die!"

But it took the jury only two and a half hours to answer the 165 questions set before them. Their verdict on every question was unanimous. Just before midnight on 4 April, Petiot was found guilty of twenty-four of the twenty-seven murders with which he stood accused.

Petiot was guillotined on 25 May, smiling as the blade fell.

Britain's Godfather
(Darby Sabini)

Edward T. Hart

Darby Sabini (1889–1950) has been called the most remarkable man in the annals of British organized crime. At the zenith of his awesome power Sabini had 300 armed men under his command. With judges, politicians and senior policemen in his pay he created the most lucrative criminal empire ever seen in Britain. The Anglo-Italian Sabini gang started as racetrack thugs who threatened bookmakers for protection and a cut of their profits. They often fought pitched battles with rival gangs for control of their pitches, while the police stood idly by. Big money was at stake. "When a gang went to a racecourse like Brighton," recalled East End gangster Arthur Harding, "they could clear £4,000 or £5,000. At Epsom, on Derby Day, it could be £15,000 or £20,000." Although known as razor gangs, the Sabinis employed other weapons, including guns, and eight people were killed during their reign of terror. Later Sabini moved into London's protection and gambling rackets before retiring to Brighton, where he kept a penthouse at the Grand Hotel. He was the model for the gangster Colleoni in Graham Greene's novel Brighton Rock. *During World War Two he and his brothers were interned as enemy aliens, and by the time they were released, rivals had carved up their West End empire. The Sabinis' ruthless exploits were chronicled by crime writer Edward T. Hart (1923–2002), a prolific contributor to British true crime magazines such as* True Detective *and* Master Detective.

"Who needs a bruised face on a Sunday morning?" – *Darby*
Sabini, attempting to reason with the Elephant gang enforcer
Monkey Benneyworth.

I t was raining in Little Italy. Pavements glittered wetly under
the lamplights, and derelicts huddled in every doorway, watching the night go by.

Darby Sabini, wrapped in some strange private world of his
own, walked in the open seemingly unaware of the wind and the
rain. The collar of his dark jacket was upturned. His check-cap
tilted over his right ear and a cigarette dangled from the corner of
his mouth. He was a powerful man with wide shoulders tapering
down to bullfighter hips. To the denizens of this square mile of
London, huddled on a hillside under the shadow of St Paul's, he
had always been something special. According to legend, he was a
direct descendant of the Sabines; and, in this band of exiles, that
gave him a kind of kingship.

The Italians, the most persecuted race in the city, looked upon
him as their protector, a saviour to lead them to better days. Mind
you, there was little about the man to suggest such a thing. He lived
in a hovel on Saffron Hill and wore the clothes of a peasant. Any
self-appointed shrink would have taken one look at Darby and
known instantly that he would never amount to much. He was too
indolent, too short of ambition, to ever be a hero.

The whalebone of pride which stiffens the back of a true man
appeared to be totally missing from this burly fellow. Admittedly
he had certain talents. As a professional fighter, he had strung up
a long unbeaten run. While still in his teens, he scored a first-
round knock-out of Fred Sutton, until then the rising star of the
middleweight division. There had even been talk of a bout for the
title. But champions are made by the sweat and the toil of
training, and this was never Darby's way. The rest of the city
would come alive with the dustcarts and the dawn. Darby would
slumber on long into the morning and then rise reluctantly at
noon.

Boxing promoter Dan Sullivan recognized this fatal flaw and
realized that Darby could never be a contender. So instead he
offered him the job of strong-arm man at the Hoxton Baths, then
the roughest and most riotous fight arena in London. It was said
that impromptu bouts between the paying customers were often

better value than those being waged between the ropes. Darby, aided by his brothers Joe and Fred, tamed that savage place within a month . . . and made the taming look easy.

But then, of course, this had been night work and Darby was one of those people who seemingly only come truly awake when the darkness wraps itself around the streets. And of all the nights of the week, Saturday night was his favourite. Now that the First World War was finally over, Little Italy had once again taken on the carnival air of its homeland.

On Saturday nights such as this, coloured lights shone out from the pubs and the clubs. Hurdy-gurdies played, and on the warm evenings there would be dancing in the streets. It was a good night on which to forget the cares of the week gone by.

As Darby reached the foot of Saffron Hill and turned left up the Clerkenwell Road, a group of Italian girls watched him go by. He barely gave them a glance. In the distance he could already see the lights of the Griffin, hear the music and the sounds spilling out. He quickened his step.

Monkey Benneyworth came into the Griffin and shook the rain from his hat. And as he did so the volume of sound around the bar ebbed for a brief second and then flowed back louder than before. He recognized the quiver for what it was. Fear! It was, after all, his stock-in-trade. Monkey Benneyworth was perhaps better known as "the Trimmer", a tag bestowed on those who "trimmed the sails" of other men, cutting them down to size. He was a huge man with huge hands, but it was the face of the Trimmer that told you most. There was violence, cruelty, brutality, written in every line. He was the strong-arm man for the Elephant Gang, based in the Elephant and Castle area of London south of the river. He was a man who enjoyed his work, and most of all he enjoyed his visits to Little Italy.

For hunters such as the Trimmer, this was the perfect hunting ground. In the line of business you could run the protection racket around the clubs, busting heads and breaking arms. You could beat up the men and rape the women in the certain knowledge that no one would ever complain to the police. The Italians were strangers in a strange land, preyed upon by every other race and creed. The police were their enemies too.

The Trimmer began to push his way across the crowded floor, knocking elbows, spilling drinks along the way. No one complained. The Trimmer's reputation ensured that. Upon reaching the bar, he ordered a pint of best bitter, ignoring the fact that there were others waiting too.

A barman came scurrying along, anxious to please. But at that moment the Trimmer spotted the latest addition to the Griffin, a young and nubile barmaid named Carmen Cardoza.

He surveyed the barman with scorn. He said, "I don't want you serving me, you little runt. I want her." And he threw a hand carelessly in the direction of the girl. Being new, she was probably the one person in the Griffin that night who didn't know the reputation of the Trimmer. Yet at twenty-one she was old enough to recognize the type, sense the menace of the man. And realizing all this she still said, "You wait your turn, Big Man, like everybody else." Something very close to joy came into the eyes of the Trimmer. In his sexual life, as in everything else, he was a plunderer with no great wish to take anything given freely. This was one of the reasons why the girls of Little Italy appealed to him so much. With their dark flashing eyes and proud ways, they represented a challenge. There was a spirit that needed to be broken. As befitting good Catholics, they were apt to cling to their virginity as though to a life raft.

He surveyed Carmen Cardoza with hooded, lecherous eyes. She was the type that seems to ripen in Mediterranean lands. In a few years, the hips would spread and she would become prematurely old like the matrons of her race. But for the time being she was in her prime, long-legged and with firm, full young breasts jigging delightfully beneath the red silk dress. She was voluptuous, essentially lush, very much the Trimmer's kind of woman. He promised himself that he would have her before the night was out. He knew that she wouldn't yield willingly. The thought gave him a certain pleasure.

The flickering lights of the Griffin came through the window of Silvio Massarda's flat, bathing the room in strange contrasting hues. The room was otherwise in darkness. Massarda lay upon the bed, still wearing his shirt and trousers. He was slowly undressing a blonde showgirl called Jeannie Harris.

He did so meticulously, placing each garment removed with care upon a nearby chair. It was a task which would normally have occupied his full attention. But tonight he felt oddly disenchanted with the whole affair.

He was one of those people who live their life upon a dream. In

his mind's eye, he would always travel first-class, surrounded by
fast exotic cars and fast exotic women. It was only occasionally on
nights such as this that reality washed away the dream. The room
had seen better days, and so too had Jeannie Harris. On the
shadowed stages of second-rate music halls she could still conjure
up a long-lost glamour. But the bright light of day betrayed her.
The face was a map of battles lost and faded hopes.

Massarda tried to make-believe that he was undressing Anne
Marlowe, the current star at the Lyceum, the focal point of his
wildest dreams. He had never actually met her and yet he was
convinced that one day they would share the good times. Mind
you, he had the style and the panache to make such things come
true. He had the looks of a matinee idol and flamboyant Italian
ways that did his cause no harm at all. He was tall, with good
shoulders and a deep chest. His dark hair was naturally waved and
the whiteness of his smile was apt to have the most devastating
effect upon women of all ages. The one feature that dented the
image was a Roman nose. Because of this he was known in Little
Italy as "Big Shonk". Few ever called him by any other name.

He slipped her panties down over rounded hips with practised
ease . . . noticing with a touch of surprise that she really was
blonde. He placed the panties upon a chair with the same care as
before and then he began to caress the plump thighs with a velvet
touch. Jeannie stretched out, arms and legs akimbo, like some well-
fed jungle cat, and the purr was feline too. Then the hands of
Massarda became still and he sighed. He had planned this as a love
feast; but in his present mood, he realized it was impossible. He
remembered that Darby would be in the pub across the road. He
wondered whether a touch of enchantment would return after a
few drinks with his friends. He slapped her carelessly along the
flank.

He said, "Come on, sweetie, get dressed. The night's too young
for this. Let's go out and howl. We can come back here later."

She sat up slowly as though scarcely believing what she'd heard.
Then she shrugged resignedly, one more battle lost.

Massarda picked up his coat and headed for the Griffin.

As Darby pushed his way through the swing doors of the pub, the
rain gusted in behind him. Immediately voices were raised in
welcome and he smiled back, gold teeth glinting in the bar lights.
Viewed thus he looked very Italian, dark eyes in a dark face.

The Trimmer watched him with open derision. He could never understand what these Raddies saw in this simple peasant. He thought it was maybe time he destroyed the last of their myths. He thought that maybe tonight could be the night.

Meanwhile Darby was running his eyes along the bar. He spotted the Trimmer and gave no sign that he had done so, then gave a brief nod as he sighted Georgie Sewell at the far end of the pub. Sewell nodded back without warmth and, not for the first time, Darby began to wonder about the man. Like Darby, he was a pro fighter who just might have been a champion if the desire had been a little greater. But there was a brand of violence in the soul of the man which could never be entirely slaked by gloved battles in the ring. Sewell was only a medium-sized fellow, a head shorter than the Trimmer and at least three stone lighter. Yet he could inspire more fear than anyone else Darby had ever met.

At the age of twenty-seven he was already a gangland legend and known as "the Cobblestone Fighter". In hand-to-hand fighting on the streets, he was considered almost unbeatable. He had made his mark as a bouncer in Soho. One night he had barred entry at a club to five members of the Rocca Family, an Italian band of enforcers based in Islington. They had told him precisely, and in graphic detail, what they intended to do to him. He had nodded matter-of-factly.

"There are five of you and so no doubt you'll carve me up," he'd said. "But take my advice. Kill me. Because if you don't, I'll hunt you down one by one if it takes me the rest of my life."

Half an hour later the police arrived to find Sewell unconscious upon the floor, his face gashed, his hands broken. Beside him lay two of his attackers equally unconscious, equally savaged. Two other members of the gang had left, supporting a battered comrade. True to his word, Sewell began hunting them down on the very next night with the stitches still holding his face together and his hands in plaster.

The trio fled the city. Their wives and families waited patiently for the return of their menfolk. When it became clear that nothing short of hell-fire would drive them back to London, the wives packed up their belongings and they too journeyed north beyond the reach of the hunter.

With such a reputation the Cobblestone Fighter would have been made welcome in any of the London gangs. He could have named his price, but that was never his way. He was a loner to be hired, but never bought. He was better at making enemies than friends. And yet in the cold heart of Georgie Sewell, there dwelt a certain morality. Only the villains were his natural prey. Honest men had nothing at all to fear from him.

The Trimmer was making his pitch for Carmen in forthright fashion. He simply positioned himself at the centre of the bar. Even on a crowded Saturday night the other drinkers preferred to stay clear of him and queue for the two barmen flanking the girl. So with little choice in the matter, she served him.

He said, "When this place closes, you're coming with me round the clubs. So don't go making no other plans."

The sheer effrontery of his approach amused her a little. She half-smiled and said tauntingly, "I'm careful of the company I keep. When I'm desperate enough to want to go out with the likes of you, I'll let you know. Until then I suggest you stop wasting your time, and mine."

The game had almost run its course as far as the Trimmer was concerned. The smile had gone. The eyes were moody and mean.

"You guinea tarts are all the same," he told her. "You behave as though the mere idea of a man touching you would make you sick to the stomach. Then once you're stripped down for action you become sheer animals, ready to eat a fellow alive. I'm an old soldier and I know, so don't think you fool me. And don't get any bright ideas about going anywhere tonight with one of these half-baked Raddies."

He swung round to survey the room, and the Italians to a man turned away.

"If any of them so much as gives you a look, I'll tear his arm off. Tonight you're gonna make it with a real man."

Massarda and several of the Italians were looking curiously at Darby, wondering whether he would intervene. He was known to be notoriously strait-laced in matters of sex. But he was staring down into his beer and it was as though he hadn't heard a single word. Seemingly the only Italian in the bar that night with any spirit was Carmen Cardoza.

She laughed into the face of the Trimmer. "No girl in her right mind would ever go out with you and I'll tell you why. You're too old (the Trimmer was, in fact, forty-two), too ugly and too dirty."

Before she could utter another word, the big hand of the Trimmer reached out, seized the top of her dress and with one savage tug ripped it all the way down to her waist. Her full breasts sprang out and she leapt back, covering them with her hands. Her face was a mixture of outrage, astonishment and fear, with fear the predominant emotion. For the Trimmer was moving towards the bar flap intent upon finishing what he had begun.

"Now we'll see the rest of you," he said. "Take some of that sass out of you."

He put out a hand to raise the bar flap and, as if by chance, found Darby barring the way.

"Look, you've had your fun," said Darby. "Now be a reasonable man, drink up and go."

His voice was an odd blend of Southern Italy and Bow Bells; his tone quiet, almost apologetic; his whole attitude that of a man who most definitely didn't want trouble.

The Trimmer paused as a new thought came to him. Why not ruin this peasant first in front of his admirers and then go after the girl?

He looked at Darby. "No one asked you to interfere, you Raddie bastard," he said, "but now you got a choice. You either step out of my way or get flattened. My guess is that you haven't enough craw to stay there."

Georgie Sewell was watching the scene closely, although nothing showed in those cold eyes of his. The Italians were watching Darby too and scarcely believing what they saw. For his head was down as though he was incapable of meeting the Trimmer's eyes.

Darby said, "Be sensible. I've nothing against you. We're just two fellows out for a Saturday night drink and a good time. We're men of the world. We don't want to fight over a girl. Who needs a bruised face on a Sunday morning?"

He looked up at last. "I'll tell you what. Drink up and I'll buy you another. What's it going to be?"

By now the Italians were staring at him with shame, wondering how they could have been so blind for so long. But there was no mercy coming from the Trimmer, and no escape for Darby.

"I'm not drinking with a gutless coward," said the Trimmer, his words carrying clearly across the silent room. And with that, he hit Darby back-handed across the face. It was little more than a slap, and yet there was enough force in the blow to spin Darby like a top and, in reaching out to prevent himself falling, he landed face down across the bar. The Trimmer lunged forward as though about to hurl himself upon the back of Darby. But the Italians formed a thin line in front of their fallen hero.

Only Carmen could see Darby's face and what she saw brought hope to her heart. For he was smiling, a smile so cold, so chilling that he looked like a different man entirely. Yet there was no hint of this as he slowly raised himself to once again face the Trimmer. Blood was dripping from the corner of his mouth and he wiped it away with the back of his hand, considering it gravely.

He said, "If you won't drink with me and you won't reason with me, you don't give me much choice."

His tone was still that of a peace-loving man. It was only the dark eyes that said otherwise. By way of reply, the Trimmer threw a big right-hand and Darby took it on the side of the face quite deliberately as though testing it for size.

That was the last punch the Trimmer would throw that night. Darby, moving fast, caught him with a left hook to the body that drove him back against the bar and followed this up with a combination of punches to the head that brought an animal-like scream from the lips of the big man. He pitched forward unconscious, and when they turned him over there was a gasp from the onlookers.

In the space of a few brief seconds, the Trimmer had been transformed into a pathetic wreck of a man. His jaw and cheekbone had been cracked, giving the face a grotesque alignment. Blood pumped steadily from the nose and a gash over the left eye. They carried him out of the Griffin on a door and up to the tram terminus at the junction of the Clerkenwell and Grey's Inn Roads, from whence he was rushed by ambulance to the Charing Cross Hospital.

Darby watched him go, shaking his head. "You just can't reason with a fellow like that," he said.

In the early hours of Sunday morning, the men of Little Italy wended their way up Saffron Hill to the door of Darby Sabini. They came to offer allegiance to their new leader. And Darby took each hand in turn, listening to the promises and nodding in reply. His was a most reluctant kingship. Yet he was realist enough to know that it was now an inevitable, even a necessary, one.

Down in the Griffin he had committed what was in gangland terms an act of war. Once the wounds had healed the Trimmer would return. Only this time he would come mob-handed with the Elephant Gang at his back.

If Little Italy wished to survive that raid, it would need to mobilize its forces. The prospect brought him no pleasure at all.

After the last caller had departed he put on his black pyjamas and, still wearing his check-cap, went to bed.

His world had been changed, and he sensed that for him life would never be quite the same again. He silently cursed the fate that had taken him to the Griffin and wondered whether he would pay for this night's work with his life. He was still wondering when he fell asleep.

The Death of the Don
(Tony Accardo)

Richard C. Lindberg

One of Capone's henchmen in the early 1930s was Antonino Leonardo (Tony) Accardo, alias Joe Batters, the son of a Sicilian shoemaker. He went on to carve himself a criminal career of unusual violence and cruelty. Accardo was just fifteen when he committed his first offence (a traffic violation), and eventually notched up a total of 27 arrests on charges including extortion, kidnapping and murder. He liked to boast that despite this roll of dishonour, the only penalty he ever paid was the occasional small fine. In 1929, Accardo was a member of Chicago's vicious Circus gang, based at the Circus Café, head-quarters of Claude Maddox, whose ties to Capone, the Purple Gang and Egan's Rats were well-known. According to Capone's biographer John Kobler, the police believed that Accardo was one of the planners of the notorious St Valentine's Day Mas-sacre of 1929. Soon after this, Accardo became a Capone bodyguard, and could sometimes be seen in the lobby of Capone's headquarters at the Hotel Lexington with a tommy gun across his knees. Accardo soon forged ahead as an important Mafioso, and by the mid-60s had replaced the expatriated Sam Giancana as the head of the Chicago syndicate. He was also a member of the Mafia's national council. Richard Lindberg (b. 1953), is a lifelong Chicago resident and the author of 11 volumes of Chicago history dealing with aspects of true crime, ethnicity, sports and politics. He is a past president of the Society of

*Midland Authors and the Illinois Academy of Criminology.
Here Lindberg, one of America's foremost historians of crime,
recalls Tony Accardo's charmed life and tough times.*

S umming up the late Tony Accardo's leadership abilities,
mobster Paul Ricca once confided to *Chicago American* columnist George Murray that "Accardo has more brains before
breakfast than Al Capone ever had all day." Possessing a nimble
mind and a canny instinct for self-preservation, Accardo boasted of
having never spent a night in jail, although he was picked up in
Miami Beach in 1929 on vagrancy charges while playing a round of
golf with Al Capone and Jack McGurn, architect of the St
Valentine's Day Massacre. Accardo's closest brush with the slam-
mer came on 24 February 1945, when he was forced to suffer the
indignity of appearing in a police line-up at the Chicago Detective
Bureau during a murder investigation. But that too, was only a
mere formality.

Even during his last years when he was consumed with cancer
and his body a thin and frail shell, this elder statesman of the
rackets was accorded a respect that was never shown other mob
figures of his generation who reaped a more bitter harvest. Nearly a
decade after his death, Tony Accardo still looms as the most
important Chicago mob figure of this era; the boss of bosses
who helped shape criminal policy making on a national level.

Anthony "Big Tuna" Accardo, a product of the Prohibition era,
ruled the rackets in Chicago for nearly fifty years before succumb-
ing to the ravages of old age and cancer on 17 May 1992. He was an
early product of the Circus Gang, a collection of Northwest Side
toughs who congregated at John "Screwy" Moore's (a.k.a. Claude
Maddox) Circus Café on North Avenue. Moore was nominally
connected to the Torrio-Capone outfit, and he willingly obliged
Scarface with a percentage of his gang's liquor revenue, and the
necessary armaments through their gun dealer Peter Von Frant-
zius.

The future gang boss, a strapping, five-nine, 200-pounder was
the son of Francesco Accardo, an immigrant shoemaker. Accardo
joined the Circus Gang while he was still in his teens. There, he
was introduced to the mob boys by "Tough" Tony Capezio, a
gambling boss and syndicate man, who plucked him off the streets
of West Town, the Grand and Milwaukee corridor, and gave him

something more "useful" to do than stealing tomatoes from pushcart vendors. By the end of the 1920s, Accardo was performing various tasks for the Capone mob while running with another gangster of future importance, his closest friend and confident, Felice De Lucia, better known as Paul "the Waiter" Ricca.

Mob media writers have always asserted that the youthful Accardo may have had something to do with Chicago's most sensational gangland killing, the 1929 St Valentine's' Day Massacre. Accardo was a very young man at the time, and may have acted as one of Capone's lookouts on Clark Street, but it is baseless speculation to place him inside the garage at the time of the actual shootings. It was after the massacre, however, when Accardo first began to make a name for himself as Al Capone's bodyguard and special enforcer. His fearsome reputation for violence and cunning was no doubt nurtured by his immediate superior and criminal mentor: "Machine Gun" Jack McGurn.

Accardo's stock and trade was vengeance and it was whispered from time to time that he was a good man with a baseball bat. In May 1929, Al Capone discovered that he was the target of a murder plot, hatched by Alberto Anselmi and John Scalise, a pair of imported Sicilian contract killers who had been on the big guy's permanent retainer for the previous five years. At a lavish dinner party given in their honor, someone – maybe it was Accardo, maybe it was Capone, no one knows for sure – swung a baseball bat to their traitorous heads, and afterward dumped the bodies in a ditch near Wolf Lake, outside Hammond, Indiana. Accardo's respectful mob associates would later pin a nickname on him that he would carry to the grave: "Joe Batters," or "Joe B."

The "Big Tuna" moniker was strictly a press invention. There are those who believe it was given to him in 1949 by the late Ray Brennan of the *Chicago Sun Times* who marvelled at the 400-pound tuna fish Accardo pulled out of the waters of Wedgeport, Nova Scotia one day. Others insist that Accardo actually landed the "big one" at Bimini during a deep-sea fishing expedition in 1955, and he continued to use the nickname as an alias while serving as a "phantom" salesman for Fox Head beer, distributed by the Premium Beer Sales Company between 1956–8.

Accardo pulled down a hefty salary of $179,000, even though he was rarely seen around the offices. When he would telephone company president Dominick Volpe, Accardo would identify himself as the Big Tuna placing a call to the "little Tuna". Volpe had accompanied Accardo on the Bimini trip, and the fish he landed was a small fry by comparison. Fish stories aside, Tony Accardo was easily pegged as one of Chicago's important gangland figures early on in his career.

In 1931, the Chicago Crime Commission was well aware of Accardo at a time when the power structure of the Chicago outfit was being revamped due to Al Capone's imprisonment for tax evasion in violation of the Federal income tax laws. Accardo expanded Capone's gambling operations across the city and suburbs, siphoning portions of this illegal revenue into various legitimate enterprises including trucking firms, lumber and coal companies, labour unions, and restaurants and hotels.

As the "old guard" slowly faded from view, Ricca and Accardo broadened their responsibilities. After Frank Nitti committed suicide in March 1943 rather than return to Federal prison, Accardo became part of a ruling triumvirate that would govern the Outfit for the next decade. He ran day-to-day operations with Paul Ricca and Jake "Greasy Thumb" Guzik, a holdover from the World War One era of crime.

Accardo functioned as Paul Ricca's second in command and always managed to defer final action to Ricca during the entire three-year period the "Waiter" spent in confinement at the Leavenworth Penitentiary. Upon his release, Accardo was handed a rich plum for his abiding loyalty: he was put in complete control of wire operations and betting parlors from northwest Indiana to the distant northern suburbs of Chicago.

Evidence of Accardo's propensity for violence, and willingness to employ whatever means necessary to effect an outcome was clearly demonstrated on 24 June 1946, when James M. Ragen was cut down in a fusillade of bullets as he drove south on State Street near Pershing Boulevard. Ragen controlled the Nationwide News Service (the name was later changed to Continental Press), a telephone wire that dispensed racetrack results to participating poolrooms across the US. The stormy history of this operation extends back to the horse and buggy era when gambling czar Mont Tennes seized control of the wire from John Payne. After Tennes was "squeezed by Capone in the 1920s, he sold his interests to publishing mogul Moses Annenberg, who launched his career in Chicago "slugging" rival news dealers on behalf of William Randolph's Hearst's newspaper, the *Chicago American*.

When Annenberg was forced to divest his gambling interests in

1939, because of tax troubles with the government, James Ragen, an aging South Side bookmaker with important ties to the Ed Kelly–Pat Nash–Jake Arvey political machine that ran Chicago, stepped in and took control. But Ragen proved intractable with the syndicate bosses, and refused to share his spoils with Accardo, who allegedly ordered his removal. When the volley of bullets failed to kill Ragen, a mob operative slipped into his hospital room in August to administer the *coup de grâce*. In the autopsy that followed, traces of mercury were found in Ragen's blood system.

A valiant Chicago police captain named William Drury doggedly tracked down every shred of evidence he could find and, when suspects were finally produced, Drury was stricken from the active duty roster on trumped-up charges by the shaken police brass who had their own separate agenda and special interests to serve. Drury, an unsung hero in the fight against organized crime in Chicago, was murdered in his garage on Addison Street in September 1950, on the eve of the Chicago phase of Senator Estes Kefauver's nationwide probe into organized crime and its control of the illegal gambling rackets.

Under Accardo's direction, Continental became the outfit's cash cow. Kefauver's Senate investigating committee called it "the life blood" of the outfit. That same year, 1950, Accardo, acting under Ricca's orders, shoved aside "Big" Jim Martin who controlled an enormous policy racket in the Twenty-Eighth ward. Political protection was provided by Alderman George Kells, and with so much revenue and "clout" at stake, Martin and his silent partner in City Hall were understandably perturbed at Ricca for demanding that they relinquish control. On November 15, Martin suffered serious gun shot wounds. The shooter missed the mark, but Accardo achieved his original purpose. Martin fled to Los Angeles, and Kells, fearful of syndicate retribution, drove to Florida never to return. The alderman told reporters at the time that he was doing it because his wife was in "poor health."

Accardo now personally controlled more than 10,000 gambling dens in Chicago, ranging from corner cigar stands right up to the lavish Loop pool rooms. He also played a role in establishing Havana, Cuba, as a new base of operations for organized crime figures following the repeal of Prohibition. The revenue from these operations netted the Outfit millions, but narcotics-trafficking was one area Accardo steadfastly refused to involve himself with. Only in recent decades has this edict been challenged by the

"Young Turk" faction, and usually with a corresponding loss of life within the ranks of the interlopers.

Accardo, like others before him, had a penchant for the good life. As his wealth, esteem, and political influence escalated in the early 1950s, he purchased a lavish mansion at 915 Franklin Street in River Forest for the sum of $150,000, this time ignoring the advice and counsel of Humphreys who told him that "the smart money don't go to the suburbs. You and your family will stick out like a sore thumb and the Feds will always know exactly where you are." Nevertheless, Accardo stocked his mansion with the most expensive furniture and tapestries. A black onyx bathtub served as his unofficial command post. Later, Accardo added a twenty-room mansion in Miami to his holdings.

Accardo's opulent lifestyle, and a celebrated European vacation he took with his devoted wife Clarice, and a well-known Chicago police lieutenant named DeGrazia in 1959, attracted national media attention compelling the government to sit up and take notice, though the Chicago Police Department didn't much care one way or the other that one of their own was acting as a personal escort and bodyguard to one of the most powerful crime bosses in the nation.

A year later he was indicted, convicted, and sentenced to six years on charges of income tax evasion. However, the US Circuit Court of Appeals later overturned by Assistant US Attorney Richard B. Ogilvie's successful prosecution of Accardo due to what they called "prejudicial newspaper coverage." In a second trial convened in 1962, the Chicago mob boss was acquitted.

Tony Accardo bragged that he never spent a night in jail, even though he was indicted no fewer than four times between 1948 and 1982. Each time the government failed in its mission to put him behind bars. In the celebrated 1982 labor-racketeering trial in Miami, Accardo and fourteen co-defendants were charged with conspiring to share in $2 million in kickbacks involving the placement of insurance business from the mob-controlled 550,000-member Laborer's International Union into the hands of a convicted swindler named Joseph Hauser of Beverly Hills, California. In stirring courtroom testimony, Hauser labeled Accardo as "the number one" power behind the union. He detailed the methods used by the Chicago mob leader to force the removal of secretary treasurer Terrance O'Sullivan in favor of his own man.

Accardo's two crack defense attorneys, Carl M. Walsh and

Eddie Kay, poked holes through Hauser's testimony and revealed that the government had paid him $105,000 as a protected witness. The Miami jury freed Accardo but sent six of his associates to jail including Al Pilotto, president of Local 5, and James Caporale, an official in the Chicago-based council. Working from behind the scenes Accardo quietly orchestrated the appointment of his son-in-law Ernest Kumerow as president of the County and Municipal Union Local 1001. Kumerow, a former star baseball player at the University of Illinois, took charge took of a Local that represented some 3,000 city street and sanitation workers. The old man's clout in organized labor was extensive and far-reaching.

The unfavorable publicity surrounding Accardo, coupled with his continuing IRS woes, compelled the nervous Ricca to make a change in the upper echelon of the outfit. In 1957 or so, Paul Ricca decided that Accardo should shun the limelight for a while, relax and take it easy in favor of Sam "Momo" Giancana, the *soto cappo* of the Outfit, and an ambitious, but maniacal killer whose modest brick bungalow in Oak Park was a far cry from the palatial estate the Big Tuna called home.

Giancana was at first considered to be a "low-profile" type, but nothing could have been further from the truth. Ricca had erred badly in this regard. Giancana took up with Phyllis McGuire of the singing McGuire Sisters act, and soon found himself more enchanted with the celebrity star-gazing than attending to his business in the manner Ricca would have preferred.

Paul Ricca succeeded in diverting the attention away from Accardo, but the publicity surrounding Giancana's own ostentatious life style forced another change in 1966, the year after "Momo" went into a self-imposed exile following a year-long stretch in prison after he refused to testify before a federal grand jury.

Accardo resumed control with Joey Aiuppa serving as his second in command. This time, Accardo seemed more than willing to avoid the mistakes of the past. He sold his home in River Forest in 1963, in favor of a more "modest" 18-room ranch house at 1407 North Ashland Avenue. It was there in January 1977 that a burglary crew operating outside of the Outfit foolishly broke into the Accardo home in search of cash and jewels. They were stalked, hounded, and ultimately tracked down by syndicate hit men who slashed the throats of the six burglars. One was castrated, and another disembowelled.

Bernard Ryan, the first of the burglary suspects was found shot to death on 20 January 1978 in Stone Park. Steven Garcia, 29, was pulled out of the trunk of a car parked in the garage at O'Hare Airport on 2 February. Vincent Moretti and Donald Swanson, two veteran second-story men, were stabbed to death on 4 February. They were found in an abandoned car in the parking lot of Esther's Place in south suburban Stickney Township. Moretti's face had been burned with an acetylene torch. John Mendell, who was considered somewhat of an electronics expert, suffered a similar fate. Police located his slashed remains in an auto trunk on the South Side on 20 February.

The sixth man suspected of complicity in the burglary, 43-year-old John McDonald, was shot to death in a North Side alley in April 1978. In the weeks that followed, a number of burglars and sneak thieves prudently decided to skip town though they were not involved in the River Forest heist. Noone was taking any chances with the old man on this one, especially after Accardo's 75-year-old houseman Michael Volpe disappeared just five days after testifying before a grand jury.

Accardo had sent an important message to all those who would question his ability to lead or willingness to mete out justice as he had done in years past. Since 1979 and up to the time of his death, Tony Accardo alternated his residence between his Indian Wells condominium located twenty miles outside of Palm Springs California, and his other home in Barrington Hills. From his location in the warm California desert, Accardo served as the outfit's "chairman emeritus" while younger men carried out his directives back in Chicago.

In the last years of his life, Accardo was beset with various legal and personal problems. In February 1983 his 40-year-old nephew John Simonelli was indicted by a DuPage County grand jury on auto theft charges.

A few months later, the Big Tuna was dragged before a Senate Subcommittee investigating labor racketeering within the Hotel Employees and Restaurant Employees International Union (HEREIU), led by Edward Hanley. Accardo was an uncooperative witness even though he was under an immunity grant from the government. His refusal to answer sensitive questions or provide clarification to the committee members resulted in a Contempt of Congress citation, handed down in February 1984.

Ill health prevented him from further testimony, as the committee concluded its hearings with this finding: "the committee finds that the mobster dominated locals of the Hotel & Restaurant Employees Union in the Chicago Area served only the purpose of giving a cloak of legitimacy to what was nothing more than a pure extortion racket." Accardo, as the press had come to expect, emerged from his Senate ordeal unscathed. Before another year had passed, Tony's niece Sheila Simonelli was busted for allegedly trying to sell $23.5 million in stolen securities. The woman's mother, Marie Simonelli, is Accardo's sister.

Then in August 1991, a federal appeals court in Chicago ruled that Accardo could not deduct $60,000 in back taxes and penalties stemming from his courtroom victory in Miami nine years earlier. While the sum of money was trifling compared to the vast fortune Accardo had amassed over the years, it was indicative of the heat the government had been putting on the ailing gang leader. Accardo's death in 1992 closed out a significant chapter in Chicago organized crime history. For all practical purposes he was the last link to Al Capone and the fabled Prohibition era that has faded into the abyss of history. Reserved and soft-spoken, Tony Accardo was without question the most powerful mob figure of his generation. Since his passing, Chicago mob watchers have failed to arrive at a working consensus as to who is really in charge of the Chicago "outfit" in the post-Accardo era.

The Great American Express Job
(Eddie Guerin)

Eddie Guerin

*Cannibalism, betrayal, revenge, attempted murder: a century
ago, the exploits of Eddie Guerin (1860–1933) set the Edwardian world agog. With the celebrated prostitute "Chicago May"
in tow, along with another crook called "Dutch Gus", Guerin
planned a spectacular heist, blowing open the safe at the Paris
office of American Express. But after the robbery Eddie was
caught on the boat train back to Calais; May pretended not to
know him, and went on to London with the money. She came
back, however, to stand by him through his trial in 1901, and
served four years' hard labour for her pains. Guerin, who had
previously served ten years' penal servitude in France, was sent
to a French convicts' settlement on Devil's Island to serve a life
sentence, and was one of the few men ever to escape it. He did so
by bribing his guards with money that May scraped together
after her release. Eddie Guerin's chance to escape came when
another lifer died and Guerin's name was substituted on the
crude wooden cross marking the grave. Officially dead, he and
two other convicts launched a makeshift canoe they'd built,
hoping to be picked up by a passing ship. Eventually they made
it home, Eddie Guerin having reputedly killed and eaten one of
his companions on the way in order to stay alive, a claim he
repudiates here. Back in London he took up with another
woman, but ran into May who tried to shoot him dead in a
jealous rage before betraying Guerin's whereabouts to the police.*

Guerin was arrested, but in the course of lengthy extradition proceedings brought by the French government, managed to prove that he was of Irish birth. Released, Guerin was cornered in Bloomsbury by a vengeful "Chicago May" and her new lover Charles Smith, both of them armed. Guerin was wounded by Smith's pistol, but his assailants were quickly arrested. At their trial, Smith was sentenced to penal servitude for life and May to fifteen years. This account of Eddie Guerin's eventful incarceration and escape appeared in 1928, in a book bearing his name as author, and purporting to be "The Autobiography of a Crook". But some years later, while being tried for cheque fraud, Guerin, now 71, disowned the book, claiming it was the work of an (unnamed) Australian journalist, and complaining of shameful persecution by the press.

What I am about to narrate now is nothing but the plain, unadulterated truth. The time has come when I can tell it, if only for the purpose of finally killing the preposterous stories that were put into circulation when I made my escape from the penal settlement in French Guiana. The wild lying that went on! It was alleged that three of us had got away from Devil's Island in a boat and that one of the party had been killed and eaten to keep the remaining two of us alive! I know I have been many things in my time, but I have not yet been reduced to the straits when I could be compelled to turn cannibal. Anyhow, with my active career in crime at an end I might just as well tell the true story of everything that happened, right from the very beginning up to the time in the Central Criminal Court in London, popularly known as the Old Bailey, when the gunman who had tried to "do" me was reviling, in the foulest language ever heard, the Judge who had sentenced him. Smith couldn't have possessed the slightest sense of the eternal fitness of things, otherwise he might have reserved his maledictions for the vindictive creature who had lured him to the length of murder.

For some time after my return to England in 1900 I succeeded in leading a fairly respectable life. I had relations in Liverpool with whom I stayed for a few months while I worked for an uncle who made a book on the racecourse. But I always found myself short of money. What I earned in the way of salary I lost backing horses, with the result that I set off to London with the feeling that I must do something to get some money.

London was much the same as I had left it. At the old Provence in Leicester Square, a famous place extensively patronized by the foreign *demi-mondaines* who were then so common in London, I found dozens of Americans I knew, kindred souls most of them, ready to take on anything. I made the acquaintance of the notorious Kid McManus, one of the best "boxmen" in America, who had crossed over to London to keep out of the way of the Pinkertons. He had heard of me and I knew all about him, with the result that we palled-up and for a time went about as two brothers.

I was in the company of Kid McManus when I first made the acquaintance of "Chicago May", the woman who subsequently played such a dramatic part in my life. Don't think I am going to paint any romantic pictures of this lady. As I am writing this story for the purpose of proving that you can't win at the crooked game, I am going to do nothing but keep to the truth. So I might just as well say straight out what "Chicago May" was.

She was already famous – or shall I say infamous? – in London. When Kid McManus first introduced me to her she would be about twenty-eight or thirty years of age, painted up to the eyes, with peroxided hair, pretty enough in a way, and no doubt quite fascinating in the manner she spoke to you. At any rate, I "fell" for her, so nothing more need be said about her charms. May's profession was the oldest one in the world, but the way in which she carried it on would have got her lynched in any decent society. She used to patrol Northumberland Avenue, a London street where there are several big hotels used by well-to-do provincial visitors. I saw her there myself many times, and I was informed, long before I knew her, that she worked in conjunction with Tim Oats, a "panel man", and his wife. So that the uninitiated may understand what a "panel man" is I will explain that he works with ladies of easy virtue who take men to their rooms with the intention of robbing them. There is a panel in the room which is slid to one side while the victim's clothes are stolen. Then the female blackmailers get to work and demand anything for the return of the clothes. Ninety-nine times out of a hundred they used to succeed, and "Chicago May" played this game for quite a long time without getting into the serious trouble she deserved.

Times without number had she been taken to the police station on the complaints of her clients, and on each occasion had she told a tale which resulted in her being discharged. As I have already said, May had a bit of a way with her. McManus introduced her to me at a flat in Tottenham Court Road.

"May," he said, "this is a doctor friend of mine from the States."

May took a good look at me. She was naturally a shrewd judge of a man and it didn't take her long to size me up.

"Doctor!" she laughed, "you're no doctor. I know who you are." And she did; she told me I was Eddie Guerin and, right from the jump, seemed to take quite a liking to me. The whisky bottle went round and round, with the result that May and I got very drunk. We decided to "get together".

Kid McManus took me on one side to warn me. "You leave that dame alone. She's dangerous. She'll rob you of everything you've got."

"Don't worry about me, Kid," I replied. "She can't get much because I've got nothing to lose" – which was the absolute truth. So, indifferent to the warning I had received, I took "Chicago May" under my wing and generally let it be known in the under-world of London that she and I were as one. I daresay it suited her book pretty well. She knew that I could get money, and if there was one thing in this world her soul craved for it was that. Money to her meant plenty of booze, as many dresses as she wanted, while it also freed her from the necessity of going out on the streets to rob men.

Originally, May had come from Chicago, like most of us. One way and another the old city turned out – and I mean in the most literal sense – some of the finest crooks in creation. If "Chicago May" wasn't exactly what I would call a good criminal she certainly knew how to batten on the blood of the men who got their living by various means outside the pale of the law. Her real name, I believe, was May Latimer, while she was also known as May Churchill – no relation of other and more distinguished families of that name. In her thirtieth year she was undoubtedly a smart piece of goods, calculated to attract the eye of any man. As she wasn't at all backward in pressing her claims upon you she did fairly well for herself while her looks lasted.

Kid McManus and I remained together in London for some two or three months waiting the opportunity for a big smash. I meant it to be something good because while you are about it you might just as well get a few years for a job that is worth while as be caught in a paltry little theft which brings you practically nothing more than the price of a meal. The Kid thoroughly agreed with me. Irish-American by birth, safe-breaker by trade and desperado by nature, there was nothing in the world he would not dare to do. He, also, had a lot of "time" behind him in America. We were what the poet calls "birds of a feather." With "Chicago May" as a consort I daresay we constituted a trio ripe for any mischief.

It must have been about January or February 1901, that there arrived in London from Paris a man whom I knew slightly, a highly educated German-American known as "Dutch Gus." His real name was Gustav Muller, but like most of the criminal fraternity he soon achieved the distinction of a nickname. Tall, fair, handsome, and the possessor of a refinement of manner which often made me wonder what had induced him to take to robbery, he was known to me by repute as one of the greatest "dan" men in the States. From being an engineer with a first-class job in Pittsburg he took to dynamiting safes all over the country. The thousands of little banks and post-offices that were scattered all over the States used to use safes that were easy to an expert like "Dutch Gus." However, the Pinkertons got him in time and Gus came over to Europe to make a fresh start. He had been temporarily engaged purloining diamond and pearl scarfpins, rings and any other small valuables he could pick up in a jeweller's shop. It is a trick called "penny-weighting"; you go in to buy something, get a few trayfuls of diamond pins and such-like in front of you, and palm one or two under the eyes of the jeweller. I will give Gus his due, whatever I have to say about him afterwards. He loathed such petty tricks. He, like the Kid and I, was on the look-out for something that would keep him in affluence for a year or two. In Paris he had found it; the offices of the American Express Company in the Rue Scribe contained a safe which might be blown open if the black caretaker could be put out of the way.

Gus, it appears, had been having letters addressed to him at the office, and from continually going into the place he had come to be very well known. He also made friends with the caretaker, and the next thing to be done was to find some one to work the job with him.

I did not hear of the matter until he had talked it over with Kid McManus, asking him if he knew of a third man who might be trusted.

"There's Eddie Guerin," said the Kid. "He's all right and he can speak French. You couldn't get a better man."

Gus gave me a very close scrutiny when the three of us met. He asked me a hundred questions, told me what it would mean if we were caught, and warned me at the peril of my life to keep my mouth shut. I told him I knew all about the danger and that as far as I was concerned he could count on me to the death. So then and there we settled the deal; the three of us should "do" the American Express Company and share and share alike.

Now, it just shows you how your good fairy may be lurking near at hand to save you from yourself. It was just about this time that I made the acquaintance of a wealthy Australian racing man who wanted to take me to the Antipodes to see a bit of the game "down under". I foolishly told him I had important work to do in Paris before I could go, but nevertheless I would run down to Naples and see him there before he left on the steamer. I kept my promise to him to the extent of travelling to Naples from Paris while we were waiting to pull off the American Express job, but circumstances made it impossible for me to board the Orient liner *Ortona* as my Australian friend wanted. Afterwards didn't I wish I had! It would have saved me a few years' suffering.

I realized, of course, the considerable risk I was running in returning to Paris. When you have served ten years' penal servitude in a country like France you would be well advised to give it the go-by for evermore. In my case I was not only well known to the Sûreté, and therefore liable to be arrested on sight, but also in danger because I had been deported and forbidden to return to France after serving my ten years in Rion. Still, I never let little things like that deter me. I decided to go and to take "Chicago May" with me. She would be what we call a good "square". If the police saw me in her company they would probably conclude I was perfectly harmless.

I told May nothing at all about the real object of the trip. Never having seen Paris, she was delighted with the idea of going, and never for one single moment suspected what I wanted her for. "Sufficient unto the day—" was always May's motto. "Dutch Gus" didn't mind her accompanying me; I fancy he was rather sweet on her himself and probably thought he might work me out. I wish he had.

All three of us got over to Paris, travelling separately, without arousing any suspicion, and we remained doggo in the city for three weeks before we attempted to make a move. I kept under cover more than the others because mine was the greater peril.

Once the police discovered I was back it would be all up as far as I was concerned. The three weeks that went by were mostly occupied in keeping observation on the American Express offices, taking turn and turn about and reporting the result of our vigil as we went back. All the time this was going on "Chicago May" blissfully enjoyed herself. Neither the Kid nor "Dutch Gus" was inclined to trust any woman with their life and liberty, any more than they believed in allowing a woman, whatever her character, to be mixed up in the dangerous job of dynamiting a safe. May and I were staying at an hotel near the Madeleine where they asked no questions. I took her around to all the stock sights of Paris, the Bois de Boulogne, the Louvre, even the Morgue. She never dreamed that I was just waiting.

Sentry duty continued. Night after night, with the glare of the street lamps still full upon us, we kept watch. We discovered that the black caretaker left the offices about seven o'clock at night and went off to the cafés drinking. He would get back about half-past nine or ten. In turns, "Dutch Gus," the Kid, and myself visited the offices almost every hour of the night, watching for anything that might undo us. We gave the place a look over at midnight, at two o'clock in the morning, at three o'clock and at six o'clock. Not a sign could we see of any watchman patrolling the premises. Evidently what happened was that the caretaker went in and straight away went to bed. It seemed that nothing could possibly happen.

The clever Gus had got hold of a duplicate key of the office. It wasn't a difficult matter to get the caretaker out drinking one night and obtain possession of his door key just long enough to make a wax impression. The key was slipped back with the caretaker none the wiser. It must have been half-way through our vigil that we were guilty of a most foolish lapse. More to while away the time than anything else, but also to provide an alibi that we were American tourists, the three of us frequently went to the offices of the American banking firm Drexel & Company in the Boulevard Haussmann. Gus had the idea in his head that he might also pick up a "mug" there, which only shows the stupidity of being too clever.

Our almost daily visits there, added to the fact that we never attempted to transact any business at the bank, aroused the suspicions of one of the attendants. He thought the matter so curious that on his own responsibility he telephoned to the Sûreté.

If I, for one, had known that my old friend Debischof, the self-same detective who had received me from the custody of Scotland Yard for the Crédit Lyonnais robbery, was following me about Paris at that time, I would have skinned off so quickly as to break all records in evacuating a battle-line. But Debischof did his work so cleverly and so quietly that none of us suspected anything wrong. The most extraordinary part of the affair was that neither he nor any of his men were ever successful in discovering the hotels where we were staying. The reason was that we always separated when we got out into the Boulevard Haussmann and, as it happened, did not go back to our hotels. The crowded Paris streets swallowed us up, with the result that Debischof had to keep continual observation at the banking office to pick us up again. Even then he did not suspect what we were in Paris for; he must have thought we were after some of the people who had business with Drexel & Company, not an unnatural assumption in view of our past records. As a matter of fact, Debischof would have done me a good turn had he pinched me then and there, but he was much too cunning for that. He knew there was something on the boards; what it was only time would reveal.

Everything had been planned out and to us there seemed no possibility of failure. We had even discussed how we should make the getaway. Kid McManus said: "I'm for Italy; it's a million to one on that we shan't be able to get back to England." "Dutch Gus" made up his mind to go to Marseilles and from there take a trip to Egypt.

"I'm with you," I said to the Kid. "We'll be nabbed in London for sure. Leach will soon know who's done this."

Unfortunately for me, I changed my mind – so did "Dutch Gus", with results that will be disclosed later. The Kid was the only one who made up his mind and kept to it.

The time came for the job to be done. Think of it, you people who lie in your bed of a night, and ask yourself whether you would like to go out at midnight for the purpose of dynamiting a safe, a job fraught with half a dozen disastrous possibilities, in my case magnified tenfold by the fact that I had already served a long term and that I would as sure as fate get at least another ten years if the police nabbed me. It is no use saying that crime doesn't require pluck and plenty of it. *I know it does*; the man doesn't breathe who can break into a place in the early hours of the morning without feeling the qualms of fear. He may be shot dead the moment he becomes a burglar. The alarm may be given while he is inside doing the job. A dog may bark, and of all the horrible sensations any housebreaker can experience let me recommend waiting inside a house, afraid to move one way or the other, with a dog incessantly barking. Then you know what it is to die a thousand deaths. If you are wise you will get out at once and chance what happens; it is nothing short of suicide to try and silence the brute.

There was nothing particularly elaborate about the scheme we had evolved. With the key in our possession there was little or no difficulty about getting into the building. Once inside we intended to gag and bind the caretaker, the Kid and I to keep guard over him and make him remain quiet while Gus blew the safe. The dynamiting was the great danger. Anything might happen. The windows might be blown out, the noise of the explosion might attract the attention of passers-by. Both Gus and the Kid were armed; if the worst came to the worst they would make a bid for life and liberty. I thought I might just as well follow suit. As time drew on it dawned upon me that we would have to be pretty lucky to get away clear.

We were certainly fortunate enough while the plans were going forward. The last time we visited the Drexel offices we were followed, entirely without our knowledge. The three of us made our way towards the Halles, McManus and I standing at the corner while "Dutch Gus" went into a chandler's shop to buy some rope which we intended to use in tying up the caretaker. The market square was crowded with people and after Gus had left the shop the detective rushed in, showed his police card to the proprietor, and asked him what the man had bought. Rope, the detective was told.

"What for?" he asked.

"How should I know?" replied the chandler, probably disliking the police as much as we did. "To tie up a trunk, I expect."

By the time the detective had finished his questioning the three of us had disappeared, so for the moment we were safe enough.

The great night arrived. Two of us stood outside the American Express office, carefully watched the caretaker go in and shut the door behind him, after which we went off, intending to return about half-past one, when the streets of Paris were quietening down. I took a trip back to my hotel to see what had happened to "Chicago May". That evening she was blind drunk – I had seen to that. I wanted her to be sound asleep all night long, so that if I were arrested she could truthfully declare that I had been with her at ten o'clock and had not left her all night. When I left her about a quarter to twelve she was speechless; I had no fear of her waking up for at least another eight hours.

I managed to slip out of the hotel without the concierge seeing me, and went round to the rendezvous where Gus and the Kid were waiting. There we stopped until it was close on the time.

Kid McManus, who had made the key, went along and opened the door. There were very few people about. Watching him from the shadows of the other side Gus and I saw him slip in unnoticed. At intervals of five minutes we followed suit, shut the door behind us, and then looked about. Everything seemed dead quiet. Except for the noise of passing cabs there was not a sound. The bank was as silent as the grave and but for the flickering lights of the arc lamps outside we might have been in a graveyard.

The black caretaker blissfully sleeping upstairs received the shock of his life when the Kid and I crept into his room and seized him. He thought at first it was some of the clerks of the office playing a joke on him! "Now then, boys," he cried, struggling to get free "stop your funny business. This ain't no time of the night to wake a man up."

"If you don't keep quiet," hissed the Kid, "I'll throttle the life out of you. This ain't no game, nigger. Shut your mouth and you'll be all right."

I have no doubt that the poor devil was petrified with fear.

"I'll keep quiet, boss, if you don't hurt me," he said, quivering with fright.

I gagged him with a handkerchief, while the Kid tied his hands and feet. The two of us were masked, even if the caretaker could see in the dark. He must have known, of course, that we were Americans, although he afterwards swore that he thought we were Germans, which only goes to show what fear will do for a man.

"Dutch Gus" had been waiting to see if we got the caretaker all right. Then he went downstairs to get his dynamite ready, leaving the Kid and me to look after the caretaker. It seemed ages before there came a tremendous explosion which rocked the whole building. I stopped upstairs, expecting any second to hear the police rushing in. Nothing at all happened. The Kid went downstairs and then called me to have a look. Gus had done his work so well that the safe door stood open, with only a twisted and distorted lock to tell what had occurred. Hovering over the place was the acrid, pungent smell of the dynamite. When I got down below Gus was busily shovelling out stack after stack of cheques and bank-notes.

Outside the day was beginning to break. We knew the staff did not get there before nine o'clock, leaving us plenty of time to divide the loot then and there. As near as we could estimate there was between £40,000 and £50,000 in the safe and about £4,000 in hard cash. Time was of no particular value. The explosion had gone by unheeded, the only danger for at least three hours was the poor caretaker upstairs. So then and there we shared out in three equal parts, stuffing the money into our pockets and congratulating ourselves on having pulled off the job so easily.

Another hour went by. Then we opened the front door and one by one sneaked out. There were but a few people passing by. We disappeared as we had entered – at intervals of a few minutes. Kid McManus, the last man out, coolly locked the door behind him without attracting the slightest attention and went off to his hotel, while I, creeping in once more unseen by the concierge, went into my bedroom to find the fair May still sound asleep.

Now for the *dénouement*!

I realized that the Paris papers would be screaming the news of the robbery before long. You can't dynamite a bank safe in the heart of a big city without the story leaking out. In the beginning, the French police concluded that a son of one of the officials must have had something to do with the affair. A short time previously this boy had broken into the office one night, prised open a couple of desks, and purloined a tidy little sum of money. When the actual culprit was discovered the matter was hushed up.

The police thought that our job had also been done by the same boy. However, they speedily discovered their mistake and, aided by the knowledge that "Dutch Gus", Kid McManus and myself had been acting suspiciously for some weeks past, went out hot on our trail.

When I got back to my hotel near the Madeleine in the early hours of the morning I had a fortune in my pockets. "Chicago May's" peroxided head peacefully reposed on the pillow. I was busy shaving myself when she woke up, blissfully ignorant of what had been happening.

That same morning I paid the bill and with May in my company moved over to the Hotel Regina in the Rue Rivoli. I carefully kept the newspapers out of May's way, and for a time at least she had no suspicion of anything wrong. She knew I had got some money from somewhere. In a foolish burst of generosity I told her to get some dresses for herself.

"What's the matter with you all of a sudden?" she demanded. "It isn't like you to be buying dresses."

"Go on," I replied, "I don't mind. What's the use of a woman coming to Paris if she doesn't get herself some clothes?"

Anyhow, a modiste came round and showed May a few dresses, but she fastidiously declined to have them and told me I had better wait until we got back to London.

My intention was to go to Italy. I had a pretty good idea in my head that the way to London might be dangerous. We stayed at the Regina for a couple of days and, of course, the papers were full of the robbery. But May never saw them; I carefully kept them out of her way, feeling it would be quite time enough to tell her the story when we reached another country. But one morning, when May and I had gone into a café in the Avenue de L'Opera to have *déjeuner*, who should come in but one of the cashiers from the American Express Offices. He knew me well enough by sight because I had repeatedly changed money in the bank.

"Morning," he said. "Heard what's happened?" I professed entire ignorance.

"Well, the bank has been robbed. There's nearly 250,000 dollars gone."

"Good heavens!" I exclaimed shocked. "As much as that?"

"We don't know for certain yet. We're just checking off the amounts, but it won't be far short of a quarter of a million."

"Dear me! How dreadful! Have the police caught anybody yet?"

"No," said the cashier, "but they think it is a gang of Russians. They'll have them soon."

He left me, went over to another table and ordered himself a drink. May shot a look at me.

"Oh," in a way that only a woman could say it, "so that's the reason why I haven't been able to see a paper for a couple of days!"

"Don't talk like a damned fool," I whispered to her, "and don't start shouting. I've had nothing to do with it."

I got her out of the place as soon as I could and took her for a walk into the Place de la Concorde, when I got another nasty surprise. Who should we see riding past in a *fiacre* but "Dutch Gus." He pulled up and made us go and have a drink with him.

Gus was in rather a vainglorious mood and anxious to show May what a hell of a fellow he was.

"Well, May," he began, "we'll be all right soon. Plenty of money for you to spend," giving her a dig in the ribs.

May, as fly as they make them, took it all in and said very little. But I could see her looking at me in a way that boded no good for me in the immediate future. However, she said nothing at the time and when we left Gus it was with the arrangement that we should meet in London a week later. The moment we got back to our hotel May let loose.

"Now, then, what's it all about? Where's the money? Either I get my share or else there'll be trouble."

When a man is between a she-devil and the deep blue sea it's no use hesitating. I produced what she wanted and her eyes glistened as only a woman's can when they see a big sum of money in front of them.

"Ah," she exclaimed, "so you thought you were going to do me, did you?" She picked up bundles of cheques and notes and began stowing them away in various parts of her clothing. Some went down her stockings – a favourite hiding-place with ladies of her profession – a lot more she secreted in her bodice. She kindly left me a bundle of French notes for my own use.

"The best thing we can do," said May, when she had secreted the money to her liking, "is to get out of here at once. We'll be nabbed for sure if we stop much longer. I'm going back to London."

I didn't care about the idea at all. Kid McManus had disappeared and I concluded he had gone to Italy, where I also meant to go. Where "Dutch Gus" intended to make for first of all I didn't know. I certainly hadn't the slightest notion that he would have tried to reach England via the Gare du Nord and Calais.

The papers were still full of the robbery when May and I took our departure from Paris – as we hoped for good. We arrived at the station at the very last minute and I don't mind confessing that I was in a devil of a funk. The first thing the police of any country do when a big *coup* has been pulled off is to watch the main exits from the city, and I had no illusions about the danger of trying to get away from Paris unrecognized.

But everything seemed to be all right. May and I sat down in the compartment anxiously watching for developments. I knew, of course, that I could be trapped in the train like a rabbit in a hole.

We sat talking for some time when suddenly I grew uneasy. Two or three people walking by the compartment looked to have police written all over them.

"Well," I thought, "it's no good stopping here if there's anything doing."

I lit a cigar and nonchalantly walked outside into the corridor. Two Frenchmen passed me and politely asked if there was a buffet at the end of the train. "I think so," I said. I walked on when suddenly they grabbed me by the neck and threw me into an empty compartment, slammed the door and forced me down on the seat.

"What's this b— game?" I panted.

"You will soon know," they replied.

They put a pair of handcuffs on me, drew the blinds of the compartment, and sat on either side of me until we reached Amiens. There they pulled me off the train and asked me, on reaching the police station, whether I would consent to being searched, if I was as innocent as I protested.

"No, you won't search me if I can help it," I replied. "You've taken me off the train, knocked me about, and treated me like a common crook. Now, tell me what it's all about?"

"You are wanted for a robbery in Paris," said one of the men. "Beyond that we can tell you nothing."

"You're making a big mistake," I exclaimed. "I'm a British citizen and you'll hear about this."

"Ah, that will be all right, Monsieur. We know who you are and we want you."

The only spark of comfort I had was that May held possession of the bulk of the money. She, wide as they make them, had heard the struggle on the train and had seen me hauled off to the police station. She didn't want me to tell her of the risk she ran.

Here was a pretty predicament! May gone with the money, "Dutch Gus" and Kid McManus out of sight. I resolved to keep a tight mouth; the bluff would begin as soon as I was taken back to Paris. The detectives in charge of me said very little, which made me realize that I was in grave danger. When the police ask you a lot of questions they know nothing; when they keep silent they know a lot.

I learnt a few things on the return journey to Paris. "Dutch Gus", like a damned fool, had gone down to the Gare du Nord to catch a train *en route* to England. Detectives watching the station recognized him as the man who had bought the rope from the chandler's shop. They at once grabbed him and took him off to the Sûreté where a little judicious questioning and the usual promise of getting him off if he would "snitch" induced him to tell the story from beginning to end.

Apparently Gus made no bones about giving the show away. He had told the police that Kid McManus and I had been in the job, how McManus lived in a flat near St Thomas's Hospital in London, and that in all probability they would find him there when he returned for his clothes. As a matter of fact, they never got the Kid. He cleared out of Europe altogether and never turned up again until some years later when he got a seven years' stretch in Canada for blowing a safe.

But they certainly had me tight enough. I spent the night in a cell with a man outside all the time. The following morning my old acquaintance Debischof came into the cell and told me I was to go before the *juge d'instruction* to be interrogated. He wanted to know whether I was going to confess.

"Confess!" I retorted. "What for? I don't know anything about it."

"Ah, ah, it is the same old Eddie," said Debischof. "What you call the American bluff, eh? We shall see."

The police court proceedings quickly demonstrated that things were pretty serious for me. The *juge d'instruction* somewhat unnecessarily informed me that I had been followed from the Drexel Bank in the Boulevard Haussmann, and that I had been in the company of "Dutch Gus" when he bought the rope. He also added that the chandler had identified the rope with which the caretaker of the American Express Company had been bound.

"What's all that to do with me?" I asked. "It doesn't prove I had anything to do with the robbery."

"Ah," the *juge* exclaimed shaking his head wisely. "We have got 'Dutch Gus'. He has confessed that you and he were confederates."

But I never believed in being bluffed myself. They might have got "Dutch Gus" in custody and again they might not. Anyhow, I wasn't owning up to anything.

"Take him away," ordered the *juge*, waving his hand, "and bring in the other man."

I was put into a cell below and while there "Dutch Gus," escorted by two gendarmes, passed by. I took the opportunity to call him a b— traitor, but he hung his head and wouldn't look at me.

Gus didn't remain long before the *juge d'instruction*. Only five minutes elapsed before a couple of men opened my cell door and took me upstairs again. I saw "Dutch Gus" in one part of the room, while I was stood on the other side in between two gendarmes. Once more the *juge* started.

"Well, Guerin, you say you know nothing about this?"

"And I do not."

"It's no use your denying it," said the *juge* angrily. "We know all about you, and this man," pointing to Gus, "has told us you were with him."

I gave a look at Gus but he would take no notice of me.

"He is a liar," I said. "He wants revenge because I took the woman he was after."

So it went on for another quarter of an hour, but I admitted nothing. Downstairs I went again and eventually was taken away to a depot prison where they tried to get my photograph. I don't think they succeeded very well. They searched me, found something like a thousand francs on me, and demanded to know what I had done with my share of the money.

"I don't know what you're talking about," was my reply. At which there was much shaking of heads and muttering of threats.

"You have given it to the woman," Debischof informed me. "Never mind, she shall be brought back here before long."

It is more than twenty-six years ago since the events I am narrating took place and I have forgotten the number of times I was brought up before the *juge d'instruction* to see if I would not confess. I had been arrested on 1 May 1901, but something like nine months elapsed before I was put on my trial. When the *juge d'instruction* finally came to the conclusion that he could get nothing out of me he ordered that I should not be allowed to have any more money. I was kept in solitary confinement in La Santé prison, idling away the time, grimly determined to confess nothing. There was always the chance of being acquitted. Some American friends of mine smuggled me in some money and with it I managed to buy odds and ends of food, cigars, and various other things to make the life bearable. The prison authorities winked at it, hoping I would let up and tell them what they wanted to know. But I didn't intend to do that.

I had been in custody for about five or six weeks when "Chicago May" did something incredibly foolish for a woman of her profession. She came over to Paris to see me and put her head right into the noose by calling at La Santé to ask whether she could see me! She could not have known, of course, that the police were looking for her, or if she suspected it she might have thought that she would take the risk and do what she could for me. Possibly she may have wanted to discover whether I had "snitched", and if so whether she would be safe in having anything more to do with the money. She certainly saw me, but that was about all. While she was at the prison the Sûreté was telephoned to and May was arrested the same night. From my point of view her action was absolutely suicidal; the only evidence against me up to then was that of "Dutch Gus". In all probability I would have been acquitted had May kept out of the way.

The French police found upon her evidence that the money had been put into a safe-deposit in Albany Street, London. Scotland Yard got the safe opened at once, but found nothing. The money had gone and only May could say where. Chief Inspector Froest, of Scotland Yard, had been following May about all over England without being able to discover the whereabouts of the missing money. When she had seen me taken off the train at Amiens she had gone on to London undetected and put up at a Bloomsbury hotel, and whilst staying there had rented a box at the safe-deposit. The watchman at the hotel said he had seen May put into her stocking a packet of cheques, but from that time, until Scotland Yard discovered that the cheques were being "put down" all over London, no trace of them could be found. Three or four men engaged in getting rid of them were arrested and held on suspicion.

I will give May the benefit of the doubt and say she was drunk most of the time, or she wouldn't have been so insane as to go over to Paris to see me. Her arrival in the Gay City coincided with a great drinking bout among the ex-jockeys and hangers-on who were to be found all round the cafés sponging on the people from the States. The fact that May had had a "touch" seemed to be no secret, and it was also generally known that the money she was throwing about came from the American Express Office. The crowd following May about were all under police surveillance, and when she took it upon herself to come and see me at La Santé the Sûreté then knew for certain where she had got her money.

Also, I believe, my old friend of years gone by, Sophie Lyons, had written to the French police telling them that "Chicago May" was in Paris and that it might be worth their while to follow her. The only wise thing May did was to keep her address a secret from

the loungers with whom she was mixing. It was only when in a
state of maudlin generosity she called at the prison that the Sûreté
were able to pick her up.

They had no direct evidence, unless she liked to give it, that she
had ever received any money from me. I continued to deny all
knowledge of the matter, May also taking the same attitude. One
day, I was sent for by the *juge d'instruction*.

"Now, then," he said to me sternly, waving a bundle of cheques
in front of my eyes, "here is the money you gave 'Chicago May'."

Everybody in the room was looking at me, no doubt hoping for
me to "blab". They couldn't catch an old bird like me.

"I never gave her any money," I replied.

"Four people have been arrested in London passing these
cheques," the *juge* informed me.

"Why don't you bring them over here? They are probably the
people who committed the burglary."

The months slipped by. May was shut up in the women's
prison at La Rocquelle, and I only saw her about three times in
nine months. I felt a bit afraid, not quite knowing what she
would do. "Dutch Gus" had already "snitched", but unless May
did the same I had a good fighting chance. To keep her "square"
I got a friend outside to engage a barrister for her, but nevertheless it was an anxious time looking forward to the day when
we would be brought up at the Seine Assizes. I had retained
Henri Robert, one of the greatest French barristers of his time,
and another lawyer who spoke English well. This man came to
me one day and said: "What is the use of going on with the case?
Why don't you plead guilty and throw yourself on the mercy of
the court?"

"I'm not going to plead guilty for what I haven't done," I
replied.

" 'Chicago May' wants to plead guilty."

"She can do what she likes. They've got nothing against me
except that I am supposed to have given 'Chicago May' the
money."

This was the occasion I discovered that Sophie Lyons, who was
in London when May returned from Paris, and naturally came to
hear that she had plenty of money, immediately informed the
French police. Scotland Yard could do nothing to her whilst she
was in England. I also found out that Sophie had written to the
Sûreté. The letter was produced at my trial; it was the same sort of

thing that she had done in 1888 when I was arrested for the robbery at Lyons.

And so the great day arrived. Kid McManus had got clear away. "Dutch Gus" and I were indicted for burglary with violence, May for receiving monies knowing them to be stolen. In the usual French fashion the police reconstructed the crime; they took a safe out on the ramparts and used dynamite upon it so that they could describe the operation in full. They might have invited me to take part in the scene, but they didn't even go to the length of asking me to participate. In fact, they never apologized for putting me on my trial. I wanted them to, but all I received was a contemptuous "Bah!"

It has been my doubtful fortune to take part in many criminal trials and this one at the Seine Assizes was certainly well done. In France, when you are charged with an offence, they get out your dossier, in which is written everything that is known about you. Your past is sifted out from childhood upwards. If your father or any of your relations were ever in trouble the facts are duly recorded against you. It is set out when, how, where and why you were born, what you have done for a living, and what your habits are. They call it the Code Napoléon, no doubt from the fact that Napoleon Bonaparte invented it as a means of keeping a check upon his enemies. My dossier certainly astonished me when it was handed to me to be read, so that I might have the opportunity of contradicting anything that was said about me.

I don't suppose there is any necessity for me to deal at length with the trial. Evidently there was considerable public interest in the case. A crowded court watched in breathless silence when "Dutch Gus", "Chicago May" and myself, were put into the dock. Gus and I had a couple of gendarmes between us, while May was on the other side of Gus. The thought flashed through my mind that she was going to give me away. The caretaker from the American Express Company contradicted the statements he had made when "Dutch Gus" and I were arrested. He had told the police in the beginning that he thought the robbers were Germans. When they showed him Gus he suddenly remembered him! When the caretaker saw me before the *juge d'instruction*, who asked him: "Is that Eddie Guerin?" he promptly replied that it was. As a matter of fact, I doubt whether he had ever seen me!

On the second day of the trial there came a dramatic interlude. "Dutch Gus" was evidently stricken with the pangs of remorse, because I received a note he had written telling me that he was sorry for what he had done and that he had only "snitched" hoping to get away with a lighter sentence. He was good enough to add that if there was anything he could do to save me from a severe sentence he would do it. One of the warders saw me in possession of the note. We had a fight for it, until I was overpowered. Eventually it got into the possession of the Commandant of the prison, but I succeeded in extracting from him a promise that it would be produced before it was too late.

The President of the court read the note and remarked that it was undoubtedly a message from one guilty man to another.

"Yes," I shouted back, "put a knife in his (Dutch Gus's) hand and he'll cut the throat of anyone in the court."

The only defence I could put forward was that of an alibi. I went into the witness-box and swore that I was at an hotel with "Chicago May" and had not left my room all night. I went to bed at ten o'clock and did not go out. I added that "Dutch Gus" had tried to implicate me in the crime owing to jealousy, and that if the court liked to have read his police record it would show that he was an old and experienced bank robber who had been guilty of many similar crimes in the past. "Chicago May" went into the box and told exactly the same story, saying I had been in her company at the time the robbery took place and furthermore that I had not given her the large sum of money I was alleged to have received.

The unfortunate part of the whole affair was that "Dutch Gus" broke down and told everything. The copy of the indictment I had been furnished with contained all sorts of statements about English and American crooks in Paris, how Kid McManus was the man who robbed the Wagon-Lit office and got away with several thousand pounds, how the Kid and three other men had committed another big robbery at the Gare du Nord offices, embellished by all the names of the men concerned in it. There were hisses in court while these statements were being read.

Henri Robert made a passionate speech to the jury on my behalf, dramatically pointing out how terrible it was that a man should be betrayed by another so that he could escape the full consequences of his misdeeds. "Chicago May's" lawyer pleaded want of guilty knowledge on her behalf. The President of the court summed up and the jury went out. We were being taken below when I made a jump at "Dutch Gus" and landed him a smash on the jaw which sent him staggering down the steps. Three or four gendarmes jumped on me to prevent further mischief, but at any rate I got the satisfaction of giving him something he would remember for a week or two.

Half an hour elapsed before we were brought back into court. I am no coward, but my heart was thumping ominously when the jury returned and delivered their verdict – all three of us guilty, with "extenuating circumstances" in the case of "Dutch Gus". One by one we came to the front of the dock to receive sentence – "Dutch Gus" and myself transportation for life, "Chicago May" penal servitude for five years. I more or less expected what I got, but I certainly did not think that "Dutch Gus" would get a "lifer". In the savage satisfaction of realizing that he was to suffer the same as myself I completely forgot what it would mean to spend the remainder of my existence in a convict settlement. It was not until I had been taken back to the depot prison that night that I got the opportunity of appreciating the terrible time before me. And in this instance I think I could truthfully say that I had made the worst blunder of my misspent life. The money from the American Express Office had not been in my possession for more than three or four days, and I had spent practically none of it. Yet here I was, doomed for evermore, for committing a barren crime. What I called myself in the seclusion of my solitary cell, as it finally dawned upon me what it all meant, I need not repeat. All night long the maddening refrain drummed itself into my head that I was to be a prisoner for the rest of my natural life.

Texas Rattlesnake
(Clyde Barrow)

Lew Louderback

Born to a dirt-poor family in Texas, Clyde Barrow (1909–34) was still a child when his cruel streak broke through. He enjoyed torturing pet animals, half-wringing the necks of chickens to prolong their agony. An anger dwelt within Clyde, wrote historian Joseph Geringer, having been born ragged and made more ragged by the Depression. As a young outlaw, he sometimes killed in cold blood, and always tried to justify the murders as if he had a right to pull the trigger, thus releasing somehow the seething that built up like a volcano deep inside him. Clyde was first arrested in late 1926, running from police who confronted him over a rental car he had failed to return on time. His second arrest, with brother Buck Barrow, came soon after, this time for possession of some stolen turkeys. Despite holding down regular jobs between 1927 and 1929, he also cracked safes, burgled stores, and stole cars. Known primarily for robbing banks, he preferred smaller jobs, robbing grocery stores and filling stations at a rate far outpacing the ten to fifteen bank robberies attributed to him and the Barrow gang. Clyde's first meeting with Bonnie Parker in January 1930 ended inauspiciously when he was arrested by police investigating a series of armed robberies in Waco. Clyde Barrow escaped from prison using a gun smuggled in by Bonnie, only to be recaptured a week later and sentenced to 14 years in the state penitentiary. Such was the brutality of the regime there that Barrow persuaded a fellow convict to chop off two toes from his foot with an axe, in the hope of a transfer; ironically, while recovering from his mutilation, Barrow learned he was to be paroled and released. But it was back in prison, in 1932, that Clyde Barrow first killed another man, a fellow prisoner named "Big Ed", alleged to have beaten and raped Clyde. A prisoner serving a life sentence took the blame willingly for this killing. A fellow inmate said that it was there that Clyde turned "from a schoolboy to a rattlesnake". Bonnie joined the Barrow gang, although there is no evidence that she ever shot or killed anyone. Clyde and many of his partners, however, would not hesitate to shoot their way out of trouble, and Clyde was the suspected gunman in some ten murders. As the fame of Bonnie and Clyde grew, they shot their way out of police loops, each time growing tighter and tighter, claiming that the "laws" they killed just happened to get in the way. Their luck ran out on 23 May 1934 when the couple were shot dead in a police ambush in Louisiana. This portrait of Clyde Barrow and his murderous gang is by the American writer Lew Louderback (b. 1930), who authored numerous true crime stories in the pulp era of the 1950s before turning to paperback novels. Now retired, he lives in New York.

"Machine Gun Kelly!" Clyde Barrow sneered the day he read of his capture in Memphis. "I've forgotten more about a Tommy gun than that phony creep ever knew."

It was probably true. The pint-sized Texan with the weak chin and the soft hazel eyes had no equal for sheer gunmanship. Guns were more than just the tools of his trade. They were objects of beauty to him, almost of veneration.

Ray Hamilton, who ran his mouth a lot after he was captured, told how Clyde was always fussing with his extensive collection of weapons, modifying them, oiling them, polishing them, holding them up to the light admiringly.

Clyde was the most heavily armed outlaw of the thirties. His arsenal included several submachine guns, a half dozen automatic rifles, and a bewildering variety of shotguns, automatics, and revolvers. When he ran low on ammunition or needed more guns, he backed his car up to a National Guard Armory and filled it – at gunpoint.

His aim was deadly. Target practice was a daily ritual with him.

Anybody who rode with him had to be good, too. He drilled them until they were. His diminutive blonde traveling companion, Bonnie Parker, was said to be able to shoot the pips out of a playing card at twenty paces. Clyde himself could slice the card sideways, shoot the head off a dove in flight.

The speed of his draw was equally phenomenal. He carried a sawed-off shotgun in a zippered compartment in his right trouser leg, and was proud of the fact that he could draw it almost as fast as he could his pistol. His gunfighting attitude was Billy the Kid's: "It's a game for two – and I get there first."

The Barrow gang robbed and killed in five states before the law finally caught up with them. They never made a big score, never, to anyone's knowledge, tried for one. Their favorite targets were gas stations, luncheonettes, variety stores, plus an occasional small-town bank. Their biggest haul was $1,500.

They moved across the countryside aimlessly, heading any-where – sometimes even in circles – to avoid their final destination. They had no political or legal connections, never had enough money to buy their way into established underworld retreats like Hot Springs and St Paul, and were unwanted in such places anyway.

They were outlaws even to the rest of the criminal world. Most big-time heist men would have turned them in on sight. To them Barrow and his crowd were "kill-crazy punks" who were ruining the business for everyone else.

Yet today Clyde and his sweetheart, Bonnie, have the bigtime reputations, while the big-leaguers of their day – the Harvey Baileys, the Eddie Bentzes and Frank Nashes – are largely for-gotten.

It's partly the work of the 1967 film: its appeal, particularly to the young, came from its portrayal of Clyde Barrow and his moll as a pair of displaced kids on the run, barreling along from crime to crime in a restless search for their place in the sun. As the screen Bonnie puts it: "When we started, I thought we were going somewhere, but we're just going."

Barrow and his girl are presented in the film as sad, murderous, dumb kids – confused neurotics rather than the old Hollywood "mad dog" stereotype. What they do is crazy and terrible, but it's never that far removed from the secret desires of a debilitated, apathetic population trapped in the economic decay of the Depres-sion.

The film's period flavour – the cheesebox sedans, the moneyless banks, the hopelessness on every face – underscores this message. So do scenes of the gang in repose – listening to Eddie Cantor on the radio, playing checkers, taking endless pictures of themselves with a Kodak. They're just folks and, like the rest of us, disorganized, confused, frustrated.

So far, so good. This is what the real Bonnie and Clyde were probably like. Even the neurotic sensualities that plagued the two star-crossed lovers are there. Granted, their sexual hang-ups have been changed a bit, but at least they're present. They would have been glossed over completely in a standard Hollywood "shoot-'em-up".

Biographically the film sticks close to the facts. The screenwriters have left out some things and have shifted others around to tighten the plot, but many of the scenes, particularly the action ones, re-create in faithful detail exactly what happened.

Where the film and reality go their separate ways, however, is in the suggestion that Bonnie and Clyde were Robin Hood figures to the poor people of the Southwest. That is simply not true. Other outlaws – Dillinger, Pretty Boy Floyd, even the Barkers – robbed the wealthy and left the poor alone. But not Bonnie and Clyde. They preyed on their fellow poor and they killed them when they got in their way. The Barrow gang was universally feared, and most of all by those likeliest to encounter them – the poverty-stricken farm folk of the Dust Bowl.

It's been argued that Bonnie and Clyde don't really deserve a place in American folklore because of this. Maybe they don't, but the argument is academic. The two of them are already there, enshrined beside Billy the Kid and Jesse James, and no amount of debunking is going to dislodge them now.

It isn't just the film's doing. It began in their own lifetime with the discovery of a handful of snapshots and one of Bonnie's poems, "The Story of Suicide Sal". The photos and the verses gave people an intimate, keyhole view of what it must have been like during those two years of driving, killing and hiding.

It struck a nerve. The poetry was bad, little more than doggerel, really. The emotions expressed were often trite and sentimental. But there was the thrill of its having been composed in the heat of action. And there was something else, too – a strangely detached, abstracted view that Bonnie had of Clyde and herself and of their crazy, pathetic ride to nowhere.

The real Clyde was born on a farm near Telice, Texas, on 24 March 1909. He was one of eight children. His father, Henry, was a tenant farmer. Clyde was farmed out to relatives when he was five, living first in Dallas, then in Corsicana and Houston. He was in trouble right from the start. At age nine he was committed to the Harris County School for Boys as an "incorrigible truant, thief, and runaway". He served three years. He was released to his parents after Henry Barrow finally gave up the land for good and moved to Dallas, finding work in a gas station.

Clyde's first serious brushes with the law involved cars. He loved them, tinkered with them, stripped them down, drove them fast. Speed intoxicated him. He never voluntarily stopped for anything, including red lights. The police started chasing him, but Clyde just drove faster. "It's easier to run than explain," he told his older brother, Ivan Marvin ("Buck") Barrow.

What he needed, he stole. Clyde had a feeling for music, so he swiped a saxophone. It went everywhere with him. Clyde had a date with a girl in San Antonio. His roadster burned out that same day. So he rented a car and kept it. He was arrested and charged with auto theft. His parents dug up the money, and he was released.

Buck, meanwhile, had been getting into trouble on his own. He had started out peddling hot turkeys, had graduated to stealing cars, and was now doing it professionally, turning the vehicles he clipped over to a hot car ring for a cut of the resale price. Clyde wanted to work with him, but Buck didn't want his kid brother in the racket. He advised him to go straight.

Clyde did – to Houston. His traveling companions were two West Dallas toughs, Frank Clause and Raymond Hamilton. Clause was a small-time sneak thief. Hamilton, the descendant of one of the Southwest's most noted outlaw families, had never seriously considered any life other than crime.

The three of them gravitated to Houston's Fifth Ward, a section so tough that oilman Glenn McCarthy would later recall that ". . . the cops were afraid of the people, and there was almost always a dead man somewhere in the street in the morning." There they enrolled in the Root Square Gang, a finishing school for burglars. Soon Clyde was hard at work with the others, learning how to break and enter, strip cars, and roll drunks.

Graduation day saw him holding up a Fort Bend gambling spa with a rusty "Saturday Night Special" that wouldn't even fire. It didn't matter, though. Before housemen could figure the odds, Clyde had lifted a couple of long-barreled .38s from two off-duty deputies. That gave him the winning hand – a pair of sixes.

The gang returned to Dallas, where an impressed brother Buck and a youth named "Dapper Dan" Black joined them. After pulling a string of robberies in the Dallas area, the group headed across the line into Oklahoma, where Hamilton had kinfolk.

They hit a whole flock of grocery stores and gas stations in the Choctaw country, high-tailing it from town to town along the back country roads. Clyde was the wheelman and a damned good one. He could maneuver their sedan along the rutted roads at eighty-five and better, bucking through the gulches between the clay cuts and the trees, sucking the dust out of the cornfields into their wake, boiling it up into a thick white cloud that choked the pursuing posses.

At Henreyetta, Oklahoma, the gang stole a new car and started back to Dallas, pulling holdups and burglaries along the way.

In Denton, Texas, they stuck up a gas station and when they couldn't open a small safe, they heaved it into the car. Outside of Lewisville a police car jumped them. Clyde was driving. He floorboarded her. The police started shooting. Bullets shattered the rear window, slammed into the metal door stanchions. Buck pitched forward. "I'm hit," he grunted as he clutched at his right shoulder.

Clyde had her up to ninety when he came to a right-angle turn with no road signs to warn him. He stood on the brakes, but it was too late. The car careened across a ditch and ploughed into the chaparral, both axles snapping. The men leaped out and started running. All except Buck escaped.

The next morning the police came for Clyde. Everybody in Dallas knew that the two brothers were working together. Clyde made a deal – the only one, it's said, of his career. He sold Clause and Black out on a burglary charge. Buck drew a five-year jolt at the Eastham prison farm. Clause and Black got suspended sentences.

Clyde went back to work with Ray Hamilton, pulling a series of jobs in the Waco area. He was arrested three more times for investigation of burglary and car theft. None of it stuck. He was only five feet, six and three-quarters inches tall and had the face of a choirboy. People simply couldn't believe that a boy like that would do anything bad.

Clyde met Bonnie Parker in January 1930. He was twenty-one, she was nineteen. They met through Ray Hamilton, who had been her husband's friend and was now hers. The husband, Roy Thornton, was chopping cotton at Eastham and would be at it for the next ninety-nine years. Bonnie had his name tattooed on her right thigh, along with two hearts, but that was the limit of her devotion. At the time she met Clyde, she was working as a waitress in Dallas and was juggling dates with several men on the side.

She was a tiny girl, less than five feet tall and weighing only ninety pounds. She had boyishly flat flanks, an angular body, and an almost pretty face that was spoiled by an overly hard mouth. She had come to Dallas from Cement City, one of those arid, innocent North Texas towns where nothing happens in even the best of times. Before that there had been another town, Rowena, where she had been born, the daughter of a bricklayer, and where nothing had happened, either.

Bonnie wanted desperately to make something happen that winter of 1930. She wasn't sure just what or how. All she knew was that she was "bored crapless" and had been most of her life. Then Clyde came along – an unimpressive little squirt who parted his hair in the middle, had long eyelashes, small delicate hands, and a slightly effeminate manner.

In the film version Clyde was pretty explicit as to what he was offering: excitement and fame. It's doubtful that the real Clyde offered Bonnie anything of the sort. Or that he even thought of himself in those terms.

Clyde Barrow, in 1930, was essentially a burglar and a car thief. He had yet to fire his gun in anger or desperation. All that would come later. After Eastham.

Bonnie saw some quality in him. What it was, we will never know. They started keeping company. They were together the night the law came for Clyde – "mooning on the sofa", according to one of the arresting officers.

It seemed that Clyde had forgotten to wear gloves on a couple of jobs in Waco. And if that didn't stick, Chief of Police Hollis Barron had him nailed on five car thefts, too.

Clyde pleaded guilty, and a McClellan County judge sentenced him to two years on each count. The court allowed the sentences to run concurrently, but that didn't cheer Clyde up any. He dreaded prison. He had a claustrophobic horror of locks and bars, a hangover from those early years he'd spent in the Harris County School.

Then, on 2 March 1930, his brother Buck came busting out of Eastham like a bull through a corral fence.

Inspired, Clyde began to make plans of his own. His cellmate in the Waco jail, William Turner, told him he had a gun hidden away in his house, a .38 Colt with a slim Bisley handle that would fit through the bars. Clyde sent Bonnie to get it. She came back with it taped to the inside of her thigh and managed to slip it to him without the guard noticing.

That night, when the jailer brought them their supper, Clyde pressed the barrel into his neck. "Open up," he said. "Fast."

Clyde and Turner went barreling out. Bonnie had a car hidden behind the K. C. dance hall. She wanted to go with them. Turner nixed the idea, and since the gun was his, the play was, too, and Clyde backed him on it.

The two of them raced to Abilene, then to Wichita Falls, where they switched to a stolen Graham coupe. It was a good car, with new tires, and they burned up the roads with it. When it ran out of gas, they abandoned it and hopped a freight. Railroad dicks grabbed them a few days later at Middleton, Ohio, and sent them back to Texas in handcuffs.

This time the law didn't kid around. Clyde was sent to replace his brother in the cotton fields at Eastham.

Back in the '30s Eastham was known among cons as the "Burnin' Hell" of the Texas prison system. Sadism was the order of the day there. Men were beaten by wardens, by trustees, by one another. In the fields whippings were regular and almost maniacally brutal. The men were underfed and dressed in tatters. They slept on bunks, jammed one against the other, in barracks that stank of excrement.

The slightest infraction of the rules meant a hitch in the "barrel cavalry". This was a roughhewn pickle barrel mounted on a sawhorse in the blazing sun. Prisoners were made to straddle the barrel for hours at a time. Even the strongest eventually collapsed. Some of the weaker ones died or "lost it" (went insane).

Clyde's sentence had been beefed up since his escape try. It no longer ran concurrently. He was in now for the full fourteen years.

In desperation he chopped two toes off his right foot with an ax. He hoped it would get him transferred to the "Walls" at Huntsville. It didn't. It didn't even get him out of the cotton fields. The guard captain reassigned him to a hoe squad as soon as his foot stopped bleeding.

At Eastham Clyde was involved in murder – his first. He and

some other cons had been sentenced to the "barrel cavalry" for gambling. They all knew who had fingered them – the barrack stoolie, Ed Crowder.

When the punishment period was over, they trapped Crowder in a secluded section of the prison yard. Clyde had a length of lead pipe. The others had homemade knives.

There were no repercussions. At Eastham one more death was hardly noticed.

Clyde had served twenty months of his sentence when Buck Barrow surrendered outside the walls at Huntsville. His mother, Mrs Cumie Barrow, had talked him into it. "I'll go back, do my time," he told her, "so long as it's not at Eastham."

Mrs Barrrow went to Austin now, where she managed to secure a personal meeting with Governor Ross Sterling. She made an impassioned plea for both her sons. The Governor promised to review their cases.

A month later Clyde was granted a parole.

It came too late, though. Eastham had done its work. He "hit the ground" on 2 February 1932, and he hit it running. It would take almost two hundred rounds of ammunition to finally stop him twenty-six months later.

Bonnie described the change in him in "The Story of Bonnie and Clyde":

> They class them as cold-blooded killers,
> They say they are heartless and mean,
> But I say this with pride,
> That I once knew Clyde
> When he was honest and upright and clean.

> But the law fooled around,
> Kept tracking him down,
> And locking him up in a cell,
> Till he said to me,
> "I will never be free,
> "So I will meet a few of them in hell."
> This road was so dimly lighted
> There were no highway signs to guide,
> But they made up their minds
> If the roads were all blind
> They wouldn't give up till they died . . .

Bonnie was exaggerating, of course. She had never known Clyde when he was "honest and upright and clean". No one had. But at the same time she was right. Clyde had gone into Eastham a burglar and a car thief who avoided gunplay. He came out the most dangerous Texan since Wes Hardin.

In March he and Bonnie went on the road together for the first time. It was a false start, though. The car was hot, and the law jumped them outside Mabank. There was a wild chase along US 175. Clyde skidded the car off the highway and onto a backcountry road, where it immediately got bogged down in mud. Clyde, Bonnie, and the kid who'd been riding with them took to the fields. Bonnie lost her shoes and was caught.

She sat for three months in the jail at Kaufman, Texas. The jailer's wife had advised her mother not to make bail. The theory was that a session in the pokey would cool Bonnie's ardor for Clyde.

To an extent it did. She was deeply hurt that he never tried to spring her. The experience probably contributed to her later poem, "The Story of Suicide Sal".

While Bonnie sat brooding, Clyde was busy robbing. He had teamed up with his old buddy, Ray Hamilton, once again. On 25 March the two of them hit the Sims Oil Company in Dallas and escaped with several hundred dollars.

Hamilton was a small, wiry youth, smaller even than Clyde. He walked with the swaying strut of a rooster about to crow. He was talkative, quick to anger, and as jumpy, a friend once said, "as a stud horse in a box stall". He had a cruel streak in him that verged at times on the sadistic. All in all, bad news, particularly for someone standing across a gun from him.

On the night of 30 April that was John N. Bucher, a 65-year-old jeweler and service station operator in Hillsboro, Texas. Bucher's wife had just opened the safe so that he could give Hamilton and his companion change of a ten. Both youths suddenly whipped out guns. "We'll take it all, old man," snapped Hamilton. Bucher's hand darted toward the drawer where he kept his gun. They blasted him. Then, after scooping just forty dollars out of the safe, they ran for the car. A third youth was waiting behind the wheel, the motor running.

Later Mrs Bucher identified her husband's killers from mug shots: Clyde Barrow and Ray Hamilton.

Clyde's relatives denied it. His mother claimed that Clyde had told her he was the wheelman on that job, that he'd been waiting out in the car when the shooting had taken place.

Maybe so. But it didn't matter now. The chase was on. Governor Sterling offered a $250 reward for Bucher's killers, a lot of money in the Depression. Dallas newspapers, meanwhile, went ahead and convicted Clyde. He was described as "the killer of John Bucher", even though he had only been charged with the crime.

The third member of the old "Root Square" trio now joined Hamilton and Barrow. Frank Clause had apparently forgiven Clyde for fingering him after the Denton job. The three of them hit several gas stations in the Lufkin area in early May, then sped back to Dallas to knock over a liquor store on May 12. The take: a spectacular $76.

In June the Kaufman Grand Jury met and no-billed Bonnie. She returned home and told her mother that she was finished with Clyde.

The gang was in Oklahoma now. Dallas had gotten too hot. They were staying with some of Hamilton's relatives near Tishomingo. Clause had been replaced by a local gunsel.

On the night of 5 August, as the three men were cruising through the Choctaw country around Atoka, they passed a barn dance. Hamilton, who was driving, sniffed the air. "Poontang," he said, grinning, and whipped the car into the parking area.

Clyde didn't want to stop. Neither did the other man. Hamilton ignored them. He was a billygoat who had to have his daily exercise. Clyde got into an argument with him. Their voices became loud.

Atoka sheriff, C. G. Maxwell, and his deputy, Eugene Moore, heard the commotion and approached. They thought the three of them were farm boys who had come out of the hills to attend the Stringtown dance. "What's going on here?" drawled Maxwell. "You boys been drinking?"

Clyde and Hamilton whirled, saw the stars on their shirtfronts and opened fire. They emptied their .45s, then reached into the car for replacement weapons.

Deputy Moore was killed instantly. The sheriff staggered back against a car, fumbling for his pistol, but he was dropped by a second barrage of bullets before he could reach it.

Several men came running out of the dance. They leaped for cover as Clyde leaned out the car window and swept the front of the building with a raking fire from a Browning automatic rifle.

Hamilton threw the car into reverse and floorboarded her. The machine hung there a second, wheels spinning in the gravel: then it shot out of the lot like a cork out of a bottle.

Hamilton spun the wheel hard left. With a clash of gears, the car roared off into the darkness.

The road was slick from a recent rain, though, and a few minutes later they went slithering off the shoulder into a ditch. Cursing, the three men climbed out and looked around. A farmhouse lay a hundred yards down the road. As they approached it Clyde spotted the silhouette of his favorite car, a Ford V-8, in the front yard. They knocked on the door and asked the farmer who answered if he would help get them out of the ditch.

The farmer nodded and climbed into his V-8. Clyde, Hamilton, and the third man piled into the seat behind him. "Never mind pulling us out," said Clyde, as he pressed the muzzle of the BAR into his neck. "Just start driving."

The farmer drove too hard. The engine soon began to sputter and clank. It had thrown a rod. Another car came along. Clyde flagged it down and asked the driver if he wanted to trade. He said he didn't. But he traded anyway and was glad to do so.

They drove the new car to Clayton, fifty miles east of Stringtown. There Clyde spotted a brand-new V-8 parked on a side street. He couldn't pass it up. He jumped the switch on it, and the gang piled in. With Clyde behind the wheel now, they roared out of town, heading through the Kiamichi mountains toward the Arkansas line.

Several days later Bonnie received a phone call. "Pack your clothes," said Clyde. "Then turn on the radio. When you hear the Neuhoff Company has been robbed, be ready to leave."

That same afternoon, 12 August, the bulletin came over the radio: two men identified as Clyde Barrow and Raymond Hamilton had just held up the Neuhoff Packing Company offices in downtown Dallas. The two, sought for the recent murder of an Atoka County sheriff and his deputy, were heavily armed. They had escaped with approximately $1,100 and at last report were driving west toward Fort Worth at high speed.

Bonnie got ready. The Parker home was on the Fort Worth Turnpike, not far from Arcadia Park. She kissed her mother goodbye and told her that she had a ride to Wichita Falls. A new cafe had just opened there, and she thought she might be able to find work.

A car honked, and Bonnie ran out to meet it. Mrs Emma Parker glanced out the window. The car was a dusty V-8 sedan with Oklahoma plates. As it pulled away Mrs Parker caught a glimpse of the two men sitting in the front seat with Bonnie. One of them looked an awful lot like Clyde Barrow.

In the car there was backslapping and laughter. It was a happy reunion. For all three of them. They decided to honeymoon in New Mexico, where Bonnie had an aunt. Clyde drove the whole distance with lead in his foot.

Bonnie's aunt gave them a big welcome when they pulled into Carlsbad the next morning. It was certainly nice of the two young men to have brought her niece all the way from Dallas for a visit. "Glad to be of service, ma'am," said Clyde, grinning. "I'll just get our things from the car."

He turned – and stopped short. A tall man wearing a gun belt was looking over their car. "Howdy," said the man. He came sauntering up the walk, and Clyde saw the silver star on his shirt-front.

Clyde and Hamilton had left their guns under the car seat. Because of that, Sheriff Joe Johns lived to tell the story to his grandchildren. "I was just passing" – the sheriff smiled amiably – "an' I saw the out-of-state plates an' wondered who was visitin' Missus –"

He felt a sudden pressure between his shoulder blades and turned. A tiny, freckle-faced blonde in a dark blue beret was holding a shotgun on him. "Don't move, damn you!" she snapped.

Clyde leaped forward, snatched the sheriff's pistol out of his holster, and prodded him in the belly with it. "Get in the car," he snarled.

The aunt stood watching from the porch, eyes wide with dis-belief. Bonnie had sighted the sheriff through the window, had raced to her uncle's room, grabbed his shotgun, and skinned out the back door to sneak up behind him – all in thirty seconds flat.

The four of them were in the car now. It roared away in a cloud of dust. The aunt went back into the house and had herself a good case of hysterics.

The trio drove the sheriff all the way to San Antonio. It was a nonstop trip with Clyde, as usual, keeping the needle hovering between ninety and a hundred.

Hamilton didn't want to release him. "We either got to kill him or keep him with us," he kept saying. But Clyde overruled him.

They couldn't take him with them, and as for killing – that was out. Clyde never killed a hostage. It was a quixotic quirk of his. He would kill in the heat of action and never think twice about it. But a hostage was different. A hostage presented no immediate threat, and Clyde, to his credit, killed only when threatened.

After dropping the sheriff off along the highway between Beckman and San Antonio, the gang drove east toward the Gulf.

In Victoria Clyde spotted a new V-8. Naturally he had to have it. He and Bonnie clouted it, and Hamilton followed them in the other car. The theft had been seen, though, and reported to the local sheriff. He got on the phone to Wharton, describing the two cars that were headed their way.

There was only one bridge across the Colorado River, a narrow trestle-like affair on US 59 just outside Wharton. A dozen armed officers hurriedly took up positions at either end of it.

The two cars came roaring along the highway. The Wharton sheriff tried to flag them down, then jumped for his life as Clyde opened up with a pistol, shooting around the edge of his windshield. The other officers returned the fire. A deadly fusillade tore into the two cars as they roared onto the bridge.

The men at the other end got ready, zeroing in on the first car. Suddenly Clyde spotted them. He threw the V-8 into second gear, cocked the wheel and hit the accelerator, bringing the rear end skidding around in a perfect 180-degree arc. It was the famous "bootlegger's turn", flawlessly executed.

He went roaring back across the bridge with a dozen pistols, rifles, and shotguns spitting hell at him. Bonnie stuck her twelve-gauge out the window and let the ambushers have it. Hamilton, still right behind them, was driving with one hand, shooting with the other.

It was Bonnie's first taste of combat, the first time she had heard the angry buzz of bullets around her head or felt the thud of buckshot ripping into glass and metal. It didn't bother her a bit. She handled herself with an easygoing skill that won the instant admiration of both men. "That Bonnie," Clyde said later, as they licked their wounds in an empty field near Yoakum, Texas, "she's sure full of piss and vinegar."

They hid out in an abandoned farmhouse at Grand Prairie for the next few weeks. From here Clyde and Hamilton raided the National Guard armory at Fort Worth, returning with boxes full of submachine guns, automatic rifles, shotguns, and extra ammunition. The Wharton ambush had taught them the importance of firepower.

From here, too, they pushed off against the Abilene State Bank on 8 October 1932. Bonnie was the wheelman on that job, Hamilton the center fielder. Clyde took the cages. It was their biggest haul so far – $1,400.

They headed north and east from Abilene, intending to swing up into the Choctaw country. At Sherman, in the Red River Valley, they stopped for food and supplies. Bonnie and Hamilton waited in the car while Clyde entered a small general store. Casually he looked around. He saw only two attendants working amid the jumble of dried sausages, meal, flour, and fly swatters – Homer Glaze, at the cash register, and Howard Hall, behind the meat counter.

After Clyde had ordered everything on his shopping list, he showed Glaze the .45 he was carrying. "Open the register," he said. Glaze's pupils shifted slightly. Clyde swung around just as the butcher leaped toward him, a meat cleaver in his hand. Three of the four shots he squeezed off found their mark. Clyde scooped $50 out of the till, grabbed his groceries, and ran. The butcher was dead on arrival at the Dennison Hospital.

The trio worked their way north, riding the back country roads by night, sleeping in the car or beside it. They lived on sandwiches and on coffee, which they brewed over an open fire. On the rare occasions when they slept in a bed, it was in remote tourist cabins or fishing resorts where there were no telephones, newspapers, or radios.

They were famous now. Newspapers in the Southwest called Clyde the "Texas Rattlesnake." Bonnie hadn't been identified by name as yet; she was simply his "quick-shooting woman accomplice." They had a good description of her, though, and they kept running it in the papers and on the radio.

So the gang stayed off the main roads as they moved north that fall, heading through the Ozarks to Illinois, and up through Indiana to the North Woods of Michigan. The car was the focal point of their lives. They relaxed only when they were in it or near it. The gas tank was kept full, the motor tuned to perfection. Their belongings were in the trunk, their arsenal on the back seat, together with a four-day supply of food, a first-aid kit, Clyde's saxophone, and a five-gallon jug of drinking water.

The outdoor life didn't appeal much to Ray Hamilton, though.

He began to get restless. Finally, in late October, he announced his decision: he was going to strike out on his own. "All right," said Clyde. "But you'll get caught, and I'll have to get you out. You ain't smart like I am."

Hamilton returned to Texas, where he recruited his former girl friend's brother, Gene O'Dare. The two of them hit the Carmine State Bank at LaGrange on 9 November, and then, with a gunsel named Les Stewart in center field, the Cedar Hill State Bank in Dallas on the 25th. The take from that job was $1,800, more than Hamilton had ever made with Bonnie and Clyde. Who was smart now?

Clyde pulled only one job during the same period – a minor one. With Bonnie behind the wheel, he took the Oronogo, Missouri, bank for a few hundred dollars on November 15. Then, because Bonnie was homesick, the two of them returned to Dallas and hid out with relatives.

While there, they shopped for Hamilton's replacement. They found him just down the street from Henry Barrow's filling station. He was a seventeen-year-old car thief named William Daniel Jones. Most people called him either "W. D." or "Deacon," a tribute to his guileless appearance.

In the film his name became "C. W. Moss," and he was supposedly picked for his mechanical skills. Actually, he didn't have any. Nor much criminal experience, either. But he had other attributes: vacant, blue-eyed good looks, an almost overbearing innocence.

"Want to take a ride with us?" Clyde was said to have asked him. "I'm Clyde Barrow and this is Bonnie Parker. We rob banks."

Awed beyond belief, the seventeen-year-old climbed into their V-8 and was swept off into thirteen months of "living hell", during which he was shot at, unnaturally assaulted by both of them, kept in chains, and forced, while fleeing from police, to fire a sub-machine gun.

That's W. D.'s story at any rate – the one he told police when he was finally picked up. His remarkable 28-page confession is a goldmine of information about Bonnie and Clyde and the way they lived while on the run. Most of it has an authentic ring to it, particularly the parts about their sex lives. W. D. was an innocent at heart, a Panhandle fundamentalist who believed that fleshly sins deserved fleshly punishment. His profound shock at some of the stuff that went on is apparent in every line of the confession.

The three of them left Dallas on December 22 and headed south.

Ray Hamilton was back in town – in police custody, just as Clyde had prophesied. Hamilton had gone tomcatting all over the country with the Cedar Hill loot and had naturally been collared. Now he was busy running his mouth for the benefit of police and press.

Clyde, Bonnie, and young Jones drifted quietly south. As they drove through Temple, Texas, on the afternoon of 23 December, Clyde spotted a new V-8 parked along a quiet, residential street. He turned to W. D. "Go get it, boy."

Jones trotted over to the Ford obediently, climbed in, and started fussing with the ignition wires. A minute passed. Two minutes. Nothing happened. Sighing, Clyde got out of the car and walked over. "Not that way," he said. "This way." But Jones was nervous now and lost the contact after the motor had turned over once with a loud growl.

That brought the Ford's owner, Doyle Johnson, charging out of his house. He'd been in the middle of dinner and was still wiping gravy off his chin. "Hey! That's my car!" he shouted. "What are you fellows doing?"

Clyde whirled, drew, and fired in one motion. Johnson dropped to his knees, a surprised look on his face. He clutched at his stomach and slowly toppled forward, dead.

Bonnie had the other car in motion, doors open. Clyde tumbled in, cursing, pushing W. D. ahead of him. Bonnie slammed the accelerator to the floor, and the car vanished around the corner, tires squealing like pigs being slaughtered.

In Dallas, meanwhile, a jury listened to the evidence against Ray Hamilton and decided that he needed to do some time in the cotton fields of Eastham. They thought two hundred and sixty-three years would be about right. Hamilton was returned to the Hill Country Jail to await transfer. While there, he hit the panic button.

Clyde had a pretty extensive communications network set up by now. He could be contacted, or make contacts, through strategically located "drops" in Texas, Oklahoma, and Louisiana.

Hamilton's message reached him in late December. It was short and to the point: "Get me out." Clyde decided that it might be a good idea. It would stop that nonstop mouth of his, at any rate. He made arrangements to visit Ray's sister in Dallas, Mrs Lillie McBride. She would be the go-between.

The McBride house was already under surveillance, though. Odell Chandless and Les Stewart had robbed the Grapevine Bank on 31 December. Texas Rangers had nabbed Stewart, and he'd told them that Chandless was supposed to visit Mrs McBride on the night of 6 January.

That was the night that Clyde decided to come calling.

The house was packed with Rangers and Tarrant County sheriffs and deputies, all heavily armed.

Clyde cruised past the darkened house twice. Instinct told him something was wrong. He had W. D. park directly in front. "Keep the motor running," he told him. He slipped a sawed-off twelve-gauge into the zippered compartment of his pants leg and told Bonnie to cover him. As he moved through the shadows and up onto the porch, Bonnie trained a .30–.30 Winchester on the front of the house.

Inside, Ranger J. F. Vannoy heard Clyde's footsteps. He tapped Ray Hamilton's 18-year-old sister on the shoulder and signaled her to go to the door and open it.

As she started forward Clyde suddenly cut loose. He hadn't heard anything, hadn't seen anyone. It was just a sudden "feeling" he had. His automatic shotgun blasted out a second-story window. Tarrant County Deputy F. T. Bradberry dropped to the floor, cut by flying glass.

Vannoy and his men opened up from inside now, firing blindly through doors and windows. As they did, Deputy Malcolm Davis raced around from the back of the house. He saw Clyde starting down the steps. He leaped onto the porch, gun in hand. "Hold on there!" he shouted. Clyde spun toward him. His twelve-gauge roared. The load of buckshot caught Davis in the chest, catapulting him backward to the ground, killing him instantly.

Bonnie opened up with the Winchester as Clyde ran for the car. The withering fire from her .30–.30 kept Vannoy and his men inside the house until the car was in motion. W. D. had them halfway down the block and pushing seventy by the time the first officers reached the street and opened fire.

Dallas County was immediately sealed off by roadblocks. Rangers and city police armed with riot guns began raiding every known gangster haunt. Clyde, Bonnie, and W. D. Jones were far away, though, roaring through the red clay cuts of Oklahoma.

Back in Texas things were looking up for Clyde's older brother, Buck. Mrs Miriam A. ("Ma") Ferguson had replaced Ross Sterling as governor in January. "Ma" was famous for granting pardons. She had issued more than two thousand of them during her first term in office back in the '20s.

Buck's wife, Blanche, mother of three children and about to give birth to a fourth, saw her chance. She hitchhiked to the state capital with the kids and made a tearful, in-person plea. "Ma" was so moved that she granted Buck Barrow a full pardon. He walked out of Huntsville on 20 March 1933 a free man.

He hung around Dallas until Blanche gave birth. Then both of them suddenly vanished, leaving all four kids behind. Mrs Cumie Barrow told police that Buck had gotten a letter from Clyde and was on his way to see him to try and talk him into going straight.

She must have got the message wrong, because Buck's next public appearance was in a jewelry store stickup in Neosho, Missouri. A few days later he and his brother popped up again, not to surrender, but to get themselves some new guns out of a federal armory in Springfield, Missouri. Three days after that they appeared once again, using their new arsenal to kick in a loan office in Kansas City.

Then they went to ground, renting a garage apartment in Freeman's Grove Addition, a suburb of Joplin, in early April.

Clyde didn't like the idea. He preferred to be in, or near, his car, with open country on all sides of him. But Blanche was still kind of "delicate". So he let himself be talked into it.

The five of them took life easy for a while, sleeping late, playing cards, admiring the Kodak snapshots they had taken of each other.

The Texas license plates were noticed, though, and a delivery boy got to wondering why the women never let him into the apartment with his packages. Both reports reached the ears of Sergeant G. B. Kahler of the Missouri Highway Patrol. He figured it for a bootleg liquor operation and decided to raid. He rounded up a highway patrolman, a Newton County constable, and two Joplin police detectives and, on the afternoon of 13 April, the five men drove out to Freeman's Grove Addition in a couple of unmarked cars.

It was around 4 p.m. Clyde and W. D. Jones were standing in the garage, checking over their Marmon sedan. Blanche was upstairs cooking. Buck was sitting in his undershirt reading a newspaper. Bonnie was hard at work on her first poem, "The Story of Suicide Sal".

Clyde spotted the two cars coming up Oak Ridge Drive and got one of his sudden "feelings". He leaped into the garage, pulled W. D. in behind him, and slammed the doors.

Sergeant Kahler brought his car to a stop a few yards beyond the driveway. The second vehicle swung in, blocking the gang's escape route. The garage doors opened a crack, and a blast from a shotgun sprayed the car with lead. Newton County Constable Wes Harryman leaped out with his pistol drawn. He managed to squeeze off one shot before his head was practically torn from his body by a second blast.

Detective Harry L. McGinnis sprinted forward, firing his pistol. Suddenly his right arm was ripped off at the elbow. Buckshot showered his face and head. He dropped to the pavement, dying.

Upstairs Buck had grabbed his submachine gun. Bonnie ran into the bedroom and snatched up two pistols. Blanche just stood there, hands over her ears, screaming. It was her first taste of combat.

Detective Thomas DeGraff had taken cover behind the car. He fired into the garage as Sergeant Kahler and Patrolman W. E. Grammer moved to the left, trying to outflank the gang.

Suddenly W. D. Jones came running out of the garage, spraying the car with fire from a Browning automatic rifle. DeGraff was forced to retreat around the east side of the building.

Jones leaped over the two bodies and struggled with the hand brake on the police car. Kahler fired at him. Jones clutched at his head and staggered back into the garage.

Buck Barrow came charging out next, spraying machine gun fire in all directions. He ran to the police car, released the brake, and gave it a push. The car coasted down the driveway, slowly gathering speed, then shot across the street, bounced over the curb, and smashed into a red oak tree.

Blanche, still screaming at the top of her lungs, burst out of the building and went racing down the driveway into the street. At that moment the garage doors suddenly swung open, and the Marmon sedan roared out, gears clashing. Kahler saw three men and a woman in it. As the lawmen peppered the car with bullets, it swung left, chasing Blanche. It slowed down as it reached her, and Kahler saw a man learn out and pull her inside. Then it roared off in a whirl of red dust.

Kahler sent Patrolman Grammer for help. An ambulance came. It was too late, though. Harryman and McGinnis were both dead. Reinforcements arrived shortly after that. Half of them were sent after the Marmon. The rest made their way cautiously into the upstairs apartment.

There they found an arsenal of rifles, machine guns, and BAR's. And snapshots. One of Bonnie holding a shotgun on Clyde. Another showing Bonnie with one foot up on a car bumper, puffing on a cigar. And on the dining room table they found Bonnie's unfinished poem:

THE STORY OF SUICIDE SAL
By "Bonnie" Parker

We, each of us, have a good alibi
    For being down here in the joint;
But few of them are really justified,
    If you get right down to the point.

You have heard of a woman's glory
    Being spent on a downright cur.
Still you can't always judge the story
    As true being told by her.

As long as I stayed on the island
    And heard confidence tales from the gals,
There was only one interesting and truthful,
    It was the story of Suicide Sal.

Now Sal was a girl of rare beauty,
    Tho' her features were somewhat tough,
She never once faltered from duty,
    To play on the up and up.

Sal told me this tale on the evening
    Before she was turned out free,
And I'll do my best to relate it,
    Just as she told it to me.

I was born on a ranch in Wyoming,
    Not treated like Helen of Troy,
Was taught that rods were rulers,
    And ranked with greasy cowboys . . .

The press went to work on the legend. The "Battle of Joplin" shared the front page with the Japanese siege of Peking. The snapshot of Bonnie with the cigar appeared alongside Amelia Earhart's photograph in one of the more prestigious newsweeklies. Excerpts from "Suicide Sal" ran in practically every paper in the country.

The gang didn't learn about their new fame immediately. They were holed up in the swamps of Lincoln Parish, Louisiana, too hot to even venture out for food, let alone a newspaper.

W. D.'s head wound was more painful than serious. They were able to treat it with their own first-aid supplies. In his confession Jones said that he ran away from the gang at this point, stole a car, and fled home to Dallas, but that Clyde and Bonnie followed him and forced him to return.

The Barrow gang struck next in Indiana. The Lucerne State Bank. A small take but plenty of fireworks: two women bystanders wounded by machine gun fire. Eight days later, on 16 May, they swooped into the First State Bank of Okabena, Minnesota. A redheaded woman stayed at the wheel of a dark green V-8 sedan. The townspeople opened fire from the sidewalks as the men came barreling out with their $1,500 take. Bullets thudded into the car as it pulled away. The gang shattered the car windows and fired back, with BAR's and shotguns. "The battle raged furiously," according to one account, "but it was impossible to face the outlaw barrage and live. Slowly the defenders fell back to the shelter of buildings, and the bandits escaped."

Bonnie was homesick. Clyde wanted to see his family, too. Buck said it was too risky. So he and Blanche were dropped off at a hideout in the Arkansas Ozarks, while Bonnie, Clyde, and W. D. ran the gauntlet into Dallas.

They met their families at an abandoned stone quarry off the Fort Worth Turnpike. There was time just for a few quick embraces, inquiries about each other's health, and a hurriedly gobbled picnic of cold chicken and homemade apple pie. Then the running started again.

Clyde raced north through the Texas Panhandle, the speedometer needle shivering, as usual, between 90 and 100 mph. They were to meet Buck outside Erick, Oklahoma, late that night.

Clyde didn't see that the bridge over the Salt Fork River north of Wellington was out. The car sailed off the edge, flipped over, and burst into flames on the dry river bed below. Bonnie was pinned beneath the wreckage. Clyde and W. D. were thrown clear.

Two farmers who had heard the crash came running. Bonnie was screaming, begging Clyde to shoot her so that she wouldn't burn to death. The farmers, Steve Pritchard and Lonzo Carter, helped Clyde and W. D. pull her free. She was badly burned. Her arms were seared to the shoulders. The lower part of her face was white with blisters. Her whole right leg was a mass of cooked flesh.

"This woman needs a doctor," said Pritchard.

"No doctor," said Clyde. "Where do you live?" Pritchard pointed, and Clyde said, "All right, carry her up there."

The two farmers looked at the automatic rifles the men were holding and did as they were told. At the farmhouse Mrs Pritchard made up a paste of baking soda and spread it on the burns. Bonnie was writhing and moaning, obviously in terrible pain.

"I'm going back for the rest of the guns," Clyde said abruptly. He turned to W. D. "Keep them covered."

W. D. had been unnerved by the whole business, though. He was careless, and Lonzo Carter got away. The farmer ran through the darkness to a neighboring house and telephoned Sheriff George Corry at Wellington. Corry picked up City Marshal Paul Hardy and the two of them sped toward the Pritchard farmhouse.

Clyde returned with the guns and W. D. told him that Carter had probably called the law. Moments later, there was a knock at the door. Clyde whirled, snatched up his shotgun and fired.

A woman screamed. He swung the door open. There stood Pritchard's daughter-in-law, her right hand shot off. Clyde herded her inside with the others. "Get down on the floor, all of you," he commanded tersely. "Don't let me hear a sound out of you." He and W. D. carried Bonnie out of the house and into the underbrush. They made her comfortable on a bed of leaves, then waited there beside her, guns ready.

Sheriff Corry's car pulled up a few minutes later. He and Marshal Hardy got out and cautiously approached the farmhouse with drawn weapons. Clyde and W. D. stepped out of the darkness, shotguns aimed at their heads. "Back into the car," ordered Clyde. He forced the two of them to hold Bonnie on their laps in the back seat while W. D. covered them from the front.

Clyde drove west to Pampa at high speed, then north toward Erick, relaxing only when he had crossed the state line. "You're in a fine pickle," he shouted over his shoulder at the two men. "I'm Clyde Barrow. Guess what that means for you?"

The officers swallowed heavily, but Clyde was just kidding

around. When they reached Buck Barrow's car and Buck asked if they were going to kill them, Clyde shook his head. "Naw," he chuckled, "I've had them with me so long I'm beginning to like them."

The officers were left bound to an oak tree with barbed wire. They managed to get loose a few hours later and limped into town to tell their story to a breathless world. "One thing's sure," said Sheriff Corry. "The woman's burned bad. She'll die if they don't get her to a doctor."

The gang knew that. They took Bonnie to an isolated tourist cabin near Fort Smith, Arkansas, and Clyde brought a doctor out to see her, explaining that his wife had been burned by an oil stove explosion at their campsite. The doctor treated her but said that she would either have to be taken to a hospital or have round-the-clock nursing. Clyde settled for the nursing. For a week he never left her bedside, day or night.

Bonnie kept begging for her mother in her delirium. So Clyde left Buck in charge and ran the gauntlet into Dallas once again. He refused to bring Mrs Parker back, though. She would be recognized by the police. He settled instead on Bonnie's younger sister, Billie Jean.

Meanwhile, the medical bills continued to pile up, eating into the gang's slim reserves. By mid-June they were broke. Leaving W. D. in charge of the three women, Clyde and Buck drove forth to scare up some cash.

They knocked over the Alma State Bank on 22 June, then raced north to hit a Piggly Wiggly store in Fayetteville. On their way back to Fort Smith on US 71 they had to pass through Alma once again. A description of their car had been phoned ahead to Alma's marshal, H. D. Humphrey. He realized that it was the same car that had been used in the bank job – a '33 Ford V-8 with Indiana plates.

He and his deputy, A. M. Salyars, jumped into their patrol car and headed north to intercept them. Two miles outside Alma they saw a car approaching. They slowed down. So did the other car. The driver waved. It was Webber Wilson, night manager of a nearby garage, on his way to work. Wilson stopped his car and leaned out the window, about to say something.

At that instant Humphrey saw the second car. It was approaching at better than 90 mph. "Better not stop," he shouted to Wilson. "That fellow will run you over." Humphrey started forward, saw that it was the V-8 they were looking for, and jammed on the brakes.

The second car went ploughing into Wilson's. Metal shrieked. Flames burst with a roar from both cars. Humphrey was sure that no one could have survived the wreck. But to his surprise he saw Wilson crawl free and the Barrow brothers, too. He and Salyars leaped out, guns drawn. "Get them up!" they shouted, racing toward the wreckage.

Buck and Clyde took shelter behind the open doors. There was a quick burst of shots as one of them opened up with a Browning. Humphrey and Salyars fired back. Then a shotgun roared, and the marshal seemed to trip over his own feet and go sprawling face down on the highway.

Salyars kept firing until he was out of ammunition. Then he ran behind the corner of a farmhouse and reloaded. Buck and Clyde came charging out. Clyde stopped and leaned over Humphrey as his brother ran toward the police car. "I ought to finish you right now," he snarled.

"Go ahead," the marshal groaned. "I think you've already finished me." (He had. Humphrey died of his wounds four days later.)

Clyde ran on, leaping into the police sedan. It roared off, passing the terrified occupants of cars in the opposite lane. Deputy Salyars peppered it with shots but to no avail. It quickly vanished into the darkness.

Buck and Clyde drove to Van Buren. There they forced a Fort Smith couple to surrender their car. Clyde took a wrong turn a few minutes later, though, and got on a dead end road that petered out at the top of Mount Vista. Quickly a half dozen posses closed in on them.

The Barrows took to the brush, making their way on foot to a cabin in the Ozarks just north of Winslow. Clyde kicked in the door and ordered Mrs John Rogers to hand over the keys to the ancient jalopy standing out in the yard. She refused. Clyde whipped out his shotgun. She still refused. The posses were so close now that the two men could actually hear them hallooing.

Buck picked up a trace chain and began to beat her with it. She still wouldn't give them the keys. Clyde tried to jump the switch meanwhile, but he wasn't familiar with a Pierce-Arrow's innards and had to give up. "Okay," he snarled, "we'll fix it so nobody can use it!" With Buck's help he gave the gave the car a shove toward a nearby cliff. The woman leaped to her feet and ran after it. Clyde leveled his shotgun at her. "Don't touch it!" he yelled.

Mrs Rogers ignored him. She leaped onto the running board and gave the steering wheel a twist that sent the car careening into a tree.

The Barrows had finally met their match: a hill woman who refused to be separated from her car.

Cussing wildly, the two of them fled into the woods in back of the cabin. Mrs Rogers heard a great trampling behind her. She swung around. Possemen came streaming out from among the trees at the far end of the clearing. "They went thataway!" she shouted. "They're only seconds ahead of you!"

They were sure they had them now. Extra men were poured into the area with instructions to shoot first, then ask. Scouts went ahead of the main body to guard against ambush. Everyone regarded a major battle as imminent. Sheriff A. H. Maxey of Crawford County rushed men up State 59 to get ahead of the outlaws and throw out a net. The Barrows slipped through like minnows through a whale net.

They made it back to the Fort Smith tourist cabin and pulled out that same night. Bonnie's sister, Billie Jean, was sent home to Dallas; the others headed across the line into Oklahoma.

When the doctor stopped by the next morning and found them gone, he got suspicious and called the police. There could be no doubt from his description – he had been treating Bonnie Parker. "They won't get far," he said. "She's an extremely sick woman. She shouldn't have been moved."

The gang surfaced next at Enid, Oklahoma, where they stole Dr Julian Fields' car in order to get his medicine kit. Within the hour they knocked over the National Guard Armory, too, escaping with fifty Army automatics and armloads of ammunition.

Fort Dodge, Iowa, was next. On 18 July three men and two women in a Ford sedan robbed three filling stations in quick succession. One of the women, a redhead, had bandages on her face and arms. It was obviously the Barrow gang.

At ten o'clock that same night the five of them pulled up in front of the Red Crown Cabin Camp at the junction of US 71 and State 59, six miles southeast of Platte City, Missouri. They rented a double brick cabin separated by two garages and paid the attendant, Delbert Crabtree, in small change. After backing the car into one of the garages and closing the doors, the group split up – three into the left-hand cabin, two into the right. A little later the bandaged redhead bought five sandwiches and five beers from Crabtree. Again she paid in small change. The next day the cabin rental was renewed, and the redhead bought five chicken dinners. The bill came to ten dollars and something. She paid it with nickels, dimes, and quarters.

Crabtree told his boss. His boss phoned the Missouri Highway Patrol. The lawmen listened to the description of the five, plus the fact that they paid for everything in silver, and realized that it was the group who had hit the Fort Dodge filling stations – and that spelled Barrows. They called Kansas City for reinforcements.

The extra men and equipment arrived shortly before midnight – sheriff's deputies, constables, and city police armed with shotguns, machine guns, automatic rifles, even an armored car mounted with searchlights. The small army moved quietly into position, confident that the gang was asleep.

Actually, every move they made was being watched.

W. D. Jones had gone into Platte City earlier that night to buy bandages and salve for Bonnie. While there, he had overhead a man in the drugstore mention "all the officers out at the highway junction".

Jones had alerted the gang, and they were now crouched in Buck's darkened cabin, watching as the armored car drove up and two helmeted figures set machine guns up behind steel shields. Suddenly the searchlights blazed on. There was a knock at the door. "Officers," a voice announced. "We want to talk to you."

"As soon as we get dressed," said Bonnie. Then, as W. D. slipped through the inside door connecting the cabin with the garage and got behind the wheel of the car, she added, "The men are on the other side."

"You had better come out," called the lawman.

The Barrow brothers were in position now: one at the window, one at the inside door. "Let the bastards have it!" yelled Clyde.

There was a sustained roar of gunfire. Bullets rattled off the steel shields as the machine gunners swung into action. Armor-piercing rounds sliced through the armored car as if it were paper. Deputy George Highfill crumpled, shot through both legs, but still shooting as he fell. Sheriff Holt Coffey went down, a bullet in his neck. His son, Clarence, pitched to the ground. Bullets had smashed his right arm, punctured his cheek.

A shotgun blast short-circuited the armored car's horn. It began a steady blast. The rest of the men thought it was a signal to charge and came rushing forward into the murderous cross fire.

A fragment of glass jammed the mechanism of one of the machine guns. "Let's get out of here," yelled Deputy James Thorpe, realizing that they were sitting ducks. He and Highfill managed to throw the armored car into reverse. They backed away from the garage doors as bullets continued to buzz around their heads like angry hornets.

Buck Barrow came charging out of the right-hand cabin now, a blazing automatic in each hand. Bonnie and Blanche were behind him, holding up mattresses as shields.

The posse directed its fire at the trio. As they did, a motor roared to life inside the garage. A man suddenly swung open the doors and hopped on the running board of the car that came shooting out. It was Clyde Barrow, hanging on with one hand and laying down a deadly barrage of sub-machine gun fire with the other. W. D. was behind the car's wheel, a cap pulled low over his face.

Bonnie and Blanche dropped their mattresses and began firing pistols as they ran toward the car. The officers returned their fire. Suddenly Buck staggered, shot through the temple. Blanche and Bonnie leaped to support him. They pulled him into the car. Blanche screaming that she'd been hit.

The car roared forward into a withering cross fire. Its windows dissoved into milky opalescence. The metal door frames seemed to actually shiver under the impact of dozens of rounds, a woman inside the car screamed in terrible, agonized pain. The vehicle swung onto the highway, careened wildly from side to side for a moment, then straightened out and disappeared in the direction of Platte City.

Though seriously wounded, Sheriff Coffey dragged himself to a telephone. Roadblocks were immediately set up on all major highways.

The gang had already swung east, though, and was traveling along backcountry roads. About halfway between Platte City and Hoover they stopped and took stock. Buck was in the most critical shape; a bullet had entered his right temple and had exited from his left. Clyde had a scalp wound. Bonnie had a bullet burn along the ribs. Blanche's eyes had been cut by bullet-showered glass; she could only see vague, shadowy shapes and was in terrible pain. W. D. alone had come through unscathed.

At this point any other gang would have retreated to a city where the fix was on. Crooked lawyers would have arranged hideouts; underworld surgeons would have treated their wounds. But the Barrows, with around $200 in nickels and dimes in their pockets, had only one alternative – keep running.

A vast manhunt was already in progress. The FBI, which had been keeping an eye on the gang since their raid on the Enid armory, sent agents to all hospitals in a five-state area, warning them to hold anyone with gunshot wounds. WDAF, the radio station of the *Kansas City Star*, broadcast detailed descriptions of the fugitives. A motorist near Mount Ayr, Iowa, just north of the Missouri line, heard one of these broadcasts. A few minutes later he spotted a car parked on a lonely side road. A man lay on the rear seat. Two men and two women were bent over a fire, burning bloody bandages. They leaped into the car and drove off the moment they saw him.

He reported what he had seen and the manhunt shifted to Iowa. Three days later a farmer came across a smoldering campfire and bloody bandages at a deserted amusement park halfway between the towns of Dexter and Redfield.

John Love, a member of the county vigilantes, hid in some nearby bushes and waited. He saw two cars drive up later that afternoon. Three men and two women got out. Love crept away and phoned Sheriff C. A. Knee of Adel. His description of the five matched the Barrows.

Knee called the sheriffs of surrounding counties and also the Iowa National Guard. By evening a good-sized army of officers had assembled at Dexter, its ranks swollen by dozens of local citizens armed with shotguns and squirrel rifles. With all possible escape roads sealed off, the posse moved in. They crept cautiously from tree to tree, slowly encircling the campsite. At dawn they began to tighten the noose.

Bonnie was brewing coffee over an open fire. Blanche was frying eggs. Clyde stood watching them, smoking a cigarette. W. D. Jones sat with Buck on the running board of one of the cars. Buck was clad only in a one-piece suit of underwear. Blanche, who wore riding breeches and boots, had a pair of dark goggles over her injured eyes.

Suddenly Clyde went diving towards his shotgun. He had caught a glimpse of movement in the tree. "The law's coming!" he shouted. The coffee spilled into the fire as the others snatched up weapons. It was too late, though. They were surrounded. A murderous fusillade was already pouring into them from all sides.

"Get the car started!" Clyde shouted, as he fired back, trying to cover the others. W. D. ran toward it but was hit by a load of buckshot and fell, momentarily stunned. Still firing, Clyde shoved him into the back seat while Bonnie ran around to the other side and climbed in.

Clyde slid behind the wheel, and the car started forward. A couple of dozen guns roared. The machine was riddled. Clyde lost control of it as a bullet ripped into his arm. The car went ploughing into a tree stump.

The three of them leaped out and ran through withering fire to the second car. As it started up, a thunderous volley smashed into it, dissolving the windows, ripping the tires to shreds. They scrambled out and plunged off into the woods on foot with half the posse on their heels while the other half stayed to shoot it out with Buck.

Buck and Blanche were trapped behind a tree stump. Both had automatics. The posse surrounded them, called on them to surrender. Buck's answer was a curse as he opened fire. Bullets laced into them from all sides. Buck was hit twice but kept firing. Blanche huddled closer to him, handing him clips of shells. He jammed them into the gun, emptied it, then loaded up again. He was hit four more times. Blanche began to scream hysterically. Buck's head slumped forward, but he managed somehow to keep firing. Finally Doctor H. W. Keller of Des Moines, a national guardsman, rushed forward and kicked the gun out of his hand.

Blanche struggled with the possemen who seized her, hitting out at them blindly with her fists, spitting and cursing as they tried to drag her away. "Don't die, Daddy," she screamed. "Don't die!"

But there wasn't much else Buck could do. Blood was pouring from his old head wound and also from six new ones – all critical. He was taken to the Kings Daughters Hospital at Perry, where he died five days later.

W. D. and Bonnie, meanwhile, were fighting their way through the woods toward a creek that skirted the north side of the park. Clyde was right behind them, laying down a covering fire. All three were wounded – Clyde in the arm, Bonnie in the fleshy part of the back, Jones with a shoulder full of buckshot.

Possemen seemed to be lurking behind every bush. No matter which direction the trio headed, they found themselves trapped.

"They fought desperately each step through the woods," an eye-witness report later stated, "darting from brush clump to brush clump. They made difficult targets and they were shooting with deadly accuracy."

They reached the stream and dived in, heading for the cornfield on the opposite side. The possemen halted at the edge of the clearing and took careful aim. Spouts of water rose around the fleeing outlaws. Bonnie screamed and sank out of sight. Clyde tugged at her but couldn't lift her because of his injured arm. W. D. gave him a push up the steep bank, then went back for Bonnie. The posse opened fire as he lifted her into his arms and carried her up the bank. W. D.'s head jerked to one side. The possemen cheered. They were sure they had gotten him. He didn't stop, though, and now the three of them were in the cornfield, and even the bravest members of the posse didn't want to go in after them.

A ring of men was thrown around the field, but it was too late. The three had already dashed out the other side, commandeered a farmer's Plymouth sedan, and fled north in it. An airplane was brought in to aid in the search. Two hundred possemen in cars followed it on the ground. Suddenly, near Guthrie Center, it dipped low, a signal that the outlaws had been sighted. An armored car was rushed to the head of the column to shield the possemen. This time they were sure they had them, but they didn't. The Plymouth ran the gamut of their fire and escaped.

They had Blanche, though. And after displaying her to the press, police tried to question her. She was incoherent. The months of running, the gun battles, her blindness, and now Buck's death had finally gotten to her. She subsequently served ten years in the Iowa State Prison for her part in the Dexter battle.

Clyde, Bonnie, and W. D. Jones stayed on the back roads that fall. They treated each other's wounds and lived on food that they stole from the fields.

The Fort Smith doctor had been right. Bonnie should never have been moved. Her burned leg had drawn up. She couldn't walk and was delirious much of the time. She had been a pretty twenty-year-old blonde only sixteen months earlier. Now, at twenty-two, she was scarred and crippled, and looked twice her age.

W. D. split with them some time in October. He made his way back to Texas and was arrested. He didn't seem unhappy about it. While awaiting trial, he dictated his twenty-eight-page confession, then pleaded for a life sentence. At least behind bars he would be safe from Bonnie and Clyde.

In early November the two of them dashed in to Dallas to see their parents. It was a foolhardy venture, but they brought it off, managing to spend almost an hour with them in a field near Grand Prairie. The parents noticed that they both seemed obsessed with thoughts of death. Bonnie even discussed funeral arrangements with her mother. When the two came home for another visit around Thanksgiving, those arrangements almost went into effect.

The Dallas County sheriff, Smoot Schmid, had heard about the last visit and had put tails on both families. When the two mothers drove to a lonely road off the Fort Worth Turnpike on the morning of 22 November, Schmid concealed a group of heavily armed deputies in the ditches and woods on each side of the car in which they were sitting.

When Bonnie and Clyde showed up, the deputies let them have it. They blasted with machine guns, rifles, shot-guns, and pistols. They put seventeen holes in their car altogether. Clyde and Bonnie were hit in the legs but managed to drive away.

Clyde was furious that his mother's life had been endangered. He sent a message to Sheriff Schmid through a Dallas newspaper, warning him that if a hair of his mother's head was ever harmed, he would personally kill him.

The audacity of the threat appealed to the underworld. News of it traveled via the grapevine to Eastham, where Ray Hamilton decided that Clyde might be in the mood to spring him. Hamilton had been boasting that he was going to be sprung ever since they had put him away back in October. On checking into Eastham, he had told Warden B. B. Monzingo: "I won't be here long. Clyde Barrow won't let me lie around no prison farm." He had said it so many times that even his fellow cons had stopped believing him.

But now Clyde received Hamilton's message and was receptive.

On the morning of 16 January 1934, a party of ninety-five convicts marched through dense fog to the brush-covered river bottom where they had been clearing land. Three mounted guards were in charge of the detail. As the cons got down to work, Ray Hamilton slipped away from his squad and joined Joe Palmer and Henry Methvin. The three edged their way over to a large pile of brush next to a drainage ditch. Quickly they reached in – and came up with the .45 automatics that Clyde had hidden there.

The three guns roared in unison. Major E. M. Crowson was hit in the stomach by a shot from Hamilton's gun and toppled out of his saddle. Joe Palmer hit Guard Olen Bozeman as B. B. Bullard, a new screw, managed to bring up his shotgun. Nine pellets of buckshot slammed into Joe Palmer but didn't stop him. He swung toward Bullard, whose horse was rearing, and fired. The shot went wild as Bullard leaped from his saddle and dived behind a stack of cordwood.

Bozeman's horse bolted, with the wounded guard still clinging to the saddle. An auto horn had begun to blare, meanwhile, somewhere beyond the fence. Hamilton, Methvin, and Palmer asked who wanted to go with them. Convicts Hilton Bybee and J. B. French stepped forward. "Let's go, then," shouted Hamilton. The five of them slipped through the drainage ditch and ran toward the road.

Clyde and Bonnie were waiting beside two cars. As the men burst through the trees, they opened up with a submachine gun and a BAR, laying down a heavy barrage of covering fire. But no guards were following them. It had gone even smoother than expected.

Convict J. B. French split a few miles away from Eastham. He wanted to be on his own. He was recaptured the next day. Hilton Bybee was let out in Amarillo. He lasted a week.

The others hit a bank at Lancaster, Texas, then raced north to Oklahoma. It was like the old days, with Clyde, Bonnie, and Hamilton riding together once again. But with a difference. Now there was no refuge anywhere. They were too hot even for Hamilton's relatives. "Keep going," they were told. And so they drove north, out of Choctaw country, heading toward the Cookson Hills.

The heavily timbered hills had been a sanctuary for bad-men since the days of Jesse James and Belle Starr. The topography favored fugitives. It was wild, inaccessible, sinister country, honey-combed with caves and crisscrossed by chasms and gorges – 2,400 square miles of roadless wilderness covered over with scrub oak and blackjack. A fugitive could step twenty feet off the main road – gravel-topped State 82 – and be in Tibet, as far as anyone could tell.

Lawmen didn't enter the hills. It was a waste of time. Not only did the topography favor the outlaws, but so did the hill dwellers. They fed and sheltered fugitives, and even refused to take money from those they liked. But they wouldn't lift a hand to help the

Barrow gang. Word had come down from the "Boss of the Hills",
Pretty Boy Floyd: shun them, starve them out, if necessary lead the
law to them. They were too hot for the Cookson Hills; they would
ruin it for the other outlaws holed up there.

The Barrows got the message. They packed up. But it was
already too late. Their two cars, as hot as their occupants, had been
sighted turning off into the hills at Muskogee. It had been the final
straw for the already hard-pressed Oklahoma authorities.

On the night of 17 February 1934, 1,000 lawmen, including four
companies of Oklahoma National Guardsmen, began surrounding
the Cookson country in drizzling rain. For the first time in history
a large body of troops would be sent sweeping through the hills in
search of outlaws. Their orders: shoot to kill.

At dawn they pushed off. Guardsmen set up Army machine
guns at all crossroads. Their instructions were to stop and search
every car moving. If they refused to stop, shoot.

It was the biggest manhunt the press had ever had a whack at.
Every newspaper in the Southwest sent reporters. Hubert Dail, of
True Detective Magazine, was lucky enough to hitch a ride with an
advance group. "Every officer was heavily armed," he reported.
"Each police car carried bright red lights and signs reading: 'Stop!
Sheriff!!' It was a weird scene, the darting cars with their red lights
and the big shadowy trucks loaded with guardsmen lumbering
along more slowly. A thin snow lay over the Hills and the dirt roads
were deep in mud. Even the chill air seemed hostile. . . . The
officers soon left all trails behind and trudged across the open
country. Occasionally the rat-a-tat-tat of machine gun fire reached
their ears. It meant that someone out along the road had refused to
stop for questioning."

But all the rat-a-tat-tatting came to naught. Only nineteen
people were caught in the dragnet, all of them small-fry. Pretty
Boy Floyd got away. The Ford Bradshaw gang escaped. And so did
the Barrow outfit.

They headed north once again, hitting banks in Michigan, Iowa,
and Indiana before Joe Palmer, who had stomach trouble, left the
gang. At Terre Haute, Clyde and Hamilton got into a squabble
over Bonnie's share of the loot, and Hamilton bowed out, too.

That left Bonnie and Clyde alone with Henry Methvin, a shy
Louisiana farm boy with blond hair and blue eyes. He was W. D.
all over again.

Keeping Methvin with them was a mistake. But Bonnie and

Clyde would never have time to regret it. They would discover their error and die in the same instant.

Death was all they could think about these days; and the news from home only confirmed the manner in which it would finally come to them.

The Texas Legislature was up in arms. Major E. M. Crowson had died of his wounds following the Eastham Prison Farm delivery, and lawmakers were talking about a "Wanted Dead" reward for Bonnie and Clyde.

T. H. McGregor, the representative from Austin, pleaded against the measure. "You are about to do in cold blood a thing which a mob does in the heat of passion," he cried.

That brought Congressman George Winningham to his feet. "I place Barrow and his gang beyond the category of human beings," he shouted angrily. "You are talking about according a trial to a beast. I say give him the same chance he gave those he murdered. Shoot him down like the mad dog he is."

A $2,500 reward was finally settled on, and the words "or alive" were added to the "Wanted Dead" posters that would be distributed. It was a victory for the moderates.

Lee Simmons, the general manager of the Texas prison system, didn't think that proclamations or rewards were going to do any good. He had his own ideas on how to get Bonnie and Clyde. He sent for Frank Hamer, a former captain of the Texas Rangers. The fifty-year-old Hamer was an almost legendary figure in Texas. An old-style lawman who always dressed in somber black, he was reputed to be the fastest draw south of the Red River. The sixty-five desperadoes he had killed in face-to-face encounters made Clyde's fatality list look pretty feeble.

Simmons gave Hamer a free hand, unlimited authority. "I don't care how long it takes," he told him. "I'll back you to the limit." And then he added, "I'd be foolish to tell you how to do your job, but the way I look at it, the best thing to do is put them on the spot, know you are right, and shoot everybody in sight."

On 10 February Hamer set out on his grim assignment. Like Clyde Barrow, he used a Ford V-8 and, like Clyde, he lived in it for days at a time. As he traveled through the Southwest Hamer stopped and interviewed anyone who had ever known Bonnie and Clyde. Slowly a picture of his quarry emerged – right down to the cigarettes they smoked, the food they ate, the kind of clothes they wore. A pattern of movement began to emerge, too. The fugitives traveled along a rough circle from Dallas to Joplin, Missouri, then over to Louisiana and back to Dallas.

In late February Hamer missed them by minutes at Texarkana. He was close again at Shreveport, then at a campsite outside Wichita Falls. Then suddenly the trail grew cold.

They had come to rest at the Methvin farm in Bienville Parish, Louisiana.

Bonnie had become obsessed with the idea of writing one last poem that would explain everything. She would send it to a newspaper and then the world would finally understand that they weren't as bad as they were painted. She sweated for some hours over the opening stanzas:

> You have read the story of Jesse James,
> Of how he lived and died.
> If you still are in need of something to read,
> Here is the story of Bonnie and Clyde.
>
> Now Bonnie and Clyde are the Barrow gang.
> I'm sure you all have read
> How they rob and steal,
> And how those who squeal,
> Are usually found dying or dead.
>
> There are lots of untruths to their write-ups,
> They are not so merciless as that;
> They hate all the laws,
> The stool-pigeons, spotters and rats.

After explaining how Clyde had been "honest and upright and clean" until the law had started hounding him, she elaborated on how every crime of the period was being attributed to them:

> If a policeman is killed in Dallas
> And they have no clues to guide –
> If they can't find a fiend,
> They just wipe the slate clean,
> And hang it on Bonnie and Clyde.

She also recorded her version of the battles of Joplin and Platte City, concluding:

> If they try to act like citizens,
> And rent them a nice little flat,
> About the third night they are invited to fight.
> By a submachine-gun rat-tat-tat.

There was also a rather shrewd comment on their fame, and what it meant to some people during the Depression:

> A newsboy once said to his buddy:
> "I wish old Clyde would get jumped;
> "In these awful hard times,
> "We'd make a few dimes
> "If five or six cops would get bumped."

Before she could finish the poem, the running began once again. State and Federal officers made a vice raid on nearby Ruston in mid-March, heating up all of Bienville and Lincoln Parishes.

Clyde, Bonnie, and young Henry Methvin drove west, crossing the Sabine River at Joaquin, Texas. They hid out in the "big piney" country for the next few weeks, then made a dash into Dallas on 1 April.

It was Easter Sunday. Bonnie had bought a baby rabbit for her sister. At around 2 p.m. they arrived at the rendezvous point, a lonely country lane a hundred yards off the Preston Road near Grapevine, Texas. They tied a ribbon around the rabbit's neck and let it out to play in the grass.

As they stood watching it two motorcycle cops roared past on State 114. The cops glanced at the trio, then swung around and came back. It's thought that the two, State Highway Patrolmen E. B. Wheeler and H. D. Murphy, were just going to ask them to move on.

Clyde watched them rack their cycles at the edge of the dirt lane and start toward them. Casually he reached inside the car for his shotgun . . .

A lot of newsboys made a lot of extra dimes that night.

The reaction to the double killing was intense. Both officers had been young – in their early twenties. Neither had had a chance to unholster his gun. Clyde was made Texas' Public Enemy Number One.

Captain Hamer wasn't far behind as the trio sped north from Grapevine along backcountry roads. At Tioga he found a campsite.

He knew it was theirs from the marks left by rabbit's teeth in some lettuce leaves. There were also stubs of Bonnie's Camels, one of them still warm. Hamer raced on.

The V-8 was found abandoned outside Cannon, Texas. There were no recent auto theft reports in the area, though, so gradually the trail began to cool.

Clyde, Bonnie, and Methvin surfaced five days later outside Commerce, Oklahoma. They were driving a new Plymouth now. As they jounced along a rutted dirt road known locally as The Lost Trail they got mired in the mud. Clyde tried to flag down a farmer, but the man caught a glimpse of the rifles stacked inside their car and sped away. He drove straight in to Commerce and told Police Chief Percy Boyd what he had seen.

Boyd picked up Constable Cal Campbell, and the two men drove out along the road until they spotted the Plymouth. They stopped and got out of their car. As they approached on foot, Clyde Barrow suddenly stepped out from behind the Plymouth. He had a Browning automatic rifle in his hands.

Campbell, a large man with a western-style mustache, was proud of his fast draw. He had his pistol out and was firing it before Clyde could get off a shot. His aim was wild, though. Clyde's wasn't. Campbell dropped, mortally wounded. Chief Boyd had also drawn and fired. He was sent spinning into the mud by a second blast from the BAR.

Barrow ran down the road while Methvin covered the two men. Clyde got a farmer in a truck to pull the Plymouth out of the ditch. Then the chief, who wasn't seriously wounded, was loaded into the back seat, and the four of them drove off.

That night they stopped at Fort Scott, Kansas, and Bonnie bought a newspaper and food, which they ate in the woods. They learned from the paper that Constable Campbell had died. "I'm sorry I killed the old man," Clyde told Boyd. "But I had to. He shouldn't have shot at me."

They released the police chief near Prescott, Kansas, an hour later. Bonnie's last words to him were that the much-publicized snapshot of her had been a joke. "Tell the public I don't smoke cigars," she called out as the car drove away. "It's the bunk."

Captain Hamer, as usual, was only a half hour behind them. He had been on their trail forty-five days now. It was a record. "Clyde Barrow," he would later tell newsmen, "was the smartest of them all. He was the most elusive and shrewdest man I ever tracked."

The FBI was too busy with the Dillinger case to waste much time on the Barrows, but one Special Agent, L. A. Kindell, had been acting as a liason between local police agencies and the Bureau.

In early April, Kindell discovered the identity of the third gang member, Henry Methvin. He took a trip to Louisiana and turned up another interesting fact – Clyde and Bonnie often visited Methvin's father, Ivan.

While poking around the Arcadia area, some eighty miles east of the Texas–Louisiana border, Kindell met Frank Hamer, who had also been drawn there by the Methvin angle. The two men went to see the Arcadia sheriff, Henderson Jordan.

He reported that Ivan Methvin had moved recently. At their request, Jordan tracked him down. Methvin was living on a rented farm about halfway between Arcadia and Gibsland. The three men went to see him. Methvin admitted that his son was involved with Bonnie and Clyde. But he refused to help them. "I've got my boy to think about," he said.

A few weeks passed, while the lawmen tried to figure out their next move. Then suddenly Ivan Methvin came to see them. Clyde and Bonnie had returned and had forced him to move once again. The four of them were holed up in an abandoned farmhouse deep in the woods. Methvin was now willing to cooperate with the law – for a price.

Hamer contacted Prison Manager Simmons and named the price. He could put Barrow and his girl on the spot, but it would take a full pardon for Henry Methvin.

Simmons went to Austin and conferred with "Ma" Ferguson. She agreed to issue the pardon if Methvin's father cooperated. Hamer passed the word on. Methvin was satisfied. He promised to help the lawmen and even suggested a plan.

The gang's routine, in the event they got separated, was to meet at the abandoned house. Methvin said he would tell his son to get lost, and when Clyde and Bonnie appeared at the rendezvous point, they could – well, be captured.

Ivan Methvin took his son aside that same night and told him the plan. Henry said they were going in to Shreveport the next day to do some shopping and that he would vanish at the first opportunity. He did. Clyde and Bonnie waited for him almost an hour. Then, figuring that something must have scared him away, they drove out to the abandoned house and waited.

Ivan Methvin sat watching them, sweat pouring down his face.
But they apparently suspected nothing. Finally Bonnie said,
"Maybe he got mixed up and went over to the rented place."

Clyde said to Methvin, "You better check on it. We'll meet you
on the road between Sailes and Gibsland tomorrow morning at
nine."

As soon as they were gone, Ivan rushed to Sheriff Jordan's
house. Jordan phoned Federal Agent Kindell, but his office said he
was out of town on an emergency assignment and couldn't be
reached. Captain Hamer was in town, though, and came right over.
With him was an old Ranger sidekick, M. B. "Manny" Gault, and
two men from Sheriff Schmid's Dallas office, Chief Deputy Bob
Alcorn and Deputy Ted Hinton.

After picking up Jordan's deputy, Paul M. Oakley, the six men
drove back and forth between Sailes and Gibsland, looking for the
best ambush spot. They finally settled on a patch of woods outside
Mt. Lebanon. The road was narrow at this point and with steep
banks on both sides. Clyde wouldn't be able to pull off his famous
U-turn.

The men got into position behind the embankment. Captain
Hamer and Sheriff Jordan had automatic shotguns. Hinton had a
BAR. Gault, Oakley, and Alcorn had Winchester repeaters. All
had a perfect field of fire.

Finally, around eight o'clock that morning, 23 May, they heard
Ivan Methvin's truck approaching. Sheriff Jordan flagged it down.
Methvin was told to pull over to the side of the road and to take the
truck's right front wheel off, as if he had a flat.

Then the waiting started once again. At nine o'clock several cars
passed. The men tensed each time, but the cars sped by without
stopping. Then, at nine-fifteen, a Ford V-8 suddenly appeared
over the rise and came speeding toward the ambush site.

Clyde was at the wheel. He wore sunglasses and was driving in
his socks. Bonnie sat beside him, munching on a sandwich. She
had on her best dress, a flashy red one that she had bought in Terre
Haute a few weeks earlier. Clyde's sawed-off twelve-gauge was
propped between them. Their usual armory was on the back seat –
eleven pistols, a revolver, three BAR's, and more than two thousand rounds of ammunition. Bonnie's overnight case was on top of
it, together with Clyde's saxophone and some sheets of music.

Bonnie's poem wasn't in the car, though. She had completed it a
few weeks earlier and had sent it to the Dallas *Evening Journal* with

instructions to publish it after her death. The poem's final verses
ran:

> The road gets dimmer and dimmer.
> Sometimes you can hardly see,
> Still it's fight, man to man,
> And do all you can,
> For they know they can never be free.
>
> They don't think they are too tough or desperate,
> They know the law always wins,
> They have been shot at before
> But they do not ignore
> That death is the wages of sin.
>
> From heartbreaks some people have suffered,
> From weariness some people have died,
> But take it all in all,
> Our troubles are small,
> Till we get like Bonnie and Clyde.
>
> Some day they will go down together,
> And they will bury them side by side.
> To a few it means grief,
> To the law it's relief,
> But it's death to Bonnie and Clyde.

Clyde saw Ivan Methvin's truck and slowed to a stop beside it.
"Got a flat?" he called out. Methvin nodded nervously. "Did you
find Henry?"

Methvin shook his head, then turned suddenly to Bonnie and
asked her for a drink of water.

"Sure," she said, and reached for the thermos. Methvin dived
behind his truck.

"Put 'em up, Clyde. You're covered!" Sheriff Jordan bellowed.

Clyde shifted into first, grabbed his shotgun, and swung the
door open – all in one movement. Bonnie already had her pistol
out.

The ambush party opened fire. Six powerful weapons poured
nonstop streams of lead into the car. Bonnie and Clyde's bodies
danced like puppets on a string. Clyde's jacket was literally torn

from his body. He sagged against the wheel. His foot slipped off the clutch pedal. The car rolled forward against the embankment and there it bounced to a stop.

"Be careful, they may not be dead," Ranger Gault shouted as Captain Hamer cautiously approached the car.

One hundred and sixty-seven slugs had ripped into the vehicle, all of them breast-high on the two occupants. Yet there was still doubt in the lawmen's minds as to whether Bonnie and Clyde were actually dead. Such was the power of their legend.

The crowds got at the bodies immediately. They tore away scraps of their clothing and snipped off locks of their hair. They gathered up the empty cartridges and bits of broken glass.

The car was towed into Arcadia with the bodies still in it.

Photographs taken at the funeral parlor show the two bodies lying riddled and leaking on adjoining stone slabs, the tools of their trade piled on their chests, as crowds file past, gaping, hungry for one last thrill.

Captain Hamer's job was over. He had finally taken them – after 102 days of tracking. "There isn't much to it," he told the chief of the Texas Highway Patrol over the telephone. "They just drove into the wrong place. Both of them died with their guns in their hands, but they didn't have a chance to use them."

The news was flashed around the world. In New York City the *Herald Tribune* observed solemnly that "society is glad that Louisiana rubbed them both out."

They were not buried side by side as Bonnie had predicted in her poem. Clyde was buried beside his brother Buck in West Dallas Cemetery. Bonnie was lowered into the ground at Fish Trap Cemetery several miles away while a quartet sang "Beautiful Isle of Somewhere." Her body was later moved to Crown Hill Memorial Park.

The authorities were busy, meanwhile, rounding up the remnants of the gang. Ray Hamilton and Joe Palmer were caught and sentenced to death for killing Major Crowson during the Eastham bust-out. They made a spectacular escape from the Huntsville death house in July 1934 but were later recaptured and electrocuted.

Henry Methvin got his pardon from Texas, but Oklahoma officers were waiting for him. He was taken to that state and sentenced to death for the murder of Constable Cal Campbell. The sentence was later commuted, and he was paroled in 1942. A train ran over him in Sulphur, Louisiana, six years later.

Mrs Cumie Barrow and many other relatives of Bonnie and Clyde served prison terms ranging from a few days to years for having given "aid and comfort" to the pair while they were fugitives.

And that was supposed to be the end of it. Time would pass and people would forget. Instead the legend grew. Around Grand Prairie and the West Dallas viaduct it got more elaborate with every passing year.

There were the poems, and there was Clyde, who had carried Bonnie with him when she was crippled and no longer pretty, and there was Bonnie herself tough and hard-mouthed, a killer, yet capable of caring for him in some furious, half-crazy way.

After Bonnie was buried at Crown Hill Cemetery, her family had a plaque put over her grave. There were some verses on it. Not Bonnie's, just those standard lines that used to come with a certain price headstone back in the Depression. They read:

> As the flowers are all made sweeter
> By the sunshine and the dew,
> So this old world is made brighter
> By the lives of folks like you.

Gorbals Boy
(Patrick Carraher)

George Blake

Drink was the downfall of Patrick Carraher, a vicious beer-house brawler and aggressive street-fighter, violent and morose. When in drink, which was often, he was arrogant and dangerous, and served several prison stretches for assault and theft. Born in 1906 in the overcrowded Gorbals district of Glasgow, an area of slum streets and festering tenements, Carraher was in and out of gaol from the age of 16, and in 1934 stood trial for murdering a young soldier, James Sydney Emden Shaw, who had died from a knife wound in the neck during an affray in the Gorbals. Found guilty only of culpable homicide (the Scottish equivalent of manslaughter), Carraher was sentenced to three years' penal servitude. In 1943 he was back inside for assault and razor-slashing. Gripped still tighter by the effects of drink, in November 1945 Carraher killed another soldier, a Seaforth Highlander named John Gordon, recently released from a German prison camp, and faced a second trial for murder. Gordon, described in evidence as "half seas over", had been stabbed to death – again in the neck – during a drunken scuffle on a street corner in Glasgow's Townhead district. In Carraher's defence, it was argued that he was a psychopathic personality, whose emotionally unstable condition had been aggravated by excessive alcoholism. There was also a suggestion of "persecution mania" arising from Carraher's morbid self-pity, and his defence invoked the doctrine of diminished responsibility – in those days,

*applicable only in Scotland – although to no avail. "Paddy"
Carraher was sentenced to death and hanged at Barlinnie
Prison in April 1946. George Blake (1893–1961) was a Glas-
gow-based author and journalist who wrote for the* Scottish
Daily Express *and the* Glasgow Herald *and who became a
familiar figure on the Scottish literary scene in the 1940s and
50s. His series of Garvel novels, set in Greenock, exemplify
Blake's abiding love of the Clyde and its ships. He also wrote
industrial histories and contributed* The Trials of Patrick
Carraher *to the* Notable British Trials *series, from which this
account is drawn. It begins with a chance late-night encounter at
Gorbals Cross, now demolished, but then the area's favourite
meeting place near the Victoria Bridge spanning the River
Clyde.*

1

At 11.15 p.m. on the evening of Saturday 13 August 1938, an
18-year-old working girl, Margaret McKay McNicol, arrived
at Gorbals Cross to meet by arrangement a 19-year-old window
cleaner called James Durie. The hour may seem late for such an
assignation, but it would still be quite light in those northern
latitudes and, as we shall see, the nocturnal habits of the Gorbals
folk are apt to be eccentric. Margaret's first encounter at the
rendezvous was with a man she knew as Paddy Carraher. He
was alone, and she perceived that he had taken drink. Carraher's
desire was that this young girl should go and act as intermediary
with a woman called Katie Morgan, a former lady-love from
whom, it appears, he had been parted by misunderstanding.

Margaret McNicol declined this delicate embassy. As she put it
in court subsequently: "Well, the two of them fell out, and I didn't
want anything to do with it." In the light of the evidence we may
imagine that this young girl, undoubtedly knowing Carraher's
criminal record and alarmed by the truculence which had come
upon him with drink, was chiefly concerned to get out of his
company as quickly as possible. She even came to know that he had
a knife about his person; and this would seem to suggest that
Carraher, in his sour mood, boasted of his lethal possession and his
intention to use it if necessary. Even at this early stage the reader
should note the overtone of theatricality in all the more desperate
utterances of Patrick Carraher.

Alarmed by her encounter with this sinister personality – a girl of 18 against an habitual criminal of 32 – Margaret McNicol looked about for succour and saw her boyfriend, James Durie, not far away. She ran towards him. But Patrick Carraher followed her and grasped at her arm, tugging her away from Durie. This young Durie caught her by the other arm and tugged in his turn: the young woman helpless between them. In the issue of this formless brawl, the girl escaped from between Carraher and James Durie, and the two men came to grips.

This was a climax of some importance as the High Court of Justiciary came to consider it later on. The burden of the evidence is that Carraher seized young Durie by the lapels of his jacket with his left hand and, with an open knife in his right, threatened him direly: the point of the knife menacingly aimed at the youth's midriff. This, if the evidence for the Crown is to be accepted, was assault in an advanced degree.

The intelligent reader will, however, study with care the relevant passages in the various testimonies. It was maintained by witnesses for the Crown that Carraher and Durie remained in this statuesque pose "for five or ten minutes", and one wonders if even a couple of film stars could have so brilliantly "held" such a powerful scene over such a great length of time. The presiding judge at the consequent trial in the High Court, the late Lord Pitman, almost contemptuously dismissed this single issue in his charge to the jury. Considering the reported case after a lapse of twelve years, the layman may reasonably feel that the Crown – in the sense of mere tactics at least – put an excessive emphasis on this episode of technical assault and thus in fact, by dividing the interest, weakened the case of murder against Patrick Carraher.

However that may be, the two young people extricated themselves from the grip of Paddy Carraher at Gorbals Cross and made towards Peggy McNicol's home in Eglinton Street, about a quarter-of-a-mile away to the West. They would have done well to leave it at that, but it appears that, after a colloquy in the close leading up to the girl's home, they decided to return to the Gorbals and continue the dispute. In fact, they made for 163 Hospital Street, where young Durie's older brother lived under the roof of his mother-in-law, Mrs Morgan. This John Dickson Durie, aged 24, was then an unemployed labourer. Hearing his brother's tale of threatened assault with a naked knife, he rose, dressed and went down with the others to Gorbals Cross. He conceived it his business to see that his junior "got a fair fight" – that is, against Carraher – but we may reasonably imagine that the Duries went out in force to maintain the family honour against a notorious troublemaker. This was a clan feud.

These Duries were not gangsters. The family record with the police was clean enough. They were rather of the class known in the *argot* of Glasgow as "Neds" – that is, the rather shiftless lads who hang about street-corners and watch and wait: without much purpose, without definitely criminal intent, but with a wary eye for the main chance: the loungers on the edge of active society.

When these two Duries got down to Gorbals Cross at a late hour of the night Paddy Carraher was not immediately in sight. They had, however, reinforced themselves. Peggy McNicol had gone home by this time and may now be forgotten; but with the Durie brothers at Gorbals Cross there were now Charles Morgan, aged 16, John Durie's brother-in-law, and Peter Howard, aged 23, and a shunter in good employment. By midnight or thereabouts the Durie clan thus felt itself no doubt ready for anything. In due course they spotted their man and went across to have it out with him.

According to the evidence of the Duries and their henchmen, their proposition to Carraher was that he should there and then agree to a fair fight with bare fists with one or other of the Durie brothers. To this Carraher would not agree, and we may share the presiding judge's view that this was only a prudent decision. He had taken a good deal of drink, and he rightly feared that, according to the code he knew so well, he might ultimately be beaten up by the Durie faction. The argument became heated; Carraher was heard to declare that if he had only two other men like himself he would "redd the corner" – that is, clear the place of the Duries and their friends. It is one of the small curiosities of this case that Carraher is more than once reported as speaking in good braid Scots instead of the debased *patois* of his native city.

There then appeared upon the scene a strangely ill-fated young man. This was a young Regular soldier, James Sydney Emden Shaw – a name of some interest to the student of naval history. Now, it is important that Shaw was little known, or not known at all, to the Carraher-Durie group. As they say, he butted into a private quarrel, perhaps with some drink in him. He appears to have overheard Carraher's brave boast of redding the corner, and he remarked to this dangerous citizen that he "spoke like an Englishman", or words to that effect. This observation, which might gratify a certain type of Scotsman, could not be construed by a man of Carraher's stamp as anything but an insult. The ball of controversy passed from the Duries to Shaw; and they were all making such a noise that the policeman on the beat intervened, telling them to "take a walk" – the Glasgow equivalent of the London Bobby's "Move on, now".

The party, Shaw still of the company, started to move eastwards from Gorbals Cross along Ballater Street, and Carraher and the soldier continued their highly personal argument. They were "throwing cracks" at each other; that is, they were insulting each other, and there is no doubt at all that Carraher was nagged and provoked by this intruder. Reaching the corner at Thistle Street, the older Durie wisely decided that he and his relatives should go home, and they started to move away. Peter Howard, however, lingered awhile on the edge of the pavement, Carraher and Shaw still wrangling in the roadway a few yards away. It appears that Shaw insisted on continuing his argument. The evidence hereabouts is somewhat obscure, but it is fairly clear that, as Howard was turning to follow the Duries, a scuffle on the roadway caused him to look back; whereupon he saw Shaw "haudin' his neck" – that is, holding his neck with his hands – and pointing towards Gorbals Cross as if he looked for succour in that direction or hoped that Howard would seek it there. Carraher had meanwhile disappeared in the darkness. It was now after one o'clock of a Sabbath morning; and Paddy Carraher had the gift of swift disappearance from scenes of violence.

Peter Howard thus became, willingly or not, the leading actor in a tragedy. He was alone with a man bleeding to death from the jugular vein. A minor complication, of which the Defence ultimately made the best it could, was the appearance on the scene of a man in a light suit. From this passer-by Howard borrowed a handkerchief to stanch the flow of blood from Shaw's neck, and then he, also, disappeared into the shadows of the Gorbals. The episode seems to make a sinister convolution in the pattern of that night's dark doings, but we may agree with the view of Lord Pitman that it was not a material point, and that any one of us, encountering such a situation late at night in a notoriously dangerous area, would readily produce a handkerchief and even more readily escape the scene of an affair so obviously involving police proceedings. The stranger in the light suit was in fact never traced.

In the meantime, Shaw had staggered to the pavement at the

corner of Thistle and Ballater Streets, and there he collapsed. It was afterwards discovered that the pool of blood at this point was even larger than that at the point on the roadway where he had been struck. Then he rose again and, according to Howard, "ran" westwards along Ballater Street towards Gorbals Cross: the trail of his blood clear to the detectives when they came to examine the scene. He passed under the viaduct that carries the railway lines across the Clyde into St Enoch Station and then, having covered some 150 yards, finally collapsed in front of a picture house. A policeman watching a shop nearby attended to him, and an ambulance duly arrived to carry the unfortunate soldier across the bridge and up the hill to the Royal Infirmary. He died as they were taking him to a ward. The detectives on the spot in the Gorbals arrested Peter Howard.

The bush telegraph of the slums works fast. Even at that small hour of a Sunday morning people were abroad, including one female witness who "decided to go for a walk along with my daughter about 12.45 on the Sunday morning". It very rapidly got about the Gorbals that a man had been killed, and that Howard had been arrested. A woman called Mary McCafferty, an unemployed domestic servant, aged 22, went out with her friend Kate Docherty to see what was afoot, saw Shaw being put into the ambulance in Ballater Street about 1.40 a.m., and gathered that Peter Howard had been arrested. This Kate Docherty was friendly with Howard's older brother, Robert, and the two women went to inform him of what had happened. Their subsequent movements are of rather curious interest.

On their way towards the house in Portugal Street where Robert Howard was saying – that is, westwards and beyond Gorbals Cross – the girls encountered Carraher. He was in Norfolk Street, near its junction with Buchan Street. He spoke to them, no doubt anxious to have the latest news of what was happening, and he went with them to the close giving entry to No. 12 Portugal Street. There, while Kate Docherty ran upstairs, he waited with Mary McCafferty but said nothing. Shortly they were joined by Robert Howard and Kate Docherty, and the strange foursome then proceeded across the Albert Bridge towards the Central Police Station not very far away. Short of this establishment, in the narrow and picturesque thoroughfare known as the Bridgegate, Carraher and the girl McCafferty lingered behind while Robert Howard and Kate Docherty went on to discover at the Police Office how matters stood with the former's young brother. An astonishing conversation ensued.

One is strongly tempted to believe that Carraher had in him that streak of vainglory which is apt to go with the temperament of the third-rate killer. With a good deal of drink in him, possibly with memories of American gangster films, he seems to have posed as the big man, the strong-armed hero who has disposed of the enemy. At all events, he told this girl whom he hardly knew that it was he who had stabbed Shaw.

> "I said, 'What for?' and he says, 'I was arguing with a fellow. He was very cheeky.' I said, 'How did you do it?' and he says, 'With a knife,' and he took a knife out of his pocket and showed me it. . . . It was like a pocket knife, a dark knife."

When the girl protested that it would now go hard with Peter Howard she had from Carraher the prompt and rather too romantic assurance: "Oh, yes, they will let Peter Howard out because I will give myself up; I won't let him swing for it."

One might think that he could then have walked into the Central and told the police what he had just told Mary McCafferty, but the heroics of Paddy Carraher were hardly so perdurable as all that. They were rejoined by Robert Howard and Kate Docherty, and back across the bridges to the Gorbals the foursome started again. Carraher walked next to the parapet, and on the way home Mary told the others what Paddy had revealed to her as they waited in the Bridgegate. "Show him your knife," she urged, and Robert Howard asked: "Have you got a knife?" To which Carraher blandly replied, "No, I have not got a knife, but I possess a razor blade. It is still in the packet."

When the detectives arrested Patrick Carraher later on that morning they found this razor blade on his person, apparently still in its original packet. They did not find a knife, for Carraher had in fact, unseen by his companions, slipped it over the parapet of the bridge.

The subsequent trial of Patrick Carraher for murder is of only limited interest as an exercise in detection. That his was the hand which raised the knife to stab young James Sydney Emden Shaw to death there is no doubt at all. He was in a drunken condition, and we may think that he believed his blow to be aimed at an older enemy than the young and foolish soldier who had crossed his path by accident. The proceedings in the High Court of Justiciary were remarkable only for the brief, not to say brusque, nature of Lord Pitman's charge to the jury. Some of the odd considerations we have reviewed – the matter of the knife over the parapet of the bridge, for instance – were not so much as mentioned by his lordship. If ever a jury was directed to reduce the capital charge to one of culpable homicide (*anglice* manslaughter) it was never more marked than in this case. It is only fair to observe that Lord Pitman had much in mind the factor of drink.

In the issue, the fifteen good men and women and true who constitute a Scots jury in criminal causes returned the unanimous opinion that Patrick Carraher should be found not guilty of assault but, by the majority verdict allowable in Scottish procedure, that he was guilty of culpable homicide. Lord Pitman thereupon sentenced Paddy Carraher to penal servitude for three years, and we may well think that the prisoner in the dock was a very lucky man.

During trial after trial over a period of at least fifteen years verdicts of culpable homicide were returned in Murder trials, and it appeared that the new mixed juries were unwilling to pronounce sentence that would lead to execution by hanging. In one notorious case of a shooting near Perth the jury found the accused guilty of rape but the charge of murder not proven, whereas it seemed obvious to those of us who sat in court throughout those days that the man in the dock could not have outraged the young woman in the case if he had not first killed her sweetheart. The embarrassment of the judge in charge of the proceedings – the then Lord Justice-Clerk, the late Lord Craigie Aitchison – was obvious as he hesitated to pronounce sentence.

It may very well be that the incalculable inclinations of the new mixed juries subtly affected the old Roman sternness with strict justice of criminal procedure in Scotland, and the hypothesis was widely debated at the time, but we merely note the fact that social circumstances and the state of the public conscience had completely changed when, in March 1946, Paddy Carraher appeared before the High Court of Justiciary for the second and last time on a charge of murder committed on a November night of 1945. It is worth recording at this point, without prejudice one way or another, the unofficial view of the City of Glasgow Police that two or three hangings during the 1945–6 period notably reduced the post-war exuberance of the local gangsters.

2

After his release from prison Carraher appears to have deserted his native Gorbals and transferred his operational headquarters to the Townhead area of Glasgow, on the other side of the river. The attraction here was a woman, Sarah Bonnar; and her brother, Daniel Bonnar, a rather notoriously aggressive citizen, became Carraher's henchman in many an escapade. Given Bonnar's adventurous temperament and Carraher's prestige as one who had done time for killing his man, this couple were at once able to exert considerable influence in their district and class and to be almost certainly destined for more serious trouble with the police.

The Townhead of Glasgow is utterly unlike the Gorbals in layout and general character. It is an older settlement by far, and it scrambles over and along the slopes of those clay drumlins, or ridges, which are so marked a feature of the city. Historic and important buildings stand in or about it. The Cathedral, the ancient house known as Provand's Lordship, and the mass of the Royal Infirmary are at hand. Allan Glen's School, the Maternity Hospital, the Royal Technical College, and even the City Chambers lie within the grouping, which also includes more than one printing establishment of international repute. Many of the older domestic buildings are of great architectural interest and even charm, but too many of them have been overwhelmed by the internal pressures that are the curse of a great industrial city with narrow boundaries and are now only festering slums. As distinct from the Gorbals of the broad level streets, the Townhead is rather a clotted congeries of twisting lanes and dark, steep streets lined with the tall, grey tenements of the industrial West. Public-houses abound.

In this favourable environment, then, in February 1943, Carraher and Bonnar enjoyed an orgy of violent misbehaviour. The Indictment at the subsequent trial charged Bonnar with breach of the peace, assault with a bottle and kicking a woman; the items against Carraher included vicious assault on a man in a public-house in George Street – punching, kicking and slashing with a razor to his severe injury – and then a turning on three women with a razor, putting them in a state of bodily fear and alarm. For about a week between 9 and 17 February that year these two men seem to have been in an extreme state of offensive madness or drunkenness. The trial, however, which took place on 11 May, is of no criminological interest. The case was a plain one of lurid hooliganism. Carraher was sent back to gaol for three years.

We may notice here how Carraher's development as a criminal was now not to be halted; it was proceeding only too rapidly. He had started in early youth with theft and assault and some clumsy burglaries; but once he had wielded a weapon and got away with it, as they say, and doubtless as he relied more and more on the stimulus of drink, arrogant brutality grew upon him. The circumstances of the period, moreover, favoured the lone wolf, the reckless enemy of society. Carraher was unfit for military service, having a weak chest and a bad stomach, and he luxuriated in an atmosphere in which easy money, deserters on the run from the Services, the black-out and psychological strain sombrely coloured low life in all British cities. Honest liquor was scarce, but the lack of it could be made up with cheap and potent wines, sometimes fortified with methylated spirit to form a cocktail of lethal strength. Shortages, controls and the black market, along with the strain on depleted police forces, completed the picture of a gangster's paradise.

We should understand, however, that Carraher was in fact not a gangster in the literal sense. He neither commanded nor belonged to a large and organized clan of law-breakers. He seemed to be content to operate with the able and enthusiastic assistance of his "good-brother", that is, brother-in-law – though it was not actually in law in this case – Daniel Bonnar. Indeed, the sensitive student of the proceedings in both trials may get from the evidence an uncomfortable sense of Carraher's essential loneliness and will certainly note the fact that in neither of his two fatal assaults was he the original provoker of the conflict. In the Gorbals case he was threatened by the Duries and nagged by the intruding Shaw; in the second and final case we are now about to study the pot of trouble was undoubtedly stirred mainly by Daniel Bonnar on one side and Duncan Revie on the other. Carraher's austere function was that of Lord High Executioner: the man with the knife or chisel, prepared at the critical moment to redd the corner. We may fairly see that he was doomed by his temperament and circumstances sooner or later to overstep the limit a fairly tolerant society imposes on its bad boys.

At the time of his last trial Carraher was nearly 40 years of age, and his person was showing the signs of wear and tear. His height was rather below the average, being 5 feet, $6\frac{1}{2}$ inches; his sandy fair hair was thinning above the temples. His eyes were the most remarkable features of his appearance. Seen in profile they were heavily lidded, hooded, so that from the front they appeared to be mere slits. It was a sinister and apparently merciless visage, so far as these outward stigmata matter at all.

It was on the night of Friday, 23 November 1945 that Carraher committed his last crime. That his was the hand which struck another fatal blow at a fellow-creature, another slash with a weapon at a man's neck, there can be little room for doubt. At the same time, the evidence is highly confused, like the topographical nature of the scene; and counsel on both sides were dealing mainly with people of indifferent education and low mentality: some of them quite obviously concerned to make a show of their own innocence. It is perhaps legitimate here, however, greatly to simplify the story and take a short cut through the tangle of testimony, described by the Advocate-Depute as "a mosaic of evidence which is rather like the disconnected pieces of a jigsaw puzzle".

3

On the afternoon of this Friday in November 1945, then, three brothers of a family called Gordon left their father's house about 4.30 p.m. These were John, Joseph and Edward Gordon: the first-named the oldest, with 18 years' service as a Regular soldier in the Seaforths and not long released from imprisonment in a German camp since Dunkirk.

These Gordons – there were eight brothers in the family – were not unknown to the police, but they had the reputation of being sufficiently clean fighters in the petty warfare of the poorer quarters, and they were not of the workshy type. It is of pathetic interest that John, the old soldier, was notoriously the quietest of the family, and it is of at least a little importance that until the evening of his last day on earth he had remained indoors and had not touched drink. Apparently the Gordons had fallen foul of the Carraher–Bonnar faction, but whether for racial, denominational or merely family reasons we do not know, and there is no evidence to show that they went looking for trouble in the first place.

Their first port of call was a house at 139 McAslin Street, in the Townhead, where there lived a sister married to one Duncan Revie

– another of those somewhat unfortunate "good-brothers" with a too highly developed sense of family loyalty. This Revie was a deserter from the Army and on the run, able to visit his wife with safety only on occasion. At the statutory hour of 5 p.m. the four men went into the "Coronation Bar" next door to 139 McAslin Street, and there remained, drinking steadily, until about 7 p.m. They then decided to go down to the Rottenrow to Cameron's public-house (now vanished in a slum-clearance scheme) where John Gordon was well known, and there again they drank until near closing time, 9.30.

There is no indication that there was any sensible pause for a bite of food. Indeed, the two younger Gordons passed out under the influence of alcohol and may now, for our present purposes, be forgotten. In Cameron's pub the Gordons had meanwhile encountered a young man called John Keatings, another deserter, but from the Navy in this case. In evidence he admitted that when he, John Gordon and Duncan Revie emerged from Cameron's pub they were all half-seas over.

In the meantime, probably unknown to the Gordons, Carraher and Bonnar had been drinking more or less steadily throughout the day and had passed the evening in Thomson's public-house, not far from Cameron's in the Rottenrow. Apparently they left this place about 8.45 p.m. and went down to Daniel Bonnar's house in the same street; with them a little man called Thomas Connelly Watt, "Wee Watt", who was to prove the absolutely fatal witness against Carraher in the subsequent trial. The Carraher–Bonnar party in the house in the Rottenrow, womenfolk among them, then decided that they should have a sing-song, and Bonnar went out to secure supplies of drink and bring in such kindred spirits as he might encounter on the way. He thus made his way up the Rottenrow and opposite Cameron's pub encountered the Gordon clan and its adherents either emerging or just emerged from the premises.

We cannot now safely surmise whether or not this meeting was foreseen or planned; we do not know exactly why the parties should have leapt so swiftly into violent action. We do know that the handsome, fair-haired boy called Keatings, of the Gordon faction, immediately roared his intention to clear the street of lesser men, and that Bonnar on his part doffed his jacket, laid it on the roadway, and prepared for battle against this obvious enemy. It is safe to surmise that both Keatings and Revie made for Bonnar, and it is certain that Bonnar ran away, pursued by Keatings at least. It is also fairly clear that there must have been an exchange of blows. After a brief chase, however, the affair fizzled out. Keatings, in a tolerably advanced state of drink, disappeared from the scene and close students of the case have little more interest in him. But he had done his bit to set the heather on fire.

Bonnar now retired to the house of a sister in College Street, his blood up, and there borrowed (a) a hatchet and (b) a woman's costume jacket to replace his own jacket that had been left on the roadway opposite Cameron's pub. Thus strangely attired and heavily armed he returned to the fray, and on the way he met Carraher and "Wee Watt" near Weaver Street. These alert citizens had been warned that the good-brother was in trouble with the Gordons, and they had come out to support their friend. A Mrs Helen Josephine Colquhoun, wife of a soldier and a temporary postwoman in her own right, had been cleaning her windows, even at 9.30 p.m., and had seen Bonnar chased along Rottenrow by Keatings. She had thus conceived it her neighbourly duty to go down to Sarah Bonnar's house in Tarbet Street and tell her that her brother was in a fair way to be seriously assaulted.

The details of the next phase of the operations will probably remain forever shadowy. It is merely a safe short-cut through the jungle of rather suspect testimony to say that, after the first encounter with Bonnar and the disappearance of Keatings, John Gordon and Duncan Revie went up from the Rottenrow into McAslin Street; and that, in the meantime, Carraher and Bonnar, with "Wee Watt" in attendance for a while at least, executed a flanking movement through the dark, dull streets and came upon their enemies again near the intersection of McAslin and Taylor Streets.

Whether "Wee Watt" was actually present or not does not matter now. It is certain that the factions then clashed. Revie went for Bonnar, and again Bonnar executed a rapid retreat downhill, pursued by John Gordon's pugnacious good-brother. It seems equally certain that John Gordon, no doubt swaying pretty hopelessly on the edge of the pavement, was pounced upon by Paddy Carraher. When next seen by a fellow-creature he had collapsed on the pavement and was bleeding copiously from a wound at the back of the neck.

Of this tragic scuffle late at night and at an ill-lit corner there were, however, four good witnesses, if from various distances.

Two more than middle-aged tradesmen, both respectable painters, had been chatting at the corner nearby. They did not claim to have heard sounds of scuffling, but they did hear voices raised in sundry incitements to violence, and they saw certain things happening. From some 60 yards away two much younger men heard the commotion and had seen very much what the painters had seen.

None of these witnesses could identify any of the men taking part in the brawl, and they differed as to the number of men involved: an agreeable symptom of their honesty. They all agreed as to the shouting of the men fighting, and they all saw two, or three, men running away down McAslin Street, one (or two) apparently in pursuit of another. They all saw still another figure advancing and "punching" the man who stood on the pavement's edge. They all agreed that, when they went to the aid of the man who had been seemingly "punched", he was bleeding copiously from a wound at the back of the neck. This man was John Gordon.

The evidence becomes slightly confused again at this point, but it is perfectly clear that some of these four witnesses started to help John Gordon to the Royal Infirmary, not far away. An unidentified sailor came to their assistance. The two ageing painters prudently disappeared from the scene. One of the two remaining witnesses – a young private in the Royal Marines called Neil Campbell – hastened to call a taxi to take the wounded man to hospital. The latter collapsed at the junction of Stanhope Street with McAslin Street as they were helping him along, but he appears to have been persuaded to his feet again. And then, an extremely odd incident, Duncan Revie reappeared, took the wounded person of his brother-in-law on his shoulder, and carried him up to the second-floor landing of the close at 139 McAslin Street, even if he might have seen that Gordon was rapidly bleeding to death.

We may surmise that Revie was in a state of high excitement and even apprehension; no doubt he had in his confused mind the notion of getting his good-brother into the care and protection of his own clan. Marine Campbell, however, had meanwhile found a taxi-cab, and Gordon was rushed to the Royal Infirmary. There he died exactly a minute after the doctor on duty at the gatehouse had made a superficial examination of his injuries.

Approximate silence then fell on the Townhead of Glasgow. From the evidence it is clear, however, that the affair had made a stir, and that sundry parties concerned continued to hang about,

awaiting developments, their sombre curiosities not unnaturally
aroused. One of the most important of these as a fatal witness
against Carraher was a tall, 27-year-old part-owner and driver of a
taxi-cab, John Douglas Stewart by name.

It was he who had been with Marine Campbell at the corner
not far from the scene of the assault. He had helped to get John
Gordon along McAslin Street towards the Royal Infirmary.
Whatever he had done with himself thereafter, at about 11.30
p.m. that night, in either Cathedral Street or its brief extension
into Stirling Road, he encountered an acquaintance, George Ross
Elliott, nicknamed "Gasser" Elliott, apparently on account of his
conversational proclivities. These two discussed what had happened, and they set off together, near midnight, to look for
Daniel Bonnar, whose name was being freely mentioned as the
author of the crime. It is merely fair to say that Stewart knew
little of the parties concerned and proved to be an intelligent and
useful witness.

Elliott and Stewart thus went first to Bonnar's house in the
Rottenrow. There was nobody there, and they proceeded to Sarah
Bonnar's home at 14 Tarbet Street. Into this dwelling they were
admitted by Bonnar after some hesitation. Men and women were
assembled in the kitchen, Carraher among them, and we get from
the evidence a strong impression of excitement, now heightened by
Stewart's intimation that Gordon was dead. It is of importance
that Stewart had never seen Carraher before. Ultimately, after a
great deal of talk backwards and forwards, the latter invited the
former into a room apart. The report then reads: –

Do you remember one of the people in the house coming up to you
and asking you to speak apart? – Yes, the accused asked me who I
was, and I told him it did not matter. He said "Where do you come
from?" and I said, "Over the road."

Where did this conversation between you and the accused take
place? – In the kitchen. That was when he asked me, and he said,
"Well, come here a minute," and he took me through a door into
another room . . .

What happened when you and the accused were in this other
room? – He told me that he was having a cup of tea in the house
when someone came and told him Bonnar was in trouble in the
Rottenrow, and he went out and met Bonnar, and the two of them
went to a close in McAslin Street, but they didn't see anyone there

and they went to the corner of Taylor Street and met the two fellows and the fight started . . .

Try and recollect the actual words the accused used? – He just said, "I gave one of them a jag and ran away when the fight started."

Bonnar was later to testify in the same sense, but this was an astonishing statement to make to a stranger. Carraher seems to have had a purpose, however, for when they returned to the kitchen and Stewart showed a clear desire to escape from this alarming situation, Carraher slipped something into his hand, saying, "Chip that away," so that when Stewart found himself in the open air again with "Gasser" Elliott he was in possession of the short, sharp blade and the wooden handle of a woodcarver's chisel.

We may wonder that Stewart did not march straight to the Central Police Station with this incriminating object, but we can make allowance for the excitement and alarm of the situation and for the presence of Elliott. In the issue, they dropped the blade down a stank in the High Street – that is, through the grating over a gutter drain – and the handle down another some yards away, having to use force to get the bulbous wooden part between the bars. These objects were recovered by the police within a few days.

This was not such absolute proof of Carraher's guilt as a judge and jury would accept out of hand, but the odds were narrowing.

Elliott followed Stewart in the witness-box and added some useful detail. He had seen Carraher draw the weapon from his hip pocket and break it into its two parts before handing it to Stewart. He had seen the accused wipe it with a dishcloth, but had not noticed any stain resulting. He had seen Bonnar take off a blood-stained shirt but understood that this was the result of one of his scraps with the Gordon faction; and Bonnar testified that he had been struck on the side of the head. Elliott had observed that Bonnar was excited, Carraher calm.

With regard to the nature of the wound of which John Gordon died there was some interesting testimony from the medical witnesses. It ran *upwards* from near the back of the neck to penetrate the cerebral canal; and at the post-mortem examination it measured four inches by the probe, whereas the effective length of the carver's tool was only about $2\frac{1}{2}$ inches. The Defence naturally sought to make the best of this disparity, but expert evidence for the Crown was able to show that (a) in the case of a blow delivered with force the surface tissues would "give" considerably under the impact, and (b) that there would ensue a considerable swelling or infiltration of the soft tissues by subsequent bleeding. Professor Allison's citation of the swelling seen in a case of mumps provided a convincing illustration. So far as the upward track of the wound is concerned, it is not difficult to see that Gordon probably crouched head downwards to receive it, and that the assailant would be pulling a clenched fist towards himself at the nadir of his stroke. The discovery of a cut on the ring finger of Gordon's right hand would surely indicate the involuntary raising of a hand to protect the vulnerable neck.

We may now return for a moment to the scene of the scuffle at the corner of McAslin and Taylor Streets, if only in order to clear away some of the confusions surrounding the figure of Carraher in that setting. Was it certainly he who was seen to "punch" Gordon in the view of the four detached witnesses?

Whatever the motives of those pugnacious "good-brothers" Revie and Bonnar, they exculpated each other in their separate testimonies. Revie was quite certain that he chased Bonnar down the street, Bonnar that he retreated before Revie, both leaving Gordon alone of his faction on the pavement; and Revie swore that he had seen Carraher menacing John Gordon. Was "Wee Watt" among those present? Bonnar insisted that he was, but the Defence, though naturally concerned to imply the possibility, made no overt suggestion that he struck the fatal blow nor suggested that he had ever been in possession of a weapon.

If Carraher was not thus indicated as the assailant beyond any reasonable doubt it was left to "Wee Watt" to tell a story of damning and lurid circumstantiality.

Poor Paddy Carraher! one is almost tempted to exclaim; he was so scurvily served in the witness-box by those who had been his cronies and sycophants. As will be seen from his evidence, Thomas Connelly Watt, aged 47, was at some pains to tell the whole truth as he knew it of the happenings during that fatal November night, and it should be observed that the keenest cross-examination could not break his story. Briefly, it went thus:

Watt was with Carraher and Bonnar in the latter's house when, after the session in Thomson's pub, it was proposed they should have a sing-song and Bonnar went out to bring in a friend. Then the news had come in that Bonnar was being chased by the young sailor, Keatings, and Carraher and Watt had emerged to see what was happening. Then, according to Watt, the carver's tool was in Carraher's breast pocket, the sharp edge showing. "He showed the blade from the top pocket," said Watt. He ran his thumb across the cutting edge, and he said to Watt, "This is the very tool for them."

If that was not enough, Carraher was to make in Watt's presence another candid confession of his guilt. This was when, the fighting over but before the arrival of Stewart and Elliott with the news of Gordon's death, the Carraher–Bonnar faction had reassembled in Daniel Bonnar's house in the first place. In this instance Carraher demonstrated how he had dealt with his enemy, dancing on tip-toe like a boxer, the right hand swinging backward and forward, and then the upraised arm and the vicious stroke downwards. "He said he did not know whether he had got him down the side of the face or shoulder," Watt testified.

The presiding judge, Lord Russell, invited Watt to demonstrate these sinister movements, and those who were present in court declare that "Wee Watt's" vivid pantomime of a vicious assault was far and away the most telling evidence the Crown produced during the three days' hearing of the case. They also report that, throughout the proceedings, Carraher bore himself coldly and glumly, like one who knows his doom is sealed, his narrow eyes hooded and never a glance towards one of his enemies or his former friends in the witness-box.

In the early morning of 24 November 1945, the Glasgow C.I.D. acted swiftly and arrested several of the principal participants in the brawl. Most of these were ultimately convicted for breach of the peace, while Carraher alone faced the charge of murder. The trial took place on Thursday, Friday and Saturday, 28 February and 1 and 2 March 1946. After the judge's careful charge it took the jury only twenty minutes to return a unanimous verdict of guilty. On 6 April 1946, after an unsuccessful Appeal, Patrick Carraher was hanged in Barlinnie Prison, Glasgow; and most of us would agree that society was thus well rid of a vicious pest.

4

Carraher was not insane. At school he was a normal pupil. The Defence invoked a legend of the traditional stepmother who put him from the house at an early age, but this romantic interpolation

must be qualified in the light of information that was not produced
in court. Paddy's dismissal from his father's house was the deliberate act of both parents, sickened and saddened by his incorrig-
ibility. The list of his convictions from first to last is a lengthy
chronicle of misdemeanour and imprisonment over some twenty
years, so that he spent much more of the second half of his life in
prison than out of it, with a spell of Borstal intervening. The man's
father was an anxious listener in court at the first trial for murder in
1938, but he made no appearance at the second and last.

There were also introduced into the proceedings certain vague
suggestions of a persecution mania. The medical witnesses for the
Defence found Carraher harbouring a general grievance against
the Law and the police, surely a familiar attitude among inveterate
criminals. There was the account of his occasional trick of looking
into cupboards for men who were not there, but if that was not a
symptom of the irritability of the chronic alcoholic, one may think
it not unnatural in one who lived with a lady who was not his legal
wife. As for the man's grievance against people "piping" him in
public-houses, who that has lingered in any East End pub does not
know the sodden wreck with a chip on his shoulder, to whom even
an accidental look is an insult to be wiped out only by abuse or
assault?

On the whole, even the layman may think that if the defence had
rested wholly on the plea of chronic alcoholism in Carraher's case
it might have availed him more than the somewhat experimental
plea of diminished responsibility, advanced by two doctors who
had not seen a great deal of him, and then only when the strict
regimen of Barlinnie had allowed the drink to work out of his
system.

The fatal brawl was undoubtedly provoked and inflamed by
drink. A telling fragment of Sarah Bonnar's evidence was to the
effect that the man would rarely face a proper meal. A close student
of this case, highly qualified to judge these matters, has privately
declared that such as Carraher probably drank rather less in the
average day than many a wealthier and better-fed man of invul-
nerable respectability, but that the absence of substantial food to
absorb and offset the effects of alcohol would tend to enclose such
as Carraher within, as it were, a glasshouse of morose illusion, into
which a stranger might break only at the risk of violent assault by
the lone wolf on guard.

The social problem symbolized by the public-house in such

clotted cities as Glasgow is a heart-breaking one indeed. In Glasgow in particular it is complicated by the fact that strong pressure by the extreme elements of the temperance movement, working over a long period of years and with influence on the licensing Bench, has tended to turn the average public-house in the poorer districts of the city into a species of penal establishment. Even the most harmless games, such as dominoes and darts, are not permitted, and the police are forced by superior instruction to exercise the strictest sort of supervision of licensed premises, while any effort by a progressive licensee to improve his premises to the standards prevailing in, say, England does not have the encouragement of the magistrates at least.

Even so, the public-house in those overcrowded districts of central Glasgow is an important part of the social structure. Given grossly overcrowded conditions of housing, the menfolk at least are simply driven out of their mean, stinking, insanitary and often bug-ridden homes. If it is not to be wholly a matter of hanging about the street corner with the other "Neds", it must be the pub, especially in a notoriously wet climate. It would be a vicious irony to suggest that the Glasgow working man's pub is his club. It is occasionally so, let us admit, but on the whole it is simply a refuge from the degradation of so many homes, from the meanness of the environment.

A terrible case has developed against those who have governed Glasgow during the past century. Throughout the long period of industrial expansion so little foresight went to the problems bound to arise when peoples of half-a-dozen races scrambled for work in an expanding city, when landowners and property-owners allowed dwellings and their sites to be divided and sub-divided, to be built over again and again, producing warrens in which the impoverished detritus of the old industrial order multiplied and festered. The maintenance of decency in such conditions is much more than a simple social duty; it is a feat.

Much has been made of gang warfare in Glasgow, and of those bands of pugnacious youths who, under fancy names, banded to fight each other on such pretexts as the old Billy and Danny rivalry, Protestants against Catholics. The pretexts are meaningless. The emergence of a Scoto-Irish breed, mainly huddled in the most degraded areas, did indeed complicate the pattern, but its basis was the essentially Scottish one of the clan system. Strong and violent youth unconsciously organized itself in groups in order, one had almost said, to fight its way out of sombre monotony. Theirs was only a special and unpleasant expression of the motive that bids millions rather more fortunately placed to sublimate their sense of frustration in blind loyalty to this or that football team. It is of touching interest that a sympathetic police official of one of the eastern divisions of Glasgow could, by 1942, show from his careful records that most of his notoriously bad boys were by then serving, if they had not already fallen, in North Africa or in the various Commando raids on the European coasts. So badly did they need a way of escape from the home environment and from the doldrums of unemployment that so terribly afflicted the industrial regions of Scotland during most years of the third decade of the 20th century!

It has been suggested here that Paddy Carraher was not cut out to be a good gangster. His morose and individualistic temperament fated him to operate within small groups and usually as the Big Man with a somewhat theatrical fondness for the part of the decisive killer: the vicious egoist *in excelsis*. It has not been suggested, despite modern psychological science, that he was aught but a rat, acute and resourceful within his limitations. It has not been claimed that he was ever involved in a case of subtle interest to students of crime. One would like to think, however, that this account of his killings, trials and subsequent punishment may assist in moving the public conscience and the authorities towards a more urgent sense of the appalling problems of housing and reconstruction, and of the gravity of the human problems arising out of bad environment, that still face many another British community besides Glasgow.

Kill the Dutchman!
(Dutch Schultz)

Ted Addy

Murderer, bootlegger, racketeer and double-crosser, Dutch Schultz was universally hated. Vicious and unpredictable, the Dutchman was basically a loner. Backed by a small army of assassins, he shot his way to the top of the newly formed crime syndicate. In the end, he was assassinated by Murder Inc. Born Arthur Flegenheimer, by 1935 Dutch Schultz was in trouble not only with the federal government for tax evasion but with rival gangs, having openly declared his intention of killing Thomas E. Dewey, newly nominated DA for New York, who'd pledged to crack down on the city's criminals. Dewey had drawn up a tax indictment against Schultz, who responded with public affirmations of "Dewey's gotta go" and "We gotta knock off Dewey". Murder Inc. did not like that kind of talk; neither did Big Six or the Syndicate, names like Luciano, Siegel and Lansky, who weren't too keen on the kind of heat that might develop if the independent and overly excitable Dutchman put Dewey on the spot. Schultz may have become a big-shot but he began as a punk, a small-time thief and burglar, becoming a hitman for Jack (Legs) Diamond, then a partner in a speakeasy in The Bronx, then Beer Baron and overlord of the Harlem policy racket, before finally ranking as Public Enemy Number 1 on the private list in J. Edgar Hoover's Federal Bureau of Investigation. In sparky tabloid prose, Ted Addy describes how Schultz, 33, turned on his own lieutenant, Abe ("Bo") Weinberg before

*moving to the climax of the story with the events of 23 October in
the back room of the Palace Chop House and Tavern in Newark.*

Dutch Schultz couldn't go back to the Bronx, nor to his
apartment in Manhattan where Frances and his two children
were staying. La Guardia still threatened to throw him in jail if he
came inside the city limits.

He went directly to Newark, rented an apartment and set up his
headquarters there. He used Lulu Rosenkrantz and Abe Landau,
his muscle men, as messengers to carry orders that could not be
transmitted by phone. Schultz's recent courtroom experience had
made him very allergic to telephone conversations.

He had expected things to be rosy, that he'd be hailed as the
biggest racketeer in the nation. Maybe he thought even the cops
would be afraid of him, but he was disillusioned.

He met new troubles at every turn.

FBI agents had shadowed him all the way down from Malone,
watching him night and day. He was still Public Enemy No. 1,
which made him the big prize for J. Edgar Hoover's boys.
Furthermore, the papers said the government was preparing to
ask for a new indictment of Schultz for income-tax evasions
subsequent to those of 1929, 1930 and 1931, for which he'd been
tried.

And the State of New York was going to prosecute Schultz for
unpaid state income taxes amounting to $36,000.

As an added insult, Governor Lehman had appointed Tom
Dewey special prosecutor in a grand jury investigation into the
rackets of New York City.

"He's my nemesis!" Schultz howled.

His position in the Syndicate was just so-so. His old friend Ciro
was a has-been, and Schultz didn't know quite how to take
Cappola. Schultz was playing ball with Cappola and, on the
surface, the two men were friendly, but Schultz, true to form,
didn't trust him.

And then Weinberg said that the numbers racket had fallen off
tremendously.

He checked the figures with Abbadabba.

"Yes, they're down some," said the accountant. "The 'bust the
rackets' campaign has made our men cautious. Some of them have

been asked to appear before the grand jury, you know, and we had to get them out of town. But we still should be making a profit. I'm afraid the trouble is bad management."

"Bad management, or sticky fingers?" Schultz asked.

"Oh, I don't think Weinberg has –"

"Well, I think so. I think Bo got the idea of taking over. He figured I'd go to prison and the Policy racket was his." Schultz slammed his fist on a table. "That's about all I'll take off Bo Weinberg. I'll kill the bastard. And I'll bet Dixie was workin' with him, tellin' him what to do. If I hadn't had a couple of good lawyers, Dixie would have thrown me to the dogs. I'll kill Davis, too!"

Sometimes fate plays curious tricks. Davis *just happened* to walk into the office at that moment. It was purely a coincidence, one of those things that happen in real life, which no writer would dare use as fiction because it wouldn't be believed. But it did happen, and Davis repeated the story three years later to an investigator of the district attorney's office. When he walked in he had no idea that Schultz was entertaining the idea of rubbing him out. As it turned out, he came in just in time to hear Schultz pronounce his death sentence.

Davis felt his blood run cold. Since he called on Bo before the Malone trial he'd suspected Bo was putting a few extra dollars in his own pocket, despite the protestations that he was the Dutchman's slave. But Dixie had had no part in this.

Davis had seen Martin's execution and it hadn't been pretty.

He turned to get the hell out but Schultz happened to come through the door at that moment. Another trick of fate.

"There you are, you son-of-a-bitch!" Schultz snarled. He drew his gun. "Don't you try to run out on me."

"Now Arthur –"

"I'm gonna kill you, you cheap chiseler!"

"I didn't take a cent off you that you didn't pay me, Arthur," said Dixie.

He suddenly realized he was begging, just as Martin had begged. He knew this wasn't the kind of plea that would win his case with Schultz. As a lawyer he knew he had to use a better defense in order to stop the trigger finger of the nation's Number One racketeer.

"The hell you didn't take my money. You and that double-crossin' Weinberg always have been thick as thieves, and you've been thievin', too."

It was the blow in the pocketbook that hurt Dutch Schultz.
Davis had to hit there to save his own life.

"You can't kill me, Arthur," he said, trying to keep his voice
cool and calm.

The sudden shift, like the deft footwork of a boxer, threw
Schultz off guard.

"I can't, huh? Why in the hell not?"

"Because it'd cost you money," said Dixie. "Don't you remember? The controlling interest in the Yonkers brewery is in my
name. If you killed me, my relatives would inherit the brewery.
You'd lose it."

It was a knockout punch – the same kind that Jim Jeffries used
on Gentleman Jim Corbett. Dutch Schultz was staggered. "You
sure?"

The gun wavered uncertainly.

"I'm a lawyer, Arthur. If you don't believe me, phone any
lawyer in town."

"Then you gotta sign your share over to me."

"Do you think I'm a moron, Arthur? Don't be crazy."

Dixie turned on his heel and started to walk out of the room.
Dutch Schultz put his gun away. "Wait a minute!" he called.

"I'm in a hurry, Arthur," Dixie called back. "Bo didn't steal
from you and I didn't, either."

Dixie didn't know whether Bo did or not, but Dixie knew it was
worth any man's life to steal from Dutch Schultz and Bo should
have sense enough to know it, too.

Bo finished his sixty-day jail sentence for contempt of court,
while Dutch continued his attempts to persuade Dixie to sell his
interest in the Yonkers Brewery. Davis refused to sell – naturally –
because it was the best insurance policy he had.

After Bo's release, Davis saw him before Schultz did, at the
Policy bank in Harlem. Davis told him about his encounter with
Dutch; and Bo, who wasn't in a very good mood after his sixty-day
forced separation from his bride, snarled, "I been through a lot for
that guy – I don't reckon he'll be too hard on me."

"He's in a nasty mood," Davis said. "He can't go back to New
York unless he sneaks in. He's taking a chance every time he
crosses the river. And he's damn sure everybody working for him
is lining their pockets."

"I've seen him like that before," said Bo. "Leave it to me, Dix.
I can handle him."

Later Schultz contacted Bo by telephone. "Frankie wants to meet you at the Bronx warehouse," he said. "He wants to bring in some slots."

"Okay," said Bo. "I'll see him."

Bo went over but Frank wasn't there. Only Dutch Schultz was around with a young punk who was in charge of the warehouse.

"I'll spit in LaGuardia's eye," said Schultz.

"Where's Frank?"

"He ain't comin'," said Schultz. "I wanted to talk to you."

"You don't have to play it cute to see me, boss," said Bo. "Just send the word and I'll meet you anywheres."

"I got some figures on the Policy game, Bo," said Dutch. "Seems to me you're about eighty-one thousand dollars short. Where is it?"

Bo's eyes grew big and round. "Eighty-one G's!"

"Yes. That much stuck to your big fat fingers."

"Now listen, boss—"

"You took it, didn't you? You didn't think I'd beat the rap at Syracuse, and you thought I couldn't beat it at Malone. You were ready to take over, Bo."

"Boss, if I'd wanted you in jail, I wouldn't have had to keep my mouth shut in Malone."

"If you'd opened your mouth," said Schultz, "you'd have been in jail with me."

"Okay," said Bo, "look at it this way. I've done a hell of a lot for you. And what have you done?"

"You've been well paid."

Bo spat on the floor. "Well paid," he said. "I stuck my neck out every day of the year, for seven long years. Look at what you did for Danny. Look at what you did for Larry. They were well paid, too."

"You shouldn't have stolen it, Bo. I'm gonna have to kill you."

Dutch moved his hand toward the pistol in his shoulder holster. But Bo wasn't going to wait for the gun to come out. He lurched toward Dutch Schultz, both fists swinging. He landed a left in Schultz's belly and then tried for an uppercut. It missed and landed on the Dutchman's nose.

Schultz squealed with pain but finished his draw just as Bo swung again. This was a haymaker to the jaw and Schultz went down, dropping the gun as he fell.

Bo stepped forward, reaching down to pick up the gun, but he forgot about the young punk.

The kid made a tackle like the whole Notre Dame backfield and Bo sprawled on the floor.

Bo kicked himself loose, grabbed the kid by the hair and held the head up as he swung his fist. The blow landed right in the guy's teeth.

Bo swung again and again till the kid just hung loose in his arms.

But he'd taken too much time settling the kid and the Dutchman had recovered from the beating he'd received. Schultz was still on the floor, crawling toward the gun he had dropped when Bo scored his third punch.

Bo dropped the kid and started toward the Dutchman, but he was too late.

The first shot brought Bo to his knees. He hung there a moment, trying to reach his own gun, when the Dutchman fired again.

Bo shook himself. With effort he grabbed the gun butt and tried to pull it out.

A third shot caught him right between the eyes.

Bo Weinberg sprawled on the floor.

Dutch Schultz got to his feet, pulled out a handkerchief and wiped the blood from his face. He walked over to the spot where the kid was lying. He shook the kid, who responded feebly. Then the Dutchman got a pail of water and threw it on him. The Dutchman spoke hoarsely.

"Get up!" he said. "We gotta mix some cement."

They stood Bo in an empty barrel, his outstretched arms supporting his weight and keeping his head out the top. Then they took some sacks of cement and mixed it with water.

They poured it around Bo Weinberg's body.

"It ought to harden before dawn," said Schultz. "Wait as long as you can, then drop it into the river."

The months rolled on. Schultz repeatedly tried to buy Dixie's interest in the Yonkers brewery; Dixie repeatedly refused to sell.

George Weinberg was in charge of the Harlem numbers racket, and he refused to discuss his brother, Bo. It was worth his life to say that he suspected what had happened to him. And he couldn't quit the mob. George's number would be up if he did.

Dewey was continuing his probe of rackets and the Policy racket was one of his big objectives. He was also talking to restaurant owners.

"What can we do about him?" Dutch asked Dixie, after his usual request for Yonkers brewery stock.

"Not a damn thing," said Dixie. "And the less we try the better off we'll be. If he indicts us, we've got to hope to beat it."

"I'll hit him," said Schultz. "That'll stop him."

Recently Schultz was threatening to kill everyone. He was more of a mad dog than Vince Coll had ever been.

The idea obsessed the Dutchman. "We gotta get that guy Dewey outa our hair," he kept repeating. "We gotta hit him."

But Dewey was not a hoodlum and to take him on a one-way ride, or to drop him into the Hudson with cement overshoes on his feet, would have caused a bigger furor than the sinking of the Maine.

Nevertheless, when Schultz slipped into Manhattan on one of his rare visits to attend a meeting of the Syndicate council, he brought it up.

The Syndicate had changed considerably since that first meeting in Atlantic City. Cappola had replaced Ciro, Luciano was now the head Mafia man in place of Maranzano, Gordon and Madden were no longer members of the committee and Capone was in jail. Moran had been out of things for a long time. Lepke was there and so was Costello. A new man was Albert Anastasia, head man at the waterfront, and Jake Gurrah, Lepke's partner, was a big shot now instead of a bodyguard. Johnny Torrio, Capone's former aide, had moved into the New York rackets.

"Dewey's after you, too," Schultz told Luciano. "Dewey says he'll get all of us."

"I've seen a lot of investigations," said Luciano. "They're staged for votes. They'll raise a little stink, maybe make a couple of arrests, then after the voters believe that the politicians are a hell of a good bunch of guys, everything will be forgotten. Nothin' to worry about."

"I suppose Capone and Gordon shouldn't worry?" Schultz asked. "And I goddamn near got in the same hotel where they are."

"I think we should wait," said Cappola. "Wait and think it over."

"Yes," said Anastasia, "it is not good to decide to kill somebody unless you know how it's to be done and how much risk is involved."

Anastasia was closely linked with Murder Inc., and he, Lepke and Gurrah were the chief hatchet men of the Syndicate.

"I'm not gonna wait till we're all in jail," said Dutch. "Why don't you case the job, Albert? See just what can be done. Then we'll meet next week and take a vote on whether we should do it."

Anastasia looked from face to face. Some favored, some opposed. Those who opposed knew that Dewey's assassination might put teeth in the investigation.

Luciano needed time to raise opinion against Schultz's proposal. "That's the best thing to do. Albert, you case it. And if you think it can be done, we'll go along with the idea. If it looks too tough, we'll drop it."

As soon as the meeting adjourned, Albert Anastasia assigned men to watch Dewey.

A child and a velocipede were borrowed and the watcher pretended to be a father taking a morning walk with his offspring in the vicinity of Dewey's apartment.

Dewey adhered to a strict schedule every morning. For four successive mornings he left the apartment in company with two police bodyguards, at almost exactly the same time. He walked a couple of blocks to a drug-store and went inside, leaving the bodyguards outside.

Anastasia's investigator learned that Dewey made a phone call from the booth in the store because he always left home before his wife was up and he didn't want to disturb her by using the phone in the bedroom. The phone call was to his office, to get his men started before he arrived.

With this information at hand. Anastasia reported back to the Syndicate the following week.

"We could hit him without much danger," he said with professional detachment. "We'd steal a car, get a gun that couldn't be traced, even license plates for the car, which we'd have near the store. Our man would be in the store when Dewey came in and it wouldn't be any trouble to knock him off in the phone booth. We'd use a silencer and the cops outside wouldn't know what went on till our man had walked out of the store and made his getaway."

"See?" said Schultz. "We can do it. Let's take a vote."

But during the week between the two meetings, Luciano had been busy, and so had Lepke. They had presented the arguments against the killing to the members who were on the fence. Until Dewey came up with something, no attempt should be made.

"I'm against it," said Luciano.

"Me, too," said Lepke. "It would bring every cop in the city down on us."

"Are we just gonna sit here and do nothin'?" Schultz asked.

"Sure. If we get indicted, we bump off the witnesses. Nobody gives a damn about witnesses. And without 'em nobody can be convicted."

"If you guys don't want to risk your goddamn precious skins," said Schultz, "I'll bump him off myself."

He got up and walked out of the meeting.

It was unfortunate that Schultz left early. As in the case of women's clubs, the first one to go gets talked about. In Schultz's case, he wasn't talked about. He was voted upon.

"We take no chances," said Luciano. "We hit him first."

Because Anastasia had favored Dewey's assassination and therefore could be considered on Schultz's side, Lepke was given the contract to wipe out Schultz.

He picked Charley "The Bug" Workman for trigger man. Mendy Weiss was to cover The Bug's retreat, and a punk called "Piggy" would drive the getaway car.

Schultz's movements were well known by the mob. He went to the Palace Chop House in Newark each Wednesday evening to check up on Policy receipts brought over from the Harlem bank. Usually Abbadabba Berman, Lulu Rosenkrantz and one or more mobsters were with him. The Bug didn't worry about the odds. He was a fast trigger and figured he'd get the drop.

The Palace was a rather large tavern, with a long bar in the main room. At the end of the bar was the men's room, and on the other side was a small alcove containing a telephone booth. In this alcove was a table, some chairs and a wooden screen fitted with coat hooks, which could be moved around to hide the business meeting from prying eyes in the main part of the room.

Schultz came to the Palace with Lulu and was joined later by Abbadabba and Abe Landau. Abbadabba had adding machine strips showing total receipts of close to half a million dollars. Dutch and Abbadabba ordered drinks and talked business. Schultz spoke of his hatred of Tom Dewey, but he hadn't figured out yet just how he'd do the job on him.

"Maybe I won't hire anybody this time," he said. "It'd be a pleasure to blast him myself." He was a little drunk perhaps.

He had been drinking enough to want to go to the toilet. Just after he went into the john, The Bug entered the tavern. He glanced at the bar, saw the bartender and a couple of customers. No one paid any attention to him and afterwards nobody could give the police a satisfactory description of what he looked like.

He was wearing a topcoat, since it was 23 October and a little cool. The coat concealed the gun he held in his hand as he opened the door to the john in order to make sure that no one would pop out and shoot him in the back.

There was a short, stocky fellow washing his hands under a running faucet. The Bug noted that the guy looked familiar, and as the fellow turned and saw The Bug, he made a move.

Dutch Schultz had seen the hand in The Bug's coat pocket and guessed what it held. The Bug looked like a torpedo and Dutch Schultz was always alert for a trigger man. He never knew just who might be trying to kill him.

Schultz grabbed for his gun, but it was too late. The Bug fired, sending a bullet through Schultz's left side. The Dutchman fell, leaving the faucet running, which was understandable.

The Bug whirled out of the door, glancing at the bar to make sure nobody there was aggressive. The bartender had ducked behind the mahogany and the two customers were stampeding toward the front door.

The Bug looked back to see Lulu Rosenkrantz coming around the screen, drawing his pistol. The Bug fired first and Rosenkrantz sprawled beside the telephone booth.

Then the Bug emptied his pistol at the other two men sitting at the table. Both men fell dead.

The Bug stood beside the screen a moment, his eyes scanning the three figures. None was Dutch Schultz. He had to get the Dutchman. That was orders. His gun was empty and he reached down and took Lulu's pistol, leaving his own – a weapon that couldn't be traced – beside Lulu. Then he remembered the guy in the washroom. That was Dutch Schultz.

The Bug knew that about four years ago, when Danny was shot, the cops had found $18,000 and more in Schultz's pocket. The Bug thought that was worthwhile loot and he went back into the washroom to search Schultz. There was a billfold with what looked like only a few dollars in it (it actually contained $1,000), and he left it.

The Bug came out of the saloon and saw people running toward the place. Mendy and Piggy were gone and he was afoot. He ducked into an alley, ran through some vacant lots and finally got back to Manhattan safely by way of the ferry. Later he reported to Lepke what had happened and Mendy and Piggy were called up on the carpet. Abandoning a comrade in such a situation was a capital offense.

Much to everyone's surprise, Mendy admitted it.

"Sure, we ran out on him," said Mendy. "People were comin' from all directions and the place was too hot. We stuck by The Bug until he'd completed the contract, which was Syndicate business. But when he went in the toilet to frisk the Dutchman and knock down a little loot, that was his business. So we took off."

Lepke upheld them. Nor was The Bug reprimanded. He'd completed his contract and individual initiative is approved of in all corporations, even Murder Inc.

Abbadabba and Landau were dead, but Schultz and Rosenkrantz, although critically wounded were both alive when police arrived. They were taken to a Newark hospital.

After police arrived, Frances, the Dutchman's wife, came to the Palace to meet her husband. She saw the crowd and assumed it was a raid. She took a train back to Manhattan. Not until she arrived there and got an early edition of a morning paper did she learn that her husband had been shot.

She wanted to go to his bedside, but she hesitated. What would the police do to her? Would they ask her questions? Would they believe her if she told them she knew nothing about her husband's activities, beyond the fact that he was in the rackets?

She thought of her two children, Nancy and John. What would happen to them if their father died? What would happen to her?

Finally she slept. When she awakened, it was noon.

The radio told her that Dutch Schultz was still alive. She must go to see him. She caught a train back to New Jersey.

On the way back she thought of her husband. He was dying. He had committed many, many sins. Her religious training as a Catholic was now uppermost in her mind. She and Schultz, strangely enough, had discussed religion a great deal. He had a thirst for knowledge about every subject. He had asked her about her religion and he was impressed by her faith.

She knew that he had carried a rosary in his pocket through the trials at Syracuse and Malone. He still had it among his effects at home.

Before she went to the hospital, she stopped and persuaded a Catholic priest to accompany her to the hospital.

Schultz was still conscious, altrough his fever was climbing.

"Arthur," she said, "will you be baptized?"

"Baptized? You mean, became a Christian?"

"Yes, dear."

"A bad Jew can be a Christian?" asked Dutch Schultz.

"We believe that baptism washes away sins," said Frances. "It is your only hope of salvation."

Dutch, his fever climbing, nodded his head. He was dying and he needed all the luck he could get. "Yes, Frances."

Arthur "Dutch Schultz" Flegenheimer was baptized.

Frances left when two police officers came into the room. One was Sergeant Luke Conlon of the Newark police and a police stenographer, F. J. Lang.

Schultz saw a newspaper in the sergeant's pocket and the headlines telling of the shooting.

"Has it been in any other papers?" he asked.

"All of them," said the sergeant. He nodded to the stenographer, who sat down at a table and began taking down the conversation. He had been instructed to write down everything the Dutchman said.

A nurse came in and took his temperature. It was 106. He was dying. Deathbed statements before witnesses can be used as evidence if the patient knows he is dying.

The nurse left and Schultz spoke in a whisper. "George, don't make no bull moves. What have you done with him? Oh mama, mama, mama. Oh, stop it. Stop it . . ."

He was delirious. The stenographer leaned forward to catch what he was saying.

"Now listen, Phil, fun is fun. Ah, please, papa. What happened to the sixteen? Oh, oh. He done it."

The stuff didn't make sense.

"John, please." Was he speaking of Johnny Torrio, the Capone aide who had recently come to New York? "Did you buy that hotel? You promised a million. Sure. Get out. I wish I knew. Please make it quick, fast and furious. Please. Fast and furious. Please help me get out." (Of the rackets?) "I'm getting my wind back, thank God. You will have to please tell him you got no case."

Dutch muttered phrases about the dot-dash system, and he gave a number, Phil 13,780. He mentioned Henry and Frankie. Then he gave what sounded like a radio commercial:

"Oh, oh, dog biscuits and when he is happy, he doesn't get

snappy. Henry, Frankie, you didn't meet him. You didn't even meet me."

After this incoherency, he stopped for breath.

Conlon leaned forward and spoke to Schultz. "Who shot you?"

"The boss himself," said Schultz weakly.

"What did he shoot you for?"

Schultz moved an arm. "I showed him, boss. Did you hear him meet me? An appertment. Appeal stuck. All right, brother."

"Was it the boss that shot you?"

"Who shot me?" Dutch asked as if he didn't know. "No one." Conlon sighed.

Schultz tried to lift himself up. "Will you get me up?" he asked the sergeant, almost lucidly. "Okay. I won't be such a big creep." The sergeant shook his head.

"I can't go through with it," Schultz went on. "Oh, and then he clips me. Come on. Cut that out. We don't owe a nickel. Hold it. Instead, hold it against him. I am a pretty good pretzler."

Schultz's voice rose in pitch. "Winifred. Department of Justice. I even got it from the department. Sir, please stop it."

"Don't holler," Conlon interrupted. "What did they shoot you for?"

"I don't know, sir," said Schultz. "Honest, I don't. I don't even know who was with me. Honest. I was in the toilet and when I reached the – the can the boy came at me. Big fellow."

"The big fellow gave it to you?"

"No. I don't know who shot me," Dutch said. "Don't, but anyone near this check. Please give me a shot. It is from the factory. I don't want harmony. I want harmony. Who give it to him? Let me in the district – fire – factory that he was nowhere near. It smoldered. There are only ten of us and there are ten million fighting somewhere of you. So get your onions up and we will throw up the truce flag. Police are here."

Schultz stopped to cough.

"Communistic . . . strike . . . baloney!" he muttered. "Honest, this is a habit I get. Sometimes I give it and sometimes I don't. The sidewalk was in trouble and the bears were in trouble and I broke it up.

"No payrolls. No walls. No coupons. That would be entirely out. Pardon me, I forgot I am plaintiff and not defendant. Look out for him. He owed me money. He owes everyone money. Why can't he just pull out and give me control?"

Once again he lapsed into silence. Then, he spoke again. "Police are looking for you all over. Be instrumental in letting us know. They are Englishmen and they are a type. I don't know what is best, they or us. Get the doll a roofing. You can play jacks. Girls do that with a softball and do tricks with it."

He sighed deeply and became poetic, "A boy has never wept, nor dashed a thousand kim."

He closed his eyes and was silent.

"How many shots were fired?" Conlon asked.

Schultz opened his eyes. "I don't know. Two thousand. Come one. Get some money in the treasury. Please, warden, what am I going to do for money? Please crack down on the Chinaman's friends and Hitler's commander."

He stared at the ceiling and said, "Mother is the best bet and don't let Satan draw you too fast."

"What did the big fellow shoot you for?" Conlon persisted.

"Him? John? Over a million. Five million dollars."

"John shot you and we will take care of John," said Conlon.

"That is what caused the trouble. I know who they are. They are French people. Oh, my memory is gone. A work relief. Police. Who gets it? I don't know and I don't want to know, but look out, it can be traced . . ."

His hands slid to the mattress and the fingers opened and shut.

"I am wobbly."

After a moment he said, "You ain't got nothing on him, but we got it on his helper."

Another fit of coughing interrupted him.

"Control yourself," said Conlon.

"But I am dying," said Schultz.

A police officer appeared in the doorway. "His wife is here, sir," he said to the sergeant.

"Send her in," said Conlon.

Frances came hesitantly into the room. She went over to the side of the bed and looked down at him. Dutch looked up at her with vacant eyes, not recognizing her.

"This is Frances," she said softly.

Schultz blinked. "Then pull me out," he said. Then suddenly recognition came into his eyes. "I'm half crazy." The recognition faded. "They dyed my shoes. Danny, please get me in the car."

Frances looked at Conlon and shook her head. Then slowly she turned and walked out of the room. She paused by the police officer who stood outside the door.

"He was always good to me," she said. "And he had the nicest smile."

In the room, Conlon worked doggedly at his task. "Who shot you?" he asked again.

"I don't know," said Schultz. "I didn't even get a look. I don't know who could have done it. Anybody." He sighed. "Please take my shoes off." His shoes were off. He wasn't dying with his boots on.

"I don't know what I'm doing here with my collection of papers. It isn't worth a nickel to two guys like you and me, but to a collector it is worth a fortune."

There was no doubt about his delirium now. His eyes were closed and he was growing weaker.

"Come on," he murmured. "Open the soap duckets. The chimney sweeps. Talk to the sword. Shut up; you got a big mouth. Please help me up. Henry . . . Max . . . come over. French-Canadian bean soup. I want to pay, Larry. Let them leave me alone."

His words were without meaning, without sense.

Arthur "Dutch Schultz" Flegenheimer slipped into unconsciousness at 6:30 on the evening of Thursday, 24 October 1935, and died two hours later. He was 34 years old.

Lulu Rosenkrantz, the fourth victim of the Palace Chop House massacre, outlived his boss by only seven hours.

Bouncer
(Charles Connolly)

Roger Francis

What happens when a hard man grows old? I met Charlie Connolly in the mid-1990s, almost half a century after his hard-knock heyday, when he was trying to prove his innocence in a famous murder. Back in 1949, he was accused of being the accomplice in the so-called Cameo case in Liverpool, in which a masked gunman shot dead two defenceless employees of a back street cinema. The police eventually arrested Connolly, claiming that he'd acted as lookout while a small-time crook called George Kelly, brandishing a gun, burst into the cinema office demanding the takings. Both men vehemently denied any involvement, but after two trials Kelly was convicted of murder and sentenced to hang; in the end, Connolly pleaded guilty to robbery in order to escape the same fate. Connolly's plea of not guilty to murder was accepted and he was jailed for ten years. On his release, Connolly continued to protest his innocence. Forty years on, he explained why to Roger Francis (b. 1948) who wrote up his story for a Sunday newspaper.

Like hundreds of bouncers, Charlie Connolly is a fighter, and proud of it. He remembers the night he knocked another doorman senseless for not letting him into a dance. But that was years ago when he was young, and quick to pile in with his fists. Now, at 73, when he smiles at the memory, you notice he's missing several front teeth. The hair may be silver and thinning, but Connolly is still tall and well set up. His easy geniality is disarming. Once, years ago, they nearly hanged Charlie Connolly for taking part in one of the most cold-blooded murders in British criminal history.

On a chilly Saturday night in March 1949, the manager of the Cameo cinema and his assistant were murdered, shot like dogs by a masked gunman in a bungled raid for the takings. After a floundering, ramshackle investigation, Connolly and a local villain called George Kelly were eventually arrested, charged and put on trial. Both protested their innocence. Kelly, identified as the gunman, was convicted and hanged. Connolly, who was supposed to have acted as lookout, was rescued from the hangman only when he was persuaded – literally on pain of death – to plead guilty to the lesser charge of robbery. He was jailed for ten years.

Almost anyone who remembers the era remembers the Cameo murder case. In an age that evokes a black and white folk memory of crime-free streets, PC Dixon and *The Blue Lamp*, it was crime of seemingly careless brutality. Confidence in the police was high. Most people thought that "if the police say he did it, he did it." But nearly fifty years on, Charlie Connolly says the police were wrong, and that he was judged and condemned simply on his reputation as a hard man. Viewed from our end of the century's telescope, the case seems pinny-and-curlers quaint, redolent of a lost England of soot and smoke in which people jumped trams and set clocks by the wireless. But Connolly has burst out of this 1940s amber with new evidence. He says it proves he was unjustly accused, the victim of a frame-up concocted by a corrupt detective. Connolly today is a man gravelled by his own conscience: did his plea of guilty to robbery seal George Kelly's fate and send an innocent man to the gallows? Nearly half a century after standing trial for a murder he says he knew nothing about, Charlie Connolly is determined to clear his name.

The facts of the killing can be stated with C major simplicity. The scene is the tiny office above the Cameo, a small back street cinema in the scruffy Liverpool suburb of Wavertree. At about 9.30 p.m. a masked gunman wearing a brown belted overcoat and a trilby hat with the brim pulled down shoots the manager Leonard Thomas and his assistant John Catterall as they cash up for the night. Thomas falls first, a bullet in the chest at point blank range and dead before he hits the floor. Catterall, walking in on the robbery, apparently tackles the gunman but falls to his knees, winged by a bullet in the hand. A second bullet rips into his chest. As he sinks to the floor, the killer fires a third shot into Catterall's back.

Downstairs, a couple of hundred people jammed in the smoky auditorium watching *Bond Street*, a noisy black-and-white thriller, hear nothing. But the sound of gunfire brings several members of the cinema staff running to the office door. As they do so, the door opens to reveal a masked man brandishing an automatic pistol. Ordering the staff to stand back, the gunman shoulders his way past, clattering down a spiral staircase to the street door below. The cinema fireman gives chase but outside, in the maze of poorly-lit streets, there's no sign of the gunman. Upstairs, the cashier and projectionist are cradling the dead and dying.

It was a frustrating and complex inquiry that unleashed one of Britain's biggest post-war manhunts: 65,000 people interviewed, 1,800 fingerprinted, 9,000 homes visited. The police came for Charlie Connolly when the inquiry seemed exhausted and spent, six months after the killings. It was 2.30 in the morning, a Friday, the last day of September. A bright pinpoint in Connolly's memory: he was making love to his wife. Then there were police cars in the street below and blue lights flashing on the bedroom window of his mother-in-law's house on the outskirts of Liverpool. "Get up and get dressed," one of the detectives said. Connolly remembers Mary, his wife, trying to conceal her nakedness from the police, clutching a limp condom and looking puzzled. At police headquarters in Dale Street, they told Charlie Connolly they were investigating the killings at the Cameo. They didn't believe he was the gunman, but they had evidence that he was the accomplice in the shadows, the unseen lookout. The proposition baffles Connolly now as much as it baffled him then. He swore then, and swears now, that he'd never been to the Cameo Cinema in his life and that he'd never met or heard of George Kelly.

When the police arrived at the cinema on the murder night, they were struck by several curious facts. The masked intruder had made his move just as the night's takings of just over £50 were being counted, so the raid seemed to have been precisely timed. The fact that the wires to the cinema's telephone had been deliberately cut, causing a delay in raising the alarm, also suggested careful planning. The gunman had fled, empty-handed, through an emergency door that couldn't be opened from the street, so he'd evidently entered the cinema from the front, maybe even queuing for and buying a ticket for 1s 6d [7½ p]. The unusual layout of the cinema (it was a converted Welsh Methodist chapel, with offices created by partitions in the original gallery) suggested that the killer must have staged some sort of reconnoitre. A casual thief, staging an opportunist raid, would surely have been defeated by such an eccentric arrangement. Whoever had done it knew his way around the cinema and the down-at-heel area in which it stood. For the Cameo killer, whoever he was, had vanished within seconds into the labyrinth of streets and alleys that criss-crossed Wavertree. The police had only the scantiest of descriptions, based on the glimpses of the four terrified cinema employees: *Man, 20 to 30 years, 5ft 8/9ins, well-built, dressed in brown tweed overcoat, brown trilby hat pulled down all round with black silk scarf used as a mask.* In a teeming seaport city of 800,000 on a Saturday night, it wasn't much to go on.

Cue the detective. Bert Balmer had been more than 20 years in the police and by the spring of 1949 was ranked at chief inspector, number two in the Liverpool CID. Quietly-spoken, with a Rotarian air of self-confidence, Balmer's instinct was to play a hunch. His first move was to call on one of his informants, a small time crook called George Kelly who, with an entourage of brothers and assorted hangers-on, liked to act the gangster, the Liverpool tough guy. Kelly was living at a cramped terraced house in Cambridge Street, set between the gasworks and railway marshalling yards at Edge Hill, not far from the Cameo Cinema. It was 11.15 a.m. when Balmer knocked, and George Kelly was still in bed. "There you are," he called to Dolly O'Malley, the woman he lived with. "Didn't I say they'd come calling?"

What Balmer wanted was information. Balmer reckoned that if there had been word on the street about the Cameo killings, Kelly would have picked it up. "Yes," nodded Kelly, "I heard all about it." Balmer knew that Kelly, 27 years old, swarthy and muscular, fitted the description of the masked gunman. "So," said Balmer, "where were *you* last night?"

Kelly immediately told Balmer that he'd spent the whole day drinking in various pubs, and that by 9.30 p.m., the time of the killings at the Cameo Cinema, he'd been "well bevvied". A search of Kelly's house revealed neither coat, mask nor gun. Right away, one of Kelly's drinking cronies backed up Kelly's story. Balmer was in two minds about George Kelly. While he regarded him as a reliable and regular source of lowlife intelligence, he knew that Kelly's criminal record, while extensive, disclosed no history of owning or using a weapon. Moreover, Kelly's alibi seemed impregnable. Bert Balmer reported back to his boss.

The head of the CID, Chief Superintendent Tommy Smith, was already gloomily reviewing the failure of his fingerprint branch to match a couple of smudged prints found at the cinema to any of the 30,000 sets of prints held in the city's police records. By Monday morning, Smith was forced to concede that "there was nothing left in the office which provided any real clue". It was a lacklustre, impoverished approach which was to typify the entire investigation. Certainly for the next two weeks, while detectives conducted hundreds of house-to-house inquiries in the Wavertree area, Smith and Balmer were unable to report any significant progress in the hunt for the Cameo gunman.

Looking back, the first breakthrough in the case seems almost risible, something torn from the pages of a cheap detective thriller. But on Monday 4 April, fifteen days after the killings, the police received an anonymous letter. It was hand-written in small child-like characters. "It says in the papers you are looking for one man," the letter observed, adding: "I know three and a girl, not including myself, who heard about his plan for the robbery." The writer offered to name the Cameo killer "if you give me your word I won't be charged." The police were instructed to guarantee this assurance in the personal column of the *Liverpool Echo*. After a hurried conference with the chief constable of Liverpool, Chief Superintendent Smith authorised an advertisement to appear in that night's edition: "Anonymous letter received. Promise definitely given." A sprat to catch a mackerel.

But no one came forward. Smith waited a day or two, then advertised again. Still nothing. Appeals in the news columns of the papers failed to flush out the sender of the mysterious letter. Just as the detectives were writing it off as the work of a crank, hungry for notoriety, events took another curious turn.

On Monday 2 May, a small-time crook called Donald Johnson told the police that he too had important information about the Cameo case. His problem was that he and his brother were locked up at Wallasey police station, across the River Mersey from Liverpool, unable to stump up bail on a mugging charge. Two detectives immediately drove to Wallasey. Don Johnson turned out to be a slim young man of 22, with a shock of long fair hair. To their amazement, Johnson, without further ado, named the Cameo gunman as a Charlie Dugan, whom Johnson had met when both men were inmates at Walton Gaol in Liverpool in 1945. Then Johnson appeared to crumple. "Oh, it's no good telling lies," he went on, apparently in some distress. "Dugan isn't his real name. But if I tell you the truth, I'll put a rope round his neck." Johnson explained that he and Dugan had gone to the Cameo on the murder night, Dugan armed with a gun. Bored with the film, Johnson had left at about 9.20 p.m., a quarter of an hour before Dugan slipped from his seat, crept up to the manager's office and shot the two men dead.

Balmer and Smith were summoned at once. Johnson explained that he was in a difficulty. He'd named Charlie Dugan as the Cameo gunman, but he'd promised Dugan "on the Holy Eucharist" that he wouldn't betray him. Johnson persuaded the detectives themselves to stand bail for him in a surety of £20 so that he could find Dugan, free himself from his promise and turn in both the gun and the gunman. Accordingly, Johnson was bailed by a magistrate and driven in a police car to Liverpool. Before turning Johnson out on to the streets, the police produced a local Catholic priest to reassure him that the promise he'd made to Dugan was, in the circumstances, not binding. This spiritual guidance was wasted on Don Johnson. Instead of producing either Dugan or the gun, Johnson spent the next few days (and nights) at the home of his brother's wife, stringing along the exasperated detectives with a series of broken promises. Eventually, Chief Superintendent Smith's patience ran out, and Don Johnson was rearrested. Johnson was remanded in custody to await trial on a charge of harbouring the Cameo gunman. It was the middle of May, Friday the thirteenth. For the investigating detectives, it seemed an unlikely moment for a lucky break. But once again, the unexpected happened. Once again, a local lowlife was asking to see Bert Balmer. This time it was a woman.

Jackie Dickson gave her age as 23. She was known to the Liverpool police as a prostitute, a Lime Street "queen" of the lowest grade. Because Dickson, a sixpence-a-trick bottle blonde, was habitually broke, she had to steal to survive and she'd been arrested that morning for shoplifting. Dickson had a proposition for the police, and it concerned that anonymous letter that had been gathering dust on Bert Balmer's desk for five fruitless weeks. Dickson announced that she'd read in the papers about the letter, and was ready to part with some information about it provided the detectives agreed to drop the shoplifting charge.

She was driven to police headquarters but Dickson, her painted face clenched with fear, refused to make a formal statement. "They've threatened to kill me if I open my mouth," she explained. Pencil poised, Balmer told Jackie Dickson to start naming names. "Go and see Charlie Connolly," she said. "He knows all about it."

Balmer was puzzled. He'd never heard of Connolly. Connolly's criminal file disclosed a brief and undistinguished history of petty crime, nothing recent. But, asking around, Balmer learned that Connolly had a reputation as a street fighter. It seemed this Connolly was a hard hitter who, when he was out of work, drifted in and out of the Lime Street snooker halls and bars, killing time. Connolly was brought in for questioning. Where had he been on the night of the Cameo shootings?

Connolly thought back to March, when he'd been employed as a packer at a seed crushing mill near the Liverpool docks. "Working at Bibby's," he said, adding that he "didn't get off until after 10 p.m." Balmer then confronted him with the anonymous letter. "I've written no letter," Connolly protested, "because I know nothing about it." But Connolly did admit knowing the prostitute Dickson, at least by sight. Unkempt and crude, she was the roughest of all the girls who cruised the bars and billiard halls of Lime Street. "Oh, I know Jackie Dickson all right," he said, picking out her mug shot in a folder. Balmer told Connolly that his alibi for the murder night would be checked. In the meantime, he was free to leave.

Guilty or not, Connolly kept his cool. But what he didn't know was the extent to which Dickson was already implicating him in the Cameo killings. According to Dickson, Connolly had gone on the Cameo job to keep "douse" [watch] for the gunman Kelly. Dickson's story was that Connolly had taken her into his confidence because he was always pestering her for sex.

She told Balmer how she'd bumped into Connolly near Lewis's department store a few days after the Cameo murders. Connolly had taken her for a cup of tea, and had pulled a handkerchief from his pocket, telling her to "give these to Kelly". Dickson could feel something folded inside, but it was only later, when she got home, that she saw that the handkerchief contained 23 rounds of ammunition. Dickson had panicked. "Give them to Kelly yourself," she told him when they met again the next day. She claimed Connolly had confessed to running off on hearing the first shots, not expecting Kelly to use the gun. Now, said Dickson, Connolly was terrified and desperate. Connolly had begged her to go with him to London, but she'd refused. As for the letter, Connolly had explained how he had devised a subterfuge to make the police think it had been written by a woman. He'd used words and phrases which he thought made the writer sound woman-like: "I'm scared . . . he wants me to go away with him." Finally he'd rubbed some lipstick on the envelope.

Meanwhile the police were checking Charlie Connolly's alibi that he'd been at work at the time of the Cameo killings. Bibby's records showed this to be untrue. Connolly was questioned again when he called, by appointment, at the CID office on the following Monday, but merely shrugged off the discrepancy. "I say I was at work," he told detectives, "and you say I wasn't. If I wasn't, then I don't know where I was. That's all there is to it." The listening police seemed to accept that Connolly may have muddled up his dates, and at this point seemed to show no interest in pursuing Connolly's alleged involvement. When Dickson saw Bert Balmer later that day, she was furious. "You've let [Connolly] go," she ranted. "I told you to get Connolly. Let him talk. If you think I'm telling lies," she added, "have a look at that letter and you'll find lipstick on it." Balmer had run forensic tests on the envelope and already knew this to be true. But a day or two later, the inquiry suffered two unexpected setbacks. Firstly, the results of tests on Connolly's handwriting showed beyond doubt that he had not written the anonymous letter. Secondly, after warning Balmer that she'd be killed if she talked, Jackie Dickson jumped bail on the shoplifting charge and vanished from her usual beat on Lime Street. Inquiries soon revealed that she'd fled Liverpool altogether.

By late May, the police were in a fix. They had two separate witnesses naming two different suspects, both called Charlie. They had two different stories, wholly irreconcilable. One concerned a man called Dugan, who couldn't be found or didn't exist. The other concerned a man called Connolly, who agreed he knew the prostitute Dickson but who seemed airily unconcerned that his alibi for the murder night had been demolished at a stroke. Who were the police to believe? At this stage they evidently believed Don Johnson's tale about Dugan, since the police continued to press a case against Johnson, accusing him of being an accessory after the fact of murder by harbouring the killer. But by the time the case came to trial in the middle of June, Johnson had retracted his story. Now he said he'd invented Dugan, had made no promises, sacred or otherwise, and had made up the line about putting a rope around his neck "to make the story more plausible". Johnson's trial lasted two short, farcical days before the case was thrown out on the direction of the judge. Mr Justice Lynskey said it was clear that by standing Johnson's bail, the police had offered him an inducement. Johnson was driven back to prison, where he'd just started a four year sentence for mugging a workman for his week's wages.

It was now three months since the double murder at the Cameo Cinema, and in spite of the massive scale of the inquiry, the publice brouhaha and the best efforts of the police and courts, no gunman had been arrested or charged. Bert Balmer had cast a suspicious eye on George Kelly scarcely twelve hours after the shooting, but his alibi seemed watertight. Charlie Connolly had been questioned in the middle of May, but since then he'd heard no more about it. The detectives had found – then managed to lose again – Jackie Dickson, the prostitute who said she'd posted the anonymous letter, but they were unable to discover either the identity of the author or Dickson's present whereabouts. It was an unimpressive result. Worst of all, the police had been made to look foolish by an out-of-work window cleaner called Don Johnson and the chimerical Charlie Dugan.

As summer wore on, the police grew increasingly frustrated. Balmer continued to watch George Kelly as he swaggered around the town with his small-time criminal cronies. Charlie Connolly had packed in his job at Bibby's and had worked for a while as a railway porter. By September, Connolly had drifted on to the dole and had been seen around the milk bars and snooker halls of Lime Street. The humiliation heaped on the police by the Johnson debacle still smouldered in the memory. Then, on a mid-September morning, the telephone rang on Bert Balmer's desk at Dale Street police headquarters. The inquiry was about to take another switchback swerve.

The caller was a police officer in the neighbouring Lancashire force. Apparently, a man called Robert Graham was asking to see Balmer concerning the Cameo murder case. Balmer drove up to Preston. Graham turned out to be a lanky, thin-faced man in his early forties. He'd just been released after serving eight months of a twelve-month sentence at Walton Gaol in Liverpool. Graham explained that in the course of his duties as a cleaner in the prison hospital, he'd got to know Donald Johnson, a prisoner from Liverpool who'd figured in the harbouring case in June. Graham told Balmer that he was willing to make a statement about this man. It seemed Johnson was no longer talking about a mystery man called Charlie Dugan. According to Graham, Johnson had confessed to carrying out the Cameo killings himself.

Graham's story was that Johnson had confided in him in the days leading up to his trial for harbouring. Johnson had said that if his lawyers failed to have the case thrown out, he'd tell the truth and confess to being the Cameo gunman. Johnson told Graham "he'd be topped any time, but he wasn't going to do life. He'd tell the truth and get it over." According to Robert Graham, when the case against Johnson collapsed, he returned to Walton in high spirits and bragged about how he did the killings at the Cameo. "I can tell you now," Johnson told Graham, "because they can't try me again . . . unless they find the gun." According to Graham, Johnson described running out of the cinema and then "mooching around the district" still carrying the gun before being stopped by a policeman who asked for his identity card.

Bert Balmer told Smith, his boss, that he was satisfied Graham was telling the truth. "Whether Johnson is," added Balmer, "is, of course, a different matter." This was a curious view for Balmer to take, since the police at Preston had warned him that Graham was an inveterate conman with an unstable mental history.

While Balmer and Smith pondered the value – if any – of Robert Graham's story of Johnson's "confession", events again took an unexpected twist. On the last Saturday in September, exactly one hundred days after the collapse of the Johnson case, the missing Jackie Dickson was traced to Manchester and arrested. She'd been living in a rundown flat with her pimp, a whey-faced young housebreaker of 23 with a lacerating stutter called Jimmy North-am. Both were terrified out of their wits at the prospect of returning to Liverpool. "I daren't tell, I daren't tell," Jackie Dickson wept, incoherent with fright. "They said they'd kill me and I know they would." Bert Balmer showed her into his office at police headquarters and tried to calm her down. For five full days, she and Northam were questioned repeatedly, but neither would make a statement. It was the cue for another deal. Following a word to the magistrate from Bert Balmer, Jackie Dickson was given a conditional discharge on the shoplifting charge, still hanging over her from the spring. In the light of Dickson's ill-health (she was said to be suffering from tuberculosis), she was also conditionally discharged for jumping bail. As soon as the case was over, Dickson sent for Balmer.

"Can the police protect me if I tell you what happened at the Cameo?"

Balmer nodded.

"Well," said Jackie Dickson, "I'll tell you the whole truth."

The men the police were looking for, she said, were George Kelly and Charlie Connolly. She knew this, she explained, because she and Northam had been in on the Cameo plot.

In lengthy statements, Dickson and Northam both admitted to being present when the raid was planned in the back room of a Liverpool pub called the Beehive. Apparently, it had been a spur-of-the-moment venture, devised by Charlie Connolly who had spoken of "a smashing place called the Cameo" which would be the ideal target for a robbery. It was Connolly, according to Dickson and Northam, who had decided that the raid would have to be an armed hold-up, but Kelly who had produced an automatic gun from his pocket. They would do it there and then, that night. Kelly would do the hold-up, Connolly would be the lookout man. Kelly, feeling chilly, borrowed Jimmy Northam's brown, belted overcoat. Northam was asked to go too, but stayed in the pub, having only been released that morning from prison after serving three months for larceny. Dickson said she walked with Kelly and Connolly as far as the tram stop but, becoming uneasy, "took a tumble to myself" and went back to join Northam in the pub where he was celebrating his release in the company of a Scandinavian prostitute called Norwegian Margie. Her contribution to the Cameo enterprise had been to lend Kelly a black silk scarf to mask his face.

The police pounced. Within an hour of Jackie Dickson signing her statement, detectives were hammering on the door of the house on the outskirts of the city where Charlie Connolly was in bed with his wife. While Mary Connolly fussed upstairs with the couple's baby daughter, Connolly himself was driven to Liverpool police headquarters. Curiously, the police made no parallel move to arrest George Kelly, the man said to have pulled the trigger.

Connolly was told he'd been arrested over the Cameo killings. He again protested his innocence, repeating that he'd never been to the Cameo in his life. "Tell me the strength," he demanded. "I have a right to know all the details." Connolly was shown to a cell and locked up. George Kelly was arrested the following morning. "I never had a gun in my life," was Kelly's indignant response. "I don't know how to fire one." Kelly was told that Charles Connolly had been arrested too. "I don't know Charles Connolly," said Kelly. That afternoon, Jackie Dickson picked Kelly out at an identity parade. On his way back to the cells, Balmer had arranged for the two suspects to confront each other. Connolly had his back turned when Kelly was led in, but straight away Kelly called out loudly: "You've never seen me in your life before, have you? You don't know me at all."

"No," Connolly replied, "I don't."

On the face of it, there was every reason why they *might* have known each other. Both came from large Liverpool-Irish families. Kelly was raised in the Bull Ring, a rookery of slum flats behind Lime Street Station. He'd been known to the police since he was ten, but he wasn't in serious trouble until 1942, when he was in the Navy. After jumping ship, Kelly had picked up a woman in a Liverpool pub. When she refused his drunken advances, he punched her in the face. As she lay bleeding on the floor, Kelly kicked her in the stomach. At war's end, he had the unusual distinction of being court-martialled twice in one day, first on five counts of desertion and again for wrecking the roof of his cell. Discharged with ignominy, Kelly drifted back into a dead-end existence in Liverpool, taking odd jobs or helping his mother at her fruit barrow near Central Station.

Connolly's family lived near Liverpool's old Chinatown. Connolly, too, was in the Navy, but an enlisted man who boasted six years' blameless service along with five campaign medals. His ships had chased enemy submarines in the Indian Ocean and drawn German artillery fire on D-Day. As an amateur boxer in the Navy, he'd fought 60 opponents and never lost a fight. Demobbed in 1946, he immediately signed on in the Merchant Navy and had only been back in civvy street just over a year before the Cameo case. Connolly's problem was that he led with his fists, and couldn't resist wading in if he saw a fight in the street. He'd run up a couple of convictions for brawling, but now that he had a working wife and young daughter, life had settled down into a comfortable routine. Connolly took labouring jobs where he could, and filled the rest of his time drifting between the snooker rooms and milk bars of Lime Street, or in dance halls.

When Connolly appeared in court the morning after his arrest, dressed in his green pullover, khaki shirt and brown jacket, he had two days' stubble growth and looked tired and drawn. Bewildered, he propped himself against the rail of the dock. "I have a right to know who's supposed to have given evidence against me and implicated me in this," he declared, before sinking on to a chair in the dock and burying his head in his hands. Connolly's tie had been confiscated. Kelly, too, appeared open-necked and unshaven in a cream shirt and light brown jacket, and sat anxiously biting his lip as the prosecutor outlined the police case against the two men.

It was pretty thin. The problem for the police was that the case turned on the evidence of Jackie Dickson and Jimmy Northam, two self-confessed accomplices in the planning of the Cameo raid who'd both been offered immunity from prosecution in return for their story. There was no corroborating evidence of any substance, and no forensic evidence to tie either man to the scene of the shootings. Bert Balmer's 25-page report on the case dropped on to Tommy Smith's desk exactly a week before the start of committal proceedings. Balmer was candid; the case would stand or fall on the testimony of Dickson and Northam, two "unfortunates" with criminal records. The unwritten thought that underpinned Balmer's *résumé* of the evidence was that the case might well be thrown out by the magistrate and that Kelly and Connolly would walk free from court.

Both Smith and Balmer were desperate for more evidence. Balmer's problem on the street was that no one would give him any. The police needed to prove that Kelly and Connolly were, in Balmer's constabularian phrase, "constant associates". Balmer had already complained that the inquiry had been hampered because none of the other raggle-taggle thieves and prostitutes the police had interviewed dared to testify. What haunted the detectives was the risk of a re-run of the Johnson fiasco, public humiliation and an empty dock. With time running out, Bert Balmer simply couldn't afford to run such a risk. He needed to shore up his case, and he needed Kelly and Connolly firmly implicated not just in the planning and execution of the Cameo raid but also in its immediate aftermath. It was Balmer's neck as well as theirs. It was time to turn the screw.

Dickson and Northam were soon busily giving additional statements to the police, supplying details which they claimed to have forgotten before. As if by magic, both of them now recalled an entirely new sequence in the story, in which everyone involved in the plot had met in the White Star pub the next day. Kelly, they said, had told them in vainglorious detail how he did the murders and had warned the others to keep quiet. He'd threatened Connolly in particular, calling him "a yellow bastard" for running away and ridiculing Connolly's gibbering plan for leaving the country. Kelly had scornfully advised him to get an alibi. Balmer was jubilant. The story sounded strong. There was even, by way of corroborating detail, a mention of Balmer's own role in events on that first Sunday. "I had that bastard Balmer up at our place this morning," Kelly is supposed to have snarled. "If I'd still had the gun, he wouldn't have stood there so cocksure of himself." In mid-October, Dickson and Northam were led, line by line, through their evidence at the proceedings to commit Kelly and Connolly for trial at the assizes. The magistrate had no hesitation in remanding the defendants to Walton Gaol while preparations went ahead for a full-scale trial. This would take place in Liverpool in the New Year.

The remand to Walton turned out to be significant. Towards the end of November, Bert Balmer heard again from Robert Graham, the nark from Preston who claimed to have heard Don Johnson's "confession" to the Cameo murders. Graham, an habitual crook, was back in Walton on remand himself, and had returned to his task as a cleaner in the hospital wing. This was where Kelly and Connolly, also remand prisoners, were being held. Robert Graham said he had some more information for Balmer, who hurried up to Walton to interview Graham. Yes, he would make a statement, and yes, he would appear as a witness. Once again, Graham's story concerned a confession. But whereas in June it had been Don Johnson confessing to the Cameo killings, now it was Kelly and Connolly who were doing the confessing.

Graham told Balmer that since Kelly and Connolly were being held in separate cells and weren't allowed to exercise together, they used him as a go-between to pass messages to each other. Graham told Balmer that both Kelly and Connolly had singly and separately confessed to him their parts in the Cameo killings. According to Graham, Kelly boasted he'd been in his local pub, the Leigh Arms, having a drink five minutes after the shooting. The way

Kelly put it, according to Graham, crystallized Kelly's plight. "My life," he'd confided, "hangs on those five minutes."

No matter that Graham was a liar with a psychiatric history, who was still being treated for an undisclosed mental condition. Here was the independent corroborative evidence that Balmer had been hoping for, evidence that stood apart from the stories of Dickson and Northam. At their trial, both Kelly and Connolly strenuously denied having anything to do with Graham. They pointed out that they had no need to use him as a messenger since they were able to hold conversations at night from their respective cells, even though the cells were separated by a corridor. The prosecution rejected this claim, leaving the entire case against Kelly and Connolly resting on the testimony of three people, Dickson, Northam and Graham, all of them criminals.

The trial began on 12 January 1950 and ran for thirteen days, to become what was then the longest criminal trial in English legal history. Public interest was intense. In the witness box, both Kelly and Connolly maintained their innocence and gave strong accounts of themselves. But the prosecution witnesses also clung to their stories, even under fierce cross-examination. The defence pointed out that everything in Robert Graham's story was already in the public domain and had been since the massively reported committal hearing. His evidence contained nothing new. As for Graham's earlier "confession" story at the Johnson trial, the judge ruled it inadmissible. The jury was confused and failed to agree.

Mr Justice Oliver ordered that Kelly and Connolly would be tried again, separately this time, and that George Kelly would be tried first. The ruling dismayed Charlie Connolly and his lawyers. The evidence against Kelly was the same, but this time a new jury found him guilty and a new judge, Cassels, sentenced him to death. Connolly was next. "I knew as soon as Kelly was convicted," he says, "that I'd got no chance."

Although no one ever suggested that he'd been anything more than a lookout, an accomplice, the position in law was that if the case against Connolly were proved, he too would be guilty of murder and would automatically face the death sentence. Although his involvement in the Cameo murders was purely on the evidence of convicted lowlifes, Connolly's prospects looked gloomy. The night before his second trial, Connolly was visited by his defence counsel, Edmund Rowson KC. Rowson told him that the court would consider a change of plea. If Charlie Connolly pleaded not guilty to murder and the jury found him guilty, he – like Kelly – would be sentenced to hang. If he pleaded guilty to the lesser charge of robbery, he'd go to prison for ten years.

Connolly's position was acute. If he stuck to his guns and pleaded not guilty to murder, he risked the same fate as Kelly. But pleading guilty to the lesser charge destroyed the credibility of Connolly's defence and blew apart his protestations of innocence. "But the result would be that my life would be saved," Connolly reflects today. "No man in his right mind would gamble with his own life." Connolly's mother went to see him, and told him she'd rather have him alive then dead.

What would be the effect of a change of plea on George Kelly's appeal? Connolly urgently put the question to his barrister. Rowson's emphatic reply was that it would have no effect at all. Kelly's appeal would be based on the ground that the judge misdirected the jury. Nothing about Connolly's case would be mentioned.

"All right," said Connolly, "I'll give it some thought."

Rowson stood up and smashed his fist on the table. "Good God, man, don't you understand? I'm trying to save your life!"

Connolly agonized all night. Only when he was in the taxi taking him to court the following morning did he make up his mind to plead not guilty to murder but guilty to robbery. Convicted, Charlie Connolly duly found himself sentenced to ten years in gaol for the theft of £50 (even though no money was actually stolen in the bungled raid on the Cameo).

The consequences for George Kelly's appeal were disastrous. Connolly's change of plea amounted to an admission of guilt and, if Connolly was guilty, then it followed that Kelly was guilty also. Robert Graham's "independent" evidence was reckoned as crucial. Lord Chief Justice Goddard declared that it put Kelly's guilt beyond doubt. Shortly afterwards, Graham, the incorrigible and mentally unstable liar, received a remission of sentence. The Crown's star witnesses, Jackie Dickson and her pimp Jimmy "Stutty" Northam, were each awarded £20 from public funds by the trial judge. Dickson went on to sell her story to the *News of the World*. George Kelly was hanged on the morning of 28 March 1950. Having promised to meet his doom singing his mother's favourite Irish ditty, in the event Kelly was seized with fear and shat himself on the scaffold.

At the suburban club where he works part time as a doorman,

Connolly has scarcely touched his orange squash. "Kelly was a very vain little man, a bragger and a boaster, who wanted to be somebody but ended up a nobody. His last words to me were: 'Look after yourself, Charlie . . .'" On the day his verdict was due, Kelly told Connolly that he knew the case the case was running against him. "Kelly was a criminal who knew how a case played. I had a different attitude. I'd never been in prison before and I knew there was no way in the world that I'd be convicted of a crime I didn't do." Five days later, Connolly changed his plea and he was sentenced to ten years. He'd effectively convicted himself, but rescued himself from the brink of the scaffold. "The strongest instinct in a man prevailed," Connolly concedes, "and I saved my own neck."

He remains uncertain about the effect of his decision on Kelly's appeal, but accepts that it destroyed the credibility of his own defence witnesses. "It also bolstered the credibility of all those narks, crooks and prostitutes who told all those lies in court."

People are starting to arrive at the club, and Charlie Connolly is nodding affably at some of the regulars. Everyone seems to know him. "I've got a reputation," he smiles. "Not a violent reputation, a popular one." He searches for all the grace a septuagenarian can muster when reminded of his reputation fifty years ago as a hard hitter on Lime Street. "I can still knock heads together if necessary, and defend myself against the best," Connolly murmurs confidentially. "But if I can avoid trouble, I believe it's better to use brain than brawn."

Charlie Connolly served six and a half years of his sentence. He was released with maximum remission for good conduct in September 1956. He maintains his innocence to this day, but accepts that his decision to change his plea and save his own neck had the effect of condemning him in the eyes of many who've watched the case and wondered. There are other qualms too. His claim to have been working at Bibby's on the night of the crime was patently false; it also turned out that Connolly had handed in his notice two days after the murders. A second alibi canvassed in court that he was at a dance taking part in a rumba competition turned out to be hopelessly vague, muddled and impossible to prove. The prosecution also produced evidence that shortly after the murders, Connolly applied for an assisted passage to Australia. The application form itself was produced, and is clearly dated 31 March, twelve days after the crime. Connolly's explanation that he'd filled the form in months before – but only posted it at the end of March – sounds feeble. On the other hand, none of these points conclusively places Charlie Connolly outside the Cameo Cinema on the murder night. Moreover, of the 44 witnesses for the prosecution at his joint trial with Kelly, the first 30 never even mentioned Connolly.

Some questions remain unanswered. Perhaps the most inconvenient, from Connolly's point of view, is this: even allowing for a muddled story about working at Bibby's on the night of the crime, it was another four months before Connolly was called on to come up with an alibi, but he failed to do so. Even when charged at the end of September, it was only when he was locked up in prison on remand that he remembered he'd been at a dance. When it turned out that his own family were almost the only people who had any recollection of this, it seemed less than compelling.

What runs in Connolly's favour? No one actually *saw* an accomplice keeping watch outside the Cameo, although the police interviewed a handful of people who all reported seeing someone leaving the cinema by the front door. But these sightings fall far short of proof. No one could identify this second man, and in any case, what was an accomplice doing coming out of the lighted foyer when he could have kept watch with greater discretion in the nearby shadows? One witness, an RAF serviceman who saw such a man leaving the cinema, not only put the time at 10 p.m. (when the place was swarming with police and any accomplice would have been long gone) but also, six months later, failed to identify Connolly. The police believed this was because Connolly had since had his hair cut and his sideburns removed, but photographs from the time don't bear this out.

Apart from the Dickson–Northam testimony, no evidence whatsoever places Connolly either at the Cameo, the Beehive on the night of the crime or the White Star pub on the day following. There was no conclusive evidence that Connolly ever knew George Kelly. The store detective at Lewis's, an ex-policeman called Sangster, obliged Balmer with a statement that the two men had knocked around Liverpool together. But while he claimed to have seen the pair together "at least six times" the same Sangster was unable to identify Connolly's wife Mary. Since Mary Connolly had worked under Sangster's nose as a waitress in Lewis's cafe, the defence had no trouble casting doubt on Sangster's powers of observation.

The Johnson case, with its ready-made solution so tantalizingly uncheckable, provides Charlie Connolly with all the answers at a stroke. In the event, it was no more than a mirage.

For years Connolly spoke of his ordeal only discreetly, not knowing how to break cover to try to clear his name. In 1990, he met a retired Liverpool businessman, Lou Santangeli, who'd read about the Cameo controversy. Santangeli set about studying the case, spending much time and money reading the documents and reports, making copies and talking to Charlie Connolly. Convinced that Connolly couldn't possibly have been on the Cameo job, Santangeli took up his cause. He set about trying to find new evidence to put the question of Connolly's guilt beyond doubt. Santangeli has been astonished by his own discoveries.

Lou Santangeli looked again at the evidence of Robert Graham, who testified at the trial of Kelly and Connolly that both men had confessed to the Cameo killings while on remand at Walton Gaol. Kelly and Connolly had repudiated Graham's tale that he had passed messages between them, pointing out that their two cells – although about twelve yards apart and separated by a passageway – were close enough together to let the man in one cell hold a conversation with the man in the other. Messengers, they argued, weren't needed. Graham, on the other hand, had testified on oath that the geography of the two cells would have made communication "absolutely impossible". The point was so vital that it had been drawn to the attention of the jury by the judge at Kelly's trial. It struck Lou Santangeli that neither judge nor jury had been allowed to test the assertion for themselves.

Two years ago, shortly before a renovation scheme changed the 1940s layout, Santangeli was given permission to visit the area of the hospital wing at Walton Gaol where Kelly and Connolly had been held more than forty years before. With Lou Santangeli went the Liverpool playwright Bill Morrison, who was researching a radio play on the Cameo case. Both men were immediately struck by the same thing. Both had anticipated that the two cells would have been furnished with heavy solid doors, and that Graham may have been right to claim that once locked up and separated even by a short corridor, Kelly and Connolly would have been *incommunicado*. What Santangeli and Morrison found demolished that notion at once. Because both defendants were remanded on a capital charge, they were classed as potential suicides and held in cells with *open barred gates* so that prison staff could keep them under surveillance. Not only was conversation between the two cells entirely possible, it was actually helped by an echo.

So much for Robert Graham's story, evidence which, according to Lord Goddard at Kelly's appeal, had put Kelly's guilt beyond doubt. So much for Goddard's ringing endorsement of Graham's evidence. So much for Balmer's belief that Graham was telling the truth. So much, perhaps, for Bert Balmer. Connolly believes that he was bent, and it's a view shared by a several villains, still living in Liverpool, who remember the case and the failure of the police to make an early arrest. Connolly has traced and talked to them; his belief is that when Balmer first questioned him in the middle of May, "the police were simply fishing to see if I *did* have anything to do with it. When the Johnson case collapsed, Balmer mapped out a plan to frame me and Kelly, and blackmailed Dickson and Northam into perjuring themselves to get a result." One of Kelly's old drinking mates, tracked down by Connolly, declared that Balmer may well have written the so-called anonymous letter himself as the first move in such a plan.

The charitable view is that Balmer was investigating a difficult case and operating in the feverish post-war atmosphere of a blitzed and bustling seaport. The city was heaving with visiting servicemen in search of a good time. In the pubs, picturedromes and fried fish shops, whores like Jackie Dickson and Norwegian Margie could pick up dozens a night. There was an air of impermanence; alliances were casual and fleeting. Rationing, even four years after the end of the war, meant a flourishing black market, with deals struck day and night in a town where everyone seemed touched by corruption. Anything could be fixed, even a murder case. Liverpool legend speaks of a corrupt and criminal relationship between Kelly and Balmer which detonated when Kelly tried to double-cross his handler over a deal. Kelly's mother is known to have run a string of black market rackets from her flower stall outside Central Station. Kelly's paramour, Dolly O'Malley, figured in it too, and Balmer was reportedly smitten by her himself. Was it fear or frustration that prompted Kelly to blurt out at one white-knuckled moment of the investigation: "If it's the last thing I do, I'll get you for this, Balmer"?

Round the rim of this story runs a suspicion that Kelly and Connolly were framed. Balmer may have been corrupt, and willing to fabricate evidence, to invent a story in order to spare the blushes of a clueless CID and to get a result. Charlie Connolly certainly thinks so. Old timers who remember Balmer agree that he was always cool, always confident. "Always a chancer," said one. "Secretive too, a man who had his own methods, his own way of doing the job. Not like the others." If Balmer thought he had the right man, he wasn't above "elaborating" a case. "But this was general," explained one retired officer who admired Balmer. "In those days, a policeman's word was law. They were different times. Nobody questioned how cases were done, and certainly not Balmer." In the 1960s, Balmer wound up deputy chief constable of Liverpool, and retired after more than forty years in the force. He died in 1970.

For nearly half a century, Charles Connolly has been asking himself why Jackie Dickson and Jimmy Northam, egged on by the police, picked on him and Kelly to be the fall-guys. But what haunts Connolly still, nearly half a century later, is the possibility that his change of plea cost Kelly his life. When Kelly appealed against the death sentence, how could Goddard, the sadistic Lord Chief Justice" with an unlovely relish for the gallows", have wiped from his mind that Kelly's alleged accomplice, Connolly, had pleaded guilty to his part in the crime? "The state blackmailed an innocent man to choose between life and death," says Lou Santangeli. "It's inconceivable that our legal system could possibly visit such a gross injustice on two totally innocent men."

After the case, both Dickson and Northam disappeared. Jimmy Northam married in 1951, changed his name, had a family and ran a successful motor business in another area of Merseyside. He died of a heart attack in 1989. Jackie Dickson, racked with tuberculosis at the time of the Cameo case, has never been heard of since. No one ever knew why she should have given the police the name of Charlie Connolly, and her word remains his only proven link to the case.

Who was the gunman? No one saw the shooting and no one saw his face. There virtually no forensic evidence in the ransacked office at the Cameo. No gun was ever found. No witnesses, aside from the discreditable Dickson and Northam – placed either Kelly or Connolly at the scene. Singularly, the police's very first suspect, George Kelly, turned out to be the man convicted of the killing and hanged a year later. "Bearing in mind the total absence of any firm, reliable and independent evidence," observes Lou Santangeli, "the odds of securing a conviction against the very first suspect must be millions to one."

If Connolly and Kelly didn't do it, who did? Connolly himself is phlegmatic, saying he could name names if he chose but it would just be speculation. It's known that Jackie Dickson lived for a time with Kelly's brother Joey. Connolly wonders if Joey may have been the lookout man. "Joey Kelly looked a bit like me, so maybe when she saw me in the street, she tried to pass me off to the police as the gunman's accomplice." That suggests that George Kelly may have known more than he let on.

What of Don Johnson? Although no further action was taken following the collapse of the harbouring case, he stayed in prison to serve four years "corrective training" for mugging the man at New Brighton. His brother George (known as Judd) was bound over for the same offence. Johnson told various people at Walton Gaol that Judd had committed the Cameo murders, but that since Judd was married with children, Johnson himself was prepared to carry the can. Speaking of Judd a few days before his harbouring trial, he told a prison officer at Walton that "he has more to lose than I have." Johnson admitted idolizing Judd's wife Florrie. Letters that have since come to light bear this out. "Judd will get off," Johnson wrote to Florrie, "I assure you on that. I made a sacrifice as you know." At the end of May, Johnson told a fellow prisoner in Walton, a man called McBride, that Judd had done it and given him the gun. "Apparently," McBride reported, "his wife knows all about it."

In September 1988, Don Johnson, by then a retired factory hand, dropped dead on a visit to the South Coast World theme park at Bognor Regis. He was 61. His criminal record dated back to 1935 when he was just eight years old. His surviving family say they knew nothing of Johnson's link with the Cameo case.

Can Connolly still clear his name? His most important piece of evidence – George Kelly – was hanged by the state. Connolly isn't the first man to claim to be innocent who confessed to a crime he hadn't committed. The late Timothy Evans, a former tenant at 10 Rillington Place, is another example. Connolly is desperate to prove he didn't take part in a wicked and callous crime. The new evidence is persuasive, but it is notoriously hard to prove a negative, especially in a case so old in which almost everyone else is dead and clues have long since frozen over. Why did he not make more of a fuss at the time? Connolly says he was poorly advised, but that was then and this is now. What might yet tip the scales in his favour is the thought that a guilty man, having served his time, would have simply put it all behind him, perhaps changed his name and started a new life. If Connolly was the lookout on the Cameo murder, why would he wish to prolong his own agony?

Nearly half a century on, does it really matter? On two counts, the answer has to be: Yes. True, both Kelly and Connolly were self-confessed petty villains and downright nuisances whom some people might have considered better off behind bars. Kelly was hanged and we can only guess at what he may or may not have become in later life. But Charlie Connolly emerged from prison a changed man. He was no longer the feckless waster of the Lime Street billiard halls, but a man of maturity with a sense of responsibility who determined to put the past behind him and to make something of his life. He wanted to earn the respect of his family, and in that he has succeeded. But he insists he was framed for his part in the Cameo case. "Until I met Lou," says Connolly, "I thought the truth would never come out. He's helped me summon up the courage to tell my grandchildren and great-grandchildren about what really happened to me all those years ago."

More important, perhaps, is the principle that everyone should be reckoned equal before the law. "Once we start *selecting* those whom we think worthy or unworthy of justice," wrote Ludovic Kennedy in 1980, "we shall all in the end be diminished; for even if justice is sometimes rough in practice, it must in theory be indivisible." There would be others who, if justice was allowed to go by default, may come to suffer like George Kelly and Charlie Connolly. Kennedy was writing of the Luton sub-post office murder case of 1969, in which two young men protested their innocence, just as Connolly does today. Kennedy had already written two books about major miscarriages of justice; the Luton case, he argued was a third. Lou Santangeli says Kennedy could be writing of the Cameo case when he declared that "justice miscarried because of the over-zealousness of CID officers who had persuaded themselves into believing (with greater or lesser justification) that the suspects they had apprehended were guilty, and who, by deliberate omission and/or fabrication of evidence, took steps to ensure that their beliefs would be confirmed by the jury."

"I know I'm innocent," says Charlie Connolly. "My conscience is clear. I can sleep soundly at night because I know I didn't do it. Neither did Georgie Kelly." All men are innocent in the eyes of the law until they are proved guilty by convincing evidence. In the case of Kelly and Connolly the evidence seems now to fall short of what can reasonably be called convincing. In 1950, justice failed Timothy Evans. In the case of Kelly and Connolly and the Cameo killings, did justice fail once more?

Charlie Connolly died in 1997, the year after this story appeared, having failed to clear his name. But the convictions of both Kelly and Connolly were finally quashed by the Court of Appeal in 2003. In March 2006, George Kelly's remains were exhumed from a prison grave and reburied on consecrated ground.

Acknowledgments and Sources

Once again, the editor wishes to express his gratitude to Jonathan Goodman and Wilf Gregg for allowing him the run of their encyclopaedic collections of true-crime books containing many of the cases featured. He wishes to thank James Morton for his expert guidance on gangs and gangsters, and Kate Fassett, head of library at the *Daily Telegraph* in London, for letting him peruse the paper's files on many of the individuals included in this book.

The editor would also like to thank the following for their kind permission to reprint the extracts indicated:

Neil Acheson-Gray on behalf of the estate of the late Edward T. Hart for "A Reluctant Kingship" from *Britain's Godfather* (True Crime Library, London 1993) © Edward T. Hart 1993; Tristan Allsop for Kenneth Allsop, "Al, We're With You" from *The Bootleggers* (Hutchinson, London 1961); Lynn Barber for *Jimmy Boyle: Is There Life After Life?*, originally published in the *Sunday Express*, 27 October 1985, and reproduced by permission of the author; Jeffrey Bloomfield for *Getting Gotti Good!*, an extended version of the original published in *The Modern Murder Year Book*, edited by Jonathan Goodman (Robinson Publishing, London 1994) © Jeffrey Bloomfield 2006; Bill Campbell, David Lister and Hugh Jordan for "Mad, Bad and Dangerous to Know", an extract from *Mad Dog: The Rise and Fall of Johnny Adair and "C Company"* by David Lister and Hugh Jordan (Mainstream Publishing, Edinburgh 2003); Carroll & Graf for "The Process of

Elimination" from *Killer: The Autobiography of a Professional Murderer* by Joey and Dave Fisher (Star Books, 1987); Keith Dovkants for "The Police Killer Without Remorse", from *Evening Standard*, London, 17 May 1995 © Keith Dovkants 2006; Roger Francis for *Bouncer*, an extended version of the original published in *Night and Day* in September 1996 © Roger Wilkes 2006; Richard Lindberg for *The Death of the Don: The Legacy of Tony Accardo*, originally published in *Illinois Police and Sheriff's News*, September 1992 © 1999–2006. All rights reserved. Reproduced by permission of the author. Website: www.richardlindberg.net; Clifford L. Linedecker for The Rack from *The Man Who Killed Boys* (St Martin's Press, New York 1980) © Clifford L. Linedecker 1980, reproduced by permission of the author; Lew Louderback for extract from *Pretty Boy, Baby Face – I Love You* (Coronet, London 1969) © Lew Louderback 2006; Margaret McConnell for Brian McConnell, extract from *The Rise and Fall of the Brothers Kray* (David Bruce, and Watson Ltd., London 1969); Bel Mooney for *Hell's Archangel*, originally commissioned (but never published) by *The Times*, and included by kind permission of the author © Bel Mooney 2002. Website: www.belmooney.co.uk; James Morton for an extract from *Mad Frank: Memoirs of a Life of Crime* (Time Warner, 1995); Sylvana Nown for Graham Nown, extract from *The English Godfather* (Ward Lock, London 1987); John Pearson for "Axe Man" from *The Profession of Violence* (Weidenfeld and Nicolson, London, 1972); Stephen Richards for an extract from *Silent Scream: The Charles Bronson Story* (Mirage Publishing, Gateshead 1999) © Charles Bronson and Stephen Richards 1999; reproduced by permission of the author; and for an extract from *Viv (Graham) – The Final Chapter Vol.3* (Mirage Publishing, 2001). Website: www.crimebiz.com; Chris Summers for "Dead Man Walking" © Chris Summers 2006; Richard Whittington-Egan for "The Ice-Cream Gang Cometh" from *The Modern Murder Year Book*, edited by Jonathan Goodman (Robinson Publishing, London 1994).

Every effort has been made to trace the original copyright holders of the following, without success; the editor and publishers would be pleased to hear from any claimants to legal copyright of:

Ted Addy, extract from *Dutch Schultz* (Belmont Tower Books, New York 1973); George Blake, Introduction to *The Trials of*

Patrick Carraher (William Hodge, Edinburgh 1951); Stephen D. Frances (Hank Janson), *Jack Spot: The Man Of A Thousand Cuts* (Alexander Moring, London 1958); Dean Jennings, *We Only Kill Each Other: The Life and Bad Times of Bugsy Siegel* (John Long, London 1968); Eddie Guerin, *Crime. The Autobiography of a Crook* (John Murray, London 1928); Billy Hill, *Boss of Britain's Underworld* (Naldrett Press, London 1955); Myron J. Quimby Jr., *The Devil's Emissaries* (Thomas Yoseloff, Ltd., London, 1969); David Rowan, "Doctor Marcel Petiot" from *Famous European Crimes* (Frederick Muller Ltd., London 1955); William Schulz, "The Shocking Success Story of Public Enemy No. 1 (Meyer Lansky)" from *Reader's Digest* (US edition) May 1970; John Toland, *The Dillinger Days* (Arthur Barker Ltd., London 1963); Marthe Watts, *The Men In My Life* (Christopher Johnson, London 1960).

Other titles available from Robinson

The Mammoth Book of Pirates **Ed. Jon E. Lewis** £7.99 [ ]
True accounts of the most notorious pirates of the seven seas. Awash with skulduggery, malice, terror and opportunism, here are nearly 30 eyewitness and first-hand adventures of history's most famous pirates and privateers, including Blackbeard, Captain Kidd, 'Calico Jack' Rackman, Anne Bonney and Jean Lafitte.

The Mammoth Book of Special Ops
Ed. Richard Russell Lawrence £7.99 [ ]
The once shadowy activities of special forces have become an increasingly exposed element of 21st century warfare and anti-terrorist activity. In this great, unputdownable volume, are 40 of the most dangerous operations of modern time.

The Mammoth Book of Heroes **Ed. Jon E. Lewis** £7.99 [ ]
Gathered together in this volume are over 70 accounts, many of them in the words of those who were there, about men and women who showed real courage, often with their lives on the line. No fictional hero can match the true courage of Ernest Shackleton, the bravery of British soldiers at Rorke's Drift or the spirit of Annie Sullivan teaching the deaf and blind Helen Keller to speak and read.

The Mammoth Book of The Edge **Ed. Jon E. Lewis** £7.99 [ ]
Eyewitness accounts of triumph and tragedy on the world's greatest mountains. Presenting 25 first-hand accounts spanning an arc in time, from the golden Victorian age of Edward Whymper to the present, this is truly an exploration of the furthest reaches of human daring and endurance.

Robinson books are available from all good bookshops or direct from the publisher. Just tick the titles you want and fill in the form below.

TBS Direct
Colchester Road, Frating Green, Colchester, Essex CO7 7DW
Tel: +44 (0) 1206 255777
Fax: +44 (0) 1206 255914
Email: sales@tbs-ltd.co.uk

UK/BFPO customers please allow £1.00 for p&p for the first book, plus 50p for the second, plus 30p for each additional book up to a maximum charge of £3.00.
Overseas customers (inc. Ireland), please allow £2.00 for the first book, plus £1.00 for the second, plus 50p for each additional book.

Please send me the titles ticked above.

NAME (Block letters) . . . .

ADDRESS. . . . .

. . . .

POSTCODE. . . . .

I enclose a cheque/PO (payable to TBS Direct) for . . . .

I wish to pay by Switch/Credit card

Number . . . .

Card Expiry Date . . . .

Switch Issue Number . . . .

Other titles available from Robinson

The Mammoth Book of SAS and Special Forces
Ed. Jon E. Lewis   **£7.99 [ ]**
This terrific collection contains 30 true and graphic accounts, including recent operations in Iraq, Afghanistan and Bosnia, with reports detailing the entire range of special
forces from SAS, Commandos and Rangers to Navy SEALS and Paratroopers.

The Mammoth Book of Famous Trials **Ed. Roger Wilkes**   **£7.99 [ ]**
Here are 30 of the most famous trials ever, as recorded by the people who were there,
including Truman Capote, Brian Masters, Damon Runyon and other star turns in true
crime writing. Among the cases featured are O.J. Simpson, Oscar Wilde and Rosemary
West.

The Mammoth Book of War Correspondents **Ed. Jon E. Lewis £7.99 [ ]**
Starting with William Howard Russell's reports from the Crimea – the birth of war
reportage – all major conflicts of the modern era are here, including George Orwell on
the Spanish Civil War, Ernest Hemingway on D-Day and Max Hastings on the
surrender of Port Stanley.

The Mammoth Book of Endurance & Adventure
Ed. Jon E. Lewis   **£7.99 [ ]**
This definitive collection comprises over 30 accounts of true-life adventures taken from
contemporary memoirs, letters and journals. They span the years from 1800 to the turn
of the twentieth century – a period than can legitimately be termed the modern age of
exploration.

*Robinson books are available from all good bookshops or direct from the publisher. Just tick
the titles you want and fill in the form below.*

TBS Direct
Colchester Road, Frating Green, Colchester, Essex CO7 7DW
Tel: +44 (0) 1206 255777
Fax: +44 (0) 1206 255914
Email: sales@tbs-ltd.co.uk

UK/BFPO customers please allow £1.00 for p&p for the first book, plus 50p for the
second, plus 30p for each additional book up to a maximum charge of £3.00.
Overseas customers (inc. Ireland), please allow £2.00 for the first book, plus £1.00 for the
second, plus 50p for each additional book.

Please send me the titles ticked above.

NAME (Block letters) . . . .

ADDRESS. . . . .

. . . .

POSTCODE. . . . .

I enclose a cheque/PO (payable to TBS Direct) for . . . .

I wish to pay by Switch/Credit card

Number . . . .

Card Expiry Date . . . .

Switch Issue Number . . . .